1850 1880 1900 1925

Mary Mapes Dodge, *Hans Brinker,* 1865

Lewis Carroll, *Alice's Adventures in Wonderland,* illus. John Tenniel, 1865

Walter Crane, *Sing a Song of Six Pence,* 1865

Louisa May Alcott, *Little Women,* 1868

Jules Verne, *20,000 Leagues Under the Sea,* 1870

Mark Twain, *The Adventures of Tom Sawyer,* 1876

Randolph Caldecott, *The House That Jack Built,* 1878

Joel Chandler Harris, *Uncle Remus, His Songs and His Sayings,* 1880

Johanna Spyri, *Heidi,* 1880-81

Carlo Collodi, *Pinocchio,* 1882

Robert Louis Stevenson, *Treasure Island,* 1883; *A Child's Garden of Verses,* 1885

Kate Greenaway, *A, Apple Pie,* 1886

Andrew Lang, Scottish collector of folklore, *The Blue Fairy Book,* 1889

Joseph Jacobs, collector, *English Fairy Tales,* 1890

Rudyard Kipling, *The Jungle Books,* 1894-95

L. Frank Baum, *The Wonderful Wizard of Oz,* 1900

Beatrix Potter, *The Tale of Peter Rabbit,* 1902

Howard Pyle, reteller, *The Story of King Arthur and His Knights,* illus. N. C. Wyeth, 1903

James M. Barrie, *Peter Pan,* 1904

Kenneth Grahame, *The Wind in the Willows,* illus. E. H. Shepard, 1908

Lucy M. Montgomery, *Anne of Green Gables,* 1909

Frances Hodgson Burnett, *The Secret Garden,* 1910

Walter De la Mare, poet, *Peacock Pie,* 1913

Carl Sandburg, poet, *Rootabaga Stories,* 1922

A. A. Milne, *Winnie the Pooh* series of stories and verse, illus. E. H. Shepard, 1924-28

Wanda Gág, *Millions of Cats,* 1928

THIRD EDITION

Literature and the Child

Literature and the Child

THIRD EDITION

BERNICE E. CULLINAN

NEW YORK UNIVERSITY

LEE GALDA

UNIVERSITY OF GEORGIA

HARCOURT BRACE COLLEGE PUBLISHERS

Fort Worth   Philadelphia   San Diego   New York   Orlando   Austin   San Antonio
Toronto   Montreal   London   Sydney   Tokyo

PUBLISHER	Ted Buchholz
SENIOR ACQUISITIONS EDITOR	Jo-Anne Weaver
DEVELOPMENTAL EDITOR	Sarah Helyar Smith
PROJECT EDITOR	Angela Williams
SENIOR PRODUCTION MANAGER	Tad Gaither
ART DIRECTOR	Peggy Young
PICTURE DEVELOPMENT EDITOR	Lili Weiner
PICTURE EDITOR	Sandra Lord

Address for Editorial Correspondence
Harcourt Brace College Publishers
301 Commerce Street, Suite 3700
Fort Worth, TX 76102

Address for Orders
Harcourt Brace & Company
6277 Sea Harbor Drive
Orlando, FL 32887
1-800-782-4479 or
1-800-433-0001 (in Florida)

ISBN: 0-15-500985-0

Library of Congress Catalogue Number: 93-79967

Printed in the United States of America

5 6 7 8 9 0 1 2   032   9 8 7 6 5 4 3

*For Kali, Jason, Trisha, Anna, and Adam
our next generation of readers,
and in loving memory of Arlene M. Pillar*

Preface

About Children's Literature

Children's literature has become increasingly important in today's schools, libraries, and homes. Since the publication of the second edition of *Literature and the Child,* the trend toward literature-based instruction in elementary and middle schools has continued to grow. Increasing numbers of teachers and librarians engage in literature-based programs; children flock to the library, read during lunch, and take home books to read with their parents. They also spend a lot of time reading during the school day. Teachers and librarians, too, spend a lot of their time reading as the world of children's books—and the magnificent possibilities inherent in that world—opens up to them.

Interest in children's books has led to a strong demand for more of them, and publishers have responded generously. Today approximately 75,000 children's books are in print, with 5,000 to 6,000 new books published each year. With this wealth of books to choose from, you, as a teacher or librarian, need to know how to select wisely. The third edition of *Literature and the Child* can help you become a knowledgeable and critical consumer of children's books.

It is our hope that this book will make you want to read as many children's books as you can get your hands on, and you will read them with clear and critical eyes. You can then pass these books on to your own students, giving them the gift of reading and responding to wonderful books. If you do this, you will give them a lifelong gift, for they will become readers in the fullest sense of the word.

About the Third Edition

The third edition has been substantially revised from the second edition. The most apparent change is its length,

which has been reduced from the standard 800 pages to a concise 600 pages. The shortened version makes the book more timeless, enabling us to focus on what to look for in a children's book rather than on listing all the books available that fit the criteria. Moreover, the chapters are reordered to reinforce the primary purpose of covering educational theory and practice as well as the literature itself. Coverage of preschool and primary grade books has been moved to each genre chapter, as applicable, instead of being concentrated in a single chapter. This change balances the book's coverage of titles for preschool through ninth grade. Visually, the use of color in the illustrations enables us to show the full skill and artistry that are devoted to children's books today.

The third edition probes fewer books in depth in order to emphasize critical thinking and reading skills; it clearly defines the criteria and demonstrates how to evaluate and select new books. Recognizing that nothing develops in a vacuum, that literature in particular reflects and projects all of life's experiences, and that significant parallels exist in the experiences of different cultures, the textbook shows how interrelated the genres are and carefully integrates books of cultural diversity in each chapter. Further, for those who want to focus on multicultural books as a distinct genre, we detail the issues in a separate chapter. In fact, the third edition carries throughout an image of a patchwork quilt to represent the varied colors and patterns of books and people who inhabit the world of children's literature.

Content

Extending the metaphor of a multicolored patchwork quilt, we divide the text into three parts: Part One, The Framework of Children's Books; Part Two, The Patterns of Children's Books; and Part Three, The Threads That Bind Children and Books. Part One begins with The Story of Children's Literature (Chapter 1), which introduces the types of children's books, discusses current trends in children's literature, and presents highlights from its history. Chapter 2, Children Reading Literature, describes the readers of children's books—the children themselves. We present the ways children read to respond, read to learn, and read to enjoy. Understanding children and their reading is crucial to success as a teacher or librarian.

Part Two focuses on specific genres: picture books, poetry, folklore, fantasy, contemporary realistic fiction, historical fiction, biography, and informational books. In each chapter, 3 through 10, we carefully define the genre, discuss reasons for its importance, and present criteria for selecting and evaluating books of that type. We then discuss at length one or two outstanding examples of the genre and demonstrate how each book reflects the appropriate criteria.

Part Three contains broader issues woven throughout the field of children's literature. Chapter 11, Literature in a Culturally Diverse World, focuses on literature from many cultures and countries. While we discuss literature that represents different cultures throughout the text, we focus on such books in Chapter 11 to call attention to the resources available for building a curriculum that fosters international understanding. In Chapter 12, Planning and Assessing the Literature Curriculum, we present ways of working with literature in classrooms, extending ideas described in Chapter 2 and the information about books presented in Chapters 3 through 11.

Like the two earlier editions, these chapters discuss exemplary children's books, list many other notable books, and suggest approximate age levels. A designation of *N* (nursery) indicates that nursery school children, from birth to approximately age 4, are the primary audience. The designation *P* (primary) indicates books for 5- to 9-year-old children in kindergarten through grade 3; *I* (intermediate) indicates books for 10- to 12-year-old readers in grades 4 through 6; and *A* (advanced) indicates books for 12- to 15-year-old readers in grades 7 through 9. These designations are suggestions; many books are enjoyed by children of many ages.

Instructional Features

Special features in each chapter reinforce the philosophy of the book. In addition to an outline to help orient you to the content, each chapter opens with a poem exemplifying a child's connection with books. The genre chapters provide a checklist of evaluation criteria to aid in critical analysis. We provide suggestions for wide reading in figures organized by theme, topic, and audience level. These graphic organizers show at a glance how subtopics relate, and they make additional titles available without adding to the length of the book. The checklists and figures are carefully coordinated and similarly designed to give an integrated overview of the genre. Profile boxes in the chapters echo the critical thinking theme by providing insights into the lives of authors and illustrators, ex-

plaining how each has influenced the field of children's literature. And teaching ideas suggest effective, engaging activities that stimulate thought and demonstrate the concepts for students.

The back matter echoes the intent of this book to serve as a primary reference tool as well as a textbook. Six appendixes contain a wealth of information to draw upon, a glossary of literary terms provides concise definitions of frequently read and used terms, separate professional and children's books reference lists provide source information for all books mentioned in the text, and separate subject and author/title indexes enable readers to locate information readily.

The *Instructor's Manual,* by Linda DeGroff of the University of Georgia, supports and extends the concepts presented in *Literature and the Child*. It provides suggestions for additional activities, essays, ideas for journal entries, test items, and supplementary reference materials for many of the activities presented earlier in the manual.

Acknowledgments

We extend special appreciation to illustrator James Ransome for the art that graces the cover and part openers of our book. His star as an illustrator of children's books is rising rapidly and appropriately—based on his excellent talent and devotion to his work. He worked with us to conceptualize the idea of a patchwork quilt as a fitting metaphor for the field and then made the idea real and visually appealing through his art.

Special thanks to Brod Bagert, poet-attorney-friend, who is a valued contributor and an eager student of the field of children's literature. His enthusiasm for the subject and zest for sharing literature with children made the task of writing more joyous. He field tested many selections on his and his wife Debby's four children.

Our work on this book was made easier by the generous help of friends and colleagues. Joel Taxel, Linda DeGroff, Carol Fisher, Ira Aaron, and JoBeth Allen at the University of Georgia and Angela Jaggar, Trika Smith-Burke, John Mayher, Nancy Lester, Gordon Pradl, and Lenore Ringler at New York University helped keep us informed about exciting developments in the field of language education and children's books. Anita Peck, Jane West, Jennifer Drewes, Deborah Wooten, Diane Person, Lesley Yeary, Jason Ream, Lisa Maestri, and Kali Ream worked hard and long to help us screen books and prepare this manuscript. Their efforts saved us many hours, freeing us to read and savor the excellent children's books we discuss here.

A special debt of gratitude goes to research assistant and colleague Ann Lovett. Ann worked beside us to edit manuscript, prepare booklists, develop teaching ideas, photograph classrooms, and review books. Finally, she undertook the onerous task of obtaining permissions for copyrighted materials. Her work, her friendship, and her steadfast faith are indispensable.

Our reviewers provided thorough and thoughtful criticism, gave us fresh insights, and significantly helped shape this edition:

Phylliss Adams, California State University, San Bernardino

Brod Bagert, author, poet

Donna Bessant, Coordinator of Instructional Materials and School Libraries, Monterey Peninsula Unified School District

Patricia Cianciolo, Michigan State University

Roger Farr, Indiana University

Ellin Greene, Library Services for Children, Rutgers University

M. Jean Greenlaw, North Texas State University

Shirley Haley-James, Georgia State University

Julie Jensen, University of Texas, Austin

Linda Lamme, University of Florida

Miriam Marecek, Boston University

Sara Miller, Librarian, Rye Country Day School

Dianne Monson, University of Minnesota

Marcia Posner, Jewish Publication Society, Jewish Book Society

Phyllis Povell, C. W. Post College, Long Island University

Laurence Pringle, author

Timothy V. Rasinski, Kent State University

Carole Rhodes, College of New Rochelle

Nancy Roser, University of Texas, Austin

Kathy Short, University of Arizona

Rudine Sims Bishops, Ohio State University

Dorothy Strickland, Rutgers University

Joel Taxel, University of Georgia

V. Ellis Vance, Fresno County Office of Education, Fresno Pacific College

Students from Miriam Marecek's Fall 1991 Children's Literature course, Boston University

Working with Developmental Editor Sarah Helyar Smith once again was an extraordinary pleasure. She had nurtured the previous edition through its development and publication and continued the process with this edition. Her good nature, subtle sense of humor, and gentle prodding made it seem a lark to stay up all night to edit manuscripts. She applies pressure with loving care.

Project Editor Angela Williams celebrated the completion of our work by getting married—to a production manager at Harcourt Brace, of course. Her happiness and good spirits throughout our manuscript preparations were only partly due to the fact that we met our deadlines.

Picture Development Editor Lili Weiner deftly guided us in the selection of illustrations and photographs. She worked tirelessly to maintain the quality of reproduction in art samples and helped us to interpret technique and medium.

Art Director Peggy Young gave us a design that both reflects and supports the beautiful illustrations in children's literature, and Production Managers Annette Wiggins and Tad Gaither steadfastly kept the book on a difficult schedule.

And Acquisitions Editor Jo-Anne Weaver, who even makes house calls, deserves a special thanks for spearheading the organizational, financial, and production plans to get the job done. Her cheerfulness and buoyant personality made it all seem possible; she was right.

Finally, our family and friends supported and encouraged us as we struggled to keep to our impossible schedule. To them—Tony Pellegrini, Anna Pellegrini, Adam Pellegrini, Janie Carley, Jim Ellinger, Jeanne Brown, Cecile Sinamal, Sandra Maccarone, Merrille Koffler, Kent and Jody Brown, and others too many to mention—we can only say, with love, thank you.

Bernice E. Cullinan
Lee Galda

About the Authors and the Illustrator

Dr. Bernice E. Cullinan

Dr. Cullinan is Professor of Early Childhood and Elementary Education at New York University, where she specializes in children's literature, language arts, and reading. Dr. Cullinan is a member of the editorial board for *The New Advocate* and a book reviewer for *The Horn Book Guide*. She taught in elementary school for 15 years before completing her doctorate at Ohio State University.

A past president of the International Reading Association, she is a member of the Reading Hall of Fame, has received the Arbuthnot Award for Outstanding Teacher of Children's Literature, and was honored with the Jeremiah Ludington Award for her contributions to educational publishing.

Dr. Cullinan is a literature consultant for HB Treasury of Literature and Passports, new literature-based programs published by Harcourt Brace and Company. Her other published works with HB include *Language, Literacy, and the Child*. She is also editor of WordSong, the poetry imprint for Boyds Mills Press. Additional publications include *Children's Literature in the Classroom: Extending* Charlotte's Web, *Children's Voices: Talk in the Classroom, Fact and Fiction: Literature Across the Curriculum, Invitation to Read: More Children's Literature in the Reading Program, Let's Read About: Finding Books They'll Love to Read, Pen in Hand: Children Become Writers,* and *Read to Me: Raising Kids Who Love Books.*

Dr. Lee Galda

After teaching in elementary and middle school for a number of years, Lee Galda received her Ph.D. in English Education from New York University and is now a professor in the Department of Language Education at the University of Georgia. A member of the National Reading Research Center project, she is researching children's engagement with literature.

Dr. Galda is an active member of the National Council of Teachers of English and the International Reading Association and was the Children's Books Department Editor for *The Reading Teacher* from 1989 to 1993. She is on the Editorial Board for *Language Arts* and also reviews for a number of journals, including *Research in the Teaching of English.* She is co-author of *Language, Literacy, and the Child* with Bernice Cullinan and Dorothy Strickland, published by Harcourt Brace College Publishers.

© Lesa Ransome.

James Ransome

Born in Rich Square, North Carolina, Mr. Ransome received his Bachelor of Fine Arts degree in illustration from Pratt Institute.

He has illustrated more than nine picture books for children including *Aunt Flossie's Hats* by Elizabeth Howard (Clarion Books), *Sweet Clara and the Freedom Quilt* by Deborah Hopkinson (Alfred A. Knopf), *Uncle Jed's Barbershop* by Margaree King Mitchell (Simon & Schuster), and *Red Dancing Shoes* by Denise Lewis Patrick (Tambourine Books).

In addition to children's picture books, he has also illustrated several book jackets for young adults including *Down in the Piney Woods* and *The Cry of the Wolf.* Paintings from these works have been exhibited in group and solo shows throughout the country. He has also completed assignments for magazines such as *Esquire, Family Handyman, Cricket,* and *Ladybug.*

Mr. Ransome lives in Jersey City, New Jersey, with his wife, Lesa, and their Dalmation, Clinton.

Table of Contents

Literature and the Child

THIRD EDITION

Part
One

The
Framework
of Children's
Books

1

The Story of Children's Literature

THE POEM ON MY PILLOW

I felt very small
And the house was dark
But those cookies kept calling from
* the kitchen*
So I tiptoed downstairs
And peeked around the corner
To make sure there were no
* monsters.*

Then I saw my dad
Alone at the kitchen table
With an open book
And a pencil and paper.
He wrote very carefully,
Then he stopped and listened . . .
And he smiled.

This morning I found this poem on
* my pillow.*

  To the Little Boy Who Hides

I listen for your breath while
  you sleep.
I follow your footsteps across
  the floor above me.
I hear the creak of wooden
  steps as you tiptoe down.
And I feel your fear of
  darkness.
Oh little son,
You need not hide from the
  night.
Speak out . . .
Your courage will make light.

When I read the poem I thought
My gosh . . . he heard me!
Was he angry?
Did he think I had been bad?
Then I noticed how he signed the
* poem . . .*
  "To My Son . . . With Love . . .
  from Dad."

Brod Bagert

ome of the world's best literature has been written for children. It surges from the hearts of people who love children and who believe that the world of tomorrow is shaped by what our children read today.

Children's literature, books written for children and books written for other audiences that children have made their own, enrich children's lives and widen their horizons. Picture 9-year-old Anna, head bent forward so her dark hair makes a tent around her face and the book she is reading, totally engrossed in the world of ***The Whisper of Glocken.*** When she gets to the part where Silky finds a little gray creature and calls him Wafer she looks up, sighs, and says, "Mom, Wafer is a perfect name for a gray kitten." She then goes back to her reading, once more lost to the world. Later, finished with the book she talks about it, wondering aloud how the Minnipins had the courage to leave their valley and venture out into the bigger world, questioning whether she would be that brave. From one

book she's found the perfect name for her new gray kitten, has experienced a dangerous journey into an unknown land, and has thought about her personal courage, all without leaving her own living room.

She's been doing this all of her life. She careened down a hill in a buggy with Max, Rosemary Wells's captivating rabbit, even as she chewed the corners of the sturdy board book. She went with another Max in his private boat to the land of the wild things, played in the rain with Peter Spier's children, and learned to understand the natural world with Joanne Ryder's imaginative nonfiction. She's laughed, cried, gathered information, experienced danger, engaged in adventures, solved mysteries, and learned a great deal about the world and about herself as she sat, dark hair falling around her face, reading book after book. Anna's a lucky child. She's been engaged with wonderful children's books all of her life.

Children's literature enables children to explore and construct life. In books children can travel down the street, across the world, or back and forth in time; they can visit other people's lives and make friends; they can explore their own feelings, shape their own values, and come to understand the feelings and values of others; they can increase their storehouse of experience, which in turn helps them to better understand new experiences. Children's books contain beautiful language and outstanding art, providing their young readers with wonderful examples of symbolic thought. The act itself of reading books develops children's facility with language as they pore over carefully crafted prose and poetry.

Children's books are a powerful force in the lives of children, and as teachers, we can take advantage of this by shaping our curriculum around children's books. The richness and diversity that typifies literature for children today mean that teachers, parents, and children have a wealth of books from which to select.

LITERATURE FOR TODAY'S CHILD

With so many good books available, how do we choose? How do we know what kinds of books are available? How do we decide which books to read? This chapter briefly discusses the types, or **genres,** of literature available for today's children, and the general criteria of "good books" that parents and teachers can use to help children select those books.

Literary forms provide a frame of reference for the student of children's literature; they help

Anna is totally absorbed in the book she is reading. A frequent traveler in the world of books, she knows the pathway well.

simplify the task of presenting literature in meaningful and varied ways. One basic distinction is that between narratives and nonnarratives. Narratives tell a story; they usually consist of a character or characters who encounter some kind of problem and work to solve that problem. The narrative is developed through the plot—the temporal events or actions that lead to the solution of the problem—progresses to a climax, or solution to the problem, and ends with a resolution, or closure to the story. Books that are not narratives do not tell a story. They may be poetry that is not narrative or nonfiction that presents concepts and information.

Literature can be divided along the lines of genre, format, and content. Genre classification groups share a number of characteristics, such as types of characters, settings, actions, and overall form or structure. This book primarily uses genre classifications, with the exception of picture books, which are based on format, and culturally diverse books, which are based on content (see Figure 1-1).

Various distinguishing features help categorize the genres. For example, ancient stories are known as *folklore;* stories focusing on events that could happen today are works of *realistic fiction;* stories that are set in the past, *historical fiction;* those that could not happen in the real world, *fantasy;* and those that might happen in the future, *science fiction.* Books that present information rather than tell stories are called *nonfiction.* A book can be fiction or nonfiction, a picture book or not a picture book. If a book is fiction it can be historical or contemporary, realistic, fantasy, or science fiction. Children discover the distinctions gradually as they read widely and have books read to them. Books can

Figure 1-1

Classification Scheme for Children's Literature

Type	Brief Description
Picture Books (Chapter 3)	Interdependence of art and text. Story or concept presented through combination of text and illustration. Division based on format, not genre. All genres appear in picture books.
Poetry and Verse (Chapter 4)	Condensed language, imagery. Distilled, rhythmic expression of imaginative thoughts and perceptions.
Folklore (Chapter 5)	Literary heritage of humankind. Traditional stories, myths, legends, nursery rhymes, and songs from the past. Oral tradition; no known author.
Fantasy (Chapter 6)	Imaginative worlds, make believe. Stories set in places that do not exist, about people and creatures that could not exist, or events that could not happen.
Science Fiction (Chapter 6)	Based on taking physical laws and scientific principles to their logical outcomes. Stories about what might occur in the future.
Realistic Fiction (Chapter 7)	"What if" stories, illusion of reality. Events could happen in real world, characters seem real, contemporary setting.
Historical Fiction (Chapter 8)	Set in the past, could have happened. Story set in an earlier time that reconstructs events of past age; events could have happened.
Biography (Chapter 9)	Plot and theme based on person's life. An account of a person's life, or part of a life history; letters, memoirs, diaries, journals, autobiographies.
Nonfiction (Chapter 10)	Facts about the real world. Informational books that explain a subject or concept.
Culturally Diverse Books (Chapter 11)	Reflect people of many cultures. Books that portray various cultural groups authentically. Not a genre; division based on content. Culturally diverse books appear in all genres.

also be classified according to grade level of children likely to enjoy reading them. In this text N = Nursery, P = Primary, I = Intermediate, and A = Advanced.

Picture Books

Picture books tell a story or demonstrate a concept through a unique combination of text and illustration. The illustrations extend and reflect the meaning conveyed by the words. The content may be realistic, fanciful, or factual; it is the format that defines a picture book. Robert McCloskey's popular classic, *Make Way for Ducklings* (P), successfully combines text and illustrations to tell a charming story about a family of ducks. Text and illustrations also work together to explore the nature of hum-

mingbirds in Joanne Ryder's ***Dancers in the Garden*** (I).

Picture books abound for young children, beginning with small books made out of cardboard that are just right for babies to hold, look at, and chew. Nursery and primary-grade children are the main readers of picture books, and most of these books are aimed at that audience, but many are appropriate for intermediate and advanced-grade readers as well. We explore picture books extensively in Chapter 3.

Poetry and Verse

Poetry is the shorthand of beauty, with its distilled language that captures the essence of an idea or experience and encompasses the universe in its vision. As Emerson suggested long ago, poetry says the most important things in the simplest way. Much poetry is rhythmic and rhymed, appealing to the ear as well as to the mind and the emotions. Taking many forms, the best poetry and verse—from nonsense rhymes and limericks through lyrical and narrative poetry—shapes a taken-for-granted ordinary experience into thoughts extraordinary.

Sometimes mystifying, often difficult to fully understand, poetry can enrich life and fire the imagination. A wide variety of poetry is available for today's children, poems that appeal to the very young child and poems that speak to the advanced reader. We explore poetry fully in Chapter 4.

Folklore

Folklore comprises stories that were passed through generations by word of mouth before they were ever written down. As such, they have no single identifiable author. As people told the stories to one another, they were changed and molded to suit the teller's style or fancy. Eventually they were written down by collectors of oral folklore such as Charles Perrault and the Brothers Grimm. Folklore represents the values of a culture; it encompasses universal experience as shaped by individual cultures. Thus folklore reflects the culture from whence it came.

There are many types of folklore. For example, **nursery rhymes,** such as those from Mother Goose, are a part of folklore. **Folktales and fairy tales,** such as Cinderella or the Anansi stories, reflect the values of a culture; they constitute another major category of folk literature. **Fables,** those simply told and highly condensed morality tales such as "The Boy Who Cried Wolf," often use animal characters to embody human virtues and vices—these, too, belong to the folklore tradition.

In addition, **mythology,** which explains the origin of the earth, the phenomena of nature, and the relation between humans and their gods, makes up a large portion of folklore. **Legends,** exaggerated hero tales grown hardly recognizable through retellings, such as **Robin Hood,** embellish an initial grain of truth. The American version of hero tales, **tall tales** about characters such as John Henry and Paul Bunyan, exaggerate the strength, the size, and the riches of America.

Folklore for today's children is appropriate for nursery through advanced-grade readers. It represents a wide variety of cultures and beliefs, reflecting the pluralistic nature of our world. We discuss folklore in Chapter 5.

Fantasy

Fantasy is distinguished by the nonrealistic nature of places, events, and characters: Animals talk in surreal worlds, inanimate objects have feelings, time follows no rules, or humans accomplish superhuman feats. Fantasy ranges from simple talking animal stories for very young children to complex novels that explore themes of eternal or universal truths which reflect human concerns. Even though fantasy stories could not possibly occur, carefully constructed plots, well-developed characters, and vivid settings make fantasy stories believable. E. B. White's **Charlotte's Web** (P–I) is a well-known fantasy, and many favorite picture books, such as Maurice Sendak's **Where the Wild Things Are** (N–P), are also fantasy. We explore the nature of fantasy in Chapter 6.

Science Fiction

Science fiction imaginatively extrapolates fact and theory: Stories project what could happen in another time through a logical extension of established theories and scientific principles. Science fiction describes worlds that not only are plausible, but may exist someday; it also considers the impact of science on life. Early science fiction writers extrapolated primarily from technology, but the genre has grown to incorporate sociology and anthropology. Science fiction themes often question the effect of progress on the quality of life and examine the values of contemporary society. Eleanor Cameron's **Wonderful Flight to the Mushroom Planet** (I) is a good introduction to science fiction. Madeleine L'Engle's **A Wrinkle in Time** (I) is considered a classic in the field. A discussion of science fiction appears in Chapter 6.

Realistic Fiction

Fiction set in modern times, with events that could occur, is called **realistic fiction** (or contemporary realism). Although the author creates and manipulates plot, character, and setting, all remain within the realm of the possible. Phyllis Reynolds Naylor's **Shiloh** (I) is an excellent example of realistic fiction.

Children's books reflect a country's social and political philosophies, and realistic fiction for children reflects the joys and the imperfections of living in today's world. Books such as Cynthia Rylant's **Missing May** (I) and Avi's **Nothing But the Truth** (A) explore serious issues like death and freedom of speech; Lensey Namioka's **Yang the Youngest and His Terrible Ear** (I) is a sensitive exploration

 **EACHING IDEA 1-1**

Helping Children Learn About Fantasy and Realism (P)

Choose two picture books on the same topic or two by the same author or illustrator. Choose one realistic book (it could possibly happen) and one fantasy (it could not happen; it is make believe). Read aloud both books; ask children to compare them on relevant points as below.

The Chalk Doll		**Will's Mammoth**
Genre:	Realistic fiction	Fantasy
Characters:	Rose, Mother	Will, Woolly Mammoths
Plot:	Mother remembers Jamaican childhood	Will imagines prehistoric world
Setting:	Rose's bedroom	Will's room and his imagination
Theme:	Childhood memories are happy	Imaginative play is fun
Details:	What did Rose's mother remember?	Where did Will go on his woolly mammoth?
	Were the dolls, dress, heels, parties real?	What kind of animals did Will see?

How did you know which story was real, and which one was make believe? Which pictures and sentences prove it?

Pomerantz, Charlotte. *The Chalk Doll*. Illus. Frané Lessac.
Martin, Rafe, *Will's Mammoth*. Illus. Stephen Gammell.

of growing up with a realistic happy ending. Picture books that are realistic fiction, such as Michael Rosen's *Elijah's Angel* (P–A), abound. Realistic fiction is available for children of all ages, with books for older readers exploring complex issues from a variety of perspectives. We discuss some of these issues in Chapter 7.

Historical Fiction

Historical fiction sets stories in the historical past, portraying events that actually did or possibly could have occurred. Authors create plot and character within an authentic historical setting. Although much historical fiction is written for intermediate and advanced-grade readers, such as Elizabeth George Speare's *The Witch of Blackbird Pond* (I–A), there are many fine picture books, such as Jane Yolen's *Encounter* (P–I) and Gloria Houston's *My Great-Aunt Arizona* (P), that bring the past to life for younger readers. We discuss historical fiction in Chapter 8.

Biography

Biography tells part or all of a real person's life. The subject of a biography is often someone who is famous or exemplary in some way. Politicians,

artists, sports figures, writers, and explorers are often the subjects of biographies that may be picture books or longer texts. Some biographies have explored the lives of ordinary people, such as Diane Hoyt-Goldsmith's *Hoang Anh: A Vietnamese-American Boy* (I). Biography bears the imprint of the author; although the story of a person's life provides the basic facts, the writer interprets, selects, and organizes elements to create an aesthetic work. Russell Freedman casts a new light in *Lincoln* (I–A), his award-winning photobiography.

Like biographies, autobiographies are stories of a person's life, but they are written by the subjects themselves. Currently we enjoy a number of autobiographies by contemporary children's authors, such as Rosemary Sutcliff's *Blue Remembered Hills* (A). Biographies are available for a wide audience from primary through advanced grades. We discuss biographies in Chapter 9.

Nonfiction

Informational books aimed at explaining a subject are categorized as **nonfiction.** Children are naturally curious about the world they inhabit. They observe and explore, question and hypothesize about how this world works. Outnumbering fiction in most children's libraries, nonfiction is available for children from nursery through advanced grades.

 **IDEA** 1-2

Helping Students Learn About Historical and Contemporary Realistic Fiction (I–A)

Choose two books by the same author or two on the same topic. Choose one with a contemporary setting and one with a historical setting. After students have read the books, ask them to compare relevant points. For example, here are two books by Avi.

	The True Confessions of Charlotte Doyle	**Nothing But the Truth: A Documentary Novel**
Genre:	Historical fiction	Realistic fiction
Characters:	Charlotte Doyle and Ship's Captain	Philip Malloy and English teacher
Setting:	On sailing ship, 1832	School, contemporary time
Plot:	Captain boondoggles crew	Philip expelled for humming
Theme:	Be true to yourself	Good guys don't always win
Details:	How did you know which one was historical fiction and which one was contemporary realistic fiction? What evidence can you cite to support your position?	

Nonfiction presents information in a variety of formats: in picture books and photographic essays, as reproductions of original documents, as how-to-do-it manuals, or as direct expository texts. Nonfiction covers diverse topics, ranging from dinosaurs to endangered species, cathedrals to igloos, triangles to probability, elements of art to book construction. Many nonfiction books are works of art as well as works of fact. David Macaulay's *Cathedral* (I–A), Ron Hirschi's *Spring* (P), and Lynne Cherry's *A River Ran Wild* (I) are all as beautiful as they are informative. We discuss nonfiction books in Chapter 10.

Culturally Diverse Books

Culturally diverse books are classified according to content. They portray diverse groups of people accurately, while demonstrating the common humanity that connects all human beings. Human needs, emotions, and desires are similar; books can help us appreciate those similarities as well as celebrate the uniqueness of cultural groups. North America was once considered a melting pot, where peoples of many nations came to live and cultural differences disappeared in favor of the new culture. Today North America is more like a patchwork quilt: patches of varying colors, textures, shapes, and sizes, all held together by a common thread (Jack-

son, 1992). Today's children live in a pluralistic world, with its rich mix of diverse cultures.

As children prepare to live in the twenty-first century, children's books offer the opportunity for building knowledge about and understanding of many cultures. Picture books, poetry, folklore, realistic and historical fiction, biographies, and nonfiction that celebrate cultural diversity are available for a wide range of readers. Books such as Mary Lankford's *Hopscotch Around the World* (P–I), Rachel Isadora's *Over the Green Hills* (P–I), and Minfong Ho's *The Clay Marble* (A) help children explore cultures around the world. Eloise Greenfield's *Night on Neighborhood Street* (P–I), Donald Crews's *Bigmama's* (P–I), and Joseph Bruchac's *Thirteen Moons on Turtle's Back* (P–A) support the goal of multicultural understanding in North America. We explore many culturally diverse books in Chapter 11.

The diversity and richness that marks children's literature today means that children's experiences with books can be infinitely varied. With so much to choose from, we, as teachers, can select only high-quality literature: books that use interesting language in interesting ways; work with ideas that are important and potentially interesting to child readers; and, if a picture book, contain illustrations that are artistically excellent. The criteria that quality literature of each genre exemplify are summarized in Figure 1-2 and discussed in subsequent chapters.

 EACHING IDEA 1-3

Culturally Diverse Literature in Many Forms (I)

When you look to literature to learn about the world, you find a wealth of material. For example, if you choose to examine an Asian culture, such as China, Japan, Korea, or Cambodia, you find books in every genre to expand your understanding.

Books portray diverse cultures in authentic ways. They are best written from a perspective inside the culture by a member of the group they portray; they are often set in the author's native land. Books about culturally diverse groups span the genres; the division is based on content, not on literary form or conventions. Students discover not only what is different but also what is similar among cultures when they read books about culturally diverse groups. These books focus on Asian cultures; you can find comparable variety from every genre for other cultural groups.

POETRY
Gordon, Ruth. *Time Is the Longest Distance: An Anthology of Poems.*

PICTURE BOOKS
Baker, Keith. *The Magic Fan.*
Kalman, Maira. *Sayonara, Mrs. Kackleman.*

FOLKLORE
Tejima, illus. *Ho-limlim: A Rabbit Tale from Japan.*

HISTORICAL FICTION
Choi, Sook Nyul. *Year of Impossible Goodbyes.*

REALISTIC FICTION
Ho, Minfong. *The Clay Marble.*

BIOGRAPHY
Say, Allen. *El Chino.*

NONFICTION
Schlein, Miriam. *The Year of the Panda.* Illus. Kam Mak.
Waters, Kate, and Slovenz-Low, Madeline. *Lion Dancer: Ernie Wan's Chinese New Year.* Photos by Martha Cooper.

SHORT STORIES
Yee, Paul. *Tales from Gold Mountain: Stories of the Chinese in the New World.* Illus. Simon Ng.
Yep, Laurence. *The Rainbow People.* Illus. David Wiesner.
Yep, Laurence. *Tongues of Jade.* Illus. David Wiesner.

Group Activity: Reading Books About Culturally Diverse Groups.

1. As a group, brainstorm all the information you know about a particular culture. Write down the "facts" without evaluating them. List contradictory "facts" if volunteered. List one category of "feelings, or attitudes" toward the cultural group. Save the list for later study.

2. After reading a variety of books, return to your original list of information and feeling statements. Add to categories of additional information. Discuss feelings or emotions to discover any changes.

3. Discuss which books contributed most to changes in emotional response to a cultural group and why.

Group Activity: After Reading Books About Culturally Diverse Groups.

1. Create a chart with relevant items for comparison across the top; list book titles down the left column.

2. Ask students to fill in the grid collaboratively. For example:

Title	Genre	Character	Conflict	Cultural Value

Figure
1-2

Criteria for Good Books by Genre

	Text	Illustration
Poetry	Rhythmic, sensory images.	Interpret beyond literal meaning.
Folklore	Patterned language, fast-paced plot. Sounds like spoken language.	Interpretive of the tale and cultural origins.
Fantasy	Believable, consistent, logical world. Clearly defined conflict. Strong characterization.	Extends fanciful elements, reflects characterization and events.
Science Fiction	Speculative, extrapolation of fact. Hypotheses about life in untraveled worlds.	Visualizes imaginative worlds, reflects characterization and events.
Realistic Fiction	Story is possible, reasonable, plausible. Well-defined conflict, strong characterization.	Verisimilitude, reflects mood, characterization, and events accurately.
Historical Fiction	Setting affects plot; details and language in keeping with period.	Authentic images of the period.
Biography	Interesting story of a person's complete or partial life.	Authentic images of life segments.
Nonfiction	Clarity, factual accuracy.	Clarifies and extends concepts.
Culturally Diverse	Authentic portrayal of culture.	Images and symbols representative of culture.

THE DEVELOPMENT OF LITERATURE FOR CHILDREN

Richness and diversity have not always been the case in children's literature. Since the first children's books were published nearly four centuries ago, the amount, kind, and quality of books for children has undergone a vast transformation. What accounts for this transformation?

The Evolution of Childhood

Books are not created in a vacuum; they are generated and shaped by the world around them. The prevailing perception of childhood is itself a part of the social, ethical, philosophic, and aesthetic forces of any given time, all of which leave their mark on children's books. Commager states it succinctly:

We have in literature not only a continuous record of childhood, but a continuous record of society as a whole, and—what is more important—of the ideas and standards that society wishes to inculcate into each new generation. (1969, pp. xvi–xvii)

The way in which adults regard children has evolved over time. Some ancient societies, such as many Native American cultures, marked the passage from childhood to adulthood by a ceremonious rite of passage. Other societies, such as those of Western Europe and North America until well into the nineteenth century, regarded children as miniature adults; society made little distinction between activities and functions for children and those for adults, and few special learning materials were provided for children.

Only gradually, beginning in the nineteenth century and evolving during the twentieth century, did the belief evolve that children are seeking, learning individuals, developmentally distinct from adults, with unique perceptions of the world and with different needs and abilities. This vision of children led to a demand for books that children could call their own, and the children's book industry blossomed. A brief recounting of major events in the development of children's literature in Western Europe and North America illustrates the profound changes that have occurred.

The Influence of Colonial Morality

When the Pilgrims settled in New England in 1620, bookmaking was a slow and costly process, and the Bible and other religious books were the chief products of the printer's craft. Books for pleasure reading were virtually nonexistent; most books were meant to inform. Further, there were few distinctions between books for children and books for adults.

During the 1600s, literature was mostly an oral tradition, shared through folktales and fables, Bible stories, ballads, epics, romances, and the performances of wandering players and minstrels. Books were scarce and relatively expensive, so few early colonists had them. In addition, colonial living conditions were harsh, with everyone, including children, working long hours. During the dark winter months, even light to read by was a luxury.

Religious Tracts and Tales

The values held by the early colonists, particularly the Puritans, reflected their desire to be obedient to the will of God and to cast off the wages of original sin in order to redeem the soul. These values were transmitted to children primarily through direct instruction by adults. The few books available to colonial children were moralistic, didactic, and riddled with sanctions. Through books of catechism and lists of duties, children were instructed to live deeply spiritual lives, to obey their parents, to prepare for death, and to avoid incurring the wrath of God. One such book, James Janeway's *A Token for Children: Being an Exact Account of the Conversion, Holy and Exemplary Lives, and Joyful Deaths of Several Young Children* (1672), was popular both in England and in the colonies. Cotton Mather's American edition of the same book, *A Token for the Children of New England, or Some Examples of Children in Whom the Fear of God was Remarkably Budding Before they Died,* was first published in Boston in 1702.

The Puritans regarded human nature as inherently sinful. According to their doctrine, children were born naturally depraved; religion led to salvation, and children were taught to read for the primary purpose of reading the Bible. The funeral elegy was a popular form of literature for children. It gloomily detailed the death of a young person who had given wise counsel on the deathbed, as in Benjamin Colman's *A Devout Contemplation On the Meaning of Divine Providence, in the Early Death of Pious and Lovely Children. Preached upon the Sudden and Lamented Death of Mrs. Elizabeth Wainwright. Who Departed this Life, April the 8th, 1714. Having just completed the Fourteenth Year of Her Age.* The first of many of its kind to come, this book contained an address to the mournful relatives of the deceased, an address to the children of the town, and the sermon at her funeral. Children were taught to be in constant preparation for death and warned that it could come at any moment.

Books from this period affirm the Puritan ethic and the role of religious guidance in children's lives. The concern for children's souls and the search for salvation appear grim and dreary to us today, but the images of fire and brimstone rife in these books were frighteningly real for Puritan children.

Isaac Watts's work stands in stark contrast to this threatening picture. Somewhat more subtle in his moralizing, Watts states in the preface to *Divine and Moral Songs for Children,* published in England in 1715, that his work is intended to "give the minds of children a relish for virtue and religion." Some of Watts's hymns are still sung today, notably "Joy to the World," "O God, Our Help in Ages Past," and "Hush, My Dear, Lie Still and Slumber."

Secular Tales: Chapbooks and Battledores

Not all was gloom and doom in England and North America, however. Decried by early spiritual leaders, **chapbooks,** crudely printed little books sold for a few cents by peddlers—or chapmen—contained poorly retold stories. Despite their cheap quality, the wide circulation of chapbooks created a readership for later books published for children. Perhaps even more important, they preserved many fairy tales and nursery rhymes for later, happier retellings.

Battledores, made of folded cardboard, had a cover embellished with crude woodcuts of animals, while the inside was filled with alphabets, numerals,

Note: Many of the historical books discussed in this chapter are no longer available except in rare book collections. Most can be found in the Pierpont Morgan Library, New York, NY; Rosenbach Collection, Philadelphia, PA; Osborne Collection, Toronto, Ontario, Canada; British Museum Library, London, England; Boston Public Library, Boston, MA; Cooperative Children's Book Center, Madison, WI; Library of Congress, Washington, DC; New York Public Library, New York, NY; Philadelphia Free Public Library, Philadelphia, PA; and Trinity Public Library, Dublin, Ireland.

[107]

A

T O K E N

F O R   T H E

C H I L D R E N

O F

N E W - E N G L A N D.

IF the Children of New-England *should not with an Early Piety, set themselves to* Know *and* Serve *the Lord* JESUS CHRIST, *the* GOD *of their Fathers, they will be condemned, not only by the Examples of pious Children in other Parts of the World, the publish'd and printed Accounts whereof have been brought over hither ; but there have been Exemplary Children in the Midst of* New-England *itself, that will rise up against them for their Condemnation. It would be a very profitable Thing to our* Child-en, *and*

[108]

highly acceptable to all the godly Parents of the Children, *if, in Imitation of the excellent* JANE-WAY's *Token for Children, there were made a true Collection of notable Things, exemplified in the* Lives *and* Deaths *of many among us, whose* Childhood *hath been signalized for what is virtuous and laudable.*

In the Church-History *of* New-England *is to be found the* Lives *of many eminent* Persons, *among whose* Eminencies, *not the least was,* Their fearing of the Lord from their Youth, *and their being loved by the Lord when they were* Children.

But among the many other Instances, of a Childhood *and* Youth *delivered from* Vanity *by serious* Religion, *which* New-England *has afforded, these few have particularly been preserved.*

Cotton Mather's foreword to the New England edition of Janeway's *A Token for the Children of New England* presented stories of pious children as models to readers. (From *Yankee Doodle's Literary Sampler of Prose, Poetry & Pictures.* Selected from the Rare Book Collections of the Library of Congress and introduced by Virginia Haviland and Margaret N. Coughlan.)

and simple reading lessons. They were intended "to instruct and amuse" and contained only vague religious references. Battledores were popular in England and North America from the mid-1700s well into the 1800s.

Books for Formal Education

Typical colonial schools were "dame schools," conducted in private homes, with children attending to their lessons while the teacher carried on her household duties. The curriculum included reading, writing, spelling, arithmetic, prayers, hymns, and catechism read from hornbooks, the Bible, and a few other books.

First used around 1550, **hornbooks** were small wooden paddles with lesson sheets attached to them, and covered with a sheet of transparent cow's horn fastened with small strips of brass. They were used to teach the alphabet and often contained a list of syllables and vowels, the Lord's

Prayer, or short verses. "In Adam's fall we sinned all" began one such alphabet verse. These instructional materials combined learning skills with religious salvation—the ultimate goal.

The New England Primer provided religious education in language children could understand. First published in London as *The Protestant Tutor* or *The Royal Primer,* its author, Benjamin Harris, was sent to the pillory in 1681 for printing the book, one of the first to depart from traditional religious catechism. Harris escaped to Boston where he reissued the book as *The New England Primer* in 1690. Pictures in the *Primer* were crude woodcuts, but they held children's attention with their gruesomely detailed accounts of burnings and other punishments.

The numerous editions of the *Primer,* although varied in subject matter, had certain features in common, including the alphabet in couplets of admonitory sentences, the catechism, and various hymns and prayers. Children were expected to study it until they had memorized it word for word.

Battledores, made of heavy, folded cardboard, offered alphabets, simple pictures, and religious precepts. (From *Yankee Doodle's Literary Sampler of Prose, Poetry & Pictures.* Selected from the Rare Book Collections of the Library of Congress and introduced by Virginia Haviland and Margaret N. Coughlan.)

The simple text of hornbooks was mounted on a wooden paddle covered with a sheet of hammered cow's horn—hence the name. (Facsimile of a hornbook reproduced by *The Horn Book.*)

Major sections of the books the colonists gave their children were filled with directives for manners and morals. Here are some typical rules for table manners:

> Grease not thy fingers or napkin more than necessity requires. Lean not thy elbow on the table, or on the back of the chair. Stuff not thy mouth so as to fill thy cheeks, be content with smaller mouthfuls. (Rosenbach, 1966, p. xxxix)

Children's behavior and manners were of great importance to the prim and unbending writers of this period. Nearly every book included instructions on proper behavior, with large doses of humility and correct manners. The didactic nature of books for children during this period established a trend that continued to influence children's literature for years to come.

Changing Ideas of Education

Throughout the colonial period of the seventeenth and eighteenth centuries, while the North American colonists were wresting a living from an untamed land and winning their political independence, the thoughts of some in Europe were moving away from the stern Puritan morality toward a child-centered system of education. These forerunners of child-centered thought were Comenius, Locke, and Rousseau.

John Amos Comenius (1592–1670), a Moravian educational reformer and theologian, believed in a

G	As runs the Glass, Our Life doth pass.
H	My Book and Heart Must never part.
I	Job feels the Rod,— Yet bleffes GOD.
K	Proud Korah's troop Was fwallowed up
L	Lot fled to *Zoar*, Saw fiery Shower On *Sodom* pour.
M	Moses was he Who *Israel's* Hoft Led thro' the Sea.

This page from a version of *The New England Primer* shows the alphabet with biblical rhymes as mnemonic devices.

uniform system of education for all children and wrote a compendium of the information he believed every child should know. His *Orbis sensualium pictus (Illustrated World of the Senses)* appeared in 1658 and is particularly noteworthy because it was the first book in which pictures were as important as the text.

A stronger and more lasting influence came from John Locke (1632–1704), the English philosopher whose *Some Thoughts Concerning Education* (1693) set forth the view that when an infant comes into the world his mind is a "tabula rasa"—a blank slate—ready to have life's experiences written on it. Accordingly, the impressions made on the child are most important. He believed that children should be treated as rational creatures, that their curiosity was an expression of an appetite for knowledge. His view of childhood as a time of special significance, as well as his stress on human reason, had widespread influence throughout the eighteenth century. Locke held out the promise of change through the careful use of rewards and punishments. He believed the strongest of these incentives to be esteem and disgrace.

Fifty years later, French philosopher Jean-Jacques Rousseau (1712–1778) startled the world with a view of child growth as inner directed. Here,

too, were implications for the education of the child. In *Emile* (1762), Rousseau set forth the idea that the child is born with an innate sense of right and wrong which is only warped and distorted by parents and teachers. Left to follow his natural impulses, the child, like the "noble savage," would develop and grow into an adulthood superior to that imposed by civilization.

Rousseau brightened the view of childhood by denying the idea of original sin and by deeming childhood important in its own right. This led to a revision in thinking about how children learn. One of the primary principles of his theory of natural education, "Do not teach but let the child instruct himself through experience," is still debated today. Another maxim, "Nature wants children to be children before they are men," embodied an affirmation of the importance of childhood and countered the miniature-adult notion prevalent for so long.

Locke and Rousseau, alike in their positions that childhood is a time distinct from adulthood, differed dramatically in their views of how the child learns. Locke's emphasis on the importance of training, discipline, and reason foretold the assertions of modern behavioral psychologists, who believe that the child's behavior is molded primarily by rewards and punishments. Rousseau's views, on the other hand, prefigured those of developmental psychologists, who assert that the child's growth is primarily the result of the development of innate abilities and personal discovery of the world.

The Beginnings of the Children's Book Industry

In 1744, a London businessman, John Newbery (1713–1767), began a venture that was to affect children not only in England but in the United States and Canada as well. Newbery, an English merchant, perhaps saw in the popularity of Charles Perrault's Mother Goose tales a potential market. He opened The Bible and Sun (originally called The Bible and Crown) where he offered for sale, along with a variety of medicines, the first book that was specifically designed to entertain as well as instruct children. *A Little Pretty Pocket-Book: Intended for the Instruction and Amusement of Little Master Tommy and Pretty Miss Polly* was a new attempt to teach children the use of the alphabet by way of diversion. It included rhymed directions and morals, games, fables, proverbs, rules of behavior, poems, and a rhyming alphabet. This publication and Newbery's bookshop earned him a place in children's literature matched by no other. The Newbery Medal, named in his honor, is given annually

Title page from *The History of Little Goody Two Shoes,* attributed to Oliver Goldsmith. After much poverty, Goody Two Shoes acquired "learning and wisdom," which she passed on to others.

for the most distinguished contribution to literature for children published in the United States. In 1765, he published ***The Renowned History of Little Goody Two Shoes.*** Attributed to Oliver Goldsmith, the bittersweet story tells of Margery Meanwell, an orphan who is taken in by a virtuous clergyman and his wife. When they buy her new shoes, she is so overcome with gratitude that she cries out, "Two shoes, Madam, see my two shoes"—and thus her name. ("Goody," a polite term for a woman of humble social standing—a "Good-woman"—was often used as a title preceding a surname.) Margery, forced to leave the house of the clergyman, persists in learning to read and goes from house to house teaching other children. Her virtue and goodness spill forth from the pages, and even today "Little Goody Two Shoes" connotes a saintly, pious, albeit saccharine child.

Darton, noted historian of children's books, places Newbery's deeds in context:

> It is no good pretending that John Newbery was consistent, or had any reasoned theory of infant psychology, or was an apostle of this or that school of educational thought. He was simply an active and benevolent tradesman, who was the first to see that, in his line of business, children's books deserved special attention and development. (1982, pp. 4–5)

Thus in a bookstore in England began what was to become a major force in children's lives—literature for pleasure as well as education.

Beyond Religion: Didacticism and Entertainment

Continuing the movement toward books for pleasure, literature for children changed considerably from the late eighteenth through the nineteenth century. The "good godly" books of the Puritans were still widespread at the beginning of this period, with characters who were noble, virtuous, and strongly religious. Gradually, fantasy, poetry, and picture books developed, and a strong movement toward entertaining realistic fiction grew.

At the end of the eighteenth century the child portrayed in books was polite, diligent, dutiful, and prudent. Adults expected children to be well informed and, to that end, to seek information doggedly. Questions by children, such as "Pray Papa, what is a camel?" would trigger a flow of factual information from the all-knowing adult. Parents, teachers, and ministers were unquestioned as ultimate sources of information and as translators of God's prescriptions for behavior.

In spite of this earnest regard for instilling in children the fundamentals of moral and righteous living, there emerged early in the nineteenth century a belief that these same ideas could be made more palatable by presenting them in the guise of entertainment. Children had already taken for their own several books that had been written for adults, but in the early 1800s a new type of book began to appear: stories written expressly for enjoyment by children.

Many of the books read by North American children were first published in Europe, then brought to the New World. A few of these, in addition to the textbooks and books of religious and moral instruction, were epics and ballads, as well as narrative accounts of explorations and stories of adventure. Several books (in particular **The Pilgrim's Progress, Robinson Crusoe, Gulliver's Travels,** and **The Swiss Family Robinson**), although not originally written for children, were widely read by them. Despite the somber, moralistic tone of some of these stories, children no doubt relished them for their departure from the rigid lessons of their textbooks.

In addition to the adult books that children adopted from mainstream literature, other stories written specifically for young people became popular, and many made their way to America. Although the stern work ethic that prevailed well into the 1800s condemned such frivolity, many children did have access to fairy tales and other books published abroad, including Charles Perrault's **Histoires ou Contes du Temps Passé avec Moralités (Stories or Tales of Times Past with Morals)** and **Contes de ma Mère l'Oye (Tales of Mother Goose),** which included "Sleeping Beauty," "Little Red Riding Hood," "Blue Beard," "Puss in Boots," "Cinderella," and "Tom Thumb." Most adults, however, did not want their children to waste time on frivolous stories; fairy tales still were considered a dangerous and corrupting influence on the child.

Building on a market that John Newbery had clearly established, some publishers commissioned authors to write expressly for children; many of these writers were women. Most of the books that they wrote were didactic and moralistic; some omitted religion entirely while others continued the link between morality and religion in their stories (Hodges & Steinfirst, 1980).

Three important women writers during this period were Sarah Kirby Trimmer (1741–1810), Anna Laetitia Aiken Barbauld (1743–1825), and Maria Edgeworth (1767–1849). These women were a product of their times: They wanted their books to be enjoyed and at the same time to teach children acceptable modes of behavior. Mrs. Trimmer, mother of twelve children, published her most popular book, **Fabulous Histories,** in 1786. The book, reissued frequently under the title **The History of the Robins,** was a collection of fables about a robin family with lessons for a human family. The father robin addresses his children Robin, Dicky, Flapsy, and Pecksy:

> You must be sensible, my dear young ones, that from the time you left the egg-shell, till the present instant, both your mother and I have nourished you with the tenderest love. We have taught you all the arts of life which are necessary to procure you subsistence, and preserve you from danger. . . . Let none of your own species excel you in any amiable quality, for want of your endeavours to equal the best; and do your duty in every relation of life, as we have done ours by you. (Demers & Moyles, 1982, p. 190)

Anna Laetitia Aiken published her first volume of adult poems in 1773 before her marriage to the Reverend Rochemont Barbauld in 1774. The newly married couple began teaching at an English boys' school where Mrs. Barbauld wrote **Easy Lessons for Children and Hymns in Prose (1786),** which were created for her adopted son Charles and her other students. The lessons came in thinly disguised stories expressing her conviction that there was a proper order for parents and children to follow. In Hymn VIII, she writes,

> See where stands the cottage of the labourer, covered with warm thatch; the mother is spinning at the door; the young children sport before her on the grass; the elder ones learn to labour, and are obedient; the father worketh to provide them food . . . his children run to meet him when he cometh home, and his wife prepareth the wholesome meal. (Demers & Moyles, 1982, p. 188)

Maria Edgeworth, the eldest daughter in a large Irish family, knew firsthand the likes and dislikes of children. Her mother died a few years after her birth; her father remarried three times and fathered 21 children, 18 of whom survived infancy. To entertain and instruct the ever-expanding Edgeworth brood Maria wrote stories, tried them out on her siblings, revised them, and then copied them over in ink (Goldstone, 1984, p. 48).

Maria Edgeworth's most famous story, though perhaps not her best, is **The Purple Jar.** The story about Rosamond first appeared in **The Parent's Assistant** in 1796. Rosamond craves a glowing purple jar in an apothecary's window, but her mother suggests a much needed new pair of shoes instead. Rosamond chooses the purple jar and her shoes grow more shabby until at last she cannot run, dance, jump, or walk in them. Her mother cannot take her on walks, and her father cannot take her with him on an outing to see a glasshouse because of her worn-out shoes. Her closing remark shows that although she is remorseful and repentant, she still recognizes her fallibility in the future:

"O mamma, . . . how I wish that I had chosen the shoes! They would have been of so much more use to me than that jar: however, I am sure—no not quite sure, but I hope I shall be wiser another time" (Darton, 1982, pp 144–145).

The story appeals because of the excellence of the narrative; we want to find out what happens despite the oppressive certainty that a calamity with a vivid moral will befall the injudicious little girl. We dislike the mother although we know she is right, and we loathe rectitude accordingly. In the end, however, we know that Rosamond is a real child (Darton, 1982).

Thomas Day (1748–1789), a contemporary of the didactic English women writers, was a fervent follower of Rousseau in his books, *The History of Sandford and Merton* (three volumes: 1783, 1786, 1789) and *The History of Little Jack* (1788). Harry Sandford, a farmer's son, is a bright, well-informed boy with no faults. Tommy Merton, from a wealthy family, is a spoiled brat, illiterate and high handed. Harry rescues Tommy, the two boys become friends, and they become students of Mr. Barlow. Harry is receptive to his teacher's guidance, but Tommy is slow to learn. Throughout the stories, the author draws contrasts between the eager learner and the simpleton who gradually learns to mend his ways. This good boy–bad boy story was repeated frequently in the literature of this period.

The Influence of National Pride

During the late eighteenth and early nineteenth century, American religious leaders continued to encourage writers to instruct the young in proper and virtuous living but other books developed a feeling of patriotism. After the Revolutionary War, Americans, struggling to become a united nation, were eager to show they were no longer a part of England. Authors tried to develop a sense of pride in their country, extolling the virtues of the new land. Many books were provincial and overstated, claiming Americans were more fortunate than others, and that other people were to be pitied because they were strange and different.

Adventure stories of travel on the American frontier and courageous battles with the Indians became a part of the material young people read. Most books were just as didactic as the earlier "teach and preach" books but added history and geography lessons as well as the new American "work hard and make good" ethic.

Good behavior and knowledge continued to be valued. Between 1825 and 1850, Samuel Griswold Goodrich, who believed books would guide children along the right path, collaborated with other writers, including Nathaniel Hawthorne, to produce the Peter Parley books. Peter Parley is a venerable old gentleman who answers—in *Tales of Peter Parley*

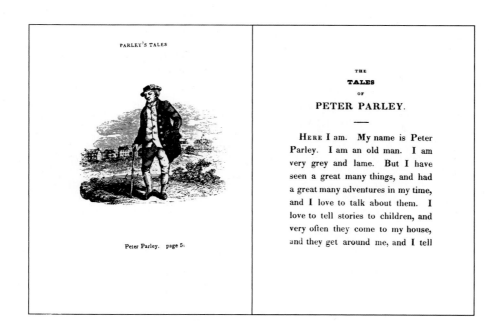

Opening of *The Tales of Peter Parley About America,* stories of travel and adventure with a wise mentor that offered lessons on geography and manners. (From *Yankee Doodle's Literary Sampler of Prose, Poetry & Pictures.* Selected from the Rare Book Collections of the Library of Congress and introduced by Virginia Haviland and Margaret N. Coughlan.)

about America (1827) and in more than a hundred titles that followed—the many questions about history, geography, and science children put to him. Although some books were designed as textbooks, most were what were then called "toy books," intended for out-of-school reading. They were simple, well illustrated, clearly printed, and inexpensive. Despite the wide approval for the information and codes of conduct in the books, the slight story frames were often criticized as contrivances that made children imaginative and indolent (Perkinson, 1978). Nevertheless, the Peter Parley books were the first of a new kind of literature for children—series books.

There was a subsequent deluge of series books, which children eagerly devoured as an alternative to their textbooks. Jacob Abbott wrote a series about a young boy who eagerly learns all he can about his world while remaining ever mindful of his supposedly superior American heritage. The series, *Rollo's Tour in Europe,* reads like a travelogue, with wise Uncle George serving as guide and mentor to young Rollo. Rollo eventually returns to America "with the satisfied consciousness of hailing from a land superior to those inhabited by foreigners" (Jordan, 1983, pp. 48–49). The democratic form of government was still budding, and authors felt obliged to tell readers they were very lucky to live in America.

Books for General Instruction

The New England Primer continued to be a popular textbook for children during the first half of the 1800s. It was revised several times, reflecting changing American values. For example, immediately followed the American Revolution a great increase in textbooks intended to develop a purely American education. Books were marked by practicality and loyalty, with Noah Webster pointing the way with his spelling book.

The United States was 60 years old before the first system of public education was established—in Massachusetts, under the leadership of Horace Mann. As the young country expanded westward, organized public education was slow to follow, so that decades passed before all children had access to schools. The textbook was the primary tool of education in early nineteenth-century America. Because school attendance was sporadic, at best, and children most often learned their lessons at home, the textbook was the one constant in a pupil's educational experience. Students always knew where they were in their studies: They had completed the Primer or were halfway through Webster; textbooks marked pupils' progress. The method of

study was always the same: Students memorized the lessons and then recited them to the teacher or monitor.

McGuffey's *Eclectic Readers* first appeared in 1834. These were a series of books of increasing difficulty and were filled with stories, poems, and information by many authors: the first American basal reader. They provided a national literature and a national curriculum for a people who sought stability, a common culture, and continuity in their rapidly changing lives.

The Need for Fantasy

Children had little time for childhood in the mid-nineteenth century. The social and economic conditions of the time dictated that many young people work, often in truly horrible circumstances. The Industrial Revolution brought with it the necessity for a plentiful supply of cheap labor; and so women, children, and immigrants were enticed to the cities to lives that were filled with unremitting drudgery and a considerable amount of danger. Women and children worked 12 hours a day, 6 days a week in the mills, and gruesome accidents were common (Holland, 1970).

The society that tolerated such horrendous conditions developed a literature that served both as a fantasy escape from the harsh workaday world and a justification of the work ethic. Although much of the fanciful literature came from England it was welcomed by many hard-working American children as well.

Alice's Adventures in Wonderland (1865) and *Through the Looking Glass* (1871), by Charles Dodgson (pseudonym, Lewis Carroll), are recognized as the first significant works of fantasy for children. Dodgson, cleric and mathematics professor who took up the pen name to avoid identification with his books, often told stories to the three Liddell girls, daughters of a minister friend at Christ Church, Oxford. On an afternoon boat ride, his favorite, Alice, asked for a story with nonsense. The story she heard that day became the world-famous one after he wrote it down for her the following Christmas.

The curious, complicated kind of nonsense Alice Liddell loved intrigues readers who become "curiouser and curiouser" along with Alice as she follows a white rabbit down a hole under a hedge. Thus begins the story of memorable madness read by generations of children and adults alike. The story, filled with subtleties that poke fun at English social customs of the time, has a satiric meaning that often eludes modern readers, but the cleverness of the story still holds them.

The tea party, drawn by John Tenniel for Lewis Carroll's *Alice's Adventures in Wonderland* and *Through the Looking Glass.* Carroll and Tenniel conferred frequently during the preparation of the drawings.

Another English writer whose fantasies were loved in America was Edith Nesbit, a talented writer who combined realism and fantasy. Her series, *The Story of the Treasure Seekers* (1899), is about the six Bastable children who had an unmistakable propensity for getting into trouble. The mixture of realism and fantasy in their chaotic adventures laid the foundations for many stories to come, notable among them P. L. Travers's *Mary Poppins* (1934).

The Budding of Poetry

In the seventeenth century, Mother Goose verses provided young children with poetic forms and lilting songs to delight the ear; a great deal of doggerel and sentimental stanzas existed as well. Riddles and traditional rhymes were also plentiful, but little poetry was written especially for children until the middle of the nineteenth century.

In children's poetry, however, as in all other literary forms, some truly great works preceded the flowering of the genre. The English poet William Blake (1757–1827) was one of the first to capture the spirit of childhood in verse. Barely noticed in his lifetime, his *Songs of Innocence* (1789) and *Songs of Experience* (1794) are masterpieces. Although not written for children, the poems in *Songs of Innocence* portray the human mind with a childlike quality. In the introduction, Blake begins:

> *Piping down the valleys wild,*
> *Piping songs of pleasant glee,*
> *On a cloud I saw a child,*
> *And he laughing said to me.*
> *Pipe a song about a Lamb. (1925, p. 65)*

Blake's poems show the child as refreshingly curious and responding intuitively to unfathomable beauty; they are a benchmark for all subsequent poetry of this kind.

Ann Taylor (1782–1866) and Jane Taylor (1783–1824), daughters of a British engraver, began writing verses when they were very young. When Ann was 22 and Jane 21, the two published *Original Poems for Infant Minds by Several Young Persons* (1804). Their memorable verses had a childlike spirit despite an intent to teach a lesson. Among those that children still learn today are "Twinkle, twinkle, little star" by Jane Taylor and "Welcome, welcome little stranger, to this busy world of care" by Ann Taylor. Rare exceptions among the now forgotten sermonlike verses typical of their time, these childlike poems live on.

Some early stories and poems became so commonly known and so widespread it is difficult to remember they are not from folklore: for example, "Mary had a little lamb" (1830) by Sarah Josepha Hale and "'Will you walk into my parlor?' said the Spider to the Fly" in *Fireside Verses* (1799–1888) by Mary Howitt.

Most nineteenth-century poets still had a strong desire to teach a lesson, but some went beyond preachy moralistic verses. A few early English poets portrayed life from a child's perspective and sang the pleasures of childhood as children saw them. The tradition begun by William Blake led to the poetic conventions we draw on today. Early poets include William Roscoe, *The Butterfly's Ball* (1806); Edward Lear, *A Book of Nonsense* (1846); William Allingham, *In Fairyland* (1870); Robert Louis Stevenson, *A Child's Garden of Verses* (1885); and A. A. Milne, *When We Were Very Young* (1924) and *Now We Are Six* (1927).

An American, Clement C. Moore, produced a poetic work, *A Visit from St. Nicholas* (1823), that would keep the magic of Christmas in our hearts. Written for his children, it appeared anonymously in the Troy (N.Y.) *Sentinel* on December 23, 1823; it was a rarity in its complete freedom from the didacticism so prevalent at the time. Children's delight in the visions his words called forth caused them to take it for their own and, as an owner's right, to rename it "The Night Before Christmas," which it shall forever remain. Moore's call

> To the top of the porch, to the top of the wall!
> Now, dash away, dash away, dash away all!
> (1823; 1971)

might have been signaling the beginning of the boundless visions future poets would paint.

Richard Doyle's imaginative illustrations complement William Allingham's imaginative poetry. (From Allingham's *In Fairyland*—1870.)

George Cruikshank's artistry brought to life the fairy folk, giants, and sprites of classic tales. (From *The History of Jack and the Beanstalk* by Cruikshank.)

Walter Crane believed that children prefer well-defined forms and bright, strong colors, so he used black line with flat, brilliant, and delicate colors. He attributed these characteristics to the influence of Japanese prints. (*An Alphabet of Old Friends*)

☞ The Development of Illustration

Book illustration has developed into a fine art through the growth of publishing specifically for children. Illustrations carry great importance because the art in books may be the only art some children ever see; certainly it is the first they see and has a lasting impact on a developing taste for beauty.

Children's book illustration began to flower during the nineteenth century, although its beginnings were in the mid-seventeenth century. Illustrated books actually began with the artless (and often anonymous) woodcuts of children's eighteenth-century catechism pages. Printers used any woodcuts they had, not necessarily ones that went with the story.

---

*T*EACHING IDEA 1-4

Comparing Old and New Picture Books (P–I–A)

Ask students to collect old picture books from parents, grandparents, relatives, neighbors, friends, librarians, antique book dealers, flea markets, or garage sales. Visit a museum or library collection of historical children's books to examine the books at close range. If you cannot locate any old books, select reprinted classics, such as *Alice in Wonderland, The Tale of Peter Rabbit, John Gilpin's Ride*, or *Peter Parley*. Choose early Newbery (1922) and Caldecott (1938) winners. At the same time, collect several recent picture books, preferably prize winners, to compare the new and the old. Prepare a chart of elements to compare. For example,

	Old Title	New Title
Color		
Style of Art		
Relation to Story		
Quality of Art as Art		
Attractiveness		
Visual Appeal		
Questions to Ask About the Books:		

Do the books reflect the year they were published?
Is the art coordinated with the text?
How were children dressed in the old/new books?
How are children expected to behave then and now?
Does the art survive as good art?
Is the layout and design appealing?

George Cruikshank (1792–1878), one of the early outstanding artists, illustrated **Grimm's Fairy Tales** in 1823. His luxuriant style extended the fancy of the tenacious tales and became the standard by which other art was judged. Cruikshank came into his own with fairy art, and **George Cruikshank's Fairy Library** (1853–54), published in four volumes, contains some of his most memorable work.

At first artists merely lightened the text with decoration or with occasional illustrations that filled gaps in the page or emphasized crucial moments in the story. Because of technical limitations they seldom achieved a perfect match between their picture images and the author's literary images. Full-fledged illustrations—by Walter Crane, John Tenniel, Kate Greenaway, and Randolph Caldecott—soon followed, however.

Walter Crane, the son of a portrait painter, abhorred the cheap, crudely illustrated books for children of his day. Despite the venture's high financial risk, publisher Frederick Warne brought out Walter Crane's first nursery picture books—**Sing a Song of Sixpence, The House that Jack Built, Dame Trot and Her Comical Cat,** and **The History of Cock**

Robin and Jenny Wren—in 1865–1866, launching Crane's productive career.

John Tenniel left his artistic mark on Lewis Carroll's **Alice's Adventures in Wonderland** (1865) and **Through the Looking Glass** (1871). His mark is so substantial that we find it difficult to think of Alice except in the ways Tenniel envisioned her.

Randolph Caldecott (1846–1886) published his illustrations in numerous magazines in England and the United States, but the turning point in his career was **The Diverting History of John Gilpin** (1878). This picture book immortalized Caldecott in the field of children's literature and was followed by 16 others. The U.S. Caldecott Award for outstanding illustration is named in his honor. A scene from *John Gilpin* appears on the medallion.

Kate Greenaway (1846–1901) is noted for renditions of prim, well-groomed children surrounded by the bouquets and garden scenes from her childhood. **Under the Window** (1878), which was her first picture book, was followed by a long and distinguished line of books marked with her unique style and charm. The Greenaway Medal, the English counterpart of the U.S. Caldecott Medal for distinguished illustration, is named in her honor.

Kate Greenaway's proper, well-groomed Victorian children, who look like miniature adults, dance to the tune of the Pied Piper's flute. (Robert Browning, *The Pied Piper of Hamelin*)

Gradually, illustrations became more integrated with the text than the early decorative panels. Artists were no longer peripheral but rather partners in the storytelling itself. The growth of literacy and improvements in printing that lowered the cost of books led to greater distribution of books as the nineteenth century progressed. New technologies enabled publishers to provide more than a frontispiece or sporadic illustration. In the 1860s, publisher Edmund Evans, who joined Walter Crane in criticizing the poor quality of art in children's books, introduced the use of color. The development of photoengraving processes in the 1880s finally freed artists from the tyranny of the hand-engraved (and distorting) translation of their art.

Illustrations in children's books were boosted in their evolution toward distinctive style and design.

➤ The Growth of Realism

The desire to instruct children in the work ethic was nowhere more evident than in the series begun by Horatio Alger in 1868. Humble characters reaped generous rewards for hard work and conscientiousness. They epitomized the work ethic and had so strong an impact that the name Horatio Alger still invokes this message today. Alger was a prolific author, turning out more than 100 stories in which the male characters acquire power and

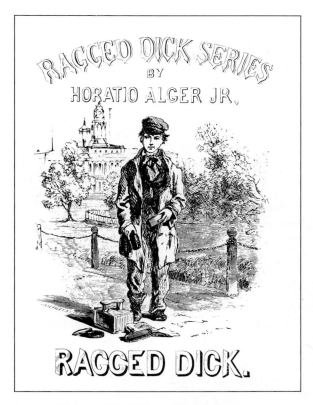

Cover of *Ragged Dick,* one of many formula stories by Horatio Alger, Jr., with the theme that hard work and good behavior are rewarded with success.

From the mid-nineteenth century, the Elsie Dinsmore stories captured the imaginations of young ladies and extolled Victorian feminine virtues. (From *Elsie Dinsmore* written by Martha Finley)

wealth through fortitude, dauntless courage, and the exercise of impeccable morality. The stories were dramatic—snatching a baby from a burning building or a damsel from the heels of a runaway horse were all in a day's work for the Alger hero— and children read them avidly. Alger broke literary tradition—for example, by setting *Ragged Dick* (1868) in a New York slum rather than in the customary rural surroundings. Subtitled "Street Life in New York with the Boot Blacks," *Ragged Dick,* like all the other books in the series, traces a poor boy's achievement of wealth and respectability.

Mass-produced series books that appeared during the middle of the nineteenth century set a trend that continues today. *Rollo Learning to Talk* (1834) by Jacob Abbott, *Boys of '76* (1876) by Charles C. Coffin, and *The Young Buglers* (1880) by George Henty signaled a torrent of such books to follow.

Whereas books for boys, filled with thrills of travel and adventure, urged them to strive and succeed, those for girls urged their readers to practice the tamer arts of homemaking and virtues of kindness, sympathy, and piety. Martha Farquharson (Finley) epitomized melodrama in the *Elsie Dinsmore* stories, wherein tears and prayers were called forth regularly. Young girls devoured these stories and eagerly followed Elsie throughout her lifetime. Elsie Dinsmore is a link in the chain of tearful, saintly girls that includes *Little Goody Two Shoes* and Rosamond (of *The Purple Jar*).

Gradually a new type of literature appeared in which characters were more human. Priggishness gave way to devilment as boys—but not yet girls— were portrayed more realistically. Thomas Bailey Aldrich's semiautobiographical *The Story of a Bad Boy* (1870) acknowledges tricks, pranks, and mischievous behavior in a "boys will be boys" spirit:

I did n't ask the Captain's leave to attend this ceremony, for I had a general idea that he would n't give it. If the Captain, I reasoned, does n't forbid me, I break no orders by going. (1870; 1976, pp. 346–347)

This book began an era of "bad boy literature" that peaked in Mark Twain's ***The Adventures of Huckleberry Finn*** (1884) but continues even now.

Girls were given an alternative to the melodrama of Elsie Dinsmore when Louisa May Alcott wrote ***Little Women*** in 1868. Although considered too worldly by fundamentalist leaders, ***Little Women*** has been called the century's most significant piece of fiction. Alcott's substantial work focused on the homespun virtues of the wholesome American family.

Girls also found pleasure in a series of family stories by Margaret Sidney (pseudonym of Harriet M. Lothrop). ***The Five Little Peppers and How They Grew*** (1880) begins a series—filled with touching sentimentality—about a widowed mother and her brave struggles to raise her children. Embedded in the idyllic family life portrayed is the idea that generosity, humility, and proper manners earn rewards, whereas the opposite end in atonement.

The last half of the nineteenth century also brought a surge of inexpensive, aesthetically poor, mass-produced books written according to a formula and printed on spongy, poor quality paper. These series books, unlike those of the early part of the century, had no literary distinction or originality to recommend them. Children, however, devoured them with the same uncritical enthusiasm as readers of today's series books. The Immortal Four—Finley, Alger, Adams, and Fosdick—all used a variety of pseudonyms under which they ground out hundreds of books. This wave of fast-paced,

*L*OUISA MAY ALCOTT grew up in "genteel poverty," as she called it. Her father, Bronson Alcott, was a visionary whose educational and social views were far in advance of his times. Their neighbors (Ralph Waldo Emerson, Henry David Thoreau, and Nathaniel Hawthorne) were among the outstanding intellectual leaders of the day and although Louisa's life was not rich in material things, it was rich in books and ideas. Louisa May Alcott's writings reflect many of her day's popular literary and social movements. Magazine stories and cheap novels in the gothic style inspired by Mary Shelley's ***Frankenstein*** were great popular favorites, and Louisa began her life's work of rescuing her beloved family from chronic poverty by scribbling these potboilers for the ever-hungry publishers.

She was deeply affected by—and involved in—the social issues of her day, particularly the emancipation of the slaves. Louisa spent several

Louisa May Alcott

months nursing wounded soldiers in a Civil War army hospital, where conditions were deplorable. With her own health impaired, Louisa returned home from this exhausting experience to produce her first serious book, ***Hospital Sketches*** (c. 1866). Its instant popularity inspired her to continue writing serious fiction. Her astute publisher, Thomas Niles, encouraged her to write

cheap, and extremely popular books provoked adult objections, but as entertainment they gained much popularity with children.

Building on the success of Horatio Alger and the Elsie Dinsmore series, other writers produced quantities of fast-moving adventure stories. One enterprising writer, Edward Stratemeyer, developed a scheme that became a vast syndicate responsible for the mass publication of millions of tawdry juvenile books—some available even today. With this scheme of mass marketing, children no longer had to read books under an adult's Sunday supervision or with clean hands; inexpensive production had made books dispensable.

After working for pulp magazines, Stratemeyer wrote **Under Dewey at Manila** shortly after the

Spanish-American War. He enjoyed writing war stories and began several series with America's wars as background. As Stratemeyer's syndicate grew, he limited his participation to outlining the stories and hired hack writers, producing in this way the Colonial Boys series, the Mexican War series, and the Pan American series. He continued with other series, including those of the Rover Boys, the Motor Boys, Tom Swift, the Hardy Boys, and the Bobbsey Twins—using the pseudonyms Arthur Winfield, Clarence Young, Victor Appleton, Franklin W. Dixon, and Laura Lee Hope, respectively. Stratemeyer produced 68 different series under 46 pseudonyms. At his death in 1935, his daughter, Harriet Stratemeyer Adams, took over the massive operation, which still produces books.

CONTINUED

"something for girls." **Little Women** (1868) was the result. In its pages and in those of the several novels and dozens of short stories that followed, readers glimpse much of the popular culture of the times. **Little Women** is one of the first and finest examples of realistic fiction.

Louisa herself was an avid reader, and through Jo (in **Little Women**) we see the influence of **The Pilgrim's Progress** and the work of Charles Dickens. We also hear the story of Rosamond (of **The Purple Jar**) retold and find occasional references to the novels of "dear Miss Yonge," one of Alcott's predecessors in writing the American family story.

Many books followed **Little Women,** namely **An Old-Fashioned Girl** (1869), **Little Men** (1871), **Work** (1873), **Eight Cousins** (1874), **Rose in Bloom** (1876), **Under the Lilacs** (1877), **Jack and Jill** (1879), and **Jo's Boys** (1886). These have been reissued and are widely read. Alcott's short stories have also been reissued: **Glimpses**

of Louisa appeared in 1968, the centennial of **Little Women;** Alcott's **An Old-Fashioned Thanksgiving** was reissued as a picture book.

Interested readers find additional information in such sources as "Louisa May Alcott and the American Family Story" in *A Critical History of Children's Literature* by Cornelia Meigs et al.; *Bronson Alcott: His Life and Philosophy* by F. B. Sanborn and W. T. A. Harris; Cornelia Meig's *Invincible Louisa;* and Gretchen Anderson's *Louisa May Alcott Cookbook.* The cookbook (Illus. Karen Milone. Little, Brown, 1985) re-creates recipes from nineteenth century cookbooks for dishes mentioned in Alcott's books. Recipes for tarts, pies, plum pudding, and steak and potatoes accompany excerpts from the novels; full-page drawings and text describe the life and work of Louisa May Alcott. A 9-year-old student in a gifted and talented class started the cookbook as a class project.

Gradually Americans could envision the world beyond our shores and provincialism waned; authors began to write about children in other lands. For example, Mary Mapes Dodge wrote **Hans Brinker; or, The Silver Skates** (1865), which, though ostensibly to teach American children about life in far-off Holland, was enjoyed most for its exciting story. Similarly, Johanna Spyri wrote **Heidi** (1884) to give a glimpse of life in Switzerland, but children loved it for its portrayal of a young girl's relationship with her grandfather.

Magazines

Many of the early magazines for children were Sunday school periodicals filled with religious sayings and anecdotes. There was *The Encourager* (Methodist), *The Children's Magazine* (Episcopal), *The Juvenile Instructor* (Mormon), and *Catholic Youth's Magazine*. Even secular ones such as *Frank Leslie's Chatterbox* (1879–1886) advertised that it intended to "improve the mind, diffuse knowledge," and provide good, healthy, and interesting literature for the young. Each sketch promised to convey a moral or some useful information in only the purest tone and language.

St. Nicholas (1873–1943) was a prestigious children's magazine that lasted for 70 years and had excellent contributing writers. Notable among them was Frank Stockton, a frequent contributor to and later associate editor of *St. Nicholas*. Another editor of *St. Nicholas,* Mary Mapes Dodge, best known for her **Hans Brinker,** actively sought established writers and artists to contribute to the magazine. The creative leadership of these two accounted for the primary position the magazine maintained for three-quarters of a century and the standards of excellence it set for the entire children's publishing world. Work by Arthur Rackham, Frances Hodgson Burnett, Howard Pyle, Rudyard Kipling, and Laura E. Richards often graced its pages. Many of the short stories were reprinted as books, and anthologies of its articles were published; some of the serialized novels remain classics today. Frances Hodgson Burnett's **Sara Crewe** (1888); Frank Stockton's **America's Birthday Party** (1876); Susan Coolidge's **What Katy Did** (1872); Louisa May Alcott's **Jo's Boys** (1873), **An Old-Fashioned Girl** (1870), and **Eight Cousins** (1875); Rudyard Kipling's **The Jungle Book** (1894); and Lucretia P. Hale's **The Peterkin Papers** (1880) first appeared in the pages of *St. Nicholas*.

The Youth's Companion (1827–1929) survived 102 years, longer than any other magazine in

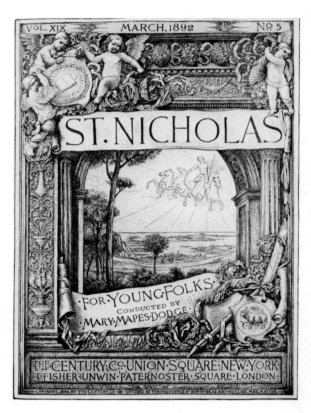

A cover from **St. Nicholas** magazine, in which many authors who became noted in the field of children's books were first published. (**Yankee Doodle's Literary Sampler of Prose, Poetry & Pictures,** introduced by Virginia Haviland and Margaret N. Coughlan)

America; in 1929, it merged with *The American Boy,* which ceased publication in 1941. From the beginning, editorial policy demanded that its content remain seemly; parents could give the weekly magazine to their children without fear of introducing them to any untoward subject. In addition to the enticement of a distinguished list of contributors— Sarah Orne Jewett, Jack London, Theodore Roosevelt, Henry Wadsworth Longfellow, Alfred Lord Tennyson, James M. Barrie, H. G. Wells, and Oliver Wendell Holmes, among others—the editors offered various premiums to its readers.

The first children's magazine published in America, *The Juvenile Miscellany* (1826–1834), was edited by Lydia Maria Child and became an immediate success. Lydia Maria Francis (later Mrs. Child) was a former teacher who wanted children to learn to read with material they could enjoy, but she found very little that answered this requirement. *The Juvenile Miscellany* filled the void, but when Lydia Maria Child spoke out vehemently against slavery, sales dropped so drastically that the

Edmund Dulac's interpretation of "The Princess and the Pea" was the beginning of a trend: Highly respected artists turned their considerable skill toward illustrating children's stories. ("The Princess and the Pea," in *Stories from Hans Andersen,* illustrated by Edmund Dulac)

magazine stopped publication in 1834. Sarah Josepha Hale's "Mary Had a Little Lamb" first appeared in this magazine.

The Early Twentieth Century

The turn of the century brought a new surge of stories for children. Although moral overtones were not forgotten, most books now contained humor, adventure, and spirit—and enough connection with rough-and-tumble to provide a firm ground for the even more true-to-life stories that were to follow.

Boys were reading adventure books like George Grinnell's *Jack Among the Indians* (1900) and George Henty's *With Kitchener in the Soudan* (1903). Girls' stories retained their emphasis on the quieter virtues of home and family. Among the favorites were Kate Douglas Wiggin's *Rebecca of Sunnybrook Farm* (1903), Lucy M. Montgomery's *Anne of Green Gables* (1908), and Frances Hodgson Burnett's books, including *Little Lord Fauntleroy* (1886) and *The Secret Garden* (1911). One story, *Pollyanna* (1912), by Eleanor Porter became so well loved that the character's name still symbolizes an ever-joyful optimistic disposition. Fantasy also continued to flourish, with stories such as the classic story-play *Peter Pan* (1904) by J. M. Barrie, loved by adults and children everywhere.

Children's book illustration continued to develop as printing processes improved. In the early 1900s, Arthur Rackham created Mother Goose characters and Beatrix Potter created Peter Rabbit, characters who became memorable because of the artists' unique interpretations and rare talents. Edmund Dulac contributed outstanding interpretations of old favorites, such as his classic painting for "The Princess and the Pea." A trend was beginning: Truly talented artists created children's books as a vehicle for their art.

Picture books as we know them today emerged around the turn of the century, when many of today's classic illustrations were published. Some of these were W. W. Denslow's pictures in Baum's *Wizard of Oz* (1900) and L. Leslie Brooke's in *The Golden Goose Book* (1905). These earn the artists a place beside Cruikshank, Crane, Tenniel, Potter, Rackham, Greenaway, and Caldecott as outstanding illustrators of early children's books.

Up to the late 1920s most picture books originated in Europe and were imported to North America. In 1927, William Nicholson's *Clever Bill* was the first picture storybook published in the United States. The still popular *Millions of Cats* (1928) by Wanda Gág followed shortly. It was at this point that an American school of illustration began, with artists using the increasingly sophisticated technology of printing to help them produce their unique visions (Meigs, Eaton, Nesbitt, & Viguers, 1969).

Children's rooms were established in public libraries early in the twentieth century and children flocked to them. At about the same time the first organized review of children's books began appearing in *The Horn Book* and *The Bookman*. Children's departments were created in publishing houses, and promotions such as Children's Book Week were inaugurated. The demand for more books grew. Fortunately, the technology grew along with the demand, and by 1930 it was possible to print low-cost large editions of illustrated books. The result was an increase in the availability of folktales, historical fiction, and poetry for young readers. During this decade Laura Ingalls Wilder began her *Little House* series, and J.R.R. Tolkien wrote *The Hobbit* (1938).

During the period of the Second World War, many talented European artists came to work and live in America. Ingri and Edgar Parin d'Aulaire (*Abraham Lincoln,* 1939), Ludwig Bemelmans (*Madeline,* 1939), and Roger Duvoisin (*White Snow, Bright Snow,* by Alvin Tresselt, 1947) are a few such artists.

During the 1940s and 1950s the children's book industry continued to grow as children's

Ludwig Bemelmans's Parisian background is reflected in scenes he painted for the *Madeline* stories.

books became an increasingly important part of libraries, schools, homes, and publishing houses. Many wonderful books were produced during this time, such as Robert McCloskey's **Make Way for Ducklings** (1941), Eleanor Estes's **The Moffats** (1941), **Johnny Tremain** (1943) by Esther Forbes, **Charlotte's Web** (1952) by E. B. White, **My Side of the Mountain** (1959) by Jean George, and the **Narnia** series by C. S. Lewis.

CHILDREN'S LITERATURE TODAY

Children's literature continues to grow and develop as a field of study. Teachers know that using children's books in the classroom enriches their curriculum. School libraries are filled with students and teachers seeking books, and in many schools the media specialist is a key figure in the classrooms as well. Public librarians see that more children—and younger children—visit libraries to participate in story hours, summer reading programs, after school programs, author visits, and other special events. New organizations and journals are founded to pursue literary criticism, to explore using literature in the classroom, and to promote the use of literature. Television programs such as *Reading Rainbow* are based on children's books, and many public radio stations include children's book reading segments in the early evening hours. More than 400 children's bookstores have opened since 1980. The enthusiasm for children's books is high. Sales of children's books continue to climb.

This enthusiasm for children's books has created new markets and increased production. Whereas approximately 2,000 children's books were published annually by 1960, 5,000 were published annually by 1990. Children's books mean business—big business—for writers, illustrators, publishers, booksellers, and literary agents.

In addition to the illustrated folklore, fantasy, realism, and poetry that marked the beginning of the twentieth century, the beginning of the twenty-first century is marked by toy books, picture books, science fiction, biography, historical fiction, and nonfiction literature for children as well as an increasing paperback market. Each of these genres has changed across the course of the twentieth century.

As the world changes, so, too, does literature for children. The ease of world travel and communication has turned children's books into a global industry. International book fairs lead to co-publishing among many nations. Children's books truly have universal appeal.

The Genres Today

The artistic possibilities in the picture book format attracted many skilled artists to the field of children's books. Marcia Brown, Maurice Sendak, and Chris Van Allsburg are among those whose work typifies the changing styles of the period. Compare Marcia Brown's early art in Perrault's **Cinderella** (1954) with her work in **Once a Mouse** (1961) and later in **Shadow** (1982) to see how she adapts the art to a story and how she has developed as an artist. Sendak's work began as cartoonlike drawings in Krauss's **A Very Special House** (1953) and developed into elaborate art in **Outside Over There** (1981). Chris Van Allsburg began as a talented draftsman in **Ben's Dream** (1982) and grew in his storytelling art in **Polar Express** (1985). Today, picture books come in a wide variety of styles and techniques, and the subject matter is as varied as the art.

Realistic fiction, too, has developed into a genre that grapples with the entire range of human conditions and emotions as the world changes. Modern problems such as addiction, divorce, and homelessness are confronted in realistic fiction as are the more traditional themes of growing up and making friends. Books like **The Language of Goldfish** (A) by Zibby Oneal, **Homecoming** (A) by Cynthia Voigt, and **Fly Away Home** (P–I) by Eve Bunting reflect the realities of life at the end of the twentieth century. Once the province of a narrow segment of the population, realistic fiction now includes children from many cultures and lifestyles, with writers like Virginia Hamilton, Walter Dean Myers, Sharon Bell Mathis, Jean Okimoto, and Lucille Clifton producing books that reflect the cultural diversity we now enjoy.

Series books continue to flourish, with today's readers enjoying modern versions of books that their grandparents enjoyed, such as **Nancy Drew** and **The Hardy Boys.** New series books, such as **The Babysitters' Club, Sweet Valley Twins,** and **Sweet Valley High** (all I–A) have enjoyed tremendous success. There also are several fine series books, such as the **Anastasia** books (I–A) by Lois Lowry and the **Bingo Brown** books (I) by Betsy Byars, written with humor and style, that appeal to today's children.

Realistic books that offer alternate paths for reading, such as the "Choose Your Own Adventure" series, have reached a responsive audience. First developed by Edward Packard and Ray Montgomery, they are now imitated for every age group and developed in every genre. Children read each book several times—until they have exhausted all the alternate routes to the end of the story.

Poetry continues to expand as a genre, reflecting a tremendous growth in interest in poetry and a concomitant increase in the number of books of poetry for children since 1975. Teachers use poetry to teach beginning reading, to expand language, and to enrich experiences across the curriculum. A great diversity of style, content, and poets mark this genre as well. The National Council of Teachers of English Award for Excellence in Poetry for Children calls attention to outstanding poets who write for children. The winners of this award can be found in Appendix A. Today, publishers create an imprint (division) devoted entirely to poetry, whereas they used to publish only one or two poetry books per year.

Folklore has also changed, with folktales from around the world indicating the increasingly international view so prevalent in American children's literature. As rapid advances in transportation technology have increased the possibility for worldwide travel and as international conflicts have increased global awareness, cross-cultural books for children that accurately reflect other lands and cultures have increased. While this growth has occurred in other genres as well, it is most notable in folklore. Similarly, as the composition of North America has become increasingly multicultural, folklore for children has expanded from a predominantly Western European tradition to include folklore of many cultures.

Many internationally known artists lend their particular vision to traditional stories as they interpret classic tales in modern ways. Verna Aardema's interpretations of African folklore, Lawrence Yep and Jeanne Lee's Chinese lore, and Julius Lester and Virginia Hamilton's African-American folklore are some of the many fine stories that reflect the global perspective of people today. The interest in the genre is so high that parodies of traditional tales, books such as John Scieszka's ***The True Story of the Three Little Pigs*** (P–I) and ***The Stinky Cheese Man and Other Fairly Stupid Tales*** (I–A) are also enjoying tremendous popularity.

Fantasy as a genre continues to grow, with many modern fantasy writers creating their own powerful stories redolent with the legacy of folklore. As advances in science led to speculations about the consequences of these advances, science fiction developed. For example, space travel has led to stories of space colonies and intergalactic wars. The time slip novel has become the vehicle of many talented authors who use the fantasy device of the time slip to entice their readers into the past, framing an historical story within a modern setting. Jane Yolen does this in ***Devil's Arithmetic*** (A).

Historical fiction has changed also, with modern writers such as Christopher and James Lincoln Collier re-creating the past for young readers in a more realistic and less laudatory style as they do in ***My Brother Sam Is Dead*** (A). The scope of this fiction has widened to include the whole sweep of history, from prehistory to the Vietnam War era. Mildred Taylor's chronicles of being African American in Mississippi during the depression such as in ***Roll of Thunder, Hear My Cry*** (A), Pam Conrad's stories of pioneer life on the prairie such as ***My Daniel*** (I), and books for younger readers such as ***Dakota Dugout*** (P–I) by Ann Turner enable today's children to read realistic and emotionally rich accounts of times past.

Biographies of important historical, political, and sports figures continue to be written as new individuals become important. New visions of historical figures, such as Russell Freedman's ***The Wright Brothers*** (A), Diane Stanley and Peter Vennema's ***William Shakespeare: Bard of Avon*** (I–A), and Scribner's ***Great Lives*** series (A) provide fresh, clear visions. Biographies are beginning to be more international in scope, with books such as Stanley and Vennema's ***Shaka, King of the Zulus*** (I–A) making historical figures from other nations known to young readers in North America.

The end of the twentieth century has seen a dramatic increase in the number and quality of nonfiction books published for children. Informational books for very young children about any topic you might imagine appear on library shelves. As topics become timely in our lives they appear in nonfiction for children; the recent increase in books about the environment reflects our growing awareness of and concern for the damage to the environment that progress represents. Outer space, world hunger, and natural science topics appear in children's books as rapidly as they appear in the daily newspaper. Illustrations within nonfiction books represent some of the best art to be found in children's books. For example, the **Eyewitness Books** combine stunning photographs and careful drawings to provide a wealth of information about many topics. Alphabet and counting books, once for the very young, have evolved into sophisticated formats for artists to demonstrate their talents. Books designed to inform have evolved into books designed to inform and delight.

Children's magazines continue to be an important part of children's reading material; the fresh surprise of each issue brings a special pleasure. Some of the most popular magazines today center on nature and the environment, with *Ranger Rick, Your Big Backyard,* and *National Geographic World* exemplifying the best. *Highlights for Children,* founded in 1946, contains stories, poems, games, informational articles, and hidden pictures. This excellent general magazine has more than 3 million subscribers. *Cricket* includes outstanding children's literature, often the published work of established authors, and has been so successful that a counterpart for preschool readers, *Ladybug,* is now available. *Cobblestone, Zillions, Sports Illustrated for Kids, U.S. Kids, Math Power, Sesame Street,* and *The Electric Company* promise a bright future for young magazine readers.

Trends in Literature Today

As children's literature has come into its own during this century it has become increasingly important in schools, as well as in libraries and at home. The growth of nonfiction is one result of the essential place of children's literature in today's schools. Easy-to-read books became plentiful during the 1970s as writers like Else Holmelund Minarik and Arnold Lobel demonstrated that young children find beautiful stories both enchanting and easy to read. So, too, today's emphasis on shared reading in schools has led to the production of Big Books, oversized editions of picture books with large print that can be easily read by a teacher and a group of children.

Keeping Up with Children's Books

A major development of the late twentieth century is a tremendous increase in the number of books published for the very young. Board books by artists such as Rosemary Wells and Helen Oxenbury are available in great numbers to delight today's babies. Toy books, such as waterproof books for the bathtub, musical books, lift-the-flap, and pop-up books now abound.

Editions of classic stories accompanied by cassette recordings made by noted actors and musicians and video versions of these same stories have also become plentiful since 1980. The Rabbit Ears productions of Kipling's *How the Camel Got His Hump* and *How the Rhinocerous Got His Skin,* narrated by Jack Nicholson with music by Bobby McFerrin, and Robin Williams's narration of *Pecos Bill* delight children of all ages. The best of these productions are faithful to the story while being cleverly interpreted by the readers and musicians.

The current widespread use of paperbacks accounts for a sizable part of the increase in children's book publishing and sales. Teachers and librarians have found that students *like* to read paperbacks even more than they like to read hardcover books. Distribution in book clubs, discount stores, drugstores, grocery stores, and airports has made children's paperbacks widely accessible.

Perhaps the most exciting trend in literature today is the increasingly culturally diverse nature of children's books. A number of small presses, like Children's Book Press, Open Hand Press, and Tundra Books, have a multicultural or cross-cultural focus, and many of the larger publishing houses are offering more titles that reflect a global perspective. Organizations such as the International Board on Books for Young People, with members from around the world, keep the spotlight on global literature.

KEEPING UP WITH CHILDREN'S BOOKS

It is clear from the voluminous body of high-quality children's literature that the field has attracted many talented writers and illustrators. Creative people continually respond to and change their world, so innovations will always be a part of the children's book world. If the number of books published continues to increase, as it probably will, selection will become even more difficult because of the sheer volume. Our job as teachers, librarians, and parents is to select the best from the vast array of books.

As poet Walter de la Mare stated more than fifty years ago, "Only the rarest kind of best is good enough for children" (1942, p. 9).

Fortunately, we as teachers have help in making informed judgments about children's books. The primary goal of this textbook is to make clear what is good literature and why it is good. We also have several review journals on which we can rely for information about good books, and we have established awards for children's books that call attention to the best in literature for children.

Review Journals and Other Resources

The best sources of information about new books are the review journals: *The Horn Book Magazine, The Horn Book Guide, Bulletin of the Center for Children's Books (BCCB), School Library Journal (SLJ), Booklist,* and *Booklinks.* Addresses for each are found in the "Book Selection Aids" appendix.

The *BCCB,* published monthly except August, and *Booklist,* published twice monthly from September through June and monthly in July and August, contain reviews of books, audiovisual materials, and computer software for children and adolescents. *The Horn Book Magazine,* published six times a year, and *SLJ,* published eleven times a year, contain discriminating reviews of high-quality new books as well as articles by authors, illustrators, publishers, teachers, librarians, critics, editors, and others interested in the field of children's literature.

Other selection resources are also available. The cumulative *Horn Book Guide* contains ratings and reviews of all books published January–June and July–December each year. The books are grouped by genre, with within-genre subheadings. There are also book-length bibliographies, like *Adventuring with Books,* which is published regularly by the National Council of Teachers of English. *Booklinks* is specially written for teachers and librarians who use literature in the curriculum. Articles center on books related to a theme or feature one author's work.

Other journals that focus primarily on classroom practices can be excellent sources of information about children's books. *Language Arts,* by the National Council of Teachers of English, and *The Reading Teacher,* by the International Reading Association, are published from September through May and have monthly children's book review columns. *The New Advocate,* published quarterly, contains articles about children's literature by teachers, librarians, authors, and illustrators and also has a review column.

Children's Book Awards

The excitement in the children's book world reaches fever pitch in mid-January when it is Newbery and Caldecott selection time. The selection committees have read all the books published during the year and meet in long sessions to decide which books will be the winners of these two prestigious awards. Waiting to hear who won the Newbery and Caldecott is like waiting for the announcement of the winner of the Pulitzer Prize for Literature. Why are these awards so important? Experts declare that the winners are the outstanding examples of children's literature for the year. The awards have significant educational, social, cultural, and financial impact. The books that receive these awards will be read by and will influence generations of children around the world. In America alone, every public and school library will purchase the award-winning books. Winning one of the awards, therefore, also guarantees considerable financial reward for the author, illustrator, and publisher. The awards receive widespread media attention, and the winning authors and illustrators usually receive numerous speaking invitations.

The John Newbery Medal

Frederic G. Melcher, editor of *Publisher's Weekly* magazine, donated and named this award as a tribute to John Newbery (1713–1767) who was the first English publisher and bookseller of books for children. The award, administered by the Association for Library Services to Children of the American Library Association, was established in 1922 and has been awarded annually ever since. The Newbery Medal is given for the most distinguished contribution to literature for children published in the United States during the year. The judgment is based on the literary quality of the text. A list of winners and honor books is in Appendix A.

The Randolph Caldecott Medal

In 1937, Frederic G. Melcher proposed an award for picture books and named in honor of Randolph Caldecott (1846–1886), the English illustrator who was one of the first to put action and liveliness into illustrations for children. This award, administered by the Association for Library Services to Children of the American Library Association, has been awarded annually since 1938. The Caldecott Medal is given to the illustrator of the most distinguished picture book published in the United States during

The Newbery Award is given annually for the most distinguished writing for children. In this 1993 winner, Cletus, Summer, and Uncle Ob watch for a sign from the heavens that they can interpret as a message from recently deceased Aunt May. (***Missing May*** by Cynthia Rylant)

the year. A list of winners and honor books is in Appendix A.

Other awards for children's books are described here, and the winners of each are listed in Appendix A.

THE HANS CHRISTIAN ANDERSEN AWARD was established in 1956 by the International Board on Books for Young People. It is given every two years to an author who has made an important international contribution to children's literature. Since 1966 an illustrator's award has been given also.

THE INTERNATIONAL READING ASSOCIATION CHILDREN'S BOOK AWARDS were established in 1975 and they are given for the first or second book of a new writer who shows unusual promise in the children's book field.

THE NATIONAL COUNCIL OF TEACHERS OF ENGLISH AWARD FOR EXCELLENCE IN POETRY FOR

The Caldecott Award is given annually for the most distinguished picture book for children. In the 1993 Caldecott Award winner, Mirette walks on the high wire and reaches out to express her courage and friendship toward a retired performer. (*Mirette on the High Wire* by Emily Arnold McCully)

CHILDREN was established in 1977. It is given every three years to a living American poet in recognition of his or her entire body of work.

THE LAURA INGALLS WILDER AWARD, administered by the Association of Library Service to Children of the American Library Association, was established in 1954. It is given every three years, to an author or illustrator who has made a substantial and lasting contribution to children's literature.

THE CHILDREN'S BOOKS: AWARDS AND PRIZES, a comprehensive listing of award winners, is published every six years by the Children's Book Council. The 1992 edition lists approximately 71 awards in the United States selected by adults and 42 selected by young readers, 25 awards granted in the British Commonwealth, 14 Australian, 19 Canadian, 4 New Zealand, and 17 international and multinational awards.

In addition to these individual awards, teachers and librarians should be aware of various lists of outstanding books published annually. The International Reading Association selects a list of new books designated as "Teachers' Choices," which represent new books that teachers feel are outstanding but will require introduction and/or guidance by the teacher if they are to be appreciated by children. The list of Teachers' Choices is published every November in *The Reading Teacher*. *Outstanding Science Trade Books for Children* is published by the National Science Teachers Association, and *Notable Children's Trade Books in the Field of Social Studies* is published by the National Council of Social Studies in the respective journals of their organizations.

Finally, children get to vote annually for books they like in Children's Choices, sponsored by the

Randolph Caldecott's art could be presented in a more appealing manner because of new technologies in color reproduction and photo-engraving processes developed for book publishing in the 1880s. (*An Elegy on the Glory of Her Sex, Mrs. Mary Blaize* by Randolph Caldecott)

𝒯EACHING IDEA 1-5

Creating Your Own Children's Choices (I–A)

1. Conduct a survey of your students' favorite books.
2. Have students write comments about favorite books on index cards.
3. Have students give book talks to promote the reading of their favorite books.
4. Create a classroom file from the index cards for students to browse through when selecting books.

International Reading Association and the Children's Book Council. This list appears annually in the October issue of *The Reading Teacher*. Further, there are many state-sponsored awards for children's books in which children get to vote for their favorites.

SUMMARY

Children's literature today has been shaped by years of history and the visions of those who are involved with children and their books. Books that children read have undergone a vast transformation from the early days of religious exhortations and crude hornbooks to the artistic excellence of children's literature today, and we are the richer for it. As our world has changed, children's books have changed as well, and today's children, poised on the threshold of the twenty-first century, have virtually unlimited opportunities available to them through children's literature.

The diversity and richness of children's literature today can seem overwhelming when you first begin to explore the field, but as you read and study children's literature, discover your personal favorites, talk to your friends about their favorites, discuss books with other teachers, and read this text and journals in the field, you will discover that the delights of the wonderful world of children's books is ample reward for hard work.

2

Children Reading Literature

THE READER VOICE

She took me to the forest
And showed me fairies, elves, and trolls.
We watched a hunter's firewood
Burn low to the glow of coals.

We met a boy who was just like me,
He tried to win each race
And cried alone in his room at home
When he finished second place.

I listened as she read each tale
And made each tale my own,
And now . . . I still hear her magic voice,
Even though I'm old and grown.

Brod Bagert

Memories of special books and those who read them to us stay with us all of our lives. Who we are makes a difference in how we read, and what we read makes a difference in who we are. The experiences we have during our lives shape and are shaped by the books that are important to us.

Many children who love to read get so engrossed in their books that the real world disappears. Parents laugh about calling and calling their children to no avail, and then discovering them curled up somewhere reading, oblivious to what is going on around them. Teachers recognize that good books excite children about reading and encourage them to read widely. Librarians are aware that exciting read-alouds lure children into the library to check out books on their own. Reading researchers have shown that the single most important activity for building the knowledge required for eventual success in reading is reading aloud to children, and that independent reading by children leads to increased fluency

When children enter the world of story, they are swallowed up by it and read independently—even while eating!

and comprehension (Anderson, Hiebert, Scott, & Wilkinson, 1985). Still others note that our vocabularies are enriched and expanded by the books we read (Baumann & Kameenui, 1991).

Children understand their world through cognitive processes; they use language and reasoning to make sense of their experiences, including their experiences with books. Cognitive psychologists realize that a narrative (or story) is structured the same way that the human mind is structured; the way we organize our minds is the way we construct stories (Bruner, 1987; Hardy, 1978). Children's social development also influences the way they make sense of their world, respond to people and books, and adopt feelings and beliefs about themselves. We search for an understanding of ourselves when we read. Child development specialists recognize that literature fosters development and helps children realize their potential.

Beyond a child's immediate world, the culture in which children live also shapes both cognitive and social development. It shapes children's attitudes and understanding about books and the ways that books function in their lives.

Teachers appreciate that a child's imagination is fostered by a story's invitation to pretend. But non-narrative books also play an important role in children's lives. Teachers see how children seek out and devour nonfiction texts and how these books enliven any area of study. Britton (1970) talks of how the language models of well-written books—

narrative, poetic, and informational texts—help form the language that children use in their own speaking and writing.

Yes, the books children read are formative in their lives; it is our responsibility to know their books. It is also our responsibility to know the children, their experiences, how they develop and learn, and how they read and respond to what they read. Useful criteria for choosing literature for children are based on an understanding of children's development and experiences, and a knowledge of children's books. We explore children as readers and classrooms as places that promote reading in this chapter; further discussion of effective classroom practices appears in Chapter 12.

A critical reason for selecting appropriate books is to foster children's connections with the books they read. When we share excellent literature with children we must be sure to consider the age of the child. No matter how wonderful the book, children don't want to be seen reading what they consider to be "baby books." If we miss the golden years of 2 to 4 when Margaret Wise Brown's **Goodnight Moon** (N) strikes a responsive chord, children may never see the charm of it later. If we lose the chance to share Maurice Sendak's **Where the Wild Things Are** (P) when children are 5 to 7, they may never appreciate its magic. Fifth-grade students will not be caught reading Arnold Lobel's **Frog and Toad Are Friends** (P) nor will junior high school students be seen reading **Tuck Everlasting** (I), but what a

Five- to seven-year-old children appreciate Max's fun during a wild rumpus. Sendak says his relatives used to come toward him and say, "I'm going to eat you up." He used them as his models. Notice they are all smiling. (***Where the Wild Things Are*** by Maurice Sendak)

shame if students miss them. There are over 75,000 children's books in print. Children could read omnivorously and still never read an outstanding book. Most importantly, unless children read some of the really good books, they will probably not get hooked as lifelong readers.

We, as teachers, can observe children's responses to literature and other media, and thus become aware of the broad patterns of intellectual organization that structure their thinking. When we come to know the children in our classrooms, we also can learn to make judgments about the appropriateness of specific books for specific children. Most importantly, when we begin to understand the cultural forces that shape our students' lives, we can begin to enlarge our perceptions of "appropriate" to include culturally diverse expressions of literacy. Figure 2-1 contains some guidelines for book selection that can help you make initial judgments about appropriate books. No guidelines, however, can substitute for knowing your students well.

A TRANSACTIONAL VIEW OF READING

Readers construct meaning as they read a text (Goodman, 1985). Instead of absorbing an elusive "one right meaning" from a text, readers rely on their own background knowledge and create unique meanings (Rosenblatt, 1938/1976, 1978).

Meaning does not reside in the text alone, waiting for a reader to unearth it, but is created in the transaction between a text and a reader. As a reader reads, personal experiences, feelings, preferences, and reasons for reading guide the selection and construction of information from the text. At the same time, the text itself—the words on the page— guide and constrain the meaning that a reader builds. Engaged readers build meaning that is shaped by the text, no matter what kind of book they are reading.

Langer (1990) and others argue that reading is temporal in nature: Readers construct meaning that is fluid and changes during the act of reading. Readers begin by "being out of and stepping into" their "envisionment" of the text. They then move through this envisionment, often stepping back and rethinking their previous understandings. Finally they step out of the envisionment and react to the reading experience (Langer, 1990, p. 238). This process occurs with all types of text. However, the emphasis and reasoning processes that readers use to construct their "envisionments" vary, depending on whether the text is informative or narrative (Langer, 1990).

Efferent and Aesthetic Reading

When people want to find information about something they usually look for an informational, or nonfiction text. A person might read a recipe to discover

Figure
2-1

Guide to Book Selection

Characteristics of Children	Features of Books	Favorite Titles
Infants and Toddlers (Birth to 2 Years)		
Explore world with eyes, ears, hands, feet, and mouth	Invite participation	*Pat the Bunny* (Kunhardt)
Enjoy bouncing rhymes, rhythm, music, and singing	Have brief, rhythmic text	*Mother Goose Songbook* (Yolen)
"Read" pictures as adult reads words; ask, "What's that?"	Are colorful and sturdy	*Max's First Word* (Wells)
Nursery—Early Childhood (2 to 4 Years)		
Understand simple concepts, counting, and ABCs	Have clear uncluttered pictures, simple concepts	ABC books, Counting books
Want to "do it myself"	Present simple plots, songs, and verse	*Goodnight Moon* (Brown)
Hold book and "read" familiar story to self	Have melodic, lilting language, animal characters	*Have You Seen My Duckling?* (Tafuri)
		Rosie's Walk (Hutchins)
Primary (5 to 8 Years)		
Become independent readers	Show eye-for-an-eye morality, strong friendships	*Where the Wild Things Are* (Sendak)
Have vivid imagination	Present phrase structure for books to read alone	*The Talking Eggs* (San Souci)
Demand strict moral judgments	Contain fantasy and realistic elements	*Chrysanthemum* (Henkes)
		Frog and Toad Are Friends (Lobel)
Intermediate (9 to 12 Years)		
Like mystery, intrigue, and humor	Present realistic view of the world	*Bridge to Terabithia* (Paterson)
Develop strength in independent reading	Develop strong characters, memorable plots	*A Wrinkle in Time* (L'Engle)
Form strong friendships outside the family	Stress growing up themes	*Tuck Everlasting* (Babbitt)
		Freaky Friday (Rodgers)
Advanced (12 Years and Up)		
Accepts responsibility for self and action	Deal with social and personal problems	*Dicey's Song* (Voigt)
Seeks role models and heroes	Show the underside of people and society	*A Wizard of Earthsea* (Le Guin)
Self-conscious; everybody's looking at me	Develop complex plots and strong characterization	*The Wright Brothers* (Freedman)

how to prepare a new dish, a manual to learn how to put a bicycle together, a factual text about dogs to discover how to care for a new puppy. Rosenblatt (1978) calls this "efferent" reading, reading done for the practical purpose of gaining knowledge from the text—much like your reading of this textbook.

Stories and poems, however, usually are read for different purposes and in a different fashion. Rosenblatt calls this kind of reading "aesthetic." Reading aesthetically involves being aware of the sound and feeling of a text, as well as of the experience of identifying with characters and participating in the story world—virtually experiencing the story. Reading aesthetically gives readers the emotional space in which to evaluate the feelings, actions, and decisions of the story world, and thus to construct their own personal values (Britton, 1970).

Efferent and aesthetic reading are not opposites, but rather two ends of a continuum, with most reading comprising a mixture of the two. Whereas efferent reading relates mainly to public, cognitive aspects of meaning, aesthetic reading relates mainly to private, affective aspects of meaning, to the lived-through experience (Rosenblatt, 1991). Different genres signal a predominant stance to a reader, but it is a reader's individual purpose for reading that decides the stance. For example, a cookbook signals an efferent stance—information about how to cook is inside the covers. However, a reader might pick up an especially enticing cookbook and read it for pure pleasure, imagining how good the various dishes might taste and what dishes might go well together; or another reader might enjoy the beautiful photographs of food or the accompanying humorous asides while following a particular recipe. It is a reader's purpose that determines the stance a reader takes. Rosenblatt argues that while both efferent and aesthetic experiences can be present in any reading, it is important that we, as teachers, are clear about the primary stance appropriate for different purposes for reading. Stories and poems, for example, are meant to be read aesthetically. If a book is meant to be "'literature' for . . . students, it must be experienced" first (Rosenblatt, 1991, p. 447).

Readers connect with narratives, whether realistic or fantasy, by becoming involved with and caring about the characters, by being engrossed in the events of the story, by experiencing the story they are reading—feeling like they are there, in the story world. One young reader described being "inhaled by books"—a metaphor which perfectly sums up the single-minded absorption that connecting with a book can provide, the perfect description of an engaged reader (Galda, 1982). But just what happens when readers read aesthetically and respond to literature?

Response to Literature

Reading and responding to stories and poems is a complex process that involves readers, texts, and the contexts in which reading occurs. Who is reading, what is being read, the purposes for reading, and the social and cultural factors surrounding reading all influence what a particular reader creates while reading a particular text. Responses are influenced by many factors and come in many forms (Galda, 1988). A text that may make one reader cry might bore another; a book read as a 10-year-old might bring a different kind of pleasure when read again as a 13-year-old; and the cultural values that permeate a text will trigger varying responses in culturally diverse readers.

Responses are often invisible, living in the moment of reading and only imperfectly captured later through writing, discussion, art, or dramatic activities. Young children in classrooms sometimes show their responses on their faces, in their bodies, in their laughter; older children often shield themselves by not expressing their responses unless encouraged to do so by a supportive classroom context.

Creating meaning with a literary text involves connecting life and text. And the act of creating meaning while reading a story or poem is at once highly individual and intensely social. This creation, however, always begins with a reader.

The Reader

Who readers are and what they have experienced influence their responses to the books they read. The places they have been, the people they know, the attitudes they hold all influence how they read. Past experience with books, both inside and outside the classroom, influences how children read and respond. For example, years of reading in a classroom in which the teacher asks questions that prompt recall of specific information from stories and poems will force young readers away from their naturally aesthetic responses into an inappropriate information-seeking stance. A parent, talking about her son learning to hate reading in school, described how he first reads the questions he has to answer at the end of each reading selection and then reads the story or poem to find the answers to those questions. Reading for information means he misses the story; never connecting with the story means he misses the pleasure that a story can bring. Missing that pleasure, he has learned to not like to read.

In contrast, children who have had an array of pleasurable experiences with books spontaneously compare stories, knowledgeably discuss authors, and bring their concepts about literature to their reading. Many researchers and teachers, such as Hickman (1981), Eeds and Wells (1989), and Short and Pierce (1990) have documented the richness of children's responses when children are in an environment that encourages exploration and consideration of books.

Readers' preferences and reading ability also influence the act of reading. Children who like science fiction approach a science fiction text with the expectation of pleasure (and with a storehouse of experience reading science fiction), whereas children who have not read and enjoyed science fiction approach the same text rather doubtfully. Children who read fluently can read with an ease that enables them to concentrate fully on the story world they are creating; children who struggle with words often lose their meaning. A group of fourth-grade readers was discussing L'Engle's *A Wind in the Door* (I–A), a complex science fantasy that contains some difficult proper nouns, when one reader remarked, "I was doing okay; then I tried to figure out the names and got all mixed up." Another reader responded by describing how he had "replaced" the hard names with familiar ones because, as he put it, "it didn't make any difference to the story" (Galda, 1990, 1992, 1993).

Differences in concepts of story certainly influence response. What readers know about literature—its creations, its forms, its purposes, and its effects—influences the meaning that they create (Galda, 1982). Applebee (1978) describes how children's concepts of story grow in complexity as they mature. As they learn more about literature, children grow in their ability to appreciate different books for different reasons, to step back from their personal preferences and view books in the larger literary context. The third-grade reader who didn't especially enjoy *Charlotte's Web* (I) may learn to appreciate the style and humor of E. B. White even if animal fantasies are not a preferred genre.

Children's Cognitive Development.   Cognitive development and learning influence responses to literature. As children grow and learn they change as people, and certainly as readers. Piaget's theories of intellectual development offer a useful framework for analyzing changes underlying thought processes. He views the acquisition of knowledge as a gradual developmental process in which children actively experience and organize concepts about their environment. Therefore, the child is seen as an active, dynamic being who interacts with the environment to create knowledge.

Piaget views development as movement through four main stages: sensorimotor, preoperational, concrete operational, and formal operational (Piaget, 1964). The **sensorimotor stage** lasts approximately the first 18 months to 2 years of life. Children learn through their senses and motor movements; they feel, grasp, taste, touch, smell, see, and hear people and objects in their environment. During this stage, books that children can hold (and chew), and are congruent with real-life experiences make sense to them. Board books containing simple stories or pictures of familiar objects, and participation books, such as Kunhardt's *Pat the Bunny* (N), incorporate experiences appropriate for this age child. Young children are also learning language rapidly. This language is learned in real-life contexts because of the needs it serves. Children learn language to tell people what they want, to relate to others, to find out about their world, and to play "let's pretend." Books provide infinite opportunities to engage a child in talk about meaningful things.

The **preoperational stage** (approximately 2 to 7 years) is characterized by rapidly developing language, thought, and symbolic representation. Books provide children with rich and varied opportunities for exploring language in many ways, finding out about their worlds, and enjoying the many virtual experiences that stories can hold. At this age, children see stories as true; they present the world as it is—not as it might be. Generally, they believe in magic and do not question contradictions. Animal fantasies and folklore are often popular with this age child.

The **concrete operational stage** (about 7 to 11 years) is a time when children distinguish between reality and fantasy in literature. They often classify literature and can be quite systematic in the way they organize their storehouse of knowledge about their world. Children in this stage, called concrete thinkers by Piaget, can comprehend some abstractions. They tolerate contradictions in their own view of reality but, at the same time, are quite firmly attached to their own ideas of the way things are and should be. Books about the here and now, about children like themselves, are often popular at this age.

Finally, around age 11 children reach the level of **formal** or **hypothetic-deductive operations;**

to it long before she can say the words. Similarly, the six-year-old who responds to a question with "I know it in my head but I can't say it," understands more than he can say. Through experience, children assimilate meaning and expand the storehouse of words they use to express meaning. Books, which provide experience beyond the immediate environment, contribute to the meaning base of language. Through books we learn to comprehend more than we actually express in speaking or writing. Books expand language by providing new words, experiences, and ideas in a context that helps children understand them. Books also provide language models in a variety of well-crafted styles.

Third, language learning never ends. As students mature, language skills increase and awareness grows in direct proportion to experiences. Students come to recognize that written material and society affect each other and that language is used in a variety of ways for a variety of purposes. Although they have been using language in a variety of ways since their early years, students come to understand and be able to talk about the persuasive uses of language, the figurative uses of language, the existence of different points of view, and the influence of literature. From wide exposure to books and many other language experiences, students extend their ability to comprehend and appreciate the subtleties and ambiguities of language.

For example, research into the stories children tell shows that their ability to tell connected stories develops over time. Applebee (1978) found that children's stories change from disconnected strings to sequential orderings and eventually to focused, sequential stories containing distinct story markers. One such marker is evident when young children signal they are telling a story by giving a title. Another appears when they begin their stories with a formal opening such as "once upon a time" and end with a closing such as "they lived happily ever after." Most children use recognizable opening and closing story frames by the time they are 5 years old. Many children at this age also use the past tense when they narrate action, and some alter their speaking tone into a dramatic "story voice," using the present tense when they are in a character role. The fact that these story markers appear regularly in children's oral language indicates the extent to which they have assimilated literature and dramatically illustrates the potential power of literature to affect linguistic as well as cognitive and affective development.

Developing a Sense of Story. Books also help children extend their understandings about story. Extensive experience with books gives children more

Duck and Frog went out to play.
"What game shall we play?" asked Duck.
"I don't know," said Frog.
"Let's go and ask Fox."

Pat Hutchins invites children to join in saying the familiar phrase that is repeated in each episode. (*What Game Shall We Play*)

resources to draw from as they build a concept of story. Children who hear many stories develop expectations about them; this is called developing a sense of story.

You can see how children's sense of story works if you read Pat Hutchins's **What Game Shall We Play?** (P), a tightly structured story with a repetitive phrase, to a group of 5-year-olds. By the time you meet the third character the children will be "reading" it with you. Hearing only the first few pages, children can recognize the story structure and predict what is coming next. They do this with any highly patterned, repetitive text they hear. They are not memorizing the text—as so many very young children do who "read and reread" their favorite story (even when it is held upside down)—but know how the story works because of their prior experiences with stories.

In addition to developing an understanding of the sequential structure of stories, children learn to use the content of stories to organize what they encounter of the world. Their vision of reality is shaped by the stories they tell themselves. Telling ourselves stories is a primary human activity, engaged in by adults as well as children. Each of us selectively perceives the world from a unique vantage point, and we tell ourselves stories about what we perceive. Children who are sent to bed in a dark room may fear the monsters that lie hidden there, and no amount of logical reassurance convinces them that the stories they have told themselves about the presence of monsters are unfounded. Philosophical treatises debate what reality actually is, but there is a consensus that one's own reality is what one perceives it to be; it is largely shaped by what we choose to believe and the stories we tell ourselves.

Britton (1970) describes "storying" as serving an assimilative function through which we balance our inner needs with external realities. Children's make-believe play and the stories they tell (often based on the stories they read) are among the activities in which they improvise freely on events in the actual world, and in so doing, they enable themselves to return and meet the demands of real life more adequately. Four-year-old Adam, in the process of learning to control his own behavior, lines up all of his stuffed animals and puts them in "time out." When they have sat for their alotted time, he seriously asks them, "Why did you have to go to time out?" Sometimes, like Peter Rabbit, they must go to bed with a dose of medicine and no supper. Play episodes like this one help Adam to manage the events of his own life.

Britton sees play and imaginative storytelling as areas of free activity that lie between the world of shared and verifiable experience and the world of inner necessity. The essential purpose of this kind of play is to relate inner needs to the demands of the external world. Children who hear or read stories of witches and fairy godmothers (symbols that may embody and work on the hate and love that are part of a close, dependent relationship) adapt or use in their own stories these symbols to accommodate their own needs.

As children mature and their experience with literature increases, their understanding about the relations between literature and life are affected. Galda (1990, 1992, 1993) found that one dimension distinguishing older readers (grades 8–9) from younger readers (grades 4–5) was the ability of most of the older children to discuss consistently the texts as works of art separate from life. The majority of the younger readers compared the characters in Betsy Byars's **The Summer of the Swans** (I) to their own lives. They complained of the lack of exact fit with their own worlds: The characters were "kind of like us," but "they don't act like we act at my house," "they don't fight like real brothers and sisters." The older readers were more objective when they criticized the book; they understood how

literature works. When one girl commented that Charlie's retardation "wasn't necessary" to the story, another countered with, "Well, the story did need it because it sort of changed the relationship between Sara and Charlie." The eighth-grade readers in the study cited earlier had the same sort of discussion about **Bridge to Terabithia** (I). One said, "She shouldn't have died," and another replied, "But it wouldn't have been the story it was if she hadn't." Rather than dismissing parts of stories they found extraneous, the older readers could go beyond their personal reactions to see how parts functioned in the story as a whole. In general, there was a more developed understanding of the interrelatedness of literary elements in the older readers than there was in the younger readers. Along with this was a diminishing tendency to judge a book according to its fit with one's personal perception of reality. Thus even fantasy came to be understood as being about recognizable people with familiar problems, as being *true* even if not *actual*.

The Text

We have discussed how different kinds of texts signal different kinds of reading, with some texts written for a predominantly efferent stance, and others a predominantly aesthetic stance. Reader preferences also influence the way that readers approach a book. We have already discussed how children change as readers over time, and certainly their preferences for different kinds of books change as well.

There are some generalizations about children's preferences that can be made, but within each generalization lies a lot of individual variation. Primary-grade children often enjoy stories with animal characters and are usually fond of folklore. As children enter middle elementary school and begin to form important friendships outside their immediate families, they often like to read stories about children "just like" themselves, especially stories that are funny and full of action. In a study of the popularity of the Newbery Award books, Schlager (1978) found that the main character's age and maturational level was an extremely important factor in children's positive responses to these books. Intermediate- and advanced-grade readers wanted to read about characters approximately their own age and rejected the books with much older or younger characters. They were more likely to choose books with characters older than they were so they could see what life would be like. They seldom chose books about younger characters.

There is a period of time during the elementary years when many readers are engrossed in

As students grow in their understanding of literature, they are able to talk about characters and books as separate from life. Readers can share Charlie's feeling of bewilderment as they stand behind the safe screen of fiction. (*The Summer of the Swans* by Betsy Byars)

mysteries, wanting "any book, by any author, as long as it's a mystery." Action, excitement, realism, and humor are preferred characteristics of books for many intermediate-grade readers. As children mature, boys and girls often show differences in reading preferences. Many advanced-grade girls prefer romance to all other types of books; often, bright advanced-grade boys are immersed in the world of science fiction and fantasy.

These generalizations, however, are just that—generalizations. There are children who never truly

like animal stories, children who do not get bitten by the mystery bug, girls who disdain romance novels and love science fiction. As each individual reader matures and reads an increasing number of books with an increasing amount of understanding, the preferences of that individual will change along lines that reflect the individual's interests, development, and experiences.

As these preferences change, so, too, does the influence of preferences on response to literature. As children read widely they seem to develop an

---

Figure
2-2

Selected Books: Children's Choices: 1991–1993

All Ages

Dakos, Kalli. *If You're Not Here, Please Raise Your Hand: Poems About School.* Illus. G. Brian Karas.

Macaulay, David. *Black and White.*

Prelutsky, Jack (selector). *Poems of A. Nonny Mouse.* Illus. Henrik Drescher.

Dr. Seuss. *Oh, the Places You'll Go!*

Wood, Audrey. *Little Penguin's Tale.*

Younger Readers

Abercrombie, Barbara. *Charlie Anderson.* Illus. Mark Graham.

Christelow, Eileen (reteller). *Five Little Monkeys Jumping on the Bed.*

Ehlert, Lois. *Fish Eyes: A Book You Can Count On.*

Henkes, Kevin. *Jessica.*

Martin, Bill, Jr., and John Archambault. *Chicka Chicka Boom Boom.* Illus. Lois Ehlert.

Walsh, Ellen Stoll. *Mouse Paint.*

Yoshida, Toshi. *Young Lions.*

Middle Grades

Blume, Judy. *Fudge-a-Mania.*

Brooke, William J. *A Telling of the Tales: Five Stories.* Illus. Richard Egielski.

Cleary, Beverly. *Muggie Maggie.* Illus. Kay Life.

Goble, Paul. *Beyond the Ridge.*

Greenberg, David. *The Great School Lunch Rebellion.* Illus. Maxie Chambliss.

King-Smith, Dick. *Ace: The Very Important Pig.* Illus. Lynette Hemmant.

Powzyk, Joyce. *Animal Camouflage: A Closer Look.*

Schwartz, David M. *If You Made a Million.* Illus. Steven Kellogg.

Older Readers

Foreman, Michael. *War Boy: A Country Childhood.*

George, Jean Craighead. *Shark Beneath the Reef.*

Hall, Lynn. *Dagmar Schultz and the Powers of Darkness.*

Janeczko, Paul B. *The Place My Words Are Looking For: What Poets Say About and Through Their Work.*

Klagsbrun, Francine. *Too Young to Die: Suicide and Youth.* Rev. ed.

Lauber, Patricia. *Seeing Earth from Space.* Illus. with photos.

Myers, Walter Dean. *The Mouse Rap.*

---

appreciation for a broad range of characters, styles, and genres, regardless of their own specific preferences. Experienced readers often look for interesting characters, and this focus seems to be linked to their developing ability to be "inhaled by a story," regardless of character age or sex, and in spite of genre differences.

It is clear that successful guesses about what readers will enjoy reading are only possible if they are based on a clear understanding of individual children and a knowledge of a wide range of books. Even then, we, as teachers and librarians, can only ask children to read books; it is entirely up to them to make books their own. In Figure 2-2 we list selected books from the Children's Choices list.

These are books that children across America have enjoyed.

The Context

It is vital to understand at least three things about the social nature of reading and responding to literature. First, learning occurs in a social context that is dependent on interaction; literature plays an important role in that context. Second, children grow in their ability to understand literature as they gain experience with life and literature. Third, a teacher's influence on children's response to literature is a powerful determinant of that response. How readers read and respond to the books they

Children who are read to from infancy choose books as a natural and necessary part of their lives. They also learn a lot about language and reading.

Parents and other caregivers who read to children provide a model of the pleasure of reading, what reading is, how language works, and new vocabulary.

read is influenced by the contexts in which they are reading. Hearing a bedtime story is different from hearing a story at a library story hour; reading on a rainy Saturday afternoon in the most comfortable chair in the house is different from reading from 8:30 to 9:00 every morning at a school desk. Reading in a classroom that is filled with books, time to read them, and other readers who support developing ideas is much different from reading a required number of pages for homework, punishment, or contests.

Children will become engaged readers when we surround them with opportunities to read and respond to a variety of genres, styles, and authors; when we appreciate individual differences and offer opportunities to explore and share diverse responses; and when we provide time and encouragement for responding in a variety of ways, such as spontaneous sharing, small group discussion, writing, art, drama, and movement.

Students need opportunities to make choices. As we discussed, responses and preferences are highly individualistic. Although you as a teacher need to be able to help students select books they will like, and certainly you can make suggestions and assign books, children need to be able to make their own choices about the books they read. They

also should be able to make choices about what they want to do when they are finished with a book. Some children might like to paint, others to talk, and others to sit quietly and think.

While response is highly individualistic, it is also intensely social. Vygotsky's (1962, 1978) exploration of language and thought clearly demonstrates how human beings use language for social purposes and learn language firmly embedded in a social world. Children learn the use, function, and power of words because language users talk to them. Children learn about books by being read to, often held on a parent's lap, and by talking about what they are doing; they learn about books by seeing what others do with them. Although reading books is often a solitary activity, the way we use and talk about books is a natural social response, one that we as readers all share. When we finish reading a good book it's quite natural to talk about it; and we usually learn from that talk.

Talking about books encourages readers to articulate their own responses and to find out how other readers responded. In many cases talking about books adds new dimensions to individual responses as the ideas of others provide new perspectives. As one young reader remarked, "I never thought about it that way, but now it makes a lot of sense," a sentiment that anyone who has discussed books with friends can understand.

Children develop feelings and beliefs about themselves and their world through interactions with those around them; this includes their interactions around books. They find out who they are and the role they are to play by interpreting the verbal and nonverbal messages significant others give to them. Children develop a positive self-concept if people around them show them they are loved and valued. In a similar way, they develop a positive attitude toward books if books are treated as a source of pleasure and knowledge. When children experience sharing books with a loving caregiver from early on, they develop positive feelings about books and the joy that can come from them. When children experience sharing books with peers and teachers in collaborative, supportive contexts,

P R O F I L E

Louise Rosenblatt

LOUISE ROSENBLATT is a remarkable woman with exceptional talent. Her work, presenting theories about the nature of reading and the literary experience, substantially shapes the teaching of English in schools and colleges.

Louise Rosenblatt brings a scholarly approach to literary criticism, combined with an active concern for the teaching of English. At a time when it was assumed that the reader's role was to passively receive the imprint of the ready-made meaning of a text, she stressed the idea of the reader actively making meaning by transaction with the text. This new vantage point helps us to understand that the reader's background and interests play an important part in the development of the ability to read. She also emphasized the difference between reading a poem or story with attention focused on what is being lived through (an aesthetic experience), and reading material with attention focused on what is to be carried away (an efferent experience), such as information or directions.

Louise Rosenblatt graduated with honors from Barnard College, Columbia University. After several years of graduate work in France, at the University of Grenoble and the Sorbonne, University of Paris, she received her doctorate in comparative literature from the Sorbonne. Her doctoral dissertation on the nineteenth-century aesthetic movement in England and France led her to see the necessity for a literate reading public. Postdoctoral work in anthropology with Franz Boas and Ruth Benedict at Columbia University inspired her feeling for the contributions of diverse cultures that encourage the creation of a democratic American society.

Louise Rosenblatt's primary professorship was at New York University where she directed the doctoral program in English education. She also taught at Barnard College, Columbia University, Brooklyn College of the

they develop positive feelings about books and about themselves as readers. The social and cultural context in which children grow and learn shapes their view of the world and the role of literature in it.

Children do not experience the same social and cultural contexts. Heath (1982, 1983) documents how three very different home cultures—in the same city in North America—influence children's experiences with and concepts about books and,

in turn, their experiences in school. She argues that children learn at home sanctioned ways of taking from their environment, which includes books. In many cases these ways of taking do not mirror the ways in which teachers present school literacy. Sensitive teachers recognize individual differences and build on the oral and literate traditions that children bring to school from home, emphasizing a multifaceted conception of literacy. They also make

CONTINUED

City University of New York, Northwestern University (summer sessions), and Rutgers University.

Louise Rosenblatt received the John Simon Guggenheim Fellowship (1943), the Great Teacher Award from New York University (1972), the Distinguished Service Award from the National Council of Teachers of English (1973), and the National Conference on Research in English Lifetime Award (1990). She was inducted into the Reading Hall of Fame by the International Reading Association in 1992. On the fiftieth anniversary of the publication of *Literature as Exploration,* the National Council of Teachers of English honored her with a full day of programs to celebrate her distinguished work. In another major text, *The Reader, the Text, the Poem,* she expands her theories and implications for practice.

In a letter dated February 7, 1993, Louise Rosenblatt states:

I believe that if in the early years youngsters get the feel of the aesthetic and efferent ways of reading, if the classroom atmosphere and teacher's interventions permit students to automatically adopt the appropriate stance, then all the other (efferent) things we do with literature—analyze, categorize, criticize, evaluate—will have real literary experiences as their subject or base. So many of the bright students who came

into my freshman and sophomore classes at the university level had learned that one reads literature in school in order to do these efferent things, (I have nothing against them in their proper place) and they had lost, if they ever had, the delight of aesthetic or literary experience. It's the cumulative effect over the years of the way literature is approached that I am concerned about.

I'm glad that you deal with both fiction and nonfiction, for example. [in *Language, Literacy and the Child,* Galda, Cullinan and Strickland, 1993] And that you point out that the aesthetic experience should usually precede and create the need for terms such as metaphor, plot, etc. Also, that the free response should not be drowned out by repeated direct questions to test whether the literal meaning has been gained, before going on to discuss and build on the story or poem as the children have created it. Some of your classroom excerpts document this point very well.

Louise Rosenblatt has been married to Sidney Ratner, scholar in philosophy and history, for 60 years. They have a grown son and a granddaughter. They spend winters in Puerto Rico where they write every morning and swim a mile a day in the Atlantic Ocean in the afternoon!

explicit additional strategies that they expect children to use in school, demonstrating, for example, how they make connections between their lives and the books they read, or among books. These teachers view reading as shaped by individual experiences; these include varied concepts about the functions of, purposes for, and appropriate stances toward literature.

Just as literature is shaped by readers' views of the world, so, too, can literature help shape readers' views of the world. Frye (1970) underscores the role of literature in educating the imagination and shows the necessity of imagination in creating a social vision. He believes that the fundamental job of the imagination in ordinary life is to produce, out of the society we *have* to live in, a vision of the society we *want* to live in. In this sense, we live in two worlds: our ordinary world and our ideal world. One world is around us; the other is a vision inside our minds, born and fostered by the imagination, yet real enough for us to try to make the world we see conform to its shape.

HELPING CHILDREN GROW AS RESPONSIVE READERS

Activities described throughout this text are chosen to help readers develop a deeper understanding of and a greater appreciation for books. Because children's literature is so rich and varied, it can be used to enhance every area of the curriculum. More important, though, are those experiences that keep literature central. The best kind of activity is one that is intended to bring readers back to books and guide them to others. The Rosens state the case well:

> It is as though there is a deep lack of confidence in the power of literature to do its work and a profound conviction that unless literature can be converted into the hard currency of familiar school learning it has not earned its keep. What will take children more deeply into the experience of the book? This is the question we should be asking rather than by what means can I use this book as a launching-pad into any one of a dozen endeavors which leave the book further and further behind, at best a distant sound, at worst forgotten entirely. (1973, p. 195)

Research and practical experience show that most children who become involved in activities related to books read more than those who do not. As Figure 2-3 suggests, the phenomenon is cyclical—reading provides practice that makes a reader more proficient. Being a better reader leads to more pleasure and a willingness to practice more frequently.

Extension activities allow children the time to savor and absorb books. It is important to ponder a book for a while before beginning another; students need a chance to linger in the spell cast by a good book. This may mean *doing nothing* or it may mean using creative learning activities. Response and reflection are important ingredients of a child's complete learning experience; give time for both.

In classrooms where there are many books and time to read and respond to them, children may respond in many ways without specific prompting by the teacher. In a naturalistic study of response across the elementary grades, Hickman (1981) described seven different types of responses that occurred in the classrooms she observed. They were as follows:

1. Listening behaviors, such as laughter and applause;
2. Contact with books, such as browsing, intent attention;
3. Acting on the impulse to share, reading together;
4. Oral responses, such as storytelling, discussion;
5. Actions and drama, such as dramatic play;
6. Making things like pictures, games, displays; and
7. Writing, by using literary models, summarizing, and writing about literature. (p. 346)

Hickman makes the point that response doesn't have to be an activity. It can range from individual thoughtfulness, to simple sharing with another reader, to a formal activity such as a group depiction of an important scene from a book. While some book encounters lead naturally into concrete projects, we should avoid overdoing a good thing, for in our zeal we may be engendering boredom instead of interest.

Children can be encouraged to respond to literature in many ways. They discover the intrinsic pleasure in extended activities when there are many to choose from. The aesthetic nature of the reading experience requires personal involvement; therefore, the impact of the book determines the response a reader makes. Reading is both a social and a private affair that calls on the emotions of the reader. Some books should be explored; others read, closed, and forever locked in the reader's heart. A sensitive teacher knows when a reader wants to make this choice.

Trust the power of literature to do its work, and give students time to savor the books they read. They need time to linger in the spell of a good book.

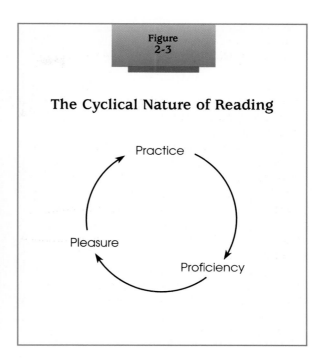

Figure 2-3

The Cyclical Nature of Reading

Practice

Proficiency

Pleasure

Time and Choice

Children need both time to read and choices about what to read, how to read, and whom to read with.

> Allowing children time to be with books in the classroom, rather than assigning them to a certain number of books to be read on their own time, teaches them to value books. When time is set aside for reading and responding to literature, students know that this is viewed as important by their teacher. So, too, does reading to and with a class help to convince students of the value and the pleasures of reading. (Galda, 1988, p. 100)

In many classrooms Sustained Silent Reading (SSR) is one way teachers build time for individual reading into their busy schedules. SSR is a plan wherein 20 to 30 minutes are set aside each day when everybody in the school reads: the principal, the custodian, the teachers, and all the students. There are many variations of the program: DEAR (Drop Everything and Read), USSR (Uninterrupted Sustained Silent Reading), and READ (Read Everything And Dream). These programs have consistently produced better readers. Even when students are not fluent independent readers, they need time to explore books independently.

We know that reading independently improves reading fluency, but research suggests that students do not have enough time to read in school. Many students spend up to 70 percent of the time allocated for reading instruction doing seatwork—workbooks and skill sheets—many of which are unrelated to reading and are actually detrimental to children's attitudes toward reading (Ingham, 1981).

A mother described her daughter storming in the door from school complaining, "Mom, I *hate* reading!" Her mother countered, "But you love reading your Little House and Beverly Cleary books here at home." "Yes, I know that, but I *hate* reading!" What she hated was the class at school called "Reading," which obviously had nothing to do with really reading books. Classroom research shows that the amount of time devoted to worksheets does *nothing* to improve reading proficiency (Leinhardt, Zigmond, & Cooley, 1981; Rosenshine & Stevens, 1984). The amount of independent silent reading children do in school, however, is significantly related to gains in reading achievement (Allington, 1984). Researchers estimate that the typical primary school child reads silently only 7 or 8 minutes per day. By the middle grades, silent reading time still only averages 15 minutes per school day. No

TEACHING IDEA 2-1

The Literature Newsletter

Read All About It, Book 'Em, The Readers' Gazette: A classroom newsletter devoted entirely to literature is a place to publish children's writing and artwork stimulated by their reading. Include items like the following:

—sharing books
—book reviews
—editorials
—crossword puzzles
—an advice column directed to book characters
—book-related cartoons
—feature articles on author/illustrator of the month

The format varies from a single sheet copied for class members (or others in the school) to a newsletter with many pages covering a variety of topics.

A newsletter requires:

—editors
—reporters
—feature writers
—book reviewers
—artists, art editors, layout designers
—ad writers

The staff is recruited from class members. Typing and copying may require help from parents or school aides, depending on the age and skills of the students.

one can become skilled at anything practiced only 7 to 15 minutes a day.

It is vitally important that students have a significant amount of time to read independently and with peers. They also need time to respond to what they have read, and they need to be able to make choices about how they respond. We discuss some of these choices later in this chapter, and Chapter 12 presents ideas for time management and grouping arrangements that promote talk about books and other ways to respond.

Teachers help students become knowledgeable about themselves as readers by providing both guidance and the freedom to choose books. Teachers of young children might present many books to the class during read-aloud time; many of these books might be highly patterned stories or stories familiar to the children. They can then read these stories independently during SSR time, approximating the teacher's reading and gradually developing their ability to read the text independently. As children become confident readers, they learn to recognize what books they can read and what books they might like to read. They begin to know which authors and illustrators they like. And they learn where to go for recommendations about books—the teacher, the librarian, family and friends, and particular colleagues in their classrooms. Good readers know how to find books for themselves.

Other ways you as a teacher can show you value literature are being a reader yourself, reading along with the children during silent individual reading, talking about books you like, reading bits of your own stories aloud to them, and, of course, reading aloud with pleasure and skill.

Reading Aloud

One primary way that teachers help children grow as engaged, responsive readers is to read aloud. Reading aloud is one of the most common and easiest means of sharing books and poetry—and a pleasurable experience for all when done well. Once considered a suitable time filler or a calming activity after lunch or recess, it is now known to have a positive impact on students' reading development (Clark, 1976; Durkin, 1966; Wells, 1986). Reading aloud not only helps young children become readers, but also helps older children become better readers. Reading aloud extends students' horizons, introduces literature they might not read on their own, offers alternate worlds and lifestyles, increases their experiential base from which to view the world, and provides a model of a good reader (Galda & Cullinan, 1991). Reading aloud to young children also demonstrates print and book handling concepts such as left to right and top to bottom directionality, page turning, and the role of print and pictures in telling a story or presenting a concept. The wealth of available evidence caused the Commission on Reading to conclude that "The single most important activity for building the knowledge required for eventual success in reading is reading aloud to children" (Anderson, Hiebert, Scott, & Wilkinson, 1985, p. 23). The many reasons for reading aloud are summarized here:

READING ALOUD

Introduces new words—vocabulary

Displays interesting sentence patterns

Presents a variety of forms of language

Students in classrooms that keep reading a central focus develop into communities of readers. They read books together and talk about books they read.

Shows various styles of written language

Develops a sense of story

Motivates children to read more

Provides ideas for students' writing

Enriches students' general knowledge

Models for students what good reading
    sounds like

Adds pleasure to the day

There are some important guidelines to consider when selecting books to read aloud, the most important of which is to select well-written stories. Books of quality abound, and it is a waste of precious time to read second-rate materials. Good books pique interest and incite children to read them, or others like them, independently. Sometimes teachers read an inferior book "because the children love it," but students will love good books even more. Select books for reading aloud that will influence and expand children's literary tastes.

Find out which books are already familiar by asking children to list their favorites, and then build from there, selecting books that children will probably not discover on their own. By all means read to them Roald Dahl's *James and the Giant Peach* (I) unless, of course, most of them have already read this book on their own. Save reading-aloud

time for the special books you want your students to know. Unless you are doing an author study, introduce children to all of an author's books by reading aloud from one of them. For example, read Beverly Cleary's *Ramona Quimby, Age 8* (P–I), create a display and give short book talks about her other books, but let students discover Cleary's other characters on their own.

Reading from outstanding examples of all types of literature—realistic fiction, historical fiction, fantasy, science fiction, folklore, poetry, biography, nonfiction—can help expand children's literary tastes. Reading some books slightly above students' reading abilities extends their language; they usually comprehend more than they can read. However, a good book can be spoiled for children by reading it to them before they can understand its subtleties. Most books can be understood on several levels, but it would be a waste to read MacLachlan's *Sarah, Plain and Tall* (I) to a first-grade class just because it's a short book. Choose books to read aloud that you want to make part of the whole-class experience, books that you want to become part of the shared knowledge in your classroom. Figure 2-4 suggests some titles for you to start with; you will discover many more on your own.

When reading aloud to children, know your material before you begin. Practice reading is important, especially when reading poetry, where the

Figure
2-4

Good Books to Read Aloud

Nursery (N)

Adoff, Arnold. *Black Is Brown Is Tan.*

Brown, Margaret Wise. *Goodnight Moon.*

Crews, Donald. *Truck.*

Clifton, Lucille. *The Boy Who Didn't Believe in Spring.*

De Brunhoff, Jean. *Story of Babar, the Little Elephant.*

Demarest, Chris. *My Little Red Car.*

Gramataky, Hardie. *Little Toot.*

Guarino, Deborah. *Is Your Mama a Llama?*

Hines, Anna Grossnickle. *It's Just Me, Emily.*

Hoban, Russell. *Bedtime for Frances.*

Primary (P)

Bang, Molly. *Ten, Nine, Eight.*

Barton, Byron. *Bones, Bones, Dinosaur Bones.*

Bemelmans, Ludwig. *Madeline.*

Brett, Jan. *Annie and the Wild Animals.*

Browne, Anthony. *Tunnel.*

Bunting, Eve. *Fly Away Home.*

Carle, Eric. *The Very Busy Spider.*

Cooney, Barbara. *Miss Rumphius.*

de Paola, Tomie. *Nana Upstairs, Nana Downstairs.*

Flournoy, Valerie. *The Patchwork Quilt.*

Fox, Mem. *Wilfrid Gordon McDonald Partridge.*

Friedman, Ina. *How My Parents Learned to Eat.*

Hall, Donald. *Ox-Cart Man.*

Hill, Elizabeth Starr. *Evan's Corner.*

Hopkins, Lee Bennett. *Good Books, Good Times.*

Howard, Elizabeth Fitzgerald. *Aunt Flossie's Hats.*

Hughes, Shirley. *Alfie Gives a Hand.*

Hutchins, Pat. *The Doorbell Rang.*

McCully, Emily. *Mirette on the High Wire.*

Young, Ed. *Seven Blind Mice.*

Intermediate (I)

Babbitt, Natalie. *Tuck Everlasting.*

Byars, Betsy. *Bingo Brown and the Language of Love.*

Fritz, Jean. *The Great Little Madison.*

Goldstein, Bobbye (selector). *Inner Chimes.*

Hamilton, Virginia. *M. C. Higgins, the Great.*

Harvey, Brett. *Cassie's Journey: Going West in the 1860s.*

Hendershot, Judith. *In Coal Country.*

Holman, Felice. *Slake's Limbo.*

Hunter, Mollie. *Sound of Chariots.*

Jacques, Brian. *Redwall.*

Lewis, C. S. *The Lion, the Witch and the Wardrobe.*

Mathis, Sharon Bell. *The Hundred Penny Box.*

Morrison, Lillian. *Whistling the Morning In.*

Naylor, Phyllis. *Shiloh.*

O'Brien, Robert C. *Mrs. Frisby and the Rats of NIMH.*

Paterson, Katherine. *The Great Gilly Hopkins.*

———. *Lyddie.*

Paulsen, Gary. *Hatchet.*

Raskin, Ellen. *The Westing Game.*

Rylant, Cynthia. *Every Living Thing.*

Steig, William. *Abel's Island.*

Taylor, Mildred. *Roll of Thunder, Hear My Cry.*

Uchida, Yoshiko. *Journey to Topaz.*

Van Allsburg, Chris. *The Garden of Abdul Gasazi.*

Yep, Laurence. *Dragonwings.*

Yolen, Jane. *Dragon's Blood.*

Advanced (A)

Cooper, Susan. *The Dark Is Rising.*

Fleischman, Paul. *Joyful Noise.*

Fox, Paula . *Monkey Island.*

Mahy, Margaret. *Memory.*

McCaffrey, Anne. *Dragonsong.*

McKinley, Robin. *The Blue Sword.*

Myers, Walter Dean. *The Young Landlords.*

Naidoo, Beverley. *Chain of Fire.*

Nelson, Theresa. *And One for All.*

O'Dell, Scott. *Island of the Blue Dolphins.*

Orlev, Uri. *Island on Bird Street.*

———. *Man from the Other Side.*

Rawls, Wilson. *Where the Red Fern Grows.*

Rostkowski, Margaret I. *After the Dancing Days.*

Rylant, Cynthia. *Fine White Dust.*

———. *Missing May.*

Sebestyen, Ouida. *Words by Heart.*

Speare, Elizabeth George. *Sign of the Beaver.*

Staples, Suzanne Fisher. *Shabanu: Daughter of the Wind.*

Sutcliff, Rosemary. *The Road to Camlann: The Death of King Arthur.*

Voigt, Cynthia. *Homecoming.*

Children can understand books they cannot read on their own. Read books aloud that are slightly above their reading level to expand their literary experiences. Story time quickly becomes the favorite part of the school day.

phrasing and cadence carry so much of the meaning. Listening to poets reading their own work on recordings can be useful; they know how it should sound. One such recording, "Poetry Parade" (Weston Woods), offers David McCord, Aileen Fisher, Karla Kuskin, and Harry Behn reading their poetry. Practice reading also helps you decide on the mood and tone that you want to set and allows you to learn special names or refrains so you won't stumble over them and thus spoil the story.

It is important to be thoroughly familiar with the content of the material read aloud. Some books contain words and incidents that might be offensive in some communities or are best kept as a private interchange between author and individual reader. You can avoid embarrassment in a group by being alert to sensitive issues. Not all books or all scenes from books are for group sharing.

When reading, use a natural voice, with inflections and modulations befitting the story. Avoid greatly exaggerated voice changes and overly dramatic gestures. Read slowly, enunciate clearly, project your voice directly, and maintain eye contact with your listeners as much as possible. Teachers who read aloud with their noses in the book soon lose their audience. Some brief guidelines for reading aloud are presented here:

TIPS FOR READING ALOUD

1. Read the book ahead of time; be familiar with it.
2. Give a brief description of the book or character to establish a context for the listeners.
3. Prune lengthy passages of description, if necessary, to keep interest high.
4. Begin reading aloud slowly; quicken the pace as listeners enter the story world.
5. Look up from the book frequently to maintain eye contact.
6. Interpret dialogue meaningfully.
7. Read entire book, if possible, or a chapter or more per day to sustain meaning.

There are different points of view about reading picture books aloud to children. Some teachers believe the illustrations are integral to the text and that children need to see them while hearing the words. Others read the text aloud and then allow children to explore the pictures independently. Your decision will rest on the qualities of the particular book you choose. If you feel the illustrations are needed to make sense of the story, hold the book open and to one side as you read.

Young children like to sit on the floor clustered close to you; this adds to the intimacy of the story experience. Face them away from distractions such as bright windows or doorways, so their full attention can be on the story. If you choose to read the book aloud and then show the pictures, this extends the enjoyment—and there is nothing wrong with rereading a favorite book either immediately or at another time; in fact, it is advisable.

Teachers who permit students to draw, read their own books, or do quiet seatwork diminish the importance of reading aloud by implying it does not deserve students' full attention. Instead, make story time a highlight of the day—a special time you share. Your enthusiasm and special preparations for the occasion set the tone; once you have begun, the magic of the story takes over.

Trelease brought the values of reading aloud to the attention of parents and educators in *The New Read-Aloud Handbook* (1991). He explains that the desire to read is not inborn, but fostered, and that daily reading aloud has an effect comparable to that of a television commercial. If a television commercial can cause children to want a particular hamburger or breakfast cereal, how much more important it is to read aloud, to feed and nurture the minds of children as they are developing curiosity, emotional strength, and imagination. Kimmel and Segel (1983) in *For Reading Out Loud!* report that

The kind of material to be read changes, but the practice of reading aloud to students continues throughout junior high school.

reading aloud from literature meaningful to children is widely acknowledged to be the most effective way to foster a lifelong love of books and reading.

Reading aloud is central to every school day and should continue through junior high school. Nursery and primary school teachers read aloud two and three times a day. Intermediate- and advanced-grade teachers read aloud at one particular time. One school has each teacher reading aloud a novel, biography, or nonfiction book at noon recess. Students choose the group they want to attend.

Connecting With Books

Sensitive teachers also help children make connections between their own lives and the books they read. Cochran-Smith (1984) documented how one preschool teacher did this with her class as she demonstrated how to make connections between text and life, and between life and text. Many teachers across the grades see this as one of the most important things they do. Asking questions and making statements like "This story reminds me of the story that you told us about your cousin, Miguel" or "Has anyone ever had an experience like this?" demonstrates to students that the stuff of their own lives is often mirrored in the books they read. Heath and Wolf (1992) describe the way two children braid the literature read to them into their daily lives.

Teachers also help students make connections among books. Learning about the "family of stories" (Moss & Stott, 1986) is an ongoing process as students come to recognize similarities and differences in plot structures, characters, and themes. Like connecting books to life, connecting books to other books adds dimension to future reading and responding. Wide reading (many varied books) and deep reading (reading many books in a particular genre, by a particular author, with a particular structure, etc.) acquaint children with the world of literature, and help them learn a lot about specific aspects of that world.

Discoveries made during interaction between readers and text can be seen in the following account of a discussion by a group of sixth-grade students who had just finished reading Ursula Le Guin's *A Wizard of Earthsea* (A) and had previously read several books in **"The Chronicles of Narnia"** series (I) by C. S. Lewis and two of Madeleine L'Engle's space fantasies, *A Wrinkle in Time* (I–A) and *A Wind in the Door* (I–A).

MICHELLE: I liked Narnia best—it was so magicky.

JON-PAUL: Well, I liked it a lot, but not the best. For me, *A Wrinkle in Time* was best—"It," you know, the Naked Brain, and the shadowed planets, and all that.

TEACHER: There was a shadow in *A Wizard of Earthsea,* and the "black thing" caused shadowed or dark planets in *A Wrinkle in Time.* Somehow, the bad thing, the evil in several of the books we read, seems to be pictured in some way by blackness or shadows.

SARAH: Except for Narnia, and there it wasn't a black witch but a white witch. The evil spell was snow and winter.

HEDY: That's because nothing could grow or be alive then. Aslan brought the Spring.

SARAH: But still whatever it appeared like, there was a battle against the forces of evil.

TEACHER: What about *A Wizard of Earthsea?*

JON-PAUL: Well, like we read, the shadow that was following Ged was really the evil in himself, but he didn't recognize it until the end. I don't really understand that very well, but I understand it some.

TEACHER: In *A Wind in the Door* you could be "x-ed" if you weren't trying to be your real self. Again, the picture the author gives us to imagine in our own minds is rather similar: If you are "x-ed" what has happened to you?

JON-PAUL: You become annihilated. You don't exist anymore. If you were a planet, where you used to be there was just a black hole of nothingness in the universe.

SARAH: And for Ged, if he didn't recognize that there *was* a bad side to his own nature, it could destroy them. He would be "x-ed" by his shadow, and he wouldn't be living anymore, but just the power of evil could live in his body.

TEACHER: We talked a lot when we were reading the books by Madeleine L'Engle about the *theme* of her books—that the central idea was the battle between good and evil in the universe. What would you say is the theme of the other fantasies?

HEDY: Well, in Narnia it was sort of the same because Aslan was good and the White Witch was evil.

SARAH: I see it! I see it! I just finished reading Susan Cooper's *The Dark Is Rising,* and it's the same theme in that book, too. It's The light against the dark. It's good against evil. *They're all about the same thing!* (Anzul, 1988)

The other children sat in silence, mulling over this idea. They understood Sarah in a way. Certainly, they understood momentarily the words she was saying, though possibly they would soon forget them. They clearly would need time to read and reflect more before they could understand deeply this aspect of literature. Try as Sarah might to explain to them the meaning of her personal insights, it is difficult if not impossible. Sarah's life has been changed, and mere explanation will not affect her classmates. She can report how the literary works affect her, but her classmates will not know the new reality Sarah has discovered until they themselves discover it.

Sarah had taken one of those rare steps to a new level of understanding. From now on, every book she reads cannot only be a delightful world in itself, but can relate in some way to other books. She is on that threshold where every human experience she reads about, and thus makes her own experience, will begin to relate somehow to all human experience, and where human experience transmuted into literature begins to relate to all other literature.

Frye explains it this way:

All themes and characters and stories you encounter in literature belong to one big inter-

Reading several books in one genre helps students to develop understandings about literature. (Ursula Le Guin, *A Wizard of Earthsea;* Madeleine L'Engle, *A Wrinkle in Time;* Madeleine L'Engle, *A Wind in the Door*)

locking family. . . . You keep associating your literary experiences together: you're always being reminded of some other story you read or movie you saw or character that impressed you. For most of us, most of the time, this goes on unconsciously, but the fact that it does go on suggests that perhaps in literature you don't just read one novel or poem after another, but that there's a real subject to be studied, as there is in science, and that the more you read, the more you learn about literature as a whole. (1970, pp. 48–49)

When children compare a particular work with others similar to it in some way, even at the primary school level, they begin to develop an understanding of the unity of all literature. Many teachers help students construct charts that compare literature along any number of dimensions such as theme, author, or structure.

Extending Frye's proposition that authors often imitate others' stories or build on the conventions and patterns from literature, Moss and Stott (1986) show how many stories are based on similar patterns. For example, in nearly all children's stories characters make physical journeys, journeys that conclude either in a new setting (linear) or at the point of departure (circular). They suggest that, in addition to the linear and circular journey patterns, the organizing principles of conflict, genre classifications, and the quest for identity provide avenues for comparing stories. We talk more about this in Chapter 12.

Young children learn to look at literature in this way when they are immersed in stories with similar patterns. They quickly see the pattern of "three" when they hear "The Three Little Pigs," "The Three Billy Goats Gruff," and "Goldilocks and the Three Bears" read aloud. They will also recognize that William Hooks's **Moss Gown** (P–I), John Steptoe's **Mufaro's Beautiful Daughters** (P–I), and Robert San Souci's **The Talking Eggs** (P–I) have elements from the "Cinderella" story they have heard before, and when they read *King Lear* later in life they may feel familiar with the story. Recognizing patterns helps children to understand and appreciate literature. It is also basic to learning; some cognitive psychologists have come to define learning as the search for patterns that connect.

Response Activities

Teachers help students become thoughtful readers when they provide time for students to think about and articulate, in one form or another, their responses to what they read. Structured and spontaneous opportunities for students to exchange and compare ideas with their peers and to build on the responses of others help children grow as responsive readers.

Students respond to literature in a variety of ways; sometimes their silence is an eloquent testimony to the power of a book. Reflection is an appropriate response at times, but at other times, you may want to encourage a tangible response by having the children participate in a creative activity. The following sections—writing, oral language, drama, and art—and many of the teaching ideas throughout this text contain suggestions. Select from them or let them trigger your own creative ideas. Other ideas for enhancing children's experiences with literature can be found in Galda, Cullinan, and Strickland's *Language, Literacy, and the Child* (1993), in *Children's Literature in the Reading Program* (Cullinan, 1989), and in *Invitation to Read* (Cullinan, 1992).

Writing

The values of literature extend far beyond appreciation and enjoyment, although these are primary. When they read on their own, children build a storehouse of language possibilities. The stories, poems, and nonfiction texts they read and hear, created by some of the most skilled writers of all times, serve as models for children in their own writing. When children write, they draw on the literature they know as they select significant details, organize their thoughts, and express them with clarity. When children write, they also read differently, or, as Smith (1982) puts it, they "read like writers."

They become sensitive to what other writers do and learn to read with a fine-tuned appreciation of the author's craft.

Writing in response to what is read helps readers to discover what they are thinking and feeling, and to make connections between life and text. Keeping a response journal helps children explore their own responses more fully in a more private fashion than talking with peers allows. Journals also serve as a record of what books students have read and how they have felt about those books, and they demonstrate how students grow as readers across time. We talk more about the importance of these kinds of records in Chapter 12.

Keeping a journal can be an in-class or an at-home activity. Each journal entry should contain the date, the title, and the author of the book under consideration. Some teachers simply tell students, "Say whatever you want to say about the book you are reading," whereas others give students specific questions to answer. Some teachers ask students to write in their journals every day, establishing a regularly scheduled journal time, whereas others ask students to write in their journals whenever they finish a book. An example of a journal written when a book was finished appears in Figure 2-5.

Teachers can read and respond to journals on a regular basis, either frequently or periodically, or can merely check to see that students are writing in their journals as requested. Some teachers make journals into dialogues—writing letters back and forth with their students or having students write to each other. An example of this kind of journal appears in Figure 2-6.

Creative Ways to Share Books

Opportunities for formal book sharing are fun when they tap children's creative potential; they are valuable when they help a child to understand a book better by clarifying thoughts and feelings. Above all, as in the activities described in this book, the prime goal is to develop in children an enduring love of literature; everything else is secondary and is aimed at achieving this goal. Being required to read a teacher-selected book and write a report about it has turned more children away from reading than perhaps any other activity. The traditional book reports we are force fed—drudgery for the child who writes them, time consuming for the teacher who reads and grades them, and boring for the children who must listen to them read aloud—subvert our main goal.

Book sharing should take children back to the book and give them a chance to linger in the spell of a good story just a little longer. Many ways of

**Figure
2-5**

Entry From a Fifth Grader's Response Journal

I'm reading Gary pallsons wood song and there is this one part were he is driving his dogs and Storm one of his dogs started to scwurt blood out of his butt and he took Storm of the harness and tied a rope to him and put him on the sled and Storm jumped off and started to pull and Gary stopped and took Storm and put him behined and he just ran ahead and started to pull and he still scwurt blood out from his butt so the only right thing he could do was let him do what he wanted to do is to let him pull and when they got home he wasn't dead.

That night gary spent the night and he saw a bear near the fire and he through a stick at the bear andthe bear and the bear came over to him and the bear just stood here with his paws over him and it seemed as if he just stood there for over a hour then he went away and Gary went in the house and grabbed a gun and went out side and pointed the gun at the bear and then he thought and said he didn't hurt me so why should I hurt him and he lowered the gun and put the gun away and said I will never hurt a animal again.

another time is when thier dogs saw a ruffed grouse and they grabbed the grouse and ran of and gary found a nest by the road and saw ten baby grouse eggs in it and he picked them up and put them in his hat and took them home and put them under their Banty hen named Hawk and Hawk pecked his hand bloody and when the chicks hatched the hen protected them like a hen protecting it's chicks.

and one other time when Gary's wife was putting the laundry up there was a chickmunk in the woods a little bit and she still had some of a cookie that she had for a snack and she remembered that chickmuncks are none to eat out of peoples hands and so she put the cookie in her hand and held her hand out and right when the chickmunk was about to eat the cookie a squirel came and took the chickmunk under the wood pile and ate it (the chipmunk).

When I read the part about the dog squirting blood out of his butt, I felt gross because I was eating.

When I read the part about him throwing the stick to the bear, I felt worried, because that is scary. It's scary because the bear put his paws over him.

When I read the part about a rough grouse on the road, that the dogs took into the woods and ate, I felt sorry for it. When I saw the eggs I felt even more sorry.

After reading this book, I though it was really beautiful.

Journal entry by Jason Ream.
Note: Journal entries are not intended for others to read, so phonetic spellings are left uncorrected.

---

sharing books are enjoyable and meaningful to the child and valuable to the teacher who can discern from them what the child has gained from the book.

Teaching Ideas 2-2 and 2-3 present some ideas certain to suggest others. Put on index cards, these ideas could become the nucleus of a literature activity box for children's projects.

Children can express themselves through reading, writing, listening, speaking, art, and music. Remember, however, that children need choices. Some may like to put themselves in imaginative situations as they discuss books read; others may prefer just to talk about a book; and still others may choose to keep the reading experience personal. Be flexible. Encourage them to use your ideas as a springboard for others that may be more important

to them. It is illuminating to put yourself in their places; if you ask yourself what a particular idea is good for, you are on the right track. If it leads to thoughtful consideration of a book by the student or to further reading, then it has a place in your plans. Ask your students: "What do you want others to understand about your book?" and then ask, "What could you do?" In a classroom that encourages many ways of responding, students will have many options for sharing books.

Oral Language

Oral language is central to many book extension activities. These range from the spontaneous recommendations of a book by its reader to structured

---

Figure
2-6

Entry From a Seventh-Grade Dialogue Journal

Seth's entry:

My parents have a special way of helping me and my sisters with our homework. Say my sister needs to think of ten childrens books, my parents might give her clues about a story, so she can think of it. Or, my parents might tell her to look in some books in order to find out some of the titles. And, most probably, my parents might ask my sister to jog her memory for all the books that she had read.

My mom would say, "Shira, what were the last ten books that you read this year?" My sister would say, "Mom-my, I can't remember. I read a lot of books this year." "Shira, don't you keep the names of the books that you read on the back of your bookmark?" "Yes, mom, but I already thought of that. I left my book in school, and the book mark was in the book."

My mom would think for awhile, and then ask me if we had any books in the house like summarized classics for children. Since I am the only one in the house who knows how to find a book I must go looking for it. First, I look on the shelves in the den. A-ha, I see a book called The Book of Illustrated Classics for children. I bring it into the kitchen, to show my mom, only to find out that it is full of nursery rhymes. Well, Shira and mom vetoed Mother Goose, they figured out that nursery rhymes were not the type of classics that her teacher was looking for.

Teacher's Response:

Seth:

Your journal entry is first rate. You set up the situation so interestingly in the beginning that I want to keep listening to you. You have a great command of "voice." The writing sounds like you: witty, specific, explanatory, chatty. When you have something to add, you have an "oh, by the way" manner of doing it that sounds like you behind the words. Do you know how long it takes a writer to develop a voice? It comes from confidence in what you are saying and a fluency from having written a lot.

I love the extended example of how your Mom deals with you and your sister. It tells me, further, that your sense of maturity and sense of responsibility didn't just happen. That doesn't mean that you don't deserve a lot of the credit. You understand that whenever you assume responsibility whether it's at age 7 or 47, it's always "cold turkey."

Nick Aversa

---

panel discussions about books by one author. Effective oral language activities may be extensive or brief, but they always help children share and explore their responses to the books they read.

Storytelling by Children. Children's writing skills seldom match their oral language skills before the end of their elementary school years. Storytelling activities contribute to their sense of story and provide opportunities for developing and expanding language. A strong read-aloud program is vital; children will use the literary language they hear in creating their own stories.

Wordless books are an excellent stimulus to storytelling. Because the story line depends entirely on the illustrations, children become much more aware of the details in the pictures; they do not make a quick scan of them. These books provide a story structure—plot, characters, theme—as with any conventional books, and so provide the necessary framework on which to build their stories. Children can tell such stories to each other, to a group, or into an audio or video recorder. Storytelling can be done with partners, in which case each takes the role of one or more of the characters as they interpret the story. In group storytelling, children take a role, each telling the story from one character's point of view. From the experience gained, children learn how the elements of the story interconnect and build on each other.

Tape recorders are indispensable for activities with wordless books. When children record their stories, these become available for other children to listen to while looking at the book. Each storyteller's

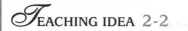 **IDEA 2-2**

Creative Ways to Share Books

- Devise a television or newpaper announcement to advertise a book. Include words and pictures.
- Make puppet characters, write a play about a book, and put on a puppet show.
- Choose a character from a book and write a new story about him or her.
- Write an account of what you would have done or how you would have acted had you been one of the characters in a book you read.
- Write about the author or illustrator of a book.
- Write a summary of a book, telling what you especially like or dislike about it.
- Compare two books about the same subject.
- Compare two books by the same author.
- Write a story about the funniest incident in a book.

Adapted from Pillar, A. "Individualizing Book Reviews." *Elementary English* (now *Language Arts*) 52 (4)(1975): 467–469.

IDEA 2-3

Book Buddies

Cross-age sharing benefits both older and younger students. Similarly, when children talk about books it increases their understanding and improves their ability to express themselves orally. Participants also gain in reading and writing achievement and in self-esteem.

Classmate Book Buddies
To implement Book Buddies in your classroom:

1. Students choose partners.
2. After completing a book, partners go off to a quiet place to talk.
3. The reader gives a brief summary, identifies good parts, and discusses the book with the partner.

Cross-Age Book Buddies
To implement Cross-Age Book Buddies, ask a friend who teaches two or three grade levels higher to join you.

1. The older students come to visit and get acquainted; they can choose their partners.
2. The older students receive training in how to select books, read aloud, engage in discussion, and plan appropriate activities.
3. Book Buddies meet on a regular schedule to read together, talk about what they read, and do related activities.

---

version of the book will be different, so that variety is thus added to the classroom collection. In addition to using tape recorders for recording stories based on books, children can use them to dictate original stories, make background sound tracks for stories read aloud, record choral speaking, create dialogue for puppet shows, and carry out other dramatic activities. Camcorders or video recorders expand the possibilities. Figure 2-7 contains a list of wordless books you can begin with.

Choral Speaking. Choral speaking—groups speaking in unison—can be adapted for any age level: For the youngest it may mean joining in as a refrain is read aloud; for older students it may involve the impromptu reading of a poem. Very young children unconsciously chime in when you read aloud passages that strike a sympathetic chord. For example, children quickly pick up and repeat the refrain when you read *Chicka Chicka Boom Boom* (P). Rhythm and repetition in language, conducive to choral speaking, is found in abundance in literature for every age group.

When introducing choral speaking, read aloud two or three times the story or poem you are using, so the rhythm of the language can be absorbed by your listeners. Encourage them to follow along with hand clapping until the beat is established. Favorite poems and refrains from stories, unconsciously committed to memory from repeated group speaking, stay in the mind as treasures to be savored for years.

Teachers in whole language classrooms use choral speaking for warm-up routines to get students to tune into the task at hand. When we draw students together in a group speaking activity it not only focuses their attention, but also gives them practice in using various patterns of oral language. Most often schools provide a great amount of practice in using written language but very little in using

Figure 2-7

Notable Wordless Books

Baker, Jeannie. *Window.*

Briggs, Raymond. *The Snowman.*

Geisert, Arthur. *Oink.*

Goodall, John. *Naughty Nancy.*

———. *The Story of an English Village.*

Hutchins, Pat. *Changes, Changes.*

Mayer, Mercer. *A Boy, a Dog, and a Frog.*

McCully, Emily Arnold. *New Baby.*

———. *School.*

Ormerod, Jan. *Moonlight.*

———. *Sunshine.*

Oxenbury, Helen. *Shopping Trip.*

Prater, John. *The Gift.*

Sara. *Across Town.*

Steptoe, John. *Baby Says.*

Tafuri, Nancy. *Do Not Disturb.*

———. *Early Morning in the Barn.*

———. *Have You Seen My Duckling?*

Turkle, Brinton. *Deep in the Forest.*

Wiesner, David. *Free Fall.*

———. *Tuesday.*

Winter, Paula. *The Bear and the Fly.*

Young, Ed. *The Other Bone.*

———. *Up a Tree.*

oral language. Choral speaking helps balance this in-equity.

Students feel comfortable taking part in choral speaking; they are members of a group. They do not risk embarrassment by being singled out. Most importantly, the students become a community of learners. Joining together in group routines solidifies the sense of community.

Leader-group response verses are fun to say. They play on the strong rhythms and melodies of our language and capitalize on the turn-taking pattern of conversation. An old favorite is "Did you feed my cow?" "Yes Mam! Yes Mam!" "Will you tell me how?" "Yes Mam! Yes Mam!" "What did

you feed her?" "Oats and hay." "What did you feed her?" "Oats and hay." Many selections have been around for generations—a testament to their universal appeal. Whole language teachers make the text visible to the participants. They print the phrases on large charts, use big books, or project them on overhead projectors. Good resources for choral speaking are listed in Figure 2-8.

Discussion. Books become a valued stimulus for discussioon, but as we have already pointed out, they can also lead to quiet contemplation; not every book needs to be probed deeply. Teachers and librarians develop the ability to recognize when discussion is appropriate and when it is not. No rules can be given for this; it is sensed intuitively by those who base decisions on knowledge of children in the group. Children themselves can also determine whether or not discussion is appropriate. Many children who participate in literature groups, discussed more extensively in Chapter 12, learn to make choices about how to respond to the books they read.

When discussion is warranted, the purpose of the discussion determines how the discussion is organized, who participates, and what the focus is. It may be that a group of children spontaneously comes together to talk about a book or books that they have been reading. These spontaneous sharings may occur on the playground, at the water fountain, or during independent reading or reading workshop time. Teachers who encourage spontaneous discussions of books notice that they occur frequently and serve important purposes. Hepler and Hickman (1982) note that children tell each other about good books to read, organize their understanding of the content of a book, and clarify their interpretations as they talk together. All of this is done without the presence of a teacher.

In their description of the "grand conversations" that fifth-grade children had in their literature study groups, Eeds and Wells (1989) demonstrate how children construct meaning together, share personal stories, question what they read, and discuss an author's style during literature discussions. Other teachers and researchers write eloquently of how children help each other to become more thoughtful and discerning readers when they work together in literature study groups (Short & Pierce, 1990). These groups are sometimes led by teachers, but often by students who have learned to work together without the presence of a teacher. Teachers demonstrate and discuss with children the kinds of questions that can be considered and the procedures that might be followed; when students

MARCH

In March the wind
blows down the door
and spills my soup
upon the floor.
It laps it up
and roars for more.
Blowing once
blowing twice
blowing chicken soup
with rice.

The repetition of the beat and the melody of the language make this delicious material for choral speaking. The sound echoes the sense and lingers in the mind. (Maurice Sendak, *Chicken Soup with Rice: A Book of Months*)

are ready to work together independently they do so.

In many cases teachers first need to learn new ways of talking about books. For many years educators have been concerned with the types of questions that teachers ask of their students. The study *Critical Reading Ability of Elementary School Children* (Wolf, Huck, & King, 1967) showed that certain types of teacher questions elicit predetermined types of student responses. Questions to clarify feelings are very different from those intended to ex-

pand understanding about literary techniques. Discussions to clarify information or to relate experiences from books to children's lives are equally valid.

Questioning is one way that teachers demonstrate what might happen in literature discussion groups; good questions elicit high-level thinking from children, and poorly framed ones invite surface thinking. The literal, interpretive, and critical levels of reading and thinking are paralleled in questioning.

Figure 2-8

Books for Choral Speaking

Anthony, Rose Marie. *Fun with Choral Speaking.*

Barton, Bob. *Tell Me Another: Storytelling and Reading Aloud at Home, at School and in the Community.*

Barton, Bob, and David Booth. *Stories in the Classroom.*

Burroughs, Margaret Taylor. *Did You Feed My Cow? Rhymes and Games from City Streets and Country Lanes.*

Krauss, Ruth. *A Very Special House.*

Kuskin, Karla. *Just Like Everyone Else.*

Milne, A. A. "The King's Breakfast": *When We Were Very Young.*

Pomerantz, Charlotte. *The Piggy in the Puddle.*

Sendak, Maurice. *Chicken Soup with Rice.*

Tashjian, Virginia. *Juba This and Juba That: Story Hour Sketches for Large or Small Groups.*

——. *With a Deep Sea Smile: Story Hour Stretches for Large or Small Groups.*

Scheer, Julian. *Rain Makes Applesauce.*

Viorst, Judith. *I'll Fix Anthony.*

Zeitlin, Patty. *Song Is a Rainbow: Music, Movement and Rhythm.*

Literal questions elicit recall of factual information explicitly stated in the printed material. Such questions based on the familiar "Goldilocks and the Three Bears" might be, Where did the three bears go? What did Goldilocks do in their house?

Interpretive questions seek information inferred from text. They are best answered by reading between the lines and synthesizing information from two or more stated facts. Interpretive questions for the Goldilocks story could be, Why did Goldilocks go into the bears' house? Why did she choose to fall asleep in Baby Bear's bed? Interpretive questions have more than one right answer—they ask for guesses and hunches.

Critical questions intended to elicit evaluation of the book invite judgments about the quality of

writing and authenticity of information (if nonfiction); they also encourage hypothesizing beyond the story—tasks requiring higher level thinking. This level of question is not answered fully by personal opinion; the basis for the judgment is also given. Critical questions for Goldilocks (where two versions have been read) could include, which version do you like best and why? What is another possible ending for the story? What did Goldilocks tell her parents when she got home? Why do you think she told them that? Does the repetition of three (three bowls of porridge, three chairs, three beds) remind you of other folktales? What other stories use the same pattern?

For many years educators thought teachers should proceed from literal to interpretive to critical questions, assuming that being able to answer literal questions is necessary before interpretation and critical evaluation can occur. This is not the case, however, as readers can have a powerful aesthetic experience with a book and be able to evaluate it critically without getting literal details (Rosenblatt, 1978).

Other kinds of questions that teachers can demonstrate involve exploring their own understanding of and responses to the books they read. The goal of a discussion might be to clarify personal responses and extend those responses by talking with others. In this case teachers would share their own responses and encourage children to share their responses, expand on what they have said, and react to others' comments. The discussion of fantasy novels excerpted in this chapter is an excellent example of a clarifying discussion. Hynds (1992) suggests that teachers ask real questions, questions they don't know the answers to, in discussions about books; encourage students to respond to each other; and pay close attention to how they respond to the answers students give. In other words, teachers respond as readers interested in discussing a book they have read with others who also have read it.

Teachers can also ask themselves questions about the books they are reading and then share these questions and answers with students during literary discussion groups. Discussion groups are wonderful opportunities for helping children learn about literature; they often present teachable moments that allow teachers to explore how literature works with interested students. Books can be explored in any number of ways. Eeds and Peterson (1991) suggest that teachers read a book twice to prepare for discussion, with the second reading focusing on structure, character, place, time, point of view, mood, and symbol as they apply to the book under consideration. Notes in the margins, Post-its, notebooks, book markers, and other devices help teachers record what they have noticed and allow them to get ready for an exciting dialogue with students in literature discussion groups. As you read in this text you will learn how literature works; this information can then be shared with your students as you read and respond with them.

Questions are not the only way to organize discussions. Other strategies like webbing allow children to find a focus in their discussions without teacher questions. Webbing enhances comprehension and learning, links reading and writing together, and promotes enjoyment and appreciation of literature (Bromley, 1991). Creating a visual representation of ideas and information and their relationships can be a powerful tool for organizing and clarifying understanding. Webs can be used to explore characters, setting, artistic elements in picture books, relationships among books, plot, and just about anything that students are interested in exploring. Figure 2-9 depicts a student-generated web and related writing.

Drama

Children engage in imaginative play instinctively. They re-create what they see on television, in everyday life, and in their stories. "Let's pretend" games are a natural way for children to express their thoughts and feelings in the guise of characters and roles. Informal dramatic play capitalizes on children's natural desire to pretend and can be the forerunner of numerous drama experiences. These experiences can promote dialogue among students and between students and teachers that allows children to control and explore their responses to literature (Edmiston, Enciso, & King, 1987; O'Neill, 1989; Verriour, 1985). Dramatic activities provide opportunities to discuss and reflect on a book.

There are many forms of drama to be explored in the classroom. Variations, often called creative dramatics, include pantomime, using body movements and expression but no words; interpreting, enacting, or re-creating a story or a scene; and improvising, extending, and extrapolating beyond a story or a poem.

Pantomime. In pantomime, a story or meaning is conveyed solely through facial expressions, shrugs, frowns, gestures, and other forms of body language. Situations, stories, or characters pantomimed should be ones the children are familiar with, recognize easily, or want to explore further.

Enacting. A good time for acting out or creating a story can be immediately following a read-aloud session. After reading aloud "The Three Billy Goats Gruff," for example, the teacher might ask, "Who wants to be the troll? . . . the big billy goat? . . . the middle billy goat? . . . the little billy goat?" Discuss with the children how the troll sounds when he asks, "Who's that tripping over my bridge?" how he shows his anger, and how each of the billy goats sounds as he answers the troll. As children learn to enact stories they can do so without teacher guidance. Children who are working together in literature study groups might decide to enact the story, or parts of the story, they are reading to explore character relationships, cause and effect, sequence, or any number of issues related to their story.

Interpretation. Interpretation involves an oral dramatic reading of a story the children are interested in. This activity builds enthusiasm for reading and develops oral reading skills. It also encourages children to discuss characters, their personalities, and how they might talk given their personalities and the situations facing them in the story.

Improvisation. Improvisation goes beyond acting out the basic story line. It begins with a supposition, often about plot or characterization, that goes beyond the story itself. What happens after Snow White and her prince get married? What is Gilly Hopkins like after living with her grandmother for a year? Well-developed characters often inspire children to extensions into new situations. Improvisation can be particularly powerful as a way for older children to explore characterization.

Role Playing. Role playing is a variation usually done with short vignettes or specific incidents from stories. Students assume a role and interact with others in roles. This activity allows students to explore and discuss meaningful episodes in stories, various characters' point of view, and characters' motivation. Brief role-playing episodes often become scenes in more fully developed presentations.

Readers Theatre. In Readers Theatre, students read orally from scripts that are based on selections from literature. Performances are not formal: Lines are not memorized; there are virtually no sets, costumes, or staging; and participants do not move about the stage. A few gestures or changes in position are permitted but the real effect must come from the readers' oral interpretation of characters and narration.

**Figure
2-9**

A Student-Generated Web

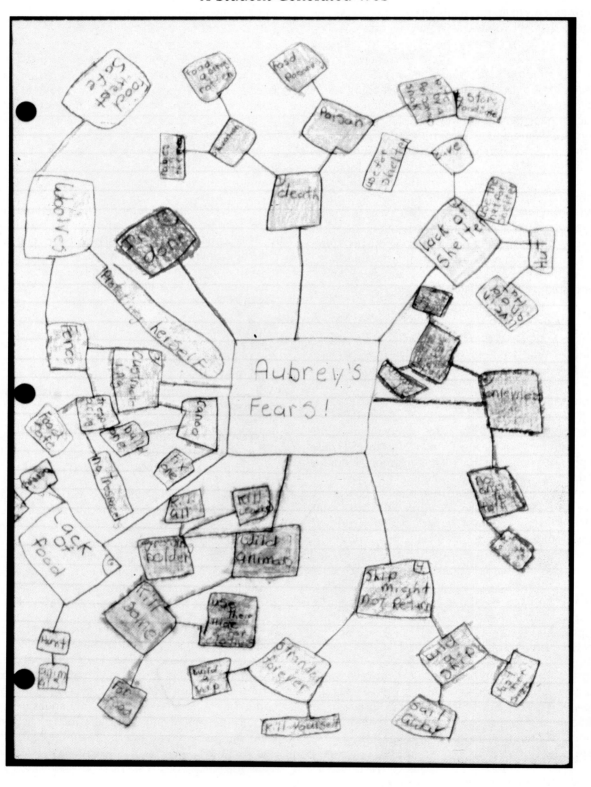

CONTINUED

Aubrey's Fears

I am stranded on a island I'm afeared I'll die. I could die from poison, get sick from a snake bite or starve from all the food being poisoned and not fit to eat. What if I get bitten by a wild animal and get rabies.

Am I going to be able to find shelter. Maybe I can find an old hut. I found a cave but it was a animals lair.

I wish somone was with me I am so lonely. No one to play with I can only sit, around. I can only play with my self and talk to my self.

What if the ship does not return. I could build a ship just my size and soul away. If I am stranded forever I will kill my self.

There are to many wild animals around I could kill the leader or kill them all. If I kill them I can use them for food and their hide for clothes.

What if I run out of food? I could hunt animals, pick berries. Fish would be okey.

Note: Each paragraph is based on a section of the web.

Students can talk about books they read by assuming the role of a character in the book.

Sloyer (1982) suggests the following steps in preparing a Readers Theatre performance:

1. Select a story with lots of dialogue and a strong plot. The best stories have a taut plot with an "and then" quality to pique your interest and make you want to know what will happen next.

2. Discuss the number of characters needed, including one or more narrators who read the parts between the dialogue.

3. Adapt the story to a play script format, deleting unnecessary phrases like "he said," and assign roles.

4. When roles are assigned, students do not need to be told to practice their oral reading; they will do so on their own, especially if they can practice with a partner or a director who can advise them on whether the character is coming through in the reading.

5. For the finished production, performers may sit or stand side by side, with the narrators off to one side and slightly closer to the audience. Readers stand statue-still holding their scripts. When not in a scene, readers may turn around or lower their heads.

Some stories, such as Bill Martin Jr and John Archambault's **The Ghost-Eye Tree,** need no adaptation to be turned into a script. These are good stories to begin with, but children learn a great deal about how stories work when they work closely with a text to make their own scripts. The titles listed in Figure 2-10 are all easily adapted to Readers Theatre.

Dramatization techniques differ depending on the students and books involved and the purposes and goals of the experience—primarily according to whether it is done as a performance for others or for the benefit of the participants themselves. A guiding rule in this area, no less than in others, is to hold the children's benefit as the highest value. This is not to say that performances for others should not be given, only that they should not be given at the cost of exploiting children as performers. Remember, the dramatic activities that students engage in begin as ways of more fully exploring the stories they are reading; keep the focus on the child and the story, and dramatic activities will be memorable learning experiences for children.

Art

Art activities can be as extensive as your creativity and energy permit. Resources expand when you have access to an art specialist; in any case, your classroom should house numerous supplies and examples of children's artistic work. Art projects related to books are used regularly, not saved for special occasions. A well-stocked art center leads to inventive projects in classrooms and libraries. Paper, fabric, yarn, buttons, socks, plastic bottles, paper bags, cardboard tubes, dowel rods, wire, plastic foam balls, egg cartons, toothpicks, and pipe cleaners all have potential in the hands of ingenious children and teachers. Needles and thread, glue and tape, and, of course, scissors, crayons, paints, paintbrushes, and markers are also needed. Items available free or for a nominal price can often be obtained from neighborhood shops, such as old wallpaper books from the local paint store. Art materials are often available to teachers who search grocery, hardware, discount, and other stores for them. Pizza rounds (cardboard trays), 5-gallon ice cream drums, boxes, and display materials, for example, often make good classroom art supplies.

What you and your students do is not as important as how what you do fits the book that has sparked the project. Art can be a vehicle for thinking more deeply about a book. Many children express themselves better in art than in oral or written language; art becomes a way of responding, a way of exploring important aspects of the reading experience. Children might labor painstakingly to depict an unusual and important setting, re-create a vivid scene, capture characterization in a portrait, or explore a favorite artist's technique. Like drama, art is a way for readers to discover what they know and how they feel about what they have read.

**Figure
2-10**

Stories and Poems for Readers Theatre

Folklore

Craig, M. Jean. *The Three Wishes.*

Galdone, Paul. *Henny Penny.*

———. *Little Red Hen.*

———. *The Gingerbread Boy.*

Oppenheim, Joanne. *You Can't Catch Me.*

Stevens, Janet. *The Three Billy Goats Gruff.*

Poetry

Bagert, Brod. *Let Me Be the Boss. . . .*

Harrison, David. *Somebody Catch My Homework.*

Kuskin, Karla. *Dogs and Dragons, Trees and Dreams.*

Picture Books

Johnson, Angela. *Tell Me a Story, Mama.*

Sendak, Maurice. *Pierre.*

Novels (Use a chapter or two)

Byars, Betsy. *The Midnight Fox.*

Hunter, Mollie. *Mermaid Summer.*

MacLachlan, Patricia. *Sarah, Plain and Tall.*

Paterson, Katherine. *The Great Gilly Hopkins.*

Students need choices in the books they read as well as in the ways they respond to literature.

EACHING IDEA 2-4

Story Theater

Story theater is oral reading plus a group to act it out. Choose narrative poems, folktales, or stories with action and little or no dialogue. Narrators read aloud while players perform the action described.

How to Prepare a Story Theater

1. Read the story to the group. Discuss it. Encourage movement/mime, for example, "Show how the frog jumps."

2. Choose from volunteers. Roles: Narrators, characters.

3. Players develop their parts as oral readers read aloud. Narrators vary their pace to match players' movements.

4. Put on final production for an audience of peers, parents, or others. Combine oral reading and mimed action.

Stories, folktales, and poems for story theater:
Bemelmans, Ludwig. *Madeline.*
Browning, Robert. *The Pied Piper.*
de Paola, Tomie. *Strega Nona.*
De Regniers, Beatrice Schenk. *May I Bring a Friend?*
Galdone, Paul. *The Gingerbread Boy.*
Harrison, David. *Never Talk to Plants.*
Nash, Ogden. *Custard the Dragon.*

EACHING IDEA 2-5

Response Activities Exploring Art

Getting children to express their response to literature through art activities invites creativity. Use the ideas here to stimulate others of your own.

Collage. An arrangement of cut or torn paper or fabric. Use Ezra Jack Keats's books *The Snowy Day* or *Whistle for Willie* as models for cut paper collages. Use Jeannie Baker's *Window* as a model for three-dimensional twigs and grass collages.

Wall Hanging. Large pieces of fabric decorated with scenes from a book and suspended from a dowel rod. Use a heavy fabric, such as burlap, for the background. Cut shapes of characters from other materials; attach to the background fabric.

Mosaic. Small bits of colored paper or tiles arranged into designs. Create figures from books. Use Leo Lionni's *Pezzetino* as a model for mosaics.

Flannel Board. A piece of flannel cloth attached to fiberboard. Cut shapes of characters or objects from other pieces of flannel or material to move about as you tell the story. Stories that work well as flannel board stories:

Hale, Irina. *Brown Bear in a Brown Chair.*
Slobodkina, Esphyr. *Caps for Sale.*
Freeman, Don. *Corduroy.*
Zemach, Margot. *It Could Always Be Worse.*
Lionni, Leo. *Little Blue and Little Yellow.*
Krasilovsky, Phyllis. *The Man Who Didn't Wash His Dishes.*
Galdone, Paul. *The Old Woman and Her Pig.*

Roller Movies. A story Illustrated in scenes on a long piece of shelf paper with each end attached to a dowel rod. Use a cardboard carton to cut a TV screen; show the appropriate scene as you tell the story.

Filmstrips and Slides. Pictures drawn on clear acetate film or slides to illustrate a story. Project them onto a screen as you tell the story.

Puppets. Figures made from paper bags, popsicle sticks, or plastic foam and fabric to represent characters. Shape the puppets to look like the characters and move them about as you say the dialogue for them.

A technique called "Sketch to Stretch" (Harste, Short, & Burke, 1988) encourages children to explore their reading through art. After having read a common book, students are asked to sketch what the book meant to them or what they "made of the reading" (p. 354). After they complete the sketches they share them with others in the group who discuss what they think the artist is trying to say. The artist then explains what he or she was trying to do. If several small groups are doing this, one sketch from each group can be put on an overhead and shared with the class. Harste and Short caution that this process may need to be repeated several times before students are comfortable. Students could also respond through music or movement by singing, playing, or dancing what a book meant to them.

Art can also be used as a way to present books to others. Talking or writing about a book are not the only ways of sharing books with others; many students enjoy sharing through art. This does not simply mean drawing a picture about a story, but using varied activities to capture the essence of a book. A wall hanging might be a perfect way to present a story with a strong episodic structure; a collage might be an effective portrayal of a character. Students need to know about and have the resources for a variety of artistic presentations. Teaching Idea 2-5 contains many ideas for unusual art projects that might be the perfect way to respond to a book. Allow your students the freedom to choose among them.

Teachers can do a great deal to help children connect with books. There are many more ideas for response activities than are presented here, and you will adapt many suggestions to suit the needs of your students. When you know your readers and the books they are reading, and when you provide a context that encourages them to explore and expand their connections with books, engaged and responsive readers flower.

SUMMARY

Reading is a transaction, with a reader actively constructing meaning under the guidance of a text. A reader brings experiences with life and literature to any act of reading; a text guides the reader as she uses prior understandings to construct new meaning. Readers select purposes for reading. Reading may be primarily efferent, in which a reader seeks to gain information, or aesthetic, in which a reader focuses on the experience he is living through as he reads. Factors inherent in readers and texts influence the aesthetic experience, as do social and cultural contexts.

Teachers can help children grow as responsive readers by allowing them time to read and respond and choices about what, how, and who they read and respond with. Literature study groups, writing, discussion, informal sharing, dramatic activities, and art offer children opportunities for connecting with books.

Part
Two

The
Patterns
of Children's
Books

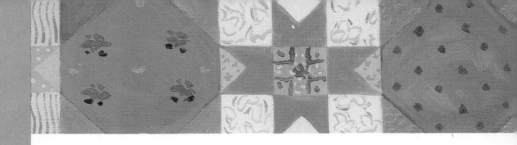

3

*P*icture Books

TRAINING WHEELS

This is my bookshelf, and these are
   my books,
I know each one by heart.
I just look at the pictures and wait
   for Dad
To give me a little start.

Some day I'll read all by myself
With confidence and speed,
But now these pretty picture books
Are everything I need.

                                          Brod Bagert

aptivated by stunning illustrations and lyrical texts, children often anticipate what comes next and eventually memorize their favorite books. This is exactly what we want them to do. They begin by approximating reading, grow in knowledge and confidence, and develop a lifelong love for books. Older children continue to enjoy picture books, finding pleasure in the unique blend of visual and linguistic symbols. For many children the picture book is their first—and perhaps only—experience with fine art.

Picture books tell a story, elaborate a concept, or impart information through a combination of words and illustrations. Picture books are the very first books children experience. Very young children grasp books made of sturdy cardboard with bright pictures designed to capture a baby's interest. Nursery and primary-grade children listen to picture books being read aloud and develop concepts about reading and literature through these experiences. Children most often hear their first stories and informational texts read aloud from picture books. Many of these books are ideally suited for reading aloud because the large pages open wide to spread across the parent-child lap or to be seen by many children at once. There are fewer picture books that are appropriate for older children, but in recent years some authors and illustrators have provided excellent books for intermediate-grade readers. Some advanced-grade teachers have come to use picture books as understandable, clear examples of literary techniques.

Children see in their picture books some of the best products of artistic talent they may ever encounter. Children are quick to judge and respond intuitively; they either like the pictures or they do not. A combination of the style, the medium used, and the images produced create an effect that can make a book acceptable or unacceptable to the reader. As children become discriminating in their tastes, they begin to develop an artistic awareness. Understanding how the lines and colors work together to form pictures they like comes gradually to children who are given a great deal of exposure to art and illustrations of all kinds. Books by illustrators such as Tomie de Paola, Leo and Diane Dillon, Jerry Pinkney, Ed Young, Chris Van Allsburg, David Macaulay, Stephen Gammell, and Amos Ferguson offer children a wide variety of artistic experiences.

Picture books are unique in the field of children's literature because format rather than content determines their definition. Picture books span the genres. They may be stories—realistic or fantastic, contemporary or historical; they also may be poetry, folklore, or informational books. They may speak to universal concerns or explore themes salient to a particular cultural group. In the chapters that follow we list and discuss quality picture books which fall within many genres. In this chapter we concentrate on books that exemplify the format which defines picture book.

Whatever the content, if the illustrations are equal or dominant partners with the text, the result is a picture book. In a picture storybook the illustrations might precisely verify the text, co-telling, with the text, the same story. Barbara Cooney's illustrations for **Miss Rumphius** (P–I) visually support her text. The illustrations in other picture storybooks might extend the text, adding visual information or meaning that are not presented through language, as Stephen Gammell does in Jim Aylesworth's **Old Black Fly** (N–P). Yet others, as in John Burningham's *Time to Get Out of the Bath, Shirley* (N–P), parallel the text, presenting visual information that creates a story within a story (Cianciolo,

1990; Nodelman, 1988). But all of these books offer reader/viewers the opportunity to create meaning through both language and art.

Books with pictures range from wordless books such as McCully's **School**, in which a story or information is conveyed entirely through the illustrations, to illustrated books. An *illustrated book* consists of both text and illustrations, but the text carries the major responsibility for depicting the story or content while the illustrations contribute significantly, but not equally, to the development and the depth and breadth of the story or content. In illustrated books, such as Nancy Burkert's **Valentine and Orson** (A), the art is used to highlight significant aspects of the setting, theme, mood, and/or characterizations. Another superb example of an illustrated book, Sharon Bell Mathis's **The Hundred Penny Box** (I–A), consists of truly accomplished illustrations by Leo and Diane Dillon and the artful use of language to explore a theme of universal social concern. While the art in illustrated books may enhance, enrich, and extend the text, these books do not qualify as picture books; in true picture books the text and the art are woven inseparably together. Words and pictures are each vital to the creation of meaning and together create a meaning that neither could create alone (Nodelman, 1988). Figure 3-1 lists books that exemplify the ways in which art and text work together.

CRITERIA FOR SELECTING PICTURE BOOKS

There are several qualities to look for in selecting picture books. Since learning is a continuous reaching out and integrating of both direct and vicarious experiences, we as teachers should select books that reflect, extend, or enrich a child's ever-expanding world. We evaluate picture books according to the literary qualities accomplished by combining words and pictures: visual art quality, artful use of language, and the characteristics of the specific genre. Look for illustrations that (1) catch and hold a child's interest and (2) have distinguished art that works with the text to enrich the story or the idea being presented. These books should also contain (1) intrinsically interesting words used in interesting ways and (2) language that has a natural internal rhythm that makes it pleasing to the ear when read aloud. A quick checklist for evaluating picture books appears in Figure 3-2.

*J*ERRY PINKNEY became interested in drawing as a child as he watched two older brothers draw pictures of airplanes and cars. His brothers drew from comic books and photo magazines; Jerry started by trying to draw what they drew. At some point he realized he would rather sit and draw than do almost anything else.

Pinkney was born in Philadelphia and grew up in its Germantown section. His mother understood him and made it clear that if art was what Jerry wanted to pursue, then that's what she wanted to have happen.

When Jerry was about 12 years old, he had a newspaper stand on a large intersection in Philadelphia. He carried his drawing pad and sketched passersby. One day an artist named John Liney, a cartoonist, noticed him and took him to visit his studio. From time to time, Liney gave Jerry art materials and supplies to work with. Liney's encouragement and example helped Pinkney see that it was possible to make a living as an artist.

After Pinkney graduated from Dobbins Vocational School, where he met his wife Gloria, he received a full scholarship to the Philadelphia Museum College of Art. Eventually he and Gloria moved to Boston. There he worked as a designer at a greeting card company and at Barker-Black, where he developed his reputation as an illustrator. Later Pinkney opened the Kaleidoscope Studio with two other artists and eventually opened his own freelance studio—the Jerry Pinkney Studio. He and Gloria moved to New York to obtain a wider range of editorial and book projects.

Jerry Pinkney teaches at the University of Delaware and works in his studio at home. He is at his drawing board between 8:30 and 9 o'clock in the morning and usually ends his day between 8:30 and 10 o'clock at night. His style and medium are tautly composed watercolor vignettes. He and Gloria have four grown children: Troy Bernadette is the director of Child Life at Jacobi Hospital and mother of their granddaughter, Gloria, who appears in a book, *Pretend You're a Cat.* Brian Pinkney is a well-known illustrator of children's books. Scott Cannon Pinkney is art director at a large advertising agency. Myles Carter Pinkney, who is studying photography, is a child-care worker at Anderson School.

Jerry Pinkney has won the Coretta Scott King award three times, and a Caldecott honor twice. His illustrations for Patricia McKissack's *Mirandy and Brother Wind* and for Robert San Souci's *The Talking Eggs: A Folktale from the American South* both earned a Caldecott Honor Book award. His other books include *Home Place* by Crescent Dragonwagon, *Further Tales of Uncle Remus* by Julius Lester, *The Patchwork Quilt* by Valerie Flournoy, *Turtle in July* by Marilyn Singer, and *Back Home,* by Gloria Pinkney.

Jerry Pinkney

Pictures and Text Work Together

Extend:

Aylesworth, Jim. *Old Black Fly.* Illus. Stephen Gammell.

Verify:

Cooney, Barbara. *Miss Rumphius.*

Parallel:

Browne, Anthony. *Hansel and Gretel.*

Burningham, John. *Time to Get Out of the Bath, Shirley.*

———. *Come Away from the Water, Shirley.*

McAfee, Analena. *The Visitors Who Came to Stay.* Illus. Anthony Browne.

Wordless:

McCully, Emily Arnold. *School.*

Illustrated:

Burkert, Nancy Ekholm. *Valentine & Orson.*

Mathis, Sharon Bell. *The Hundred Penny Box.* Illus. Leo and Diane Dillon.

Evaluating Literary Quality

Picture storybooks that are good literature exemplify the same qualities as all good stories. They need strong characterization, an engaging plot, a memorable theme, and well-crafted language. They also need to contain excellent art that works with the text to tell the story. Informational picture books must convey a meaningful message with clarity and style through a lucid text and artful illustrations. Since picture books are slender volumes—often no more than 32 pages—authors must hone the text to use the very best word in every case, and illustrators must capture mood, characterization, plot, setting, information, or concepts in carefully wrought art.

Art

Art in children's picture books involves the entire range of media, techniques, and styles used in art anywhere. The *medium*—the material used in the production of a work—may be watercolors, oils, acrylics, ink, pencil, charcoal, pastels, tissue paper, acetate sheets, or fabric. The *technique* may be painting, etching, wood and linoleum cuts, airbrush, collage, photography, and many other means. It is the individual artist's style, combined with the medium and technique, that evoke the mood presented in the book.

When illustrating a picture book, artists make many choices in addition to the media and techniques they use. They must decide about color, style, and composition in their illustrations. They make choices about line, shape, placement on a page, the use of negative space, and texture. (See the glossary for definitions of these terms.) Book illustration is an art; as such, it must go beyond the appeal of the literal to visual communication. Illustrations must be not only interesting and appealing but also imaginative and dramatic.

A beautifully illustrated children's book is a masterful work of art. Arranging the elements of art and text on a page requires an artist's eye. If the composition is awkward or unbalanced, if there is not enough white space to set off the various parts of the picture, or if the illustration does not balance well with the text, it detracts from the work. From the first look at the dust jacket and the endpapers to the close scrutiny of the art on the pages, it should be apparent that the book has been illustrated with skill and care.

The artist works with the basic elements of art—line, shape, color, and texture—and the principles of design—rhythm, balance, variety, emphasis, spatial order, and unity—to create a unified whole to convey meaning.

Line. Line is a mark on paper or where different colors meet. Lines can be straight or curved, thick or thin, sharp or soft, and can move in any direction. Lines catch the viewer's eye and force the viewer to look in a particular direction. They also convey properties such as delicacy (thin lines) or stability (thick lines).

Peter Parnall's distinctive use of a firm but delicate line and space results in a clear, uncluttered feeling. His work is scientifically accurate; it appears in *Scientific American* and *Audubon Magazine*. In *The Daywatchers* (I) his birds are meticulously realistic and in Byrd Baylor's *The Way to Start a Day* (I) he paints with reverence and dignity.

Bold carbon pencil drawings result in a sense of mass and the play of light and shadow in Chris Van Allsburg's *Jumanji* (I). A heavy use of parallel lines, architectural forms, and an exploration of perspective mark his work in *Ben's Dream* (I).

Figure
3-2

Checklist for Evaluating Picture Books

Text

Fiction:

- ❑ Is there a good story? Do you like it? Is the story lively, moving, funny, or surprising?
- ❑ Are characters well developed and delineated? How would a character react in a new situation?
- ❑ What is the theme? Is it developed in lively language and engaging illustrations?

Nonfiction:

- ❑ Are ideas presented in a logical sequence?
- ❑ Are concepts presented in understandable terms? Are terms defined? Are examples given?
- ❑ Is the writing direct and straightforward?

Both fiction and nonfiction:

- ❑ Is the book appropriate for the child? Does it meet cognitive and intellectual level interests?
- ❑ Are racial, cultural, and gender stereotypes avoided? Are groups portrayed accurately?
- ❑ Is the language of high quality? Is it appropriate? When it is read by an adult, can a child understand it?

Illustrations

Fiction:

- ❑ Do the illustrations establish the mood, theme, characters, and setting of the story?

- ❑ Are subplots contained in the illustrations for children to discover?
- ❑ Is the visual interpretation unique, yet valid? Does it enable the reader to view the story in a new and truly artistic way?

Nonfiction:

- ❑ Do the illustrations add or clarify information?
- ❑ Do the illustrations contribute to understanding?

Both fiction and nonfiction:

- ❑ Do illustrations enrich or conflict with the text?
- ❑ Does the artist use line, shape, and color to add to the meaning? Do black-and-white or monochromatic illustrations meet the same standards: Are they well crafted and distinguished?
- ❑ Is the composition well balanced? Does the arrangement add to the meaning?
- ❑ Is the artistic style appropriate to the content?

Format

Both fiction and nonfiction:

- ❑ Is the size of the book appropriate to its content and use?
- ❑ Do the dust jacket, cover, and endpapers express the book's content and purpose?
- ❑ Are the paper, typeface, and other design elements appropriate to the content and the age group?
- ❑ Does the title page foreshadow the content to come?

Note: Although guidelines are presented separately for text, art, and format, unity is crucial. Text, illustrations, and design are expressions of art; together they create a richer experience than any do separately.

The overarching question is, How artfully do they work together? First, read just the words without looking at the illustrations. Try to evaluate the words by themselves. Later, reread looking at the art. How much does the art expand and enrich the story? How does the design enhance the experience? How artfully is it done?

Select from the suggested questions; not all questions are appropriate for every book.

Shape. Shape is an area or form with a definite outline. Along with line, shape controls the direction of the viewer's eye movements. Shapes can be geometric (circles, triangles, squares); organic (less defined shapes such as clouds); or biomorphic (the shapes of living organisms). The use of shape contributes to the volume, or three-dimensional quality of an illustration. In some illustrations shapes seem to jut out from the front, or plane of the picture, coming toward the viewer. Artists make decisions about the placement of shapes (positive space) in the background (negative space).

Peter Parnall creates the feeling of vast open spaces by using a strong but delicate line and creating uncluttered pages. (*I'm in Charge of Celebrations* by Byrd Baylor)

Chris Van Allsburg's art shows an incredible use of bold line and shading to achieve a sense of architectural form and solidity. This is a spectacular example of chiaroscuro—shading using dark and light. (*Jumanji*)

Lois Ehlert uses geometric shapes to convey a sense of vitality in **Moon Rope** (P). Her books are marked by bright colors, clear, vivid lines, and shapes that seem to jump off the page. By transforming natural shapes into geometric forms she calls attention to the essential shape of the objects she depicts.

Trina Schart Hyman often uses geometric print borders to frame her meticulously detailed illustrations, as she does in **Little Red Riding Hood** (P) and **Saint George and the Dragon** (I). The borders confine her richly detailed paintings and increase the sense of lush romanticism. Vera Williams uses borders that repeat patterns in her illustrations to create a sense of loving coziness in **A Chair for My Mother** (P).

Texture. The surface of an illustration, whether actual or illusory, is its texture. Some illustrations

When they returned, the birds said,
"Your rope is ready." Fox started
climbing, paw over paw, eager
to be first on the moon.
Mole followed,
claw over claw.

Cuando regresaron los pájaros,
dijeron: — Ya está listo el lazo. —
El Zorro empezó a subir,
pata por pata, pues quería ser
el primero en llegar a la luna.
El Topo le siguió, garra por garra.

Lois Ehlert's strong graphic designs use geometric shapes and vivid color
to achieve a sense of vitality. (*Moon Rope*)

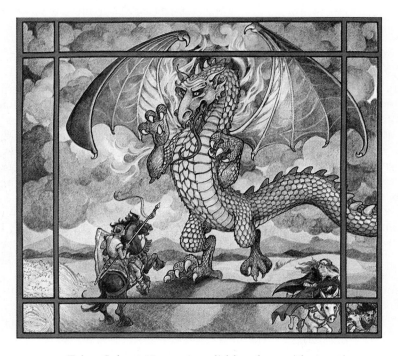

Trina Schart Hyman's solid borders with no stip-
ling or cross-hatching make it seem as if we are
looking through a window. Her technique draws
us into the picture and action. (*St. George and
the Dragon*)

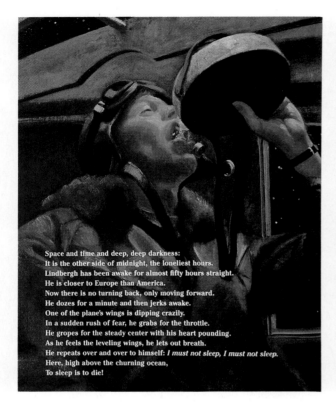

Space and time and deep, deep darkness:
It is the other side of midnight, the loneliest hours.
Lindbergh has been awake for almost fifty hours straight.
He is closer to Europe than America.
Now there is no turning back, only moving forward.
He dozes for a minute and then jerks awake.
One of the plane's wings is dipping crazily.
In a sudden rush of fear, he grabs for the throttle.
He gropes for the steady center with his heart pounding.
As he feels the leveling wings, he lets out breath.
He repeats over and over to himself: *I must not sleep, I must not sleep.*
Here, high above the churning ocean,
To sleep is to die!

Mike Wimmer creates the illusion of water—a realistic image of its texture that flows from the water jug in Robert Burleigh's biography of Charles Lindbergh, **Flight.**

The Dillons's art conveys an opulent iridescent quality that exists in opera. The marble columns and shimmering fabrics add dignity and richness to the scenes. (**Aïda** retold by Leontyne Price, illus. by Leo and Diane Dillon)

seem smooth, others rough; some, like collage, do have a rough texture in the original art. Texture conveys a sense of reality; interesting visual contrasts or patterns suggest movement and action, roughness or delicacy.

In Robert Burleigh's **Flight** (I), artist Mike Wimmer makes the water look realistically liquid. Leo and Diane Dillon give a diaphanous, iridescent quality to fabrics in Leontyne Price's **Aïda** (A). And in Bert Kitchen's **Animal Alphabet** (N–P) the animals look as rough or fuzzy as they are in real life.

Color. Artists use color—or the lack of it—to express mood and emotion. Color conveys temperature (warm and cool colors), personality traits, tastes, and feelings. Color can vary in *hue*—ranging across the rainbow of colors—and *intensity.* Dull colors can express weariness, boredom, serenity whereas intense colors evoke feelings of energy, vibrancy, and excitement. Colors can also vary in *value,* or the amount of light and dark. A range of

values creates drama or movement; an absence of contrast creates a quiet or solemn mood.

Uri Shulevitz's stunning watercolors in **Dawn** (P–I) range from the dark indigo of night to the bright green and yellow of the sunrise. The gradual lightening of the illustrations creates a sense of anticipation that is richly rewarded with the drama of daybreak.

Brian Wildsmith's distinctive bright, contrasting colors in a harlequin pattern have a strong visual impact in **The Little Wood Duck** (P), **Daisy** (P), and **Give a Dog a Bone** (P).

Principles of Design. Artists use the basic elements we have discussed to create meaning and feeling. They manipulate these elements through the principles of design to express their own unique visions. Artists work to achieve unity, or a meaningful whole, through the *composition* of their art. To achieve unity, artists make use of balance, repeating rhythms, variety, emphasis, and spatial order (Greenberg & Jordan, 1991). Balance means

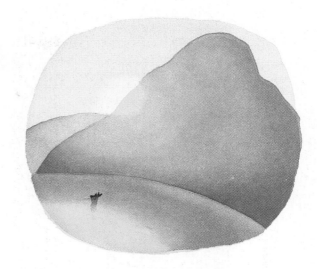

Uri Shulevitz achieves a sense of dawn breaking and the day growing brighter by using less paint and lighter watercolors. (*Dawn*)

Bert Kitchen achieves an amazing depth of texture in *Animal Alphabet.* The animals seem to be alive as they are presented in bold colors against a white background.

giving equal weight to the lines, shapes, textures, and colors in a picture; without it the picture seems awkward (Greenberg & Jordan, 1991). Repetition in art helps to achieve visual harmony and balance, whereas variety sets up oppositions and progressions that lead the eye from one point to another. Artists use emphasis to draw attention to a particular part of their piece; size, placement, color, and line can work together to force our eyes to notice a particular part of an illustration first.

Peter Parnall's use of white space focuses the viewer's eye on the elements Parnall wants to stress. Lois Ehlert's bright contrasting colors, shapes, and hard lines emphasize the objects she is exploring. Chris Van Allsburg uses perspective to emphasize objects in *Two Bad Ants* (P), as Don Wood does in Audrey Wood's *The Napping House* (P).

In picture books, principles of design relate to the overall design of a book as well as to individual pictures, and are integrated with the content. In *Strega Nona* (P) Tomie de Paola uses sturdy figures

And a nice big bone.
Stray jumped.

Brian Wildsmith's illustrations appear in brilliant contrasting colors with strong representational shapes. His abstract tendencies allow text and art to exist without the other. (*Give a Dog a Bone*)

The *Napping House* is made all the more inviting by the use of colors once removed from real life. The twilight scenes say "Welcome, it's safe to come inside." (*Napping House,* by Audrey Wood, illustrated by Don Wood)

arranged almost as if they were on a stage setting. This reflects the sturdy folktale he retells and the pasta-eating grandmother.

The cover design, text placement, typography, endpapers, illustrations, and white space are all elements of the total design. Arrangement and sequencing of design elements lead the eye effectively through a book. Lane Smith uses every inch of available space to increase the feeling of delighted shock in Jon Scieszka's **The Stinky Cheese Man** (I–A). The cover, title page, dedication page, table of contents, and typeface are all playfully manipulated to achieve a sense of violating conventions. The text consists of hilarious versions of familiar folktales; the surrealistic art heightens the mockery of folktale conventions. Beyond that, the text and illustrations play with the format of the picture book itself, achieving a remarkable unity of text and illustration.

Media and Technique. Artists also make choices about the media, techniques, and styles they work in. Media refers to the material used in the production of a work. Technique refers to the method of creating art. Artists can work with virtually any medium—clay, wood, metal, watercolors, oils, fabric, acrylics, ink, pencil, charcoal, pastels—or combination of media. They can also use a variety of techniques—painting, etching, wood and linoleum cutting, airbrush, collage, photography. Some artists become known for their work with a particular technique or medium, like Ezra Jack Keats for his collages, Brian Pinkney for his scratchboard art, or Ken Robbins for his photographs. For **Bridges** (P–I–A) Robbins began with black-and-white photographs of various bridges and then hand colored them to produce exquisitely beautiful illustrations of real bridges. The hand coloring produces a soft romantic mood.

Other artists range across a variety of media and technique, selecting what best suits the text they are illustrating. Figure 3–3 lists some examples of the media and techniques that can be found in picture books; illustrations for Figure 3–4 provide examples.

Style. Style reflects the individuality and artistic strength of the artist and is influenced by both the content and mood of the text and the intended audience (Cianciolo, 1976). The styles available in books for children are many and varied. *Representational art* consists of literal, realistic depictions of characters, objects, and events. James Ransome works from photographs and live models to achieve realism in his paintings. His representational paintings for Denise Lewis Patrick's **Red Dancing Shoes** (P) are perfect for expressing the familiar emotional content of the story.

Expressionistic art is more abstract, conveying the artist's subjective emotions rather than seeking to imitate reality. Emily Arnold McCully's paintings in **Mirette on the High Wire** (P–I) convey the almost lighter-than-air vitality of young Mirette; nineteenth-century Paris is romanticized with light and color.

Surrealism contains "startling images and incongruities" that often suggest an "attitude or

Tomie de Paola's comical cutout characters dance across the stage of the layout and seem slightly less alive than the spaghetti—which is all the funnier for it. (**Strega Nona**)

Jon Scieszka and Lane Smith play topsy-turvy with the traditions for telling folk tales, for art, and for book making. Their nontraditional art and stories show children that adults can break the rules when retelling old folktales and putting together a book. It says "You can make books and language a play thing, too." (**Stinky Cheese Man** by Jon Scieszka, illus., by Lane Smith)

Figure 3-3

Media Used in Illustration

Woodcuts

Brown, Marcia. *Once a Mouse.*

Emberley, Ed. *Drummer Hoff.*

Geisert, Arthur. *Pigs from A to Z.*

———. *Oink.*

Tejima. *Owl Lake.*

Wolff, Ashley. *A Year of Birds.*

Scratchboard

Albert, Burton. *Where Does the Trail Lead?* Illus. Brian Pinkney.

Cooney, Barbara. *Chanticleer and the Fox.*

Hooks, William. *Ballad of Belle Dorcas.* Illus. Brian Pinkney.

Collage

Baker, Jeannie. *Window.*

———. *Home in the Sky.*

Bang, Molly. *Paper Crane.*

Brown, Marcia. *Shadow.*

Carle, Eric. *The Very Hungry Caterpillar.*

Fox, Mem. *Hattie and the Fox.* Illus. Patricia Mullins.

Keats, Ezra Jack. *The Snowy Day.*

Lionni, Leo. *Little Blue and Little Yellow.*

———. *Inch by Inch.*

Young, Ed. *Seven Blind Mice.*

Watercolors

Bunting, Eve. *The Wall.* Illus. Ronald Himler.

Lyon, George Ella. *Come a Tide.* Illus. Stephen Gammell.

McCloskey, Robert. *Time of Wonder.*

Wiesner, David. *Tuesday.*

Williams, Vera. *A Chair for My Mother.*

Acrylics (plastic paints)

Cooney, Barbara. *Miss Rumphius.*

Opaque Paint

Brown, Margaret Wise. *The Little Island.* Illus. Leonard Weisgard.

Politi, Leo. *Song of the Swallows.*

Tempera

Sendak, Maurice. *Where the Wild Things Are.*

Pastels

Hendershot, Judith. *In Coal Country.* Illus. Thomas B. Allen.

Chalk

Grifalconi, Ann. *Osa's Pride.*

Grease Pencil

Goble, Paul. *Where the Buffaloes Begin.* Illus. Stephen Gammell.

Conte Pencil

Van Allsburg, Chris. *Jumanji.*

Oil Paints

Patrick, Denise Lewis. *Red Dancing Shoes.* Illus. James Ransome.

Zelinsky, Paul. *Rumpelstiltskin.*

Photographs

Hopkins, Lee Bennett (compiler). *Through Our Eyes: Poems and Pictures About Growing Up.* Photos by Jeffrey Dunn.

Hoban, Tana. *Spots, Feathers, and Curly Tails.*

Robbins, Ken. *Bridges.*

---

mockery about conventionalities" (Cianciolo, 1976, p. 40). As we discussed, Lane Smith's surrealistic paintings for **The Stinky Cheese Man** (I–A) are clever accompaniments to the brassy challenge of the text. His illustrations are full of garishly funny details, such as the Little Red Hen's feet coming out of the giant's mouth as he picks his teeth with a feather.

Impressionistic artists emphasize light and color, placing small bits of color close together to create images. The softly blurred lines of Carole

Byard's acrylic paintings in Sherley Anne Williams's **Working Cotton** (I) suggest images of a day in the cotton fields, and the strength and exhaustion of those picking. Byard's paintings suggest rather than sharply define reality.

Folk art simplifies, exaggerates, and distorts reality, but in a way that is characteristic of the traditional art of a culture. This is often realized through the use of traditional motifs, symbols, and techniques (Cianciolo, 1990). Deborah Nourse Lattimore's illustrations for **The Dragon's Robe** (I) make

Jeannie Baker's collages are made from bits of fabric and twigs. They look so real we want to feel the texture. The three-dimensional look of the collages gives that textural impression. (***Where the Forest Meets the Sea;*** collage)

Hoban's photographs capture color, line, shape, and texture to illustrate concepts in a book for the very young. (***Dots, Spots, Speckles, and Stripes*** by Tana Hoban

use of traditional Chinese motifs and symbols and reflect the art that marks the period of Chinese history in which the story is set.

Naive art is technically unsophisticated but is marked by an artist's clear, intense emotions and visions. Naive art presents the essence of experiences and objects in a simplified fashion; it is generally not marked by concerns with perspective (Cianciolo, 1990). Faith Ringgold's illustrations for ***Tar Beach*** (P) simply burst with joy and vitality as young Cassie flies up from the roof of her apartment building and out over New York City.

Cartoon art depicts incongruities or incompatibilities, often through exaggeration, and the result is humor (Cianciolo, 1976). Steven Kellogg is a master of cartoon humor, and his classic ***Pinkerton, Behave*** (P) exemplifies this style. A Great Dane who flunked obedience school, a burglar, and a quick-thinking dog owner create a situation as hilarious as the illustrations.

All of these styles can be found in picture books. The illustrations shown here are examples of art in an assortment of styles. Notice the variety of techniques and media as well.

When evaluating the art in picture books look for (1) the artistic quality of the illustrations, (2) how the illustrations reflect the words to tell the story or present the information, (3) how the illustrations extend the story or elaborate the concept, and (4) how each illustration presents a unique, fresh visual interpretation that enables a reader to view aspects of a story, poem, or concept in a new, truly artistic way.

Language

The language, or style, of picture books is as essential to a successful book as the art. The most fully developed and beautiful forms of language are found in literature. Literature *is* language at its most graceful, and children's language grows through experience with literature. Children learn naturally in an environment that is filled with language in use; they learn the language they hear or read. It follows that the richer the environment, the more fully developed a child's language will be.

The influence of the language of literature on children's own language can be heard when children mimic words and phrases they meet in books, such as when 2½-year old Trisha, after hearing Kevin Henkes's ***Chrysanthemum*** (N–P), mimicked "absolutely poifeck." Even when children do not directly imitate book language, its influence is still there as the beautiful words they hear become part of their life experience. Children who make language their toy when they are young become adults who value the nuances in beautiful word images.

Picture books contain rich language because they are usually meant to be read aloud to children

---

**Figure
3-4**

Styles of Art in Picture Books

Naive Art

Aldersen, Sue Ann. *Ida and the Wool Smugglers.* Illus. Ann Blades.

Bryan, Ashley. *Sing to the Sun.*

Cooney, Barbara. *Island Boy.*

Goffstein, M. B. *An Artist.*

Ringgold, Faith. *Tar Beach.*

———. *Aunt Harriet's Underground Railroad in the Sky.*

Representational

Greenfield, Eloise. *Nathaniel Talking.* Illus. Jan Spivey Gilchrist.

Grifalconi, Ann. *Flyaway Girl.*

Hopkinson, Deborah. *Sweet Clara and the Freedom Quilt.* Illus. James Ransome.

Mathis, Sharon Bell. *Hundred Penny Box.* Illus. Leo and Diane Dillon.

McKinley, Robin. *Rowan.* Illus. Donna Ruff.

Patrick, Denise Lewis. *Red Dancing Shoes.* Illus. James Ransome.

Impressionistic Art

Christiansen, Candace. *Calico and Tin Horns.* Illus. Thomas Locker.

Williams, Sherley Anne. *Working Cotton.* Illus. Carole Byard.

Expressionistic Art

Baylor, Byrd. *I'm in Charge of Celebrations.* Illus. Peter Parnall.

Brodsky, Beverly. *The Story of Job.*

Conrad, Pam. *The Lost Sailor.* Illus. Richard Egielski.

Farber, Norma. *Return of the Shadows.* Illus. Andrea Baruffi.

McCully, Emily Arnold. *Mirette on the High Wire.*

Stanley, Diane, and Peter Vennema. *Bard of Avon: The Story of William Shakespeare.* Illus. Diane Stanley.

Surrealistic Art

Browne, Anthony. *Tunnel.*

———. *Changes.*

———. *Piggybook.*

McAfee, Annalena. *The Visitors Who Came to Stay.* Illus. Anthony Browne.

Van Allsburg, Chris. *Jumanji.*

———. *The Mysteries of Harris Burdick.*

———. *Polar Express.*

Cartoon Art

Bucknell, Caroline. *One Bear in the Picture.*

Kellogg, Steven. *Pecos Bill.*

Krauss, Ruth. *A Very Special House.* Illus. Maurice Sendak.

Marianne (pseud. Marian Foster Curtis). *Miss Flora McFlimsey and the Baby New Year.*

Noll, Sally. *I Have a Loose Tooth.*

Steig, William. *Dr. De Soto.*

Wellington, Monica. *Mr. Cookie Baker.*

Folk Art

Clement, Claude. *The Painter and the Wild Swans.* Illus. Frederic Clement.

Lattimore, Deborah Nourse. *The Dragon's Robe.*

Sabuda, Robert (reteller). *Saint Valentine.*

---

long before they are read individually by children. Picture books are most often introduced to children by an adult reading *to* the child. The language in the books is language that adults can *read* and children can *understand.* Thus it is not appropriate to look for simple, easy-to-read language in picture books, as most are not meant to be beginning reading material, although many may certainly be used effectively in this way. (We discuss this later in this chapter and in Chapter 12.) Instead, look for (1)

interesting words used in interesting ways that build excitement, drama, images, or concepts, and (2) language that has an internal rhythm and melody. If it sounds natural when read aloud, it's probably well written.

Content

The content of a picture book determines its structure and genre. Picture books designed to present

Young children find it comforting to look at Eric Carle's big blocks of color. His naive art collages are symbolic, not representational. They help children accept symbols that represent objects and meaning—a necessary part of learning to read. (*All Around Us;* naive art)

Carole Byard uses acrylic colors to represent light in its various forms, almost as Monet or Cezanne did. Her daubs of color combine to give the impression of reality. (*Working Cotton* by Sherley Anne William; impressionistic art)

information and develop concepts differ from those designed to tell a story or present a poem.

Nonfiction Picture Books. Nonfiction picture books should address a subject of interest to a child, and should present information in a way that is understandable, appropriate to the age of the child, and helps the child form a concept. For example, a book about trucks for young children might be a combination of pictures and labels or brief text,

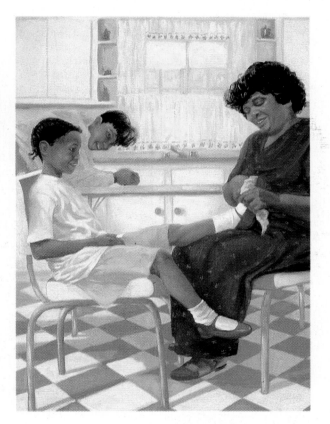

James Ransome is a rare talent who works with oils and uses live models. His representational art carefully balances pattern and movement to capture the essence of emotions. (*Red Dancing Shoes* by Denise Lewis Patrick; representational art)

McCully uses watercolors to borrow from Toulouse-Lautrec deliberately, even including Jane Avril—one of his subjects. When children see Toulouse-Lautrec's theater posters, they will have a sense of familiarity because of their love for Mirette on the high wire. (***Mirette on the High Wire*** by Emily Arnold McCully; expressionistic art)

Surrealists portray "over reality" to stress experiences that are hidden in normal life (or hyperreality to create a sense of actuality). Van Allsburg uses conte pencil and conte dust to paint in the style of Magritte, showing clouds floating over intricate subjects and architectural reality. (***Jumanji;*** surrealistic art)

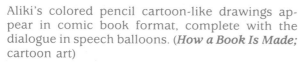

Aliki's colored pencil cartoon-like drawings appear in comic book format, complete with the dialogue in speech balloons. (***How a Book Is Made;*** cartoon art)

McDermott uses gouache and ink to create symbols from the folk art of Native Americans in highly stylized repetitive patterns. The leader of the Dance of Life wears the cross-cut pattern of an ear of corn as a chest shield. (***Arrow to the Sun;*** folk art)

TEACHING IDEA 3-2

Explore Art Media

Experiment with the media and techniques artists use to illustrate books. Collect books that contain the various media and techniques as models for your experiments.

Paper

Feelings, Tom. *Moja Means One. Jambo Means Hello.*
     tissue paper, oil, inks, tempera.

Keats, Ezra Jack. *The Snowy Day. Peter's Chair.*
     cut paper from textured paper

Lionni, Leo. *Pezzetino.*
     torn paper, mosaic tile.

Use tissue paper, construction paper, magazines, newspaper, wallpaper, gift wrap paper for book illustrations, collages, mosaics, and paper sculptures.

Watercolors

McCloskey, Robert. *Time of Wonder.*

McDermott, Gerald. *Arrow to the Sun.*

Shulevitz, Uri. *Dawn.*

Use watercolor paints, tempera, gouache, and water-base paint for book illustration projects, landscapes, crayon resist painting, seascapes, skyscapes, and backgrounds.

Crayons and Pastels

de Paola, Tomie. *Bonjour, Mr. Satie.*

Hogrogian, Nonny. *Always Room for One More.*

Spier, Peter. *Rain. Noah's Ark.*

Use crayons, Craypas, pastels, water crayons, and markers for book illustration projects, including crayon scratch drawings, crayon resist, chalk paintings, crayon texture drawings, or any combination of media.

Printing Techniques

Emberley, Ed. *Drummer Hoff.*

Haley, Gail. *A Story, A Story.*

Lent, Blair. *The Wave.*

Lionni, Leo. *Swimmy.*

Tejima, Keizaburo. *Owl Lake.*

Use paper doilies, linoleum blocks, woodblocks, potato prints, plastic foam, cardboard, sandpaper, and yarn for book illustration projects. Create shapes to dip into paints and stamp onto paper. Make relief prints, etching, cardboard cuts, and potato prints.

Cartoons

Peet, Bill. *Bill Peet: An Autobiography.*

Sendak, Maurice, and Matthew Margolis. *Some Swell Pup or Are You Sure You Want a Dog.*

Comic Strips

Ardizzone, Edward. *Little Tim and the Brave Sea Captain.*

————. *Tim All Alone.*

Spiegelman, Art. *Maus I.*

————. *Maus II.*

Use speech balloons to hold the dialogue spoken by the characters. Illustrate the action. Share your work with classmates.

---

presenting information about various types of trucks; children a bit older would want more information about what various trucks are for; even older children might want a book that details the uses and the internal mechanics of trucks.

Nonfiction picture books vary in structure, with the information itself determining the order of presentation. The illustrations must be accurate and exactly match the text, and should provide extra details that enhance the verbal information. For example, Bruce Brooks describes several functional structures that animals build in **Nature by Design** (I). He begins by describing a personal experience

of discovering a wasp nest stuck against barn eaves and gradually helps us appreciate the intricacy of the construction by revealing more information about it. He shares his own wonder at each discovery and includes clear color photographs to portray the wonder for us. The gradually expanding revelations in text and photographs draw us into the subject as it informs us because the author shares his passion as well as his knowledge of the topic.

The many types of nonfiction picture books include picture book biographies as well. Gwen Everett's **Li'l Sis and Uncle Willie: A Story Based on the Life and Paintings of William H. Johnson**

The exquisite detail in the photographs answers many questions but also raises new ones. Viewers share the author's sense of wonder about the beauty and intricacy of designs in nature. (***Nature by Design*** by Bruce Brooks)

Good nonfiction books present accurate information about interesting topics. Mary Barrett Brown's ***Wings Along the Waterway*** conveys clear information about 21 wetland birds through text and illustrations.

(I–A) is beautifully illustrated with reproductions of paintings by the subject. Diane Stanley and Peter Vennema's ***Bard of Avon: The Story of William Shakespeare*** (I–A) situates Shakespeare in the political and social climate of Elizabethan England. Stanley's accurate paintings provide details of dress and custom.

Children of all ages enjoy learning how to do things, and how-to-do-it picture books are very popular. Constance Nabwire and Bertha Montgomery's ***Cooking the African Way*** (P) is realistically illustrated with photographs by Robert and Diane Wolfe. The clearly written directions in Joan Irvine's ***How to Make Super Pop-Ups*** (I–A) are easy to follow because of Linda Hendry's step-by-step illustrations.

The content of nonfiction picture books also includes areas such as mathematics and music. Bruce McMillan's ***Eating Fractions*** (P) is illustrated with close-up focused photographs that explain why fractions are important in real life! Marjorie Pillar's photographs for ***Join the Band!*** (I) demonstrate the hard work and excitement of being in a school band.

When evaluating the content of nonfiction picture books, look for (1) interesting topics presented in an understandable fashion for the intended audience, (2) clear structure with illustrations that confirm and extend the verbal information, and (3) accuracy in text and illustrations. A book that reflects all of these qualities is Mary Barrett Brown's

---

Figure 3-5

Nonfiction Picture Books:
Science, Social Studies, Math, Art, Music, and Movement

Allen, Thomas B. *On Grandaddy's Farm.* (P–I)

Arnosky, Jim. *Secrets of a Wildlife Watcher.* (P–I)

Axelrod, Alan. *Songs of the Wild West.* Arrangements by Dan Fox. Color photos. (A)

Blizzard, Gladys S. *Come Look with Me: Exploring Landscape Art with Children.* (P–I)

Burleigh, Robert, and Mike Wimmer. *Flight: The Journey of Charles Lindbergh.* (P–I)

Cole, Joanna. *Magic School Bus at the Waterworks.* Illus. Bruce Degen. (P–I)

Cummings, Pat (editor). *Talking with Artists.* (I–A)

Fisher, L. E. *The Oregon Trail.* (I–A)

Freedman, Russell. *An Indian Winter.* (I–A)

Hammerstein, Oscar II. *A Real Nice Clambake.* Illus. Nadine Bernard Westcott. (P–I)

Hoyt-Goldsmith, Diane, and Lawrence Migdale. *Pueblo Storyteller.* (P–I)

Langstaff, John. *Climbing Jacob's Ladder: Heroes of the Bible in African-American Spirituals.* Illus. Ashley Bryan. (P–I)

Lauber, Patricia. *Get Ready for Robots.* Illus. True Kelley (P)

———. *Seeing Earth from Space.* (I–A)

Lavies, Bianca. *Backyard Hunter: The Praying Mantis.* (P–I)

Lourie, Peter. *Amazon: A Young Reader's Look at the Last Frontier.* Photos by Marcos Santilli. (P–I)

Macaulay, David. *Cathedral.* (I–A)

———. *Pyramid.* (I–A)

———. *Castle.* (I–A)

———. *The Way Things Work.* (P–I–A)

McDonald, Megan. *Is This a House for Hermit Crab?* Illus. S. D. Schindler. (P)

Musgrove, Margaret. *Ashanti to Zulu.* Illus. Leo and Diane Dillon. (P–I)

Richmond, Robin. *Introducing Michelangelo.* (I)

Schick, Eleanor. *I Have Another Language: The Language Is Dance.* (P)

Schwartz, David. *If You Made a Million.* Illus. Steven Kellogg. (I)

Simon, Seymour. *Volcanoes.* (P–I)

Skira-Venturi, Rosabianca. *A Weekend with Degas.*

Sweet, Melissa. *Fiddle-i-Fee: A Farmyard Song for the Very Young.* (N–P)

Yoshida, Toshi. *Young Lions.* (P–I)

Butterfly and Moth: Eyewitness Book. Dorling Kindersley. (I–A)

Visual Dictionary of the Human Body: Eyewitness Books. Dorling Kindersley. (I–A)

Wings Along the Waterway (I–A). Brown discusses 21 wetlands birds, describing each bird and its habits in a lucid text that accompanies painstakingly detailed paintings. The paintings range from double-page spreads to close-ups of a particular body part, elaborating the information the text is presenting. Brown's gentle epilogue about the importance of conserving our wetlands is made powerful because the previous text and illustrations have made readers appreciate these birds as much as Brown obviously does.

Examples of other fine nonfiction picture books are listed in Figure 3-5 and discussed in Chapter 10.

Poetry and Song Picture Books. Some picture books present an artist's visual interpretation of

Picture books of poetry extend the lyrical text through art and illuminate their emotional content. (**Heartland** by Diane Siebert, illustrated by Wendell Minor)

a song, poem, or verse. In these books the artist arranges the text across the pages, often one or two lines per page, and then illuminates each thought being expressed. In Ann Turner's **Rainflowers** (N–P), illustrator Robert Blake's vivid paintings display the power and splendor of the rainstorm that Turner captures in words. The paintings are full color double-page spreads, with the text superimposed at varying places, giving the effect of being surrounded by the storm. The paintings extend the poem, as they show a young boy going to pick a pumpkin, being caught in the storm, running to shelter in a barn, and resuming his walk home with his pumpkin when the storm subsides. Words and pictures combine to create a powerful picture book.

The song, poem, or verse should be interesting to and understandable by the intended audience. Brief, rhythmic verses, narrative verses, children's songs, and folksongs make excellent picture book texts. Some books contain several separate texts; others present single poems or songs. In beautifully designed picture books the arrangement of the text across the pages reflects the natural breaks in the meaning and sound of the original. Further, illustrations depict both action and feeling, matching the mood established by the author, as interpreted by the artist.

When evaluating the content in poetic picture books, look for (1) interesting ideas or stories presented in lyrical language, and (2) illustrations that interpret the text and illuminate its emotional content. Diane Siebert's **Sierra** (I–A), illustrated by Wendell Minor, is an excellent example of a poem illuminated by illustrations. The dramatic paintings, framed by a narrow black line, spill over 1 1/2 pages, with the text printed in the remaining space. Like the poem, the illustrations focus on both the vast and the intimate beauty of these mountains. Two visions of the Sierra, one expressed in words and the other in art, combine to present an experience made richer by both. Other examples are listed in Figure 3-6 and discussed further in Chapter 4.

Picture Storybooks. Most of the picture books that are read aloud to children are narratives—books that tell a story. These narratives may be folklore, fantasy, contemporary realistic fiction, science fiction, or historical fiction. They may reflect multicultural values and concerns. Whatever the type of narrative, picture storybooks should contain the best possible combination of art and language.

In addition to the visual art and the style, picture storybooks, as narratives, also are judged on their literary elements of setting, character, plot, and theme (see glossary), although specific criteria may vary a bit across the genres.

Setting in picture storybooks is usually presented briefly, often in the illustrations, because details about place and time can be visually portrayed quite easily and economically. Young children are usually bored with lengthy descriptions of

Figure
3-6

Picture Books of Poetry, Verse, and Song

Primary

Aliki. *Go Tell Aunt Rhody.*

Brown, Marc. *Play Rhymes.*

Clifton, Lucille. *Some of the Days of Everett Anderson.* Illus. Evaline Ness.

Field, Rachel. *General Store.* Illus. Nancy Winslow Parker.

Greenfield, Eloise. *Under the Sunday Tree.* Illus. Amos Ferguson.

————. *Night on Neighborhood Street.* Illus. Jan Spivey Gilchrist.

Griego, Margot C., Betsy L. Bucks, Sharon S. Gilbert, and Laurel H. Kimball (eds. and trans.). *Tortillitas para Mama: And Other Nursery Rhymes, Spanish and English.* Illus. Barbara Cooney.

Hart, Jane (comp). *Singing Bee: A Collection of Children's Songs.* Illus. Anita Lobel.

Hopkins, Lee Bennett. *Good Books, Good Times.* Illus. Harvey Stevenson.

————. *Still as a Star.* Illus. Karen Milone.

Lobel, Arnold. *Whiskers & Rhymes.*

Martin, Bill, Jr., and John Archambault. *Up and Down on the Merry-Go-Round.* Illus. Ted Rand.

Prelutsky, Jack (selector). *Poems of A. Nonny Mouse.* Illus. Henrik Drescher.

Raffi. *Everything Grows.* Illus. Bruce McMillan.

Zemach, Harve, and Margot Zemach. *Mommy, Buy Me a China Doll.*

Zemach, Margot. *Hush, Little Baby.*

Goldstein, Bobbye. *Inner Chimes: Poems About Poetry.* Illus. Jane Breskin Zalben.

Gunning, Monica. *Not a Copper Penny in Me House.* Illus. Frané Lessac.

Harrison, David. *Somebody Catch My Homework.* Illus. Betsy Lewin.

Janeczko, Paul B. *Brickyard Summer.* Illus. Ken Rush.

Krull, Kathleen. *Gonna Sing My Head Off!* Illus. Allen Garns.

Livingston, Myra Cohn. *Sea Songs.* Illus. Leonard Everett Fisher.

————. *Sky Songs.* Illus. Leonard Everett Fisher.

————. *Space Songs.* Illus. Leonard Everett Fisher.

Longfellow, Henry Wadsworth. *Hiawatha.* Illus. Susan Jeffers.

————. *Hiawatha's Childhood.* Illus. Errol le Cain.

————. *Paul Revere's Ride.* Illus. Nancy Winslow Parker.

————. *Paul Revere's Ride.* Illus. Ted Rand.

Metropolitan Museum of Art. *Go In and Out the Window: An Illustrated Songbook for Young People.* Music arranged and edited by Dan Fox. Commentary by Claude Marks.

O'Neill, Mary. *Hailstones and Halibut Bones.* Illus. John Wallner.

Siebert, Diane. *Mojave.* Illus. Wendell Minor.

Spier, Peter. *The Fox Went Out on a Chilly Night.*

Intermediate–Advanced

Buffett, Jimmy, and Savannah Jane Buffett. *The Jolly Mon.* Illus. Lambert Davis.

the setting. They want to know the time—present, past, or future—in which the tale is told and the place—real or make-believe. If the setting is fantastic, the details will be also, as in Jane Yolen's *Eeny, Meeny, Miney Mole* (P), illustrated by Kathryn Brown. The characters in Yolen's tale are moles and the text tells us they live "at the bottom of

a deep, dark hole." Kathryn Brown supplies the details—chairs, beds, tables, toys, and roots growing through the ceiling.

Historical settings, such as that in Patricia MacLachlan's *Three Names* (P–I), should accurately reflect life as it was lived in the time period. Alexander Pertzoff's paintings depict the vast emptiness

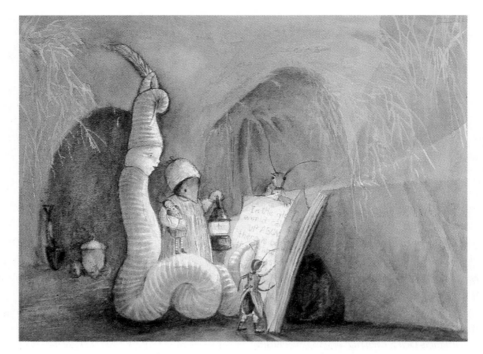

Picture books prove the axiom that a picture is worth a thousand words, especially in establishing setting. Kathryn Brown's illustrations vividly show that the characters in Jane Yolen's *Eeny, Meeny, Miney Mole* live in a deep dark hole.

Paul Goble's illustrations capture the traditions and folk art of the Native-American people whose tales and legends he retells. (*Buffalo Woman*)

and wove a wicked web as Anansi the Spider.

Caroline Binch expresses the real and make believe by showing the contrast between figure and background. Grace shows that we can become anything we want to be. (*Amazing Grace* by Mary Hoffman, illustrated by Caroline Binch)

Gloria Houston conveys Arizona's youthful exuberance by showing her dancing at the center of a circle of neighbors dressed in their turn-of-the-century garb. (*My Great Aunt Arizona*)

of the nineteenth-century prairie and the details of life there—the dress, the wagons, the animals, and the customs. As children read the story, they see both MacLachlan and Pertzoff's visions of what life was like 100 years ago.

In folklore, illustrators may decide to portray the ethnic and cultural traditions associated with the origins of the tale. But they must be careful that the details in the illustrations, and sometimes even the style of the illustrations, reflect those traditions. Paul Goble's illustrations of traditional Native American tales, such as **Buffalo Woman** (I), exemplify this. His bold, colorful illustrations incorporate both the folk motifs and the artistic style of the Plains Indians whose legends he retells.

Characters in picture storybooks also vary according to genre. In folklore, characters are usually stereotypes (one dimensional, flat)—the good princess, the brave prince, the wicked stepmother. In well-written realistic or fantasy narratives the characters are well-developed personalities that often show some evidence of growth and change across the story. Many picture storybook fantasies contain personified animal characters, with habits, behav-

iors, thoughts, and feelings that are human rather than animal, such as Arthur in the popular books by Marc Brown. Brown's characters dress and act like people, but they have the heads of various small animals. Their feelings are also human, as exemplified in **Arthur's Baby** (P), when Arthur overcomes his mixed feelings about his new baby sister to become her proud and competent big brother.

Realistic books, whether contemporary or historical, contain recognizably human characters, such as young Grace in Mary Hoffman's **Amazing Grace** (P), illustrated by Caroline Binch. Grace, the main character, loves stories and acting them out. When her friends tell her she can't be Peter Pan because he's a boy and he isn't black, she sets her mind to be such a good Peter Pan that her classmates will give her the part. The expressive realistic illustrations create the feeling that Grace is someone you know.

Gloria Houston's **My Great-Aunt Arizona** (P–I) is set in the late nineteenth- and early twentieth-century Blue Ridge Mountains. Susan Lamb's illustrations present the character Arizona as a

Subtly colored drawings, which fade in and out on the page and turn from startling detail to a suggestion of being there, bring another dimension to this tale of invisibility. (**Possum Magic** by Mem Fox, illustrated by Julie Vivas)

young girl who enjoys life—singing, dancing, playing—just as contemporary children do. Through the illustrations we see her mature and age. We also see her essential goodness, her joyful nature, and her intelligence in each of Lamb's paintings.

Whether animal or human, characters in picture storybooks are usually childlike. They reflect the actions, thoughts, and emotions of children in the narration, the dialogue, and the art. Well-developed characters in picture storybooks are active rather than passive, interacting with their story worlds to solve their own problems.

Young children find it natural to identify with storybook characters. They recognize themselves and their friends in the books they encounter, and this recognition helps them become aware of who they are and how they feel. Thus it is important for picture storybooks to contain characters (1) that are well developed in text and illustration, and (2) who actively make things happen.

Plot in picture story books is usually presented in a straightforward chronological order. Young children find it difficult to follow complex, convoluted plots with flashbacks and subplots. Neither do children like long, descriptive monologues; they want things to happen and happen fast. The plot usually centers around some problem or conflict, which is generally one that children recognize. Be-

ing too young, too small, or too scared to do something; changes in family structure; and new experiences are examples of some familiar problems found in many picture storybooks. Children also like definite, recognizable endings. If a problem is confronted, then it needs to be resolved, and in a manner that is logical according to the constraints of the story. In Mem Fox's **Possum Magic** (N–P) Grandma Poss uses her magic to make little Hush invisible but can't find the right spell to reverse the condition. She only remembers it has something to do with people food, so the two go off to search for just the right thing. Some foods make parts of Hush visible, but the story doesn't end until Hush is once again her fully recognizable self.

The plot should be (1) clear, moving forward logically, (2) visible in both text and illustration, and (3) contain a recognizable climax and a satisfying resolution.

Themes, like plots and characters in well-written stories, reflect the world of children. While themes can be and are interpreted differently by different readers, there are usually one or two main threads in a story that most readers understand as the unifying concept. Picture storybooks for children are often organized around the theme of growing up—increasing independence and self-reliance, increasing ability, increasing understanding. Good themes

---

Figure
3-7

Outstanding Picture Story Books

Nursery–Primary

Bemelmans, Ludwig. *Madeline.*

Brooke, L. Leslie. *Johnny Crow's Garden.*

Burton, Virginia Lee. *The Little House.*

————. *Mike Mulligan and His Steam Shovel.*

Carle, Eric. *The Very Hungry Caterpillar.*

de Paola, Tomie. *The Legend of the Indian Paintbrush.*

Flack, Marjorie. *The Story About Ping.* Illus. Kurt Wiese.

Gág, Wanda. *Millions of Cats.*

Gramatky, Hardie. *Little Toot.*

Hoban, Russell. *Bread and Jam for Frances.* Illus. Lillian Hoban.

Keats, Ezra Jack. *The Snowy Day.*

Lionni, Leo. *Little Blue and Little Yellow.*

McCloskey, Robert. *Blueberries for Sal.*

McKissack, Patricia C. *Mirandy and Brother Wind.* Illus. Jerry Pinkney.

Potter, Beatrix. *The Tale of Peter Rabbit.*

Rey, H. A. *Curious George.*

Ringgold, Faith. *Tar Beach.*

Say, Allen. *Bicycle Man.*

Sendak, Maurice. *Where the Wild Things Are.*

Slobodkina, Esphyr. *Caps for Sale.*

Wiesner, David. *Tuesday.*

Wisniewski, David. *The Warrior and the Wise Man.*

Intermediate–Advanced

Goble, Paul. *Crow Chief: A Plains Indian Story.*

————. *Death of the Iron Horse.*

Lasker, Joe. *Merry Ever After.*

Macaulay, David. *Black and White.*

McCunn, Ruthanne Lum. *Pie-Biter.*

Rylant, Cynthia. *Appalachia: The Voices of Sleeping Birds.* Illus. Barry Moser.

Sendak, Maurice. *Outside Over There.*

Steig, William. *Amos and Boris.*

Steptoe, John. *Stevie.*

Thurber, James. *Many Moons.* Illus. Marc Simont.

Van Allsburg, Chris. *The Garden of Abdul Gazasi.*

————. *The Polar Express.*

Willard, Nancy. *A Visit to William Blake's Inn.* Illus. Alice and Martin Provensen.

---

are neither blatantly stated, as in an explicit moral to the story, nor so subtle that they elude young readers.

Picture storybooks should have (1) a readily identifiable theme that evolves naturally from plot and character, and (2) illustrations that extend the theme and establish the mood. The titles of some outstanding picture storybooks appear in Figure 3-7, and other titles are listed in subsequent sections of this and other chapters.

A Close Look at *The Tale of Peter Rabbit*

A picture storybook that has stood the test of time and is as beloved by children today as it was when it was published in 1902 is Beatrix Potter's **The Tale of Peter Rabbit** (N–P).

Synopsis

Peter is a young rabbit with three sisters and a mother; they all live near Mr. McGregor's vegetable garden, a tempting but dangerous place where Peter's father met an untimely death. When Mrs. Rabbit goes to the baker's, disobedient Peter immediately squeezes under the garden gate and gorges himself on the treasures of the garden. Mr. McGregor spots him and chases Peter through the garden and into a shed where Peter eludes him. Peter finally finds his way out of the garden and back home, where he is put to bed to recuperate from his excesses.

Peter turns his back to his family and faces the viewer, suggesting that he may not be listening to his mother's instructions. (**The Tale of Peter Rabbit** by Beatrix Potter)

Setting

As in many fantasy narratives for young children, the setting in *Peter Rabbit* is briefly presented with words and detailed in the illustrations. Potter introduces the story as follows:

> Once upon a time there were four little rabbits, and their names were—Flopsy, Mopsy, Cottontail, and Peter. They lived with their Mother in a sand-bank, underneath the root of a very big fir-tree. (p. 9)

This description is accompanied by a delicate, realistic watercolor illustration of the four rabbits and their mother peering at the reader from their fir-tree home. Ears and tree trunk stand straight up, pulling the viewer's eye upward; the colors are muted browns and greens. Mother is foregrounded, with her back to the viewer and her head turned to look, much like a real rabbit would do if startled by a person. Three small faces appear around the roots of the tree. One set of hind legs and a tail are visible under the left-hand root; we infer later that this is Peter. The rabbits appear to be realistic—that is, they look like wild rabbits. The very next illustration shows the rabbits dressed in pink and blue human clothes, against a white background, with the three girls clustered around Mother and Peter with his back to his family, facing the viewer. His little blue jacket hides his front paws. The text contains Mrs. Rabbit's warning to her children to stay away from Mr. McGregor's garden. Thus by the second page of the book, both text and illustration establish the place and the genre—this is a fantasy. Potter's fantasy, however, is special. Her animal characters may dress in human clothes and use

Mother Rabbit makes sure that Peter hears her admonition as she buttons the top button of his jacket: "Run along and don't get into mischief." (***Peter Rabbit*** by Beatrix Potter)

We are aware of Peter Rabbit's small size and his vulnerability as we see him knocking over flower pots when he tries to escape from Mr. McGregor's big foot. (***Peter Rabbit*** by Beatrix Potter)

language, but they act like animals. Everything that Peter does is possible for a rabbit to do, but his personality is that of an irrepressible child.

Characters

The first three pages also establish the characters. In the first illustration we see the faces of three of the bunnies, the tail of the fourth. Once readers get to know Peter, they guess the tail must be Peter, as he is the naughty one. The second illustration shows Mrs. Rabbit leaning down to talk to her three daughters; Peter is turned away, obviously not listening. The third illustration again places the rabbits in the woods, but they are still in their human clothes. Mrs. Rabbit is leaning down toward Peter, whose head is tilted back, buttoning the top button of his jacket while Flopsy, Mopsy, and Cotton-tail are already going down the path. The text, "Now run along, and don't get into mischief. I am going out" (p. 13) is obviously directed toward Peter, the only one close enough to Mrs. Rabbit to hear her admonition. It is only by seeing the illustration and reading the text that the full implications of this double page can be understood.

Just in case the implications haven't been understood, the sixth illustration shows Peter, ears upright, squeezing under a gate, and the accompanying text reads, "But Peter, who was very naughty,

ran straight away to Mr. McGregor's garden, and squeezed under the gate!" (p. 18). Thus a combination of text and illustration presents Peter as a naughty but endearing young rabbit, who is very recognizable as a human child—curious and apt to ignore a mother's restrictions to find out about the world. He not only goes into the garden, but also loses his clothes—"The second little jacket and pair of shoes that Peter had lost in a fortnight!" (p. 54). Later in the story readers see him escaping from great danger and finding his way home again, all by himself.

Plot

The plot of *Peter Rabbit* is straightforward, clear, and logical. Peter gets into the garden, eats a bit too much, is spotted by McGregor, is chased, gets caught in a gooseberry net, hides in a watering can in a shed, escapes out the window, hides until McGregor gives up, finds the gate, and makes a mad dash for freedom and the safety of home, where Mrs. Rabbit puts him to bed with a spoonful of medicine, just as any good mother would. Readers view the action as they read it, seeing Peter eating carrots, coming face to face with McGregor, caught in the net, diving into the watering can, leaping out the window just as McGregor's boot is about to come down on him, and collapsed on the

Peter lies exhausted but relieved while Mother prepares food. The feeling of being safe at home brings comfort. (***Peter Rabbit*** by Beatrix Potter)

floor of the rabbit hole. Once he has lost his jacket he looks once again like the wild rabbit he is. The excitement builds twice: once when he is chased by McGregor, and once again as he finds his way out of the garden. The resolution is clear—he is home, he is safe, and he is exhausted.

As the adventure occurs the illustrations heighten the sense of panic, using perspective to indicate how small Peter really is. When Peter is in the garden Potter is careful to place him with objects that make his small size apparent; we see him among plants, flowerpots, a watering can, and Mr. McGregor himself. Perhaps the most vivid image of his vulnerability is when he flees out of a window, knocking over pots of geraniums, pursued by Mr. McGregor's hobnailed boot.

Theme

The theme, or themes, are identifiable and understandable to young readers, established by the text and extended by the illustrations. The temptation to mischief, very real in the lives of children, is exciting precisely because it is dangerous. Returning home to mother is reassuring. Both emotions are familiar ones to young readers, and these readers can see the excitement and the relief in the illustrations.

Illustrations

The illustrations are delicate, carefully wrought watercolors that, as we have seen, work in conjunction with the words to express the action,

A tear leaks out of a remorseful Peter's eye. His ears droop; he puts one foot on top of another. He could easily be chewing on his paw while he reflects upon his misbehavior and adventure. (*Peter Rabbit* by Beatrix Potter)

characterization, and theme. The delicacy and beauty of the illustrations are such that the publisher, Frederick Warne, has recently published new editions using a more sophisticated printing technique that allows them to capture the true colors of the original watercolors more closely.

Potter was a keen observer of nature, and this is apparent in the detail that graces her illustrations. Peter always looks like a real rabbit, even when he is dressed in human clothes. The position of his ears, for example, is both realistic and indicative of his emotions. When Peter is crying beside the locked door he is standing like a sad child, one foot on top of the other with a paw in his mouth; like a tired and scared rabbit his ears are back rather than straight up (as they are throughout most of the story).

Potter's accurately detailed realistic style, delicate lines, and jewel-toned glowing watercolors are unsurpassed. Other illustrators have adapted Pot-

ter's story; none can compare with the original. Those who hear the story without seeing Potter's pictures do not experience the full meaning of *The Tale of Peter Rabbit.*

Language

Potter uses interesting words in interesting ways and makes this story a delight to read aloud. "Mischief," "naughty," "dreadfully frightened," and "exert" are but some of the interesting words that Potter provides for her young readers. The onomatopoetic words she uses—"kertyschoo" for a sneeze, "lippity" for a slow hop, "scr-r-ritch" for the sound of a hoe—all increase the vivid quality of the story. One sentence from the middle of the story, when Peter is caught in the gooseberry net, illustrates the complex and interesting quality of the language of this story: "Peter gave himself up for lost, and shed big tears; but his sobs were overheard by some friendly sparrows, who flew to him in great excitement, and implored him to exert himself" (p. 33). Children, delighting in these interesting words, will walk around chanting: "I implore you to exert yourself" after hearing this story.

Beatrix Potter's *The Tale of Peter Rabbit* exemplifies the criteria for excellent picture storybooks. Created through pictures and words, the story is captivating and understandable. The characters, seen through Potter's keen artistic eye, are vivid and engaging and the theme is important and identifiable. Unifying story, characters, and theme, the pictures and the words are strong and elegant. It is books like this that offer children opportunities for wonderful experiences with literature.

BOOKS FOR DEVELOPING CHILDREN

Picture books are seminal forces in children's language development. Books provide models of language in use; they demonstrate the meanings of concepts and represent aspects of the world a child is coming to know. Books that children like and can understand enrich their concept development, their language development, and their storehouse of experiences. Considering children's voracious appetite for language and learning, almost any book could be a source for learning. We have so many books available to us, however, that we can be selective in those we choose, finding only the best for our children.

Notable Illustrators

Read books by the following illustrators and respond to their art. See if you can recognize the artist's style when you cover up the names. Play "Name that Illustrator" in a Jeopardy game format: Hold up an illustration. Ask classmates to say, "Who is (the name of the illustrator)?"

Mitsumasa Anno	Leo Lionni
Jose Aruego	Arnold Lobel
Eric Carle	David Macaulay
Barbara Cooney	Robert McCloskey
Tomie de Paola	Helen Oxenbury
Leo and Diane Dillon	Peter Parnall
Gail Haley	Peter Spier
Tana Hoban	William Steig
Susan Jeffers	James Stevenson
Ezra Jack Keats	Chris Van Allsburg
Steven Kellogg	Brian Wildsmith

Note: Pat Cummings, Compiler-Editor. *Talking with Artists*. Bradbury, 1992. Reference book includes interviews with Victoria Chess, Pat Cummings, Leo and Diane Dillon, Richard Egielski, Lois Ehlert, Lisa Campbell Ernst, Steven Kellogg, Jerry Pinkney, Lane Smith, Chris Van Allsburg, and David Wiesner.

Books for Very Young Children

Baby Books

Books for babies are usually 10 to 12 pages long and are aimed at 1- to 3-year-olds. These books have increased in both availability and quality over the past few years. There are cloth books, shape books, pudgy books, lift-the-flap books, toy books, and bathtub books, in addition to the most popular cardboard books. Books of this type are appropriate for children who are in the labeling and identification stage, as well as for those in the earliest stages of reading—pointing to pictures and labeling them. Eric Hill's **My Pets** (N) consists of seven 5 by 5-inch cardboard pages with brightly colored realistic pictures of common pets. Adults who read this with children often label, or ask children to label, the pets portrayed, and can also comment on what the baby bear is doing on several pages. **Animals** (N) by Valerie Greeley is a bigger cardboard book with more detail and some text. Each page contains two detailed illustrations framed by white space. Beneath each picture is a simple label of the animal that is portrayed. The illustrations are richly detailed

and so realistic that it seems possible to feel the prickles on the hedgehogs.

Participation Books

Participation books provide concrete visual and tactile materials for children to explore—textures to touch, flaps to lift, flowers to smell, and pieces to manipulate. Dorothy Kunhardt's **Pat the Bunny** (N), a favorite for 50 years, asks children to look in a mirror, play peekaboo, and feel a scratchy beard; babies love touching this book.

Some participation books rely on visual rather than tactile participation, asking young readers to find something on the pages, such as Janet and Alan Ahlberg's **Each Peach Pear Plum** (N) that asks readers to look for familiar folkloric characters hidden in the illustrations. These books involve young readers in the act of reading, requiring their active participation in the process. Some excellent participation books are listed in Figure 3-8.

Storybooks and Poems

Stories to begin on have a simple plot line, are about familiar childhood experiences, and contain clear illustrations. Toddlers who enjoy participation books also enjoy simple stories, such as Rosemary Wells's **Max's Breakfast** (N), in which a clever younger brother manages to outwit his bossy older sister in just a few pages. These books introduce children to stories that are designed to capture and hold their interest, even if they have a short "sitting span," and are often the books that children turn to when they decide to "read" to themselves or their toys. Some simple storybooks for young readers are also listed in Figure 3-8.

There are many simple storybooks and poems that appeal to children who have outgrown baby books but are not yet ready for longer stories. These books generally have a brief text and very engaging illustrations, such as Sarah Hayes's **This Is the Bear** (N), illustrated by Helen Craig. This simple rhyming story about a bear who goes off in the rubbish and is rescued by his young owner has clear realistic illustrations that depict the action and elaborate on the emotions. The small speech balloons in the illustrations add to the story line. Some other examples are listed in Figure 3-8.

Books for Nursery and Primary-Grade Children

As children mature and their worlds expand, the number of books available to them also expands.

Figure 3-8	

Books for Very Young Children

Participation Books

Ahlberg, Janet, and Allan Ahlberg. *Each Peach Pear Plum.*

———. *Peek-a-boo.*

Brown, Margaret Wise. *Goodnight Moon.* Illus. Clement Hurd.

Hill, Eric. *Spot Goes Splash!*

———. *Where's Spot?*

Isadora, Rachel. *Babies.*

———. *Friends.*

Kunhardt, Dorothy. *Pat the Bunny.*

———. *Which Pig Would You Choose?*

Miller, Margaret. *Whose Hat?*

———. *Who Uses This?*

———. *Whose Shoe?*

Pomerantz, Charlotte. *Flap Your Wings and Try.* Illus. Nancy Tafuri.

Board Books, Caption Books

Isadora, Rachel. *I See.*

———. *I Hear.*

———. *I Touch.*

Oxenbury, Helen. *I Can.*

———. *I Hear.*

———. *I See.*

———. *I Touch.*

Wells, Rosemary. *Max's Bath.*

———. *Max's Birthday.*

———. *Max's Breakfast.*

———. *Max's First Word.*

———. *Max's New Suit.*

———. *Max's Ride.*

Simple Storybooks and Concept Books

Baer, Gene. *Thump, Thump, Rat-a-Tat-Tat.* Illus. Lois Ehlert.

Barton, Byron. *Bones, Bones, Dinosaur Bones.*

———. *I Want to Be an Astronaut.*

Brown, Margaret Wise. *Red Light, Green Light.* Illus. Leonard Weisgard.

Crews, Donald. *School Bus.*

———. *Truck.*

Ehlert, Lois. *Red Leaf, Yellow Leaf.*

———. *Color Farm.*

———. *Color Zoo.*

Gibbons, Gail. *Trucks.*

Hoban, Tana. *Exactly the Opposite.*

———. *Of Colors and Things.*

Jonas, Ann. *Color Dance.*

McMillan, Bruce. *Super Super Superwords.*

Noll, Sally. *Watch Where You Go.*

Oxenbury, Helen. *The Important Visitor.*

———. *Mother's Helper.*

———. *Good Night, Good Morning.*

Rockwell, Anne. *Bikes.*

Serfozo, Mary. *Who Said Red?* Illus. Keiko Narahashi.

Tafuri, Nancy. *Spots, Feathers, and Curly Tails.*

Children in the nursery and primary grades have their choice of concept books, alphabet books and counting books, books that support their early attempts at independent reading, and books that relate to every facet of their world.

Concept Books

Concept books are simple nonfiction books. Nursery and primary school children are busy learning about the world, and a number of concept books engage these young readers. They contribute to the child's expanding knowledge and language by providing numerous examples of an idea. Some present abstract ideas such as shape, color, size, or sound through many illustrations, such as Lois Ehlert's *Color Zoo* (N–P). Ehlert uses bold colors and geometric shapes to form various animals, adding a shape at a time to create different animal faces. Children enjoy working with this book, and often experiment with creating images through shapes and color on their own.

Other books tell a story based on concepts such as time or emotions, such as Ellen Kandoian's *Is Anybody Up?* (P), which explores time zones. When young Molly wakes up on the East Coast of the United States, she wonders who else is up. The answer takes readers north to Baffin Bay and south to Antarctica, to different cultures and different languages. Much of the information about these other places is supplied through the illustrations. Some other outstanding concept books are listed in Figure 3-9.

Alphabet Books

Some nonfiction books help children learn the fundamentals of language—we call them alphabet books. Alphabet books serve many useful purposes, only one of which is related to learning the alphabet. Two- to 4-year-old children will point to and label objects on the page; 5-year-olds may say the letter names and words that start with each letter; and 6-year-olds may read the letters, words, or story to confirm their knowledge of letter and sound correspondences. Whichever way they are read, alphabet books help to develop children's awareness of words on a page, and they play a useful part in language learning in addition to the pleasurable hours they provide a child.

No one need settle for a mediocre alphabet book because there are magnificent ones available, such as Helen Oxenbury's *The ABC of Things* (N), an enduring favorite. The elongated shape and simple format appeals to young readers. Each double-page spread contains both upper and lowercase letters, one or more words beginning with the letters, and the objects associated with those words. Children enjoy how the illustrations place the objects in humorous situations, such as a cat and a cow sitting on a chair while a crow carries in a cake full of candles. Jane Yolen's *All in the Woodland Early* (N–P), illustrated by Jane Breskin Zalben, features birds, animals and insects of the North American woodland. As a girl wanders through the woods she meets a young boy who tells her he is going hunting. As she follows him they accumulate 26 animals. It turns out that they're hunting for friends, a happy surprise ending. Zalben's illustrations are delicately jewel-toned and glowing, scientifically accurate, the uppercase letters are clearly written, and the story in song (the music is included) is happily memorized by young readers. See the list of many other excellent examples in Figure 3-9.

Counting Books

Other nonfiction books help children learn numbers. Many counting books are available for the nursery and primary grades, and range from books with simple pictures reflecting the progression from 1 to 10 to those with complicated illustrations like those in Arthur Geisert's *Pigs from 1 to 10* (P–I). Geisert hides the numerals 0 to 9 in pictures that detail the quest of 10 pigs searching for a special place. Children enjoy looking for the numerals as well as telling the story.

Other books count backward, like Molly Bang's *Ten, Nine, Eight* (N–P), in which a father helps his daughter into bed, counting from 10 toes to 1 sleepy child. The illustrations depict the bedtime activities, inviting young readers to find the numbered objects as well as to enjoy the visual story. Other books count well beyond 10, or in sets such as *Anno's Counting Book* (P–I), which moves from 0 to 12, January to December, and an empty landscape to a small village with 12 houses, 12 adults, 12 children, going to church at 12 P.M. and spotting 12 reindeer in the sky. Counting books help children develop concepts of quantity and seriation through fine visual portrayal of numerical concepts. The best illustrations for young children avoid distracting clutter so the objects can be identified and counted without confusion. Some of these are listed also in Figure 3-9.

Other books about numbers present other mathematical concepts, such as Joy Hulme's *Sea Squares* (I), illustrated by Carol Schwartz. This book illustrates squared numbers from 1 to 10 and also presents a wealth of information about the ocean. The illustrations allow older children to see and count as the verse explains the numbers.

Books for Emerging Readers

As children mature, their taste for books matures along with their cognitive and linguistic capabilities and needs. Learning to read and being able to unlock the secrets of print on a page mark an important step toward maturity. Many books are available for developing readers, including those just discussed. There are also special kinds of storybooks—wordless books, predictable books, and beginning-to-read books, as well as easy illustrated chapter books—that support children's attempts at independent reading.

Wordless books are appropriate for children who are developing a sense of story and learning language rapidly. Predictable books are well suited to the child who is beginning to pay attention to print. Beginning-to-read books are perfect for children who have just become independent readers but still need the support of simple but interesting texts. Easy chapter books help newly independent readers make the transition from beginning-to-read material to full-length novels.

Wordless Books.   *Wordless books,* discussed briefly in Chapter 2, tell a story through illustration alone. Very young children who do not yet read can retell the gist of the story from looking at the pictures; beginning readers, through their developing concept of story, are able to narrate the story with character and narrator voices. Good wordless storybooks contain the elements important in good storybooks—minus the language; that is supplied by the reader. Some of the best wordless books available are listed in Figure 2-7 in Chapter 2.

Wordless books provide many opportunities for exploring how stories work. The narration that children produce for wordless books can be written on large charts and become their reading instruction material. Moreover, children who watch their own words being put onto paper learn intuitively the relation between print and sound. Literature experiences that are shared and recorded in handmade books or on large charts provide a strong base for beginning reading, since the words used are integral to students' listening and speaking vocabularies. This means of teaching, called the language experience approach, provides a meaningful foundation for reading, especially when accompanied by a strong reading-aloud program based on good literature.

Older children can also enjoy wordless books. Intermediate-grade students use them as models for story writing; junior high school students use them to delineate the elements of fiction. Emily Arnold McCully's **School** (N–P) can be enjoyed by a range of readers, each for different purposes. Young children enjoy retelling this story of a young mouse who finds a way to go to school with her older siblings. Primary-grade children can supply narration and dialogue. The conflict-resolution structure of this story along with the character development provides a good model for writers, and students can also explore the illustrations for the vivid visual characterization that McCully provides.

Patterned Books.   *Patterned books* have a highly patterned structure, which enables children to anticipate what is going to happen next. Many 4- and 5-year-old children use their predictions and their knowledge of phonics to read these books on their own after hearing them read aloud only once. The books are structured through strong language patterns, such as repeated phrases, rhyme, and rhythm; story structures that add, or accumulate, information; and familiar concepts, songs, or sequences (like days of the week). Detailed illustrations reinforce the patterns, providing a visual reproduction of the text that is often also interpreted and extended by the artist.

Reading involves sampling, predicting, and confirming (Goodman, 1985; Smith, 1978). Readers select the most useful information from print in order to predict what it says. They hypothesize the most probable meaning based on the information sampled and then confirm it by checking to see if it makes sense, matches the letter-sound correspondences, and sounds like real language. Patterned books are ideal fare for beginning readers because they match expectations every step of the way. Through repetition, cumulative structure, and familiar concepts, Pat Hutchins's **What Game Shall We Play** (N–P) invites beginning readers to chime in as familiar animals search for one another *through* the grass, *in* the wall, and so on, all the while wondering what game they should play together. As the animals accumulate, it becomes obvious they are playing the game that owl suggests in the end— hide and seek! The illustrations invite close scrutiny and depict what is happening in the text. Children can see small bits of the animal being searched for, allowing them to find it, too. The pictures also illustrate the spatial relationships of in, under, and so on, that the text uses. Other outstanding patterned books are listed in Figure 3-9.

Beginning-to-Read Books.   *Beginning-to-read books* are ones that newly independent readers can enjoy on their own; they combine controlled vocabulary with creative storytelling. Some early books of this type were stilted and bland, but gradually authors mastered the form so we now have many excellent beginning-to-read books that tell good stories in a natural way.

Many of these books have strong characterization, worthy themes, and tight plots. The sentences are generally simple, without a lot of embedded clauses, and the language is often direct dialogue. The lines are printed so that sentence breaks occur according to natural phrasing, with meaningful chunks of language grouped together. Illustrations that depict the characters and the action both reflect and extend the text, which contains a limited number of different words and tells an interesting story. Arnold Lobel's wonderful series, including **Frog and Toad Are Friends** (N–P), has been a favorite with

Figure 3-9

Books for Nursery and Primary Age Children

ABC, Counting, and Concept Books

Anno, Mitsumasa. *Anno's Alphabet.*

Aylesworth, Jim. *The Folks in the Valley: A Pennsylvania Dutch ABC.* Illus. Stefano Vitale.

———. *Old Black Fly.* Illus. Stephen Gammell.

Bowen, Betsy. *Antler, Bear, Canoe: A Northwoods Alphabet Year.*

Ehlert, Lois. *Eating the Alphabet.*

Fisher, Leonard Everett. *The ABC Exhibit.*

Grossman, Virginia. *Ten Little Rabbits.*

Kellogg, Steven. *Aster Aardvark's Alphabet Adventures.*

Kitamura, Satoshi. *From Acorn to Zoo: And Everything in Between in Alphabetical Order.*

Lobel, Arnold. *On Market Street.*

MacDonald, Suse. *Alphabatics.*

Martin, Bill, Jr., and John Archambault. *Chicka Chicka Boom Boom.* Illus. Lois Ehlert.

McMillan, Bruce. *Beach Ball—Left, Right.*

Merriam, Eve. *Halloween A B C.* Illus. Lane Smith.

Owens, Mary Beth. *A Caribou Alphabet.*

Paul, Ann Whitford. *Eight Hands Round: A Patchwork Alphabet.* Illus. Jeanette Winter.

Rankin, Laura. *The Handmade Alphabet.*

Sloat, Teri. *From Letter to Letter.*

Ziefert, Harriet. *Big to Little, Little to Big.* Illus. Susan Baum.

———. *Clothes On, Clothes Off.* Illus. Susan Baum.

———. *Count Up, Count Down.* Illus. Susan Baum.

———. *Empty to Full, Full to Empty.* Illus. Susan Baum.

Primary–Intermediate

Anno, Mitsumasa. *Anno's Math Games.*

———. *Anno's Math Games II.*

———. *Anno's Math Games III.*

Wordless Books

Anno, Mitsumasa. *Topsy-Turvies.*

Aruego, José. *Look What I Can Do.*

de Paola, Tomie. *Pancakes for Breakfast.*

Goodall, John. *Little Red Riding Hood.*

Hutchins, Pat. *Changes, Changes.*

Keats, Ezra Jack. *Kitten for a Day.*

Mayer, Mercer. *Frog Goes to Dinner.*

———. *Hiccup.*

McCully, Emily Arnold. *Picnic.*

———. *School.*

Ormerod, Jan. *Sunshine.*

———. *Moonlight.*

Patterned Books

Carlstrom, Nancy White. *Better Not Get Wet, Jesse Bear.*

———. *Jesse Bear, What Will You Wear?* Illus. Bruce Degen.

Ehlert, Lois. *Feathers for Lunch.*

Fleming, Denise. *In the Tall, Tall Grass.*

Fox, Mem. *Guess What?* Illus. Vivienne Goodman.

———. *Hattie and the Fox.* Illus. Patricia Mullins.

Guarino, Deborah. *Is Your Mama a Llama?* Illus. Steven Kellogg.

Hennessy, B. G. *Jake Baked the Cake.* Illus. Mary Morgan.

Hutchins, Pat. *What Game Shall We Play?*

Katz, Michael Jay. *Ten Potatoes in a Pot: And Other Counting Rhymes.* Illus. June Otani.

Kovalski, Maryann. *The Wheels on the Bus.*

MacDonald, Amy. *Rachel Fister's Blister.* Illus. Marjorie Priceman.

Mahy, Margaret. *17 Kings and 42 Elephants.* Illus. Patricia MacCarthy.

———. *The Horrendous Hullabaloo.* Illus. Patricia MacCarthy.

Martin, Bill, Jr. *Brown Bear, Brown Bear, What Do You See?* Illus. Eric Carle.

———. *Polar Bear, Polar Bear, What Do You Hear?* Illus. Eric Carle.

CONTINUED

Martin, Bill, Jr., and John Archambault. *Chicka Chicka Boom Boom.* Illus. Lois Ehlert.

Marzollo, Jean. *Pretend You're a Cat.* Illus. Jerry Pinkney.

Neitzel, Shirley. *The Jacket I Wear in the Snow.* Illus. Nancy Winslow Parker.

Robart, Rose. *The Cake That Mack Ate.* Illus. Maryann Kovalski.

Rosen, Michael. *We're Going on a Bear Hunt.*

Shaw, Nancy. *Sheep in a Shop.* Illus. Margot Apple.

Stow, Jenny. *The House That Jack Built.*

Suteyev, Vladimir. *Chick and the Duckling.* Trans. Mirra Ginsburg. Illus. Jose Aruego and Ariane Dewey.

Walsh, Ellen Stoll. *Mouse Count.*

———. *Mouse Paint.*

Zelinsky, Paul. *The Wheels on the Bus.*

Beginning to Read Books

Baer, Gene. *Thump, Thump, Rat-a-Tat-Tat.* Illus. Lois Ehlert.

Brown, Marc. *Play Rhymes.*

Browne, Anthony. *I Like Books.*

———. *Things I Like.*

Byars, Betsy. *The Golly Sisters Go West.*

Goennel, Heidi. *My Dog.*

Lobel, Arnold. *Days with Frog and Toad.*

———. *Frog and Toad All Year.*

———. *Frog and Toad Are Friends.*

———. *Frog and Toad Together.*

Marshall, James. *The Cut-Ups Crack Up.*

Martin, Bill, Jr., and John Archambault. *Here Are My Hands.* Illus. Ted Rand.

Marzollo, Jean. *Pretend You're a Cat.* Illus. Jerry Pinkney.

Minarik, Else. *Father Bear Comes Home.* Illus. Maurice Sendak.

Noll, Sally. *Watch Where You Go.*

Parish, Peggy. *Scruffy.* Illus. Kelly Oechsli.

———. *Teach Us, Amelia Bedelia.* Illus. Lynn Sweat.

Porte, Barbara Ann. *Harry in Trouble.* Illus. Yossi Abolafia.

Rosen, Michael. *We're Going on a Bear Hunt.* Illus. Helen Oxenbury.

Rylant, Cynthia. *Henry and Mudge: The First Book.* Illus. Sucie Stevenson.

———. *Henry and Mudge Get the Shivers.* Illus. Sucie Stevenson.

———. *Henry and Mudge and the Forever Sea.* Illus. Sucie Stevenson.

———. *Henry and Mudge in Puddle Trouble.* Illus. Sucie Stevenson.

———. *Henry and Mudge Under the Yellow Moon.* Illus. Sucie Stevenson.

———. *Henry and Mudge in the Green Time.* Illus. Sucie Stevenson.

———. *Henry and Mudge in the Sparkle Days.* Illus. Sucie Stevenson.

———. *Henry and Mudge and the Happy Cat.* Illus. Sucie Stevenson.

———. *Henry and Mudge Take the Big Test.* Illus. Sucie Stevenson.

———. *Henry and Mudge and the Long Weekend.* Illus. Sucie Stevenson.

———. *Henry and Mudge and the Bedtime Thumps.* Illus. Sucie Stevenson.

Shaw, Nancy. *Sheep in a Shop.* Illus. Margot Apple.

Van Leeuwen, Jean. *Oliver, Amanda, and Grandmother Pig.* Illus. Ann Schweninger.

———. *Oliver Pig at School.* Illus. Ann Schweninger.

newly independent readers for many years. Frog and Toad are humorous, realistic characters who have interesting, understandable problems; the theme of friendship pervades all of the intriguing stories. The illustrations depict the action as well as provide a lot of emotional details about the characters. Lobel chooses his words wisely, creating an easy-to-read story that is so well written that it is also pleasant to read aloud. Other excellent beginning-to-read books are suggested in Figure 3-9.

As children grow in their reading ability, they move beyond these early materials to easy chapter books and then full-length texts. However, even though children outgrow reading about Frog and Toad and other vivid characters from their early reading experiences, they remember their happy, successful experiences with these books. These strong positive experiences propel them into more close and happy encounters with literature.

FORGING CONNECTIONS BETWEEN LIFE AND LITERATURE

Just as children's language abilities develop rapidly from birth through the primary grades, their social abilities develop rapidly as their worlds expand. As children grow, they learn about themselves and their families. They begin to develop social knowledge and competence as they form friendships and go to school. They also come to know the natural world and the aesthetic world of art, music, dance, and literature. Their imagination, already an important part of their lives, is fed by new experiences with life and literature. Many picture books support and enrich this development, offering opportunities for virtual experiences and providing a wealth of information and imaginative resources, as well as rich and varied language experiences.

The Child's Inner World

In a supportive environment, children soon come to know that they are unique and capable of expressing themselves and of making choices. As children develop, they begin to understand they are not the only people who have needs and feelings. They gradually learn that others perceive things differently from them, and they begin to develop a concept of self based on reflections from others. Many picture books address these important self-concepts.

Children in the preschool years are busy learning about themselves—who they are and what they can do—and about others. Their self-concept develops as a direct result of interaction with the environment, including the reactions of others to their own actions. When children see their actions meet with approval, they are encouraged to explore, to express themselves, and to discover their world. Books mirror the primary experiences that shape children's actions, reactions, and feelings and can help children reflect on them. Books can play an important role for the child experiencing the conflicts of growing up; they enrich understanding when they relate to life. In addition to providing new experiences, stories also show children that their thoughts, feelings, and reactions are not unusual—that the children are like other people and a part of the human race. Issues such as sex-role stereotyping, childhood fears, and moral reasoning are some of the ideas that can be found in picture storybooks for children. Kevin Henkes explores the idea of feeling special (and liking your name) in **Chrysanthemum** (P). When Chrysanthemum is born, her parents think she is perfect, and she grows up feeling quite special. Once she goes to school, however, she begins to have doubts, especially about her name. With words and pictures Henkes explores an emotional issue that is familiar to many children. Other picture books that can support children's developing understandings about themselves are listed in Figure 3-10.

The Child's Family World

The home is the child's first school; it has a lasting influence on every child's intellectual, personal, and social development. Children's lives are affected by new babies, adoption, mothers working outside the home, day care, divorce, grandparents, stepparents, homelessness, and the death and aging of family members. Books are available that address these and many other people and events which impact on families. The best of these books sensitively explore issues related to families and present realistic pictures of the variety of loving relationships that are possible in any number of circumstances. Many books for young children explore the relationship between the youngest and oldest members of a family. Elizabeth Fitzgerald Howard depicts one such special relationship in **Aunt Flossie's Hats (and Crab Cakes Later)** (P–I). Young Sarah and Susan visit their great-great-aunt Flossie each Sunday afternoon, eager to have her show them her hat collection and tell them stories of her own girlhood. James Ransome's oil paintings capture the love between aunt and nieces and provide interesting historical details that enhance Aunt Flossie's remembrances. Other books that explore family life are listed in Figure 3-10.

The Child's Social World

Social development intersects all other areas of growth; it both reflects and influences the child's total development. Friendships with others develop slowly and may not really be possible until children develop an identifiable self-concept. By the time children enter school, they are beginning to know how to interact with others; identification with and success in a peer group follow as children slowly begin to sort out special friends within the group.

Friendship is a mixture of good and bad times and usually encounters many stumbling blocks. Oftentimes there are internal and external conflicts as children try simultaneously to declare their independence as people and develop relationships with others. There are many picture storybooks that portray friendships. Rebecca Jones's **Matthew and Tilly** (P) tells the story of best friends who do everything together, including having occasional arguments. They discover, however, that playing alone is not as much fun as playing together, so they apologize to each other and resume their friendship. Beth Peck's paintings chronicle both their activities and their emotions. Other fine picture books about friendship are listed in Figure 3-10.

Going to school expands the child's social world, and many children's books, such as Amy Schwartz's **Annabelle Swift, Kindergartner** (P), recreate the excitement and fears about school as well as familiar classroom experiences. Annabelle thinks she is all ready for school because her third-grade sister has coached her. When she gets there, however, she finds that some of the things Lucy has told her to say and do only make the other children laugh at her. She redeems herself, and her pride, and astonishes her teacher when she counts the milk money all by herself. Children recognize Annabelle's fear of being different and her pride at being the best at something. Other stories about school are listed also in Figure 3-10.

The Child's Natural World

Children learn about nature as they explore their ever-widening worlds. Firsthand experiences are primary, of course, but books can deepen and extend children's awareness of the natural world. Books can draw attention to nature in sensitive and

TEACHING IDEA 3-4

Write a Book: An Autobiography

Write your autobiography. Sections may include favorite things to do, family, friends, favorite food, favorite books, goals, and a special moment.

Value the small details of life and realize that such details are important enough to write about. Read some of the following books to see how other authors write about special moments:

Brinckloe, Julie. *Fireflies.*

Carrick, Carol. *Left Behind.*

Cooney, Barbara. *Miss Rumphius.*

Friedman, Ina. *How My Parents Learned to Eat.*

Keats, Ezra Jack. *Peter's Chair.*

McPhail, David. *Lost!*

Rockwell, Anne. *My Doctor.*

Zolotow, Charlotte. *Someone New.*

thoughtful ways; many do not tell a story as much as establish a mood or celebrate natural beauty through both words and pictures. Books explore seasonal change, special habitats and ecosystems, natural phenomena, and animals, offering children the opportunity for experiences with the natural world they wouldn't otherwise have and confirming their growing knowledge about nature that results from their own life experiences. Illustrations often offer children visions of natural life that they wouldn't otherwise see, helping them to understand and appreciate the complex beauty of the natural world. Barbara Juster Esbensen's **Great Northern Diver: The Loon** (I–A), illustrated by Mary Barrett Brown, goes beyond presenting a lot of information. A detailed and passionate text and exquisite paintings evoke the mystery and majesty of this bird so that readers who have never heard the cry of a loon might still care about their survival. Other books about the natural world are suggested in Figure 3-11.

The Child's Aesthetic World

As children's interests broaden, the aesthetic environment—music, dance, literature, and art—can add immeasurably to their overall sense of belonging. It is through literature that many children first

> **Figure 3-10**

The Child's Inner, Family, and Social Worlds

THE CHILD'S INNER WORLD
PRIMARY
Loose Tooth, Tooth Fairy

Birdseye, Tom. *Air Mail to the Moon.* Illus. Stephen Gammell.

McCloskey, Robert. *One Morning in Maine.*

Self-Esteem, Pride in One's Name

Anholt, Catherine, and Laurence Anholt. *All About You.*

Henkes, Kevin. *Chrysanthemum.*

Martin, Bill, Jr., and John Archambault. *Knots on a Counting Rope.* Illus. Ted Rand.

Resourcefulness

Holabird, Katharine. *Angelina and Alice.* Illus. Helen Craig.

———. *Angelina's Birthday Surprise.* Illus. Helen Craig.

McKissack, Patricia. *Flossie and the Fox.* Illus. Rachel Isadora.

McPhail, David. *Emma's Pet.*

———. *Emma's Vacation.*

———. *Fix-it.*

———. *Pig Pig Gets a Job.*

Schwartz, Amy. *Annabelle Swift, Kindergartner.*

Segal, Lore. *Tell Me a Mitzi.* Illus. Harriet Pincus.

———. *Tell Me a Trudy.* Illus. Rosemary Wells.

Seuss, Dr. *Oh, the Places You'll Go!*

Steig, William. *Brave Irene.*

Viorst, Judith. *Earrings!* Illus. Nola Langner Malone.

Wells, Rosemary. *Shy Charles.*

Fears

Bunting, Eve. *Ghost's Hour, Spook's Hour.* Illus. Donald Carrick.

Carrick, Carol. *Left Behind.* Illus. Donald Carrick.

Conrad, Pam. *The Tub People.* Illus. Richard Egielski.

Grifalconi, Ann. *Darkness and the Butterfly.*

Henkes, Kevin. *Sheila Rae, the Brave.*

McPhail, David. *Lost!*

Stolz, Mary Slattery. *Storm in the Night.* Illus. Pat Cummings.

Wells, Rosemary. *Max's Dragon Shirt.*

Humor

Dumbleton, Mike. *Dial-a-Croc.* Illus. Ann James.

Hale, Lucretia. *The Lady Who Put Salt in Her Coffee.* Adaptor and illus. Amy Schwartz.

Kellogg, Steven. *Prehistoric Pinkerton.*

Khalsa, Dayal Kaur. *How Pizza Came to Queens.*

Macaulay, David. *Why the Chicken Crossed the Road.*

Mahy, Margaret. *The Great White Man-Eating Shark: A Cautionary Tale.* Illus. Jonathan Allen.

Noble, Trina Hakes. *The Day Jimmy's Boa Ate the Wash.* Illus. Steven Kellogg.

Bedtime Books

Brown, Margaret Wise. *Goodnight Moon.* Illus. Clement Hurd.

Ginsburg, Mirra. *Asleep, Asleep.* Illus. Nancy Tafuri.

Hurd, Thacher. *The Quiet Evening.*

Fun, Special Events

Ehlert, Lois. *Circus.*

Goennel, Heidi. *The Circus.*

THE CHILD'S FAMILY WORLD
PRIMARY
Grandparents

Ackerman, Karen. *Song and Dance Man.* Illus. Stephen Gammell.

Anderson, Lena. *Stina.*

———. *Stina's Visit.*

Dorros, Arthur. *Abuela.* Illus. Elisa Kleven.

Farber, Norma. *How Does It Feel to Be Old?* Illus. Trina Schart Hyman.

Fox, Mem. *Night Noises.* Illus. Terry Denton.

CONTINUED

————. *Wilfrid Gordon Mc-Donald Partridge.* Illus. Julie Vivas.

Griffith, Helen V. *Grandaddy's Place.* Illus. James Stevenson.

Johnson, Angela . *When I Am Old with You.* Illus. David Soman.

Stevenson, James. *We Hate Rain!*

Williams, Barbara. *Kevin's Grandma.* Illus. Kay Chorao.

Siblings

Browne, Anthony. *The Tunnel.*

Graham, Bob. *Has Anyone Here Seen William?*

Henkes, Kevin. *Julius, the Baby of the World.*

Hutchins, Pat. *Very Worst Monster.*

————. *Where's the Baby?*

Sheffield, Margaret. *Where Do Babies Come From?* Illus. Sheila Bewley.

Wells, Rosemary. *Max's Chocolate Chicken.*

Williams, Vera B. *''More More More,'' Said the Baby.*

————. *Stringbean's Trip to the Shining Sea.* Illus. Vera B. Williams and Jennifer Williams.

Yorinks, Arthur. *Oh, Brother.* Illus. Richard Egielski.

Parents and Family as a Unit

Browne, Anthony. *Piggybook.*

Bunting, Eve. *The Mother's Day Mice.* Illus. Jan Brett.

Keller, Holly. *Horace.*

Loh, Morag. *Tucking Mommy In.* Illus. Donna Rawlins.

McPhail, David. *Emma's Vacation.*

Rayner, Mary. *Mrs. Pig Gets Cross: And Other Stories.*

Scott, Ann Herbert. *On Mother's Lap.* Illus. Glo Coalson.

Steig, William. *Spinky Sulks.*

Weiss, Nicki. *On a Hot, Hot Day.*

Wynott, Jillian. *The Mother's Day Sandwich.* Illus. Maxie Chambliss.

PRIMARY–INTERMEDIATE

Ancestors, Intergenerational

Cooney, Barbara. *Hattie and the Wild Waves.*

————. *Island Boy.*

————. *Miss Rumphius.*

Houston, Gloria. *The Year of the Perfect Christmas Tree.* Illus. Barbara Cooney.

Johnston, Tony. *Yonder.* Illus. Lloyd Bloom.

Polacco, Patricia. *The Keeping Quilt.*

Pomerantz, Charlotte. *The Chalk Doll.* Illus. Frané Lessac.

Say, Allen. *Tree of Cranes.*

THE CHILD'S SOCIAL WORLD
PRIMARY–INTERMEDIATE

Belpre, Pura. *Santiago.* Illus. Symeon Shimin.

Cohen, Miriam. *It's George!* Illus. Lillian Hoban.

————. *See You in Second Grade!* Illus. Lillian Hoban.

————. *Will I Have a Friend?* Illus. Lillian Hoban.

Dugan, Barbara. *Loop the Loop.* Illus. James Stevenson.

Fleischman, Sid. *Scarebird.* Illus. Peter Sis.

Hughes, Shirley. *The Snow Lady.*

————. *Wheels.*

Kellogg, Steven. *Best Friends.*

Mathers, Petra. *Sophie and Lou.*

Tsutsui, Yoriko. *Anna's Secret Friend.* Illus. Akiko Hayashi.

Vincent, Gabrielle. *Merry Christmas, Ernest and Celestine.*

Winthrop, Elizabeth. *Bear and Mrs. Duck.* Illus. Patience Brewster.

————. *The Best Friends Club: A Lizzie and Harold Story.* Illus. Martha Weston.

encounter the cultural arts. Through books, children can be introduced to the aesthetic world at an early age. Early and continued exposure to the arts lays a firm foundation on which children build an ever-increasing appreciation for their aesthetic world.

Picture books about the arts may be storybooks that contain a problem or theme related to the arts, such as a child wanting to practice an art, a child's effort to become good at an art, or a story in which the arts play an integral part in the main character's life. Books about the arts may also be nonfiction, explaining concepts related to a particular art. Whether fiction or nonfiction, these picture books use both illustrations and text to create meaning. The illustrations may elaborate events and emotions, such as Emily Arnold McCully does in *Mirette on the High Wire* (P–I) a story about a young girl's struggle to practice her art and restore her teacher's confidence in himself. They may also help convey information, as they do in Ann Hayes's *Meet the Orchestra* (P) in which Karmen Thompson's whimsical watercolors help young readers to see the instruments being described.

Music is an integral part of an aesthetic life. Almost from the time they hear their first lullaby, young children can hum or follow along with favorite melodies. Every culture is replete with songs of its people. Many books offer lavish visual interpretations of those rhymes or songs, publishing them as single-edition picture books or collections. Ashley Bryan is noted for his illustrations of African-American spirituals, such as *All Night, All Day: A Child's First Book of African-American Spirituals* (P–I). Bryan's beautiful interpretive illustrations accompany the words and arrangements for 20 spirituals, celebrating this musical form and the culture that created it.

Other books about music explore musical instruments, organizations, and musicians' lives. Jill Krementz's photographs and lucid text present the life of *A Very Young Musician* (I) as he tries to decide whether or not to pursue a career as a trumpet player. Krementz presents this young man so readers see him with his family and friends, in the rigors of rehearsal, and at his most memorable musical moments.

Expressive movement is natural to children; they sway, tap their feet, and bounce, impelled by the pure joy of moving. Music, stories, and poems invite expressive participation on the part of children. Stories about dance and dancers intrigue young readers who wonder what it would be like. Eleanor Schick tells the story of one young girl communicating through movement in *I Have Another*

Language, The Language Is Dance (I). As the text tells us what the young dancer is doing and thinking, the soft illustrations capture the body movements of the dancers, making it seem as if readers can actually see them moving.

Children are also sensitive to the visual art that surrounds them, and much of that art is contained in picture books. When children have the opportunity to read and savor many picture books they quickly come to recognize individual artists' styles and develop their own taste. Many children become interested in the lives of artists; there are some fine biographies of both contemporary children's book artists as well as important artists of the past.

As they learn to be sensitive to design and artistic effect, children can profit from a study of styles, techniques, and media, as we discussed earlier in this chapter. Children can experiment with a variety of artistic techniques, and can also explore books that discuss art, such as *The Painter's Eye: Learning to Look at Contemporary American Art* (I–A) by Jan Greenberg and Sandra Jordan. This book discusses the elements of art and principles of design that artists work with in a remarkably understandable fashion; the text is supported by illustrations from contemporary art that demonstrate the authors' points.

Picture books can enrich all facets of a child's aesthetic world. Some of the best books for doing this are listed in Figure 3-11.

The Child's Imaginary World

Children's imaginative lives are an important part of their early years. Adults can sometimes catch a glimpse of that fantasy world by observing the child at play with an imaginary friend, a favorite toy that has been invested with life, or other children. During these play episodes children create their own imaginative narratives. Parents and teachers can contribute to an environment that is conducive to children's imaginative play by playing "let's pretend" games, discussing dreams, and making up stories. They can also read imaginative stories.

Adults who fear too much fantasy will affect a child's sense of reality need not worry; a lively imagination is a central part of the developmental process. Imaginative stories provide a source of pleasure as well as a focal point for children's developing imagination and sense of story. In fact, children who have been deprived of traditional tales and other imaginative stories will create their own (Chukovsky, 1963). Some of the most distinguished literature for children builds on the imaginative life of the central characters. In these stories stuffed animals come to life, fancy runs free, creatures hide under beds, and imaginary friends are real.

Imagination is central to *Louise Builds a Boat* (P) by Louise Pfanner. When Louise decides to build a boat, she includes all sorts of wonderful things like a gangplank for diving, and plans to sail around the world to visit all of her friends. The text is spare; the details and emotion are portrayed through the illustrations as she gradually constructs and enjoys the boat. Other books that explore the imagination are listed in Figure 3-11.

BOOKS FOR OLDER READERS

Although the vast majority of picture books are written for nursery and primary-grade children to enjoy, many picture books appeal to older readers. The text in these books is usually longer and more complex than in books for younger readers and the themes more abstract or emotionally demanding. Sometimes these books are more like illustrated books than true picture books, as the text actually carries most of the weight in the storytelling process. In Byrd Baylor's *Hawk, I'm Your Brother* (I–A), Peter Parnall's illustrations highlight the essence of young Rudy's struggle to tame a wild hawk and learn to fly. They brilliantly portray the hawk's longing to be free, and reflect the culture and land in which the story is set. The text, however, is a lyrical, beautiful poem that could stand alone. The very real dilemma that Baylor poses and the emotional struggle Rudy undergoes is one that older readers recognize and empathize with.

Sometimes a picture book for older readers is a visual tour de force, a stunning example of an artist's vision, such as Thomas Locker's *Mare on the Hill,* Chris Van Allsburg's *The Polar Express* and *The Wretched Stone,* and David Macaulay's *Black and White* (all I–A). The text of *The Wretched Stone* consists of excerpts from a fictional ship's log and tells a strange tale of men transformed into apes by staring at a glowing stone they have brought on board ship from a strange island. The illustrations tell the rest of the story, with wonderful details about the ship, the island, and the crew's transformation, and provide humor as well. Older readers enjoy discussing the symbolism of the stone, easily relating it to their own lives. Many other picture books that appeal to older readers are listed in Figure 3-12.

PICTURE BOOKS IN THE CLASSROOM

Picture books of all kinds are a staple in primary-grade classrooms, and many intermediate- and upper-grade teachers are now beginning to discover that picture books have an important place on their classroom library shelves as well. Picture books offer a unique opportunity for children to experience outstanding visual art, well-crafted language, and intriguing content. Picture books can support every area of the curriculum.

Excellent fiction, nonfiction, and poetry in picture book format are essential to any reading/writing program. Children naturally use the books they read as material for their own thinking and writing; picture books become resources for children's language production. Picture books are a natural source for examples of the author's craft. Excellent nonfiction gives children models for their own expository writing just as excellent stories and poems provide models for other modes. Literary devices such as imagery, foreshadowing, parody, simile, and analogy are all found in picture storybooks and poetry. Talking about these devices can become a natural part of discussing favorite books when children are writers as well as readers; they constantly notice the choices that authors and illustrators make. Hall (1990) provides a source list of titles of picture books that are good examples of a number of literary devices.

Picture books that support learning in social studies, science, art, music, and mathematics also abound; many are discussed in Chapter 10. These books not only provide fine models of writing in these various fields, they explain concepts, present information, and encourage critical thinking.

Children respond enthusiastically in classroom contexts that are rich with books and with the opportunity to read and respond to those books. In a year-long study of elementary school children responding to picture books in literature-rich classrooms, Kiefer (1986) discovered that a supportive, enriched classroom environment was an important factor in children's responses. Teachers read aloud often, talked with children about the books, and made frequent comparisons to other books and real life. They talked about authors and illustrators, referring to them by name, discussed information on the end flaps, and often studied the works of single authors and illustrators. The teachers in her study discussed all aspects of books—dedication pages, copyright page, title page—and used stylistic terminology when discussing the language and the visual art.

Figure 3-11

The Child's Natural, Aesthetic, and Imaginary Worlds

The Child's Natural World (P-I-A)

Aragon, Jane Chelsea. *Winter Harvest.* Illus. Leslie Baker.

Baker, Leslie. *The Third Story Cat.*

———. *The Antique Store Cat.*

Baylor, Byrd. *The Desert Is Theirs.* Illus. Peter Parnall.

Bjork, Christina. *Linnea in Monet's Garden.* Trans. Joan Sandin. Illus. Lena Anderson.

———. *Linnea's Windowsill Garden.* Trans. Joan Sandin. Illus. Lena Anderson.

Cazet, Denys. *A Fish in His Pocket.*

Gibbons, Gail. *Farming.*

———. *Zoo.*

Hadithi, Mwenye. *Crafty Chameleon.* Illus. Adrienne Kennaway.

Hoban, Tana. *Dots, Spots, Speckles, and Stripes.*

Keats, Ezra Jack. *The Snowy Day.*

Lewison, Wendy Cheyette. *Going to Sleep on the Farm.* Illus. Juan Wijngaard.

Locker, Thomas. *Family Farm.*

Lyon, George Ella. *Come a Tide.* Illus. Stephen Gammell.

McPhail, David. *Farm Boy's Year.*

Rogers, Jean. *Runaway Mittens.* Illus. Rie Munoz.

Tejima, Keizaburo. *Owl Lake.*

Yolen, Jane. *Owl Moon.* Illus. John Schoenherr.

The Child's Aesthetic World (I–A)

Agee, Jon. *The Incredible Painting of Felix Clousseau.*

Blizzard, Gladys S. *Come Look with Me: Exploring Landscape Art with Children.*

de Paola, Tomie. *The Art Lesson.*

Everett, Gwen. *Li'l Sis and Uncle Willie.*

Greenberg, Jan, and Sandra Jordan. *The Painter's Eye: Learning to Look at Contemporary American Art.*

Greenfield, Eloise. *Under the Sunday Tree.* Illus. Amos Ferguson.

Hoban, Tana. *Look! Look! Look!*

Lyttle, Richard B. *Pablo Picasso: The Man and the Image.*

Newlands, Anne. *Meet Edgar Degas.*

Sufrin, Mark. *George Catlin: Painter of the Indian West.*

Turner, Robyn Montana. *Georgia O'Keefe.*

Zhensun, Zheng, and Alice Low. *A Young Painter: The Life and Paintings of Wang Yani—China's Extraordinary Young Artist.* Photos by Zheng Zhensun.

Both Kiefer (1986) and Cianciolo and Quirk (1993) note that, most importantly, teachers provided the time and the opportunity for children to explore their own responses to the books they read—how they felt and what they were thinking about. This personal connection to a book seemed to be a necessary first step to critical aesthetic response (Cianciolo & Quirk, 1993). After teachers encourage children to clarify their understandings, reflect on what they liked and disliked, and talk about feelings and personal connections, then children are ready to go "back to the book" to discover the artistry in the language and the illustrations.

When they connect with a book, children respond in a great many ways. Variation occurs in the way children select books, look at books, and respond to books. Some children, especially younger ones, respond physically, moving their bodies in rhythm and saying the words they are reading or hearing (Kiefer, 1986). Children often choose to respond through drama, spontaneously reenacting a favorite story or planning a more elaborate production. Some children write in journals; others extend the language of books to their own writing. And many children choose to respond to picture books through art.

Learning About Art

Not only do children often draw and paint in response to the books they read, they learn how to view and talk about art through reading and

CONTINUED

The Child's Imaginative World (P–I–A)

de Paola, Tomie. *Bonjour, Mr. Satie.*

Dorros, Arthur. *Tonight Is Carnaval.*

———. *Abuela.* Illus. Elisa Kleven.

Fox, Mem. *Possum Magic.* Illus. Julie Vivas.

Gordon, Gaelyn. *Duckat.* Illus. Chris Gaskin.

Gordon, Jeffie Ross. *Six Sleepy Sheep.* Illus. John O'Brien.

Hines, Anna Grossnickle. *It's Just Me, Emily.*

Hoffman, Mary. *Amazing Grace.* Illus. Caroline Binch.

Howard, Elizabeth. *Aunt Flossie's Hats (and Crab Cakes Later).* Illus. James Ransome.

Jeffers, Susan. *Brother Eagle, Sister Sky: A Message from Chief Seattle.*

Joosse, Barbara, and Barbara Lavallee. *Mama, Do You Love Me?*

Joyce, William. *Bently and Egg.*

———. *Dinosaur Bob & His Adventures with the Family Lazardo.*

———. *George Shrinks.*

Kellogg, Steven. *Jack and the Beanstalk.*

Lobel, Anita. *The Dwarf Giant.*

Martin, Jacqueline Briggs. *Good Times on Grandfather Mountain.* Illus. Susan Gaber.

Martin, Rafe. *Will's Mammoth.* Illus. Stephen Gammell.

Pearce, Philippa. *Emily's Own Elephant.* Illus. John Lawrence

Ringgold, Faith. *Tar Beach.*

Steig, William. *Doctor De Soto Goes to Africa.*

Van Allsburg, Chris. *The Wretched Stone.*

Waber, Bernard. *Lyle, Lyle Crocodile.*

Willard, Nancy. *Pish, Posh, Said Hieronymus Bosch.* Illus. Leo and Diane Dillon.

Yolen, Jane. *Piggins and the Royal Wedding.* Illus. Jane Dyer.

Yorinks, Arthur. *Hey Al.* Illus. Richard Egielski.

responding to beautiful picture books. Certainly children use the illustrations in picture books to help them follow the story, understand the concepts, and, in some cases, read the text. Further, Kiefer (1986) found that children were careful and critical viewers, noticing the "secrets" that artists often put in their illustrations, such as the small white dog that appears in many of Chris Van Allsburg's books.

Just as children notice the craft of the writer, they notice the craft of the artist and discuss it. Kiefer (1986) heard children of all ages talking about the elements of design. First graders discussed line, shape, texture, and color with ease; older children also considered the expressive qualities of the illustrations. In every case the children's teachers provided the classroom time for children to explore books, discover and develop their individual responses, and share those responses with others. The teachers also provided many books and many varied opportunities for response while sharing their knowledge of the elements of language and visual art and their own critical aesthetic responses.

We often think of selecting books that contain similar themes, structures, or literary devices. We can also choose books that demonstrate similarities and differences in visual art. Careful selection can lead to children comparing the use of line and color, for example, or noting how different artists use texture, light, and space. A thoughtful assortment/ collection of books that demonstrate particular qualities of visual art can educate children's eyes as well as their minds and hearts.

**Figure
3-12**

Picture Books for Older Children

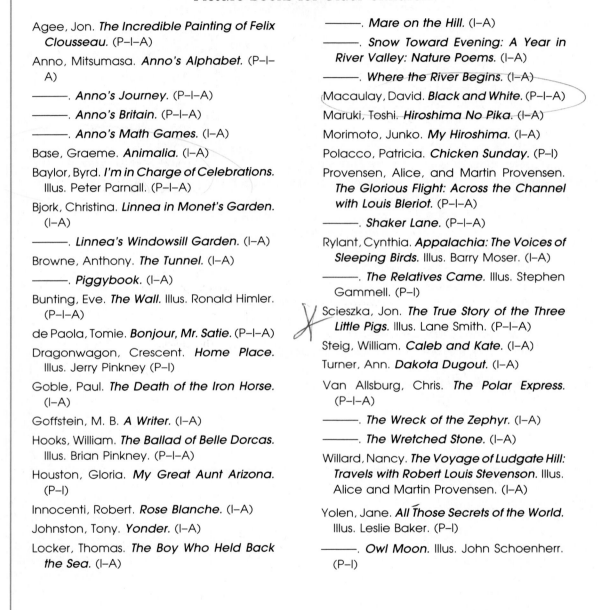

Agee, Jon. *The Incredible Painting of Felix Clousseau.* (P–I–A)

Anno, Mitsumasa. *Anno's Alphabet.* (P–I–A)

———. *Anno's Journey.* (P–I–A)

———. *Anno's Britain.* (P–I–A)

———. *Anno's Math Games.* (I–A)

Base, Graeme. *Animalia.* (I–A)

Baylor, Byrd. *I'm in Charge of Celebrations.* Illus. Peter Parnall. (P–I–A)

Bjork, Christina. *Linnea in Monet's Garden.* (I–A)

———. *Linnea's Windowsill Garden.* (I–A)

Browne, Anthony. *The Tunnel.* (I–A)

———. *Piggybook.* (I–A)

Bunting, Eve. *The Wall.* Illus. Ronald Himler. (P–I–A)

de Paola, Tomie. *Bonjour, Mr. Satie.* (P–I–A)

Dragonwagon, Crescent. *Home Place.* Illus. Jerry Pinkney (P–I)

Goble, Paul. *The Death of the Iron Horse.* (I–A)

Goffstein, M. B. *A Writer.* (I–A)

Hooks, William. *The Ballad of Belle Dorcas.* Illus. Brian Pinkney. (P–I–A)

Houston, Gloria. *My Great Aunt Arizona.* (P–I)

Innocenti, Robert. *Rose Blanche.* (I–A)

Johnston, Tony. *Yonder.* (I–A)

Locker, Thomas. *The Boy Who Held Back the Sea.* (I–A)

———. *Mare on the Hill.* (I–A)

———. *Snow Toward Evening: A Year in River Valley: Nature Poems.* (I–A)

———. *Where the River Begins.* (I–A)

Macaulay, David. *Black and White.* (P–I–A)

Maruki, Toshi. *Hiroshima No Pika.* (I–A)

Morimoto, Junko. *My Hiroshima.* (I–A)

Polacco, Patricia. *Chicken Sunday.* (P–I)

Provensen, Alice, and Martin Provensen. *The Glorious Flight: Across the Channel with Louis Bleriot.* (P–I–A)

———. *Shaker Lane.* (P–I–A)

Rylant, Cynthia. *Appalachia: The Voices of Sleeping Birds.* Illus. Barry Moser. (I–A)

———. *The Relatives Came.* Illus. Stephen Gammell. (P–I)

Scieszka, Jon. *The True Story of the Three Little Pigs.* Illus. Lane Smith. (P–I–A)

Steig, William. *Caleb and Kate.* (I–A)

Turner, Ann. *Dakota Dugout.* (I–A)

Van Allsburg, Chris. *The Polar Express.* (P–I–A)

———. *The Wreck of the Zephyr.* (I–A)

———. *The Wretched Stone.* (I–A)

Willard, Nancy. *The Voyage of Ludgate Hill: Travels with Robert Louis Stevenson.* Illus. Alice and Martin Provensen. (I–A)

Yolen, Jane. *All Those Secrets of the World.* Illus. Leslie Baker. (P–I)

———. *Owl Moon.* Illus. John Schoenherr. (P–I)

*E*D YOUNG, born in Tientsin, China, grew up in Shanghai and later moved to Hong Kong. He came to the United States on a student visa to study architecture at the University of Illinois. His father, dean of engineering at St. John's University in Shanghai and senior partner in a construction company, had hoped Ed's talent would develop along the lines of his own trade. But after three years at Illinois, Young transferred and graduated from Los Angeles Art Center College. He worked in advertising while he studied graphic arts and industrial design at Pratt Institute and taught at Pratt and later at Naropa Institute, Yale University, and the University of California at Santa Cruz.

Ed Young's interest in the art forms of his native country shows up in his work. For example, **Yeh Shen: A Cinderella Story from China** (by Ai Ling Louie) and **Lon Po Po: A Red Riding Hood Story from China** incorporate ancient Chinese panel art. In Jane Yolen's **The Emperor and the Kite,** Young uses an intricate Oriental papercut style. In some books, as in **All of You Was Singing** (by Richard Lewis), he uses rich, misty, swirling abstractions from which representational forms emerge. In **The Other Bone,** he uses vigorous pencil drawings—with humor—to tell a wordless story. Young sees Rafe Martin's book, **Foolish Rabbit's Big Mistake,** as a breakthrough book for him. In that book he broke the Indian miniature format in favor of the power of bigger images and brighter colors.

Ed Young won the Caldecott Award in 1990 for **Lon Po Po.** He received a Caldecott Honor Book Award in 1993 for **Seven Blind Mice.** In his Caldecott acceptance speech, he said,

Ed Young

. . . if **Lon Po Po** is the fruit of the tree, and I the branch that produced the fruit, where, then, I ask myself, is the tree? What is, in turn, the earth that nourished the tree, the air and rain and the sun that strengthened the earth? The collaboration of many is what makes this one remarkable fruit. All the hundreds of heroes and ideals are the rays of my sun. Those happy childhood days in my father's house, a true haven for friends and relatives in wartime China, is the ground of my earth. My world of associates—neighbors, students, fellow artists past and present, friends, and above all my teachers, my wife and family—is the source of my air and water.

Lon Po Po is but one fruit among many, and I am but one twig in the orchard, and this is only one season in time immemorial. Still, it is one precious moment. It is our opportunity to celebrate the wisdom of our belonging to something greater, of facing our adversities as a chance for growth, and of giving hope and beauty to our future.

Ed Young's art adds to the hope and the beauty that all of us experience as we enjoy his books.

Acceptance speech: Copyright, 1990, Ed Young. Reprinted in *Journal of Youth Services in Libraries,* Summer 1990. American Library Association, 50 E. Huron Street, Chicago, IL 60611.

 EACHING IDEA 3-5

Presenting Literary Concepts Through Picture Books

Picture books make it easy to study literary concepts:

- books are slender well-crafted pieces of literature
- literary elements are visible
- concepts are understandable
- concepts appear in a sparse text

The following books illustrate aspects of literature. Look at them as examples of the literary concept.

Setting

The time and place (setting) are clearly identified and interact with the plot in good literature. The following books illustrate an effective use of setting:

Baylor, Byrd. *I'm in Charge of Celebrations.* Illus. Peter Parnall.

Cameron, Ann. *The Most Beautiful Place in the World.* Illus. Thomas B. Allen.

Carrick, Donald. *Dark and Full of Secrets.*

Cooney, Barbara. *Miss Rumphius.*

Martin, Bill. Jr., and John Archambault. *The Ghost Eye Tree.* Illus. Ted Rand.

Yolen, Jane. *Owl Moon.* Illus. John Schoenherr.

Character and Setting

Character (who the story is about) is often shaped by the setting (where it takes place); further, character is revealed by the setting. All literary elements are intertwined—one affects another and they combine to affect still others. In the following books, characters are representative of the setting—they are, in fact, a part of their environment.

Hendershot, Judith. *In Coal Country.* Illus. Thomas B. Allen.

Radin, Ruth Yaffee. *High in the Mountains.* Illus. Ed Young.

Ringgold, Faith. *Tar Beach.*

Rylant, Cynthia. *When I Was Young in the Mountains.* Illus. Diane Goode.

Schroeder, Alan. *Ragtime Tumpie.* Illus. Bernie Fuchs.

Surprise Endings

Surprise endings—a plot device that suddenly upends everything that was anticipated—leave the reader gasping with delight and shock. Picture book authors and illustrators engage in clever surprises in the following books:

Charles, Donald. *Paddy Pig's Poems.*

Greene, Carol. *The Golden Locket.* Illus. Marcia Sewall.

Heide, Florence Parry. *The Shrinking of Treehorn.* Illus. Edward Gorey.

Kuskin, Karla. *Just Like Everyone Else.*

Martin, C. L. G. *The Dragon Nanny.* Illus. Robert Rayevsky.

Steptoe, John. *Mufaro's Beautiful Daughters.*

Udry, Janice May. *Let's Be Enemies.* Illus. Maurice Sendak.

Viorst, Judith. *Alexander and the Terrible, Horrible, No Good, Very Bad Day.* Illus. Ray Cruz.

———. *The Tenth Good Thing About Barney.* Illus. Erik Blegvad.

Zolotow, Charlotte. *The Quarreling Book.* Illus. Arnold Lobel.

Point of View

The point of view (who narrates) affects the telling of a story; it all depends on whose vantage point is used. These books illustrate how differently characters see things when events are told from their unique point of view:

de Paola, Tomie. *Helga's Dowry.*

———. *The Quicksand Book.*

Friedman, Ina. *How My Parents Learned to Eat.* Illus. Allen Say.

Lionni, Leo. *Fish Is Fish.*

Scieszka, Jon. *The True Story of the Three Little Pigs.* Illus. Lane Smith.

CONTINUED

Van Allsburg, Chris. *Two Bad Ants.*

Viorst, Judith. *I'll Fix Anthony.* Illus. Arnold Lobel.

———. *Rosie and Michael.* Illus. Lorna Tomei.

Plot Structure

Authors and illustrators manipulate plot structures to add variety, intrigue, and interest to their work. For example, in *Black and White*, David Macaulay continues four parallel stories that subtly become interrelated. In *Thirteen*, Remy Charlip presents 13 different illustrations on each double-page spread—numbered in reverse from 13 to 1—which are part of 13 wordless stories. The following books contain plot devices, such as foreshadowing, parallel stories, flashbacks:

Charlip, Remy and Jerry Joyner, *Thirteen.*

Macaulay, David. *Black and White.*

McCloskey, Robert. *Blueberries for Sal.*

Ness, Evaline. *Sam, Bangs, and Moonshine.*

Van Allsburg, Chris. *The Garden of Abdul Gasazi.*

Yorinks, Arthur. *Louis the Fish.* Illus. Richard Egielski.

Theme

The theme (an underlying message) is realized in many ways; the same or similar theme appears in very different stories. Read the following stories to see how the theme of memories can be visualized and dramatized:

Ackerman, Karen. *Song and Dance Man.* Illus. Stephen Gammell.

Fox, Mem. *Wilfrid Gordon McDonald Partridge.* Illus. Julie Vivas.

Martin, Bill Jr. and John Archambault. *Knots on a Counting Rope.* Illus. Ted Rand.

Mathis, Sharon Bell. *The Hundred Penny Box.* Illus. Leo and Diane Dillon.

SUMMARY

Picture books are artful books that hold a special place in the lives of children who read them. They are often children's main experience with fine art. They can enrich and extend children's worlds, providing opportunities for experiences through picture and print that allow children to confirm their own worth, to learn about others, and to learn about the world. Picture books also provide stunning examples of art and language that become resources from which children draw as they develop their own abilities to shape and reshape their world.

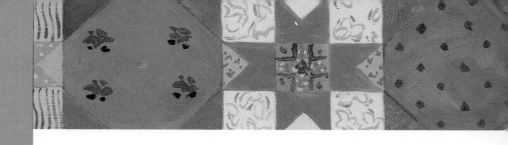

4

Poetry and Verse

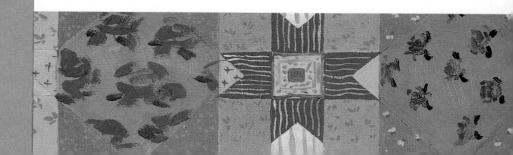

MY POEMS

I write my dreams.
I discover the laughter.
I share the things I think.
My body grows old and fails me,
But my soul lives on in ink.

Brod Bagert

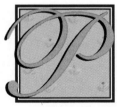oets shape an ordinary everyday experience into an emotional universal that calls to readers, "Come sing with me; come feel with me." Readers of all ages respond with joy, discovering poems that they make their own.

Poetry is a poet's intuition of truth. It combines richness of meaning with the sound of language arranged in its most beautiful form. Poetry is filled with carefully selected words that are arranged to call attention to experiences we have not known or fully recognized. We can say more easily what poetry does than what it is; poetry eludes precise definition. We know that poetry can make us chuckle or laugh out loud. It can startle us with insight or surprise us with clarity. It can also bring a peacefulness and a sense of repose. Some poems express feelings that we did not even know we had until we read them; then we say, "Yes, that's just how it is." Poetry deals with truth—the essence of life and experience. Poetry, says Gregory Corso (1983), is "the opposite of hypocrisy."

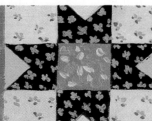
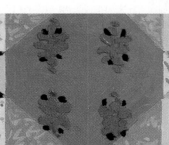

Poets Go Wishing

Poets go fishing
with buckets
of words,
fishing
and wishing.

Using a line
that's loose or
tight
(Maybe this time
a rhyme is
right.)

Unreeling
unreeling
the words till they
match
the feeling the poet is
trying to
catch.

Lilian Moore

Jane Breskin Zalben paints a jewel-toned picture of a writer fishing for words to express feelings he is trying to catch. This art for Lilian Moore's poem, "Poets Go Wishing," is found in Bobbye Goldstein's collection, *Inner Chimes.*

Understanding poetry is a continual process built only on experiences that are both wide and broad. Children develop better understanding the more they internalize poetry. They profit little from verbal definitions and descriptions. It is the first-hand experience of listening to, reading, writing, and discussing poetry that contributes the most to fostering their love of it. Children who live with poetry in their homes and in their schools turn to poems again and again for pleasure.

As teachers, we need to go beyond the surface of poetry, such as poetic elements, form, or the way it looks on a page, and consider a deeper understanding of what poetry is and what a poet does. Lilian Moore (1992) writes of a poet's work in "Poets Go Wishing."

POETS GO WISHING

Poets go fishing
with buckets
of words,
fishing
and wishing.

Using a line
that's loose or
tight
(Maybe this time

a rhyme is
right.)
Unreeling
unreeling
the words till they
match
the feeling the poet is
trying to
catch.

Lilian Moore

Although poetry's words can be familiar ones, they are carefully chosen and placed in such a way as to capture the imagination. The experience captured in poetry may be commonplace, but it becomes extraordinary when seen through the poet's eye. As Frye says, "The poet's job is not to tell you what happened, but what happens: not what did take place, but the kind of thing that always does take place" (1964, p. 63).

Poets themselves are often the best source for a definition of poetry. Many poets write about poems and the act of creating them. Bobbye Goldstein collected many of these poems in **Inner Chimes: Poems on Poetry** (P–I–A). Eve Merriam, for instance, captures the essence of poetry and reveals some of its characteristics as she describes what is "Inside a Poem" (I). She says poetry has a beat that repeats, words that chime, and images we have not imagined before. Eleanor Farjeon (1951) gives a less tangible definition in her **Poems for Children:**

What is Poetry? Who knows?
Not the rose, but the scent of the rose;
Not the sky, but the light in the sky;
Not the fly, but the gleam of the fly;
Not the sea, but the sound of the sea;
Not myself, but what makes me
See, hear, and feel something that prose
Cannot: and what it is, who knows?

Eleanor Farjeon

Poetry can make us laugh, give us something to think about, and help us put our feelings into words. Poetry captures the essence of experience.

CRITERIA FOR SELECTING POETRY

While some poetry from the past still speaks to today's children, a wealth of excellent poetry has been written since the 1960s. Figure 4-1 lists questions to ask yourself as you evaluate poetry. Search out new poems instead of relying on those you memorized in your childhood, and keep the questions in Figure 4-1 in mind when selecting poetry.

Poetry Is Understandable

Children like poems they can understand. They also enjoy poems that stretch their understanding, those that need to be read and discussed in the company of peers and adults also interested in exploring poetry. Children respond to a careful selection of poems that are geared to their intellectual development and ones that speak of their experiences. Poetry can evoke laughter, create images, and express feelings when it is about subjects and experiences that children understand.

Poems Make Us Laugh

There are poems for any brand of humor. The humor is derived from word play, preposterous situations or events, or unexpected perspectives on everyday concerns; it is never malicious or hurtful. The laughter that humorous poems evoke can be delight in the absurd or rueful recognition of the funny side of life. John Ciardi's (1993) "The Hairy-Nosed Preposterous" evokes gales of laughter from primary-grade children who enjoy word play.

THE HAIRY-NOSED PREPOSTEROUS

The Hairy-Nosed Preposterous
Looks much like a Rhinosterous,
But also something like a tank—
For which he has himself to thank.

His ears are the size of tennis shoes,
His eyes the size of pins.
And when he lies down for a snooze
An orchestra begins.

It whistles, rattles, roars, and thumps,
And the wind of it comes and goes
Through the storm-tossed hair that grows in clumps
On the end of his capable nose.

John Ciardi

Many poems for readers of all ages will evoke a response ranging from a chuckle to a loud shout of laughter. These poems are truly funny and often are a child's first happy experience with poetry. Many of the best collections of humorous poems are listed in Figure 4-2.

Poems Create Images

Many poems create sensory images. Poets craft words in such a way that readers almost see, smell, taste, touch, or hear what a poem describes. Lilian

---

Figure 4-1

Checklist for Selecting Poetry

❑ Can children understand it? Can they understand it with help from adults?

❑ Does the poem stir emotions? (delight, sadness, nostalgia)

❑ Does it create images of sight, touch, smell, taste?

❑ Does it play with the sounds of language? Does the sound echo the sense?

❑ Does the rhythm reinforce the meaning?

Moore's (1967) "Until I Saw the Sea" evokes the sight and sound of the ocean.

UNTIL I SAW THE SEA

Until I saw the sea
I did not know
that wind
could wrinkle water so.

I never knew
that sun
could splinter a whole sea of blue.

Nor
did I know before,
a sea breathes in and out
upon a shore.

Lilian Moore

See Figure 4-2 for suggestions of poetry collections that contain many sensory poems.

Poems Express Feelings

Sometimes poems express our feelings in ways we have never thought about before. Never trite or sentimental, fine poetry can help readers understand themselves and their emotions. Whether we are experiencing joy, happiness, sadness, anger, jealousy, or loneliness, there is a poem that puts these emotions into words, as Mary Ann Hoberman (1991) does in "My Father."

MY FATHER

My father doesn't live with us.
It doesn't help to make a fuss;
But still I feel unhappy, plus
I miss him.

Figure 4-2

Poems That Stir Emotions

Laughter

Bagert, Brod. *Let Me Be the Boss.* (P–I)

Cole, William (compiler). *Beastly Boys and Ghastly Girls.* (I)

—— (compiler). *Oh, Such Foolishness!* Illus. Tomie de Paola. (I)

—— (compiler). *Oh, That's Ridiculous!* (I)

—— (compiler). *Oh, What Nonsense.* (I)

—— (editor). *Poem Stew.* Illus. Karen Weinhaus. (I)

—— (compiler). *A Zooful of Animals.* (I)

Harrison, David. *Somebody Catch My Homework.* Illus. Betsy Lewin. (P–I)

——. *Never Talk to Plants.* Illus. Betsy Lewin. (P–I)

Kennedy, X. J. *The Forgetful Wishing Well: Poems for Young People.* Illus. Monica Incisa. (I–A)

——. *Fresh Brats.* (I)

——. *Ghastlies, Goops & Pincushions: Nonsense Verse.* Illus. Ron Barrett. (I–A)

Lobel, Arnold. *Whiskers and Rhymes.* (P)

Prelutsky, Jack. *The Baby Uggs Are Hatching.* Illus. James Stevenson. (P)

—— (selector). *For Laughing Out Loud: Poems to Tickle Your Funnybone.* (P–I–A)

——. *The New Kid on the Block.* Illus. James Stevenson. (P–I–A)

——. *Rolling Harvey Down the Hill.* Illus. Victoria Chess. (P–I)

Silverstein, Shel. *A Light in the Attic.* (P–I–A)

——. *Where the Sidewalk Ends.* (P–I–A)

Smith, William Jay. *Laughing Time: Collected Nonsense.* (I–A)

Steig, Jeanne. *Consider the Lemming.* (I–A)

Sensory Images

Adoff, Arnold. *Black Is Brown Is Tan.* (P)

——. *In for Winter; Out for Spring.* Illus. Jerry Pinkney. (P–I)

Baylor, Byrd. *Hawk, I'm Your Brother.* Illus. Peter Parnall. (P–I)

Bennett, Jill (compiler). *Spooky Poems.* (P–I)

Bierhorst, John. *In the Trail of the Wind: American Indian Poems and Ritual Orations.* (I–A)

Brooks, Gwendolyn. *Bronzeville Boys and Girls.* (P–I)

Bryan, Ashley. *Sing to the Sun.* (I–A)

de Regniers, Beatrice Schenk. *The Way I Feel . . . Sometimes.* (P–I)

Dunning, Stephen (compiler). *Reflections on a Gift of Watermelon Pickle & Other Modern Verse.* (A)

Esbensen, Barbara Juster. *Words with Wrinkled Knees: Animal Poems.* (P–I)

——. *Who Shrank My Grandmother's House?* Illus. Eric Beddows. (P–I)

Fisher, Aileen. *Always Wondering.* Illus. Joan Sandin. (P–I)

My father doesn't live with me.
He's got another family;
He moved away when I was three.
    I miss him.

I'm always happy on the day
He visits and we talk and play;
But after he has gone away
    I miss him.

Mary Ann Hoberman

Whatever the feelings expressed there should be a ring of thoughtful truthfulness. Whether evoking laughter, telling a story, or expressing an emotion, a poem is good only if its reader can understand it. Figure 4-2 lists some books containing poems that express feelings.

Poetry Is Appealing

When children are first introduced to poetry they generally prefer humorous poems with strong rhythm and rhyme over free verse with abstract symbolism. They enjoy narrative poetry because it

CONTINUED

Gasztold, Carmen Bernos de. *Prayers from the Ark* (new ed.).

Giovanni, Nikki. *Spin a Soft Black Song: Poems for Children.* (P–I)

Goldstein, Bobbye (selector). *Inner Chimes.* Illus. Jane Breskin Zalben. (I–A)

Greenfield, Eloise. *Honey, I Love: And Other Poems.* Illus. Leo and Diane Dillon. (I–A)

———. *Nathaniel Talking.* Illus. Jan Spivey Gilchrist. (P–I)

———. *Night on Neighborhood Street.* (P–I)

———. *Under the Sunday Tree.* Illus. Amos Ferguson. (P–I)

Gunning, Monica. *Not a Copper Penny in Me House.* Illus. Frané Lessac. (P–I–A)

Heard, Georgia. *Creatures of Earth, Sea, and Sky.* Illus. Jennifer Owings Dewey. (I–A)

Hoberman, Mary Ann. *Fathers, Mothers, Sisters, Brothers.* (P–I–A)

Hopkins, Lee Bennett (selector). *Still as a Star: A Book of Nighttime Poems.* (P–I–A)

Huck, Charlotte (editor). *Secret Places.* (P–I)

Livingston, Myra Cohn. *Poems for Mothers.* (P–I)

———. *There Was a Place & Other Poems.* (I–A)

———. *Sea Songs.* Illus. Leonard Everett Fisher. (I)

Margolis, Richard J. *Secrets of a Small Brother.* Illus. Donald Carrick. (P–I)

Merriam, Eve. *Fresh Paint.* (I)

Moore, Lilian (selector). *Sunflakes: Poems for Children.* Illus. Jan Ormerod. (P–I–A)

Moore, Lilian. *Something New Begins.* (I–A)

Morrison, Lillian. *Whistling the Morning In.* Illus. Joel Cook. (I–A)

Pomerantz, Charlotte. *If I Had a Paka: Poems in Eleven Languages.* Illus. Nancy Tafuri. (P)

———. *The Tamarindo Puppy and Other Poems.* Illus. Byron Barton. (P)

Prelutsky, Jack. *Nightmares: Poems to Trouble Your Sleep.* (I)

Shea, Pegi Deitz. *Bungalow Fungalow.* Illus. Elizabeth Sayles (P)

Sneve, Virginia Driving Hawk. *Dancing Tepees.* Illus. Stephen Gammell. (I–A)

Worth, Valerie. *All the Small Poems.* Illus. Natalie Babbitt. (I–A)

Zolotow, Charlotte. *Everything Glistens and Everything Sings.* Illus. Margot Tomes. (I–A)

---

is based on their natural love of story. Children's responses to poetry depend heavily on the way it is introduced to them. If initial encounters with poetry are happy ones, then a love for and understanding of poetry can grow over a lifetime.

Poetry is the natural language of childhood. Certainly infants and toddlers respond to being bounced on a knee and hearing "Ride a little horsie up and down a hill. If you don't watch out, you'll take a little spill." During the early childhood years, they hear jingles and readily commit them to memory. They sing songs as they play and will join in on refrains with delight. Many happy experiences with rhythm, rhyme, humor, and story shape children's preferences for poetry.

Research on Poetry Preferences

Researchers have studied the kinds of poems children like as well as the kinds of poems teachers read to them. For example, in two national surveys, Terry (1974) studied the poetry preferences of students in the upper elementary grades and Fisher and Natarella (1982) replicated Terry's study with primary-grade children. These researchers found that children like:

1. Contemporary poems;
2. Poems they can understand;
3. Narrative poems;
4. Poems with rhyme, rhythm, and sound; and
5. Poems that relate to their personal experiences.

They also found that children dislike poems that have much figurative language and imagery. They dislike highly abstract poems that do not make sense to them. Haiku were consistently disliked. Girls like poetry more often than boys do. Favorite poems were humorous and about familiar experiences or animals. John Ciardi's poem "Mummy Slept Late and Daddy Fixed Breakfast" in **You Read to Me, I'll Read to You** (P–I) and limericks of all sorts were tops among the children's choices.

The Effect of Classroom Experiences. McClure (1990) extended Terry's study and found that children respond much differently to poetry in a supportive literary environment. In such an environment, children responded more positively to a wider variety of poetry, showing that teachers' attitudes make a tremendous difference. In other words, what you do with poetry in the classroom makes a difference in the way your students respond to poetry.

Immerse Students in Poetry. Begin with poems that research has shown to be favorites: humorous poems and narrative poems with strong rhyme, rhythm, and sound elements. Then gradually expand children's experiences with poetry by exposing them to a broader range of forms. As they are hearing and reading poetry, encourage them to experiment with oral interpretation, such as choral reading. Some poems, such as those in Paul Fleischman's (1988) **Joyful Noise: Poems for Two Voices** (I–A) are perfect for this.

FIREFLIES

Light	*Light*
	is the ink we use
Night	*Night*
is our parchment	
	We're
	fireflies
fireflies	*flickering*
flitting	
	flashing
fireflies	
glimmering	*fireflies*
	gleaming

glowing	
Insect calligraphers	*Insect calligraphers*
practicing penmanship	
	copying sentences
Six-legged scribblers	*Six-legged scribblers*
of vanishing messages,	
	fleeting graffiti
Fine artists in flight	*Fine artists in flight*
adding dabs of light	
	bright brush strokes
Signing the June nights	*Signing the June nights*
as if they were paintings	*as if they were paintings*
	We're
flickering	*fireflies*
fireflies	*flickering*
fireflies.	*fireflies.*

Paul Fleischman

Children enjoy experimenting with poetry in their own writing and exploring how poetry works by studying what poets do. Providing opportunities for students to play with various styles and elements of poetry also helps children learn to understand and enjoy a wide variety of poetry.

Children enjoy collecting their own favorite poetry, perhaps copying it onto file cards or into a looseleaf binder. Primary-grade teachers might put favorite poems on charts to be read over and over; intermediate- and advanced-grade teachers might encourage their students to create their personal anthologies of favorite poems, adding to them over the year. These personal anthologies can be part of the classroom library so that peers can read and discuss each other's favorites. As the anthologies grow, students can experiment with classifying the contents.

When poetry is part of the daily life of the classroom children often memorize their favorite poems spontaneously. Do *not* require them to memorize and recite poems. Instead, casually recite your own favorites, letting your students know they are welcome to do the same. They will soon be eager to share a poem with others. We discuss working with poetry in the classroom at the end of this chapter.

Poetry is becoming increasingly popular; much more poetry is being published in appealing formats. The Children's Choices survey shows that children have selected poetry books as favorites every year since the project began in 1973. The results are even more encouraging when we realize that these preferences surfaced in the midst of opportunities to choose hundreds of other picture books, novels, and nonfiction. Children continue to choose witty poems about things familiar to them as well as ones that puzzle and astonish them.

TEACHING IDEA 4-1

Choose Your Own Poetry Award Winner

Acquaint others with the National Council of Teachers of English (NCTE) Award for Excellence in Poetry for Children: It is given for the entire body of a poet's work. Read widely from the collected works of poets who have received the NCTE Award.

Conduct a selection process among your peers. State why you think a certain poet should win, read the poems, discuss why you like this poet's work. See if your choice matches the next NCTE Committee's choice due in 1994. Who will it be? See if you can beat the experts.

Variation: Adopt a Poet. Find out where your poet was born and grew up. What books were published? What do people say about the poet? What awards were won? Why did you choose this poet?

General preferences continue to reflect Terry's findings. Figure 4-3 lists some recent children's choices.

We may not always know why a particular poem appeals to children, but we do know that the ones read aloud with enthusiasm are likely to become their favorites. Select poems you like, too, so your enthusiasm and enjoyment will be apparent to your students.

Poetry Contains Language Used in Interesting Ways

Poets manipulate the elements of sound, rhythm, and meaning to create an impact more powerful than any found in prose. Sound and rhythm are more pronounced in poetry than in prose, and meaning is more condensed. Poets use language in such a special way that there are many specialized terms used to describe it. These terms are described here and listed in the Glossary. Although you would not want to ask children to learn all of these terms and their definitions, you should be familiar and comfortable with them so you can answer children's questions when they begin to explore the techniques of their favorite poets. If, for example, children comment on the repetition of initial consonant sounds, you might want to say, "That's called

---

Figure 4-3

Children's Poetry Choices, 1974–1993

de Paola, Tomie. *Tomie de Paola's Book of Poems.* (P–I)

de Regniers, Beatrice Schenk. *Sing a Song of Popcorn: Every Child's Book of Poems.* (P–I–A)

Griego, Margot C., et al. (selectors and trans.). *Tortillitas para Mama.* (P)

Hoberman, Mary Ann. *A House Is a House for Me.* (P)

Hopkins, Lee Bennett. *Good Books, Good Times.* (P)

——. *Surprises.* (P)

Lee, Dennis. *Alligator Pie.* (P–I)

Merriam, Eve. *Blackberry Ink.* (P–I)

Milne, A. A. *When We Were Very Young.* (P–I)

——. *Now We Are Six.* (P–I)

Moore, Lilian. *See My Lovely Poison Ivy.* (I)

Morrison, Lillian (compiler). *Best Wishes, Amen: Autograph Verse.* (I–A)

Moss, Jeffrey. *Butterfly Jar.* (I–A)

Prelutsky, Jack. *The Mean Old Mean Hyena.* (I)

——. *Nightmares: Poems to Trouble Your Sleep.* (I)

—— (selector). *Poems of A. Nonny Mouse.* (P–I)

Thayer, Ernest Lawrence. *Casey at the Bat.* Illus. Wallace Tripp. (I)

Withers, Carl (compiler). *Rocket in My Pocket: The Rhymes and Chants of Young Americans.* (I)

Worth, Valerie. *More Small Poems.* Illus. Natalie Babbitt. (I–A)

Nancy Roser and Margaret Frith, editors. *Children's Choices: Teaching with Books Children Like.* International Reading Association, 1983.
Kids' Favorite Books: Children's Choices 1989–1991. International Reading Association, 1992.
Children's Choices lists in *The Reading Teacher.* October issue each year.

'alliteration.' Let's see how it works in this poem." Teachers who understand how poetry works are wonderful guides for children interested in exploring poetry.

Words as Sound

Of all the elements of poetry, sound offers the most pleasure to children. The choice and arrangement of sounds make poetry musical and reinforce meaning. Alliteration, assonance, onomatopoeia, and rhyme are among the language resources of sound.

Rhyme refers to words whose ending sounds are alike (despair/fair). Although poetry need not rhyme, children often prefer rhyme. Rhyme is not as fashionable with adults as it once was, but children still enjoy reciting it. It sticks better in the mind and lingers longer on the tongue. Generation after generation repeats the same jump rope jingles and rhyming street games.

Poets' ears are tuned to the *repetition* of consonants, vowels, syllables, words, phrases, and lines, separately and in combination. Anything may be repeated to achieve effect. Repetition is like meeting an old friend again; children find it reassuring. Repetition underscores meaning, establishes a sound pattern, and is a source of humor in many rhymes, as in this chant from David McCord (1925):

III

The pickety fence
The pickety fence
Give it a lick it's
The pickety fence
Give it a lick it's
A clickety fence
Give it a lick it's
A lickety fence
Give it a lick
Give it a lick
Give it a lick
With a rickety stick
Pickety
Pickety
Pickety
Pick

David McCord

Alliteration refers to the repetition of the initial consonant sounds of words at close intervals. Karla Kuskin (1962) uses alliteration effectively in her poem "The Meal."

THE MEAL

Timothy Tompkins had turnips and tea.
The turnips were tiny.
He ate at least three.

And then, for dessert,
He had onions and ice.
He liked that so much
That he ordered it twice.
He had two cups of ketchup,
A prune, and a pickle.
"Delicious," said Timothy.
"Well worth a nickel."
He folded his napkin
And hastened to add,
"It's one of the loveliest breakfasts I've had."

Karla Kuskin

Rhoda W. Bacmeister (1952) uses *assonance,* the repetition of vowel sounds at close intervals, and alliteration in the verses of "Galoshes":

GALOSHES

Susie's galoshes
Make splishes and sploshes
And slooshes and sloshes,
As Susie steps slowly
Along in the slush.

They stamp and they tramp
On the ice and concrete.
They get stuck in the muck and the mud;
But Susie likes much best to hear

The slippery slush
As it slooshes and sloshes,
And splishes and sploshes,
All around her galoshes!

Rhoda Bacmeister

She also makes use of *onomatopoeia,* or words created from natural sounds associated with the thing or action designated. For example, the word *murmur* resembles somewhat the sound of murmuring. Other words that sound like what they mean are hiss, bang, snap, and crack. Rhoda Bacmeister uses the onomatopoetic words *slush, slooshes, sloshes, splishes,* and *sploshes.* Onomatopoeia in combination with other sound resources can achieve poetic effect to light up any child's eyes.

An example of *end rhyme*—in which the rhyming words are at the ends of lines—is Joy Hulme's (1993) "Elephant."

ELEPHANT

An elephant's trunk is a useful tool
For squirting water to keep him cool,
For lifting up logs, or testing the trail,
Or holding hands with his mother's tail,
For sucking up peanuts, or hugging up hay,
Or feeding himself in an elephant's way.

But why is it called a TRUNK? Who knows?
It isn't packed for carrying clothes!

Joy N. Hulme

P
R
O
F
I
L
E

One of my teachers told me, "Never let a day go by without looking on three beautiful things." I try to live up to that and find it isn't difficult. The sky in all weathers is, for me, the first of these three things.

David McCord worked at Harvard University for 37 years serving as fundraiser, alumni editor, and historian but, all the while, he continued to write poetry for children. He is the author or editor of 50 books of poetry, essays, history, medicine, light verse, and verse for children. He is also an artist and has had several one-man shows of watercolor landscapes. He lives at the Harvard Club and is an avid fan of the Boston Red Sox.

McCord was awarded the first honorary degree of Doctor of Humane Letters ever granted at Harvard; it was conferred on him at the same ceremonies at which President John F. Kennedy received an LL.D.

In 1983, Simmons College in Boston, Massachusetts, presented McCord with a Doctor of Children's Literature degree. The citation states:

As a poet who has dedicated your life to the creation of poetry which opens the ears of children to the nuances of language and to the splendors of the world which language represents, you have spoken in a

David McCord, 1977

unique voice. You have brought to bear upon your work your long and thorough investigation of and fascination with the natural world, the social world, the world of the intellect, and the world of the imagination. . . . You have helped awaken adults to the sounds of the child's world. . . . The poet John Ciardi has said, "One is too few of [you] and there is, alas, no second."

David McCord was born on November 15, 1897, near Greenwich Village, New York City. He grew up on Long Island, in Princeton, New Jersey, and on a ranch by the Rogue River in Oregon. He received the NCTE Award in 1977.

When rhyme spills over from the end of one line to the beginning of the next it is called *runover rhyme*. David McCord (1986) gives us a beautiful example of this (together with end rhyme) in his "Runover Rhyme":

RUNOVER RHYME

Down by the pool still fishing,
Wishing for fish, I fail
Praying for birds not present,
Pheasant or grouse or quail.

Up in the woods, his hammer
Stammering, I can't see
The woodpecker, find the cunning
Sunning old owl in the tree.

Over the field such raucous
Talk as the crows talk on!
Nothing around me slumbers;
Numbers of birds have gone.

Even the leaves hang listless,
Lasting through days we lose,
Empty of what is wanted,
Haunted by what we choose.

David McCord

If children are provided with many opportunities to experience a variety of rhyme schemes, they will come to see how the use of rhyme can add to and enhance the meaning of a poem.

Words as Rhythm

Children respond to rhythm; they learned it by listening to their mothers' heartbeats before they were born. Rhythm is everywhere in life—in ocean waves, in the tick of a clock, in hoofbeats, in one's own pulse. In poetry, *rhythm* refers to recurrences of syllables and accents, in the rise and fall of words spoken or read. All good poetry is rhythmical, just like other forms of high art. The rhythm in painting, sculpture, and other visual arts is seen in the repetition of line, form, or color. Rhythm in dance is apparent in the flow of the body movements and the graceful flow of motion. In music it is evident in the beat. Well-written prose has rhythm, too, although it is less evident or regular than in poetry.

Rhythm is usually manifest in poetry in alternating accented and unaccented syllables. It is what Eve Merriam calls "the repeat of a beat . . . an inner chime that makes you want to tap your feet or swerve in a curve" (1964).

PROFILE

When I was young there was still quite a bit of logging nearby, and my brother and I used to follow the iced logging roads. . . . [Now] I live in Boulder, Colorado, at the edge of town on a dead-end street, close to Flagstaff Mountain. The highlight of each day is a walk with my dog and a friend and her dog on one of the many trails nearby. This keeps me in touch with the weather, the wildlife, and the wonderful scenery in every direction.

Aileen Fisher likes to work with wood she finds in the forest; she doesn't change its shape but looks for shapes that are already in the wood, then she polishes the wood and mounts it to bring out its characteristics. This is similar to the way she works with words when she writes poetry; she searches for just the right word and then polishes it to bring out the spirit of the poem.

Fisher built her own cabin; she also built her own fireplace and furniture. In her cabin, the fireplace and cookstove provide heat; kerosene lamps provide light; and a gasoline motor pumps water from a spring in the gulch. The view from her cabin of the mountains of Colorado provides Fisher with a constant source of inspiration. For though she had always written in college and

Aileen Fisher, 1978

in the city, she is truly at home in the country. She is a nature poet. Her verse recaptures, as few ever have, that special wonder children feel when they discover nature for the first time.

Aileen Fisher was born September 9, 1906, in Iron River, Michigan. She attended the University of Chicago and received her bachelor's degree in journalism from the University of Missouri. She worked at the Women's Journalistic Register and the Labor Bureau of the Middle West before she devoted herself to writing full time. Fisher lives in Boulder, Colorado. She received the NCTE Award in 1978.

The rhythm in poetry is most often metrical. *Meter* is ordered rhythm, in which certain syllables are regularly stressed or accented in a more or less fixed pattern. Meter means "measure," and metrical language in poetry can be measured. The meter in poetry can run from that of tightly structured verse patterns to loosely defined free verse. Whatever it is, rhythm helps to create and then reinforce a poem's meaning. In ***Circus*** (N–P), Jack Prelutsky (1974) adjusts his rhythms to the subject:

> *Over and over the tumblers tumble*
> *with never a fumble*
> *with never a stumble,*
> *top over bottom and back over top*
> *flop-flippy-floppity-flippity-flop.*

But the tumblers pass and are followed by the elephants, whose plodding walk echoes in the new rhythm:

> *Here come the elephants, ten feet high,*
> *elephants, elephants, heads in the sky,*
> *Eleven great elephants intertwined,*
> *one little elephant close behind.*

> *Jack Prelutsky*

and the rhythm plods along in the way elephants walk.

Word order, too, contributes to the rhythm of poetry. Arranging words is central to the making of a poem. Teachers, and perhaps interested students, should be aware of the ways poets manipulate syntax to make poetry distinctive from prose. One noticeable feature of poetic language is the way it varies from the straight declarative sentence. In Stevenson's "Where Go the Boats?" (1905) the poet states:

WHERE GO THE BOATS

> *Dark brown is the river*
> *Golden is the sand.*
> *It flows along forever,*
> *With trees on either hand.*

> *Robert Louis Stevenson*

The literal meaning of the poem could probably be communicated in this way:

> *The river is dark brown,*
> *The sand is gold.*
> *The river keeps on flowing forever,*
> *With trees on both sides.*

---

*T*EACHING IDEA 4-2

Poems for Beginning Readers

Children learning to read need certain qualities in a text that support their initial efforts to decode print:

> a small number of words on a line
> phrase-structured text (words that one would say in a single phrase placed together)
> words that flow naturally from the tongue
> words that are predictable, words that follow logically
> words that rhyme

This describes poetry. Rhymed text helps children learn to read. Some collections are especially suited to beginning readers.

Easy-to-read poetry collections

Domanska, Janina. *If All the Seas Were One Sea.*
Hopkins, Lee Bennett. *Surprises.*
———. *More Surprises.*
Kuskin, Karla. *Roar and More.*
———. *Soap Soup.*
———. *Something's Sleeping in the Hall.*
Martin, Bill, Jr. *Brown Bear, Brown Bear, What Do You See?*
———. *Polar Bear, Polar Bear, What Do You Hear?*

Retaining most of Stevenson's words but rearranging the word order totally distorts the visual image. Poets manipulate syntax until they find an order and rhythm pleasing to them and one that communicates more than the literal message. For children, the inverted sentence order used for poetic effect can at first interfere with meaning; however, they grow in their ability to comprehend inverted sentences as they hear poetry read aloud.

Words as Meaning: Imagery

Poetry often carries many layers of meaning and, as in other literature, is subject to many different interpretations. The meaning children create is directly proportionate to what their experience has prepared them to understand.

One teacher (Terry, 1974) read William Jay Smith's "The Toaster" to children of varying levels of development and asked them to draw a picture of what the poem was about. The poem describes the toaster as a "silver-scaled dragon who sits at my elbow and toasts my bread" (1955, p. 20). Children in the primary grades interpreted the poem as an actual dragon and drew fiery-mouthed dragons, showing they understood the poem at the literal, concrete level. Older children, above the fourth grade, drew pictures of toasters that resembled dragons, suggesting they understood the figurative language Smith used in the poem.

Not all poems have hidden meanings, but it is true that some poems bear subtle messages. Most poems, however, are descriptions of character, expressions of emotions, or accounts of events. We chance losing our students if we continually send them searching for hidden messages. It is perfectly acceptable to assert, as Alice did, after reading "Jabberwocky": "Somehow it seems to fill my head with ideas, only I don't know exactly what they are."

Poetic devices used to convey meaning include figurative language, imagery, denotation, and connotation. Through them poets suggest that more is meant than meets the ear. What is left unsaid is often as important as what is put down on the page, as in this poem by Lillian Morrison (1992).

DAILY VIOLENCE

Dawn cracked;
*   the sun stole through.*
Day broke;
*   the sun climbed over rooftops.*
Clouds chased the sun,
*   then burst.*
Night fell.
The clock struck midnight.

Lillian Morrison

Figurative language produces a meaning beyond the literal one of the words used. In poetry, figurative language appears frequently and affects meaning in unique ways; metaphor, simile, and personification make the language of poetry different from that of prose. As poets create vivid experiences, they use language metaphorically; they help us to see or feel things in new ways. It is not enough just to have the idea; poets must also have the words. The special and particular words often involve figurative language.

Children need experience in using and understanding figurative language before they can fully appreciate poems that rely on it. How well they understand this use of language in a poem depends on their background. Young children understand the comparisons made on a physical plane but not a psychological one. Snow-covered bushes that look like popcorn balls and cars that look like big fat raisins are more likely to make sense to these children than a prison guard's heart of stone. Young children interpret such a prison guard's heart as being physically made of stone. When they become more sophisticated language users at a later age, they recognize that the comparison refers to a psychological state.

As children gain an understanding of how figurative language contributes to meaning, poetry assumes a deeper dimension. Recognizing contrast, comparison, and exaggeration on a psychological plane provides richer interpretations. More complex comparisons can be made using the devices of metaphor and simile, which compare one thing to another or view something in terms of something else. The comparison in a *simile* is stated and uses the words *like* or *as* to draw the comparison. A comparison in a *metaphor* is inferred; something is stated as something else.

Eve Merriam (1964) makes a comparison unmistakable by entitling her equation of morning with a new sheet of paper, "Metaphor":

METAPHOR

Morning is
a new sheet of paper
for you to write on.

When I watched my young daughter trying to learn how to roller-skate, I wrote "74th Street." "Hey, this little kid gets roller skates./ She puts them on./ She stands up and almost/ flops over backwards. . . ."

My daughter starting, then falling, then starting again with many kinds of movements inspired a different sort of poem. . . . The words, the sound of them, needed to fit the content of what they said.

Myra Cohn Livingston was born on August 17, 1926, in Omaha, Nebraska. She began writing poetry at age 5; she later wrote plays and showed talent for music and sculpture. Myra's family moved from Omaha to Los Angeles when she was eleven years old; there she worked on the school newspaper. After graduating from Sarah Lawrence College, Livingston returned to Beverly Hills, California, where she lives today.

Myra Cohn Livingston, 1980

Myra Cohn Livingston received the NCTE Award in 1980.

Whatever you want to say,
all day
until night
folds it up
and files it away.
The bright words and the dark words
are gone
until dawn
and a new day
to write on.

                                   Eve Merriam

Personification refers to the representation of a thing or abstraction as a person. When we say "Fortune smiled on us" or "If the weather permits," we are giving human qualities to an idea like fortune or to a force of nature like the weather. Poets often give human feelings or thoughts to plants and animals. Valerie Worth (1987, p. 41) uses personification to make ideas more vivid or unusual.

CRICKETS

Crickets
Talk

In the tall
Grass
All
Late summer
Long.
When
Summer
Is gone,
The dry
Grass
Whispers
Alone.

                                   Valerie Worth

Langston Hughes's (1932, p. 8) "April Rain Song" also employs personification:

APRIL RAIN SONG

Let the rain kiss you.
Let the rain beat upon your head with silver liquid
*   drops.*
Let the rain sing you a lullaby.

                                   Langston Hughes

I've sometimes spent weeks looking for precisely the right word. It's like having a tiny marble in your pocket, you can just feel it. Sometimes you find a word and say, "No, I don't think this is it. . . ." Then you discard it, and take another and another until you get it right. I do think poetry is great fun. That's what I'd like to stress more than anything else: the joy of the sounds of language.

Eve Merriam was born in Philadelphia and graduated from the University of Pennsylvania. She did graduate work at the University of Wisconsin and Columbia University. After graduation from college, Eve worked as a sales clerk in a department store and as a fashion copywriter at **Glamour** magazine. She was also a playwright; several of her plays have been produced as Broadway and off-Broadway

musicals. Merriam lived in Greenwich Village, New York City; she loved the rhythms and sounds of the city. She died in 1992, and received the NCTE Award in 1981.

Poets create *imagery* through the use of words in ways that arrest our senses; we can imagine we almost see, taste, touch, smell, or hear what they describe. Little escapes the poet's vision; nothing limits the speculations on what he sees. Lilian Moore (1966) uses both imagery and personification to create her vision of autumn.

SEPTEMBER

Something is bleeding
into the
pond,
the stains are freshly
red.
Look—
beyond
and overhead.
The maple

is crimson spattered.

Summer is fatally wounded.
Soon, soon
dead.

Lilian Moore

Denotation refers to the literal meaning of a word or phrase. *Connotation* refers to the suggested meaning associated with the literal one—the overtones of meaning. Connotations can vary with the individual person. Water, for instance, may have connotations of refreshment, cooling, beauty, pleasure, or cleansing, depending on which of its many aspects you are thinking of and where you have enjoyed water the most. But it might also arouse feelings of terror in a person who has been in danger of drowning.

Poetry makes use of both denotative and connotative meaning, saying what it means but saying

Poetry and learning are both fun, and children are full of an enormous relish for both. My poetry is just a bubbling up of a natural foolishness, and the idea that maybe you can make language dance a bit.

John Ciardi (1916–1986) taught at the University of Kansas City, Harvard University, and Rutgers University. He served as director of the Bread Loaf Writers' Conference at Middlebury College, received international acclaim for his translation of Dante's **The Divine Comedy,** served as poetry editor of **Saturday Review** (1956–1972), served as host of the CBS show "Accent," and wrote the definitive textbook on poetry, **How Does a Poem Mean?** (1959). He received the Prix de Rome from the American Academy of Arts and Letters in 1956 and the NCTE Award for Excellence in Poetry for Children in 1982.

Ciardi, the only son of Italian immigrants, graduated magna cum laude from Tufts University in 1938 and re-

John Ciardi, 1982

ceived his M.A. in English literature from the University of Michigan the following year. Although he died in 1986, he lives on in the hearts of children because of the delight in language he shared with them through his poetry. John Ciardi received the NCTE Award in 1982.

much more. Connotation enriches meaning. Sometimes the sounds of words combine with their connotations to make a very pleasing pattern. Georgia Heard (1992) uses the connotation of stained glass windows to make us think about dragonflies in a new way.

DRAGONFLY

It skims the pond's surface,
searching for gnats, mosquitoes, and flies.
Outspread wings blur with speed.
It touches down
and stops to sun itself on the dock.
Wings flicker and still:
stained-glass windows
with sun shining through.

Georgia Heard

Good poets make use of the elements of poetry that help them best express what they are trying to say. Children who hear and read poetry that contains excellent examples of these poetic elements will come to understand and appreciate their use, and will use them as tools for their own writing.

Poetry Comes in a Variety of Forms

Individual poems can be judged on how understandable they are, on their appeal, and on their use of poetic elements. We can also judge the overall nature of our selections in terms of the diversity of content, moods, and language use, as well as the variety of forms that it contains. Although teachers may begin with narrative poetry or brief humorous verses, gradually exposing children to a broader range of forms will expand their experiences with poetry, thus increasing the potential for greater interest and understanding.

It is evident to the beginning reader that poetry comes in many forms. Poems look different; the visual form, which reflects the pattern, affects the way the poem is to be read and contributes to meaning. Poetic patterns are clearly defined, although poets manipulate the conventional patterns as often as they manipulate word meanings.

Narrative Poems: Poetry as Story

Think about stories from childhood that you first heard through poetry. Perhaps "The Pied Piper of Hamelin," "Casey at the Bat," "Hiawatha," "Paul Revere's Ride," or another rhyme story comes to mind. Many children enjoy narrative verse, and this is not surprising—they enjoy and are familiar with

stories of all kinds. A narrative poem tells a story. A book-length narrative poem (one that is longer than a picture book) is called an *epic,* but most story poems for children are relatively short and relate one or more episodes.

Narrative poetry sets a story—with characters, plot, and theme, like any other story—into a poetic framework, which can make even a humble story memorable. A. A. Milne, Aileen Fisher, Henry Wadsworth Longfellow, and Rosemary and Stephen Vincent Benét are known for their narrative poems. Contemporary narrative poets include Jack Prelutsky, Aileen Fisher, and Shel Silverstein.

When poetry is read aloud, the words can truly sing, and listeners can fully savor the musical quality of the verse; narrative poetry is most appreciated in oral presentations. Listening to story poems helps children develop a sensitivity to the charm of the spoken word and the tune of verse.

Poets are experimenting with the narrative form, and several new books, such as Arnold Adoff's **In for Winter, Out for Spring** (P–I), illustrated by Jerry Pinkney, contain a series of short poems which, taken together, tell a story. Books like this, plus many beautifully illustrated single editions of narrative poems are listed in Figure 4-4. With these books available we no longer need settle for the simple, dull, and standard verses of textbooks.

Limericks and Riddles

Limericks, a form of light verse, have five lines and a rhyme scheme of a a b b a. The first, second, and fifth lines (which rhyme) have three feet (in poetic meter), whereas the third and fourth (which rhyme) have two feet.

Limericks appeal to children because they poke fun and have a definite rhythm and rhyme scheme. Edward Lear (1812–1888) is given credit for making limericks popular, although he did not create the form. His **Book of Nonsense** (I), published in 1846, is still popular today. Part of the lasting appeal of limericks lies in their tendency to make fun of those who take themselves too seriously.

Students who enjoy a playful brand of humor devour limericks. Some limericks are in the stream of folklore, and their original authorship is lost. One such is the following:

A flea and a fly in a flue
Were imprisoned, so what could they do?
Said the fly, "Let us flee."
Said the flea, "Let us fly."
So they flew through a flaw in the flue.

Anonymous

There was an Old Man of the Hague, whose ideas were excessively vague;
He built a balloon to examine the moon,
That deluded Old Man of the Hague.

Edward Lear, an accomplished watercolorist, made highly accurate, beautiful paintings of birds for the London Zoological Society. He illustrated the *Book of Nonsense* with birdlike characters to amuse the grandchildren of his patron, the Earl of Derby.

Children laugh at the nonsense primarily because the verses break the conventions of language; limericks encapsulate a joyful absurdity. Figure 4-4 lists some popular collections of limericks.

Children also enjoy rhyming riddles. These appear in the folklore of many cultures, and many contemporary writers employ this form as well. William Jay Smith and Carol Ra (1992) have compiled some rhyming riddles in **Behind the King's Kitchen** (I), such as this one:

> *Runs all day but never walks,*
> *Often murmurs, never talks.*
> *It has a bed, but never sleeps.*
> *It has a mouth, but never eats.*
>
> *(a river, traditional)*

Other collections of rhyming riddles are listed in Figure 4-4.

Concrete Poems

Concrete poetry uses the appearance of the verse lines on the page to suggest or illustrate the poem's subject. Children call these poems *shape* (or *picture*) *poems*. The actual physical form of the words depicts the subject, so the whole becomes an ideogrammatic statement; the work illustrates itself as the shapes of words and lines take form as in the two poems here. Figure 4-4 lists some books containing concrete poetry.

Lyric Poems: Statements of Mood and Feeling

Lyric poetry offers a direct and intense outpouring of thoughts and feelings. Any subjective, emotional poem can be called lyric, but most lyric poems are songlike and expressive of a single mood. As its Greek name indicates, a lyric was originally sung to the accompaniment of a lyre. Lyrics have a melodic lyrical quality to this day; they are songs.

Eleanor Farjeon's (1951) "The Night Will Never Stay" is a good example.

THE NIGHT WILL NEVER STAY

> *The night will never stay,*
> *The night will still go by,*
> *Though with a million stars*
> *You pin it to the sky;*
> *Though you bind it with the blowing wind*
> *And buckle it with the moon,*
> *The night will slip away*
> *Like a sorrow or a tune.*
>
> *Eleanor Farjeon*

Many children's poems are lyrical because they have a singing quality and are personal expressions of feeling. Older students, with a rich understanding of symbolism, have a better appreciation for this type of poetry. Lyric poems, above all others, are meant to be read many times over. That children must come to trust their own feelings and learn there is no single right interpretation when it comes to poetry is particularly the case with the lyrical

A SEEING POEM

A SEEING POEM HAPPENS WHEN WORDS TAKE A SHAPE THAT HELPS THEM TO TURN ON A LIGHT IN SOMEONE'S MIND

Robert Froman defines concrete poetry in "A Seeing Poem:" It is words taking shape to help turn on a light in someone's mind. (*Seeing Things: A Book of Poems*)

mode. Some collections of lyric poetry are listed in Figure 4-4.

Haiku and Cinquain

The word *haiku* means "beginning." It generally refers to nature, a particular event happening at the moment, and an attendant emotion or feeling, often of the most fragile and evanescent kind. This Japanese verse form consists of three lines and 17 syllables: the first line containing 5 syllables; the second line, 7; and the third, 5. A haiku usually focuses on an image that suggests a thought or emotion, as in the following examples:

> Take the butterfly:
> Nature works to produce him.
> Why doesn't he last?

> All these skyscrapers!
> What will man do about them
> When they have to go?

> (McCord, 1986, pp. 482–483)

Poets who master the haiku form sometimes stretch its boundaries by varying the 5-7-5 syllable count while maintaining the essence of its meaning. Issa (1969, unpaged), a noted Japanese poet, demonstrates the beauty of haiku in these variations:

> Where can he be going
> In the rain,
> This snail?

> Little knowing
> The tree will soon be cut down,
> Birds are building their nests in it.

Although haiku is a favorite with teachers, Terry's study of children's preferences in poetry shows that it is *not* always a favorite with children—a signal for teachers to handle haiku with care. Myra Cohn Livingston recommends that teachers who want to know the essence of haiku read *Wind in My Hand, The Story of Issa* (I) by Hanako Fukuda. Collections of haiku by Issa and others listed in Figure 4-4 provide excellent examples for children.

A *cinquain* consists of five unrhymed lines usually in the pattern of two, four, six, eight, and two syllables. A simplified variation that has five lines of one, two, three, four, and one word is manipulated easily by children in the intermediate grades. The pattern can be as follows:

Line 1: One word, the title, usually a noun

Line 2: Two words describing the title

Line 3: Three words that show action

Line 4: Four words that show emotion

Line 5: One word, a synonym for the title.

The following is a variation of a cinquain that a 9-year-old child wrote after studying the form:

SNIFFLES AND SNEEZES

Coughing
Sneezing a lot
Missing school, missing friends
I would feel bad at home a lot
Feel bored

> Roy Studness

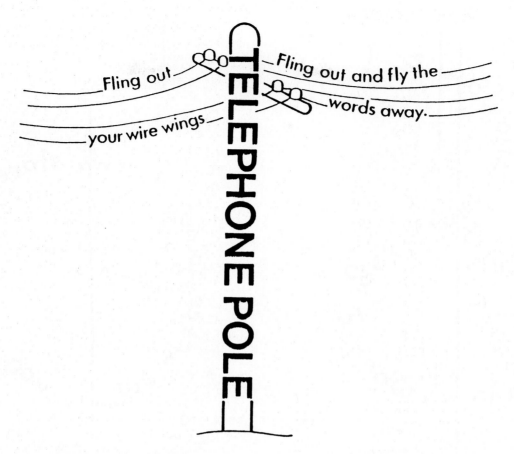

The shape echoes the sense when telephone poles fling out their wire wings and fly the words away. (*Seeing Things: A Book of Poems* by Robert Froman)

𝒯EACHING IDEA 4-3

Concrete Poems

Learn about concrete poetry by reading many examples and looking at the pictures the poems make. Concrete poems not only communicate meaning through both words and the ways the words are placed on the page. For example, if the poem is about a snake, the words may be written out in a long wavy line to look like a snake. If the poem is about a tree, the words may be placed in the shape of a tree.

Remember that poems are supposed to

> create images
> convey feelings
> communicate through associations

Work alone or with a partner to create poetic images in words and shapes.

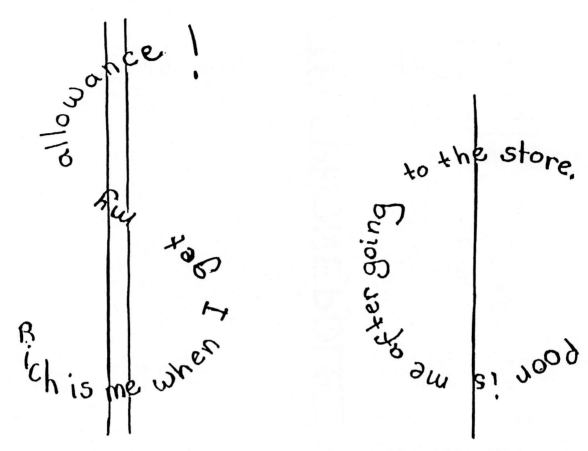

Marilyn Scala's students add meaning to their words about money by placing them in the shape of dollar and cents signs. (Munsey Park School, Manhasset, NY)

Haiku and the cinquain are probably the most abstract poetry children will encounter. Since their symbolism and imagery are elusive for many children, they need to have wide exposure to other forms before they meet these. Even then, they need a lot of opportunities to explore the form.

Ballads and Sonnets

A *ballad* is a story told in verse that is usually meant to be sung. Ballads are relatively short narrative poems adapted for singing—or giving the effect of a song. Usually written in stanzas, ballads are characterized by lyricism and a story line relating a single incident or subject through dialogue in the telling of the story and repeated refrains.

There are folk ballads and literary ballads. *Folk ballads* have no known author; they are composed anonymously and transmitted orally. "John Henry" is a well-known folk ballad. *Literary ballads* are composed by known writers who are imitating folk ballads. Billy Joel, Bruce Springsteen, Paul Simon,

Harry Chapin, and Dan Fogelberg, for example, have written contemporary literary ballads.

Generally, ballads sing of heroic deeds and of murder, unrequited love, and feuds—bawdy subjects. Carl Sandburg's ***The American Songbag*** (A) is a classic collection of the ballads of railroad builders, lumberjacks, and cowboys. Ernest Lawerence Thayer's ballad "Casey at the Bat" (I) begins

The outlook wasn't brilliant for the Mudville nine
   that day:
The score stood four to two, with but one inning more
   to play,
And then when Cooney died at first, and Barrows did
   the same,
A pall-like silence fell upon the patrons of the game.

A straggling few got up to go in deep despair. The rest
Clung to that hope which springs eternal in the hu-
   man breast;
They thought, "If only Casey could but get a whack at
   that—
We'd put up even money now, with Casey at the bat."

Ernest Lawrence Thayer

The Red Dragonfly

Add some wings to a pepper pod that's red
And you'll have
A red dragonfly instead.

—*Bashō, 1644–94*

Basho's red dragonfly takes on new life when aligned with Demi's visual interpretation. Demi revitalized the ancient Japanese poetic form of haiku by illustrating *In the Eyes of the Cat* with verve and color.

SUMMER

Joyful Crickets

O leaping crickets,
Watch what you do!
You might land and split
These emeralds of dew.

—*Issa, 1763–1827*

The "Joyful Crickets" look like the emeralds of dew that Issa speaks about in his haiku verse. Demi blends crickets, dew drops, and blades of grass in an artful arrangement with the words. (*In the Eyes of the Cat*)

Figure 4-4

Poetry in Many Forms

Narrative Poems

Browning, Robert. *The Pied Piper of Hamelin.* Illus. Kate Greenaway. (I–A)

Coleridge, Samuel T. *The Rime of the Ancient Mariner.* Illus. Ed Young. (A)

Field, Rachel. *General Store.* (P)

Fisher, Aileen. *Listen, Rabbit.* (P)

————. *Going Barefoot.* (P)

————. *Like Nothing at All.* (P)

————. *Anybody Home.* (P)

————. *Sing Little Mouse.* (P)

————. *In the Middle of the Night.* (P)

Lear, Edward. *Owl and the Pussycat.* (P–I)

Longfellow, Henry Wadsworth. *Paul Revere's Ride.* (P–I) Illus. Ted Rand. Also illus. Nancy Winslow Parker.

Moore, Clement C. *The Night Before Christmas.* Illus. Tasha Tudor. (P–I–A)

————. *The Night Before Christmas.* Illus. Tomie de Paola. (P–I–A)

Nash, Ogden. *The Adventures of Isabel.* (P–I)

————. *Custard the Dragon.* Illus. Quentin Blake. (P–I–A)

Noyes, Alfred. *The Highwayman.* Illus. Charles Mikolaycak. (A)

Prelutsky, Jack. *The Mean Old Mean Hyena.* (P–I)

Seabrooke, Brenda. *Judy Scuppernong.* (A)

Limericks and Riddles

Ciardi, John. *The Hopeful Trout and Other Limericks.* (I–A)

Lear, Edward. *A Book of Nonsense.* (I–A)

Lewis, J. Patrick. *A Hippopotamusn't: And Other Animal Verses.* (P–I)

Lobel, Arnold. *The Book of Pigericks.* (P–I)

McCord, David. *One At A Time.* (includes limericks) (I–A)

Nims, Bonnie Larkin. *Just Beyond Reach and Other Riddle Poems.* Photos by George Ancona. (I–A)

Smith, William Jay, and Carol Ra (compilers). *Behind the King's Kitchen: A Roster of Rhyming Riddles.* Illus. Jacques Hnizdovsky. (I–A)

Swann, Brian. *A Basket Full of White Eggs: Riddle Poems.* Illus. Ponder Gombel. (I)

Concrete Poems

Froman, Robert. *Seeing Things.* (I–A)

Livingston, Myra Cohn. *O Sliver of Liver.* (I–A)

Merriam, Eve. *Out Loud.* (I–A)

Morrison, Lillian. *The Sidewalk Racer and Other Poems of Sports and Motion.* (I–A)

Some ballads for children are listed in Figure 4-4.

Unlike other ancient poetic forms that became archaic, such as the rondeau and the triolet, sonnets continue to be well known. *Sonnets* are lyric poems of 14 lines, usually written in rhymed iambic pentameter (a line consisting of 5 metrical feet with each foot composed of a short syllable followed by a long or an unstressed syllable) and expressing a single idea or theme. They follow two models: the *Petrarchan,* an 8-line stanza followed by a 6-line stanza; and the *Shakespearean,* three 4-line stanzas followed by a rhyming couplet. Perennial themes for sonnets—love, friendship, time, and the mean-ing of life—are skillfully expressed within the rigidity of the rhyme scheme and meter. The lineage of some of our most famous sonneteers, W. H. Auden, Louise Bogan, John Berryman, and Edna St. Vincent Millay, can be traced to William Wordsworth, Percy Bysshe Shelley, and John Keats. Helen Plotz, foremost anthologist, has collected 130 poems in ***This Powerful Rhyme: A Book of Sonnets*** (A). The title comes from Shakespeare's prophetic sonnet that begins "Not marble, nor the gilded monuments/Of princes, shall outlive this pow'rful rhyme."

The lure of this fragile form is as durable as Circe's enchantment. Phyllis McGinley's (1979,

CONTINUED

Lyric Poetry

Baylor, Byrd. *The Other Way to Listen.* Illus. Peter Parnall. (I–A)

de la Mare, Walter. *Peacock Pie.* (P–I–A)

Frost, Robert. *You Come Too: Favorite Poems for Young Readers.* (I–A)

Hoberman, Mary Ann. *A House Is a House for Me.* (P–I)

Larrick, Nancy. *I Heard a Scream in the Street.* (I–A)

Lewis, J. Patrick. *Earth Verses and Water Rhymes.* Illus. Robert Sabuda. (I–A)

O'Neill, Mary. *Hailstones and Halibut Bones.* (P–I–A)

Singer, Marilyn. *Turtle in July.* Illus. Jerry Pinkney. (I–A)

Haiku and Cinquain

Atwood, Ann. *Haiku: The Mood of Earth.* (I–A)

———. *Haiku Vision: In Poetry and Photographs.* (I–A)

———. *My Own Rhythm: An Approach to Haiku.* (I–A)

———. *Fly with the Wind, Flow with the Water.* (I–A)

Demi. *In the Eyes of the Cat.* (I–A)

Fukuda, Hanako. *Wind in My Hand, The Story of Issa.* (I–A)

Livingston, Myra Cohn. *Sky Songs.* (I)

Ballads and Sonnets

Child, Lydia Maria. *Over the River and Through the Wood.* (P–I)

de Paola, Tomie. *Tomie de Paola's Book of Christmas Carols.* (P)

Fox, Dan (arranger). *We Wish You a Merry Christmas: Songs of the Season for Young People.* (P–I–A)

Key, Frances Scott. *The Star Spangled Banner.* (P–I–A)

Plotz, Helen. *As I Walked Out One Evening: A Book of Ballads.* (A)

———. *This Powerful Rhyme: A Book of Sonnets.*

——— (compiler). *A Week of Lullabies.* (A)

Free Verse

Adoff, Arnold. *Black Is Brown Is Tan.* (P–I)

———. *Chocolate Dreams.* (I)

———. *Eats.* (I–A)

———. *In for Winter, Out for Spring.* (P–I)

———. *Sports Pages.* (I–A)

Janeczko, Paul. *Pocket Poems.* (A)

Rylant, Cynthia. *Soda Jerk.* (A)

———. *Waiting to Waltz.* (A)

Soto, Gary. *Fire in My Hands.* (I–A)

---

p. 218) "Good Humor Man" seems up to the minute with this classical form as she likens the ice cream man to the Pied Piper:

GOOD HUMOR MAN

*So, long ago, in some such shrill procession
Perhaps the Hamelin children gave pursuit
To one who wore a red-and-yellow fashion
Instead of white, but made upon his flute
The selfsame promise plain to every comer:
Unending sweets, imperishable summer.*

Phyllis McGinley

Other sonnets appear in books listed in Figure 4-4.

Students nurtured on poetry can make meaningful experiences from linguistically complex adult forms such as ballads and sonnets. Like Wordsworth's "Michael," building stone by stone, students building poem by poem can reach a gratifying eminence, for poetry once possessed is forever a wellspring of joy.

Free Verse

Free verse is unrhymed verse that has either no metrical pattern or an irregular pattern. The arrangement on the page, the essence of the subject, and the density of thought distinguish free verse from prose. Teachers often encourage children to write in free verse when they are experimenting with poetry; it helps children avoid some difficulties of trying to rhyme.

Gary Soto's (1990) collection, **A Fire in My Hands** (A) contains poems written in free verse, such as the following:

LEARNING TO BARGAIN

Summer. Flies knitting
Filth on the window,
A mother calling a son home . . .
I'm at the window, looking
Onto the street: dusk,
A neighbor kid sharpening
A stick at the curb.
I go outside and sit
Next to him without saying
A word. When he looks
Up, his eyes dark as flies . . .
I ask him about the cat, the one dead
Among the weeds in the alley.
"Yeah, I did it," he admits,
And stares down at his feet,
Then my feet. "What do you want?"
"A dime," I say. Without
Looking at me, he gets
Up, goes behind his house,
And returns with two Coke bottles.
"These make a dime." He sits

At the curb, his shoulders
So bony they could be wings
To lift him so far. "Don't tell."
He snaps a candy into halves
And we eat in silence.

Gary Soto

Although children often initially prefer rhymed, metered poetry, exposure to the many excellent examples of free verse increases their appreciation of this form. Figure 4-4 lists some books containing fine examples of free verse.

BUILDING A POETRY COLLECTION

Poetry is available in many different shapes and sizes. Many memorable poems are published in single volumes with beautiful illustrations accompanying them. Children who read picture books enjoy hearing and reading poems in this familiar format. Some outstanding examples of single-volume editions of poems are listed in Figure 4-5. These books provide children with the opportunity to explore not only the fine poetry that they present, but also individual artist's visual interpretations of those poems. Evaluating this kind of book is discussed in Chapter 3.

 **IDEA** 4-4

Play With Poetry: Act It Out

Children readily become poetry performers if we invite them into the process by making it fun and nonthreatening. First, as teachers we perform a poem—we model it for students. Next we invite students to recite a few poems as a group. After they have fun saying group poems, we can invite individuals to do short poems and, finally, encourage individuals to recite poems of their own choosing. At all stages, children hold a copy of the poem in their hands—to use or not to use as they choose—this is not a memory test. Brod Bagert says, in *Invitation to Read*, if children make the right face when they are ready to say a poem, everything falls into place. He suggests we search for what a poem means and ask, "What face should I make when I say these words?" When we or children make a face to express feelings, we are bound to give the right expression to the words.

Here are some poems that beg to be dramatized:

Bagert, Brod. *Let Me Be the Boss.*
Ciardi, John. *Mommy Slept Late and Daddy Fixed Breakfast.*
Fleischman, Paul. *Joyful Noise: Poems for Two Voices.*
———. *I Am Phoenix: Poems for Two Voices.*
Service, Robert. *The Cremation of Sam McGee.* Illus. Ted Harrison.
———. *The Shooting of Dan McGrew.* Illus. Ted Harrison.

**Figure
4-5**

Poems in Picture Books

Primary–Intermediate Grades

Ciardi, John. *Someone Could Win a Polar Bear.* Illus. Edward Gorey. (I–A)

Clifton, Lucille. *Some of the Days of Everett Anderson.* Illus. Evaline Ness. (P–I)

Fields, Julia. *Green Lion of Zion Street.* Illus. Jerry Pinkney. (P–I)

Fleischman, Paul. *I Am Phoenix: Poems for Two Voices.* (I–A)

———. *Joyful Noise: Poems for Two Voices.* (I–A)

Frost, Robert. *Birches.* Illus. Ed Young. (I–A)

———. *Stopping by Woods on a Snowy Evening.* Illus. Susan Jeffers. (I–A)

Harrison, David. *Somebody Catch My Homework.* Illus. Betsy Lewin. (P–I)

———. *Never Talk to Plants.* Illus. Betsy Lewin. (P–I)

Hopkins, Lee Bennett. *Voyages: Poems by Walt Whitman.* (I–A)

Hughes, Langston. *The Dreamkeeper and Other Poems.* (I–A)

Lindbergh, Reeve. *Legend of Johnny Appleseed: A Poem.* Illus. Kathy Jacobsen. (I)

Longfellow, Henry Wadsworth. *Hiawatha.* Illus. Susan Jeffers. (P–I)

———. *Paul Revere's Ride.* Illus. Ted Rand. (P–I)

Morrison, Lillian. *Whistling the Morning In.* Illus. Joel Cook. (I–A)

Noyes, Alfred. *The Highwayman.* Illus. Charles Mikolaycak. (I–A)

Rylant, Cynthia. *All I See.* Illus. Peter Catalanotto. (P–I)

Siebert, Diane. *Heartland.* Illus. Wendell Minor. (A)

———. *Mojave.* Illlus. Wendel Minor. (A)

———. *Sierra.* Illus. Wendell Minor. (A)

Steig, Jeanne. *Consider the Lemming.* Illus. William Steig. (I–A)

Thayer, Ernest Lawrence. *Casey at the Bat.* Afterword by Donald Hall. Illus. Barry Moser. (I)

Willard, Nancy. *The Ballad of Biddy Early.* Illus. Barry Moser. (A)

———. *Pish Posh, Said Hieronymous Bosch.* Illus. Leo and Diane Dillon. (I–A)

———. *Visit to William Blake's Inn: Poems for Innocent and Experienced Travelers.* Illus. Alice and Martin Provensen. (I–A)

Yolen, Jane. *Birdwatch: A Book of Poetry.* Illus. Ted Lewin. (I)

Anthologies and collections are invaluable. To provide variety in poetry and yet hold collections to a manageable size, teachers and librarians need anthologies. Poems are often easier to locate in themed collections than when shelved individually by author.

Three types of anthologies are particularly useful in the classroom: the specialized anthology, with work by several poets on one subject; the generalized anthology, with works by many poets on many subjects; and the individual anthology, the work of only one poet.

Specialized anthologies are gaining in popularity. The plethora of collections of poems and verses about holidays, monsters, dinosaurs, horses, and other special topics bears witness to this. Three noted anthologists, Lee Bennett Hopkins, Nancy Larrick, and Jane Yolen, have added immeasurably to the wealth of resources. Lee Bennett Hopkins has a distinguished group of more than 50 collections from easy-to-read verse to collections of Carl Sandburg and Langston Hughes. Nancy Larrick brings the visions of many fine poets to *Bring Me All of Your Dreams* (I–A) and her other collections. Jane Yolen has given us multicultural collections in *Street Rhymes Around the World* (P–I) and *Sleep Rhymes Around the World* (P–I). *Alphabestiary* (P–I), *City Scape, Sky Scrape* (P–I–A), and

Silence in the court,
The monkey wants to speak,
No laughing or talking
Or stamping your feet.

Alvin Schwartz organized his collection of American folklore around autograph rhymes, work songs, story poems, and nonsense rhymes in *And the Green Grass Grew All Around*, as illustrated by Sue Truesdell.

Weather Report (P–I) are among other Yolen anthologies that enrich poetry collections tremendously.

A very different kind of theme organizes Alvin Schwartz's (1992) ***And the Green Grass Grew All Around*** (P–I–A). This collection of more than 250 folk poems contains autograph rhymes, work poems, story poems, nonsense, and much more. Other specialized anthologies are listed in Figure 4-6.

The classic generalized anthology, May Hill Arbuthnot's ***Time for Poetry,*** now incorporated into ***The Arbuthnot Anthology of Children's Literature*** edited by Zena Sutherland, is a complete volume with verse on many subjects. Best-loved poems of childhood include those about people, animals, adventures, games, jokes, magic and make-believe, wind and water, holidays and seasons, and wisdom and beauty. The anthology is essential for librarians and teachers who consider poetry central to children's lives. Other generalized anthologies are less comprehensive and more inviting to child readers. One such book, X. J. and Doro-

thy Kennedy's (1992) ***Talking Like the Rain*** (P–I) contains poems arranged under nine headings. The illustrations by Jane Dyer help make the book a pleasure to read. Several generalized anthologies are listed in Figure 4-6.

David McCord's ***One at a Time*** (all ages) is an individualized anthology comprised solely of his work. An impressive volume, it is a collection of most of his poetry. McCord's wit and thoughtful perception sing in the music of his words. ***One at a Time*** is a wonderful resource for cultivating poetic taste, to produce children who will read poetry for pleasure.

When you find a poem that delights you and your students, look for others by the same poet; you may be surprised to find an entire anthology devoted to your favorite poet. Brewton's ***Index to Poetry*** (1978) will hasten the search. Every classroom needs several specialized, generalized, and individualized anthologies of poetry such as those listed in Figure 4–6, as well as individual children's personal anthologies. Teachers who know and love poems can do justice to the privileged task

---

Figure
4-6

Specialized, General, and Individual Anthologies

Specialized Anthologies (by several poets on one subject)

Bober, Natalie. *Let's Pretend: Poems of Flight and Fancy.* (I–A)

Carter, Anne (selector). *Birds, Beasts, and Fishes: A Selection of Animal Poems.* (P–I)

de Regniers, Beatrice Schenk. *So Many Cats!* (P–I)

Hopkins, Lee Bennett. *Click, Rumble, Roar: Poems About Machines.* (I)

Knudson, R. R., and May Swenson. *American Sports Poems.* (I–A)

Larrick, Nancy. *Cats Are Cats.* Illus. Ed Young. (P–I)

———. *Mice Are Nice.* Illus. Ed Young. (P–I)

Livingston, Myra Cohn (selector). *Cat Poems.* (P–I)

———. *Dog Poems.* (P–I)

Generalized Anthologies (by many poets on many subjects)

Arbuthnot, May Hill. *Time for Poetry.* (P–I–A)

Cole, Joanna. *A New Treasury of Children's Poetry: Old Favorites and New Discoveries.* (P–I–A)

Hall, Donald. *The Oxford Book of Children's Verse in America.* (I–A)

Hopkins, Lee Bennett, collector. *Side by Side: Poems to Read Together.* Illus. Hilary Knight.

Prelutsky, Jack. *The Random House Book of Poetry.* (P–I–A)

Sutherland, Zena and Myra Cohn Livingston (editors). *The Scott, Foresman Anthology of Children's Literature.* (P–I–A)

Individualized Anthologies (work of one poet)

Adoff, Arnold. *Sports Pages.* (I–A)

Bodecker, N. M. *Water Pennies: And Other Poems.* (P–I)

Cassedy, Sylvia. *Roomrimes.* (I–A)

Ciardi, John. *Doodle Soup.* (P–I)

Kuskin, Karla. *Dogs and Dragons, Trees and Dreams.* (P–I)

Lenski, Lois. *Sing a Song of People.* (I–A)

Lewis, Claudia. *Up in the Mountains and Other Poems of Long Ago.* (I)

Livingston, Myra Cohn. *Space Songs.* (I)

McCord, David. *One at a Time.* (P–I–A)

Prelutsky, Jack. *Ride a Purple Pelican.* (P–I)

———. *Beneath a Blue Umbrella.* (P–I–A)

Siebert, Diane. *Mojave.* (I–A)

Willard, Nancy. *A Visit to William Blake's Inn: Poems for Innocent and Experienced Travelers.* (I–A)

---

of passing on the beauty of language from one generation to the next.

Although every teacher and every class will have personal favorites, there are some poets whose works we believe to be basic to the curriculum. These are listed in Figure 4-7 according to the age group for whom they hold greatest interest, although age designation should be considered flexible. Poetry, especially, appeals to a wide age range.

Reading reviews in professional journals and noting the winners of the NCTE Award for Excel-lence in Poetry for Children are ways to keep current in poetry for children. The award is given to poets considered to be the *very best;* it is given for the entire body of their work, not just a single collection or poem. The award was given once a year from 1977 to 1982; now it is given every three years. Teachers and librarians celebrate the award winners: David McCord, 1977; Aileen Fisher, 1978; Karla Kuskin, 1979; Myra Cohn Livingston, 1980; Eve Merriam, 1981; John Ciardi, 1982; Lilian Moore, 1985; Arnold Adoff, 1988; and Valerie Worth, 1991.

Figure 4-7

A Basic Poetry Collection

Primary Grades

Hoberman, Mary Ann. *A Fine Fat Pig and Other Animal Poems.*

Hopkins, Lee Bennett. *More Surprises.*

Prelutsky, Jack (compiler). *Read-Aloud Rhymes for the Very Young.*

———. *Something Big Has Been Here.*

Royds, Caroline (editor). *Poems for Young Children.*

Stevenson, Robert Louis. *A Child's Garden of Verses.* Illus. Jessie Willcox Smith.

———. *A Child's Garden of Verses.* Illus. Henriette Willebeek le Mair.

Sutherland, Zena (selector). *The Orchard Book of Nursery Rhymes.*

Intermediate Grades

Elledge, Scott (editor). *Wider Than the Sky: Poems to Grow Up With.*

Hall, Donald (selector-editor). *The Oxford Book of Children's Verse in America.*

Kennedy, X. J. *Knock at a Star: A Child's Introduction to Poetry.*

Lear, Edward. *The Complete Nonsense of Edward Lear.*

Livingston, Myra Cohn. *I Like You, If You Like Me.*

———. *Higgledy Piggledy: Verses and Pictures*

Silverstein, Shel. *A Light in the Attic.*

———. *Where the Sidewalk Ends.*

Stevenson, Robert Louis. *The Land of Nod and Other Poems for Children.*

Advanced Grades

Berry, James. *When I Dance.*

Gordon, Ruth. *Time Is the Longest Distance.*

Hearne, Betsy. *Polaroid and Other Poems of View.*

Hopkins, Lee Bennett. *Voyages: Poems by Walt Whitman.*

Janeczko, Paul B. *Brickyard Summer.*

———. *The Place My Words Are Looking For: What Poets Say About and Through Their Work.*

———. *Preposterous: Poems of Youth.*

Livingston, Myra Cohn (editor). *Why Am I Grown So Cold? Poems of the Unknowable.*

Strauss, Gwen. *Trail of Stones.*

It is important for students to feel comfortable using the books that you gather; display the fronts of some books to attract readers. Other books can be shelved by author or subject, depending on the interests of your students. Students need space to browse, to pull out several volumes at once, and to compare poems or look for favorites. Tape recorders close by encourage oral interpretation of favorite poems. Students also need time to use the poetry collection and to understand they are expected to be familiar with poetry books. Encourage them to browse through the poetry area during free time or to look up a poem for a particular occasion or for independent reading. Allowing and encouraging students to use the poetry area together, and to talk quietly while doing so, forges strong bonds among a community of readers. It also helps students learn how to read poetry and increases contact with poetry and poets.

EXPLORING POETRY WITH CHILDREN

Many children learn to hate poetry when someone insists they search for an elusive meaning or rhyme scheme that makes no sense to them. Close attention to children's comments can supply a basis for thought-provoking questions that will lead children to discover the substance of poetry for themselves. The object is to develop a child's liking for the music of words; detailed analysis divests poetry of its splendor. Explanation that destroys appreciation is no better than misconceptions. The magic that the words exercise on the imagination, more valuable than accuracy at beginning stages, leaves a telling mark. Appropriate discussions of poetry take children back to the poem, not away from it.

A love of poetry is contagious. How you read and respond to poetry has a tremendous effect on

P
R
O
F
I
L
E

Poetry should be like fireworks, packed carefully and artfully, ready to explode with unpredictable effects. When people asked Robert Frost—as they did by the hundreds—what he meant by "But I have promises to keep / And miles to go before I sleep / And miles to go before I sleep," he always turned the question aside with a joke. Maybe he couldn't answer it, and maybe he was glad that the lines exploded in so many different colors in so many people's minds.

Lilian Moore was born on March 17, 1909, in New York City. She attended New York City schools, Hunter College, and did graduate work at Columbia University. She taught school in New York City and worked in a publishing house. She now lives on a farm in

Lilian Moore, 1985

upstate New York. Lilian Moore received the NCTE Award in 1985.

how students read and respond. If students see teachers enjoying poetry, they will be more likely to approach poetry with the expectation of pleasure. If they see you turning to poetry to comment on the events of your life, they will be more likely to do so. If they see you responding to poetry as connected to real experiences and feelings, they will be more likely to make those connections. Perhaps the most important thing that teachers do with poetry is to read it as a person, to make a human connection with a poet's words.

Poetry is valuable for the full realization of life. Only by hard work can we participate in the imaginative experience of others—and thereby understand our own experiences better. The more readers participate, the more they themselves create, and the more personal and enjoyable the experience of poetry becomes. The rewards are more than worth the effort.

Immerse Children in Poetry

Teachers who want to develop an appreciation for poetry in their students immerse them in it. They collect poems they and children like, read them

Karla Kuskin designed the medallion for the National Council of Teachers of English Award for Excellence in Poetry for Children, an award she later won. The award is given for a distinguished poet's entire body of work; the seal may appear on each of the poet's books.

 **EACHING IDEA** 4-5

Celebrate With Poetry

No matter what the occasion, use poetry to celebrate. Celebrate a holiday, the season, the weather, writers and poets. Poems make celebrations special.

Celebrate the Holidays

Hopkins, Lee Bennett. *Good Morning to You, Valentine.* Illus. Tomie de Paola. (P)

Livingston, Myra Cohn. *Halloween Poems.* (P)

Moore, Clement C. *The Night Before Christmas.* Illus. James Marshall. (P)

Yolen, Jane. *Best Witches: Poems for Halloween.* (I)

Celebrate the Seasons

Fisher, Aileen. *Listen Rabbit.* Illus. Symeon Shimin. (P)

Hopkins, Lee Bennett. *Easter Buds Are Springing.* Illus. Tomie de Paola. (P)

Morrison, Lillian. *Whistling the Morning In.* Illus. Joel Cook. (I)

Singer, Marilyn. *Turtle in July.* Illus. Jerry Pinkney. (P–I)

Updike, John. *A Child's Calendar.* Illus. Nancy E. Burkert. (I)

Yolen, Jane (selector). *Weather Report.* Illus. Annie Gusman. (I)

Celebrate Writers—Child and Adult

Merriam, Eve. *Blackberry Ink.* (P) Illus. Hans Wilhelm.

Smith, William Jay and Carol Ra. *Behind the King's Kitchen: Riddles.* Illus. Jacques Hnizdovsky. (I)

---

aloud several times a day, put poems on charts for group reading, and sprinkle poetry throughout the curriculum. They do what Beatrice Schenk de Regniers (1983) suggests:

KEEP A POEM IN YOUR POCKET

*Keep a poem in your pocket
and a picture in your head
and you'll never feel lonely
at night when you're in bed.*

*The little poem will sing to you
the little picture bring to you
a dozen dreams to dance to you
at night when you're in bed.*

*So—
Keep a picture in your pocket
and a poem in your head
and you'll never feel lonely
at night when you're in bed.*

Beatrice Schenk de Regniers

Children in the Cypress-Fairbanks School District in Houston, Texas, benefit when their teachers respond to a questionnaire each fall from the dis-

trict's language and reading coordinator, asking if they would like to receive the monthly newsletter *Poetry Supplement.* There are two requirements: Teachers must (1) establish a personal (not team) poetry card file to keep poems at their fingertips for convenient use, and (2) return the form with their name and school. Each month, the *Poetry Supplement* contains 15 to 20 poems on a theme with suggested activities for each. Patricia Smith, the creator of the newsletter, explains, "I gather an assortment of poems intended to promote an appreciation of poetry and at the same time facilitate teaching the essential elements of speaking, listening, reading, and writing."

Smith introduced the March issue by saying:

March is sometimes marked as a month of contrasts. It enters loudly and goes out quietly. Your *Poetry Supplement* is organized into pairs of poems this month in a manner that will promote connections and reflections on likenesses and differences. The model for the pairs was inspired by Bernice Wolman who compiled pairs of poems for her wonderful new collection,

Taking Turns. Please consider asking your students to hunt for pairs of poems. The similarity might be topic, style, or poet. The reading and critical thinking for this task will be immense. (1992, p.1)

Following this introduction are seven pairs of poems with teaching suggestions for each.

We communicate expectations through body language, gestures, and how and what we say. Observe someone who loves poetry and one who does not love it read a poem aloud; the differences in behavior are startling. If we read poems in a spirited, enthusiastic manner, with a twinkle in the eye, children respond positively. If the reader is boring, children are bored.

Familiarize students with the poetry you enjoy by reading poems frequently throughout the day. Students unfamiliar with poetry need to hear a lot of it in pleasurable situations. Read or recite the poem and then go on to what you need to do next. Soon students will "think poetry" as things that they see and do remind them of poems they have read or heard you read.

Set aside a regularly scheduled time for sharing poetry. If you comment on the poems you read, just as you would on a book you read, students will begin to feel they can understand poems just as they can understand books. They can learn to feel the emotions and see the images of the poems they read and hear. As they become familiar and comfortable with hearing and commenting on

PROFILE

Most of the time, almost all of the time, I want my poems to do more than prose can do. So if I want to just say, "Dear Mom, I am fine at camp," I don't have to write a poem. But if I'm going to be a poet, if I'm poeting, if I'm writing poems, I want to do more in my poems than just present facts or feelings or communicate. I want my poems to sing as well as to say.

Arnold Adoff has a love affair with food. Since he works at home he is able to cook at the same time he is composing poems; he sometimes pauses from his work to stir the soup or punch down the bread. His passion for food is evident in his collections of poems ***Eats, Greens,*** and ***Chocolate Dreams.*** Once he was eating peanut butter while he was typing. He got peanut butter in the typewriter and a repairman had to come and fix it.

Adoff was born July 15, 1915, in the East Bronx section of New York City. He received his B.A. from City College and attended Columbia University and the New School for Social Research. He was a teacher in the New York Public

Arnold Adoff, 1988

Schools in Harlem and the Upper West Side. He has taught at New York University and Connecticut College. He and his wife, author Virginia Hamilton, live in Yellow Springs, Ohio. Their two grown children, Leigh and Jamie, are both involved in the world of music. Arnold Adoff received the NCTE Award in 1988.

poetry, you can begin to introduce discussions about how poetry works.

Help Students Explore How Poetry Works

Children who have the opportunity to hear and read lots of poetry will want to discover how poetry works. Exploring poetry can link the experiences of listening to, orally interpreting, silently reading, and writing poetry. Experiences with poetry build on each other—listening to a poem being read well provides insight into how poetry works, what a poem might mean to a reader, techniques for oral interpretation, and strategies for reading that can be employed silently. Writing poetry, best accomplished on a firm foundation of reading and listening experiences, in turn helps children appreciate how poetry works. Poetry writers read poetry with greater understanding than nonwriters. Exploring poetry, perhaps more than any other genre, requires both oral and written language activities.

PROFILE

Never forget that the subject is as important as your feeling: The mud puddle itself is as important as your pleasure in looking at it or splashing through it. Never let the mud puddle get lost in the poetry—because, in many ways, the mud puddle *is* the poetry.

Readers say that Valerie Worth's poems are crystal clear images. They are luminous jewels in the homely guise of coins, pebbles, or marbles. Her small poems are witty but not ostentatious. Their gravity is their grace. Things, plants, animals are enchanted by her contemplative mind.

Worth says that Natalie Babbitt, a well-known writer of fantasy, "discovered" her. They shared a writer's group and when Natalie heard Valerie read some of her poems, she asked if she could show them to her editor. Natalie's editor, did, indeed, like Valerie's poems and published her work. When it was time to select an illustrator for the first book of small poems, Valerie asked Natalie Babbitt if she would do the illustrations; that is the way their collaboration began.

Worth says, "Occasionally, I send her a small magnet or a tiny copper bell I own—objects that inspired the creation of the small poems."

Valerie Worth, 1991

Valerie Worth was born October 29, 1933, in Philadelphia. Her father taught biology at Swarthmore College and joined the Rockefeller Foundation as a field biologist to study typhus. The family traveled to Bangalore, India, so her father could study malaria. Valerie attended one year of high school in Bangalore but later returned to Swarthmore for her bachelor's degree in English. She currently resides in Clinton, New York. Valerie Worth received the NCTE Award in 1991.

 EACHING IDEA 4-6

Word Play and Poetry

Poets are wordsmiths—they play with the infinite possibilities of language. They listen to the repetition of similar sounds, they probe the double or triple meanings of words, they look for surprises that unusual combinations of words can achieve. Poets savor language and try to pack their poems with multiple meanings. They work to make poems that are well crafted. You can become sensitive to the nuances of words, too.

Look at word books.

Discover what they offer.

Here are some examples:

McMillan, Bruce. *Play Day: A Book of Terse Verse.*

Merriam, Eve. *Chortles: New and Selected Wordplay Poems.*

————. *A Poem for a Pickle: Funnybone Verses.*

Terban, Marvin. *Time to Rhyme: A Rhyming Dictionary.*

————. *A Dove Dove.*

————. *Hey Hay.*

Create word maps, word balloons, word sunbursts. Put one word in the middle of a page. Encircle it with all the other words it makes you think of. Cluster words that go together. Play with the words. See if they suggest a poem or verse. Try different arrangements to see if they establish a tone or mood.

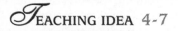 EACHING IDEA 4-7

Make Poetry a Part of Every Day

Read a poem every day.

Print it out on a large chart and display it.

Collect poems around a theme: weather, sports, holidays.

Choose a poet of the week or month. Read that poet's work.

Do impromptu choral readings of poems.

Play music (bells, drum, cymbal) as a background to reading a poem.

Act it out. Do group presentations. Invite individual presentations.

Stage a poetry happening. Let everyone do a poem.

Based on Nancy Larrick's *Let's Do a Poem.*

Choral reading can help students discover how important sound is to many poems as they experiment with ways of reading, exploring how pitch, stress, and rate influence the overall effect of the reading of a particular poem. These kinds of experiences lead naturally to discussions of rhythm, and of other elements of sound.

The rhythm of poetry is a natural springboard into movement. Young children move spontaneously to the beat of highly metrical poetry and older children can be encouraged to clap or tap pencils as they hear the beat in the poems they read. These experiences can lead to discussions of variations in rhythm, how rhythm contributes to meaning and

Figure 4-8

Resource Books for the Poetry Teacher

Brown, Bill, and Malcolm Glass. *Important Words: A Book for Poets and Writers.* Heinemann, 1991.

Denman, Gregory A. *When You've Made It Your Own: Teaching Poetry to Young People.* Heinemann, 1988.

Grossman, Florence. *Listening to the Bells: Learning to Read Poetry by Writing Poetry.* Heinemann, 1991.

Heard, Georgia. *For the Good of the Earth and the Sun: Teaching Poetry.* Heinemann, 1989.

Hopkins, Lee Bennett. *Pass the Poetry, Please.* rev. ed. HarperCollins, 1987

Kennedy, X. J., and Dorothy M. Kennedy. *Knock at a Star: A Child's Introduction to Poetry.* Little, Brown, 1982.

Larrick, Nancy. *Let's Do a Poem.* Delacorte Press, 1991.

Myra Cohn Livingston. *Climb into the Bell Tower. Essays on Poetry.* HarperCollins, 1990.

————. *Poem-Making: Ways to Begin Writing Poetry.* HarperCollins, 1991.

McClure, Amy, with Peggy Harrison and Sheryl Reed. *Sunrises and Songs: Reading and Writing Poetry in an Elementary Classroom.* Heinemann, 1990.

Taxel, Joel (editor). *Fanfare: The Christopher-Gordon Children's Literature Annual.* Vol. 1. Christopher-Gordon Publishers, Inc. 1993.

to individual readers, especially when these readers are writers as well.

Children who read a lot of poetry will want to try writing it themselves. In the introduction to **Dogs and Dragons, Trees and Dreams** (I), Karla Kuskin says,

> The poetry reader often becomes a poetry writer. What could be better? No imagination is freer than a child's, no eye is sharper. The conversation of young children is a constant reminder that they are natural poets. But fitting unrestrained thoughts into rigid forms can be discouraging and may cramp the eccentric voice that makes a child's work (any work) unique. Read rhymes to children, but encourage them, as they begin to write, to write without rhyming. To write any way at all. And to read everything, anything . . . more poetry. (1980)

Just as children try on other forms of writing to suit their own purposes, they will try on a poet's cloak when they feel comfortable with poetry. Sensitive teachers will encourage, but not require them to do so. Some professional references for teachers and children who are engaged in writing poetry are listed in Figure 4-8.

Creative teachers find many ways to involve children in poetry. One group noticed primary grades' interest in studying weather and asked, "Why not have poetic as well as meteorological reports?" The teachers asked a poetry reporter to select a poem that best expressed the foggy, sunny, windy, or rainy day; the poems extended the meaning of the weather symbols attached to the classroom calendar. Now Jane Yolen hastens their search with **Weather Report** (P–I), a collection of poems about fog, rain, snow, wind, and sun.

Poets themselves have good suggestions for aspiring poets. In her acceptance speech for the 1981 NCTE Award for Excellence in Poetry for Children, Eve Merriam encouraged children:

> Read a lot. Sit down with anthologies and decide which pleases you. Copy out your favorites in your own handwriting. Buy a notebook and jot down images and descriptions. Be specific; use all the senses. Use your whole body as you write. It might even help sometime to stand up and move with your words. Don't be afraid of copying a form or convention, especially in the beginning. And, to give yourself scope and flexibility, remember: It doesn't *always* have to rhyme. (1981)

Gimmicks, elaborate plans, and detailed instructions are not needed: A lot of poetry, time to savor it, and pleasurable experiences are what is needed to give your students the gift of a poet's words.

overall effect, and how word choice relates to rhythm.

Artful drawing in response to poems can help children formulate their own meanings. (See Chapter 2 for a discussion of "Sketch to Stretch.") Poems that are rich in figurative language can lead to discussions of metaphors, similes, and imagery. Discussions of "how" a poem means can spring naturally from discussions of "what" a poem means

SUMMARY

Hearing, reading, and writing poetry helps us to learn about the world, about ourselves, and about the power and potential of language. Poems make us laugh, create memorable images, and express feelings in an understandable way. Poets make use of devices of sound, rhythm, and meaning to present their own unique visions. Poetry comes in varied forms, and is available in many formats. Children are attracted to poetry and teachers can build on this attraction, providing experiences with poetry that will lead children to enjoy poetry and thus to consider how poetry works. Children who experience a poetry-rich environment will become lifelong readers of poetry.

5

Folklore

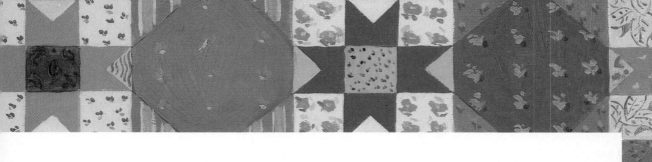

BEAUTY AND THE BEAST

There was a dark castle,
And a courageous girl,
And a prince trapped
In the body of a beast,
And a wilting rose to scent the air
Of an untouched wedding feast.

As I read these fairy tales
I begin to understand,
They speak a truth as lasting
As the sky
And the sea
And the land.

Brod Bagert

In our generation we have come to understand what Joseph Campbell calls "the power of the myth." Though fairy tales and folklore are sometimes infected with anachronisms and old prejudices, they often bear the seed of truth. When children read folklore, they are baptized in the eternal sea of the human unconscious.

Folklore, the body of literature that has no known authors, has been told through the generations and enhanced with variations bestowed by many story-tellers. The legacy of this literature includes Mother Goose and nursery rhymes, folktales, fables, myths, legends and tall tales, and folksongs. Each type is distinctive, but all echo the beliefs, customs, and eternal dreams that appeal to people across time.

THE ORIGINS OF FOLKLORE

Theories about the origin and function of folklore come from the work of cultural anthropologists, who study beliefs, celebrations, and ceremonies of primal societies. Ruth Sawyer, a well-known twentieth-century storyteller, draws on collections of such materials in her description of the beginning of storytelling: "The first primitive efforts at conscious storytelling consisted of a simple chant, set to the rhythm of some daily tribal occupation such as grinding corn, paddling canoe or kayak, sharpening weapons for hunting or war, or ceremonial dancing" (1962, pp. 45–46).

In addition to composing songs and tales about their daily work, their hunting, and their warfare, primal societies created stories about the world around them. Wonder and awe at the power of nature and speculation about the supernatural forces that might be at work behind it led to those tales we classify as myths. And as time passed and the tribes grew, so did the impulse to preserve the stories of their ancestors. Legends and hero tales of the mighty deeds of those who had gone before were passed from one generation to the next and became the cultural heritage.

The roots of folklore exist in all societies from all times. The story of civilization shows a continual quest to shape a harmonious balance between the physical world and the mortal's place in it. Through creative imagination, people transform outer reality into a vision of life that they control through analogy and metaphor. The lore they create is a rich source of literature for children. (See Figure 5–1.)

At one time, common belief held that all folklore emerged from one prehistoric civilization. The Grimm brothers, who collected tales from all over Germany, held this view of singular origin, speculating that as people migrated they took their stories with them. This theory would account for regional differences in some folktales, such as the evolution of West Africa's trickster "Ananse the Spider" to "Anansi" in the Caribbean, and to "Aunt Nancy" in the southern United States. But as folklorists studied the tales of many diverse cultures, it became apparent that some stories must indeed have originated in a number of places. "The themes were . . . those concerning human beings everywhere and the stories were bound to be invented wherever communities developed" (Cole, 1982, p. xix).

According to Jung, the collective unconscious is a part of the mind from which come dream, fantasy, imagination, and vision. Jung perceived this as a substratum of mind common to all people, and he attributed the commonality of the stories of diverse peoples to the universal nature of the unconscious. Whatever the explanation, it is clear that similar elements are found in the myths, legends, and folktales of all people across time and place. The reappearing themes, or archetypes, are clearly visible in folklore. For example, the archetype of the hero's quest—slaying a dragon or winning a princess—is seen as the psychological expression of the normal process of maturing. The good mother (fairy godmother), the bad mother (wicked stepmother or old witch), and the shadow (evil underside in every person) are vivid examples of archetypes familiar to us all.

Today, cultural anthropologists believe that both theories about the origin of folklore are correct: Some did indeed spread among cultures, whereas others with similar themes appeared spontaneously in a number of separate places. Iona and Peter Opie, in **The Classic Fairy Tales,** note that no one theory "is likely to account satisfactorily for the origin of even a majority of the tales. Their wellsprings are almost certainly numerous, their ages likely to vary considerably, their meanings—if they ever had meanings—to be diverse" (1974, p. 18).

FOLKLORE IN CHILDREN'S LIVES

In the same way that folklore explained the world to early people, it helps young children understand their own world today. Preschool children often believe that magic accounts for the things they cannot understand; they attribute human characteristics to inanimate objects artlessly. André Favat explains:

> The characteristics of the child and the characteristics of the fairy tale permit a fairly clear observation: just as magic and animism suffuse the world of the fairy tale, so do they suffuse the world of the child; just as a morality of constraint prevails in the fairy tale, so does it prevail in the moral system of the child; just as the fairy tale world and its hero become one in achieving his ends, so do children believe their world is one with them; and just as causal relations remain unexpressed in the fairy tale, so do they remain unexpressed in the child's communication. (1977, pp. 38, 50)

Innumerable interpretations are given to the role of folklore: According to Freud, fairy tale characters symbolize subconscious urges during a child's emotional development; Jung sees the mythical figures and conflicts as archetypes of racial memories. Bettelheim's views, much like Freud's, are that fairy tales tap deep unconscious wishes and desires—the wellsprings of repressed emotions. Bettelheim reasons that fairy tales help children deal with emotional insecurities by suggesting images—more easily dealt with—for their fantasies. Isaac Bashevis Singer points out that children love a good story, above all.

Applebee (1979) explains children's fascination with stories from another perspective. He sees children engaged in a search for meaning, a search for structures and patterns that will suggest order and consistency in the world around them. The patterns of meaning they find are transmitted by a range of social devices—stories among many others. Pleasure comes through mastery of the rules, a particularly important factor in highly patterned, stereotyped formula stories such as folktales and fairy tales.

Author Jane Yolen (1981) writes of the importance of folklore, suggesting four ways that folklore can function in children's lives. First, folklore provides "a landscape of allusion" (p. 15), presenting archetypal characters that children become familiar with and use to understand other literature. Familiarity with folklore is, she argues, "necessary for any true appreciation of today's literature" (p. 15), especially fantasy. Secondly, folklore provides a way of seeing another culture. Third, folklore is a form of therapy, with the old tales allowing wishes and fears to surface safely and be managed. Finally, she argues, folklore provides a framework for individual belief systems, "stating in symbolic or metaphoric terms the abstract truths of our common human existence" (p. 19).

Whatever the reason, children of today respond with enthusiasm to the folklore of long ago. The folktales, fables, myths, legends, and songs that enchanted people from all around the world before the written word was available still enchant people around the world today. Many contemporary writers and illustrators choose to retell or adapt traditional tales, shaping the folktales of yesterday for today's children.

CRITERIA FOR SELECTING FOLKLORE

Because folklore is a part of culture, it is easily and readily published in a variety of forms. Unfortunately, many unimaginative and inferior editions by their sheer number can overshadow the truly excellent ones that do exist. Therefore, look for certain qualities when evaluating books of folklore. Language is the primary criterion, for the old tales are best when they reflect their oral origins. Look for language that (1) sounds natural, with authentic-

---

TEACHING IDEA 5-1

Archetypes in Folklore

Wide reading of folklore develops a sense of its basic elements. Gradually you become aware of archetypes in the folklore you read. Make notes on the archetypes and titles of stories in which you found them. Compare and discuss the tales as you read.

Some elements to search for in folklore and novels:

Hero's Quest:

St. George and the Dragon.

Story of King Arthur (Pyle)

String in the Harp (Bond)

Fairy Godmother:

Cinderella

Missing May (Rylant)

Wicked Witch/Wicked Stepmother:

Hansel and Gretel

Dinky Hocker Shoots Smack (Danziger)

Benevolent Crone:

Strega Nona

Memory (Mahy)

Shadow/Evil underside of Human Nature/Good Versus Evil:

Tam Lin

Where the Wild Things Are (Sendak)

Wrinkle in Time (L'Engle)

Wizard of Earthsea (Le Guin)

As you read, be aware of conventions, tasks, refrains, magical objects, and other folkloric elements. Many elements appear in the same folktale. For example, in Tomie de Paola's **Strega Nona** you find a noodlehead, an overflowing pot, a chant, a benevolent old crone, among other elements.

---

sounding dialogue and melodious rhythms; (2) maintains the cultural richness of early retellings; and (3) is structured to quickly involve a reader or listener in the action. Avoid simplified controlled-vocabulary versions that dilute the stories to trite episodes. (See Figure 5–2.)

**Figure
5-1**

Folklore From Around the World

The Americas

Aardema, Verna (reteller). *Borreguita and the Coyote: A Tale from Ayutla, Mexico.* (Mexico) (P–I)

Brusca, Maria Cristina and Tona Wilson. *The Cook and the King.* Illus. Mari'a Cristina Brusca. (Argentina) (P–I)

Bryan, Ashley. *The Cat's Purr.* (West Indies—Antilles) (P–I)

———— (reteller). *Turtle Knows Your Name.* (West Indies) (P–I)

De Armond, Dale (adapter). *The Seal Oil Lamp.* (Eskimo) (P–I)

Goble, Paul. *Crow Chief: A Plains Indian Story.* (P–I)

Hooks, William. *Moss Gown.* Illus. Donald Carrick. (United States) (P–I)

Hunter, C. W. *The Green Gourd. A North Carolina Folktale.* (P)

Martin, Rafe. *The Rough-Face Girl.* Illus. David Shannon. (P)

McKissack, Patricia C. *The Dark-Thirty: Southern Tales of the Supernatural.* Illus. Brian Pinkney. (African-American) (I–A)

Oughton, Jerrie. *How the Stars Fell into the Sky: A Navajo Legend.* Illus. Lisa Desimini. (P)

Rodanas, Kristina. *Dragonfly's Tale.* (Zuni) (P)

Rounds, Glen. *Three Little Pigs and the Big Bad Wolf.* (P)

San Souci, Robert D. *Sukey and the Mermaid.* Illus. Brian Pinkney. (South Carolina) (P)

————. *The Talking Eggs.* Illus. Jerry Pinkney. (African-American) (P–I)

Europe, Africa, and the Middle East

Cauley, Lorinda Bryan (reteller-illustrator). *The Pancake Boy: An Old Norwegian Folk Tale.* (Norway) (P)

Climo, Shirley (adapter). *The Egyptian Cinderella.* Illus. Ruth Heller. (Egypt) (P)

Cooper, Susan (reteller). *Tam Lin.* Illus. Warwick Hutton. (Scotland) (P–I)

de Paola, Tomie. *Tony's Bread.* (Italy) (P)

Greene, Jacqueline Dembar. *What His Father Did.* (Europe) (P)

Grifalconi, Ann. *The Village of Round and Square Houses.* (Africa) (P)

Haley, Gail E. *A Story, A Story.* (Africa) (P–I)

Hutton, Warwick. *The Trojan Horse.* (P–I)

McDermott, Gerald. *Tim O'Toole and the Wee Folk.* (Ireland) (P)

McVitty, Walter (reteller). *Ali Baba and the Forty Thieves.* Illus. Margaret Early. (Arabia) (I–A)

Olson, Arielle North. *Noah's Cats and the Devil's Fire.* Illus. Barry Moser. (Romania) (P)

Rayevsky, Inna (reteller). *The Talking Tree: An Old Italian Tale.* Illus. Robert Rayevsky. (Italy) (I)

Shute, Linda (reteller). *Clever Tom and the Leprechaun.* (Ireland) (P–I)

Steptoe, John. *Mufaro's Beautiful Daughters: An African Tale.* (Africa) (P–I)

Williams, Sheron. *And in the Beginning.* Illus. Robert Roth. (Swahili) (P)

Wisniewski, David. *Elfwyn's Saga.* (Iceland) (I) (Africa) (P–I)

Illustrated versions of folklore are abundant; they vary from slick cartoon drawings to the studied work of talented artists. Comic strips that portray Snow White as a simpering beauty queen or Zeus as a Superman hero destroy the authenticity of the ancient lore. Illustrators have the opportunity to present an immense amount of cultural detail in their illustrations that the language of the tales often does not provide. Further, since the tales often contain scant details about setting and character, illustrators have a unique opportunity to create their own visions. Look for illustrations that (1) complement and extend the narrative with accuracy and details that reflect the culture of origin; (2) enrich the narrative with details of setting and character; and (3) are artistically excellent.

CONTINUED

Yolen, Jane. *Tam Lin.* Illus. Charles Mikolaycak. (Scotland) (I)

Western Asia

Afanasyev, Alexander Nikolayevich. Retold by Lenny Hort. *The Fool and the Fish.* Illus. Gennady Spirin. (Russia) (I)

Bider, Djemma. *A Drop of Honey.* Illus. Armen Kojoyian. (Armenia) (I)

Brett, Jan (adapter). *The Mitten: A Ukrainian Folktale.* (Ukraine) (P)

Ginsburg, Mirra. *Good Morning, Chick.* Adapted from story by Kornei Chukovsky. Illus. Byron Barton. (Russia) (P)

Hodges, Margaret (reteller). *The Little Humpbacked Horse: A Russian Tale Retold.* Illus. Chris Conover. (Russia) (P)

Hogrogian, Nonny. *The Contest.* (Armenia) (P)

———. *One Fine Day.* (Armenia) (P)

Kismaric, Carole (adapter). *The Rumor of Pavel Paali: A Ukrainian Folktale.* Illus. Charles Mikolaycak. (I–A)

Ransome, Arthur (reteller). *The Fool of the World and the Flying Ship: A Russian Tale.* Illus. Uri Shulevitz. (Russia) (P–I)

Sherman, Josepha (reteller). *Vassilisa the Wise: A Tale of Medieval Russia.* Illus. Daniel San Souci. (Russia) (I)

Tresselt, Alvin R. (reteller). *The Mitten: An Old Ukrainian Folktale.* Illus. Yaroslava. Retold from version by E. Rachev. (Ukraine) (P)

Winthrop, Elizabeth (adapter). *Vasilissa the Beautiful.* Illus. Alexander Koshkin. (Russia) (P–I)

The Far East

Demi (reteller-illustrator). *The Empty Pot.* (China) (P)

———. *The Magic Boat.* (China). (P–I)

Ginsburg, Mirra (adapter). *The Chinese Mirror.* Illus. Margot Zemach. (China) (P–I)

Heyer, Marilee (reteller-illustrator). *Weaving of a Dream: A Chinese Folktale.* (China) (I)

Ishii, Momoko (reteller). *The Tongue-Cut Sparrow.* Translated from Japanese by Katherine Paterson. Illus. Suekichi Akaba. (Japan) (I)

Johnston, Tony (adapter). *The Badger and the Magic Fan.* Illus. Tomie de Paola. (Japan) (I)

McDermott, Gerald. *The Stonecutter: A Japanese Folktale.* (Japan) (P)

Paterson, Katherine (reteller). *The Tale of the Mandarin Ducks.* Illus. Leo and Diane Dillon. (Japan) (P–I)

Quayle, Eric (reteller). *The Shining Princess and Other Japanese Legends.* Illus. Michael Foreman. (Japan) (I)

Yacowitz, Caryn (adapter). *The Jade Stone: A Chinese Folktale.* Illus. Ju-Hong Chen. (China) (I)

Yep, Laurence. *Tongues of Jade.* Illus. David Wiesner. (China) (I–A)

Yolen, Jane. *The Emperor and the Kite.* Illus. Ed Young. (China) (I)

Young, Ed. *Seven Blind Mice.* (India) (P)

A Close Look at *The Rough-Face Girl*

Folklore that is structured around the basic Cinderella tale type is common; approximately 1,500 versions of the tale have been recorded by folklorists. Rafe Martin retells the Algonquin Indian version of Cinderella in **The Rough-Face Girl** (I), illustrated by David Shannon. In this retelling both the Algonquin culture and the voice of the storyteller are apparent in both illustrations and words.

Synopsis

The story begins "long ago" in a "village by the shores of Lake Ontario." Many women of the village want to marry the Invisible Being, but first they

Ashley Bryan conveys the spirit of family unity and the celebration in song and dance that he brings from his West Indies background. (*Turtle Knows Your Name*)

must be able to see him and answer questions that his sister asks. Two of the village women are cruel and haughty sisters who torment their younger sister, forcing her to keep the fire going, a job that results in scars on her face and hands. After the sisters fail in their attempt to marry the Invisible Being, the younger sister goes to his tent. When questioned by the Invisible Being's sister, the girl answers correctly. She is married to the Invisible Being and "they lived together in great gladness and were never parted."

Structure

The simple structure of an oral tale is preserved in this retelling. The story begins with a simple statement of setting and moves immediately to the problem: Only the woman who can see the Invisible Being can marry him. On the third page we are introduced to the characters: a poor man with three daughters, two cruel and heartless, one sweet and submissive. The story then moves immediately to the action, briefly detailing the unsuccessful at-

Tomie de Paola's folk art is just as appropriate and appealing in three dimensions, here shown in *Giorgio's Village,* as it is in the two-dimensional illustrations for *Strega Nona* and other folktales.

tempts of the haughty sisters to convince the Invisible Being's sister that they have seen him and the subsequent triumph of the Rough-Face Girl. This economy of detail reflects the oral origins of the tale: Brief statements of setting and the use of stereotypical characters allow the teller to get right to the exciting part—the action—thus holding the attention of his audience.

Language

The language, too, reflects the oral origins of the tale. There is dialogue and the use of prosodic features such as tone and volume when the sister of the Invisible Being speaks:

> "All right," she said quietly, "if you think you've seen him, then tell me, WHAT'S HIS BOW MADE OF?" And suddenly her voice was swift as lightning and strong as thunder!

There is also repetition: The Rough-Face Girl asks her father what her older sisters have already asked, she makes the same journey they did, and she is asked the same questions by the sister. Sharp contrasts between them are drawn: Her father has nothing to give her, the villagers laugh at her as she

---

Figure 5-2

Checklist for Evaluating Folklore

Language:

❑ Does it retain the flavor of the oral form?

❑ Does it have natural, easily spoken rhythms?

❑ Does it reflect the integrity of early retellings?

❑ Does it avoid controlled, diluted, or trite vocabulary?

Illustrations:

❑ Do they complement and extend the narrative?

❑ Do they portray the traditional character of the tale?

❑ Do they maintain the cultural heritage of the tale?

walks in her odd clothing, and she answers the questions correctly. By repeating the events and the important dialogue, the storyteller heightens the drama of the tale.

Perhaps the most moving passage comes when the Invisible Being enters his wigwam and sees the Rough-Face Girl:

> And when he saw her sitting there he said, "At last we have been found out." Then, smiling kindly, he added, "And oh, my sister, but she is beautiful." And his sister said, "Yes."

Read aloud, these words ring with emotion.

Illustrations

The voice of the storyteller comes through the words, but the culture of the people comes through both the words and the beautiful full-color realistic paintings that illustrate this tale. The first page, on which the setting is introduced in one sentence, exemplifies how text and illustrations work together. Above the text is a painting of an Algonquin village. If you look closely you can see men in canoes and carrying game, women carrying water, tending fires, scraping skins, and cooking, and children playing. Surrounding the village are tall pines and firs with mist rising from the lake. Thus in one

PROFILE

*I*SAAC BASHEVIS SINGER, the son and grandson of rabbis, was born in Radzymin, Poland, in 1904. Although he was a student at the Rabbinical Seminary in Warsaw, he chose not to become a rabbi and went to work as a journalist for the Yiddish press in Poland after completion of his studies. He immigrated to America in 1935 and was a prolific writer: journalist, memoirist, children's storyteller, and novelist. Although he originally wrote in Hebrew, Singer adopted Yiddish as his medium of expression and personally supervised the translation of his works into English.

Singer received many literary awards. In 1978 he was awarded the Nobel Prize for Literature; in 1980 he received the Medal of Honor for Literature given by the National Arts Club in New York; in 1970 he received a National Book Award in Children's Literature for *A Day of Pleasure;* and in 1974, another National Book Award in fiction, for *A Crown of Feathers.*

Singer's works have been translated into numerous languages and read by people around the world. When asked

Isaac Bashevis Singer

if he would take a guess about why people appreciate what he writes, he said, "The guess is that there is a kinship between souls. Souls are either close to one another or far from one another. There are people who, when they read me, they like what I say." Discussing the appeal of literature across national borders, Singer explained,

line the story is set, and the setting is elaborated in the detailed illustration.

In subsequent illustrations we see wigwams and their symbolic decorations, details of clothing, and beautiful natural images that inspired much of Algonquin folklore. These images speak of the people and the culture that first told this haunting tale. We also see the pride and meanness of the two sisters, the humility of the Rough-Face Girl, and the awesome nature of the Invisible Being. Thus the illustrations not only reflect but elaborate and extend the story, providing readers with details that are not easily incorporated in a brief oral text.

The Rough-Face Girl exemplifies the close rela-tionship among reteller, artist, and original tale. The combination of a riveting tale, a skillful retelling, and beautiful detailed illustrations result in a book that children remember and return to.

TYPES OF FOLKLORE

Folklore has many categories. Those most commonly available to children include nursery rhymes, folktales, fables, myths, legends, and folksongs. Beginning in infancy, children delight in nursery rhymes. As they develop they come to understand and enjoy folktales, legends, and mythology and to

CONTINUED

. . . to enjoy a book you don't really have to go there and to know the land and the people, because human beings, although they are different, also have many things in common. And through this you get a notion which writer says the truth and which writer is fabricating. . . .

When I sit down to write a story, I will write the kind of stories which I write. It's true that since I know the Jewish people best and since I know the Yiddish language best, so my heroes, the people of my stories, are always Jewish and speak Yiddish. I am at home with these people.

Isaac Bashevis Singer did not begin writing for children until he was well over 60 years old. He had, of course, been writing all his life, so the transition was not a difficult one for him. Once he started, he found it very rewarding. He said,

There are five hundred reasons why I began to write for children, but to save time I'll mention only ten of them.

1. Children read books, not reviews. They don't give a hoot about the critics.

2. Children don't read to find their identity.

3. They don't read to free themselves of guilt, to quench their thirst for rebellion, or to get rid of alienation.

4. They have no use for psychology.

5. They detest sociology.

5. They don't try to understand Kafka or *Finnegans Wake*.

7. They still believe in God, the family, angels, devils, witches, goblins, logic, clarity, punctuation, and other such obsolete stuff.

8. They love interesting stories, not commentary, guides, or footnotes.

9. When a book is boring, they yawn openly, without shame or fear of authority.

10. They don't expect their beloved writer to redeem humanity. Young as they are, they know that it is not in his power. Only the adults have such childish illusions.

Isaac Bashevis Singer's writings make children's literature much richer. He died at the age of 87 in 1991.

appreciate the morals encoded in fables. Although schoolchildren are often first introduced to folktales, subsequently move to legends, and study mythology in the upper grades, the wide-ranging appeal of folklore makes such age distinctions unnecessary. Many primary-grade children enjoy mythology when it is presented in an appealing format; when they study mythology later they have a foundation on which to build more sophisticated understandings. Likewise, many advanced-grade children enjoy and profit from a study of folktales, especially if they are familiar with the tales from childhood.

Mother Goose and Nursery Rhymes

Mother Goose rhymes are the foundation of a rich literary heritage. The rhythm and rhyme of the language, the compact structure of the narratives, and the engaging characters all combine to produce the perfect model for young children who are learning language. There are phrases to chant, nonsense words to mimic, and alliterative repetitions to practice. Poet Walter De la Mare attests to their importance. Mother Goose rhymes, he declares,

> free the fancy, charm the tongue and ear, delight the inward eye, and many of them are tiny masterpieces of word craftsmanship. . . . Last, but not least, they are not only crammed with vivid little scenes and objects and living creatures, but, however fantastic and nonsensical they may be, they are a direct short cut into poetry itself. (1962, p. 21)

Mother Goose rhymes have come under attack many times through the years, but they have always survived the criticism and have continued to play an important role in the lives of children. As early as the seventeenth century, our stern forefathers considered many of the verses unfit for childish ears. Their adult perceptions saw brutality, dishonesty, and irresponsibility rather than silly whimsy and nonsensical fun. In more recent years, harsh criticism has been leveled at the apparent sexism and violence in the verses. Some of these charges may indeed be valid from an adult perspective, but it seems that young children value the rhymes for their rhythm, rhyme, fanciful language, and nonsense, and seem to pay little attention to other aspects. Further, these rhymes are but a part of the literary experience of children and other things that they read and hear reflect more modern perceptions of gender equity and nonviolence.

David Shannon's art quickly establishes the setting of a village by the lake. The time of "long ago" is reflected in the shelter and food preparation scenes. (*The Rough-Face Girl* by Rafe Martin)

Origins

As is true of all folklore, there is no conclusive evidence about the events that generated the Mother Goose rhymes or about the existence of an actual person with that name. Iona and Peter Opie, authors of two definitive works, **The Oxford Nursery Rhyme Book** and **The Oxford Dictionary of Nursery Rhymes,** display a healthy skepticism about the origin of the anonymous rhymes and the diverse referents ascribed to them:

> Much ingenuity has been exercised to show that certain nursery rhymes have had greater significance than is now apparent. They have been vested with mystic symbolism, linked with social and political events, and numerous attempts have been made to identify the nursery characters with real persons. It should be stated straightaway that the bulk of these speculations are worthless. Fortunately the theories are so numerous they tend to cancel each other out. (1951, p. 27)

Some rhymes may have been composed to teach children to count, to learn the alphabet, or to say

David Shannon captures the relationship between the human-sized Rough-Face Girl and the overwhelming grandeur and beauty of nature. (***The Rough-Face Girl*** by Rafe Martin)

their prayers, while others—riddles, tongue twisters, proverbs, and nonsense—were simply for amusement.

The name *Mother Goose* seemingly was first associated with an actual collection of tales in 1697 with Charles Perrault's publication of ***Histoires ou contes du temps passé, avec des moralités (Stories or tales of times past, with morals)***. The frontispiece shows an old woman spinning and telling stories, and is labeled ***"Contes de ma Mère l'Oye" (Tales of Mother Goose)***. The exact origin of the name, like the authors of the verses, is lost in the past, but the vitality of the rhymes assures their appeal even today.

Characteristics

The dominant feature of this type of folklore is the *powerful rhythm* of the verses; the strong beat resounds in the ear and invites physical response. Long before meaning is attached to the sounds, the cadence of the language and bounce of an adult's knee undergird a child's developing rhythm. Northrop Frye emphasizes this physical aspect:

> Ideally, our literary education should begin, not with prose, but with such things as "this little pig went to market"—with verse rhythm reinforced

---

TEACHING IDEA 5-2

Folklore Theater

Folklore is ideal material for readers theatre, puppetry, story theater, or choral reading. Folktales contain clean plot lines, a limited cast of characters, and decisive endings.

1. Ask book talk groups to choose folktales to read.

2. Have them choose a folktale they want to share through a form of creative drama.

3. Have them prepare a script for readers theatre, a puppet play, story theater, or choral reading.

4. Share the performances with the total class group.

by physical assault. The infant who gets bounced on somebody's knee to the rhythm of "Ride a Cock Horse" does not need a footnote telling him that Banbury Cross is twenty miles northeast of Oxford. He does not need the information that "cross" and "horse" make (at least in the pronunciation he is most likely to hear) not a rhyme but an assonance. He does not need the value judgment that the repetition of "horse" in the first two lines indicates a rather thick ear on the part of the composer. All he needs is to get bounced. (1963, p. 25)

The pronounced beat of the Mother Goose rhymes reinforces the child's developing sense of rhythm. Even more crucial are the audible beat, stress, sound, and intonation patterns that establish themselves in memory and contribute to rhythm in the child's developing language. Who can chant

> Hickory, dickory, dock,
> The mouse ran up the clock.
> The clock struck one,
> The mouse ran down,
> Hickory, dickory, dock.

without some form of toe tapping, head nodding, or other physical accompaniment?

A second major characteristic of Mother Goose is the *imaginative use of words and ideas*. Nothing is too preposterous or ridiculous to form the content of a verse. Children delight in the images suggested by

> Hey diddle, diddle,
> The cat and the fiddle,
> The cow jumped over the moon;
> The little dog laughed
> To see such sport,
> And the dish ran away with the spoon.

The fanciful visions of "Three wise men of Gotham who went to sea in a bowl," and "There was an old woman tossed up in a basket, nineteen times as high as the moon," spark creativity and enrich the developing imagination. Nothing is impossible, anything can happen in the young child's unfettered world, and the verses feed the fancy.

A third characteristic of Mother Goose rhymes is the *compact structure*. The scene is established quickly and the plot divulged at once. In four short lines we hear an entire story:

> Jack Sprat could eat no fat,
> His wife could eat no lean,
> And so between them both, you see,
> They licked the platter clean.

Undoubtedly, as in all folklore, the consolidation of action and the economy of words result from being said aloud for many generations before being set down in print. As they were passed from one teller to the next, they were honed to their present simplicity.

Another quality that accounts for the popularity and longevity of Mother Goose verses is the *wit and whimsy of the characters*. Nonsense is so obvious that the child is in on the joke in

> Gregory Griggs, Gregory Griggs,
> Had twenty-seven different wigs.
> He wore them up, he wore them down,
> To please the people of the town;
> He wore them east, he wore them west,
> But he never could tell which he loved best.

The humor appeals to both the children and the adults who share the verses with them. Surprise endings provide a clever resolution as in

---

𝒯EACHING IDEA 5-3

Cut Loose With Mother Goose

Teachers find that Mother Goose rhymes serve as excellent reading material for beginning readers. The verses have rhythm, repetition, and rhyme—the qualities needed in predictable texts for emerging readers. Use the books listed in Figure 5-3 to locate children's favorite rhymes.

1. Copy favorite Mother Goose rhymes onto large charts.
2. Read the verses as a group many times.
3. Point to words as the group says them.
4. Ask children to
    put their hands around words they know,
    locate words that begin with the same letter,
    locate words that sound alike.
5. Let children point to the words as the group says them.
6. Make individual copies of each rhyme for children to illustrate and create their own book.
7. Send the handmade books with each child as take-home reading material.

"Oh! Mother Dear, we greatly fear
Our mittens we have soiled."

Galdone puts children's expressions on kittens' faces as they explain what happened to their mittens. His bold colors and cartoon-like art extend the make-believe and whimsical tone of the verses. (***Three Little Kittens***)

A, B, C, tumble-down D,
The cat's in the cupboard
And can't see me.

Jerry Hall, he was so small,
A rat could eat him,
Hat and all.

Upstairs, downstairs, upon my lady's window,
There I saw a cup of sack and a race of ginger,
Apples at the fire and nuts to crack,
A little boy in the cream pot up to his neck.

Peter Piper picked a peck of pickled pepper,
A peck of pickled pepper Peter Piper picked.
If Peter Piper picked a peck of pickled pepper,
Where's the peck of pickled pepper Peter Piper picked?

28

Alice and Martin Provensen display their command of palette, composition, and perspective in their whimsical interpretation of *Mother Goose*.

This is the man all tattered and torn,
That kissed the maiden all forlorn,
That milked the cow with the crumpled horn,
That tossed the dog,
That worried the cat,
That killed the rat,
That ate the malt
That lay in the house that Jack built.

Marguerite de Angeli conveys the humor and folkloric qualities in sketches for the cumulative verse "The House That Jack Built" in *Book of Nursery and Mother Goose Rhymes.*

Peter, Peter, pumpkin eater,
Had a wife and couldn't keep her;
He put her in a pumpkin shell,
And there he kept her very well.

Selecting Mother Goose Books

Because we share Mother Goose rhymes by reciting them, and their essence lies in the words, language is a crucial factor in selecting a collection. The verses should maintain the original poetic, robust vocabulary. Rewritten or abridged verses should be avoided, for the value lies in the quality and vigor of the language.

Most Mother Goose books are illustrated, so the quality of the art should also be considered. The normal function of illustrations—to help visualize the action and characters and to amplify and extend the text—is no simple task. Some illustrators develop an entire book around a single Mother Goose rhyme; others focus a collection of rhymes around a single topic as Paul Galdone does in **The Three Little Kittens** (P), and still others present a general collection interpreted by their particular artistic vision. One such collection, Alice and Martin Provensen's **Mother Goose** (P), has been a favorite for many years. Small humorous illustrations accompany the diverse rhymes that represent a rich sampling of nursery lore. The large format is appealing; never busy, each page gives children a lot to look at. Leonard Marcus and Amy Schwartz have gathered several rhymes for **Mother Goose's Little Misfortunes** (P–I), humorously illustrated by Schwartz with cartoonlike illustrations that underscore the essentially ridiculous nature of the situations presented in the rhymes.

Collections of Mother Goose rhymes are more abundant than books based on the individual verses, but they vary in quality of selections and illustrations. Ideally, the illustrations should extend the verses without overpowering them. Another outstanding example—Marguerite de Angeli's **Book of Nursery and Mother Goose Rhymes** (N-P)—combines a comprehensive collection of verses with exquisite illustrations. The verses are a mixture of pathos, joy, and nonsense, and they retain the rhythmic language of the old versions. The adult reader and child viewer share a work of art as they look at spacious pages graced with finely crafted illustrations. De Angeli captures the whimsy of some verses and the tenderness of others. Both single verse and collections are listed in Figure 5-3. Nursery school and primary classrooms should have many of the standard Mother Goose collections listed in the figure for children to read, hold, share, and love.

Folktales

Children and adults have shared and enjoyed the same literature for centuries. Folktales, which include talking beast, noodlehead, cumulative, and wonder, or fairy tales, have been handed down from one generation to the next, with each storyteller adding slight variations. Some Eastern stories appeared in print as early as the ninth century. Straparola collected Italian tales in mid-sixteenth-century Venice in his **Piacevoli Notti,** followed by Basile's **Pentameron or Entertainment for the Little Ones** in seventeenth-century Naples. With the French publication, in 1697, of Perrault's **Histoires ou contes du temps passé,** folk literature began to flourish in Europe. Among the tales included were "Sleeping Beauty," "Little Red Riding Hood," "Cinderella," and "Puss in Boots." During the course of the eighteenth century, La Fontaine's **Fables,** Countess d'Aulnoy's **Fairy Tales,** and Madame de Beaumont's **Beauty and the Beast** were published.

Toward the end of the eighteenth century, philologists began to examine folklore as a source of information about the customs and languages of different societies. In Germany, two brothers, Jacob and Wilhelm Grimm, traveled through the country asking people to tell the stories they remembered. The Grimms did eventually write both a German dictionary and a book of grammar, but they are remembered for retellings of the stories they heard. The two volumes of the first edition of *Kinder- und Hausmärchen* were published in 1812 and 1815, respectively.

Many of the tales collected by the Grimm brothers were translated into English in 1823. **German Popular Stories,** with pictures by the noted illustrator George Cruikshank, became an instant success and raised the respectability of the old tales among scholars and educators who had held them to be "an affront to the rational mind" (Opie & Opie, 1974, p. 25).

Over the years, hundreds of translations of folklore have been published; many contain outstanding illustrations by respected artists. Walter Crane illustrated **Household Stories** in 1886, and Wanda Gág translated and illustrated **Tales from Grimm** in 1936. Of those published more recently, **The Juniper Tree and Other Tales from Grimm** (I), illustrated by Maurice Sendak, is one of the best. The translations by Randall Jarrell and Lore Segal retain the vigor and charm of the original language. Also noteworthy are **Popular Folk Tales: The Brothers Grimm** (I), translated by Brian Alderson and illustrated by Michael Foreman, and **Favorite Tales from Grimm** (I), retold by Nancy Garden and illustrated by Mercer Mayer.

Enthusiasm for collecting folklore spread around the world: Joseph Jacobs and Andrew Lang collected folktales in England. Jacob's **Ardizzone's English Fairy Tales** includes some of the best-loved stories. Lang's series, identified by color—**The Blue Fairy Book,** for example—have long served as the primary source of British tales. Norse scholars Peter

---

Figure
5-3

Mother Goose and Nursery Rhymes

Conover, Chris (reteller-illustrator). *Mother Goose and the Sly Fox.*

Cooney, Barbara. *Chanticleer and the Fox.*

Craig, Helen. *I See the Moon, and the Moon Sees Me.*

de Paola, Tomie. *Tomie de Paola's Mother Goose.*

———. *Tomie de Paola's Favorite Nursery Tales.*

Edens, Cooper (selector). *The Glorious Mother Goose.* Illus. reproductions.

Girling, Brough. *I Know an Old Lady.*

Larrick, Nancy (compiler). *Songs from Mother Goose.* Illus. Robin Spowart.

Lobel, Arnold (editor-illustrator). *Random House Book of Mother Goose.*

———. *Whiskers and Rhymes.*

Marcus, Leonard, and Amy Schwartz (compilers). *Mother Goose's Little Misfortunes.* Illus. Amy Schwartz.

Marshall, James (Illustrator). *Old Mother Hubbard and Her Wonderful Dog.*

———. *James Marshall's Mother Goose.*

Mother Goose. *The Real Mother Goose.* Illus. Blanche Fisher Wright.

Opie, Iona, and Peter Opie. *The Oxford Dictionary of Nursery Rhymes.*

——— (compilers). *Tail Feathers from Mother Goose: The Opie Rhyme Book.* Illus. by various artists.

Spier, Peter. *To Market! To Market!*

Sutherland, Zena (selector). *The Orchard Book of Nursery Rhymes.* Illus. Faith Jaques.

Watson, Wendy. *Wendy Watson's Mother Goose.*

———. *Father Fox's Pennyrhymes.*

Yolen, Jane (editor). *Jane Yolen's Mother Goose Songbook.* Music by Adam Stemple. Illus. Rosenkrans Hoffman.

Christian Asbjørnsen and Jorgen E. Moe collected most of the Scandinavian tales we have today. Asbjørnsen and Moe published a notable collection, **East O' the Sun and West O' the Moon** (I), during the 1840s. These tales were rendered into English by George Webbe Dasent in translations that retained the vitality of the spoken language. Many of the same tales appear in Ingri and Edgar Parin d'Aulaire's **East of the Sun and West of the Moon** (I), whose illustrations echo Norwegian folk art.

Characteristics

Folktales are *narratives* in which heroes and heroines demonstrate virtues like cleverness and bravery, or lovable vices like supreme silliness to triumph over adversity. They have an artistic yet simple form attributable to their oral tradition. The *plot* lines are clean and direct: The first paragraph establishes characters and setting, the body develops the problem and moves toward the climax, the ending resolves the problem without complications.

There is little ambiguity in folktales: The good are supremely good, the evil are outrageously evil, and justice prevails without compromise. The problem, or conflict, is identified early, and only incidents that build the problem or add complexity have survived oral transmission. The problem resolution is decisive, with little denouement; characters live happily ever after.

Characters in folktales are delineated economically, with intentional stereotyping to quickly establish character traits. Subtleties are seldom found, since folktales are concerned more with situation than character. The foolish, the wise, the wicked, or the virtuous immediately crystallize as characters who will perform in predictable ways. These little-developed characters are stock figures, either altogether good or altogether bad, who seldom change during a story. Names represent a group—Jack, for example, for any lad.

Themes in folktales, obvious although not stated explicitly, express the values of the people who created them and reflect their philosophy of life. The *language* is direct, vivid vernacular uncluttered by awkward constructions or convolutions. Colloquialisms add to the flavor and reflect the heritage of the tale; they are tempered to the tongue, having been pruned and polished through centuries.

The *setting* of folktales is geographically vague, leaving an impression of worlds complete in themselves. Stories occur at unidentified times in places defined by the minimal physical detail necessary to the events. Because children accept the idea that there was a different range of possibilities in the past, the stories are believable to them. Young children may know that giants do not live in today's world, but they readily accept the possibility that they lived at one time. Figure 5-4 summarizes these characteristics.

Types of Folktales

Fairy Tales. Fairy tales, like all folktales, are structured by an unvarying sequence of episodes, but they are unique among folktales in the deeply magical character of their events. In some, the action of the story is carried forward by the intervention of wee people, a fairy godmother, or a magical being. Filled with enchantment, these stories nonetheless present a vision of life based on fundamental truths. Children see courage, hard work, and resourcefulness rewarded and the good living happily ever after. "Fairy tales," says Hazard, "are like beautiful mirrors of water, so deep and crystal clear. In their depths we sense the mysterious experience of a thousand years" (1967, p. 157).

The Rough-Face Girl (I), discussed earlier, is an example of an excellent presentation of a fairy tale. So, too, is Robert D. San Souci's **The Talking Eggs** (I), an adaptation of a Creole variant of the Cinderella story that is stunningly illustrated by Jerry Pinkney. Other exemplary editions of fairy tales are listed in Figure 5-5.

Talking Beast Tales. In this type of tale animals talk with human beings or with each other. Like human characters, the talking animals may be good or evil, wise or silly, and those who are good and wise get rewarded. Nursery and primary-grade children especially enjoy talking beast tales, and many are perennial favorites such as "The Three Little Pigs," "The Three Billy-Goats Gruff," "Henny Penny," "Brer Rabbit," and the Anansi spider stories. Eric Kimmel's retelling of a West African trickster tale, **Anansi Goes Fishing** (P), humorously illustrated by Janet Stevens, is wonderful to read aloud. The rhythmic language is appealing to listen to and the humorous situation makes children laugh with delight. Other talking beast tales are listed in Figure 5-5.

Noodlehead Tales. Another type of tale is the noodlehead story about a character who is pure-hearted but lacks good judgment. In **Noodlehead Stories from Around the World** (I), M. A. Jagendorf describes a noodlehead as a simple, blundering person who does not use good sense or learn from experience.

Every cultural group has its noodlehead stories: the wise men of Gotham in England, the fools of

---

Figure 5-4

Folktale Characteristics and Types

Characteristics:

Heroes and heroines represent traits such as cleverness, bravery, or supreme silliness to triumph over adversity

Plot lines are clean and direct

Stories contain very little ambiguity: Good is good, evil is outrageously evil

Conflict is identified early

Resolution is decisive

Characters are delineated economically

Themes express values of people who created them

Language is direct, vivid, vernacular

Setting is geographically vague and the time vague

Types:

Fairy tales

Talking beast

Noodlehead

Cumulative

Chelm in Poland, Juan Bobo in Puerto Rico, the Connemara man in Ireland, and the Montieri in Italy. Children enjoy the good-natured fun and laugh heartily at the silly blunders of noodlehead characters.

One favorite noodlehead character, Jack, appears in several stories currently available for children. Noodlehead stories are listed in Figure 5-5.

Cumulative Tales. Children recognize the cumulative pattern of some folktales—such as the particularly conspicuous one of "This Is the House That Jack Built"—wherein each incident grows from the preceding one. Cumulative folktales, characterized by their structure, are often called chain tales, since each part of the story is linked to the next. The initial incident reveals both central character and problem; each subsequent scene builds onto the original one. The accumulation continues to a climax and then unravels in reverse order or stops with an abrupt or surprise ending. "The Old Woman and Her Pig" exemplifies repetition and chaining. "The Gingerbread Boy" and its variants "Johnny Cake," "The Pancake," and "The Bun" illustrate the chain tale with a repetitive phrase—in this case, "Run, run as fast as you can. You can't catch me. I'm the Gingerbread Man." Nursery and primary

Anansi worked hard all day pulling the net out of the river while Turtle lay back, getting very, very tired.

Janet Stevens's art exaggerates the humor of the talking beast tale by showing Anansi the Spider working very hard while Turtle takes life easy. (***Anansi Goes Fishing*** by Eric Kimmel)

Figure 5-5

Types of Folktales From Around the World

Fairy Tales

Grimm, Jacob and Wilhelm. *Snow White and the Seven Dwarfs.* Trans. Randall Jarrell. Illus. Nancy Ekholm Burkert. (Germany)

——. *The Shoemaker and the Elves.* Illus. Adrienne Adams. (Germany)

——. *Rumpelstiltskin.* Illus. Paul O. Zelinsky. (Germany)

——. *Rapunzel.* Adapted by Barbara Rogasky. Illus. Trina Schart Hyman. (Germany)

——. *Hansel and Gretel.* Trans. Elizabeth Crawford. Illus. Lisbeth Zwerger. (Germany)

Ness, Evaline. *Tom Tit Tot.* Illus. by reteller. (England)

Perrault, Charles. Adapted by Nancy Willard. *Beauty and the Beast.* Illus. Barry Moser (France)

Talking Beast Tales

Asbjørnsen, Peter C. and Jorgen Moe. *The Three Billy Goats Gruff.* Illus. Marcia Brown.

Galdone, Paul. *The Three Little Pigs.* (England)

Grimm, Jacob and Wilhelm. *The Bremen Town Musicians.* Reteller and illus. Ilse Plume. (Germany)

Perrault, Charles. *Puss in Boots.* Illus. Marcia Brown. (France)

——. *Puss in Boots.* Illus. Fred Marcellino. Trans. Malcolm Arthur. (France)

Stevens, Janet (reteller and illustrator). *The Three Billy Goats Gruff.* (Norway)

Noodlehead Tales, Droll Tales

Asbjørnsen, Peter C. and Jorgen Moe. *The Squire's Bride.* (Norway)

Cole, Joanna (reteller). *It's Too Noisy!* Illus. Kate Duke.

Hague, Kathleen and Michael Hague. *The Man Who Kept House.* Illus. Michael Hague.

Lurie, Alison. *Clever Gretchen & Other Forgotten Folktales.* Illus. Margot Tomes. (Germany)

Singer, Isaac Bashevis. *Mazel and Shlimazel, or The Milk of a Lioness.* Illus. Margot Zemach. (Israel)

Cumulative Tales

Aardema, Verna. *Bringing the Rain to Kapiti Plain: A Nandi Tale.* Illus. Beatriz Vidal. (Africa)

Asbjørnsen, Peter C. and Jorgen Moe. *The Pancake.* Illus. Anita Lobel. (Norway)

——. *The Runaway Pancake.* Illus. Otto S. Svend. Trans. Joan Tate.

Butler, Stephen. *Henny Penny.* (England)

Galdone, Paul. *The Gingerbread Boy.* (England)

Hogrogian, Nonny. *One Fine Day.* (Armenia)

Stobbs, William. *The House that Jack Built.* (nursery rhyme)

---

grade children especially enjoy cumulative stories. Some examples of cumulative tales are listed in Figure 5-5.

Patterns in Folktales

Teachers and librarians can help children recognize the patterns, or archetypes, in folktales if they provide both exposure to a wide array of stories and a structure on which the children can build their understanding.

Conventions. Literary devices called *conventions* are the cornerstone in folktales and contribute to

a child's sense of story. The story frame, the repeated use of the concept of three, and the formulaic pattern of the plot and characters are conventions that children identify early in their literary education. They recognize the story frames of "once upon a time" and "they lived happily ever after" and adopt them in the stories they tell. Some tales open with variations of these story frames or markers, such as "Long ago and far away." These variations contribute to children's ability to generalize the patterns.

The use of the number three is one of the easiest folkloric conventions for children to recognize. In addition to three main characters—three bears, three billy goats, three pigs—there are usually three events. "Goldilocks and the Three Bears," for example, contains three bears, of course, but also three more sets of three: bowls of porridge, chairs, and beds. Many folktales follow this pattern of three, whether the story involves adventures, tasks, magical objects, trials, or wishes. The number seven appears frequently, too, as in "Snow White and the Seven Dwarfs," "The Seven Ravens," and "The Seven Swans."

Motifs. A *motif* is an element that has something distinctive about it; it may be a symbol, an image, a device—a thread that runs through a story to accentuate the theme. Familiar motifs appear in stereotypic characters—gods, witches, fairies, noodleheads, or stepmothers. Children learn to predict that these stereotypic characters will behave in certain ways. Witches and wolves, of course, are evil; they try to eat children. Often it is a stepmother who becomes the witch, as in "Hansel and Gretel" and "Sleeping Beauty." In **Little Red Riding Hood** (P), the wolf eats the grandmother and the child.

A second kind of motif—magical objects, spells, curses, or wishes—serves as a chief mechanism of some plots. Beans tossed carelessly out the window lead the way to a magical kingdom in "Jack and the Beanstalk." "The Magic Porridge Pot" and its variants hinge on a secret ritual.

Sometimes the magical element in a story is a spell or enchantment. Both Snow White and Sleeping Beauty are victims of a witch's evil curse when they are put to sleep until a kiss from a handsome prince awakens them. In some stories, the evil spell causes a transformation, and only love and kindness can return the frog, or donkey, or beast to its former state. "The Frog Prince," "The Donkey Prince," "The Seven Ravens," "The Six Swans," "Jorinda and Joringel," and "Beauty and the Beast" are all transformation tales.

Trickery or outwitting another is an oft-played element in many tales. For example, a spider man is the trickster in African and Caribbean tales. Trickery and cunning also appear in French and Swedish folktales like "Stone Soup" and "Nail Soup."

The wiliest trickster of all times, Brer Rabbit, has traveled in one form or another in tales from Africa through Jamaica and to the rural South. While many of the tales were popularized by Joel Chandler Harris, the characters appear in many guises in stories told around the world. One of the most outstanding renditions of five of the tales is found in Van Dyke Parks's adaptations of Joel Chandler Harris's tales, for example, **Jump! The Adventures of Brer Rabbit** (I) and **Jump Again! More Adventures of Brer Rabbit** (I), both illustrated by Barry Moser.

---

*T*EACHING IDEA 5-4

Folklore Numbers

Folktales contain numbers that supposedly have magical qualities. Tales use every number up to twelve (or more); those for numbers three and seven are most plentiful. Use numbers as an entry to folktale study.

1. Ask students to search for folktales with numbers.

2. Categorize folktales by the number they use.

3. Read the folktales.

4. Compare the folktales for each number.

Suggested Folktales

One: *Puss in Boots*

Two: *Jorinda and Joringel*

             Perez and Martina

Three: *Three Wishes*

             Three Little Pigs

             Three Billy Goats Gruff

             Goldilocks and the Three Bears

Four: *Bremen Town Musicians*

             Four Gallant Sisters

Five: *Five Chinese Brothers*

Six: *Six Foolish Fishermen*

Seven: *Seven Blind Mice* (Ed Young)

             Her Seven Brothers (Paul Goble)

             Seven at One Blow

             Snow White and the Seven Dwarfs

Julius Lester's retellings of these traditional tales, **The Tales of Uncle Remus, More Tales of Uncle Remus,** and **Further Tales of Uncle Remus** (I–A), are also marked by melodious language patterns that reflect the authentic speech patterns of the culture which gave rise to these stories.

As children read widely, they soon begin to recognize these recurring patterns in the folklore of many countries. Characters, events, and resolutions appear over and over again, and students begin to make predictions and build their own conceptions of folkloric elements.

*T*RINA SCHART HYMAN, born in Philadelphia, Pennsylvania, grew up in a rural area about 20 miles north of the city. The woman who owned a nearby farm was an artist who painted portraits; Trina at age 6 made one of her first drawings for this woman and submitted it to her timidly. She was encouraged and sustained her early interest in art, went to art school in Philadelphia after high school graduation, and wandered through the art museum often. Hyman lived in Sweden and bicycled 2,800 miles around Sweden before she settled in Boston to raise her daughter Katrin. Hyman later moved to a farm in New Hampshire where she still lives.

Trina Schart Hyman's interest in folktales began very early. She describes her attachment to "Little Red Riding Hood" as a child.

She (my mother) read to me from the time I was a baby, and once, when I was three or four and she was reading my favorite story, the words on the page, her spoken words, and the scenes in my head fell together in a blinding flash. I could read! The story was *Little Red Riding Hood*, and it was so much a part of me that I actually became Little Red Riding Hood. My mother sewed me a red satin cape with a hood that I wore almost every day, and on those days, she would make me a "basket of goodies" to take to my grandmother's house. (My only grandmother lived in Rhode Island, three hundred miles away, but that didn't matter.) I'd take the basket and carefully negotiate the backyard, "going to Grandmother's house." My dog, Tippy, was the wolf. Whenever we met, which in a small backyard had to be fairly often, there was an intense confrontation. My father was the woodsman, and I greeted him when he came home each day with relief and joy. I was Little Red Riding Hood for a year or more.

Trina Schart Hyman

Trina Schart Hyman's version of *Little Red Riding Hood* (P), in full color reflects New England farmland, houses, and characters. Borders containing relevant side scenes frame the text on pages that face magnificent full-page paintings of the major events. The paintings of Little Red Riding Hood are self-portraits of the artist as a child. The forest scenes and the wolf look mysterious and foreboding, to add just the right scariness to the tale.

Hyman won the Caldecott Medal and a New York Times Best Illustrated Book Award for *Saint George and the Dragon* (retold by Margaret Hodges). She also won a Caldecott Honor book award and the Golden Kite Award for *Little Red Riding Hood.* She received the Boston Globe–Horn Book Award for *King Stork.*

Trina Schart Hyman is noted for the quality of her illustrations for fantasy, nonfiction, picture books, historical fiction, realistic fiction, poetry and folklore. Her characters exude strength and vitality: beautiful princesses, wicked stepmothers, charming princes, and valiant knights wear their character on their faces and in their bearing.

Themes. The *themes* in folktales evolve around topics of universal human concern. The struggle between good and evil is played out time and again in folklore. Hate, fear, and greed are contrasted with love, security, and generosity. The themes are usually developed through stereotyped characters that personify one trait. For example, the bad fairy in "Sleeping Beauty," the witch in "Hansel and Gretel," and the stepmother in "Snow White" all represent evil. In each story, the evil one is destroyed and the virtuous one rewarded—satisfying endings to affirm that goodness prevails and evil is crushed. Such themes are reassuring to young children. Evil characters appear in the folklore of all cultures.

The theme of the struggle between good and evil is also shown as a contrast between surface appearance and the deeper qualities of goodness in transformation and enchantment tales. As we have seen, a curse is cast on a handsome prince who must then live as a monstrous beast, frog, donkey—as in "Beauty and the Beast," "The Frog Prince," and "The Donkey Prince." The loathsome spell is broken by love—that of a beautiful princess who sees the goodness of the prince hidden beneath the gruesome exterior. In other stories, such as some versions of "Sleeping Beauty," the entire world is under an evil spell, veiled and hidden from clear view until goodness prevails.

The search for happiness or lost identity in order to restore harmony to life is a recurring quest theme. In many stories, the hero succeeds only after a long journey, repeated trials, much suffering, and extended separation. Themes of courage, gallantry, and sacrifice also appear in folktales.

The more children read the traditional tales, the more they will discover the intricate threads and themes woven throughout them. There are many ways to look for patterns in folklore. As you read folklore with your students, the conventions, motifs, and themes you discover will become literary knowledge that your students can build on as they continue to read.

Variants of Folktales

Although the origins of folktales are clouded in prehistory, variants of some can be traced to many cultures. Folklorist Cox uncovered an amazing number of variants of the Cinderella story. She gives brief excerpts and comparisons in *Cinderella: Three Hundred and Forty-Five Variants* (for adults). In a foreword to this collection, Andrew Lang states, "The märchen [fairy tale] is a kaleidoscope: the incidents are the bits of coloured glass. Shaken, they fall into a variety of attractive forms; some forms are fitter than others, survive more powerfully, and are more widely spread." (1893, p. x)

A familiar version of "Cinderella," based on Perrault's tale, is a romantic rags-to-riches love story. This version has been illustrated in single-edition format by several noted artists; those by Marcia Brown, Susan Jeffers, and Errol Le Cain are among the best. In contrast, the German version illustrated by Nonny Hogrogian takes on a macabre tone. In order to make their feet fit into the tiny glass slipper, one stepsister cuts off her toe and the other cuts off her heel. In the end they are blinded while their mother dances to her death in iron shoes. There are also readily available Vietnamese, Chinese, Egyptian, and American Appalachian versions of this story, in addition to the Algonquin and Creole variants discussed earlier in this chapter.

In *Once Upon a Time: On the Nature of Fairy Tales,* Lüthi (1970) presents an insightful analysis of the many variants of "Sleeping Beauty." Lüthi speaks of fairy tales as remnants of primal myths, playful descendants of an ancient, intuitive vision of life and the world. For example, Sleeping Beauty, mysteriously threatened and suffering a sleep similar to death but then awakened, parallels the story of death and resurrection. In much the same vein, the awakening of the sleeping maiden can represent the earth's awakening from winter to live and blossom anew when touched by the warmth of spring.

Lüthi shows that the story of Sleeping Beauty is more than an imaginatively stylized love story portraying a girl whose love breaks a spell. The princess is an image for the human spirit: The story portrays the endowment, peril, and redemption, not of just one girl but all of humankind. Sleeping Beauty's recovery symbolizes the human soul that, suffering repeated setbacks, is yet revived, healed, and redeemed. Human feelings, such as longing, grief, and joy, are expressed in the story. The fairy tale is a universe in miniature that not only reflects the wisdom of the ages but also presents that wisdom in an enchanting tale. Although such elaborate analysis is not for children, it can provide teachers with information they may wish to share with their students.

The story of the little man who, for a cruel fee, helps the poor girl spin straw or flax into skeins of gold is a well-loved folktale that has many variants in many countries. From Germany comes the best-known version, Grimm's **Rumpelstiltskin** (P), a tale in which the dwarf spins straw into gold. In the version from Suffolk, England, an impet (dwarf) spins five skeins of gold from flax in the story called

Set in the South, William Hooks's *Moss Gown,* a version of Cinderella, portrays Cinderella's ball-gown spun from filmy strands of Spanish moss. Donald Carrick incorporates images of the South, including a fairy godmother as a witch woman who protects the helpless.

Tom Tit Tot (P), retold by Evaline Ness. In Devonshire and Cornwall, England, the devil knits stockings, jackets, and other clothing for the Squire, as recounted in the tale *Duffy and the Devil* (P), retold by Harve Zemach. The corresponding character of Rumpelstiltskin is called Trit-a-Trot in Ireland and Whuppity Stoorie in Scotland.

"Jack and the Beanstalk" first appeared in Joseph Jacob's collection of English folktales and has been illustrated by many contemporary artists (see Figure 5-6). Lorinda B. Cauley's beanstalk is a lush green forest that evokes a sense of danger and foreboding; her people are serious. In contrast, Paul Galdone's characters are oafish bunglers who create a more lighthearted story.

Folktales adapted by different cultural groups show corresponding differences in language and setting. Many Americanized versions of Old World tales are known as "Jack Tales," and revolve around a boy named Jack. One of the most familiar is a variant of "Jack and the Beanstalk" and is known as "Jack's Bean Tree," found in Richard Chase's *The Jack Tales* (I). *Jack and the Wonder Beans* (P–I) by James Still is another variant. Appalachian dialect permeates these versions of the familiar tale.

For example, the giant's refrain in *Jack and the Wonder Beans* is "Fee, fie, chew tobacco, I smell the toes of a tadwhacker."

Gail Haley's *Jack and the Bean Tree* (P) is another Appalachian retelling, this time set within the context of a storyteller's tale. Family and neighbors gather round Grandmother Poppyseed who gives a local flavor to her tales, such as a banty hen that lays the golden eggs and the giant that chants "Bein' he live or bein'/he dead,/I'll have his bones/To eat with my pones." Haley's illustrations are bold and energetic, painted on wood in brilliant colors that reflect the various intensities of light and shadow.

A parody of the Jack Tales is *Jim and the Beanstalk* (P–I) by Raymond Briggs. In this version, the giant has grown old and has lost his appetite and his eyesight. Jim helps by getting him false teeth and glasses.

There are many variants of common tales readily available to young readers. Many teachers at all grade levels find that studying folktale variants adds to their students' understanding of folklore, culture, literary structures, and genre characteristics. Several variants of familiar tales are listed in Figure 5-6. We discuss working with variants later in this chapter.

Fables

The *fable* is a brief didactic comment on the nature of human life that is presented in dramatic action to make the idea memorable. One factor distinguishing the fable from other traditional literature forms is that it illustrates a moral, which is stated explicitly at the end. Many common sayings and phrases come from fables: "Better beans and bacon in peace than cakes and ale in fear," "Slow and steady wins the race," "Sour grapes," and "Don't cry wolf." Such injunctions, explicitly stated as morals, are taught by *allegory;* animals or inanimate objects represent human traits in stories that clearly show the wisdom of the simple lessons.

Folklorists relate the fable to the beast tales (in which characters are animals with human characteristics), which were used for satiric purposes and in some cases to teach a moral. In the single incident story typical of the fable, we are told not to be vain, not to be greedy, and not to lie. Fables originated in both Greece and India. Reputedly, a Greek slave named Aesop used fables for political purposes, and though some doubt he ever lived, his name has been associated with fables since ancient times. Early collections made in the East derive from the "Panchatantra" (Five Tantras, or

Figure 5-6

Variants of Folktales

Three Little Pigs

Bucknall, Caroline. *Three Little Pigs.*

Hooks, William H. (reteller). *The Three Little Pigs and the Fox.* Illus. S. D. Schindler. (Appalachian)

Marshall, James. *The Three Little Pigs.*

Scieszka, Jon. *The True Story of the Three Little Pigs.* Illus. Lane Smith.

Zemach, Margot (reteller-illustrator). *The Three Little Pigs: An Old Story.*

Red Riding Hood

de Regniers, Beatrice Schenk, *Red Riding Hood.* Illus. Edward Gorey.

Grimm, Jacob. *Little Red Cap.* Trans. Elizabeth Crawford. Illus. Lisbeth Zwerger.

———. *Little Red Riding Hood.* Retold and illus. Trina Schart Hyman.

Langley, John. *Little Red Riding Hood.* (England)

Perrault, Charles. *Little Red Riding Hood.* Illus. Beni Montresor.

Young, Ed (translator-illustrator). *Lon Po Po: A Red Riding Hood Story from China.*

Collections of Variants

Brooks, William. *A Telling of the Tales.*

Kaye, M. M. *The Ordinary Princess.* (not a collection but a generalized fairy tale—a princess who is ordinary)

King-Smith, Dick. *The Topsy Turvy Storybook.* (Skinny Thinderella and Her Lovely Sisters, Bear and the Three Goldilocks)

Scieszka, Jon. *The Stinky Cheese Man and Other Fairly Stupid Tales.* Illus. Lane Smith. 1993 Caldecott Honor Book.

Cinderella

Climo, Shirley. *The Egyptian Cinderella.* Illus. Ruth Heller.

Hooks, William. *Moss Gown.* Illus. Donald Carrick.

Huck, Charlotte. *Princess Furball.* Illus. Anita Lobel.

Jacobs, Joseph (reteller). *Tattercoats.* Illus. Margot Tomes.

Jungman, Ann. *Cinderella and the Hot Air Balloon.* Illus. Russell Ayto.

Louie, Ai-Ling. *Yeh Shen: A Cinderella Story from China.* Illus. Ed Young.

Martin, Rafe. *The Rough-Face Girl.* Illus. David Shannon. (Algonquin Indian)

Frog Prince

Isadora, Rachel. *The Princess and the Frog.* Grimm version.

Ormerod, Jan, and David Lloyd (retellers). *The Frog Prince.* Illus. Jan Ormerod.

Scieszka, Jon. *The Frog Prince Continued.* Illus. Steve Johnson.

Goldilocks and the Three Bears

Marshall, James (reteller-illustrator). *Goldilocks and the Three Bears.*

Muir, Frank. *Frank Muir Retells Goldilocks and the Three Bears.* Illus. Graham Philpot.

Tolhurst, Marilyn. *Somebody and the Three Blairs.* Illus. Simone Abel.

Turkle, Brinton. *Deep in the Forest.*

Rumpelstiltskin

Grimm, Jacob. *Rumpelstiltskin.* Retold and illus. Paul O. Zelinsky. (Germany)

Sage, Alison (reteller). *Rumpelstiltskin.* Illus. Gennady Spirin.

Note: Grade designations are not listed because these can be used at all grade levels—just vary the amount of depth one goes into at different levels.

Books), a famous collection from India known to English readers as the Fables of Bidpai and Jataka Tales. The Jatakas are stories of Buddha's prior lives as various animals—each tale told to illustrate a moral principle.

A seventeenth-century French poet, Jean de La Fontaine, adapted many of Aesop's early fables into verse form. Several of these have been beautifully illustrated by Brian Wildsmith: *The Lion and the Rat, The North Wind and the Sun,* and *The Rich Man and the Shoemaker* (all P) will enrich any fable collection.

Noted illustrators of children's books have chosen to interpret fables artistically, although there are only a few single editions. However, there are several collections of fables, some of them intended for younger children. Examples of both individual and collected fables appear in Figure 5-7.

Figure 5-7

Fables

Aesop. *Androcles and the Lion.* Illus. Janet Stevens.

Anno, Mitsumasa (reteller-illustrator). *Anno's Aesop: A Book of Fables by Aesop and Mr. Fox.*

Bierhorst, John. *Doctor Coyote: A Native American Aesop's Fables.* Illus. Wendy Watson.

Cauley, Lorinda Bryan. *The Town Mouse and the Country Mouse.*

Clark, Margaret (reteller). *The Best of Aesop's Fables.* Illus. Charlotte Voake.

Hastings, Selina. *Reynard the Fox.* Illus. Graham Percy.

Holder, Heide. *Aesop's Fables.* Illus. Heide Holder.

La Fontaine, J. D. *The Hare and the Tortoise.*

————. *The Lion and the Rat.*

————. *The North Wind and the Sun.*

Lobel, Arnold. *Fables.*

MacDonald, Suse. *Once Upon Another: The Tortoise and the Hare—The Lion and The Mouse.* Retold and illus. Suse MacDonald and Bill Oakes.

Paxton, Tom (reteller). *Aesop's Fables.*

———— (reteller). *Belling the Cat and Other Aesop's Fables.* Illus. Robert Rayevsky.

Stevens, Janet. *The Tortoise and the Hare: An Aesop Fable.*

————. *The Town Mouse and the Country Mouse: An Aesop Fable.*

Storr, C. *Androcles and the Lion.*

Wang, M. L. *The Ant and the Dove: An Aesop Tale Retold.*

There is very little evidence, however, that primary-grade children understand the subtle abstractions on which the fables hinge. Because fables are very short and their language simple, many teachers mistakenly give fables to children who are too young to comprehend or fully appreciate them. Pillar, for instance, found that 7-year-olds often missed the point of widely used fables (1983). Since fables are constructed within the oblique perspective of satire, allegory, and symbolism, their intent may elude young children's literal understanding (see Chapter 2 for a discussion of children's cognitive development).

Mythology

Myths are symbolic stories created by the ancient peoples to explain their world. When the ancient Greeks, for instance, were frightened by and did not understand thunder, they created a story about a god that was angry and shook the heavens; when they did not understand how and why the sun moved, they invented a story about a god that drove a chariot across the sky. Native American, Aboriginal, Chinese, African, Aztec, and other cultures all told stories to explain natural phenomena. Pierre Grimal notes in his comprehensive **Larousse World Mythology** (I–A) that we humans lose our fear of things that we can identify and explain:

> Given a universe full of uncertainties and mysteries, the myth intervenes to introduce the human element: clouds in the sky, sunlight, storms at sea, all extra-human factors such as these lose much of their power to terrify as soon as they are given the sensibility, intentions, and motivations that every individual experiences daily. (1965, p. 9)

Myths comprise a sizable part of our literary and cultural heritage. They are exciting stories with well-defined characters, heroic action, challenging situations, and deep emotions. They offer readers magic, beauty, and strong visual images. They expand experience and transmit ancient values; from mythology we inherit language, symbols, customs, and law.

As folktales, fables, songs, and legends developed, a special group of stories, the ones we call myths, crystallized at the center of the verbal culture. The stories are taken seriously because they express the meaning of beliefs and portray visions of destiny. The myths, unlike other stories, relate to each other and together build a mythology of an imaginative world (Frye, 1964).

Look for retellings of myths that contain interesting language; the myths have a stately dignity that the language should reflect. Valid retellings do not change the myths from tales of grandeur into sentimental stories. Some retellers interpret characters and events in a unique mode, with variations that strikingly illustrate the effect of style on language. In myths, as in all folklore, much depends on the telling. Much depends on the illustrating, as well, and myths offer artists a wonderful opportunity to present their own images of these elemental stories.

Some of the most popular myths suitable for children are the creation and nature myths that describe both the origin of the earth and the phenomena that affect it. These are the tales that tell, for example, how the earth began and why the seasons change. Several books contain collections of creation myths from around the world; others focus on myths from one culture. Many of the best collections of mythology are listed in Figure 5-8.

The simplest of these myths are pourquoi stories. Pourquoi, or "why," tales explain certain traits or characteristics as well as customs and natural phenomena. Many of these tales are retold in stunning picture book versions of single tales, such as Verna Aardema's *Why Mosquitoes Buzz in People's Ears* (P), illustrated by Leo and Diane Dillon. Pourquoi tales are included in Figure 5-10.

Farmer, translator and interpreter of many myths, describes their purpose:

> Myths have seemed to me to point quite distinctly—yet without ever directly expressing it—to some kind of unity behind creation, not a static unity, but a forever shifting breathing one.
>
> . . . The acquisition by man of life or food or fire has to be paid for by the acceptance of death—the message is everywhere, quite unmistakable. To live is to die; to die is to live. (1979, p. 4)

Figure 5-8

Collections of Mythology

Colum, Padraic. *Children of Odin: The Book of Northern Myths.*

Connolly, James E. (collector). *Why the Possum's Tail Is Bare and Other North America Indian Nature Tales.* Illus. Andrea Adams. (I)

Crossley-Holland, Kevin. *Norse Myths.*

d'Aulaire, Ingri Parin, and Edgar Parin d'Aulaire. *Ingri and Edgar Parin d'Aulaire's Book of Greek Myths.*

——. *Norse Gods and Giants.*

Fisher, Leonard Everett. *Olympians: Great Gods and Goddesses of Ancient Greece.*

Hamilton, Virginia. *In the Beginning: Creation Stories from Around the World.* Illus. Barry Moser.

——. *The Dark Way: Stories from the Spirit World.* Illus. Lambert Davis.

Philip, Neil (selector-reteller). *Fairy Tales of Eastern Europe.* Illus. Larry Wilkes.

Russell, William F. *Classic Myths to Read Aloud.*

This great archetypal theme appears again and again throughout all cultures. Children are familiar with the rebirth of flowers and trees in the spring. Most of them have buried a seed in the ground and watched for it to sprout. In image and symbol, mythic themes reappear under many guises, and children can recognize them through their study of myth.

Mythology has given us a rich heritage of images, symbols, language, and art. Isaac Asimov explores the roots of hundreds of *Words from the Myths* (I), a handy reference for students interested in etymology. Penelope Proddow compiled the fascinating book, *Art Tells a Story: Greek and Roman Myths* (I–A), which is a collection of myths accompanied by photographs of art works that were inspired by the ancient stories. Students do not read the myths for their deep levels of symbolic meaning, however. They read them because they are compelling stories of love, carnage, revenge, and mystery.

Literature throughout the ages echoes the themes of the ancient myths; certain motifs, or recurring patterns, are clearly identifiable. Frye traces the origins of all literature, and of the archetypal themes we may identify in it, back to one central story that explains

> how man once lived in a golden age or a garden of Eden or the Hesperides, or a happy island kingdom in the Atlantic, how that world was lost, and how we some day may be able to get it back again. . . . Literature is still doing the same job that mythology did earlier, but filling in its huge cloudy shapes with sharper light and deeper shadows. (1970, pp. 53, 57)

Exploring mythology through recurring themes and motifs leads to endless discoveries.

**Figure
5-9**

Greek and Roman Gods

Aphrodite	Goddess of love	Venus
Apollo	God of the sun	Apollo
Ares	God of war	Mars
Artemis	Goddess of the moon	Diana
Athena	Goddess of wisdom	Minerva
Demeter	Goddess of grain	Ceres
Dionysus	God of wine	Bacchus
Eros	God of love	Cupid
Hades	God of the underworld	Dis
Hephaestus	God of fire	Vulcan
Hera	Goddess of women	Juno
Hermes	Messenger of the gods	Mercury
Hestia	Goddess of home and hearth	Vesta
Kronos	God of time	Saturn
Persephone	Goddess of spring	Proserpine
Poseidon	God of the sea	Neptune
Zeus	King of the gods, Lord of the sky	Jupiter

Greek Mythology

The mythology that comes to us from the ancient Greeks is often studied in school and frequently alluded to in literature. Myths are only tenuously related to historical fact and geographical location. They played an important role, however, in the lives of the ancients, and their influence permeates the art, music, and architecture of ancient Greece—in fact, all of Greek culture. Myths enrich historical study.

The ancient Greeks believed that gods and goddesses controlled the universe. Zeus was the most powerful god. He ruled not only the weather, with its lightning and thunder, but also all the other gods who lived atop Mount Olympus as well as the mortals who lived around it. Figure 5-9 lists the Greek gods and goddesses, the functions and powers attributed to them, and the names later given to them by the Romans, who adopted the Greek deities as their own.

Greek myths are replete with wondrous monsters. Children are fascinated with these half-human, half-beast creatures who frightened early people and wreaked havoc on their lands. Just as young children delight in hearing tales of witches and giants, older students, too, love to read about Medusa, who grows hissing snakes on her head instead of hair, and Cerberus, the huge three-headed dog. The horrible one-eyed Cyclops appears in children's art whenever they are studying the myths.

Stories of individual heroes appear in many books. They tell of great adventures, tests, victories, and losses of the gods. They also feature the relationships between gods and mortals and show how life must be lived with morality and conscience. Love stories interest people of all times; countless myths concern love between a god or goddess and a mortal. The unusual love story of Cupid (named Eros by the Greeks, but commonly known today by his Roman name) and Psyche is well known. Psyche, a mortal, incurs the wrath of Venus (Aphrodite) because she is declared the more beautiful. Venus, in a jealous rage, summons her son Cupid to destroy Psyche by having her fall in love with a monster. Instead of following his mother's orders, Cupid falls in love with Psyche. Students who know this myth will recognize its presence in many modern romances.

A good way for a beginner, whether teacher or student, to select versions of the myths is to turn to recognized translators who are good writers. These include Alfred J. Church, Penelope Farmer, Leon Garfield, Doris Gates, Roger Lancelyn Green,

Charles Kingsley, Andrew Lang, Barbara Picard, Ian Serraillier, and Rex Warner, among others. Inclusion of the name of the translator or adapter on the title page of a book of myths or folklore is an indication that the book is an authentic version. Their books, and others, are listed in Figure 5-10.

Myths are seldom appreciated fully until the later years of elementary school, and even then not by all students. The stories of King Midas, Pandora's box, and Jason and the Golden Fleece are basic material for students' literary education.

Norse Mythology

The mythology of all cultures is replete with tales of bravery and courage. Origin, or creation, myths abound in all societies, as do tales of adventure. We have been focusing on tales from Greek mythology, and some of their Roman adaptations, but there are equally rich stories among other groups, most notably the Vikings.

The tales that grew from the cold, rugged climate of northern Europe are filled with exciting stories of human's struggles against the cruelty of nature and against the powerful gods and monsters who ruled the harsh land. Padraic Colum, an Irish poet and master storyteller, first published *The Children of Odin: The Book of Northern Myths* (I) in 1920; it remains available today to tell the magic and majesty of the Norse sagas. Excellent versions of Norse myths are listed in Figure 5-10.

Mythology From Other Cultures

Although Greek, Roman, and Norse mythology have been the most readily available and studied mythology in the past, today we have available mythology from many cultures. Mythology from Africa and the Orient has taken its place alongside the European stories, and hauntingly beautiful versions of Native American and Inuit tales are being published with increasing frequency. Richard Lewis retells the Aztec myth that explains how music came to earth in *All of You Was Singing* (I–A), structuring his retelling as a poem and infusing it with his own interpretation. Ed Young's illustrations combine Lewis's images, Aztec cultural motifs, and his own vision. The result is a stunningly beautiful book that echoes the splendor of creation.

Students who are given the opportunity to explore myths from many cultures often make surprising discoveries about similarities across cultures while learning to appreciate the differences among them as well. Some of the best editions of myths from non-European cultures are listed in Figure 5-10.

TEACHING IDEA 5-5

Allusions From the Myths

A liberally educated person recognizes common allusions drawn from mythology. Classical allusions, such as an Achilles heel, Pandora's box, the Midas touch, the Trojan horse, and the face that launched a thousand ships appear in our language, literature, and culture; they are part of everyday vocabulary. A winged horse appears on gas stations, Mercury delivers flowers, Vulcan repairs our tires, and Venus emerges from her shell to advertise the sea.

The English language reflects Greek, Roman, and Norse myths: *erotic* comes from Eros, *titanic* comes from the Titans, *cereal* from Ceres, *hubris* is too much pride. Names of the days of the week are based on myths: Sunday = Sun day; Monday = Moon day; Tuesday = Tiu's day (Germanic); Wednesday = Odin's day (Norse); Thursday = Thor's day; Friday = Freya's day; Saturday = Saturn's day. Isaac Asimov, in *Words from the Myths*, presents more words with origins in the myths:

1. Search for words, symbols, and allusions to myths.

2. Keep a list of the words and their mythological referents.

3. Find out who Odysseus, Medea, Achilles, Antigone, Oedipus, and Hector are and why their names are important to us today.

4. Use the information you gather to prepare a Trivial Pursuit (cultural literacy) quiz.

Hero Tales

Epics, also known as hero tales, recount the courageous deeds of mortals as they struggle against each other or against gods and monsters. They reveal universal human emotions and portray the eternal struggle between good and evil. These hero tales contribute to an appreciation of world history and literature, to an understanding of national ideals of behavior, and to a knowledge of the valor, heroism, and nobility of humanity. Epics include the stories of King Arthur and Robin Hood as well as the celebrated account of the Trojan War told in Homer's

Figure
5-10

Mythology From Many Cultures

Greek and Roman

Barth, Edna. *Cupid and Psyche: A Love Story.* (A)

Colum, Padraic. *Golden Fleece and Heroes who Lived Before Achilles.* (A)

Espeland, Pamela. *Story of Cadmus.* (A)

Evslin, Bernard. *Hercules.* (I)

———. *Scylla and Charybdis.* (I)

———. *Theseus and the Minotaur.* (I)

Gates, Doris. *Lord of the Sky: Zeus.* (I–A)

———. *Two Queens of Heaven: Aphrodite and Demeter.* Illus. Trina Schart Hyman. (I–A)

Hawthorne, Nathaniel. *King Midas and the Golden Touch.* (P–I)

Hodges, Margaret. *Arrow and the Lamp.* (I)

Hutton, Warwick. *Theseus and the Minotaur.* (I)

Lattimore, Deborah Nourse. *The Prince and the Golden Ax.* (I)

McDermott, Gerald. *Daughter of the Earth: A Roman Myth.* (I)

Weil, Lisl. *Pandora's Box.* (P–I)

African

Aardema, Verna. *Why Mosquitoes Buzz in People's Ears: A West African Tale.* Illus. Leo and Diane Dillon. (P–I)

——— (adapter). *Rabbit Makes a Monkey of Lion: A Swahili Tale.* Illus. Jerry Pinkney. (P–I)

——— (reteller). *Traveling to Tondo: A Tale of the Nkundo of Zaire.* Illus. Will Hilldebrand. (P–I)

——— (reteller). *Princess Gorilla and a New Kind of Water.* Illus. Victoria Chess. (P–I)

Dayrell, Elphinstone. *Why the Sun and the Moon Live in the Sky: An African Folktale.* (P–I)

Dixon, Ann. *How Raven Brought Light to People.* Illus. James Watts. (P–I)

Gerson, Mary-Joan (reteller). *Why the Sky Is Far Away.* Illus. Carla Golembe. (P–I)

Kimmel, Eric A. *Anansi and the Moss-Covered Rock.* Illus. Janet Stevens. (P–I)

Knutson, Barbara. *Why the Crab Has No Head.* (P–I)

Lester, Julius. *How Many Spots Does a Leopard Have?: And Other Tales.* Illus. David Shannon. (P–I)

Mollel, Tololwa M. *The Orphan Boy: A Maasai Story.* Illus. Paul Morin. (P–I)

Troughton, Joanna. *How Stories Came into the World: A Folk Tale from West Africa.* Retold and illus. Joanna Troughton. (P–I)

Norse

Barth, Edna. *Balder and the Mistletoe: A Story for the Winter Holidays.* (A)

Crossley-Holland, Kevin. *Beowulf.* Illus. Charles Keeping. (A)

De Gerez, Toni (adapter). *Louhi, Witch of North Farm.* (Kalevala) Illus. Barbara Cooney. (P–I)

Mayer, Marianna. *Iduna and the Magic Apples.* Illus. Laszlo Gal. (I)

Native American

de Paola, Tomie (reteller and illus.). *The Legend of the Bluebonnet: An Old Tale of Texas.* (P–I)

Esbensen, Barbara Juster (reteller). *Ladder to the Sky: How the Gift of Healing Came to the Ojibway Nation.* Illus. Helen K. Davie. (P–I).

Goble, Paul. *Story Boy.* Retold and illus. Paul Goble. (P–I)

———. *Her Seven Brothers.* (P–I)

———. *Iktomi and the Boulder: A Plains indian Story.* (P–I)

Lattimore, Deborah Nourse (adapter-illustrator). *Why There Is No Arguing in Heaven; A Mayan Myth.* (P–I)

Oughton, Jerrie. *How the Stars Fell into the Sky: A Navajo Tale.* Illus. Lisa Desimini. (P–I)

Troughton, Joanna. *How Rabbit Stole the Fire: A North American Indian Folktale.* Retold and illus. Joanna Troughton. (P–I)

———. *How the Birds Changed Their Feathers: A South American Indian Folktale.* Retold and illus. Joanna Troughton. (P–I)

Iliad and *Odyssey*. Some classic stories are listed in Figure 5-11.

Epics are sometimes written in verse and consist of a cycle of tales that center around a legendary hero. Other hero tales that are not technically epics are often referred to as legends. The legendary heroes may be real or imaginary people; they may have some basis in fact, but they are largely embroidered with fancy. It is difficult to tell where fact stops and imagination takes over because the stories come to us by way of all folklore—word of mouth. What may have started as a report of what nearly happened soon became an account of what *did* happen; many storytellers elaborated reports of a hero's exploits until the stories became full-blown legends. The result is an intricate interweaving of fact and fiction, with a grain of truth at the core.

Each country has its folk heroes who exemplify the character traits its people value. A peculiarly American form, *tall tales* are a combination of history, myth, and fact. Davy Crockett, Johnny Appleseed, and Daniel Boone were real people, but their stories have made them larger than life. They accomplished feats no mortal would dare. Mythic men, such as John Henry, Pecos Bill, and Mike Fink, vivify the Yankee work ethic, the brawn and muscle required to develop America. These folk heroes were created by people who needed idols and symbols of strength as they built a new country. Thus their heroes are the mightiest, strongest, most daring lumberjacks, railroad men, coal miners, riverboat drivers, and steelworkers possible.

Although tall tales gave early settlers symbols of strength, they also served another need, offsetting the harsh realities of an untamed land. The exaggerated humor and blatant lies in tall tales added zest to and lightened a life of hard labor.

Children love the exaggerated humor and lies that mark the tall tales. They laugh when Paul Bunyan's loggers tie bacon to their feet and skate across the huge griddle to grease it. The thought of Slewfoot Sue bouncing skyward every time her bustle hits the ground produces giggles. And when Pecos Bill falls out of the covered wagon, children can picture the abandoned infant scrambling toward the coyote mother who eventually raises him with the rest of the coyote pack. Paul Bunyan's folks could not rock his cradle fast enough so they put it in the ocean; the waves still pound because of the strength of Paul's kicking. Because the hero in tall tales is all-powerful, readers know that he will overcome any problem. The suspense is created, then, in *how* the problem will be solved.

There are very few single editions of tall tales, although more are available each year. These are listed in Figure 5-11.

Figure 5-11

Hero Tales and Epics

Gretchen, Sylvia (adapter). *Hero of the Land of Snow.* Illus. Julia Witwear. (I)

Hodges, Margaret (reteller). *The Kitchen Knight: A Tale of King Arthur.* Illus. Trina Schart Hyman. (P–I)

———. *St. George and the Dragon.* Illus Trina Schart Hyman. (P–I)

Jaffrey, Madhur (adapter). *Seasons of Splendour: Tales, Myths, and Legends of India.* Illus. Michael Foreman. (A)

Malory, Sir Thomas. *Le Morte d'Arthur.* (A)

McKinley, Robin (adapter). *The Outlaws of Sherwood.* (A)

Pyle, Howard. *The Merry Adventures of Robin Hood of Great Renown in Nottinghamshire.* Illus. author. (A)

———. *The Story of King Arthur and His Knights.* Illus. author. (A)

Sutcliff, Rosemary. *The Light Beyond the Forest.* (I–A)

———. *The Road to Camlann.* Illus. Shirley Felts. (I–A)

———. *The Sword and the Circle: King Arthur and the Knights of the Round Table.* (I–A)

American Tall Tales

Arnold, Caroline. *The Terrible Hodag.* (P–I)

Blair, Walter. *Tall Tale America: A Legendary History of Our Humorous Heroes.* Illus. Glen Rounds. (I)

Dewey, Ariane. *Gib Morgan, Oilman.* (P–I)

———. *Pecos Bill.* (P–I)

Gleiter, J. *Paul Bunyan and Babe the Blue Ox.* (I)

Kellogg, Steven. *Paul Bunyan, A Tall Tale.* (P–I)

Rounds, Glen. *The Morning the Sun Refused to Rise: An Original Paul Bunyan Tale.* (I)

Stoutenberg, Adrien. *American Tall Tales.* Illus. Richard M. Powers. (I)

———. *American Tall-Tale Animals.* (I)

Figure 5-12

American Folklore

Bang, Molly. *Wiley and the Hairy Man.* (P–I)

Durell, Ann (compiler). *The Diane Goode Book of American Folk Tales & Songs.* Illus. Diane Goode. (P–I–A)

Forest, Heather. *The Baker's Dozen: A Colonial American Tale.* Illus. Susan Gaber. (I)

Hamilton, Virginia. *The People Could Fly: American Black Folk Tales.* Illus. Leo and Diane Dillon. (I–A)

———. *In the Beginning.* Illus. Leo and Diane Dillon. (I–A)

Harris, Joel Chandler. *Jump! The Adventures of Brer Rabbit.* Adapted by Van Dyke Parks and Malcolm Jones. Illus. Barry Moser. (I)

———. *Jump Again! More Adventures of Brer Rabbit.* Adapted by Van Dyke Parks. Illus. Barry Moser. (I)

———. *Jump On Over!: The Adventures of Brer Rabbit and His Family.* Adapted by Van Dyke Parks. Illus. Barry Moser. (I)

Lester, Julius (reteller). *The Tales of Uncle Remus: The Adventures of Brer Rabbit.* Illus. Jerry Pinkney. (P–I)

———. *More Tales of Uncle Remus: Further Adventures of Brer Rabbit, His Friends, Enemies, and Others.* Illus. Jerry Pinkney. (P–I)

———. *Further Tales of Uncle Remus: The Misadventures of Brer Rabbit, Brer Fox, Brer Wolf, the Doodang, and Other Creatures.* Illus. Jerry Pinkney. (P–I)

San Souci, Robert D. (adapter). *The Talking Eggs: A Folktale from the American South.* Illus. Jerry Pinkney. (Creole) (P–I)

Schwartz, Alvin (compiler). *I Saw You in the Bathub and Other Folk Rhymes.* Illus. Syd Hoff. (P–I–A)

Alvin Schwartz has contributed a wealth of material that enriches a study of American folklore. Through careful research in language, superstition, and folk history, he has produced several books that delve into America's legendary past. *Whop-*

pers: Tall Tales and Other Lies (I), *Flapdoodle: Pure Nonsense from American Folklore* (I), and *Witcracks: Jokes and Jests from American Folklore* (I) are valuable resources for study and tremendously entertaining books to read for pure enjoyment. Other books of American lore are listed in Figure 5-12.

Folksongs and Work Songs

Ballads and folksongs inform and persuade; they foster agreement and unify people through song. Still popular today, folksongs are found in many places. Work songs, often developed as a diversion from boring work, capture the rhythm and spirit of the labor in which their creators were engaged. The songs sing of the values and the lifestyles of the people who laid the railroads, dug the tunnels and canals, sailed the ships, and toted the bales.

B. A. Botkin observed in *A Treasury of American Folklore* that singing folksongs is a functional activity; we sing them for self-gratification, for power, or for freedom (1944, pp. 818–819). We also sing them to lighten our labor, to fill our leisure time, to record events, and to voice praise or protest. Songs are used to teach young children to count or to say the ABCs and, most often, to soothe them and sing them to sleep.

Civil rights marchers led by Martin Luther King, Jr., singing "We Shall Overcome," were united in spirit and intent by the song's moving words. The power of the song and its singers focused our nation's attention on the march toward equality. Songs are powerful persuasion in both shaping and preserving our cultural heritage.

Excellent single editions of nursery songs, folksongs, and patriotic songs are available. The best include guitar or piano musical scores, historical notes, and good illustrations coordinated with the text. Robert Quackenbush, Aliki, Glen Rounds, John Langstaff, and Peter Spier offer many excellent sources.

Jane Hart compiled 125 songs in a splendid book, *Singing Bee! A Collection of Favorite Children's Songs* (P–I), beautifully illustrated by Anita Lobel. This very attractive book includes nursery rhymes, lullabies, and finger plays and cumulative, holiday, and activity songs with piano accompaniments and guitar chords for each selection. Lobel appropriately used historical settings and eighteenth-century garb for many of the traditional songs; she also expressed her interest in the theater by creating stage production settings around many songs. Both single editions and collections are listed

Meg, yergoo, yergunnas;

Yerec, chors, choranas;

Hinc, vets, vernas;

Yoten, ooten, ooranas;

Innin, dacenin, jam yertas;

Dacen yergoo, hats geran.

One, two, grow tall.

Three, four, round as a ball.

Five, six, reach up high.

Seven, eight, don't scratch the sky.

Nine, ten, time for mass.

Eleven, twelve, lunch at last.

—*counting rhyme*

Children around the world play similar ball-bouncing games and say the same kind of jump rope rhymes. Jane Yolen's collection, **Street Rhymes Around the World,** shows the rhymes in the native language as well as English. She invited artists from each country to interpret the rhymes visually.

in Figure 5-13. Favorite songs, individually presented or collected and handsomely illustrated, enrich the store of materials we can draw on for music and early reading programs as well as for studies of folk heritage.

The Bible as a Form of Literature

One of the earliest forms of Western cultural literature is found in the Bible, and there are many reasons that forms of this traditional heritage should

---

**Figure
5-13**

Folksongs

Aliki. *Hush Little Baby: A Folk Lullaby.* Illus. Aliki. (P)

Axelrod, Alan (compiler). *Songs of the Wild West.* Arrangements Dan Fox. (I–A)

Bryan, Ashley (selector-illustrator). *All Night, All Day: A Child's First Book of African-American Spirituals.* (P–I)

Durell, Ann (compiler). *The Diane Goode Book of American Folk Tales and Songs.* Illus. Diane Goode. (P–I–A)

Glazer, Tom. *Eye Winker, Tom Tinker, Chin Chopper: Fifty Musical Fingerplays.* Illus. Ronald Himler. (P–I)

Krull, Kathleen. *Gonna Sing My Head Off! American Folk Songs for Children.* Illus. Allen Garns. (I)

Langstaff, John (selector-editor). *Climbing Jacob's Ladder: Heroes of the Bible in African-American Spirituals.* Illus. Ashley Bryan. Music arranged by John Andrew Ross. (P–I)

———. *What a Morning! The Christmas Story in Black Spirituals.* Selected and edited by John Langstaff. Illus. Ashley Bryan. (P–I)

Larrick, Nancy (compiler). *The Wheels of the Bus Go Round and Round: School Bus Songs and Chants.* Illus. Gene Holtan. (P–I)

Plotz, Helen (compiler). *As I Walked Out One Evening: A Book of Ballads.* (A)

Sharon, Lois, and Bram Sharon (compilers). *Elephant Jam.* Rev. ed. Illus. David Shaw. (P–I)

Staines, Bill (author-composer). *All God's Critters Got a Place in the Choir.* Illus. Margot Zemach. (P–I)

Watson, Clyde, and Wendy Watson. *Father Fox's Feast of Songs.* Illus. Wendy Watson. (P)

Yolen, Jane. *Jane Yolen's Song of Summer.* Illus. Cyd Moore. (P–I)

———. *The Lullaby Songbook.* Arrangements Adam Stemple. illus. Charles Mikolaycak. (P)

———. *Street Rhymes Around the World.* Illus. native artists. (P–I)

---

be a part of literary study. The universality of this body of literature is evident because the Bible is still the best-selling book in the world, printed in every language, known by all peoples, basic to all other literature, and a common denominator around the world.

Teachers and librarians distinguish between the use of biblical stories to teach a religious doctrine and the use of them to explore their literary content. In secular education, the literary content is stressed. From the obvious symbolism of the parables to the basic forms underlying all other literature, there is an abundant literary content to be explored. Northrop Frye contends,

> If we don't know the Bible and the central stories of Greek and Roman literature, we can still read books and see plays, but our knowledge of literature can't grow, just as our knowledge of mathematics can't grow if we don't learn the multiplication table. (1964, p. 70)

One approach to biblical stories amenable to public schools and libraries is to examine how a contemporary author retells a Bible story. How does the author interpret the old tale? How is the character presented? How is the period portrayed? Or how is the theme realized? Since the source of the tale is the Bible itself, early versions of each story are available for comparisons.

Some sections of the Bible reflect the oral tradition more dramatically than others: The use of lyric poetic forms, repetition, and the measured metric schemes were aids to memory before the stories were set down in writing. Although the verses·may not rhyme in English, they probably did in Hebrew, and although the metric scheme may vary in English, it was measured and pronounced in Hebrew as a way of remembering.

From a literary perspective, the Bible contains myths, legends, fables, parables, short stories, essays, lyrics, epistles, sermons, orations, proverbs,

Figure
5-14

Bible Stories

Adler, David. *A Picture Book of Hanukkah.* Illus. Linda Heller. (P–I)

Bach, Alice, and J. Cheryl Exum. *Miriam's Well: Stories About Women in the Bible.* Illus. Leo and Diane Dillon. (I–A)

———. *Moses' Ark: Stories from the Bible.* Illus. Leo and Diane Dillon. (I–A)

Bible. *The Nativity.* Illus. Julie Vivas. (P–I)

Bierhorst, John (trans). *Spirit Child: A Story of the Nativity.* Illus. Barbara Cooney. (P–I)

Cohen, Barbara. *The Donkey's Story: A Bible Story.* Illus. Susan Jeanne Cohen. (P–I)

Cole, Joanna. *A Gift from Saint Francis: The First Creche.* Illus. Michele Lemieux. (P–I)

de Paola, Tomie. *Francis: The Poor Man of Assisi.* (P–I)

———. *The Lady of Guadalupe.* (P–I)

Fisher, Leonard Everett. *The Seven Days of Creation.* (I)

———. *The Wailing Wall.* (I)

Hodges, Margaret. *Brother Francis and the Friendly Beasts.* Illus. Ted Lewin. (P–I)

———. *St. Jerome and the Lion.* Illus. Barry Moser. (P–I)

Hutton, Warwick (adapter). *Adam and Eve: The Bible Story.* (P–I)

Jonas, Ann. *Aardvarks, Disembark!* (P)

Kuskin, Karla. *Jerusalem, Shining Still.* Illus. David Frampton. (I)

Laird, Elizabeth. *The Road to Bethlehem: An Ethiopian Nativity.* (I)

Muhlberger, Richard (commentator). *The Christmas Story: Told through Paintings.* Illus. reproductions. (P–I–A)

Rice, Edward. *The Five Great Religions.* Photos by author. (I–A)

Segal, Lore (adapter). *The Book of Adam to Moses.* Illus. Leonard Baskin. (I–A)

Winthrop, Elizabeth (adapter). *A Child is Born: The Christmas Story.* Illus. Charles Mikolaycak. (P–I)

Noah Stories

Baynes, Pauline. *Noah and the Ark.* (P–I)

Hogrogian, Nonny. *Noah's Ark.* (P–I)

Ludwig, Warren. *Old Noah's Elephants.* (P–I)

Olson, Arielle. *Noah's Cats and the Devil's Fire.* Illus. Barry Moser. (P–I)

Ray, Jane. *Noah's Ark: Words from the Book of Genesis.* (P–I)

Singer, Isaac Bashevis. *Why Noah Chose the Dove.* Illus. Eric Carle. (P–I)

Spier, Peter. *Noah's Ark.* (P–I)

Stevens, Janet. *How the Manx Cat Lost Its Tail.* Retold and illus. Janet Stevens. (P–I)

---

history, biography, prophecy, and drama. The stories of Samson have even been called "tall tales." Teachers and librarians have a wealth of material to draw from. Books based on Bible stories are listed in Figure 5-14.

FOLKLORE IN THE CLASSROOM

Some children have at least a general acquaintance with the most familiar Mother Goose rhymes and folktales. Unfortunately, many have never even heard "Humpty Dumpty" or "Baa Baa Black Sheep."

Others may know nothing about Little Red Riding Hood or Goldilocks, Ananse or Raven the Trickster. Because traditional literature is a foundation for future literary understanding, it is of utmost importance to spend time reading from the vast body of folklore if we are to give children some of the necessary tools to build their literary knowledge.

Children who do not know the significance of the wolf in folklore will not understand the meaning of the wolf-shaped bush in Anthony Browne's *Piggybook* (P–I). They will not know the reason for their classmates' "uh-ohs" when they see that the babysitter in Mary Rayner's *Mr. and Mrs. Pig's*

Jan Brett uses her art to enrich the setting and ethnic background of the characters in *Goldilocks and the Three Bears*. She uses borders to convey additional information and as a frame for the art. (New York: Dodd, Mead, 1987.)

Evening Out (P) is a wolf. And they will not understand the humor of folktale parodies, like Jon Scieszka's *The True Story of the 3 Little Pigs* (P–I), if they do not know the original story. Modern references to folklore are countless, and we shortchange children if we deny them the background information necessary to understand the contemporary books. Phrases from Aesop's fables are common; children need to know the meaning of "sour grapes" and "slow and steady wins the race." Mythology, too, has given us many key phrases that children should know, such as Pandora's box or the Midas touch.

There are many ways to teach children about folklore, some of which are presented as Teaching Ideas in this chapter. The most important consideration is to read to them and with them, to immerse them in traditional stories until they begin to recognize similarities, see patterns, and make predictions. Children who have heard many folktales will tell you that they begin "once upon a time" and end "they lived happily ever after," the good people win, and the youngest son gets the princess. This response shows that children recognize the motifs, themes, and story conventions that are so plentiful in folklore. Awareness of these patterns develops through repeated experience and becomes the foundation for building a literary education.

TEACHING IDEA 5-6

Identify Folklore Style

Many original contemporary stories are written in a style based on folklore; they contain folklore elements, themes, conventions, and motifs. Learn to recognize folklore elements, patterns, motifs, symbols, devices, and allusions. Encourage students to work in book talk groups.

1. Read several stories in folklore style.

2. Discuss folklore elements—what suggests folklore?

3. Have students work in groups to discover folklore elements.

4. Compare the devices, allusions, and patterns you find in the stories.

5. Make a list of commonly used folklore elements.

Suggested Books

Arnold, Caroline. *The Terrible Hodag*. Illus. Lambert Davis.

Croll, Carolyn (adapter-illustrator). *The Three Brothers*.

French, Fiona (author-illustrator). *Anancy and Mr. Dry-Bone*.

Grant, Joan. *The Monster That Grew Small*. Illus. Jill Karla Schwarz.

Kimmel, Eric. *Hershel and the Hanukkah Goblins*. Illus. Trina Schart Hyman.

Mayer, Marianna. *The Prince and the Princess: A Bohemian Fairy Tale*. Illus. Jacqueline Rogers.

Morris, Winifred. *The Magic Leaf*. Illus. Ju-Hong Chen.

Wisniewski, David. *The Warrior and the Wise Man*.

Good teachers give children opportunities to discover recurring patterns; they do not *tell* them what to recognize. Understanding children's sense of story and knowing labels for conventions informs good teaching; but for the child being taught, it can in no way substitute for having the literary experience itself. By introducing folklore with its abundance of repeatable patterns, teachers can

A group of second-grade students compared different versions of the "Three Little Pigs." The teacher, Sandy Stoessel, modeled the process by discussing a version and filling in the comparison categories with the total group. Students then worked in small groups to compare other versions independently. (John Philip Sousa Elementary School, Port Washington, NY)

facilitate students' discovery of archetypes; as the children absorb them, the patterns become the structural framework for viewing all literature as one story.

In addition, children who have been exposed to the folklore of many cultures begin to see recurring themes in all of them. The values, hopes, fears, and beliefs of each culture are evidenced in its folklore; by knowing its stories we can begin to build a bridge of understanding about that society. Thus folklore provides a unique opportunity to increase multicultural understanding.

Working with folktale variants, such as those listed in Figure 5-6, offers children the opportunity to make interesting comparisons, looking across tales at variations in characters, themes, motifs, language, structure, and other elements of the tales. These comparisons lead to discussions of similarities and differences among tales in which children quite naturally discuss the elements of literature in a meaningful way.

Folklore also offers unique opportunities for language development. The oral origins of folklore make it a wonderful resource for dramatic oral readings and planned or spontaneous dramatic performances. Children who read and hear a lot of folklore often spontaneously use the patterns and conventions of folklore in their own writing, borrowing folkloric frameworks for their own personal narratives or exploring the conventions of the genre through writing new versions of old favorites.

Children from nursery through advanced grades can benefit from reading and studying folklore, building knowledge about literature as they enjoy a riveting story.

SUMMARY

The folklore that we read today began as stories and poems told across the generations as people sought to explain natural phenomena and transmit cultural values. Folklore helps us understand ourselves and those from other cultures.

There are many types of folklore, each with its own characteristics. Rhythmic and rhymed, Mother Goose and nursery rhymes appeal to young children. Folktales, which include fairy tales, talking beast tales, noodlehead tales, and cumulative tales, have universal themes and motifs and appear in different guises in cultures around the world. Fables contain explicit moral statements to guide behavior. Myths from all cultures explain the origins of the world and natural phenomena; hero tales reveal cultural beliefs and values. Folklore also includes folksongs, which reveal the values and circumstances of those who first sang them, and the Bible.

Teachers of all grades recognize that folklore is a valuable resource for developing language, learning about literature, and learning about other cultures. As it did in the distant past, folklore both educates and entertains today.

6

Fantasy and Science Fiction

VISION

I flew a star ship deep in space
To a place where I could see
A world of alien beings
All in perfect harmony.
It's a beautiful picture in my head
As I begin to feel
That if I can learn to have great
  dreams
I can learn to make them real.

                              Brod Bagert

FANTASY

Fantasy and science fiction are imaginative narratives that explore alternate realities. Science fiction explores scientific possibilities. Fantasy suspends scientific explanations and natural laws; it contains some element not found in the natural world. Some of it is pure lighthearted fun; some considers a deeper reality and eternal truth, probing inner journeys and truths and following the path of the hero. Fantasy and science fiction differ from folklore in that they are written by an individual author, rather than handed down by word of mouth.

Great writers of fantasy—J.R.R. Tolkien, C.S. Lewis, Eleanor Cameron, and Elizabeth Cook—use different words to describe qualities unique to fantasy. Tolkien says that *faerie* refers to a quality of feeling called *heart's desire,* a yearning for a romantic visionary world. C.S. Lewis describes feelings of *joy* evoked as an aesthetic response to fantasy. Eleanor Cameron characterizes her response while reading about the death of King Arthur as an unutterable poignancy, a sadness mixed with longing—yet a sense of exaltation, of having touched something very fine and powerful and strength giving. And Elizabeth Cook expresses that undefinable mysterious quality of wonder we have while reading fantasy with the word *numinous*—an unseen and majestic presence that inspires both dread and fascination.

The Role of Fantasy in Children's Lives

Fantasy opens doors to worlds of imagination not found in the real world. It enriches and illuminates children's lives because the stories deal with the great complexities of existence: the relativity of size, time, and space; good versus evil; the strength and courage of the individual; and self-integrity. Fantasy treats problems of the universe with a high seriousness. Yet fantasy can also deal lightheartedly with capricious supernatural events, such as cars that fly through the air, as in **Chitty Chitty Bang Bang** (I) by Ian Fleming, or stuffed animals that talk, as in Margery Williams's **The Velveteen Rabbit** (P–I).

For many children fantasy is the first literature they love. Children in preschool and primary grades love books with animal characters who act like human beings. William Steig's **Sylvester and the Magic Pebble** (P), Russell Hoban's **Bread and Jam for Frances** (P), Rosemary Wells's **Max's First Word** (N), and many other beloved books for young children are fantasies—in this case books about characters who could not really exist. Children have no trouble understanding what those stories are about and the questions that they raise about real life.

As they mature, children experience many kinds of literature. Sometimes during the elementary school years some children become enraptured with realistic fiction, giving themselves completely over to this genre. Others become avid consumers of nonfiction and biography. Some continue to enjoy fantasy, moving from picture books to more fully developed narratives. Advanced-grade readers are often sharply divided in their preferences; those who enjoy fantasy and science fiction are avid readers of it while those who prefer realism do not ever voluntarily read fantasy. As one reader commented, "I don't like fantasies and science fictions [sic]." For some these genre preferences may last the rest of their lives; others will become more eclectic with development and will again enjoy fantasy.

Why do some readers prefer this unrealistic and sometimes disturbing literature over any other genre? Susan Cooper, noted fantasy writer, speaks of fantasy as "the metaphor through which we discover ourselves" (1981, p. 16). She argues that rather than escaping out of our own selves and into a fantasy world, fantasy draws readers into themselves, pushing them to consider who they are, and what the world is. Serious fantasy "is probably the most complex form of fiction [readers] will ever find" (p. 16), and demands a great deal from its readers.

Children don't expect fantasy to help them solve their daily social problems, but rather read and enjoy fantasy because it reaches for their souls (May, 1984). Lloyd Alexander, himself a much honored writer of fantasy, talks about the power of fantasy to encourage social change. He says, "The let's pretend of literature can have both an immediate and long-range impact upon our lives . . . [it] influences our view of society and raises questions about it" (1970, p. 96). Fantasy literature can be a vital force for moral and spiritual growth.

The Roots of Fantasy

This potential for moral and spiritual growth is one manifestation of the links between fantasy and folklore. Folklore encodes a culture's morality; the roots of fantasy grow directly from folklore. Modern fantasy builds on and derives its strength from traditions established in ancient myths and legends. Just as our ancestors created a myth to describe how Apollo drove a chariot of fire across the sky to explain the sun's movement, so modern fantasy writers spin imaginative tales to explain things we do not fully understand; they create fantasies to probe the dimensions of areas we do not know.

Just as the heroes of ancient legend confront great danger and rise to impossible challenges, modern fantasy heroes take on a larger than life nature as they are depicted in stories. For example, Ged's inner and outer struggles with the evil shadow that would possess his soul—in Ursula Le Guin's **The Wizard of Earthsea** (A)—is both physical and emotional, as was King Arthur's legendary quest.

Modern fantasy writers use structural patterns found in the oral tradition. Characters may go on a quest that turns out differently from what they expected; they rise to the occasion and return home a different person. Taran in Lloyd Alexander's **Taran Wanderer** (I–A) sets out to discover his identity. In **The High King** (I–A), the last book in the series, he learns that greatness is not a matter of birth but of wisdom, humility, and responsible choice.

> ### Figure 6-1
>
> ## Checklist for Evaluating Fantasy
>
> - ❏ Is the fantasy world believable within the context of story?
> - ❏ Is there an original and imaginative concept?
> - ❏ Are the fantasy elements logically integrated?
> - ❏ How does the magic work? Is it consistent?
> - ❏ Can you visualize a well-established setting?
> - ❏ Are characters true to themselves?
> - ❏ Does their motivation make sense in context?

> ## 𝒯EACHING IDEA 6-1
>
> ### Believable Settings
>
> Good fantasy writers try to establish fully believable settings carefully. Since the fantasy world is created in the minds of readers and writers, it is spelled out in vivid detail. There are some scenes so vivid you can smell them.
>
> Read outstanding fantasies to savor the descriptive language used to portray/establish the settings. If you are working with children, read scenes to them and ask them to create dioramas, paintings, or three-dimensional visual scenes of the ones described. Discuss the examples in a writing workshop to show the effect of writing on the reader's response.
>
> Suggested books and pages that contain vivid scenes:
>
> Grahame, Kenneth. *Wind in the Willows*, page 9: "The Mole had been working. . . ."
>
> Jansson, Tove. *Tales from Moominvalley*, page 11: "The brook was a good one. . . ."
>
> White, E. B. *Charlotte's Web*, page 13: "The barn was very large. It was very old."

There is a significant difference, however, between stories that came to us through oral tradition and ones we now call fantasy. Ancient tales were shaped and honed through cultural belief and the voice of the storyteller. Modern fantasy is shaped through the author's artistic vision and stylistic choices. Egoff (1981) says this is the difference between a public dream (folklore) and a private and metaphorical vision (modern fantasy). For example, the appearance of the Holy Grail in *Le Morte d'Arthur* was not taken as fantasy in the fifteenth century; it was a public dream—meant to be believed. Modern fantasy writer Susan Cooper uses the Holy Grail as a fantasy device in *Over Sea, Under Stone* (I) to shape her own private vision. We judge the quality of a writer's private vision by how thoroughly it convinces us of its reality: how long it haunts our memory and how deeply it moves us to new insights.

Criteria for Selecting Fantasy

As with all quality narrative literature, good fantasy tells an interesting story, has well-developed characters, an engaging plot, and an identifiable theme. Authors manipulate these elements, particularly setting, character, and time, to create a fantasy world. If the fantasy writer is successful, readers willingly suspend disbelief. Noted fantasy writer Eleanor Cameron points out the task that fantasy writers face. Figure 6-1 lists criteria for evaluating fantasy.

With fantasy I believe that the author is required in the very beginning to establish a premise, an inner logic for his story, and to draw boundary lines outside which his fantasy may not wander. Without ever having to think about it, the reader must feel that the author is working consistently within a frame of reference. (Cameron, 1983, pp. 23–24).

Believability of Setting

Settings are believable, no matter how fantastic they are, when an author provides rich details that enable a reader to envision the setting. Some authors provide detailed maps of fantasy lands, complete with place names that are consistent with the fantasy. Others gradually lead readers from the real world into the fantasy world through some device, such as a magic door or a magic object. Look for fantasies that contain (1) detailed descriptions of the setting that (2) result in believability.

Believability of Plot

What happens in a fantasy must be logically consistent within the story world. If characters move through time, they do so for a reason; they may walk through a door, press a magic button, or visit a particular place. If the fantastic operates in the real world, then there must be consistency in how real people are affected by the fantastic events. Look for stories with (1) events that are logical and consistent within the story world; and (2) story elements that appeal to the imagination yet remain within the realm of the plot.

Believability of Character

Excellent fantasy contains characters that are multidimensional personalities who behave consistently, respond to events in a believable fashion, and grow and change across the course of the story. If a character who lives in the realistic story world enters a fantasy situation, the character does not magically change, but remains consistent across both worlds. Even if characters are superheroes within a story, they are so carefully delineated that readers accept their otherworldly powers. Look for characters (1) that are well developed, and (2) with behavior that is consistent and logical within the story world.

Style

How a writer chooses to tell a story—structure, syntax, word choice—makes the difference between a mediocre book and an excellent one. In fantasy, style works to establish the setting; rich images and vivid figurative language help readers envision the created world. Style makes the characters and the plot believable; authentic dialogue and clear structure help readers build characterizations and follow the action. Look for books that (1) contain vivid, interesting images and figurative language, and (2) are clearly structured.

Theme

Many fantasies consider ideas of great import: the struggle between good and evil, what it means to be human, the consequences of pride. These themes are woven throughout the story, logically radiating from character and plot. Other fantasies are more lighthearted, using humor to reveal the absurd in the human condition. Look for themes (1) that are meaningful for readers, and (2) arise naturally from the characters and the plot.

A Close Look at *Tuck Everlasting*

Natalie Babbitt's **Tuck Everlasting** (I) is an outstanding example of a novel for intermediate-grade students that illustrates the criteria for fantasy quite well.

Synopsis. Ten-year-old Winnie Foster struggles for independence against an overprotective mother and grandmother who devote full time to supervising her. Winnie lives beside a small forest and one day as an act of courage ventures into its woods. There she comes across a boy, Jesse Tuck, uncovering a fountain of water flowing from the ground, and although he takes a drink, he does not allow Winnie to drink from the spring. Jesse's family kidnaps Winnie to explain to her how they discovered the magical powers of the spring: Water from the fountain bestows eternal life on those who drink it. The Tucks also explain to Winnie the mixed blessing of everlasting life and leave her to make the choice about whether or not she will drink from the fountain.

Setting. The setting is credible. Natalie Babbitt uses a prologue to create a misty surreal period of time when anything might happen, when people do things they might not normally do:

> The first week of August hangs at the very top of summer, the top of the live-long year, like the highest seat of a Ferris wheel when it pauses in its turning. The weeks that come before are only a climb from balmy spring, and those that follow a drop to the chill of autumn, but the first week of August is motionless, and hot. It is curiously silent, too, with blank white dawns and glaring noons, and sunsets smeared with too much color. Often at night there is lightning, but it quivers all alone. There is no thunder, no relieving rain. These are strange and breathless days, the dog days, when people are led to do things they are sure to be sorry for after.
>
> One day at that time, not so very long ago, three things happened and at first there appeared to be no connection between them.

Babbitt creates suspense by suggesting that this is an eerie time and foreshadowing things to come. Phrases such as "one day at that time, not so very long ago" establish a story set in the not-so-distant past—yet in times gone by, a distancing that gives the illusion of a dream and the feeling of once upon a time. The amount of time covered by the entire story is brief, perhaps a week, but that week will never be forgotten.

Characterization. Winnie is believable and changes in believable ways in the process of the narrative; like a real girl she affects and is affected by the events of the story. Babbitt presents Winnie as a realistic character, one that a reader can believe in. She is troubled and upset with her parents—a realistic picture of a young person straining for independence. It is this very situation that helps a reader believe in the magic that is introduced into Winnie's life once she meets the Tucks. Winnie is open to something new and different; she's fed up with being sheltered. We watch her gathering her courage to take a forbidden walk in the woods. As Winnie sits on the bristly grass just *inside* the fence she speaks to a large toad squatting across the road.

> "I will, though. You'll see. Maybe even first thing tomorrow, while everyone's still asleep."

Babbitt also shows why Winnie is exasperated with too much adult supervision in her life:

PROFILE

*I*N ***Tuck Everlasting,*** Natalie Babbitt asks if the dream of an eternal life is really a blessing. For Tuck, who is explaining the cyclical nature of life to young Winnie Foster, there is no spoke on the wheel, for he has drunk from the spring granting everlasting life. Many of Natalie Babbitt's stories blur the line between fantasy and reality, leaving the reader to ponder the nature of truth.

Speaking about children and literature, Natalie Babbitt has said:

I have the greatest respect for the intelligence, sensitivity, and imagination of young people. They are the true and unfettered audience, and as such deserve the best efforts of everyone who writes for them. Nothing can be good enough, but we can try.

Natalie Babbitt grew up in Ohio. During her childhood, she spent many hours reading fairy tales and myths. She would often pretend she was a librarian, stamping her books and checking them in and out to herself. She also liked to draw and, since her mother was an amateur landscape and portrait artist, had access to lots of paints, paper, and pencils. She studied art at Laurel School in Cleveland and at Smith College. Soon after graduation, she married Samuel Fisher Babbitt, who later became president of Kirk-

Natalie Babbitt

land College and now serves as an administrator at Brown University. The Babbitts have three children—Christopher, Tom, and Lucy—all grown.

Natalie Babbitt collaborated on her first book with her husband, but then decided to write and illustrate on her own. In addition to the several books she has written, she has illustrated books of poems by Valerie Worth and the book jackets of her own novels. Told by a child interviewer how beautiful he thought the jacket illustration for *The Eyes of the Amaryllis,* she answered, "That's the nicest thing anyone ever said to me." Children's literature is enriched by Natalie Babbitt's work.

Natalie Babbitt's prologue in *Tuck Everlasting* foreshadows story events to come. Its language sounds like a legend and establishes the over-arching metaphor of a turning wheel to represent the cycle of life and revolving seasons.

Her grandmother: "Winifred! Don't sit on that dirty grass. You'll stain your boots and stockings."

And another, firmer voice—her mother's—added, "Come in now, Winnie. Right away. You'll get heat stroke out there on a day like this. And your lunch is ready."

Winnie explains to the toad:

"See? That's just what I mean. It's like that every minute. If I had a sister or a brother, there'd be someone else for them to watch. But, as it is, there's only me. I'm tired of being looked at all the time. I want to be by myself for a change." She leaned her forehead against the bars and after a short silence went on in a thoughtful tone. "I'm not exactly sure what I'd do, you know, but something interesting—something that's all mine. Something that would make some kind of difference in the world. It'd be nice to have a new name, to start with, one that's not all worn out from being called so much. And I might even decide to have a pet. Maybe a big old toad, like you, that I could keep in a nice cage with lots of grass, and. . . . Do you know they've hardly ever let me out of this yard all by myself? I'll never be able to do anything important if I stay in here like this. I expect I'd better run away. . . . You think I wouldn't dare, don't you? I will, though. You'll see. Maybe even first thing in the morning, while everyone's still asleep."

When Winnie does venture into the woods she—and the reader—is ready for adventure.

Babbitt creates such a believable character that when she reveals the element of make-believe—a sip of water from a spring that gives eternal life—we accept its truth because we have already accepted the character.

Winnie reacts to the magical water as a real person might react. As she learns about the life-giving powers of the spring water, she realizes her own immortality and blurts out, "I don't want to die."

"No," said Tuck calmly. "Not now. Your time's not now. But dying's part of the wheel, right there next to being born. You can't pick out the pieces you like and leave the rest. Being part of the whole thing, that's the blessing. But it's passing us by, us Tucks. Living's heavy work, but off to one side, the way *we* are, it's useless, too. It don't make sense. If I knowed how to climb back on the wheel, I'd do it in a minute. You can't have living without dying. So you can't call it living, what we got. We just *are,* we just *be,* like rocks beside the road."

Winnie may not fully understand the concept that Pa Tuck explains so vividly but she thinks about it again and again. She—and the reader—begins to understand the complex issues involved in everlasting life.

Plot. What happens in ***Tuck Everlasting*** is logical and consistent. Winnie is unhappy, meets the Tucks, and enters the fantasy world in which one sip of water from the spring brings eternal life. But the real world is still apparent as the Tucks worry about being found out and so move regularly around the country. The boys can't marry and have a happy family life because they don't age but their families do. And when Ma Tuck is put in jail, Winnie has to get her out, because if the authorities try to hang her, she won't die. The events in the story are all logically consistent with the magic—the results of drinking the spring water—and operate within the contraints of the real world.

Style. Babbitt's vivid language makes the setting, characters, and plot believable. Vivid images and figurative language, like that in the prologue just quoted, paint a picture of a place and time when magic might happen. Authentic dialogue builds characters that are plausible. And images, like Tuck's image of life as a wheel, help to build a powerful theme.

Theme. The main idea that ***Tuck Everlasting*** considers is eternal life. Like Winnie, we see the possibility of eternal life and ask ourselves, would we drink from the spring? We see the consequences that eternal life has had for the Tucks, the greed with which some pursued it, and the consequences for the toad when he is sprinkled with water from the spring. Readers, drawn into the fantasy along with Winnie, are pushed to consider life, death, and the consequences of immortality.

Babbitt's ***Tuck Everlasting*** combines beautiful language, well-developed characters, a logical and consistent plot, and a richly detailed setting. The result is a believable and emotionally satisfying fantasy.

Types of Fantasy

Fantasy can be arbitrarily divided into two major categories: high fantasy and low, or light, fantasy. High fantasy lies closely beside ancient folklore and contains archetypal themes. High fantasies are often literary folktales or quest stories. They may use devices such as a time slip, fully developed unreal world settings, or supernatural characters to create the fantasy. Low, or light, fantasy uses a film of unreality to disguise the real world. It may be as simple as talking animals or as complex as fully developed miniature worlds that reflect real life with a small twist. It is often marked by wordplay, humor, and wit.

The Literary Tale

Fantasy that bridges ancient and contemporary literature and bespeaks its ancestry most vividly is the *literary tale*—a story deliberately crafted by a writer who intentionally imitates the traditional qualities of ancient folklore. A writer of high fantasy, Mollie Hunter acknowledges her links with folklore, a "chain of communication through the centuries—

---

*T*EACHING IDEA 6-2

Everlasting Questions From Tuck

Powerful discussions arise from reading ***Tuck Everlasting.*** Book group discussion topics:

Would you want to live forever? What age would you choose to be?

If someone promised you everlasting life, would you do what they said to get it? What would you do?

Why does Winnie Foster confide to the toad?

How does the toad help Winnie make up her mind about drinking the spring water promising eternal life?

What does the man in the yellow suit represent?

How does the Tuck family feel about Winnie Foster?

Do you think Winnie made the right choice?

What would you say to Winnie if you could meet her?

Trina Schart Hyman portrays realistic details about the people, markets, and villages of the central-African country of Cameroon in *The Fortune-Tellers,* by Lloyd Alexander. (Literary tale)

the long unbroken line of folk memory stretching . . . from Megalithic times to the present day" (1976, p. 65).

Stories that have a haunting mythic quality and echo the sounds from storytellers' tongues of ages past are literary lore. Some of its most able practitioners are Hans Christian Andersen, Jane Yolen, Natalie Babbitt, and Isaac Bashevis Singer, as well as Mollie Hunter, Susan Cooper, and Rosemary Sutcliff. Jane Yolen's **The Dragon's Boy** (I–A) describes young Artos as he searches for wisdom.

In **A Stranger Came Ashore** (I), Mollie Hunter captures on the very first page a timeless moment reflecting this mythic quality:

It was a while ago, in the days when they used to tell stories about creatures called the Selkie Folk. A stranger came ashore to an island at that time—a man who gave his name as Finn Learson—and there was a mystery about him

which had to do with these selkie creatures. Or so some people say, anyway. . . . (1975, p. 1)

Figure 6-2 lists other outstanding examples of literary lore.

Quest Stories

Archetypal themes from folklore become vividly evident in *quest fantasies*. Here again is the misty outline of a story in which we search for the golden age or lose—and seek to regain—our identity. Victory in the battle between good and evil depends on finding the missing heir, recognizing a prince or princess in disguise, or achieving utopia under the rule of a king whose coming has been foretold.

Quest stories that are most memorable describe characters' outer and inner struggles and may involve Herculean journeys where overcoming obstacles vanquishes evil. Quests often become a search for an inner, rather than an outer, enemy. Inner strength is required as characters are put to a variety of tests that oftentimes seem endless and unconquerable. It is the indomitable goodness of character that prevails.

Weaving legends from Arthurian days into the fabric of modern life, Susan Cooper dramatizes the risks of not standing up for what is right and just. The multilayered reality of her series *The Dark Is Rising* (all I–A) epitomizes tales dealing with the interconnection between visible and sensed reality. Cooper bases her stories on English and Celtic myth, beginning with *Over Sea, Under Stone* and continuing with *The Dark Is Rising, Greenwitch, The Grey King,* and *Silver on the Tree.* Cooper's skillful manipulation of myth and reality is unparalleled.

Figure 6-2 contains the titles of some quest stories that exemplify the criteria for excellent fantasy.

*J*ANE YOLEN is a gifted, accomplished, wonderfully warm human being with endless energy. She is an editor, writer, poet, wife, mother, speaker, musician, cook, and collector of dragons. She writes fantasy *(Dragon's Blood),* poetry *(Weather Report),* picture books *(Owl Moon),* historical fiction *(The Devil's Arithmetic),* mysteries *(Piggins),* easy to read stories *(Commander Toad* series), music *(The Lullaby Songbook),* retells folklore *(The Girl Who Cried Flowers & Other Tales),* nonfiction *(Encounter),* and nursery rhymes *(Jane Yolen's Mother Goose Songbook).* She has written about 150 books and has edited many more. She has her own imprint, Jane Yolen Books, at Harcourt Brace! She's terrific!

Jane Yolen was born February 11, 1939, into a publishing family in New York City. Her father, Will Yolen, was a writer. Jane and her family lived in New York until she was thirteen, when they moved to Westport, Connecticut. She graduated from Smith College and worked in several different roles for publishers, learning the trade from the inside out. She married David W. Stemple in 1962, and they had three children: Heidi, Adam, and Jason.

Jane Yolen

Jane's autobiography, *A Letter from Phoenix Farm,* shows her daily routine of writing, editing, answering letters, and enjoying time with her family.

Jane says, "I come from a line of storytellers. My great-grandfather was the Reb, the storyteller in a small village in Finno-Russia, my father an author, my mother a mostly unpublished writer. From early childhood I have written. In fact, in first grade I was the heralded author of the class musical about talking vegetables. I played the chief carrot and our grand finale was a singing salad."

From *Something About the Author,* page 357.

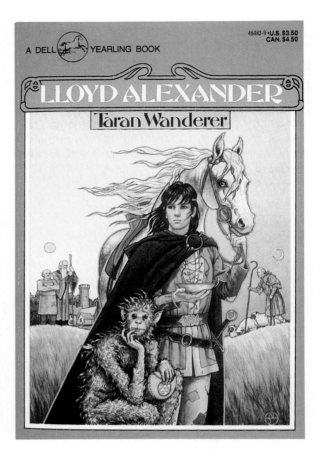

The young hero on a quest stands courageously at full center with his white horse. His serious expression denotes the gravity of his task. (*Taran Wanderer* by Lloyd Alexander; quest tale)

Time Slip

In some stories, time is the element that is carried beyond the world of everyday experience, as characters move freely between their current reality and other times and places. For many writers, the past and future are part of the present; by challenging our understanding of time as sequential, these authors are making a statement about the meaning of time itself. One such writer, Eleanor Cameron (1969), describes a globe of time in which the past, present, and future are perceived as a whole.

Authors of time fantasy invent a dazzling variety of devices to permit their characters to move in and out of conventional time. Madeleine L'Engle in **A Wrinkle in Time** (I–A) moves her characters from the here and now to other parts of the universe by "tessering" or "wrinkling time." The children in **The Lion, the Witch and the Wardrobe** (I) by C. S. Lewis enter the land of Narnia through a wardrobe door.

The time travelers in Anne Lindbergh's **Travel Far, Pay No Fare** (I) enter the world of stories with the help of a magic bookmark. Parsley's father is marrying Owen's mother, and they are not happy about this new family arrangement. When Parsley finds that she can enter the world of whatever story she happens to be reading by placing her bookmark in the book and beginning to read, she begins to visit various stories in an attempt to prevent the marriage. Owen gradually learns that Parsley really means it when she says her cats are borrowed from Beatrix Potter, Charles Perrault, and Beverly Cleary.

Several time-slip fantasies focus on a central character who is going through a difficult adjustment period; loneliness, alienation, and extraordinary sensitivity seem to be associated with time travel. Many new time fantasies have a carefully researched, vivid historical story embedded within the time slip. Novels such as David Wiseman's **Jeremy Visick** (I–A) and Jane Yolen's **The Devil's Arithmetic** (A) use the device to propel readers into the past where they confront the realities of history.

Young Hannah in **The Devil's Arithmetic** is feeling alienated from her family; she wants to be with her friends rather than at the family Seder.

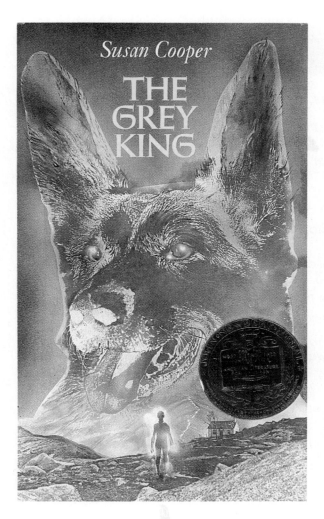

An image of darkness overwhelms the light and yet the young boy's strength is visible in the sheath of armor light that surrounds him. The blood in the wolf dog's eye denotes still greater evil. (*The Grey King* by Susan Cooper; time slip fantasy)

Feeling chagrined at being asked to perform such a childish task, she goes to the front door to open the door for Elijah and steps out of America in the late twentieth century and into Poland at the beginning of World War II. Her experiences there as Chaya, a young Jewish girl, vividly re-create the horror of the Holocaust. Figure 6-2 lists other excellent examples of time fantasy.

Animal Fantasies

Children attribute human thought, feeling, and language to animals dressed like people. Actually, young children may invest anything with life. Because books that extend and enrich such normal developmental tendencies strike a responsive chord in children, animal fantasy is a well-loved

---

𝒯EACHING IDEA 6-4

The Power of a Name

Some believe that to know something's true name is to possess power over it; to know a person's name is to hold that life in your keeping. In many high fantasies (quest novels) the secrecy of a name or the true identity of the hero is heavily guarded. Heroes do not give their true name without a great deal of consideration and trust. Read books in which names/naming are integral to the plot.

Suggested titles (all Advanced):

Alexander, Lloyd. *The Book of Three.*

———. *The Black Cauldron.*

———. *The Castle of Llyr.*

———. *Taran Wanderer.*

———. *The High King.*

L'Engle, Madeleine. *Wind in the Door.*

Le Guin, Ursula. *The Farthest Shore.*

———. *Tombs of Atuan.*

———. *Wizard of Earthsea.*

Sutcliff, Rosemary. *The Road to Camlann.*

Discussion questions for your book talk group:

If those who knew your name held power over you, to whom would you give your name?

What characteristics do these people (to whom you would give your name) share?

What kind of people would you keep your name from?

---

form. Like the folktale, it becomes part of children's literary experiences before they make clear distinctions between fact and fancy. This early pleasure in animal fantasy often continues as children mature into reading novels.

Some of the most memorable characters from children's literature are created in animal fantasy. Wilbur, Peter Rabbit, Babar, and Winnie the Pooh call to mind many of the modern classics of this genre. Some animal fantasies for older readers create an allegorical world in which the human scene is replayed to amuse and, often, to instruct. Authors of books like **Charlotte's Web** (I) by E.B. White, **Mrs. Frisby and the Rats of NIMH** (I) by Robert O'Brien, **Ratha's Creature** (A), by Clare Bell, and

To po_ minimum

Figure
6-2

Literary Tales, Quest Tales, and Time-Slip Fantasy

Literary Tales

Alexander, Lloyd. *The Fortune Tellers.*

Andersen, Hans Christian. *The Emperor's New Clothes.* (P)

———. *The Princess and the Pea.* (P)

———. *The Ugly Duckling.* (P)

Cooper, Susan. *The Selkie Girl.* (I)

Gág, Wanda. *Millions of Cats.* (P)

Hamilton, Virginia. *The Magical Adventures of Pretty Pearl.* (A)

Hunter, Mollie. *A Stranger Came Ashore.* (I)

Kipling, Rudyard. *The Just So Stories.* (P)

———. *The Elephant's Child.* (P)

Singer, Isaac Bashevis. *Zlateh the Goat.* (I)

Thurber, James. *Many Moons.* Illus. Louis Slobodkin. Also illus. Marc Simont. (P)

Wrightson, Patricia. *The Nargun and the Stars.* (A)

Yep, Laurence. *Dragon of the Lost Sea.* (A)

Yolen, Jane. *The Emperor and the Kite.* (I)

———. *The Girl Who Loved the Wind.* (I)

Quest Tales

Adams, Richard. *Watership Down.* (A)

Alexander, Lloyd. *The Black Cauldron.* (A)

———. *Book of Three.* (A)

———. *The Castle of Llyr.* (A)

———. *The High King.* (A)

———. *Taran Wanderer.* (A)

Le Guin, Ursula. *The Farthest Shore.* (A)

———. *The Tombs of Atuan.* (A)

———. *Wizard of Earthsea.* (A)

McKinley, Robin. *The Blue Sword.* (A)

———. *The Hero and the Crown.* (A)

Sutcliff, Rosemary. *The Sword and the Circle.* (A)

———. *The Light Beyond the Forest.* (A)

———. *The Road to Camlann.* (A)

Tolkien, J. R. R. *The Hobbit.* (A)

———. *The Lord of the Rings.* (A)

Time-Slip Fantasy

Bosse, Malcolm. *Cave Beyond Time.* (A)

Cooper, Susan. *The Dark Is Rising.* (A)

———. *Greenwitch.* (A)

———. *The Grey King.* (A)

———. *Over Sea, Under Stone.* (A)

———. *Silver on the Tree.* (A)

L'Engle, Madeleine. *A Swiftly Tilting Planet.* (I)

———. *A Wrinkle in Time.* (I)

Lunn, Janet. *The Root Cellar.* (I)

Ormondroyd, Edward. *Time at the Top.* (I)

Park, Ruth. *Playing Beatie Bow.* (I)

Paton Walsh, Jill. *Chance Child.* (A)

Pausacker, Jenny. *Fast Forward.* (I)

Pearce, Philippa. *Tom's Midnight Garden.* (I)

Watership Down (A) by Richard Adams use the vehicle of animal fantasy to comment on the human condition.

Dick King-Smith examines issues of freedom and tolerance in *Martin's Mice* (I). Martin, a farm cat, loves mice—as pets instead of dinner. After he becomes involved in protecting and feeding a brood of mice he begins to realize that having pets brings responsibility as well as pleasure. When he becomes a pet himself, he learns about freedom. And when he escapes from his owner and returns to the farm, he learns how to stand up for himself and take pride in being different. Figure 6-3 contains a list of other memorable animal fantasies.

Miniature Worlds

Every cultural group has its folkloric sprites, elves, trolls, hobbits, or leprechauns, which go unseen about houses and villages. Fantasies about toys or miniature beings highlight human emotions by displaying them in action on a minuscule scale. From

"Hello, Drusilla," said Martin. "I hear you're expecting another happy event. Many congratulations! I'm sure you'll be glad when it's all over—it must be so tiring for you. I don't know if you'd like it, but I've brought you a nice fresh juicy blackberry."

Drusilla squeezed herself out of the hole.

"Oh, Martin!" she said. "There never was a cat like you!"

Martin the cat is a loveable, fuzzy creature who plays with mice. The artist shows the whimsy in the soft texture, contrasting lines, and expressions on the animal's faces. (***Martin's Mice*** by Dick King-Smith; animal fantasy)

Beth and Joe Krush reveal a great deal in their illustration: the contrast in sizes between the boy and the Borrowers; the clever use of discarded objects; and the space under the floorboards where the Borrowers, miniature people, live. (***The Borrowers*** by Mary Norton; miniature worlds tale)

Arriety in ***The Borrowers*** (I) by Mary Norton, to the Minnipins in ***The Gammage Cup*** (I) by Carol Kendall, the best and worst in human nature is magnified against a lilliputian backdrop where characters are memorable because of their size.

Like animal fantasy, fantasy worlds inhabited by inanimate objects and fanciful creatures with human thought, language, and feelings are real to young children. The soldier in Hans Christian Andersen's ***Steadfast Tin Soldier*** (P–I) appears all the more heroic because he is a tiny toy with no power over his own fate. Similarly, Andersen's ***Thumbelina*** (P–I) blossoms with dignity through her search for happiness. Respect for life, woven into the stories, says to small children that a person is a person no matter how small.

Just as older readers continue to enjoy novel-length animal fantasy, they also continue to respond to the call of the miniature. Miniature worlds, like animal fantasy, often reflect the best and worst of the human condition. They can be lighthearted looks at what life in miniature would be like, or serious explorations of human needs and desires.

A secret world-within-a-world where dolls live ***Behind the Attic Wall*** (I–A) is created in Sylvia

Cassedy's novel of a lonely, belligerent girl. Maggie, an incorrigible 12-year-old rebel who has been expelled from numerous boarding schools for "poor adjustment," hears whispers behind the walls and explores. These whispers gradually lead her to two dolls who welcome her to their strange secret life. The contrast between the tenderness Maggie shows to the dolls and her scathing response to humans around her is stark. In Figure 6-3 we list some memorable fantasies that are set in miniature worlds.

Magic

Many fantasy stories make use of magic and humor, and children avidly respond to both. Whether delighting in the antics of Astrid Lindgren's ***Pippi Longstocking*** (I) or enjoying William Steig's ***Sylvester and the Magic Pebble*** (I), children recognize the possibilities that magic entails and enter into a

"Take us back, take us back!" Eddie quacked. "I don't want to be a bird!"

Magic begins to happen slowly on the island of paradise as Al and his dog, Eddie, gradually turn into birds (*Hey, Al* by Arthur Yorinks, illustrated by Richard Egielski; magic)

world that doesn't operate by natural laws. In Bruce Coville's ***Jeremy Thatcher, Dragon Hatcher*** (I) Jeremy enters a shop that is magic, both literally and figuratively, and leaves with a dragon egg. When the egg hatches and he has to care for the dragon, he learns about responsibility, good and evil, and personal integrity. Figure 6-3 lists other fantasies that make use of magic.

SCIENCE FICTION

Science fiction is speculative fiction based on some scientific possibility; it asks "what if" and explores the potential impact of science on life as we know it. Science fiction, set most often in the future, deals

with the impact of technology and science on humans, humanoids, or other creatures. Some science fiction considers major questions such as the aftermath of nuclear war or the results of global pollution; some centers around technology, such as intergalactic travel and space wars.

In many books, the distinctions between fantasy and science fiction are blurred; these books are sometimes called science fantasy. This blurring of the genres reflects the similarities between them: Both are often set in worlds that do not correspond to present realities. Yet science fiction differs from fantasy in that the future realities it depicts are based on extrapolation from scientific principles. Highly respected science fiction writer Robert A. Heinlein describes it this way. In science fiction,

Figure 6-3

Talking Animals, Miniature Worlds, and Magic

Talking Animals

Adams, Richard. *Watership Down.* (A)

Burningham, John. *Mr. Gumpy's Outing.* (P)

De Brunhoff, Jean. *The Story of Babar.* (P)

Freeman, Don. *Corduroy.* (P)

Grahame, Kenneth. *Wind in the Willows.* (A)

King-Smith, Dick. *Babe: The Gallant Pig.* (I)

Lawson, Robert. *Rabbit Hill.* (A)

Lobel, Arnold. *Frog and Toad Are Friends.* (P)

Milne, A. A. *Winnie the Pooh.* (I)

O'Brien, Robert C. *Mrs. Frisby and the Rats of NIMH.* (A)

Potter, Beatrix. *The Tale of Peter Rabbit.* (P)

Selden, George. *Cricket in Times Square.* (I)

White, E. B. *Charlotte's Web.* (I)

Miniature Worlds

Carroll, Lewis. *Alice's Adventures in Wonderland.* (I)

Cassedy, Sylvia. *Behind the Attic Wall.* (A)

———. *Lucie Babbidge's House.* (A)

Conrad, Pam, *The Tub People.* Illus. Richard Egielski. (P)

Hoban, Russell. *The Mouse and His Child.* (A)

Jansson, Tove. *Finn Family Moomintroll.* (I)

Joyce, William. *George Shrinks.* (P)

Kendall, Carol. *The Gammage Cup.* (I)

Norton, Mary. *The Borrowers.* (I)

Magic

Dahl, Roald. *James and the Giant Peach.* (I)

de Paola, Tomie. *Big Anthony and the Magic Ring.* (P)

Fleming, Ian. *Chitty, Chitty, Bang, Bang: The Magical Car.* (A)

Fox, Mem. *Possum Magic.* (P)

Nesbit, E. *Five Children and It.* (I)

Steig, William. *The Amazing Bone.* (I)

———. *Sylvester and the Magic Pebble.* (P)

Turkle, Brinton. *Do Not Open.* (P)

Van Allsburg, Chris. *The Garden of Abdul Gasazi.* (P)

Yorinks, Arthur. *Hey Al.* Illus. Richard Egielski. (P)

[t]he author takes as his first postulate the real world as we know it, including all established facts and natural laws. The result can be extremely fantastic in content, but it is not fantasy; it is legitimate—and often very tightly reasoned—speculation about the possibilities of the real world. (1953, p. 1118)

The Role of Science Fiction in Children's Lives

As some of the prophecies made by earlier science fiction writers came true, such as the atomic age, space travel, and the computer revolution, science fiction attained credibility; it had long been considered merely sensationalist. Not only was the content now believable, the quality of the writing and the seriousness of the ideas explored improved. Contemporary science fiction writers are introspective, often dealing with the interaction of human beings and some aspect of science, technology, or the natural world that does not exist at the present time. They suggest hypotheses and ask probing questions about the future of humankind and the nature of the universe.

As children mature they either move toward science fiction or avoid it entirely. By sixth or seventh grade, reader preference shows up markedly in science fiction (Cullinan, Harwood, & Galda, 1983; Galda, 1990). Those who like science fiction love it, and those who do not like it will hardly try it. Those who do try it are rewarded by the riveting stories and memorable characters, as well as the profound and challenging questions that science fiction explores. The imaginative speculation that marks science fiction stretches the minds of readers as they consider ethical dilemmas as well as physical and technological problems.

These stories set in worlds never before known deal with problems that children may someday face—the rights of extraterrestrials whose planets are colonized, the sharing of diminishing resources in a world of rapidly growing populations—and cause readers to rethink the choices and directions of our society. Science fiction, a literature about change and the attendant moral issues that change brings, is very appropriate for children of a rapidly changing world.

Criteria for Selecting Science Fiction

The science fiction community has established its own awards to recognize outstanding writers. The Nebula Award, given for a short story, novelette, novella, or novel, is chosen by a vote of the membership of the Science Fiction Writers of America. The Hugo Award is named in honor of Hugo H. Gernsback, who is credited with the development of modern science fiction. Both awards are given annually to books in several categories.

Generally, the criteria for science fiction follow those for fantasy presented earlier in this chapter. Good science fiction has a tightly woven, logical plot, well-developed characters, memorable themes, and is written with grace and style. In good science fiction, facts do not encumber the plot, and the hypothetical situation is internally consistent. If in another time or place, the setting is often richly detailed. Characters, whether human or nonhuman, are recognizable beings with strong emotions; readers can easily understand and identify with them.

The themes in science fiction make us consider the emotional, psychological, and mental effects of futuristic ideas, conflict, and change. They help us keep an open mind to consider unlimited possibilities and to raise questions about other forms of life. Gifted writers such as Isaac Asimov, Arthur C. Clarke, Robert Heinlein, H. M. Hoover, John Christopher, and Louise Lawrence have elevated science fiction to an art form dealing with serious themes in which moral issues are not neglected. Figure 6-4 summarizes the criteria for evaluating science fiction.

A Close Look at *Children of the Dust*

Louise Lawrence unfolds the chilling story of the fate and evolution of three generations of one family after a nuclear holocaust in **Children of the Dust** (A).

Summary. The novel, divided into three parts, shows nuclear missiles roaring toward Gloucestershire and the Cotswold Hills in England while Sarah and her family try to barricade themselves inside their home. Sarah watches all the members of her family die except for Catherine, a younger sister, whom she takes to a safe house before going back to face her own death.

Catherine is the only survivor, and in the second part, she is a mature woman living in a rebuilt rural community. Their father, who was away from home at the time of the bombing, has remarried, believing that none of his family has survived and lives in an underground base where inhabitants seek to live as they did in the past. One day, Catherine meets her young half sister, Ophelia. In the third part of the book, Ophelia's son, Simon, returns to the farm settlement from the underground base when the technology they needed for survival fails. Simon is horrified to discover that the young people he meets have mutated and are white-eyed and covered with a fine furry down. He finally realizes they are strong, competent, and the hope of the new world.

Believability. Lawrence begins her story in the world as it is today, with ordinary things happening—school, sunshine, flowers, and birds. But bombs had already begun to fall across Europe and the mad panic that Sarah and others are thrown into is a sharp contrast to the beautiful spring day. Recognizing that Sarah is a real person with familiar feelings increases the believability and the horror of what happens to her. The small details of the immediate aftermath of the bombing that Lawrence provides also heighten the realism. Having depicted a very realistic present, Lawrence then moves logically from the time of the bombing into the future, following the fate of these real human characters. Throughout the story Lawrence provides vivid details about life that create a feeling of reality.

Theme. This profoundly moving and disturbing book does not end on a fatalistic or depressing note, however, as Lawrence speculates on the possibilities for human survival in a postnuclear world. The contrast between the lives of those living in the bunkers, clinging to old perceptions and animosities, and those who adapt to the new world—the

Figure 6-4

Checklist for Evaluating Science Fiction

- ❑ Are characters recognizable beings with strong emotions?
- ❑ Can readers identify with the characters?
- ❑ Does the author extrapolate from known fact?
- ❑ Does the author explore the consequences of current behavior and practices?
- ❑ Does the story begin with established scientific, natural, and social laws?
- ❑ Is there a clearly described, well-imagined setting?
- ❑ Is the plot logical and tightly woven?
- ❑ Is the theme memorable?
- ❑ Is the hypothetical situation internally consistent?

The mood and the message of this illustration is driven by the dark desolate colors. The horror is relieved through a ray of hope—the castle planted in the midst of the mushroom cloud. (**Children of the Dust** by Louise Lawrence; nuclear holocaust horror)

children of the nuclear dust—forces readers to consider questions about what it means to be human. More than just a novel about nuclear war, **Children of the Dust** is a novel about the evolution of humanity.

Science Fiction for All Readers

Many children are introduced to science fiction by reading some of the lighter, suspenseful stories. Science fantasy, that blend of fantasy and science fiction, often set in other worlds but uncomplicated by elaborate scientific theories, provides a good entrée for beginning science fiction readers. As they read and enjoy these stories they will become interested in moving on to more complex stories that explore significant issues.

In a beautifully written story by Jill Paton Walsh, young Pattie takes **The Green Book** (I) with her when she and her family escape from the dying planet Earth. When they arrive at their new settlement Pattie and her friends explore their new world. Their courage and perseverance lead the community to find a way to exist in their new world, and Pattie's green-covered blank book becomes the place where the community can write the story of

their survival. The occasional soft illustrations by Lloyd Bloom help describe what life was like in Shine. Figure 6-5 lists some other good stories to begin with.

Another way to introduce science fiction to young readers is through the short story. If they are going to like it, they find out quickly, and if not, they do not have to read an entire novel to make their judgment. Numerous good collections of short stories are available. As Eleanor Cameron states, "if we do not quibble over fineness of categories, we then avoid the danger of becoming one of that company of scholars (some of the folklorists among them) who seem to care less about experiencing the truth and beauty of a tale than in being 'correct' in putting it into this compartment or that," (Cameron, 1969, p. 12). "In addition, she says, "Science fantasy is playful, lighthearted . . . a blend between science fiction and fantasy . . . light science fiction." Some are listed in Figure 6-5.

Vicky, bitterly disappointed with the gift of a doll-house for her birthday, experiences real terror when she is drawn into the house and the lives of its inhabitants. Trina Schart Hyman's illustrations convey the emotional struggle between Vicky and the antique dolls. (*Among the Dolls* by William Sleator; science fantasy)

Types of Science Fiction

As with any category system, dividing science fiction into types is often arbitrary; many novels can easily fit more than one classification. There are, however, three broad classifications that most science fiction falls into.

Mind Control

Several science fiction writers deal with themes of mind control, telepathy, ESP, and other forms of communication across time and space. As computers, television, and other forms of communication reach more and more people across the globe, and advances in medicine make possible genetic and nervous system alterations, the potential for mind control on a grand scale grows.

One of the early examples is John Christopher's White Mountain trilogy. This trilogy about extraterrestrial invaders of Earth appeals to today's readers

in the upper elementary grades. *The White Mountains* (I–A), *The City of Gold and Lead* (I–A), and *The Pool of Fire,* (I–A), a blend of science fiction and fantasy, are set in the twenty-first century in a world ruled by the Tripods, dreaded robots. When humans are 14, the Tripods implant steel caps in their skulls that keep them submissive, docile, and helpless. Will and his two friends learn that free people live in the White Mountains and make a hazardous journey to join them. Humane characters are pitted against hostile aliens in a series of bizarre encounters. Christopher's narrative impels readers to ponder the values of life and science. Many other science fiction stories are crafted around the problem of mind control; Figure 6-6 contains the titles of some of these.

Tomorrow's World

Many stories examine anthropological and sociological aspects of life in the future, considering questions of individual commitment and ethical behavior. The results of aggression and competition versus peace and cooperation, a consideration of what it means to be human, comparisons among cultures at different levels of development, and finding one's purpose and place in life are all ideas that science fiction writers explore.

Helen Hoover has contributed a sizable body of science fiction addressing sociological themes. In *The Shepherd Moon* (I–A), 13-year-old Merry Ambrose watches, in the forty-eighth century, for the rise of the five full moons circling the Earth. Four of the moons were satellites built as space habitats; one, the Shepherd Moon, Terra II, was the first of the space satellites sent from Earth hundreds of years earlier. Mikel Goodman, the product of genetic engineering on Terra II, lands near Merry's home and initiates his plan to rule the Earth. His innocent appearance belies his malevolent amorality, and although he does not succeed in taking over the Earth, his questions cause Merry to become aware of many social problems on Earth. Hoover raises questions about the nature of the interaction between life on Earth and life in space. Figure 6-6 lists other books that explore these kinds of issues.

Survival

Some writers' gloomy outlook on the future is apparent in the literature of survival. Although most nuclear scenarios are both all-encompassing and extremely depressing, an entire body of books exists that show children surviving a nuclear war.

JOHN CHRISTOPHER   95¢
THE WHITE MOUNTAINS

The three boys are desperate to escape the mind control devices the Tripods want to implant in their heads. A look of desperation shines from their eyes. (*The White Mountains* by John Christopher; science fiction)

Postnuclear holocaust books, like Louise Lawrence's **Children of the Dust** (A), have proliferated. It will be interesting to see if these books are less frequently written and read as the world adjusts to life without the Cold War.

But stories about survival are not limited to the horrors of life after a nuclear war. The problems of life as it is today—the overcrowding, the pollution, the extinction of animal and plant species, and the questions of an adequate food supply—provide science fiction writers with unlimited opportunities to project how humans will survive on Earth. Some propose that the new frontier lies in outer space. Others propose that if we remain here on Earth, the new frontier might be what we could do to make Earth more livable.

Figure 6-5

Science Fantasy and Short Stories

Primary

Marshall, Edward. *Space Case.*

Marzollo, Jean. *Jed and the Space Bandits.*

——. *Ruthie's Rude Friends.*

Standiford, Natalie. *Space Dog the Hero.* Illus. Kelly Oechsli.

Yolen, Jane. *Commander Toad in Space.*

Intermediate

Alcock, Vivien. *Monster Garden.*

Asimov, Isaac. *Norby the Mixed-Up Robot.*

Atwater, Richard. *Mr. Popper's Penguins.* Illus. Richard and Florence Atwater.

Hildick, E. W. *Ghost Squad Breaks Through.*

Pearce, Philippa A. *Who's Afraid? and Other Strange Stories.*

Sargent, Sarah. *Watermusic.*

Service, Pamela F. *Stinker from Space.*

Slote, Alfred. *Omega Station.* Illus. Anthony Kramer.

Advanced

Alcock, Vivien. *Ghostly Companions.*

Asimov, Isaac, Martin Harry Greenberg, and Charles Waugh (editors). *Time Warp.*

Corbett, Scott. *Deadly Hoax.*

Hitchcock, Alfred. *Alfred Hitchcock's Supernatural Tales of Terror and Suspense.*

——. *Witch's Brew.*

Rubinstein, G. *Space Demons.*

Ryan, Mary C. *Me Two.* Illus. Rob Sauber.

Sleator, William. *Among the Dolls.* Illus. Trina Schart Hyman.

——. *The Duplicate.*

Yolen, Jane (editor). *Things That Go Bump in the Night: A Collection of Original Stories.*

TEACHING IDEA 6-5

Technology Changes the World

Fantasy and science fiction writers believe that each small change in our world results in a chain reaction of changes. List some changes in the technology you use. Are any described in futuristic novels? Consider the pros and cons of their use. How will they affect life? How would you write about life in the future by extrapolating on the changes the new technology has brought? Discuss, for example:

List of Inventions	Good Changes	Bad Changes
Computers		
Fax Machines		
Portable Telephones		
CD Players		
Plane Travel		

Pattie records the events on the planet Shine in *The Green Book,* a journal she carries with her when her family leaves planet Earth far behind. One day when they go for a picnic to Boulder Valley, the stones begin to move, heave, shudder, and tear open. Moth people hatch and crawl out of their stone-like eggs. New questions arise about the way they are treated. (Jill Paton Walsh; tomorrow's world)

Caroline Macdonald sets **The Lake at the End of the World** (A) in the year 2025. The world has been environmentally devastated and one family—young Diana and her parents—think they are the only survivors until Diana sees a boy, Hector, near the mouth of a cave. Told in alternating chapters, the two young protagonists narrate the story of how Hector and some of his people escape from the underground colony in which they have been living. Issues of mind control and power intertwine with environmental issues in this fast-paced, exciting story. Figure 6-6 lists some other books that explore survival themes.

FANTASY AND SCIENCE FICTION IN THE CLASSROOM

Once children have enjoyed and made their own the many picture books that can also be classified as fantasy, it is an easy step into longer, more complex stories. Many children will find these stories on their own, moving naturally from books like Mem Fox's **Possum Magic** (N–P) to books such as E. B. White's **Charlotte's Web** (I) or Natalie Babbitt's **Tuck Everlasting** (I–A). As they develop as readers and thinkers, they discover the intellectual enchantment of Ursula Le Guin's **Tehanu: The Last Book of Earthsea** (A), Robin McKinley's **The Hero and the Crown** (A), or Meredith Ann Pierce's **A Gathering of Gargoyles** (A) and the powerful questions that Sylvia Engdahl asks in **Beyond the Tomorrow Mountains** (A) and Mary Caraker considers in **The Faces of Ceti** (A).

Some children, however, will leave fantasy behind as they grow older and will never discover the joys of science fiction unless they are helped into these genres by knowledgeable teachers. In many cases reading aloud is the very best way to encourage readers to expand their interests. We discuss earlier in this chapter how intermediate-grade teachers might want to read some of the lighter

---

**Figure
6-6**

Mind Control, Future, Survival

Mind Control

Christopher, John. *The White Mountains.* (I)

——. *When the Tripods Came.* (I)

Cohen, Barbara. *Unicorns in the Rain.* (A)

Engdahl, Sylvia. *Enchantress from the Stars.* (A)

Key, Alexander. *Escape to Witch Mountain.* (I)

Lawrence, Louise. *Children of the Dust.* (A)

——. *Star Lord.* (I)

Mahy, Margaret. *Aliens in the Family.* (A)

Marshall, James. *Merry Christmas, Space Case.* (P)

Marzollo, Jean. *Jed's Junior Space Patrol.* (P)

Ormondroyd, Edward. *Time at the Top.* (I)

Seuss, Dr. *Yertle the Turtle, and Other Stories.* (P)

——. *The Lorax.* (P)

——. *Sneetches, and Other Stories.* (P)

Slote, Alfred. *My Trip to Alpha I.* (I)

Life in the Future

Asimov, Isaac. *Fantastic Voyage: A Novel.* (I)

Brooks, Bruce. *No Kidding.* (I)

Hoover, H. M. *Orvis.* (I)

Paton Walsh, Jill. *The Green Book.* (I)

Pinkwater, D. M. *Alan Mendelsohn, the Boy from Mars.* (I)

Survival

Blackwood, Gary. *Beyond the Door.* (A)

Christopher, John. *Empty World.* (A)

O'Brien, Robert C. *Z for Zachariah.* (A)

---

science fantasy books and upper-grade teachers might want to select science fiction short stories to read aloud. Actually, teachers at any grade level can make a conscious effort to include fantasy and science fiction in their read-aloud programs. The books we discuss and list in this chapter are well written and thought provoking and are excellent choices to read aloud.

Fantasy and science fiction books can also be read and discussed by literature study groups (discussed in Chapter 12). These books fit well into genre studies as well as many thematic units. The kinds of questions about values, selfhood, good and evil, and courage that fantasy writers consider are also treated in some contemporary realism and historical fiction. Looking at books from various genres that contain similar themes can be a powerful reading experience. Science fiction, too, is easily adapted into a thematic approach, since writers probe questions such as a search for life on other worlds, eternal life, conflict of cultures, mind control, and life after a nuclear holocaust.

Benefits of fantasy and science fiction include the flexibility of imagination they encourage and the important questions that they push readers to consider. As children read stories about people and events that are real and familiar to them they also need to read stories which make them wonder, cause them to consider, and stretch their souls. Fantasy and science fiction can do just that.

SUMMARY

Fantasy is concerned with people, places, or events that could not occur in the real world. Science fiction is concerned with the impact of scientific possibilities on the world of the future. In both genres we find many excellent stories that are well written, with multidimensional characters engaged in exciting plots and profound themes. Although some children move naturally from their favorite picture book fantasies into more complex fantasies and science fiction, some need to be helped into the more complex books by their teachers. In either case the rewards are well worth the effort.

7

Contemporary Realistic Fiction

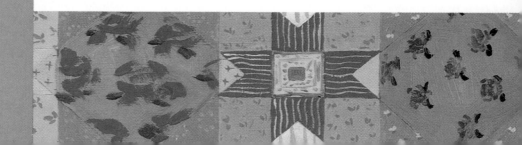

JUST LIKE ME

I read a book about a kid
As weird as he could be,
And as I turned each page I thought,
This kid is just like me.

It's good to know I'm not alone,
I'm not the only one
Who likes to eat bananas
With hot chili on a bun.

Brod Bagert

Character is the soul of great literature. When readers discover their own feelings in the character of a book, they experience the events of the story as though they were happening to them. Thus, through the magic of fiction, children accumulate the experience of many lives and grow wise beyond their years.

Realistic fiction has a strong sense of actuality. Its plausible stories are about people and events that could actually happen. Good contemporary realistic fiction illuminates life, presenting social and personal concerns in a fully human context.

Realistic fiction portrays the real world in all its dimensions; it shows the humorous, the sensitive, the thoughtful, the joyful, and the painful sides of life. By its very nature, it deals with the vast range of sensitive topics prevalent in today's world. "The raw materials of story," says Lloyd Alexander, "are the raw materials of all human cultures. Story deals with the same questions as theology, philosophy, psychology. It is concerned with polarities: love and hate, birth and death, joy and sorrow, loss and recovery" (1981). Life's raw materials, questions, and polarities appear most starkly in realistic fiction. Consequently, more controversy surrounds realistic fiction than any other genre.

Good literature does not resolve complex problems with easy answers; it considers these problems with the seriousness they require. Since literature reflects the society that creates it, children's contemporary realistic fiction reflects many of the problems our society is concerned with today: drugs, alcoholism, divorce, abortion, death, homelessness, and child abuse. It also reflects what we value in our lives: love, personal integrity, family, and friends. Thus many realistic novels are problem laden, but many are also stories of courage in which people are not beaten down by life, but transform it into something worthwhile through inner strength.

No definition of realism is simple, and to say that realism is fiction that could happen in the real world—as opposed to fantasy, which could not—is simplistic. Every work of fiction, like the stories we tell ourselves, is part fanciful and part realistic. We selectively remember and reshape events of our past and present; the same thing happens in books. A realistic story is an author's vision of what might happen (the plot) in a particular time and place (the setting) to particular people (the characters).

REALISTIC FICTION IN CHILDREN'S LIVES

For many young readers the sense of actuality in realistic fiction makes it easy to live the story as it is being read, to have a virtual experience. Realistic fiction presents stories that can act as windows, through which we see the world, and as mirrors, in which we see ourselves. Readers who relate to these stories often report seeing themselves in a realistic fiction story: "The whole time I was reading I was thinking, 'Yes, that's right. That's exactly how I feel.'" This intense connection with a book causes many young readers to prefer realistic fiction above other genres.

National surveys and librarians' reports (Monson & Sebesta, 1991) repeatedly show that intermediate-grade students choose realistic stories far more than any other type. Children unabashedly ask for books "about someone just like me" who is confronting familiar issues. The connection between the book and the reader, however, hinges not on age, time, or place, but on the validity of the emotions presented. Feelings must ring true in the reader's mind; they are more important than surface actuality. Children who read widely, testing and tasting from alternative lifestyles, have many opportunities to try out roles vicariously through realistic books. When children read books that show others searching for self, they find they are not alone. They learn that life will be what they make of it. Children search for an identity and look for a yardstick against which to measure themselves, and they turn to realistic fiction to help them define the person they want to become.

While reading, we unconsciously participate in a story, drawing analogies between what we are reading and the stories that, in effect, we tell ourselves about our own lives. These experiences through stories help us understand our lives and prepare us for the future by creating expectations and models. The expectations influence our reactions to real events. A fifth grader talked about doing just that when she said, "When I wasn't reading, I was thinking what it would be like if that really happened, because it's such a big thing that happened, . . . like if it happened to me or something. Like if I had a sister, or if my mother died or something, how that would affect me." Younger readers might not be so explicit about the connections they make between realistic fiction and life, but they will ask questions or make statements which let you know that they, too, are thinking about "what it would be like if." As one young reader expressed after hearing Lucille Clifton's ***My Friend Jacob*** (P), "Mommy, if I had a friend who needed extra special help, I'd be very nice to him."

Stories are both mirrors and windows of life; realistic stories can cause us to reflect on life as well as illuminate alternative lifestyles that through literature we can try on for size. Realistic fiction helps us experience things we would never experience in real life, or practice what we might someday experience. Realistic fiction allows us many experiences in the safety and security of our role as a reader: We can sail around the world without fear of shipwreck or suffer blindness without loss of sight while still probing the emotions of the moment. We can also rehearse experiences we might someday have: We can meet new friends and experience love and sorrow. And we can discover that others living in different environments have done, thought, and felt the same things that we ourselves have done, thought, and felt.

CRITERIA FOR SELECTING REALISTIC FICTION

Realistic fiction, like many other genres, should be evaluated in terms of the setting, characters, plot, theme, style, and the point of view selected by the author, as well as the quality of the illustrations in a realistic picture book. General criteria apply to a range of genres, but some are specific to realistic fiction. The plausibility of characters, plot, and setting, realized in both text and illustration, is especially important to this genre. It is this very quality of realism that also requires us to consider community standards when selecting these stories.

Realism and Censorship

In realistic fiction for children from nursery school through high school we can find explicit language, earthy dialogue, unseemly behavior, and sensitive issues. Some adults prefer to shield children from subjects that are too mature. Others believe that children can benefit from reading and having a safe experience once removed from reality. Both positions have merit. It is important to consider books in light of what they *say* about the subjects they explore. For example, if a story is about young people who take drugs, what happens to them? Are drugs seen as good or bad? Is the general idea that children shouldn't take drugs because they're dangerous? Often adults who complain about a book that examines a controversial subject haven't looked to see what the author is saying about that topic. In many cases the message in a controversial realistic book is actually one that the community would approve.

Giblin (1987), editor and author of children's books, looks for writers who portray reality authentically but in a way that is appropriate to their audience. He feels that almost any subject can be presented to children if it is dealt with sensitively and honestly. He expects an author to portray both sides of a conflict and to depict characters as multidimensional, not as one-sided personalities. He finds that writers who care deeply about a subject convey their ideas with emotion and thoughtfulness. As our society becomes increasingly complex, thoughtful writers are more important than ever.

Individual parents and communities will interpret the standards of what they believe to be suitable for their own children. We, as teachers and librarians, need to be sensitive to the standards of our community, while at the same time protecting children's right to read books that stimulate, inform, and delight. This is an important and difficult task, and we discuss ways to combat censorship sensitively in Chapter 12 because it is an issue that confronts teachers and librarians of all grades and concerns all genres.

When selecting realistic fiction look for books that (1) contain topics that are developmentally ap-

propriate, and (2) use language, events, and themes that are in keeping with the community's standards. Also consider the literary quality of such books, and evaluate setting, characters, plot, theme, and style.

Evaluating Literary Quality

Setting

Authors of realistic stories choose a time and place that actually does or could possibly exist as a setting. In some stories the setting is almost irrelevant; broad brushstrokes paint a picture of rural or urban, home or school, wealthy or poor, and details are

---

TEACHING IDEA 7-1

Keep a Journal

Authors of realistic fiction portray real people and their feelings in plots they develop. They observe themselves and others living their lives and record their observations in journals—not only when they are working on a story—but every day. Ask students to collect material for future stories and reflections on life by recording their observations.

Have students:

1. Read several books in which the character keeps a journal or record of thoughts and feelings.

2. Start their own journal. Record events that happen to them and events they observe. Record their feelings about what they see happening.

3. After they have kept a journal for a period of time, have them go back through their notes and highlight items that might lead to a story.

4. Make notes about what they want to watch for in future observations.

Books in which character keeps a journal:

Cleary, Beverly. *Dear Mr. Henshaw.*

Conford, Ellen. *Jenny Archer, Author.*

Fitzhugh, Louise. *Harriet the Spy.*

Lowry, Lois. *Anastasia Krupnik.*

Marsden, John. *So Much to Tell You.*

Mazer, Norma Fox. *After the Rain.*

not necessary. Picture books with this kind of setting offer artists the opportunity to create images that the text does not define, presenting their own vision of the physical surroundings of the story. In other stories setting is very important; details about a particular city or part of the country, a special home or school are important to the development of the characters and the plot. Authors like Virginia Hamilton write with the clarity that such detail demands. Many realistic picture books supply this information through the illustrations, with the art setting the background the story demands. When evaluating setting in realistic fiction, look for (1) credibility or authenticity in time and place, and (2) logical connections between the time and place and the events of the story.

Characters

Characters in realistic fiction reflect human beings we know; they are circumscribed by the natural powers and failings of a real person in a real world. Like real people, realistic characters are multidimensional with varied strengths and weaknesses, and, over the course of time, they grow and change. Their personalities are evident from what they do

PROFILE

*V*IRGINIA HAMILTON has been honored with every prestigious award that exists for writers of children's books. She has received the Newbery Award, the American Book Award, the Coretta Scott King Award, the Boston Globe–Horn Book Award, the National Book Award, and the Hans Christian Andersen Award. Her books are frequently placed on the American Library Association list of Notable Books and Best Books for Young Adults. She raised the standards for children's literature with her graphic descriptions of emotional and physical landscapes.

Virginia Hamilton says, "I've written things down since the time I could put words together to make sentences. I suspect I was in second or third grade. But I remember *really* writing more than a page or two by the age of nine. I grew up reading as well. I don't remember the moment I knew what words meant, but, one day, I could read—that's what I remember clearly. And a whole world seemed to open before me. It was as if I were sucking life in through my eyes" (Harcourt Brace promotional material).

Virginia Hamilton

Virginia Hamilton was born and raised in Yellow Springs, Ohio, an old station on the Underground Railroad where her grandfather settled after escaping from slavery. She was educated at Antioch College and the Ohio State University and studied literature and writing at the New School for Social Research. She lived in New York for fifteen years and now lives in Ohio with her husband, Arnold Adoff, a poet.

I work in my study at my desk, looking through sliding glass doors at a hundred-

or say, what others say about them or to them, what others do to them, and by what the narrator reveals. In the case of realistic picture storybooks, character is also revealed by the illustrator who interprets the characters' thoughts and actions. When evaluating characterization in realistic fiction, look for main characters that (1) are credible and authentic, (2) are fully developed as multidimensional human beings, and (3) show change or development during the course of the story. This change or development is most often due to the events that occur as the characters seek to resolve some kind of problem.

Plot

Today's readers want action in a story; they want something to happen, and happen fast. Most often, the plot is told in a straightforward chronology, but sometimes authors use a flashback, episodic, or alternating plot. Flashbacks provide background information about earlier events that led to the creation of the problem the character currently faces. Episodic plots highlight particular events in characters' lives, and alternating plots enable authors to tell stories from different points of view. When selecting realistic fiction, look for (1) plot structures

CONTINUED

year-old osage orange hedgerow. In summer, I can hear all the birds, and I watch squirrels and chipmunks play there in the tall old trees. My house sits in a field bordered on one side by the hedgerow. The field is the last part of my mother's and father's farm. Generations of my family have lived in this village in southwestern Ohio. When I look out at the trees, the land, and the farmhouses, I see not only through *my* eyes, but through my mother's and my grandmother's eyes as well. I feel deeply attached to the land and the very air of the countryside. It feels to me as if the well of my creativity in writing comes somehow out of my love of the rich earth. Mornings, I sit here, simply sigh, take a sip of my tea, and look over my sweep of 'hopescape.' I breathe in the sundrenched air and once again, I begin . . . (Harcourt Brace promotional material).

Virginia Hamilton has distinguished herself by her artistic integrity as a writer of realistic fiction *(M. C. Higgins, the Great)*, historical fiction *(The House of Dies Drear)*, folklore *(In the Beginning: Creation Stories from around the World)*, fantasy *(Dustland)*, and biography *(W. E. B. Du Bois)*. She says,

The making of any fiction for me is foremost a self-viewing that becomes a force for life and living. The fiction becomes greater than the sum of fact, memory, and imagination that create it. At the last, it stands independent from the self and is often more mysterious than anything the writer of it may have experienced herself.

That is why I so often say that life is continuous, going in a circle. And everyone who is black who has lived and those now living have something to say to me and have something to do with the person I am. It must be that all people who have lived and those now living hold our common knowledge as humans and make us one people. That is why, although I generally write of the black experience, I place no restriction on whom or what kind of people I may write about. Writers must remain free to write as readers must have freedom of choice in order to read. Writing has to be fun for me, the writer, in the hopes that readers will respond to it with enthusiasm. Therein is an interchange of thought and feeling which has a way of bringing us together in communication. (Twentieth-Century Children's Writers. page 353)

ᴛᴇACHING IDEA 7-2

Interview Book Characters

Ask a student to volunteer for the part of an emcee (MC) on a talk show (Oprah Winfrey, Phil Donahue, Geraldo Rivera). Other students will need to play the parts of Summer in *Missing May* by Cynthia Rylant and Jimmy Little in *Somewhere in the Darkness* by Walter Dean Myers.

ANNOUNCER: Hello. Today you're going to meet two characters from books: Summer and Jimmy. They appear in *Missing May* and *Somewhere in the Darkness*, books by Cynthia Rylant and Walter Dean Myers.

MC: Today I'd like you to meet two young people who have interesting stories to tell. These young people have taken some hard knocks in life and yet they have a pretty healthy outlook. Let's start with you, Jimmy. Tell us about your life up to the time your book begins.

JIMMY:

MC: How about you, Summer, tell us what happened in your life before your book begins?

SUMMER:

MC: It seems you both learned about life the hard way and you both had to learn it very young. But each of you had someone who really loved you. Tell us about that person—the one who made you feel loved.

SUMMER:

JIMMY:

MC: Now, let's get to the parts of your story covered in these books. Tell us about what happens to you.

JIMMY:

SUMMER:

MC: You both had someone who made you feel loved and wanted and you both had people that kind of let you down. Can you tell us what you think kids need from grown-ups?

SUMMER:

JIMMY:

MC: That's it for today. Maybe some adults will be listening and learn about the kinds of things kids want and need from them.

---

that can be understood by the readers most interested in the story content, (2) fast-paced action that moves toward the resolution of the problem, and (3) events that are probable given the setting and characters of the story.

Theme

Often a theme is the reason authors write in the first place: A story allows them to say what they want to say. Realistic fiction is frequently grouped by theme, which is how we discuss it later in this chapter. Readers can gain a sense of the way authors view life through the themes of their stories. Given individual differences among readers, a group of readers rarely offers the same interpretation of a theme. More often, themes vary among readers, with each one internalizing the theme in an individual way. When selecting realistic fiction, look for books with themes (1) that are woven intrinsically into the story situation, (2) that matter to children's lives, and (3) that children can understand and will want to mull over long after they have read the book.

Style

A tale is all in the telling, so style is an all-important criterion. The style needs to reflect the time, place, and character, and yet strict adherence to current slang can quickly date a book, making a good story seem slightly ridiculous. Good dialogue sounds natural, and descriptions are vivid and fresh. Look for books with a language style that (1) engages the reader, and (2) has a rhythmic, melodic quality appropriate to the theme, the setting, and the characters.

Point of View. Many realistic fiction novels are told through the voice of the central character who reports events in a first-person narrative, solely from his or her point of view. This allows readers to understand thoroughly the thoughts of the central character and often provokes a strong identification with that character. However, a first-person point of view limits the information an author can convey to what the central character could logically know. Further, this point of view can sometimes provide an experience that is too intense for many readers. Some fifth-grade readers who enjoyed the first half of Constance Greene's *Beat the Turtle Drum* (I) were unable to cope with the narrator's anguish upon her sister's death. Omniscient narrators, ones who are all-knowing, can reveal the thoughts and inner feelings of several characters. They can move about in time and space to report events from an unbiased position. This point of view allows readers to know a great deal about what all of the characters are thinking and doing. It also puts more distance between the reader and the main character, since the reader is viewing the protagonist through the narrator's eyes rather than viewing the story world through the protagonist's eyes.

Authors generally select one point of view and stick with it throughout the story, although some might alternate between two narrators as Paul Zindel does in *The Pigman* (A), or among several narrators as Alice Childress does in *A Hero Ain't Nothin' But a Sandwich* (A) and as Avi does in *Nothing But the Truth* (A). In a well-written story the point of view (1) provides a believable perspective that enriches the story, and (2) is clear, arising naturally in the telling, and consistent throughout the story.

Figure 7-1 summarizes the criteria for evaluating a piece of realistic fiction.

A Close Look at *Bridge to Terabithia*

Katherine Paterson's *Bridge to Terabithia* is a shining example of a beautifully written realistic book. Winner of the 1978 Newbery Medal, *Bridge to Terabithia* has been read by thousands of intermediate-grade students. What makes this book such an enduring favorite? Clearly, the Newbery committee felt this book was of outstanding literary merit according to the criteria presented earlier.

Synopsis

The central character, Jess, is in the fifth grade and not very happy. He does not get along with his older sisters or his mother, and his father is often away from home. He has no close friends until Leslie moves in next door. The two create the make-believe kingdom of Terabithia, and Leslie's knowledge and imagination expand Jess's world and his self-confidence.

The story is filled with small meaningful events, school encounters, and the growth of the strong friendship between Leslie and Jess. The magical kingdom of Terabithia lies across a gully that they reach by swinging on a rope. When they are in Terabithia, they are its king and queen and rule their imaginary subjects with royal dignity and grace. One day, crossing to Terabithia alone over a rain-swollen creek, Leslie falls, is knocked unconscious, and drowns. Jess's happiness ends that day, too. Initially, Jess cannot accept her death but eventually finds enough strength in himself to continue the kingdom of Terabithia as a tribute to Leslie's life.

Figure 7-1

Checklist for Evaluating Realistic Fiction

Characters

- ❑ Do characters act like real people or real animals?
- ❑ Is the emotional landscape realistic—can readers recognize that the characters' feelings are authentic, genuine—similar to theirs?
- ❑ Do the characters change and develop over time? Are they different at the end of the story from what they were at the beginning?
- ❑ Are the characters multidimensional? Do they avoid stereotypes? Do they represent an individual, not a group?

Setting

- ❑ Do the events occur in a place that could be (exist) in the known world?
- ❑ Is the setting vividly portrayed? Can you visualize a scene when you close your eyes? Would you know the place if you came upon it?

Plot

- ❑ Could the events actually happen in the real world?
- ❑ Are the problems believable and solved in realistic ways?
- ❑ Does the plot respect cultural values, unique ways of dealing with issues?
- ❑ Can the intended age group understand the plot structure?
- ❑ Does the plot move toward resolution at a fast pace?

Theme

- ❑ Does the author make a clear statement about theme?
- ❑ Is there a memorable comment—or an uplifting value?
- ❑ Does the theme shed any light on your own life?
- ❑ Does the theme respect the diversity of cultural groups?

Jess and Leslie create a make-believe world called Terabithia in the midst of a pine wooded area near their rural community, south of Washington, DC, in Katherine Paterson's book *Bridge to Terabithia*. Leslie lifts her arms to speak as the queen of the worthy subjects who inhabit their make-believe world. (Illustrated by Donna Diamond)

Setting

The setting in **Bridge to Terabithia** is Lark Creek, a small rural community south of Washington, D.C. We begin to discover what the community and Jess's family are like in the opening paragraph of the book:

> *Ba-room, ba-room, ba-room, baripity, baripity, baripity, baripity*—Good. His dad had the pickup going. He could get up now. Jess slid out of bed and into his overalls. He didn't worry about a shirt because once he began running he would be hot as popping grease even if the morning air was chill, or shoes because the bottoms of his feet were by now as tough as his worn-out sneakers.
>
> "Where you going, Jess?" May Belle lifted herself up sleepily from the double bed where she and Joyce Ann slept.
>
> "Sh," he warned. The walls were thin. Momma would be mad as flies in a fruit jar if they woke her up this time of day.

He patted May Belle's hair and yanked the twisted sheet up to her small chin. "Just over the cow field," he whispered. May Belle smiled and snuggled down under the sheet.

What do we know about the setting after reading this? We know the family is probably poor: The pickup truck doesn't always start easily, Jess's sneakers are so worn that he runs barefoot, Jess sleeps in a room with his two younger sisters, and the walls are thin. We also know they live in the country. Phrases such as "popping grease" and "flies in a fruit jar" alert the careful reader to the southern Appalachian setting.

As the story continues we learn that the local school "was short on everything," and that the community was narrow-minded and "it took them a long time to accept there what everyone could see by their TV's was OK anywhere else." Subtly and carefully, Paterson builds a picture of an authentic setting that reflects directly on the central character and the events that occur.

Characterization

The opening page tells you as much about Jess's character as it does about the setting. We learn he has enough self-discipline to get up early to run barefoot and shirtless, he is wary of his mother, and he is kind to his younger sister. In the following pages we find out he doesn't much like his older sisters, loves but gets exasperated with his younger sisters, likes to draw, and wishes his father would hug him. We see him being slow to wash before breakfast, working in the bean patch, making peanut butter sandwiches for his little sisters' dinner, drawing pictures alone on his bed, picking on May Belle, and milking the cow. In short, we see a hardworking, kind, frustrated, irritable, wistful young boy, all in the first 16 pages of the story.

Because the story is written from a third-person limited omniscient point of view, we also hear Jess's thoughts as he daydreams about his music teacher, thinks about how much he loves to draw, and longs for his father's approval. From the beginning, Jess is a fully credible, multidimensional boy, combining good and bad attributes just as real boys do.

As the story progresses and Jess becomes friends with Leslie, he begins to understand the possibilities in the world that his family's television had only hinted at. He becomes more self-confident, more willing to stand up for himself and what he loves, more able to love and pity his family. We see this growth by what he does in Terabithia with Leslie, what he does in school, and the way he acts with his family. We hear it happening as we read his thoughts, and by the end of the story we realize that Jess, too, knows he has grown and changed.

> He thought about it all day, how before Leslie came, he had been a nothing—a stupid, weird little kid who drew funny pictures and chased around a cow field trying to act big—trying to hide a whole mob of foolish little fears running riot inside his gut.
>
> It was Leslie who had taken him from the cow pasture into Terabithia and turned him into a king. He had thought that was it. Wasn't king the best you could be? Now it occurred to him that perhaps Terabithia was like a castle where you came to be knighted. After you stayed for a while and grew strong you had to move on. . . .
>
> Now it was time for him to move on. She wasn't there, so he must go for both of them. It was up to him to pay back to the world in beauty and caring what Leslie had loaned him in vision and strength.

Jess has grown and changed over the course of the story. Meeting Leslie and becoming her friend made a tremendous difference in his life, and her accidental death forced him to confront his own life purpose.

Plot

Meeting Leslie, creating Terabithia, and coming to terms with Leslie's death change Jess. These events form the framework, the plot of the story. Told in 13 chapters, the book is filled with small details, commonplace events—races at school, fooling the school bully, going to church—that, combined, form the experience which alters Jess's life. The problems Jess encounters are problems familiar to many children—lack of confidence, worry, adults who don't understand, and bullies. The experience that changes his life—friendship—is also something most children know well. Paterson's plot moves chronologically and quickly, fueled by daily events; readers are caught up in it.

Style

Bridge to Terabithia is filled with vivid similes and with dialogue that evokes the setting and the experiences of the characters. In the opening quoted segment, you find two colorful phrases: "hot as popping grease" and "mad as flies in a fruit jar." These similes not only infer the setting, they also evoke vivid, remarkable images for ordinary feelings. These kinds of images continue throughout the story. Leslie's running reminds Jess "of the flight of wild ducks in the autumn. So smooth," and the swollen creekbed was

> like in *The Ten Commandments* on TV when the water came rushing into the dry path Moses had made and swept all the Egyptians away, the long dry bed of the creek was a roaring eight-foot-wide sea, sweeping before it great branches of trees, logs, and trash, swirling them about like so many Egyptian chariots, the hungry waters licking and sometimes leaping the banks, daring them to try to confine it.

Vivid images such as these help readers create pictures in their heads as they read; they also make the story memorable.

The point of view that Paterson selects, third-person limited omniscient, also contributes to the overall impact of the story. We need to know what Jess is thinking or we wouldn't be able to understand the enormity of his early weakness, his loss, and his subsequent strength. However, to be inside of Jess's head in first-person narration and to have to bear the sorrow of Leslie's death would be too strong for most young readers. Conversely, knowing only the thoughts of others in the story, rather than focusing on Jess, would weaken the impact. The limited omniscient point of view enhances the power of Paterson's story.

Theme

As with most outstanding books, multiple themes are woven through **Bridge to Terabithia.** Many young readers respond to the ideas about self-respect and self-worth that permeate the story. Some focus on the power of friendship to change one's life, others on growing up, and yet others on the need to accept and go beyond one's experiences, both good and bad. These themes are all understandable by intermediate-grade children and, indeed, are some of the issues these children are facing today.

Friendship, growing up, and coming to terms with oneself are all things that children experience; Paterson's book helps them experience these turning points more intensely while safely immersed in the world of the book. By telling the story of one ordinary boy's transformation, Paterson offers young readers a vision of what they can become as well. In many classes **Bridge to Terabithia** becomes a talisman book, one that is talked about long after the last word is read.

*K*ATHERINE PAT-ERSON, a superior writer, has won the Newbery Award twice: for *Bridge to Terabithia* in 1978 and *Jacob Have I Loved* in 1981. She won the National Book Award in 1977 and has been the U.S. nominee for the Hans Christian Andersen Award. She was born in China, the daughter of missionaries from the American South, and lived in China, Virginia, North Carolina, West Virginia, and Tennessee while she was growing up. She attended 13 different schools before graduating from high school. She is married to a minister; they have four grown children.

Katherine describes the process of writing *Bridge to Terabithia:*

A friend of mine who writes history books said to me that he thought that the two creatures most to be pitied were the spider and the novelist—their lives hanging by a thread spun out of their own guts. But in some ways I think writers of fiction are the creatures most to be envied, because who else besides the spider is allowed to take that fragile thread and weave it into a pattern? What a gift of grace to be able to take the chaos from within and from it to create some semblance of order.

I only know one writer really well, and since she is the one making these observations, I must before I am through apply what I have been saying to her.

I can't tell you exactly when the story began, somewhere among the catacombs of childhood's fears, but it began to grow in the early months of 1974 along with a tumor, which, after a lifetime of blooming health, invaded my body. The cancer was removed, the prognosis hopeful, but by

Katherine Paterson

that time I had heard the bell toll. I could no longer pretend to be immortal. Before either I or my family had had time to recuperate from my illness, our [son] David's closest friend, a winsome, humorous little girl of eight, was struck and killed by lightning. The two events were almost more than we could bear. Every time John or I left town, the children were sure we'd never return. I was known to wonder myself. David went through all the classical stages of grief and invented a few, including one in which he was sure that God was punishing him by killing off his loved ones, one by one. He had even worked out the order of demise. I was second on the list, right after his younger sister.

In the middle of all this I went to one of the regular monthly meetings of the Children's Book Guild in Washington. By some fluke I was seated at the head table with the guest speaker, who was Ann Durell, the editor for children's books at Dutton. During the polite amenities at the beginning of the meal, one of my fellow guild members said innocently, "How are the children?" To which, as you all know, the

CONTINUED

answer is "Fine." I muffed it. I began to really tell how the children were, which led me and my rather startled dinner mates into the long tale of David's grief.

When I finally shut up, the guest of honor said quietly, "I know this sounds just like an editor, but you ought to write that story," I thought I couldn't. The rule is, as you may know, that a writer should wait fifteen years before writing about an incident of personal history. It hadn't been five months. But I began to try. It became a way of dealing with my inability to comfort my child.

After many false starts I began to write a story in pencil in a used spiral notebook, so that if it came to nothing, I could pretend that I'd never been very serious about it. Gradually, I was encouraged by the emergence of thirty-two smudged pages to transfer from the tentative pencil to the typewriter, and the book moved forward, gathering momentum, only to become absolutely frozen. I found I couldn't let my fictional child die. I wrote around the death. I even cleaned the kitchen—anything to prevent this death from taking place.

Finally I confessed to a close friend of mine what was happening. "I guess I can't go through Lisa's death again," I concluded. She looked me straight in the eye. "I don't think it's Lisa's death you can't face, Katherine. I think it's yours."

Speaking of that "compelling inward ring" I went back to my study and closed the door. If it was Lisa's death I couldn't face, that was one thing, but if it was mine, by God, I would face it. I finished the chapter and, within a few weeks, the draft, with cold sweat rolling down my arms. And I did what no professional writer would ever do—I mailed it off to my editor before the sweat had evaporated.

I wish for every writer in the world an editor like Virginia Buckley. She did not brush aside that fragile thread spun from my guts. "I laughed through the first two thirds," she told me, "and cried through the last." So it was all right. She understood, as she always has, what I was trying to do. But a thread is not a story, and in children's novels we still expect a story with a beginning, a middle, and an end. And this is what Virginia gently prodded me into weaving.

I love revisions. Where else in life can spilled milk be transformed into ice cream? We can't go back and revise our lives, but being allowed to go back and revise what we have written comes closest. By now I had some distance from the book. My heart had stopped pounding, my palms were dry, my head cool, and my eye cooler. I was far enough away from the facts to see the truth from which they sprang. I was now ready to write fiction.

If the early drafts had been conceived in fear and grief, this revision was born in joy. In the mere rearrangement of words upon a page, I had passed through a valley of the shadow and come out singing. In fact, when I sent Virginia the revision, I wrote her that I was sure love was blind, for I had just mailed her a flawless manuscript.

My vision, you'll be glad to know, has since been restored. I no longer believe that **Bridge to Terabithia** is without flaws. But to this day when a child asks me if it is true, I answer, trying not to tremble too conspicuously, "Oh, I hope so."

This excerpt is from Katherine Paterson "Yes, but Is It True?" in *Gates of Excellence: On Reading and Writing Books for Children*. Elsevier/Nelson, 1981, pages 60–63.

Katherine Paterson's story brings tears but it also brings hope to its readers.

Strikingly dramatic watercolors evoke a sense of wonder on the cold, silent night that a young girl goes with her father to search for owls. John Schoenherr's art conveys the bitter coldness and the silence of the moonlit night in Jane Yolen's *Owl Moon*.

A Close Look at *Owl Moon*

Picture storybooks can also be excellent realistic fiction, and Jane Yolen's **Owl Moon** (P–I) is a perfect example of a realistic story rendered outstanding by carefully selected words and beautiful emotional illustrations. Yolen tells the story of a father and his young child going out late one night to see owls. They walk together quietly into the woods, the father imitates the call of a great horned owl, and they see the owl. Afterward, they walk back home.

The story is deceptively simple, for poetic prose evokes powerful images of the cold, dark winter night, the silence, the beauty of the woods white with snow, and the adventure that child and father undertake. John Schoenherr's Caldecott-winning illustrations take these images and transform them into an intensely beautiful visual experience. His pictures correspond to what the text is saying, but they also transcend it. His use of white and light space is extraordinary, making the dark spruce woods and winter night seem lit from within by a shining light. In most of the pictures the father and child are small, insignificant intruders in the forest of towering trees and pristine snow. In contrast, the mysterious majesty of the owl fills three-quarters of a double-page spread, poised for flight, intensely staring, allowing himself to be glimpsed by father and child and also by the reader.

The final picture shows the father carrying the child whose arms are twined around his neck as they return to their farmhouse. The text is framed by two bare saplings, reaching to the top of the white page like supplicating arms around the words:

> *When you go owling*
> *you don't need words*
> *or warm*
> *or anything but hope.*
> *That's what Pa says.*
> *The kind of hope*
> *that flies*
> *on silent wings*
> *under a shining*
> *Owl Moon.*

Text and pictures work together to create an unforgettable experience that many children will never have—unless they read this book.

Many other picture books contain wonderful realistic stories. Some are listed along with novels for intermediate- and advanced-grade readers in the accompanying figures.

Special Types of Contemporary Realism

Like other genres, realism includes a variety of types of literature. While much realistic fiction, such

5
Personality's Final Adventure

PERSONALITY WASN'T LIKE any ordinary turtle. He was an explorer. He liked to walk across the ledge of the Kanes' shiny new bathtub. He liked to crawl up Harry's blue jeans to the top of Harry's knee. Harry was sure that Personality thought he was climbing a mountain.

"He likes adventure," said Dorothy, watching Personality explore Harry's potted plant.

"He thinks he's hiking," explained Harry. "He takes after me."

Judith Caseley portrays a slice-of-life story in *Hurricane Harry*. We follow enthusiastic Harry Kane through his kindergarten year when his family moves into a new house, he earns money for his mother's birthday present, and he visits his grandmother in the hospital.

as *Bridge to Terabithia,* considers the events of daily life, many stories are special types of realism such as adventure stories, mysteries, animal stories, sports stories, humorous stories, romance, and series books. Additionally, some books fall into more than one category, such as a mystery that is combined with an adventure story. No matter what type, good books for young readers measure up to the criteria discussed here. Books that take a realistic look at daily life are listed in Figure 7-2.

Adventure Stories

Marked by an especially exciting, fast-paced plot, *adventure stories* captivate and hold readers who can't wait to see what happens. Often the central problem is a conflict between person and nature. The best adventure stories also contain multidimensional characters who control much of the action and who change as a result of the action.

Figure 7-2

Slice of Life Stories

Primary and Primary–Intermediate

Cleary, Beverly. *Beezus and Ramona.* (P–I)

Clifford, Eth. *The Remembering Box.* (P–I)

Clifton, Lucille. *The Boy Who Didn't Believe in Spring.* (P)

MacLachlan, Patricia. *Seven Kisses in a Row.* (P–I)

McCloskey, Robert. *One Morning in Maine.* (P)

———. *Time of Wonder.* (P–I)

Intermediate and Intermediate–Advanced

Blume, Judy. *Are You There God? It's Me, Margaret.* (I)

———. *Blubber.* (I)

Casely, Judith. *Hurricane Harry.* (I)

Lord, Bette B. *In the Year of the Boar & Jackie Robinson.* (I)

Mohr, Nicholasa. *Felita.* (I)

———. *Going Home.* (I)

Montgomery, Lucy Maud. *Anne of Green Gables.* (I–A)

Park, Barbara. *Kid in the Red Jacket.* (I)

Wosmek, Frances. *A Brown Bird Singing.* (I)

Advanced

Ellis, Sarah. *Pick-Up Sticks.* (A)

Fox, Paula. *Portrait of Ivan.* (I–A)

———. *The One-Eyed Cat.* (I–A)

Magorian, Michelle. *Goodnight, Mr. Tom.* (I–A)

Myers, Walter Dean. *Fast Sam, Cool Clyde and Stuff.* (A)

Yep, Laurence. *Child of the Owl.* (I–A)

Many young readers prefer adventure stories, enjoying the compelling nature of the plot.

In Gary Paulsen's *Hatchet* (A), an exciting adventure story set in the North woods of eastern Canada, 13-year-old Brian must land a plane alone when the pilot dies of a heart attack. Even worse,

He walked with his toes
pointing in, like that:

11

Peter has an adventure exploring his neighborhood on a snowy morning in Ezra Jack Keats's book, *The Snowy Day*. Keats cut shapes from different kinds of paper to create the vivid contrasts in the collage paintings.

Brian must survive in the wilderness with nothing but a hatchet to help him.

Donald Crews captures the sights, sounds, and feelings of a hair-raising adventure in *Shortcut* (P). Even though the children have been told not to walk on the railroad tracks, they decide to take the shortcut home, down the tracks. When they hear the whistle of an approaching train, they have to decide what to do. Do they go back to the turnoff? Do they run forward? Or do they jump into the briers and the snakes? When they jump and the train moves past, Crews fills the double-page spreads with dark oversized images of the train moving, and the words "klak-klak-klak-klakity." It is impossible to look at the pictures and not feel the wind and hear the noise of the train as it passes. The titles of many other outstanding adventure stories are listed in Figure 7-3.

Mysteries

A *mystery* is marked by suspense—will the mystery be solved? The focus in a mystery story is a question—who did it, where is it, or what happened—and the action centers on finding the answer to that question and thus solving the mystery. The best mysteries revolve around an intriguing problem and contain characters who are well developed and work to solve the problem, fast-paced action, and

What Could Go Wrong?
WILLO DAVIS ROBERTS

Cousins Charlie, Eddie, and Gracie fly from Seattle to San Francisco on what should be a simple trip. But when they discover that they are being followed and that they are involved in a deadly serious illegal matter, it turns into a frightening mystery. Willo Davis Roberts turns realistic fiction into mysterious experiences in *What Could Go Wrong?*

a logical solution that is foreshadowed through the careful presentation of clues. Many children go through a phase in which mysteries are all they want to read. Fortunately, there are some excellent mysteries for children of all ages.

Young readers enjoy reading mysteries such as Elizabeth Levy's *"Something Queer"* (P) series. Other series books, such as David Adler's *Cam Jansen* (P–I), Donold Sobol's *Encyclopedia Brown and the Case of the Disgusting Sneakers* (I) and Seymour Simon's *Einstein Anderson, Science Sleuth* (I) provide younger readers with brief exciting mysteries that satisfy their desire to figure things out.

Older readers also have a lot to choose among. Willo Davis Roberts writes stories that keep children reading and guessing. *To Grandmother's House We Go* (I) tells the story of three young children who search for the answer to a family mystery that

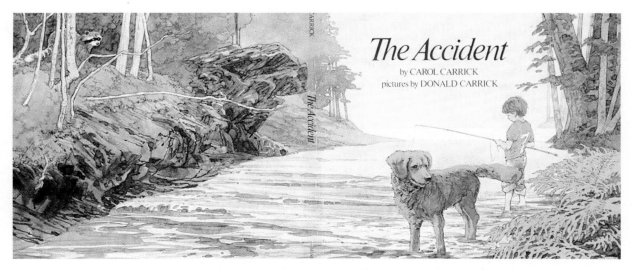

Although bright colors evoke a happy tone, the apprehensive look on the dog Bodger's face warns of impending trouble. (*The Accident* by Carol Carrick, illustrated by Donald Carrick)

threatens their own safety and happiness. James Howe's popular Sebastian Barth series provides children with well-written alternatives, such as ***Dew Drop Dead*** (I–A), to augment the many formula mystery series, such as the Nancy Drew and Hardy Boys books. Some of the best mystery stories available are listed in Figure 7-3.

Animal Stories

Animal stories are about realistic relationships between human beings and animals, most commonly horses or dogs. Although they focus on an animal-human relationship, this relationship is usually a vehicle for maturation by the central human character. Good animal stories have engaging characters who grow and change as a result of their experience with an animal. Many of these books are very moving, often provoking a strong emotional response.

Many picture books for younger readers tell stories about children and the animals they love. Donald and Carol Carrick's books about young Christopher and his dog Bodger, ***Sleep Out*** (P), ***Lost in the Storm*** (P), and ***The Accident*** (P), won the hearts of generations of young readers. Older readers also enjoy animal stories. Many intermediate-grade readers devour horse stories; others are not particular about the kind of animal they are reading about as long as the story is gripping, the character believable, and the relationship between the human and animal characters a special one. The 1992 Newbery Award winner, ***Shiloh*** (I–A) by Phyllis Rey-

nolds Naylor, is a beautiful story of a young boy's struggle to protect a mistreated dog. As Marty and the rescued dog grow to love each other, Marty grapples with increasingly complex issues of right and wrong. Children readily identify with Marty's struggle to do what's right in an adult world structured by law instead of love. Figure 7-3 lists some of the best animal stories available today.

Sports Stories

In *sports stories* the action revolves around a sport and the thrills and tensions accompanying that particular sport. Like mysteries, many sports stories are available that are not particularly well written but are devoured by young enthusiasts. Stories range from books about team sports, like baseball, to books about individual sports, like swimming, tennis, or gymnastics. An increasing number of sports books with girls as the central character increase the scope of the genre, and some recent sports stories examine social issues like sexism. The best of these books balance the descriptions of the sport with the development of the story, with the central character growing in some way as a result of the challenges he or she faces because of participation in the sport.

Philip Hanft's ***Never Fear, Flip the Dip Is Here*** (P) tells the story of a boy who loves baseball, but is such a bad player that the other kids won't let him play. When he meets an artist who is a former minor league player, he begins to learn how to

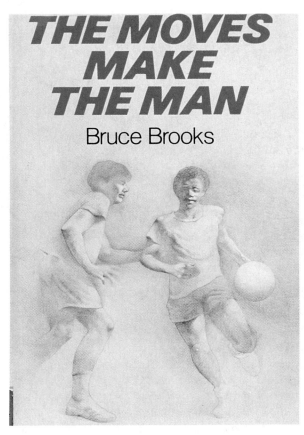

Bruce Brooks gives us much more than competition and close scoring games in his realistic sports novel, *The Moves Make the Man.* The dust jacket foreshadows events: The boys' closed eyes suggest lack of self-knowledge, but the way the watercolor, pen, and ink drawings define the boys' bodies prepares us for their potential self-discovery. The way one boy holds on to the other suggests mutual dependence—or success through united effort.

Aldo and DeDe masquerade in their fake mustaches while the full moon in the background sends a message that strange happenings will occur. (*Aldo Applesauce* by Johanna Hurwitz)

catch, throw, and hit; he also learns about friendship and self-confidence. Thomas B. Allen's soft illustrations capture the emotions of the characters and the physical exertions of the game.

Intermediate-grade readers appreciate the dilemma Andy confronts in Alfred Slote's **The Trading Game** (I). Andy tries to build a competitive ball team by enlisting his grandfather, a former major league player, as a visiting coach. He is also involved in trading baseball cards, having inherited an excellent collection from his deceased father. As he learns about his grandfather's competitive temper, he begins to understand his father a little more, and in the end he also learns a lot about himself, those he loves, and his relationships with them. Books like Bruce Brooks's **The Moves Make the**

Man (A) and Tessa Duder's **In Lane Three, Alex Archer** (A) are examples of excellent stories for older readers. Duder presents Alex as a character whose life revolves around her swimming, but who has common adolescent desires, fears, and problems as well. Even those who aren't involved with sports can appreciate and understand Alex as a believable human being. Other books that could be classified as sports books are listed in Figure 7-3.

Humorous Stories

Humorous stories present characters involved in funny situations, and the action that follows only heightens the humor. Monson (1966) studied the

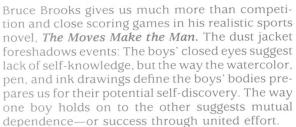

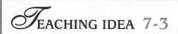

TEACHING IDEA 7-3

Study an Author's Works and Life

Choose an author who writes realistic novels and who has also written an autobiography, for example, Jean Little. Jean Little's autobiographies, *Little by Little* and *Stars Come Out Within*, tell about her life before, during, and after writing particular books. Read the books and discuss with your students how events in her life influenced the books she wrote. As a group, make a time line of Jean Little's life. List the books she wrote at various dates. List major events in her life as described in her autobiographies.

Books by Jean Little:

Different Dragons.
From Anna.
Mama's Going to Buy You a Mockingbird.
Mine for Keeps.
Hey, World! Here I Am.

Questions to begin the discussion:

1. What were the major influences in Jean Little's life?
2. How did events from her real life influence her writing? Can you find parallels between her stories and her life?
3. How did getting a Seeing Eye dog change Jean's life?
4. Who do you think has had the strongest influence on Jean?
5. What would you say to Jean if you met her?

humor found in children's books and categorized five types: (1) character humor, (2) humor of surprise, (3) humor of the impossible, (4) humor of words, and (5) humor of a ridiculous situation. Each of these types can be found in contemporary fiction.

The real world has both laughter and tears, both happiness and sadness; children's books reflect them all. A world made up of all problems and no joy is just as unrealistic as the vision of the happily-ever-after world we gave children a generation ago, when so many books displayed the happy-ending-no-matter-what syndrome. Children need humorous books, and they want them. When you ask children, "What kinds of stories do you like to read?" the majority will answer, "*Funny* stories!" Many teachers choose a humorous story to read

aloud to remind children of the pure pleasure of enjoying a good book. In the annual field test of newly published books, the Children's Choices sponsored by the International Reading Association and the Children's Book Council, humorous books such as Ken Adams's *When I Was Your Age* (P–I–A) repeatedly top the list.

Some of the best known humorous stories for the elementary grades are Beverly Cleary's Ramona books, such as *Ramona Quimby, Age 8* (P–I) in which Ramona cracks what she *thinks* is a hard-boiled egg over her head in the school cafeteria. Jerry Spinelli's books, such as *The Bathwater Gang* (I) make readers laugh and ask for another book by Spinelli. Figure 7-3 lists some of the best humorous stories available today.

Romance

The action in *romance stories* centers on falling in love. Often an element of self-discovery accompanies the action as an intense relationship with another person helps the central character to come to know himself or herself better. Upper elementary and middle-school aged children, most especially girls, often prefer romance stories, and there are a myriad of mundane, formula romance series, such as Sweet Valley High, for them to read. There are also some superbly crafted stories that can be classified as romance stories, such as the classic *Up a Road Slowly* (A) by Irene Hunt. In the best of these books the main character is a well-developed, vivid personality, one that young readers can identify with and care about. Kate Brewer is such a character. She learns about herself and her relationship with her father as she falls in love in Zibby ONeal's *In Summer Light* (A). Figure 7-3 lists other well-written romance novels.

Books in Series

Books that contain the same characters in varying situations across many different books are called *series books*. Obviously, series books are also animal, sports, humorous, adventure, mystery, romance, or "slice of life" stories, but their main characters appear in several books rather than just one. The best of these books contain memorable, vivid characters that readers remember from book to book.

Many children like to read series books; the familiarity makes them comfortable. Feitelsen and colleagues (1986) studied the effects of reading series books on first-grade readers. They found that

Figure 7-3

Types of Contemporary Realistic Fiction

Adventure Stories

Anno, Mitsumasa. *Anno's Journey.* (P)

Crews, Donald. *Bigmama's.* (P)

———. *Shortcut.* (P)

Dorros, Arthur. *Abuela.* (P)

George, Jean Craighead. *Julie of the Wolves.* (I)

———. *My Side of the Mountain.* (I)

Hahn, Mary Downing. *Dead Man in Indian Creek.* (I)

Hoffman, Mary. *Amazing Grace.* Illus. Caroline Binch. (P)

Holman, Felice. *Slake's Limbo.* (I)

Houston, James. *Frozen Fire.* (A)

Howard, Elizabeth F. *Aunt Flossie's Hats (and Crab Cakes Later).* Illus. James Ransome. (P)

Keats, Ezra Jack. *The Snowy Day.* (P)

———. *Whistle for Willie.* (P)

Medaris, Angela Shelf. *Dancing with the Indians.* (P)

Paulsen, Gary. *Dogsong.* (A)

———. *Hatchet.* (I)

———. *The Voyage of the Frog.* (A)

———. *Woodsong.* (A)

Ringgold, Faith. *Tar Beach.* (P)

Shura, Mary Frances. *Gentle Annie.* (I)

Sperry, Armstrong. *Call It Courage.* (I)

Voigt, Cynthia. *Homecoming.* (A)

———. *Dicey's Song.* (A)

Wagner, Jane. *J. T.* Photos by Gordon Parks. (I)

Watkins, Yoko Kawashima. *So Far from the Bamboo Grove.* (A)

Watson, Harvey. *Bob War and Poke.* (A)

Wild, Margaret. *Let the Celebrations Begin.* (I)

Mystery Stories

Adler, David. *Cam Jansen & the Mystery of the Dinosaur Bones.* (P)

Avi. *Windcatcher.* (I)

Bauer, Marion Dane. *Ghost Eye.* (I)

Bawden, Nina. *A Handful of Thieves.* (I)

———. *The Robbers.* (I)

———. *Rebel on a Rock.* (I)

———. *The House of Secrets.* (I)

———. *The Witch's Daughter.* (I)

Bellairs, John. *Curse of the Blue Figurine.* (I)

Bonsall, Crosby. *The Case of the Cat's Meow.* (P)

———. *The Case of the Hungry Stranger.* (P)

Brittain, Bill. *My Buddy, the King.* (I)

Conford, Ellen. *Jenny Archer.* (I)

Cross, Gillian. *Wolf.* (A)

Duncan, Lois. *Down a Dark Hall.* (A)

———. *Third Eye.* (A)

———. *Stranger with My Face.* (A)

George, Jean Craighead. *Who Really Killed Cock Robin?* (I)

Konigsburg, Elaine. *From the Mixed-Up Files of Mrs. Basil E. Frankweiler.* (I)

L'Engle, Madeleine. *The Arm of the Starfish.* (A)

Levy, Elizabeth. *Something Queer Is Going On (a Mystery).* (P)

Nixon, Joan Lowery. *Deadly Game of Magic.* (A)

Parish, Peggy. *Ghosts of Cougar Island.* (P)

Pearce, Philippa. *The Way to Sattin Shore.* (A)

Powell, Pamela. *The Turtle Watchers.* (I)

Pullman, Philip. *The Broken Bridge.* (A)

Raskin, Ellen. *The Westing Game.* (I)

Roberts, Willo Davis. *What Could Go Wrong?* (I)

———. *The View from the Cherry Tree.* (I)

Sharmat, Marjorie W. *Nate the Great & the Missing Key.* (P)

Simon, Seymour. *Einstein Anderson: Science Sleuth.* (I)

Sobol, Donald. *Encyclopedia Brown Takes the Cake.* (I)

Taylor, Theodore. *The Weirdo.* (A)

Townsend, John Rowe. *Tom Tiddler's Ground.* (A)

Trease, Geoffrey. *Flight of Angels.* (A)

Wells, Rosemary. *When No One Was Looking.* (A)

Wright, Betty Ren. *Rosie and the Dance of the Dinosaurs.* (I)

CONTINUED

———. *The Scariest Night.* (I)

———. *Ghosts Beneath Our Feet.* (I)

Animal Stories

Blades, Ann. *Mary of Mile 18.* (P)

Boston, Lucy. *A Stranger at Green Knowe.* (I)

Brett, Jan. *Annie and the Wild Animals.* (P)

Burnford, Sheila. *The Incredible Journey.* (A)

Byars, Betsy. *The Midnight Fox.* (I)

Eckert, Allan. *Incident at Hawk's Hill.* (A)

Ets, Marie Hall. *Just Me.* (P)

———. *Play with Me.* (P)

Farley, Walter. *The Black Stallion.* (I)

George, Jean Craighead. *The Cry of the Crow.* (I)

Henry, Marguerite. *Misty of Chincoteague.* (I)

———. *Stormy, Misty's Foal.* (I)

———. *King of the Wind.* (I)

Knight, Eric. *Lassie Come Home.* (I)

London, Jack. *Call of the Wild.* (A)

Mowat, Farley. *Owls in the Family.* (A)

Naylor, Phyllis Reynolds. *Shiloh.* (I)

North, Sterling. *Rascal.* (I)

Parnall, Peter. *Marsh Cat.* (I)

———. *Rock.* (P)

Rawlings, Marjorie Kinnan. *The Yearling.* (I)

Rawls, Wilson. *Where the Red Fern Grows.* (A)

Sewell, Anna. *Black Beauty: The Autobiography of a Horse.* (A)

Smith, Marya. *Winter Broken.* (I)

Tafuri, Nancy. *Do Not Disturb.* (P)

Thomas, Joyce Carol. *Golden Pasture.* (A)

Williams, Sue. *I Went Walking.* (P)

Sports Stories

Christopher, Matt. *Catch that Pass.* (I)

———. *Catcher with a Glass Arm.* (I)

———. *Dirt Bike Racer.* (I)

———. *Great Quarterback Switch.* (I)

Cohen, Barbara. *Thank You, Jackie Robinson.* (I)

Duder, Tessa. *In Lane Three, Alex Archer.* (A)

Dygard, Thomas J. *Forward Pass.* (A)

———. *Quarterback Walk-On.* (A)

Friend, David. *Baseball, Football, Daddy and Me.* Illus. Rick Brown. (P)

Kessler, Leonard. *Here Comes the Strikeout.* (P)

———. *Last One In Is a Rotten Egg.* (P)

Killien, Christi. *The Daffodils.* (I)

Knudson, R. R. *Zanballer.* (A)

———. *Zanbanger.* (A)

———. *Zanboomer.* (A)

Lipsyte, Robert. *The Brave.* (A)

———. *The Contender.* (A)

Slote, Alfred. *Finding Buck McHenry.* (I)

———. *Hang Tough, Paul Mather.* (I)

———. *Make-Believe Ball Player.* (I)

———. *Rabbit Ears.* (I)

———. *The Trading Game.* (I)

Smith, Robert Kimmel. *Bobby Baseball.* (I)

Spinelli, Jerry. *There's a Girl in My Hammerlock.* (A)

Tunis, John R. *Go, Team, Go!* (A)

———. *Rookie of the Year.* (A)

———. *Keystone Kids.* (A)

———. *World Series.* (A)

———. *Highpockets.* (A)

Humorous Stories

Allard, Harry. *Miss Nelson Is Missing.* Illus. James Marshall. (P)

Bechard, Margaret. *My Sister, My Science Report.* (I)

Blaine, Marge. *Terrible Thing That Happened at Our House.* Illus. John Wallner. (P)

Blume, Judy. *Fudge-a-Mania.* (I)

Burch, Robert. *Ida Early Comes Over the Mountain.* (I)

———. *Christmas with Ida Early.* (I)

Byars, Betsy. *The Cybil War.* (I)

———. *The Not-Just-Anybody Family.* (I)

———. *The Burning Questions of Bingo Brown.* (I)

———. *Bingo Brown and the Language of Love.* (I)

———. *Bingo Brown, Gypsy Lover.* (I)

Conford, Ellen. *If This Is Love, I'll Take Spaghetti.* (A)

CONTINUED

Gilson, Jamie. *Hobie Hanson, You're Weird.* (I)

Hall, Lynn. *Dagmar Schultz and the Powers of Darkness.* (A)

———. *Dagmar Schultz and the Green-Eyed Monster.* (A)

Hurwitz, Johanna. *Aldo Applesauce.* (I)

———. *Adventures of Ali Baba Bernstein.* (I)

———. *Once I Was a Plum Tree.* (I)

Kline, Suzy. *Herbie Jones and the Class Gift.* (P)

———. *Horrible Harry and the Green Slime.* (P)

Korman, Gordon. *I Want to Go Home!* (A)

———. *No Coins Please.* (A)

———. *Zucchini Warriors.* (A)

Lowry, Lois. *Anastasia Has the Answers.* (A)

MacLachlan, Patricia. *Seven Kisses in a Row.* (P)

McCloskey, Robert. *Homer Price.* (A)

Nabb, Magdalen. *Josie Smith at School.* (I)

Naylor, Phyllis Reynolds. *Alice in Rapture, Sort of.* (A)

Park, Barbara. *The Kid in the Red Jacket.* (I)

———. *Skinnybones.* (P)

Paulsen, Gary. *The Boy Who Owned the School.* (I)

Peck, Richard. *The Ghost Belonged to Me.* (A)

Porte, Barbara. *Fat Fanny, Beanpole Bertha, and the Boys.* (I)

———. *Ruthann and Her Pig.* (I)

Robertson, Keith. *Henry Reed's Baby-Sitting Service.* (A)

Rockwell, Thomas. *How to Eat Fried Worms.* (I)

Segal, Lore. *Tell Me a Mitzi.* Illus. Harriet Pincus. (P)

Twain, Mark. *Adventures of Tom Sawyer.* (A)

Romance Stories

Burnett, Frances Hodgson. *The Secret Garden.* (I)

Cleaver, Vera. *Trial Valley.* (A)

Cole, Brock. *Celine.* (A)

Greene, Bette. *Philip Hall Likes Me. I Reckon Maybe.* (I)

Greenwald, Sheila. *Give Us a Great Big Smile, Rosy Cole.* (I)

———. *It All Began with Jane Eyre.* (A)

———. *Rosy's Romance.* (I)

———. *Secret in Miranda's Closet.* (A)

———. *Valentine Rosy.* (I)

Hamilton, Virginia. *A Little Love.* (A)

Mazer, Norma Fox. *Taking Terri Mueller.* (A)

MacLachlan, Patricia. *Unclaimed Treasures.*

McDonnell, Christine. *Friends First.* (I)

Montgomery, Lucy M. *Anne of Green Gables.* (A)

———. *Anne of Avonlea.* (A)

Newton, Suzanne. *Where Are You When I Need You?* (A)

Oneal, Zibby. *In Summer Light.* (A)

Peck, Richard. *Are You in the House Alone?* (A)

Sachs, Marilyn. *Almost Fifteen.* (A)

———. *Fourteen.* (A)

series books facilitate reading comprehension because the reader knows the character and setting, the framework, and the background of the story. Knowing characters and what to expect from them makes reading easier; it's like meeting a good friend again. Recognizing that other books in the series are good stories increases the anticipation; if the first book was good, then the new one is sure to be.

Although some series books are formula fiction, several high quality series are available, such as Cynthia Rylant's *Henry and Mudge* books (P), Beverly Cleary's *Ramona* (P–I) books, Lois Lowry's *Anastasia Krupnik* (I) series, and the *Aldo* (P–I) books by Johanna Hurwitz. Other excellent series books are listed in Figure 7-4.

No matter how a realistic fiction book is labeled, a well-written story contains vivid characters, logical action, an understandable theme, and in the case of picture books, appropriate quality illustrations.

Unclaimed Treasures

by Patricia MacLachlan

Eleven-year-old Willa dreams of romantic love, but she realizes that many people close to her are lovable but as yet "unclaimed treasures." Patricia MacLachlan's *Unclaimed Treasures* illustrates the contemporary realistic romance novel.

THEMES IN CONTEMPORARY REALISM

The themes in contemporary realism are as many and as varied as life itself, and most books explore more than one theme. How would you classify *Bridge to Terabithia?* Is it a "friendship book" or a "death book" or a "growing-up book?" It is all of these, and more, depending on the story an individual reader creates during reading. It is helpful, however, to group books loosely by themes, since children often want to read several books that relate to a single theme; many teachers, too, enjoy constructing thematic units (discussed in Chapter 12) with their students. Some common themes in realistic fiction for children center around issues embedded in growing up, peer relations, family relations, and societal concerns.

Growing Up

Not surprisingly, some of the most popular books for children are about growing up. Because our society has few of the formalized rites of passage of primal societies, the way to adulthood is less clear for our children; they must mark their own paths. Books that portray a character struggling toward adulthood allow readers to see themselves reflected and provide a rehearsal for real life. There are numerous picture storybooks for primary-grade readers that depict realistic characters trying to cope with growing up. Many of these books deal with children's increasing independence from adults and the fear and delight accompanying that independence.

Young readers enjoy the stories Lucille Clifton writes about **Everett Anderson** (P). Within each book we see Everett working his way through a new challenge as he grows. Barbara Ann Porte's series of books about Harry, such as **Harry in Trouble** (P), are just right for newly independent readers. Harry learns to be responsible for his own actions, like repeatedly losing his library card, and children readily identify with him. We discuss some of these books in Chapter 3, and Figure 7-5 lists others.

Older readers continue to struggle for independence, often confronting conflicting feelings, difficult moral choices, and personal challenges along the way. Young people are engaged in a process of trying to find out who they are, what they like and do not like, and what they will and will not do. They are passionately preoccupied with themselves and may look to literature for solutions to or escape from their preoccupations. They enter into books in ways they cannot with television, making reading a more personal and creative experience. When students want to understand themselves, they create images of themselves behaving nobly and are left with important memories. Stories that hinge on the personal integrity of a character draw readers instinctively into grappling with envisaged tests of their own mettle.

Paula Fox's **One-Eyed Cat** (I–A) is a sensitive and gripping story. Eleven-year-old Ned gets an air rifle for his eleventh birthday but his father, a minister, forbids him to use it and packs it away in the attic. Temptation to hold the gun just once to see how it feels is too strong; Ned sneaks into the attic while his parents sleep and takes it out into the dark of night. He shoots when he sees something move and then returns the gun to the attic, feeling great guilt. When he discovers a cat that has had one eye shot out he feels even guiltier and very remorseful. Afraid to tell his family, he struggles

---

**Figure
7-4**

Books in Series

Primary

Allard, Harry. *Miss Nelson Has a Field Day.*

———. *Miss Nelson Is Back.*

———. *Miss Nelson Is Missing.*

Rylant, Cynthia. *Henry and Mudge and the Long Weekend.*

———. *Henry and Mudge in the Green Time.*

———. *Henry and Mudge Under the Yellow Moon.*

Smith, Janice Lee. *It's Not Easy Being George.*

———. *The Show-and-Tell War: and Other Stories About Adam Joshua.* Illus. Dick Gackenbach.

———. *The Monster in the Third Dresser Drawer.*

———. *The Kid Next Door and Other Headaches.*

Intermediate

Byars, Betsy. *Blossoms and the Green Phantom.*

———. *Blossom Promise.*

———. *Blossoms Meet the Vulture Lady.*

———. *Not-Just-Anybody Family.*

Cameron, Ann. *Stories Julian Tells.*

———. *Julian, Dream Doctor.*

———. *Julian's Glorious Summer.*

———. *More Stories Julian Tells.*

Cleary, Beverly. *Dear Mr. Henshaw.*

———. *Strider.*

Cleary, Beverly. *Ramona, the Brave.*

———. *Ramona and Her Mother.*

———. *Ramona and Her Father.*

———. *Ramona Quimby, Age 8.*

Cleary, Beverly. *Henry and Beezus.*

———. *Henry and Ribsy.*

———. *Henry and the Paper Route.*

———. *Henry Huggins.*

———. *Ribsy.*

Enright, Elizabeth. *Four Story Mistake.*

———. *Saturdays.*

———. *Spiderweb for Two.*

Estes, Eleanor. *Moffat Museum.*

———. *Moffats.*

———. *Rufus M.*

Haywood, Carolyn. *"B" Is for Betsy.*

———. *Betsy and Billy.*

———. *Betsy and the Boys.*

———. *Snowbound with Betsy.*

Haywood, Carolyn. *Eddie's Friend Boodles.*

———. *Eddie and the Fire Engine.*

———. *Eddie's Menagerie.*

———. *Eddie's Valuable Property.*

Hurwitz, Johanna. *Aldo Applesauce.*

———. *Aldo Ice Cream.*

---

with his feelings until he finally confesses what he did to an elderly neighbor who is dying. Ned's ability to come to terms with the truth is a step toward self-determination and taking control of his own life. Some books for intermediate and advanced readers that explore issues in growing up are listed in Figure 7-5.

Peer Relationships

Part of growing up involves learning to interact with ever-widening worlds and a broad variety of people.

Books that explore peer relationships mirror many of the concerns of young readers about their own lives. You may remember reading books as a child that pictured friendships as idyllic relationships of loyalty and noble sacrifice. Today's books explore a wide range of relationships among peers, with some characters noble, some loyal, but most simply human—warts and all. Because young people value acceptance by their friends, they are highly susceptible to peer pressure. The literature reflects their vulnerability and their strengths. Understandably, a number of realistic books dealing with peer rela-

CONTINUED

————. *Aldo Peanut Butter.*

————. *Much Ado About Aldo.*

Hurwitz, Johanna. *Russell and Elisa.*

————. *Rip-Roaring Russell.*

————. *Russell Rides Again.*

————. *Russell Sprouts.*

————. *School's Out.*

Kline, Suzy. *Herbie Jones and the Class Gift.*

————. *Herbie Jones and the Monster Ball.*

Lowry, Lois. *Anastasia Krupnik.*

————. *Anastasia Has the Answers.*

————. *Anastasia's Chosen Career.*

————. *Anastasia at Your Service.*

————. *Anastasia on Her Own.*

————. *All About Sam.*

McDonnell, Christine. *Toad Food and Measle Soup.*

————. *Lucky Charms & Birthday Wishes.*

Robertson, Keith. *Henry Reed's Think Tank.*

————. *Henry Reed, Inc.*

————. *Henry Reed's Baby-Sitting Service.*

————. *Henry Reed's Big Show.*

————. *Henry Reed's Journey.*

Simon, Seymour. *Einstein Anderson Lights Up the Sky.*

————. *Einstein Anderson Makes Up for Lost Time.*

————. *Einstein Anderson Sees Through the Invisible Man.*

————. *Einstein Anderson Shocks His Friends.*

————. *Einstein Anderson: Science Sleuth.*

Taylor, Sydney. *All of a Kind Family.*

————. *All of a Kind Family Uptown.*

————. *All of a Kind Family Downtown,*

————. *Ella of All of a Kind Family.*

Advanced

DeClements, Barthe. *Breaking Out.*

————. *Five Finger Discount.*

————. *Monkey See. Monkey Do.*

Greene, Constance. *A Girl Called Al.*

————. *I Know You, Al.*

————. *Your Old Pal Al.*

————. *Al(exandra) the Great.*

————. *Just Plain Al.*

Pascal, Francine. *Sweet Valley Slumber Party.*

Voigt, Cynthia. *Homecoming.*

————. *Dicey's Song.*

————. *Came a Stranger.*

————. *The Runner.*

---

tionships are set in school or revolve around a school-related problem.

Many picture storybooks involve peer relationships (see Chapter 3 and Figure 7-6). Making new friends, going to school, and learning to share are some of the things that children learn to do as they widen their circle of friends. Books such as Steven Kellogg's **Best Friends** (P) or John Steptoe's **Stevie** (P) can provide validating, illuminating experiences. In **Best Friends** Kathy is jealous when her best friend goes away for the summer and seems to be having too much fun without her. The difference between her fantasies and what really happens are humorously apparent in Kellogg's detailed illustrations. Steptoe's book shows that we may not appreciate a friend until he has moved away.

Many books about peer relationships for intermediate-grade students are easy to read and offer humor and satisfaction as well as reassurance that boys and girls are not alone in their feelings. These kinds of books can be read quickly and with ease by developing readers. They also form a solid foundation for the more complex stories and relationships that students will encounter as they mature.

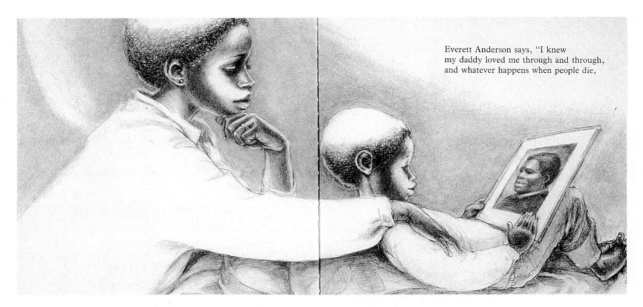

Everett Anderson says, "I knew
my daddy loved me through and through,
and whatever happens when people die,

Ann Grifalconi's charcoals convey a mother's strength and compassion, as evident in her face and her comforting touch. Both help Everett Anderson deal with his grief as he mourns his father's death. (*Everett Anderson's Goodbye* by Lucille Clifton)

Steptoe's warm tones next to strong black lines provide the appropriate medium for the mood of competition for love. Robert's aching need for affection is apparent when he lingers in the doorway to watch his mother hug little Stevie, a child she babysits for. (*Stevie* by John Steptoe)

Figure 7-5

Books About Growing Up

Primary

Cooney, Barbara. *Island Boy.*

———. *Miss Rumphius.*

de Paola, Tomie. *The Art Lesson.*

Garelick, May. *Just My Size.*

Henkes, Kevin. *Grandpa and Bo.*

———. *Jessica.*

Hutchins, Pat. *Happy Birthday, Sam.*

———. *Titch.*

———. *You'll Soon Grow into Them Titch.*

Johnston, Tony. *Yonder.*

Keats, Ezra Jack. *Peter's Chair.*

McMillan, Bruce. *Step by Step.*

Yashima, Taro. *Crow Boy.*

Zolotow, Charlotte. *The Hating Book.*

———. *I Like to Be Little.*

———. *Someone New.*

———. *William's Doll.*

Intermediate

Bauer, Marion Dane. *On My Honor.*

Blume, Judy. *Are You There God? It's Me, Margaret.*

———. *Then Again, Maybe I Won't.*

———. *Deenie.*

Burch, Robert. *King Kong and Other Poets.*

Cassedy, Sylvia. *Lucie Babbidge's House.*

Cohen, Barbara. *213 Valentines.*

Corcoran, Barbara. *The Potato Kid.*

Greenwald, Sheila. *Here's Hermione: A Rosy Cole Production.*

———. *Alvin Webster's Surefire Plan for Success (and How It Failed).*

Haseley, Dennis. *Shadows.*

Korman, Gordon. *The Twinkie Squad.*

Lisle, Janet Taylor. *Afternoon of the Elves.*

Naylor, Phyllis Reynolds. *Alice in Rapture, Sort of.*

———. *The Agony of Alice.*

———. *Reluctantly Alice.*

Lyon, George Ella. *Red Rover, Red Rover.*

Advanced

Arter, Jim. *Gruel and Unusual Punishment.*

Bauer, Marion Dane. *Face to Face.*

Geras, Adele. *Happy Endings.*

Hathorn, Libby. *Thunderwith.*

Hermes, Patricia. *Mama, Let's Dance.*

Little, Jean. *Home from Far.*

———. *Mama's going to Buy You a Mockingbird.*

Lowry, Lois. *A Summer to Die.*

———. *Rabble Starkey.*

MacLachlan, Patricia. *The Facts and Fictions of Minna Pratt.*

McDonnell, Christine. *Friends First.*

Thesman, Jean. *The Rain Catchers.*

Writers who excel in capturing the spirit of an elementary classroom include Johanna Hurwitz, Robert Burch, Barthe DeClements, Patricia Reilly Giff, Barbara Park, and Jamie Gilson. In one of Hurwitz's books, Lucas Cott has the reputation of being the *Class Clown* (P–I) in his third-grade room. After a series of escapades, Lucas decides to turn over a new leaf and become the perfect student, but it is not as easy as he thinks. Other books of this type are listed in Figure 7-6.

As children mature, their relationships become more complex. Often the unevenness of the onset of adolescence creates gulfs between good friends: One is interested in the opposite sex, one isn't; one is physically mature, one isn't. Adolescence also brings with it increasing pressures to experiment with the dangerous side of life—drugs and alcohol, sex, brushes with the law—and books for advanced readers often contain characters who struggle with a personal crisis as they seek to stand up for what they value while at the same time maintain their friendships.

Because adolescents are concerned with these sensitive issues, books for adolescents examine them. This necessitates careful selection by teachers and librarians. Some books might not be suitable for reading aloud or class discussions; they might be best read independently. As discussed

---

Teaching idea 7-4

Mothers and Fathers in Realistic Novels

Parents are portrayed in both positive and negative ways in realistic novels. Have students read the following books and compare the image of parents, discussing these questions:

1. How do the girls get along with their fathers? Mothers?
2. How do the boys get along with their mothers? Fathers?
3. How would you describe the best parents? The worst?
4. Choose phrases from each book to best describe the parents.

Fathers:

Bawden, Nina. *Robbers.*

Brooks, Bruce. *Midnight Hour Encores.*

Cleary, Beverly. *Ramona and Her Father.*

Fleischman, Paul. *Rear-View Mirrors.*

Fox, Paula. *The Moonlight Man.*

——. *Portrait of Ivan.*

Grindley, S. *Knock, Knock! Who's There?*

Hamilton, Virginia. *A Little Love.*

Houston, Gloria. *Littlejim.*

Oneal, Zibby. *In Summer Light.*

Peck, Richard. *Father Figure.*

Sebestyen, Ouida. *Words by Heart.*

Thomas, Joyce Carol. *Golden Pasture.*

Yep, Laurence. *Dragonwings.*

Mothers:

Bauer, Marion Dane. *Like Mother, Like Daughter.*

Brooks, Bruce. *The Moves Make the Man.*

——. *What Hearts.*

Bunting, Eve. *Is Anybody There?*

Cleary, Beverly. *Ramona and Her Mother.*

Colman, Hila. *Rich and Famous Like My Mom.*

Duder, Tessa. *Jellybean.*

Henkes, Kevin. *Words of Stone.*

Lowry, Lois. *Rabble Starkey.*

Paterson, Katherine. *The Great Gilly Hopkins.*

——. *Park's Quest.*

Rylant, Cynthia. *A Fine White Dust.*

Sebestyen, Ouida. *IOU'S.*

Smith, Doris Buchanan. *Return to Bitter Creek.*

Van Leeuwen, Jean. *Dear Mom, You're Ruining My Life.*

Voigt, Cynthia. *A Solitary Blue.*

---

earlier, the standards of your community are important to consider. In addition, it is useful to ask yourself, are the sensitive issues in this book treated realistically or graphically? If a book is graphic—dwelling on an issue through an excess of detail—then perhaps it is not appropriate or well written.

Robert Cormier's classic, **The Chocolate War** (A), is a beautifully written book which grapples with some sensitive issues and shows that in some cases a person who stands up for his beliefs may stand alone. When Jerry refuses to participate in a school fund-raising sale of chocolate bars, he faces the opposition of Archie, the school gang leader, and Brother Leon, the power-hungry headmaster. Between the two of them they give Jerry a physical and psychological beating, but he stands firm

against the tyranny of power and peer pressure. Some excellent books for older readers are listed in Figure 7-6.

Family Relationships

Contemporary children's books present a varied picture of family life and probe new dimensions of realism. Not only are traditional families portrayed, but also communal, one-parent, and extended families, as well as families headed by divorced or separated parents, children living alone without adults, and homeless families. Although there have always been books in which each family member stays in culturally assigned roles, books about nontraditional households appear with increasing frequency, answering children's need to see life like it really is. Modern readers find both mirrors and windows in the wealth of family stories available today.

Family stories have changed in other ways as well. Fathers receive increasing attention in books for children and adolescents. Where they had once been ignored, they are now recognized as viable literary characters; their relationships, especially with daughters, are never simple. Fictional mothers now run the full range of likeable to despicable characters just as they do in real life.

Stories about siblings have also changed with the times. Children growing up in the same home must learn to share possessions, space, and parents or guardians. Stories of the idyllic relationships portrayed in **Little Women** (A) or **Little House on the Prairie** (I) are seldom found in today's books. More often, sibling rivalry or learning to accept stepsisters, stepbrothers, or wards in foster homes is treated in contemporary novels, such as Byars's **The Pinballs** (I–A) or Katherine Paterson's **The Great Gilly Hopkins** (I–A). In addition to happy, well-adjusted children from safe, loving homes, children are portrayed as victims of child abuse, abandonment, alcoholism, neglect, and a whole range of society's ills. These characters are often cynical, bitter, disillusioned, and despondent, but sometimes courageous and strong.

Jean Little portrays an unusual big and little sister relationship in **Jess Was the Brave One** (P). Claire's overactive imagination results in so many fears that her younger sister assumes a protective role toward her. When some bullies threaten Jess, Claire's love for her sister helps her overcome her fear while her imagination helps her find a perfect way to scare off the bullies.

Patricia MacLachlan's **Journey** (I–A) explores a sad and sensitive topic—rejection by one's own parent. When 11-year-old Journey's mother leaves him and his sister with their grandparents, he is upset, unhappy, and looking for someone to blame. Photography helps him make painful discoveries about himself, his mother, and his past. He comes to accept his mother for what she is and to understand just how much his grandfather has always loved him.

Some books about family relationships for primary-grade readers are presented in Chapter 3. Figure 7-6 contains additional titles for these readers as well as books appropriate for intermediate- and advanced-grade readers.

Older relatives and friends, too, are increasingly visible in realistic stories for children. Often these friends and relatives die, and the central character must learn to accept this, as in Kevin Henkes's **Words of Stone** (A) and Cynthia Rylant's **Missing May** (A), the 1993 Newbery Award winner. Rylant's story opens in sorrow: May, beloved mother-aunt and wife, has died, and mourning has overwhelmed Ob, her husband, and Summer, her daughter-niece. As the story progresses, we go both backward, to when Summer came to live with May and Ob, and forward, to the time when sorrow abates and loving memories begin.

Sometimes an older relative or friend moves in with the character's family to create a new and sometimes difficult situation with which the character must cope, as in Mazer's **A Figure of Speech** (A). Other books explore the rich and vital relationships possible between young and old. Books about relationships with the elderly are listed in Figure 7-6.

Societal Concerns

Many books for children demonstrate society's increasing awareness of the accomplishments and special needs of the disabled. Disabled characters appear with increasing frequency in children's books: The trend has been from nearly absolute neglect, to an occasional secondary character, to the present realistic distribution of disabled characters reflective of their incidence in our population. In today's novels, disabled characters do not always recover or improve, miraculously; they sometimes die. Attitudes of those around the disabled do not always improve; they often remain narrow and cruel. Happy endings are no longer automatic in children's books, and devoted attempts to teach, train, or help a disabled character do not always result in progress, as they would have two decades ago. Early novels with disabled characters often contained episodes of miraculous cures, but in today's books we find gradual improvement and partial resolution of problems, or totally open-ended novels. A character's progress results from training programs, therapy, rehabilitation programs, or schools, rather than from the actions of some deus ex machina. Moral strength and personal determination, however, continue to be attributes of the characters who succeed.

Contemporary realistic fiction portrays many kinds of disabilities: physical, mental, and emotional. Physical impairments range from minimal

The background movement in color and tone suggests that Clay, the central figure, is trying to escape into the unknown. Clay searches for survival, and his clenched fists and apprehensive look foretell his determination to overcome difficult odds. (*Monkey Island* by Paula Fox)

muscular dysfunction to total paralysis, with as many causes as there are limitations on the disabled person's ability to move about. Orthopedic problems are central or peripheral elements in children's books more frequently than any other type of disability. Physically disabled children have dreams and aspirations like any child; overprotection and patronage, no matter how well intended, can destroy these. Judith Caseley's **Harry and Willy and Carrothead** (P) makes the point that Harry, born with no left hand, can still do lots of things. He's especially good at baseball and at being a good friend.

Deafness and hearing impairment are an invisible disability; there are no obvious signs, and as a result, misunderstandings are frequent. Because the deaf look like everybody else, they are expected to cope with the environment normally. When this does not happen, strange inferences are made—most often about their intellectual abilities. Visually disabled children range from those who are totally blind and read braille to those who are visually

Figure
7-6

Books About Relationships With Others

Peers

Aliki. *We Are Best Friends.* (P)

Blume, Judy. *Blubber.* (I)

———. *Just as Long as We're Together.* (I)

Doherty, Berlie. *White Peak Farm.* (A)

———. *Class Dismissed.* (A)

Graham, Bob. *Crusher Is Coming.* (P)

Henkes, Kevin. *Chester's Way.* (P)

———. *Words of Stone.* (I)

Hughes, Shirley. *Wheels.* (P)

Kellogg, Steven. *Best Friends.* (P)

Lowry, Lois. *Autumn Street.* (I)

MacLachlan, Patricia. *Seven Kisses in a Row.* (I)

Orgel, Doris. *Nobodies and Somebodies.* (I)

Robins, Joan. *Addie Meets Max.* (P)

Rylant, Cynthia. *Missing May.* (A)

Sharmat, Marjorie. *Gladys Told Me to Meet Her Here.* (P)

Slepian, Jan. *The Broccoli Tapes.* (I)

Steptoe, John. *Stevie.* (P)

Viorst, Judith. *Rosie and Michael.* (P)

Zolotow, Charlotte. *The Hating Book.* (P)

Family Relationships

Bawden, Nina. *Rebel on a Rock.* (A)

———. *The Outside Child.* (A)

Blume, Judy. *Fudge-a-mania.* (I)

———. *One in the Middle Is the Green Kangaroo.* (P)

———. *Pain and the Great One.* (P)

———. *Superfudge.* (I)

———. *Tales of a Fourth Grade Nothing.* (I)

Bunting, Eve. *Sharing Susan.* (I)

Cassedy, Sylvia. *M. E. and Morton.* (I)

Cleaver, Vera. *Belle Pruitt.* (I)

Conrad, Pam. *My Daniel.* (I)

Doherty, Berlie. *White Peak Farm.* (I)

Fenner, Carol. *Randall's Wall.* (I)

Geringer, Laura. *Silverpoint.* (A)

Gleitzman, Morris. *Two Weeks with the Queen.* (A)

Honeycutt, Natalie. *Ask Me Something Easy.* (I)

King-Smith, Dick. *Sophie's Snail.* (P)

Koertge, Ron. *Mariposa Blues.* (A)

Littke, Lael. *Blue Skye.* (I)

MacLachlan, Patricia. *Arthur, for the Very First Time.* (I)

———. *The Facts and Fictions of Minna Pratt.* (A)

———. *Unclaimed Treasures.* (I)

Paterson, Katherine. *The Great Gilly Hopkins.* (I)

———. *Jacob Have I Loved.* (A)

Paulsen, Gary. *The Winter Room.* (A)

Sachs, Marilyn. *The Bear's House.* (I)

———. *Circles.* (A)

———. *Just Like a Friend.* (A)

Smith, Doris Buchanan. *Karate Dancer.* (A)

Stevenson, Laura C. *Happily After All.* (I)

Personal Integrity

Avi. *Nothing But the Truth: A Documentary Novel.* (A)

Cole, Brock. *Celine.* (A)

Cross, Gillian. *A Map of Nowhere.* (A)

Ferguson, Alane. *Cricket and the Crackerbox Kid.* (I)

Fox, Paula. *Blowfish Live in the Sea.* (A)

———. *One-Eyed Cat.* (A)

———. *A Place Apart.* (A)

Little, Jean. *Hey World, Here I Am!* (I)

Lowry, Lois. *Rabble Starkey.* (A)

MacKinnon, Bernie. *Song for a Shadow.* (A)

Mahy, Margaret. *Memory.* (A)

Paterson, Katherine. *Come Sing, Jimmy Jo.* (A)

———. *Park's Quest.* (A)

Shusterman, Neal. *Speeding Bullet.* (A)

Smith, Marya. *Across the Creek.* (A)

Snyder, Zilpha Keatley. *Libby on Wednesday.* (I)

CONTINUED

Spinelli, Jerry. *Maniac Magee.* (I)

Strommen, Judith Bernie. *Grady the Great.* (I)

Williams-Garcia, Rita. *Fast Talk on a Slow Track.* (A)

Relationships With Older People

Aliki. *A Special Trade.* (P)

———. *The Two of Them.* (P)

Brooks, Bruce. *Everywhere.* (I)

de Paola, Tomie. *Nana Upstairs and Nana Downstairs.* (P)

———. *Now One Foot, Now the Other.* (P)

Doherty, Berlie. *White Peak Farm.* (A)

Fox, Mem. *Wilfrid Gordon McDonald Partridge.* Illus. Julie Vivas. (P)

Gould, Deborah. *Grandpa's Slide Show.* (P)

Hartling, Peter. *Old John.* Trans Elizabeth Crawford. (I)

Mazer, Norma Fox. *A Figure of Speech.* (A)

Okimoto, Jean Davies. *Take a Chance, Gramps!* (I)

Rylant, Cynthia. *Missing May.* (I)

Wrightson, Patricia. *Balyet.* (A)

Zolotow, Charlotte. *My Grandson Lew.* Illus. William Pène duBois. (P)

---

impaired and read large print or with the aid of special magnifying lenses or optical scanners. Fiction portraying the deaf and the blind coping with their disability offers many fine stories, such as Jean Little's *Listen for the Singing* (I).

Mentally retarded characters appear in children's books less often than blind or emotionally disturbed ones, or those with orthopedic problems, but more often than the deaf or speech impaired. Mental retardation was among the first special needs topics to appear in children's books. Books that portray mentally retarded characters often explore friendships between disabled and nondisabled characters, or family adjustment to a disabled family member. Lucille Clifton's *My Friend Jacob* (P) is a sensitively written picture book that portrays a relationship between a young boy and his older mentally retarded friend.

Emotional disturbance is often poorly understood, misdiagnosed, and feared. This happens because it is such a complex syndrome, with bizarre and idiosyncratic manifestations. There are a few fine books that accurately portray this disability, such as Phyllis Naylor's *The Keeper* (A), which describes a family with a manic-depressive father. Specific learning disabilities suffer from lack of

definition and clarification in schools as well as in children's books. This lack of clarity of definition spills over into literature with few books of literary quality accurately portraying a learning disabled character.

Figure 7-7 lists books that explore issues related to disabilities that are appropriate for primary through advanced readers.

Many other books explore current social issues such as homelessness and the drug culture. The types of issues explored in realistic fiction reflect the current concerns of society; a few years ago books about religious cults abounded, and in the 1960s books about desegregation were numerous. Homelessness is an issue in several children's books, from Eve Bunting's *Fly Away Home* (P) to Stephanie Tolan's *Sophie and the Sidewalk Man* (I) to Paula Fox's *Monkey Island* (A). Bunting and Tolan present homelessness from a young child's perspective. In *Fly Away Home,* the story is narrated by a young boy who lives with his father at an airport. Ronald Himler's illustrations heighten the terrible sadness of being homeless. In Tolan's story a young girl is moved by the plight of a homeless man she sees regularly. Eventually, she gives him half of the money she has saved to buy herself

---

Figure
7-7

Books About Social Issues

Disabilities

Byars, Betsy. *Summer of the Swans* (I)

Clifton, Lucille. *My Friend Jacob.* (P)

Covington, Dennis. *Lizard.* (I)

Dale, Mitzi. *Round the Bend.* (A)

Fassler, Joan. *Howie Helps Himself.* (P)

Holland, Isabelle. *The Man Without a Face.* (A)

Lasker, Joe. *He's My Brother.* (P)

Little, Jean. *From Anna.* (I)

———. *Listen for the Singing.* (I)

———. *Mine for Keeps.* (I)

Naylor, Phyllis Reynolds. *The Keeper.* (A)

Patterson, Nancy Ruth. *The Shiniest Rock of All.* (I)

Sachs, Marilyn. *The Bears' House.* (I)

———. *Fran Ellen's House.* (I)

Smith, Doris Buchanan. *Voyages.* (I)

Voigt, Cynthia. *Homecoming.* (A)

———. *Dicey's Song.* (A)

———. *Izzy Willy-Nilly.* (A)

Social Concerns

Bunting, Eve. *Fly Away Home.* Illus. Ronald Himler. (P)

Byars, Betsy. *The Pinballs.* (I)

———. *Cracker Jackson.* (I)

Davis, Jenny. *Checking on the Moon.* (A)

Fox, Paula. *Monkey Island.* (A)

Hamilton, Virginia. *M. C. Higgins, the Great.* (A)

———. *Zeely.* (A)

Herzig, Alison Cragin, and Jane Lawrence Mali. *Sam and the Moon Queen.* (I)

Hill, Elizabeth. *Evan's Corner.* (P)

Mennen, Ingrid, and Niki Daly. *Somewhere in Africa.* Illus. Nicolaas Maritz. (P)

Smith, Marya. *Winter Broken.* (A)

Tolan, Stephanie S. *Sophie and the Sidewalk Man.* (I)

---

something that she really wants. Neither book is simplistic; both present homelessness as a serious problem with no easy answers.

In *Monkey Island,* Paula Fox explores what it might be like to be a young boy and be homeless and alone. When Clay's mother disappears he escapes from the welfare hotel they were living in, preferring to live on the streets rather than in a foster home. Clay's one of the lucky ones, though, because he meets Buddy, a young African American, and Calvin, an older man, who become his family. However, when cold weather sets in and their city park home is attacked by young men carrying chains and baseball bats, the three must find new shelter. Clay ends up in the hospital with pneumonia, eventually goes to a foster family, and is finally reunited with his mother. Some of the best recent books that reflect contemporary societal concerns are listed in Figure 7-7.

CONTEMPORARY REALISM IN THE CLASSROOM

Children enjoy contemporary realism, and this genre is often a way to entice reluctant readers to taste the joys of a good book. The books are often ones passed around from reader to reader as children discover books they can see themselves in. These books can also open windows on other people and other worlds, offering children the opportunity to try on other lives for the space of time it takes them to read a book.

Reading and discussing contemporary realism provides an opportunity to connect children's lives with the classroom, as children use their own experiences to help them understand the books they read. Many teachers find that discussing contemporary realism opens new paths of communication

Teaching Idea 7-5

Create a Jackdaw

The term *jackdaw* comes from the name of an English bird that fills its nest with all sorts of objects. We use it to refer to a collection of items that relate to a book. Such items make a book talk more interesting. Collect items that relate to a contemporary realistic novel. You might include the following:

Maps of the setting.
Songs, dances, poems the character might say or do.
A letter the character might write or receive.
Biographical notes about the author.
A hat the character might wear.
A time line of events in the plot.

Use the items to give a book talk to your students. Invite students to give their own jackdaw book talk.

Teaching Idea 7-6

Animals in Realistic Novels

Wild animals and pets appear in realistic novels frequently. Read several stories about animals. Discuss questions like these with your students:

1. How do the authors make you like the animal?

2. What kinds of problems do the animals face?

3. What does the animal do to solve the problems?

4. How does the animal show loyalty to humans?

Dogs:

Burnford, Sheila. *The Incredible Journey.* (I)

DeJong, Meindert. *Hurry Home, Candy.* (I)

Knight, Eric M. *Lassie Come Home.* (I)

Naylor, Phyllis Reynolds. *Shiloh.* (I)

Rawls, Wilson. *Where the Red Fern Grows.* (I)

Horses:

Bagnold, Enid. *National Velvet.*

Corcoran, Barbara. *A Horse Named Sky.*

Farley, Walter. *The Black Stallion.*

Henry, Marguerite. *Misty of Chincoteague.*

———. *King of the Wind.*

Sewell, Anna. *Black Beauty.*

among students and between students and teachers.

Contemporary realism can also acquaint children with other cultures and communities. Reading contemporary realism that is set in different parts of the country or the world, contains characters that are culturally diverse, and explores the lives of a variety of people helps children learn about others. Knowing people from diverse cultures through books is a first step toward building understanding and tolerance. It is also a first step toward recognizing our common humanity—the wishes, fears, and needs we all share, regardless of culture. Many culturally diverse titles are discussed in Chapter 11.

Any well-stocked classroom library contains many contemporary realistic fiction titles. These books should represent a wide range of reading levels, a diversity of authors, and a range of types and themes. Comparing books of similar types or themes can help students learn about literature and writing as they closely examine how different authors approach comparable tasks. Reading a wide range of books can also help students develop a knowledge of their own preferences.

Having many titles on hand means that teachers can readily incorporate realistic fiction in thematic units, building on students' interests or curricular demands by making available numerous appropriate and timely books.

Fine contemporary realistic fiction rings with truth. It offers readers multiple lenses through which to view the world and themselves, allowing them to become finer people, more compassionate, more knowledgeable, more heroic than they are in real life. Britton (1970) argues that the virtual experience possible through reading fiction is an important vehicle for constructing personal values. Freed from the necessity of action that real life demands, readers engaged with stories can contemplate feelings, consider actions, and make value judgments. Realistic fiction can be the mirror and the window in which we readers see our better selves.

SUMMARY

Books of contemporary realistic fiction are plausible stories set in today's world. The characters often seem like people we know, and the plots consist of events and actions that could and do occur in everyday life. Realistic fiction includes stories about ordinary lives, adventure stories, mysteries, animal stories, sports stories, humorous stories, and romances. Several series are extremely popular with young readers, each with a memorable character who ties the books together. Contemporary realism explores a number of themes, among them growing up, peer and family relationships, and current social concerns. Sometimes sensitive issues are raised and discussed. Children enjoy realistic fiction, and teachers find the books an essential part of any classroom library.

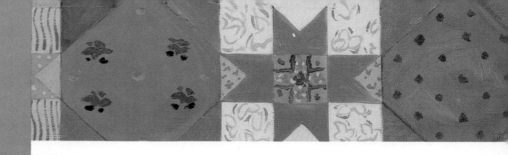

8

Historical Fiction

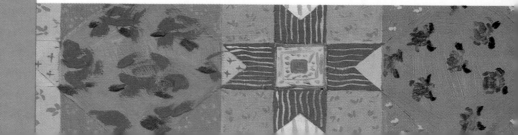

HISTORY HELP

He made us learn the names,
He made us memorize each date.
He said,
    "History repeats itself.
    Learn now! It's not too late."

OK . . . I'll learn my history,
Even though the past is done,
But isn't there some simple way
To help make history fun?

                                        Brod Bagert

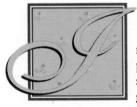

n historical fiction the events of the past occur as the story of people who seem real to us. As history becomes a story about someone we know, it becomes as interesting as classroom gossip.

History is a story, the story of the world and its people and cultures that rise and fall across time. Historical fiction tells the stories of history; as a distinct genre it consists of imaginative stories grounded in the facts of our past. It is not biography (discussed in Chapter 9), which focuses on the life of an individual; historical fiction has a wider scope. Historical fiction differs from nonfiction (discussed in Chapter 10), in that it not only presents facts or re-creates a time and place, but also weaves the facts into a fictional story. Historical fiction is realistic—the events could have occurred and people portrayed could have lived —but it differs from contemporary realistic fiction because these stories are set in the past rather than the present.

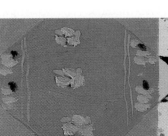

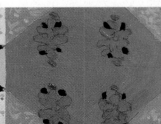

Some books we now classify as historical fiction began as contemporary realism. In 1868 Louisa May Alcott's *Little Women* (A) was a contemporary work of realism. The intervening years have made the story historical. This is a special property of historical fiction that does not occur in other genres; time does not change other genres.

Some historical fiction stories are more factual than others, as authors include real events and/or people in their imaginative stories. Ann Turner bases *Grasshopper Summer* (A) on a real event in the Dakota Territory during the Westward Expansion—the plague of grasshoppers that swarmed through the Great Plains eating everything in sight and creating great hardships for many farmers. However, the particular story she tells and the characters she creates are entirely fictional. Irene Hunt's *Across Five Aprils* (A) is a classic story of the Civil War with names, dates, newspaper accounts of real battles, and realistic political and social detail woven into a moving fictional story.

Other stories are memoirs of the authors' own lives or the lives of their relatives, sifted, artistically arranged, and presented as engaging stories. Mattie Lou O'Kelley's *From the Hills of Georgia* (P–I), Thomas B. Allen's *On Grandaddy's Farm* (P), Alice McLerran's *Roxaboxen* (I), and Laura Ingalls Wilder's *Little House* (I) books are all beautifully woven memories. McLerran's story is based on her mother's childhood and she used her mother's childhood manuscript, memories of relatives, letters, and maps of former Roxaboxenites to construct her story of an imaginary town built in the desert by a group of children.

Some authors set their stories in times past but do not specifically connect them with any particular historical events or people. Still, these authors know a great deal about the time and place of their story's setting; it is the authentic social details that make the stories good history. World War II is the setting for Deborah Kogan Ray's *My Daddy Was a Soldier* (P) and Mary Downing Hahn's *Stepping on the Cracks* (A), and each of these stories is filled with details about daily life in World War II America. Ray's book includes a great deal of visual detail in the illustrations.

No matter what type of story it is, outstanding historical fiction shows that history is created by people, that people living now are tied to those who lived in the past through a common humanity, and that human conditions of the past shape our lives today. Historical fiction offers readers the opportunity to travel across time and place and thus to find themselves.

HISTORICAL FICTION IN CHILDREN'S LIVES

History is made by people—what they do, what they say, and what they are—people with strengths and weaknesses who experience victories and defeats. Authors of books set in the past want children to know historical figures as human beings—real people like ourselves who have shortcomings as well as strengths. Historical events affected the common people perhaps even more than they did kings and battle leaders; the way the common folk responded to traumatic events shows adaptability and gives modern children a sense of reality of times past. Today's children have a hard time imagining life without computers, video technology, rapid transportation, and modern communication. They have learned to expect that problems be solved in the 30 minutes of a TV sitcom.

When they read good historical fiction, children can imagine themselves living in another time and place. They can speculate about how they would have reacted and how they would have felt. They can read about ordinary people acting heroically. By doing so, they begin to build an understanding of the impact one person can have on history.

Reading historical fiction is like listening to a grandmother's stories; there are strong links between children's family histories and the historical fiction they read. Children are interested in finding out about what life was like in the "olden" days. Knowing stories of grandmother's childhood, of great-great-grandfather's escape from slavery through the Underground Railroad, or of a great-aunt's journey across the ocean to America is knowing history. Just as family stories help children discover their own place in the history of their family, historical fiction can help children discover their own place in the history of their world; it can give them a sense of the historical importance of their own lives. Well-written historical fiction can make the past alive, real, and meaningful to children who are living today and who will shape the world of tomorrow.

Historical fiction relates to children's lives both in and out of school. Stories of life in the past set in the place that they live help children to see their home with new eyes. Knowing the details of daily life in the past enables children to understand and appreciate the magnitude of the industrial, technological, and medical advances that shape their lives. Katherine Paterson's *Lyddie* (A) is replete with details that re-create life in Lowell, Massachusetts, during the Industrial Revolution. The excitement

The sun-drenched land of a make-believe village is alive with activity. The Roxaboxenites each have roles to play as they walk the stone-marked pathways of their community. (***Roxaboxen*** by Alice McLerran, illustrated by Barbara Cooney)

Lyddie feels at the prospect of being her own person and earning her own wages is tempered with the exhaustion, fear, and danger she suffers. We see Lyddie as a real girl trying to help herself to a better life, and we understand the hidden costs of changing from an agricultural to an industrial society. So many good historical stories are available that the study of virtually any time in history can be enriched.

By relating trade books to topics in social studies, we enrich children's understanding with a wealth of material that far exceeds the limited view of any single text. We can do the same in other curricular areas, for example, reading stories set in times during which important scientific breakthroughs occurred. Biography and nonfiction, discussed in Chapter 9 and 10, can also support historical fiction and extend children's understandings about our past. Books about important events in the history of science, mathematics, art, language, medicine, and many other fields provide factual information to add to the emotional information historical fiction conveys. Historical fiction provides insights into the panoply of history; it is

> ### Figure 8-1
>
> ## Checklist for Evaluating Historical Fiction
>
> Does the work meet criteria for all good narratives?
>
> **Historical Accuracy**
>
> ❏   Is the story grounded in facts but not restricted by them?
> ❏   Are events consistent with historical evidence?
> ❏   Do characters reflect the values of the period?
> ❏   Are social issues portrayed honestly without condoning racism and sexism?
>
> **Setting**
>
> ❏   Does the text evoke a vivid historical setting?
> ❏   Is the setting consistent with historical and geographical evidence?
> ❏   Do plot events and characters ring true to the setting?
>
> **Language**
>
> ❏   Is dialogue in keeping with the time and place?
> ❏   Are colorful words retained to reflect the culture?
>
> **Characterization**
>
> ❏   Do characters represent people of the historical time?
> ❏   Do characters' feelings and values reflect the period?
> ❏   Do characters believe and behave according to standards of the time in which they lived?
>
> **Plot and Theme**
>
> ❏   Is the plot credible within the historical period?
> ❏   Is there an engaging story to hold readers' interest?
> ❏   Does the theme have universal appeal?
> ❏   Do events stay within possibilities of the period?
> ❏   Does the story avoid anachronisms and distortions?
>
> **Illustrations**
>
> ❏   Are the illustrations historically accurate?
> ❏   Do the illustrations extend the story?
> ❏   Do the illustrations enhance an understanding of plot, setting, and characterization?

a lively and fascinating way to transmit the story of the past to the guardians of the future.

CRITERIA FOR SELECTING HISTORICAL FICTION

The best historical stories come from good storytellers who are well acquainted with the facts; good historical fiction is grounded in facts but not restricted by them. An author may use historical records to document events, but the facts merely serve as a framework for the story. Many books that present historical facts do not qualify as literature. To do so, historical fiction must meet the criteria for *all* good narratives—it must have well-developed characters, integral themes, and tell an engaging story with well-crafted language and, in the case of picture books, beautiful and accurate art. Beyond this, it must meet criteria that are particular to the genre. Figure 8-1 contains a brief list of questions to ask when evaluating historical fiction.

Historical Accuracy

Historical fiction should be consistent with historical evidence. The story, though imaginative, must remain within the limits of the chosen historical background, avoiding distortion and anachronism. Historical accuracy, however, presents an interesting dilemma, one we discuss again in Chapter 9. While we can know so-called facts about our past, we know these facts only in light of the present. Every generation of historians, to some degree, reinterprets the past by using the concerns of the present as a lens. For example, a book such as Esther Forbes's Revolutionary War story, *Johnny Tremain* (A), written during a time of great patriotic fervor (1946), is not at all critical of war. James Lincoln Collier and Christopher Collier's *My Brother Sam Is Dead* (A), written during the Vietnam conflict (1974), presents a very different picture of the same war (Taxel, 1984). Both stories deal with the same set of facts, but the implications are radically different. Any presentation of history is an interpretation, but good historical fiction presents as true a picture of the past as an author can craft.

Historical accuracy can create problems of racism and sexism also. When writing about periods of time in which racism and sexism abounded, authors must take care to portray these social issues honestly while at the same time not condoning them. In Ann Turner's *Nettie's Trip South* (I) the issue of slavery is foregrounded; it is slavery that marked the South before the Civil War, and it is slavery that sickens young Nettie. Ossie Davis's *Just Like Martin* (A) is set in Alabama in the early days of the civil rights movement. Racism is a crucial part of the story, but it is presented as ugly violence. Historical fiction may have to portray racism and sexism for historical accuracy, but the stories themselves should not be racist or sexist.

Noteworthy historical novels do not *overgeneralize*; they do not lead the reader to believe, for example, that all Native Americans are like one portrayed in any one story. Each character is unique, just as each of us is, and although the novelist focuses on one person in a group, it is clear that it *is* only a person, and not a stereotype.

When evaluating historical fiction, look for (1) values and attitudes that are consistent with the time period and (2) stories that avoid generaliza-

---

ᵀEACHING IDEA 8-1

Compare Literary Descriptions of Historic Sites

Authors and illustrators describe historical settings in narratives, biographies, poetry, and nonfiction. Select books to compare literary descriptions of historical sites.

Ask your students to:

1. Read several books that describe the same region or historical period.
2. Compare selections and illustrations.
3. Discuss which descriptions are more evocative? Which ones help them understand the place best?
4. Describe the place in their own words.

Illustrative Books:

Cooney, Barbara. *Island Boy.* (P)

Dragonwagon, Crescent. *Home Place.* (P) Illus. Jerry Pinkney.

Dunrea, Olivier. *Skara Brae: The Story of a Prehistoric Village.* (I–A)

Lewis, Claudia. *Long Ago in Oregon.* (I–A) (poetry)

Macaulay, David. *Castle.* (I–A)

————. *Cathedral: The Story of Its Construction.* (I–A)

————. *City: A Story of Roman Planning and Construction.* (I–A)

————. *Pyramid.* (I–A)

McLerran, Alice. *Roxaboxen.* Illus. Barbara Cooney. (P)

---

tion, including stereotypes of gender or of ethnic or racial groups.

Setting

Setting is a crucial element in evaluating historical fiction, since it is this feature that distinguishes it most dramatically from other literary forms. Details of setting must be spelled out so clearly that readers can create a mental image of the time and place in which the events occur. These elements are integral to the plot of historical fiction; they determine characters' beliefs and actions. The setting must also be authentic and consistent with historical and geographical evidence. In evaluating historical books, we look for settings that are (1) integral to the story, and (2) authentic in historical and geographical detail.

Language

Language should be in keeping with the period and the place, particularly in dialogue. A problem arises in the case of words of the past that would not be understood by today's readers. This can be dealt with by synthesizing language that has the right sound for a period but is understandable to contemporary readers. Rosemary Sutcliff explains how she works the language into her writing:

> I try to catch the rhythm of a tongue, the tune that it plays on the ear, Welsh or Gaelic as opposed to Anglo-Saxon, the sensible workmanlike language which one feels the Latin of the ordinary Roman citizen would have translated into. It is extraordinary what can be done by the changing or transposing of a single word, or by using a perfectly usual one in a slightly unusual way: "I beg your pardon" changed into "I ask your pardon." . . . This is not done by any set rule of thumb; I simply play it by ear as I go along. (1973, pp. 307–308)

The character's thoughts should also reflect the time and place. Any metaphors, similes, or images that describe what a character is thinking or feeling must be appropriate to the setting. In Michael Dorris's **Morning Girl** (I–A), set in 1492 on a Bahamian Island that will soon be visited by Christopher Columbus, Morning Girl, a young Taino, thinks about her brother:

> . . . the world fits together so tightly, the pieces like pebbles and shells sunk into the sand after the tide has gone out, before anyone has walked on the beach and left footprints.
>
> In our house, though, my brother was the footprints.

Morning Girl's world is bounded by the sand and the sea; it is fitting that she think of life in those terms.

When evaluating language in historical fiction, therefore, look for (1) authentic language patterns that sound right for the time period and (2) dialogue that rings true to the characters.

Characterization

Characters in historical fiction should *believe* and *behave* in ways that are in keeping with the times in which they live. Authors who attribute contemporary values to historical figures run the risk of creating an anachronism, mistakenly placing something in a historical period. When actual historical figures appear in historical fiction, careful writers do not attribute dialogue to them unless there is some documentary evidence or record of what they said. Therefore, in evaluating characterization in historical fiction, look for persons who (1) behave according to the standards and mores of the time and (2) speak and believe in ways that are appropriate to the period.

Plot and Theme

History is filled with a tremendous amount of *raw material* for exciting plots and themes. Yet the abundance of historical facts may overburden a story. In *Talent Is Not Enough,* Mollie Hunter, noted writer of historical fiction and other books, says that a writer needs the facts of the past to create a story, but it is the author's sense of history and knowledge of people's dreams, realities, and passions that recreate some part of the past as a living link in the chain of human experience. None of the facts of the historical situation, she continues, may be relevant except that they serve the main function of source material—which is to yield a theme with universal application and appeal (1976, pp. 40–41).

Therefore, in evaluating historical fiction, look for books that (1) blend factual background as subordinate to the story and (2) contain a theme with universal application and appeal.

Illustrations

In recent years a number of excellent historical fiction picture storybooks have been published. These books contain not only well-written riveting stories, but also beautiful illustrations that support and enhance the story. The illustrations in picture storybooks of historical fiction must meet the criteria for quality of illustration in any picture book. In addition, they must be historically accurate, providing realistic details of life in the historical period as well as reflecting and interpreting character and action. Look for illustrations that (1) support and enhance the plot and character development and (2) provide accurate, realistic details of the historical period.

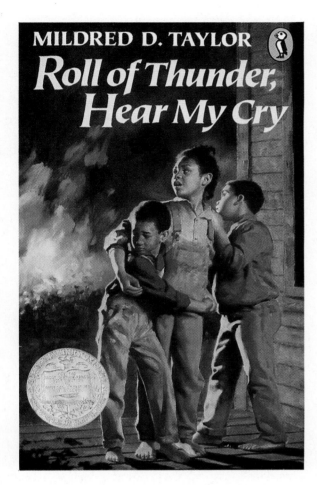

Cassie Logan tries to shelter her brothers from the racism and hatred that enflame her 1930s rural neighborhood. (*Roll of Thunder, Hear My Cry* by Mildred Taylor)

A Close Look at *Roll of Thunder, Hear My Cry*

Synopsis

Roll of Thunder, Hear My Cry (A), the Newbery Award–winning novel by Mildred Taylor, chronicles the life of Cassie Logan and her family in rural Mississippi during the Depression. Young Cassie, her grandmother, mother, father, older brother Stacey, and younger brothers Christopher-John and Little Man live on their own farm. Owning their own land, unusual for an African American in that place and time, is a source of pride for Cassie. However, she doesn't really understand why it is so important to her parents that her father leave the family in search of work. As the story unfolds it is apparent that Cassie, free and indomitable

---

TEACHING IDEA 8-2

Compare Treatment of a Topic in Textbooks, Newspapers, Encyclopedias, and Trade Books

Ask your students:

1. Choose a topic, such as homelessness, and find out how textbooks, newspapers, encyclopedias, and trade books treat it.

2. Research articles, chapters, and selections that discuss the topic.

3. Compare treatment of the topic in textbooks, newspapers, and encyclopedias with that in trade books.

4. Evaluate depth, coverage, quality of writing, voice, and insight in the various sources.

Illustrative Books on Homelessness:

Berck, Judith. *No Place to Be: Voices of Homeless Children.* (A)

Bunting, Eve. *Fly Away Home.* (P–I)

Corcoran, Barbara. *Stay Tuned.* (I–A)

DiSalvo-Ryan, DyAnne. *Uncle Willie and the Soup Kitchen.* (P–I)

Fox, Paula. *Monkey Island.* (I–A)

Rosen, Michael J. *Home: A Collaboration of Thirty Distinguished Authors and Illustrators of Children's Books to Aid the Homeless.* (P–I–A)

Tolan, Stephanie S. *Sophie and the Sidewalk Man.* (P–I)

---

among her own people, also doesn't really understand the prejudice and hatred that surround her. It is only after she is publicly humiliated by a white girl, watches her mother lose her teaching job because of prejudice, sees her brother's friend arrested, and hears stories about the horrors of the night men that Cassie realizes the truth about where she lives and the reasons for holding on to the land.

Historical Accuracy

Taylor portrays the world in which Cassie lives as it would have seemed to African Americans living at that time. Indeed, much of Taylor's story is based on family stories heard from her father and her extended family, many of whom lived in the South when they were growing up. Much of the historical context in **Roll of Thunder** is a matter of record. We know, for example, that most African Americans did not own land in the South, that many sharecroppers—both black and white—had to eke out an existence for their families any way they could, and that the Klan terrorized the southern countryside, brutally killing African Americans. The small details of Cassie's life ring true within this larger historical context, in part because of the vividly painted setting, the authentic language, the well-developed characters, and Taylor's power as a storyteller.

Setting

Taylor's words paint such a vivid picture that it is hard not to imagine you have seen a photograph of the land and the house. The story opens as Cassie and her brothers make the long walk to school, stirring up red dust with each step.

> Before us the narrow, sun-splotched road wound like a lazy red serpent dividing the high forest bank of quiet, old trees on the left from the cotton field, forested by giant green and purple stalks, on the right. A barbed-wire fence ran the length of the deep field, stretching eastward for over a quarter of a mile until it met the sloping green pasture that signaled the end of our family's four hundred acres. An ancient oak tree on the slope, visible even now, was the official dividing mark between Logan land and the beginning of a dense forest.

Everything that Cassie sees we see, as the story is told from her point of view. We see the well-kept grounds of the white children's school, the shabbiness of the black school, "a dismal end to an hour's journey," and the Logan living room.

> It was a warm, comfortable room of doors and wood and pictures. From it a person could reach the front or the side porch, the kitchen, and the two other bedrooms. Its walls were made of smooth oak, and on them hung gigantic photographs of Grandpa and Big Ma, Papa and Uncle Hammer when they were boys, Papa's two eldest brothers, who were now dead, and pictures of Mama's family. The furniture, a mixture of Logan-crafted walnut and oak, included a walnut bed whose ornate headboard rose halfway up the wall toward the high ceiling. . . .

The wealth of physical details that Taylor supplies help anchor this story in a real time and place, populated by real people. The details of actions and events that are revealed through the plot and the character development create an emotional reality as well.

Characterization and Language

Told through Cassie's eyes, this story must sound like Cassie as well. Cassie and the other characters speak in a natural dialect. Taylor carefully allows her characters to sound realistic without making the dialogue difficult for readers to understand. As they walk to school, the Logan children meet their friend, T.J., who tells them about a neighbor who's been burnt by night riders:

> "I betcha I could give y'all an earful 'bout that burnin' last night."
> "Burning? What burning?" asked Stacey.
> "Man, don't y'all know nothin'? The Berrys' burnin'. I thought y'all's grandmother went over there last night to see 'bout 'em." . . .
> "What Berrys he talking 'bout, Stacey?" I asked.
> "I don't know no Berrys."

T.J., more interested in excitement than school, drops his final g's; Stacey and Cassie, children of a teacher, do not. They all speak in a dialect, but even within that dialect Taylor is careful to delineate the distinctive voice of each character.

Cassie, as the narrator, must tell readers what she sees, thinks, and feels. Taylor is careful to keep within the boundaries of what a young girl would say.

Because we are privy to Cassie's thoughts and feelings we get to know her quite well. We feel her fear when the night riders come. We share her outrage when she is shamed by the storekeeper and forced off the sidewalk by Lillian Jean and her father. We certainly share her joyful satisfaction when she gets even with Lillian Jean in a way that is absolutely appropriate to her personality and the time in which she lives. Cassie seemingly apologizes to Lillian Jean, carries her books, and acts like her servant until one day when she lures her into the woods with the promise of a surprise. Once she gets Lillian Jean into the woods Cassie throws her books on the ground. When told by Lillian Jean to pick them back up Cassie quietly says, "Make me."

> "What?" The shock on her face was almost comical.
> "Said make me."
>
> Her face paled. Then, red with anger, she stepped daintily across the clearing and struck

Mildred Taylor

*B*Y THE TIME I entered high school, I was confident that I would one day be a writer. . . . Once I had made up my mind to write, I had no doubts about doing it. It was just something that would one day be. I had always been taught that I would achieve anything I set my mind to.

In a talk co-sponsored by the International Reading Association and the Children's Book Council, Mildred Taylor described her childhood memories of vibrant countryside and the vitality of black community life, with its revivals and courtings, prayer meetings and picnics. Where there was beauty, however, there was also insufferable hatred and bigotry. She and her sister attended local schools, and she recalls how each book was marked, not only with previous owners' names, but with their race as well. Even as a child she sensed some wrong, so she scratched out the information.

As a child, Taylor wondered why the history books contained no stories about African Americans, when the stories from her own family's past were filled with heroic men and women who fought against oppression and indignities with valor. Her desire to tell the story of strong African-American families facing difficulties heroically and with integrity led her to write *Song of the Trees; Roll of Thunder, Hear My Cry,* winner of the 1977 Newbery Medal and 1977 National Book Award; *Let the Circle Be Unbroken; Gold Cadillac* (I); *The Road to Memphis* (A); *Mississippi Bridge* (A); and *The Friendship* (I).

She decries the depiction of black ghettos only as slums. The ghetto in which she grew up was not a slum, and she has no recollection of fatherless families; rather, she remembers the protective presence of strong adults— somewhat like the Logans' protection of Cassie and her brothers in the *Roll of Thunder* series.

From her Peace Corps experience in Ethiopia, Taylor learned the price independence exacts from the individual. Although her writing carries powerful themes about survival in a hostile society, Taylor's messages radiate rather than pummel:

It is my hope that to the children who read my books, the Logans will provide those heroes missing from the schoolbooks of my childhood: Black men, women, and children of whom they can be proud.

Throughout, the strength and importance of the family is central. Taylor credits her father, a master storyteller, with having a powerful influence on her life. Her values and principles were shaped in a wholesome and loving family with strong and sensitive parents. Pride in one's heritage is a universal theme meaningful for all readers.

me hard across the face. For the record, she had hit me first; I didn't plan on her hitting me again.

I flailed into her, tackling her with such force that we both fell. . . .

After Cassie wins the fight, pinning Lillian Jean down and yanking on her hair, she makes her apologize for the torment she made Cassie endure.

And she apologized. For herself and for her father. For her brothers and her mother. For Strawberry and Mississippi, and by the time I finished jerking at her head, I think she would have apologized for the world being round had I demanded it.

Cassie's pride, one of her primary traits, had been damaged, and she found a way to make it whole again.

When Lillian Jean threatens to tell her father what Cassie has done, Cassie has an answer for that too. She threatens to tell everyone all of the hateful secrets that Lillian Jean has been telling her. Proud of herself, and secure in her safety from retaliation, Cassie begins to leave

when Lillian Jean asked, bewildered, "But, Cassie, why? You was such a nice little girl. . . ."

I stared at her astonished. Then I turned and left the forest, not wanting to believe that Lillian Jean didn't even realize it had all been just a game.

This is just one of many incidents that reveal Cassie's pride, intelligence, and determination to hold her head high in a society that demanded she look down.

Plot and Theme

The events that occur in this story are events that could, and did, happen in Mississippi during the Depression. The main action centers around the Logan family's struggle to live as decent human beings in a forbidding society, to maintain their pride, their dignity, and their very lives. The land they seek to hold on to symbolizes their struggle for decency.

The events of the story are linked to the drama of the struggle played out against the backdrop of a racist society. When Mrs. Logan loses her job rather than use textbooks that are offensive to her, she stands for pride in being African American. When Cassie and her brothers turn the tables on

the white school-bus driver who torments them, they are fighting for their sense of pride. Faced with what seem to be unresolvable problems of prejudice and poverty, Cassie asks her father if they are "giving up too." David replies:

"You see that fig tree over yonder, Cassie? Them other trees all around . . . that oak and walnut, they're a lot bigger and they take up more room and give so much shade they almost overshadow that little ole fig. But that fig tree's got roots that run deep, and it belongs in that yard as much as that oak and walnut. It keeps on blooming, bearing good fruit year after year, knowing all the time it'll never get as big as them other trees. Just keeps on growing and doing what it gotta do. It don't give up. It give up, it'll die. There's a lesson to be learned from that little tree, Cassie girl, 'cause we're like it. We keep doing what we gotta, and we don't give up. We can't."

Setting, plot, and characterization work together to present a family caught in a desperate struggle for their existence as human beings. In this family we recognize ourselves.

PRESENTING HISTORICAL FICTION BY CHRONOLOGICAL PERIOD

Historical fiction can be studied through its themes, by chronological period, or according to topics on school social studies curricula. In any case, well-written stories "establish human and social circumstances in which the interaction of historical forces may be known, felt, and observed" (Blos, 1992). We present historical fiction chronologically and then consider how to explore themes across history.

Prehistoric Times

Prehistoric times, the ancient period before written records were kept, are wrapped in the shrouds of antiquity. Scientists theorize about the daily life and culture of ancient peoples by observing fragments of life and making inferences from bits of pottery, weapons, or scraps of bone. Authors draw from the findings of archaeologists, anthropologists, and paleontologists to create vivid tales of life as it might have been.

Many novels of prehistoric times are set in distant lands around the Mediterranean Sea or in ancient Britain. The best fiction about prehistoric people does more than re-create possible settings and events of the past. It engages itself with themes basic to all persons everywhere—the will to survive, the need for courage and honor, the growth of understanding, the development of compassion. One such book is William O. Steele's *The Magic Amulet* (I–A), a story about a child of an early nomadic band that roamed what is now the southeastern United States. Left behind by his tribe because of an injury, Tragg vows that he will recover and find a new family band to join. Tragg's determination to survive his ordeal and find new companions are themes that echo throughout history. Other stories of prehistoric times are listed in Figure 8-2.

Ancient Times

Stories of ancient times often focus on life in the Mediterranean civilizations. Children are fascinated by the pyramids and mummies of ancient Egypt and by the ruins and myths of ancient Greece and Rome. Viewing museum treasures, such as those from the tomb of Tutankhamen, can heighten this interest. Some stories of ancient civilizations merge with mythology (Chapter 5), but some authors attempt to retain a more factual base for their work. Still other writers explore life in different parts of the world.

Rosemary Sutcliff is distinguished among historical fiction writers for her ability to re-create an authentic picture of life in early Britain. She wrote knowledgeably about people and places in a way that fills in many of the missing pieces of ancient Britain during the years it was occupied by Norsemen, and later by Romans, Normans, and Saxons. In *Song for a Dark Queen* (A) Sutcliff tells Boudicca's (Boadicea's) story through an old harpist who recalls her life and the fate of her people, the Iceni, during the time of the Roman occupation of Britain. Lady Boudicca is remembered as the warrior queen, defeated in a final battle and choosing her own death. The historical detail is integrated smoothly in a superb story of Roman Britain.

The ring of authenticity is not the sole distinguishing feature of Sutcliff's work. While her novels of ancient Britain are masterful evocations of their time, they also provide sensitive insights into the human spirit. Each story reverberates with an eternal truth and lasting theme. Sutcliff's heroes live and die for values and principles we hold today. Her stories reveal the eternal struggle between light—that which we value—and darkness—the forces that work to destroy it. Sutcliff's books and other fine stories of ancient times are listed in Figure 8-2.

The Middle Ages

The dissolution of the Roman Empire marks the beginning of the part of the medieval period sometimes referred to as the Dark Ages. There is little recorded history of these times, which were marked primarily by the battles of barbarian tribes that swept across Europe. Writers breathe life into the shadowy figures of the novels set in this period—novels that blend fact and legend.

Fourteenth-century England is the backdrop for Marguerite de Angeli's *The Door in the Wall* (I–A), a magnificent Newbery Award–winning story about a crippled boy. Robin is waiting to be taken as a page to Sir Peter de Lindsay when he is stricken by the crippling plague. Brother Luke rescues Robin and takes him to the monastery to nurse him back to health, teaching him to walk with crutches, read, write, swim, and most important of all, to have patience. Brother Luke continually reminds Robin that whenever there is an obstacle—a wall—there is someplace, a door in the wall, where one can go beyond the problem. Robin learns to search for and work for the doors in walls that face him. The author shows the castles, churches, monasteries, and pageantry of the medieval period in stark contrast to the bitterness of life among the common folk. As readers enjoy a gripping story, they learn a great deal about life in medieval England. Other fine stories set in medieval times are listed in Figure 8-2.

The Age of Exploration

Whether in real life or in books, mysterious or dangerous explorations of the unknown mesmerize us. Accounts of the navigators of the earlier world intrigue today's children as much as travels to the moon or to Mars. Explorers of the past and present need the same kind of courage and willingness to face the unknown. Stories of explorations range from tales of the early Vikings, such as Erik Haugaard's *Hakon of Rogen's Saga* (I), to stories set in the age of European exploration—Columbus and after.

From the early fifteenth to the mid-sixteenth centuries, adventurers from many European countries actively explored the world, with the Portuguese, Spanish, and English dominating the seas. In

De Angeli creates a Breughel-like painting of a historical village. Young, lame Robin rides astride a horse while Brother Martin considers the lessons the young boy must learn. De Angeli portrays a fourteenth-century English village as the background setting for a story of personal courage. (*The Door in the Wall* by Marguerite de Angeli)

many schools, Christopher Columbus's "discovery" of America in 1492 is parroted as fact, but most books today provide a broader historical perspective. FitzGerald (1979) comments on some of the changes in viewpoint:

> Poor Columbus! He is a minor character now, a walk-on in the middle of American History. Even those books that have not replaced his picture with a Mayan temple or an Iroquois mask do not credit him with discovering America—even for the Europeans. The Vikings, they say, preceded him to the New World, and . . . having lost or forgotten their maps, simply neglected to cross the ocean again for five hundred years. (pp. 8–9)

The 500th anniversary of Columbus's famous voyage—1992—brought forth many books to mark the anniversary. Some of them tell the story of the Native Americans who were present when Colum-

bus landed. Such books present the other side of the story, and a more balanced picture of the impact of the age of exploration.

Jane Yolen's **Encounter** (I–A) presents an account of the first meeting of Columbus and the Tainos, the people who were living happily and fruitfully until they were "discovered." Told from the point of view of a Taino boy, this story is both profoundly moving and deeply disturbing. The Taino greet the explorers with courtesy and gifts of friendship, only to be rewarded with baubles and slavery. The boy is frightened, for he sees the Europeans smiling with "the serpent's smile," but no one will listen to him. Taken aboard the boat against his will, he slips over the side and swims to freedom. The message he carries—beware the strangers—is ignored by all he meets. Yolen's story and David Shannon's illustrations contain details that reflect what little we know of the lost Taino culture.

Pam Conrad's **Pedro's Journal** (I) recounts the voyage of Christopher Columbus through the voice

**Figure
8-2**

Stories of Prehistoric, Ancient, and Medieval Times

Prehistoric

Brett, Jan. *The First Dog.* (P–I)

Denzel, Justin. *The Boy of the Painted Cave.* (I–A)

Dyer, T. A. *A Way of His Own.* (I–A)

Garcia, Ann O'Neal. *Spirit on the Wall.* (I–A)

Pryor, Bonnie. *Seth of the Lion People.* (I)

Steele, William O. *The Magic Amulet.* (I–A)

Sutcliff, Rosemary. *Warrior Scarlet.* (A)

Turnbull, Ann. *Maroo of the Winter Caves.* (I)

Turner, Ann. *Time of the Bison.* (I)

Wibberley, Leonard. *Attar of the Ice Valley.* (A)

Ancient Times

Carter, Dorothy. *His Majesty, Queen Hatshepsut.* (I)

Haugaard, Erik Christian. *The Rider and His Horse.* (I–A)

———. *The Samurai's Tale.* (A)

Lord, Bette Bao. *Spring Moon.* (I–A)

Manniche, Lise. *The Prince Who Knew His Fate.* (I)

McGraw, Eloise Jarvis. *Mara, Daughter of the Nile.* (A)

Paterson, Katherine. *The Sign of the Chrysanthemum.* (A)

Paton Walsh, Jill. *Children of the Fox.* (I–A)

———. *Crossing to Salamis.* (I)

Speare, Elizabeth George. *The Bronze Bow.* (A)

Sutcliff, Rosemary. *The Eagle of the Ninth.* (A)

———. *The Lantern Bearers.* (A)

———. *The Shining Company.* (A)

———. *Flame Colored Taffeta.* (A)

———. *Knight's Fee.* (A)

———. *Song for a Dark Queen.* (A)

Yarbro, Chelsea Quinn. *Locadio's Apprentice.* (I–A)

Medieval Times

Aliki. *A Medieval Feast.* (P–I)

Beatty, John, and Patricia Beatty. *Master Rosalind.* (A)

Chaucer, Geoffrey. *Canterbury Tales.* Trans. by Barbara Cohen. (I–A)

Colum, Padraic. *Taliesen.* (I)

De Angeli, Marguerite. *The Door in the Wall.* (I)

Eliot, George. *Romola.* (A)

Goodall, John. *The Story of an English Village.* (P–I)

Gray, Elizabeth Vining. *Adam of the Road.* (A)

Hieatt, Constance. *Arthurian Legends.* (I)

Hilgartner, Beth. *A Murder for Her Majesty.* (A)

Hunt, Jonathan. *Illuminations.* (P–I)

Kelly, Eric P. *The Trumpeter of Krakow.* (A)

Kingsley, Charles. *Westward Ho!* (A)

Langstaff, John. *Early Ballads.* (P–I–A)

Lasker, Joe. *Merry Ever After: The Story of Two Medieval Weddings.* (P–I)

———. *A Tournament of Knights.* (A)

McGraw, Eloise. *The Striped Ships.* (A)

O'Dell, Scott. *The Road to Damietta.* (A)

Picard, Barbara. *One Is One.* (A)

Stolz, Mary. *Bartholomew Fair.* (I)

Trease, Geoffrey. *The Red Towers of Granada.* (A)

Vining, Elizabeth (Gray). *I Will Adventure.* (A)

of young Pedro, a cabin boy aboard the *Santa Maria*. Readers feel the danger and thrill of the perilous sea voyage and, when the ships land in the new world, the sorrow and shame of the way Columbus and his men behaved. These stories and others are listed in Figure 8-3.

Colonial and Revolutionary Times

Immigrants began sailing to America in the late sixteenth century, some seeking adventure and financial gain, some escaping religious persecution, some hoping to convert the natives, and some seeking political freedom. Economic and social condi-

P R O F I L E

*P*AM CONRAD says, "I began writing when I was seven and had the chicken pox. My mother gave me some paper and colored pencils to draw with, but instead of drawing I began writing poetry that sounded a lot like A. A. Milne. From then on, whenever I had a fever, I would write poems. This must have been quite often, because when I was twelve my father published a private collection of them all, called *Tea by the Garden Wall*."

When Pam grew up and gave her own daughter paper to write poems on, Sarah drew pictures. Sarah now studies art and book illustration at Cooper Union; they hope to do a book together someday.

Pam Conrad attended Hofstra University and received her Bachelor of Arts degree from the New School for Social Research. She is a member of the Society of Children's Book Writers, PEN, and the Author's Guild. Her essays and articles have appeared in *Publisher's Weekly, McCalls, Newsweek, Newsday,* and *The New York Times*. Pam lives on Long Island and is on the faculty of Queens College in New York.

Pam met author Johanna Hurwitz at a Writer's Conference at Hofstra University and decided to try her hand at writing children's books. With Johanna's encouragement, she wrote *I Don't Live Here!* and, after twelve

Pam Conrad

submissions, sold the manuscript to E. P. Dutton.

Now Pam says, "I love to write. I don't think I could not write. I find out so much about my characters as I'm writing, it's like finding out about myself."

Pam said,

My first historical novel was *Prairie Songs,* and I did not do research for it. Teachers go nuts when I say this to groups of kids—they want me to say I did five years of research.

When I was growing up I read all the *Little House* books. When I was in junior high I was reading Willa Cather. I lived out West when I was married; my husband was in the Air Force. I read published journals of pioneer women. I never thought I was doing research. I thought I was reading

tions made the New World attractive to people willing to sacrifice the known for the possibilities of a promising unknown. The settlements by the English at Roanoke, Jamestown, Plymouth, and Boston are vivid settings for stories based on early colonial life.

By 1692, the early settlers were well estab-lished in their new communities and were stern guardians of their religious views, pious behavior, and moral standards. In Salem, Massachusetts, several young girls were enthralled by colorful tales recounted by Tituba, a slave from Barbados. The girls interpreted these tales according to their rigid puritanical beliefs, and though they may have

CONTINUED

what I loved to read.

I have always loved to read—not just about pioneers but about survivors. I love movies about people who survive a holocaust and are the last family left on earth. . . .

I really didn't start out wanting to write historical novels. I was not thinking about that. I was going to writers' conferences. I was taking writing courses. I was trying to write. I wanted to make a living. I didn't know how I was going to do it. I wanted a career. In my first book I imitated Beverly Cleary. . . . And then I thought, . . . there's something that's been haunting me that I have to write about. I wanted to write about a woman who had lived in Nebraska in the late 1800s and had gone mad. . . . I can't explain how I did it, except I had a passion for it. I loved it, I loved prairies. . . .

Once ***Prairie Songs*** was published it won a lot of awards. When my editor asked me if I could write another Nebraska book, I said, "No. I've written everything I can about it. It's over."

I started to write books about contemporary times. Then, early one morning, before I went to work at my desk, I was taking a shower, and words started to come to me. I jumped out of the shower and wrote stuff down. I'd get back in the shower, and more would come. It was as if something was speaking to me . . . [In writing ***My Daniel***] there was a wisdom that came to me that goes beyond understanding. I think we all can have it, if we will just open ourselves to it.

Another historical novel that I wrote came to me a different way: ***Pedro's Journal.*** It's the story of the ship's boy on the Santa Maria. Kent Brown [an editor] had actually come to me with this idea. He knew I love boats and love sailing. He asked me if I would like to do captions for a book he had in mind. It was going to be a picture book of what was supposed to be the sketch book of the ship's boy on the Santa Maria. I thought, "Ugh! Columbus." I just didn't have it in me. "Columbus" meant third grade bulletin boards, with the *Nina,* the *Pinta,* and the *Santa Maria* . . . I ended up writing a novel. I was just carried away with the idea.

I could not imagine being a 12-year-old boy climbing into the *Santa Maria* and going off the edge of the earth—that would terrify me. But I had my own little 22-foot Catalina that I would get in and head toward Block Island, and I would be terrified. So I knew terror on a smaller scale. I realized I knew what it was like—to go to the unexplored. . . .

Writing is to me an almost metaphysical thing that happens and that I love. It adds to my life; in fact it feels more like my life than my real life sometimes, to tell you the truth. . . .

Pam Conrad has more than 18 books published or under contract, including novels, picture books, adult novels, and biographies. ***Prairie Songs*** won the 1986 International Reading Association Children's Book Award, and ***Stonewords*** won the 1991 Edgar Allen Poe Award.

Jane Yolen's *Encounter* portrays events from the point of view of the Taino Indians who welcomed Christopher Columbus and his men in 1492. The narrator states: "Our chief said, 'We must see if they are true men.' So I took one by the hand and pinched it. The hand felt like flesh and blood, but the skin was moon to my sun." David Shannon vividly illustrates the experience.

started as innocent storytelling, they ultimately caused the death of 20 people convicted in the infamous Salem witch trials.

Patricia Clapp uses a first-person narrator in ***Witches' Children*** (A) to bring a sense of immediacy to the terrifying events in Salem. Mary Warren, a bound girl, is only mildly interested in the tales and fortune-telling she hears Tituba spinning for others. However, she is aware that another girl is craftily pushing Tituba to wild extremes. Mary tells the story of mass hysteria and witch trials from her own point of view, a literary device that makes it all seem possible and comprehensible.

In Elizabeth George Speare's ***The Witch of Blackbird Pond*** (I–A), winner of the 1959 Newbery Award, Kit befriends an old woman living outside the village and discovers the principle of guilt by association when she is accused, together with the old woman, of being a witch. These books and others listed in Figure 8-4 artfully blend fact and fiction to create a vivid picture of people and their lives during colonial times.

The beginning of the discontent that marked the American Revolution is not clearly marked in time. Some colonists resented paying taxes to England when they were not represented in the English Parliament. Many, however, remained loyal to King George III and fully disapproved of the rebellious leaders who agitated for the independence of the colonies. Fiction set in this period frequently involves divided loyalties in colonial families or communities. Authors often tell the story through the eyes of a child or an adolescent character who supports the rebels but whose parents remain loyal to Britain.

James Lincoln Collier and Christopher Collier tell of one family caught in conflicting loyalties in ***My Brother Sam Is Dead*** (I–A). The father, a Connecticut tavern keeper, thinks the colonists have a few legitimate complaints against England but nothing serious enough to cause bloodshed. Twelve-year-old Tim idolizes his older brother Sam, who reports in detail on his debates when he comes home from college. Tim begs for Sam's stories, savoring the clever "telling points" Sam makes against his opponents. Conflict begins when Sam arrives home wearing a rebel uniform, and it increases in intensity as the family becomes enmeshed in the struggle between loyalists and rebels. Sam is accused of stealing cattle, and an ironic turn of events leads to the bitter outcome foretold in the title.

Stories of the American Revolution are usually told from the patriots' point of view, but Ann Turner employs the Tory viewpoint for **Katie's Trunk** (P). Katie and her family leave home to hide from Patriots who are coming to ransack their home, but her anger leads her back into her house. When the Patriots arrive she hides in her mother's trunk. A Patriot who had been a friend finds her there but doesn't tell those with him. He leaves the lid of the trunk open just enough for Katie to breathe and manages to get his companions out of the house. Katie learns there are good people on both sides of battle lines. Ron Himler's lovely paintings detail period dress, furniture, and architecture. Other stories set in the Revolutionary War period that illuminate the human conflict are listed in Figure 8-4.

The history of America is incomplete without stories of Native Americans. Often their story was told by white men who characterized them in stereotyped ways—as ferocious savages or as downtrodden people who suffer nobly. Although many books perpetuate this teepee-and-feathers image, a growing number now give more accurate portrayals of Native American culture and a more objective picture of the 500-year clash between the European and Native American cultures.

Stories for younger children often present a simple view of the interaction between Europeans and Native Americans, but this view need not rely on stereotypes. Stories for older readers often consider the complexities inherent in the clash between two cultures, such as Elizabeth George Speare's compelling novel about a faltering friendship of a white boy and an Indian boy in the 1700s, **Sign of the Beaver** (I–A). Thirteen-year-old Matt's father leaves him behind to guard the log cabin they had built in the Maine wilderness while the father returns to Massachusetts to get the rest of the family. Alone in the wilderness, Matt tries to survive by hunting, but a renegade tramp who asks for shelter steals his gun. Matt has few other resources for finding food in the forest. When he meets proud, resourceful Attean, grandson of the chief of the Beaver Clan, he is dubious about the relationship. Attean makes it obvious that he has been encouraged against his will to meet Matt. The friendship flourishes, however, as Matt teaches Attean to read and Attean teaches Matt how to fish, hunt, and survive in the forest. Matt's respect for the Indian culture grows as he learns more about it. Several other stories describe the turmoil of people caught between two cultures. These and other stories about Native American peoples during the early days of America are listed in Figure 8-4.

---

*T*EACHING IDEA 8-3

Compare Versions of the First Thanksgiving

1. Collect several books that describe the first Thanksgiving.

2. Read the different versions with your students.

3. In small groups compare accounts:

   Who was there?

   What did they eat?

   How were they dressed?

   Do you hear an author's voice?

4. Which source is the most reliable and accurate? How do you know?

   What are the author's qualifications to write about this topic?

   What evidence does the author provide to assure accuracy of information?

5. Which book would you use with 5- to 7-year-olds, 9- to 11-year-olds?

Illustrative Books:

Anderson, Joan. **The First Thanksgiving Feast.** Photos by George Ancona. (P–I)

Cohen, Barbara. **Molly's Pilgrim.** (P–I)

Dalgleish, Alice. **The Thanksgiving Story.** (P–I)

San Souci, Robert. **N. C. Wyeth's Pilgrims.** (I)

Sewall, Marcia. **People of the Breaking Day.** (P)

Waters, Kate. **Sarah Morton's Day.** (P–I)

Watson, Wendy. **Thanksgiving at Our House.** (P–I)

The Civil War

Slavery was a part of American life until the Emancipation Proclamation. Many chapters of American history are grim, but those involving slavery and the Civil War are among the worst; the war was a long savage contest, costly not the least in human lives. Books about this period offer students accounts of the turmoil and tragedy of the bloody period and of its reverberations still felt today. The

Figure 8-4

Stories of Colonial and Revolutionary War Times

Colonial Times

Bulla, Clyde Robert. *A Lion to Guard Us.* (I)

——. *John Billington: Friend of Squanto.* (I)

Campbell, Elizabeth. *Jamestown: The Beginning.* (I)

Dillon, Ellis. *The Seekers.* (A)

Latham, Jean Lee. *This Dear-Bought Land.* (I)

Levitin, Sonia. *Roanoke: A Novel of the Lost Colony.* (I–A)

Monjo, F. N. *The House on Stink Alley.* (I)

Mott, Michael. *Master Entrick.* (A)

Petry, Ann. *Tituba of Salem Village.* (I)

Sewall, Marcia. *The Pilgrims of Plimoth.* (P–I)

Speare, Elizabeth George. *The Witch of Blackbird Pond.* (I)

——. *Sign of the Beaver.* (I)

Spier, Peter. *The Legend of New Amsterdam.* (P–I)

Revolutionary War

Avi. *The Fighting Ground.* (I)

Brady, Esther Wood. *Toliver's Secret.* (I)

Brown, Drollene P. *Sybil Rides for Independence.* (I)

Caudill, Rebecca. *Tree of Freedom.* (A)

Collier, James Lincoln, and Christopher Collier. *My Brother Sam Is Dead.* (I)

——. *War Comes to Willy Freeman.* (I)

Edmonds, Walter. *Drums Along the Mohawk.* (A)

Forbes, Esther. *Johnny Tremain.* (I–A)

Forman, James. *The Cow Neck Rebels.* (A)

Fritz, Jean. *Early Thunder.* (A)

——. *Will You Sign Here, John Hancock?* (P–I)

Gauch, Patricia Lee. *This Time, Tempe Wick?* (I)

Haley, Gail. *Jack Jouett's Ride.* (P)

Haugaard, Erik. *Cromwell's Boy.* (A)

Lawson, Robert. *Ben and Me, Benjamin Franklin as Written by His Good Mouse Amos.* (I)

——. *Mr. Revere and I.* (I)

McGovern, Ann. *Secret Soldier: The Story of Deborah Sampson* (I)

O'Dell, Scott. *Sarah Bishop.* (A)

Quackenbush, Robert. *Old Silver Legs Takes Over: A Story of Peter Stuyvesant.* (P)

Rappaport, Doreen. *The Boston Coffee Party.* (P)

Rinaldi, Ann. *Time Enough for Drums.* (A)

Roop, Peter and Connie Roop. *Buttons for General Washington.* (I)

Siegel, Beatrice. *Sam Ellis's Island.* (P)

Wibberley, Leonard. *John Treegate's Musket.* (I)

years immediately preceding the Civil War were a bleak period in American history, although there were individual acts of compassion and heroism. A notable children's book that has captured the antebellum period is Ann Turner's **Nettie's Trip South** (I), which depicts the horror of slavery through the eyes of a white girl from the North on a train trip to the South. The slave auctions she witnesses are grim.

Stories set during the Civil War focus on the horrors of war, especially that of countryman fighting countryman, and, in some cases, brother fighting brother. Books written about this period do not paint an exciting picture or romanticize the battles; instead, they focus on the impact of these battles on individual lives, on injury and death, divided loyalties, and, frequently, the anguish of those who wanted no involvement in the war.

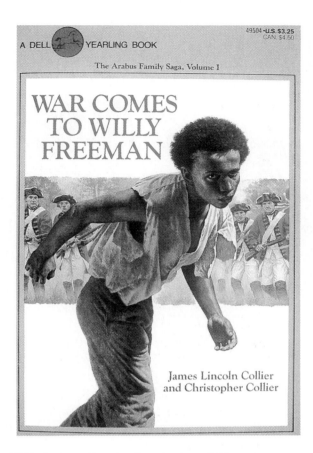

A DELL YEARLING BOOK

49504 - U.S. $3.25
CAN. $4.50

The Arabus Family Saga, Volume I

WAR COMES TO WILLY FREEMAN

James Lincoln Collier and Christopher Collier

Wilhelmina, disguised as the boy Willy, witnesses her father's death fighting the Redcoats and finds that her mother has been captured and taken aboard a prison ship in New York harbor. Willy goes to New York where she works for the owner of Fraunces' Tavern and helps her uncle win his freedom. (*War Comes to Willy Freeman* by James Lincoln Collier and Christopher Collier)

Irene Hunt's **Across Five Aprils** (I–A) describes the tragic involvement of Matthew Creighton's family, which has loved ones on both the Confederate and Union sides. In April 1861, Matthew's 9-year-old son Jethro, too young to join either army, thinks that war is exciting and wonderful. One by one Jethro's brothers and a beloved schoolmaster join the Union Army, but his favorite brother, Bill, feels he must join the Confederates. Jethro experiences the war through letters from his brothers and teacher as well as through newspaper accounts but mostly by word of mouth. News spreads through the county quickly as neighbors share news of disasters, battles, and lost sons. Jethro's enthusiasm for war changes to hatred for the cruelty and senseless loss of lives. Hunt paces the story deftly by using the critical five Aprils of the title to structure the

novel. She also catches the language of Civil War years in the dialogue of her characters. Other notable stories about the Civil War period are listed in Figure 8-5.

Life on the Frontier

Frontier life required great physical strength and an unlikely counterpart: the ability to endure loneliness. Pioneer families worked hard by necessity, providing their own food, clothing, shelter, and entertainment. Themes of loneliness, hardship, and acceptance of what life deals out are threaded through many excellent novels about the pioneers and their struggle to tame a wild land.

Among the best is the 58-page Newbery Award winner by Patricia MacLachlan, **Sarah, Plain and Tall** (P–I–A). Anna and Caleb live with Papa in a small sod house on the prairie of the Nebraska frontier. Momma died the morning after Caleb was born, and Anna has served as surrogate mother and housekeeper despite her tender years. Caleb often asks Anna about their mother and begs her to sing him the songs their mother sang. He says, "Maybe . . . if you remember the songs, then I might remember her, too." Both children are surprised when Papa announces that he has put an advertisement in the newspaper for help. Anna thinks he means a housekeeper but Papa says slowly, "Not a housekeeper. . . . A wife." Caleb stared at Papa. "A wife? You mean a mother?" . . . "That, too," said Papa. After Papa reads aloud the letter he has received in response to his advertisement for a mail-order bride, Caleb is smiling and Anna says, "Ask her if she sings." More letters are exchanged until a final one arrives, saying, "I will come by train. I will wear a yellow bonnet. I am plain and tall. (signed) Sarah." Sarah is a proud independent woman who desperately misses her home by the sea in Maine. Papa is a quiet gentle man who waits patiently for those he loves. Caleb and Anna fear that Sarah is leaving them the day she takes the horses and wagon from the homestead. When she returns Anna voices her fear, but Sarah says, "I will always miss my old home, but the truth of it is I would miss you more." The beauty of MacLachlan's spare prose and the simplicity of naive love make this a book to treasure. A film sequel, "Skylark," was presented on network television. A third story to complete the trilogy is expected.

Picture storybooks set during the frontier time include Jean Van Leeuwen's **Going West** (P). Van Leeuwen captures the excitement, fear, loneliness, and thrill of leaving home for a new life in a new

And Addie, at any time we could be sold
by a fat man in a white hat
in a tight white suit
and we'd have to go, just like that.

The man in the white suit determines the future of the slaves in his custody. As the slave auctioneer, he stands grim-faced and forbidding as he ignores the human tragedies and pain of slaves being auctioned. (*Nettie's Trip South* by Ann Turner, illustrated by Ronald Himler)

land. Thomas B. Allen's evocative chalk-like illustrations help readers picture the experiences that a young pioneer family might have had as they created a new home with love and hard work. Other books about this period are listed in Figure 8-5.

Within recent decades we have developed a new consciousness about Native Americans and the differences between their concepts and those of the European settlers. Native Americans believed, for example, that the land belonged to all; the European settlers brought with them the idea of individual ownership. This clash of cultural values resulted in great conflict—from grisly battles, in which hundreds were killed, to inner conflicts, in which individuals who had come to know each other as friends had to choose between friendship and loyalty to their own people.

The stories of the Native Americans who were pushed out of their homes by the westward expansion are tragic and moving. Noted writer Scott O'Dell's final novel, **Thunder Rolling in the Mountains,** (A), tells the moving story of Chief Joseph and the Nez Perce people who were forced to leave

their lands in the Wallowa Valley and resettle on a reservation. Some refused to go, choosing instead to flee to freedom in Canada. Their doomed flight and the battles that marked it are recounted through the eyes of the chief's daughter who comes to understand why her father would vow, "I will fight no more forever." This and other stories about the westward expansion are listed in Figure 8-5.

The New Century: Immigration and the Industrial Revolution

The Industrial Revolution changed the fabric of America, profoundly altering both economic and social structures. As jobs in factories became available, people left their family farms to seek their fortune in the cities. Unfortunately, what they found was not exactly fortunate. Katherine Paterson tells the story of one young girl who leaves her Vermont farm to find a new and better life in **Lyddie** (A). Lyddie goes to Lowell, Massachusetts, to become a factory girl and earn the money she thinks will

Thomas B. Allen uses pastels to convey the hardship that encouraged family unity and strength in pioneering families going West. (*Going West* by Jean Van Leeuwen)

free her from debt and from being controlled by others. She finds that with the money come new problems of dangerous working conditions, evil supervisors, and radical friends. Lyddie's struggle to be her own person is intensified by the social changes that marked the Industrial Revolution.

The story of America includes the story of immigration. Millions of immigrants have come from distant lands dreaming of freedom and hoping to seek a better life. Their stories are our stories repeated at family gatherings where young children gather around the older members asking them to "tell us what it was like back in the olden days." Historical fiction contains a wealth of immigrant stories for all ages.

Many books describe the conditions in another country that led families to migrate to America, and others focus on the difficulties and hardships endured during immigration. Evelyn Wild Mayerson's **The Cat Who Escaped from Steerage** (I) is the story of a 9-year-old Polish girl and her family as they travel—steerage class—to America. Young Chanah's spunk, intelligence, and determination make her an engaging and realistic character. The conditions in which the immigrants travel and the mixture of fear and hope with which they approach Ellis Island are vividly portrayed.

Only a few stories deal with the arduous circumstances that immigrants faced after their arrival. Joan Sandin's books for young readers, **Long Way to a New Land** (P) and **The Long Way Westward** (P), recount the story of how Carl Erik and

---

TEACHING IDEA 8-4

Compare the Literary Treatment of a Geographic Feature

Rivers, trails, and mountains provide settings for historical novels. Students might compare the way these setting are described in various trade books.

1. Collect several books that involve one geographic feature.

2. Read the books and compare them on the following points:

   Which is most scientifically accurate?

   Which is the most appealing description?

   How would you use each type of book?

Rivers

Ancona, George. **Riverkeeper.** (P–I)

Flack, Marjorie. **The Boats on the River.** (P)

Locker, Thomas. **Where the River Begins.** (P–I)

Lourie, Peter. **Hudson River.** (P–I)

Michl, Reinhard. **Day on the River.** (P–I)

Peters, Lisa Westberg. **Good Morning, River!** Illus. Deborah Kogan Ray. (P–I)

Twain, Mark. **The Adventures of Tom Sawyer.** (I–A)

Trails and Roads

Field, Rachel. **Road Might Lead to Anywhere.** (I)

Gibbons, Gail. **New Road!** (P–I)

O'Dell, Scott. **Black Star, Bright Dawn.** (I–A)

————. **Sing Down the Moon.** (I–A)

Mountains

Aylesworth, Jim. **Shenandoah Noah.** (P–I)

Cleaver, Vera. **Where the Lilies Bloom.** (A)

Hamilton, Virginia. **M. C. Higgins, the Great.** (I–A)

Lyon, George Ella. **Borrowed Children.** (I–A)

Radin, Ruth Yaffe. **High in the Mountains.** (P–I)

Rylant, Cynthia. **When I Was Young in the Mountains.** (P–I)

Showell, Ellen Harvey. **Our Mountain.** (P–I)

Spyri, Johanna. **Heidi.** (I–A)

White, Alana. **Come Next Spring.** (I–A)

Figure 8-5

Stories of the Civil War Period and Westward Expansion

Civil War Period

Alcott, Louisa May. *Little Women*. (A)

Beatty, Patricia. *Charlie Skedaddle*. (A)

———. *Jayhawker*. (A)

———. *Turn Homeward, Hannalee*. (A)

———. *Wait for Me, Watch for Me, Eula Bea*. (I–A)

———. *Who Comes with Cannons?* (A)

Carter, Peter. *Borderlands*. (I)

Cox, Clinton. *Undying Glory*. (I)

Fahrmann, Willi. *The Long Journey of Lucas B.* (A)

Fox, Paula. *The Slave Dancer*. (A)

Fritz, Jean. *Brady*. (A)

Hunt, Irene. *Across Five Aprils*. (I–A)

Hurmence, Belinda. *Tancy*. (I–A)

Josephs, Anna C. *Mountain Boy*. Illus. Bill Ersland. (I)

Keith, Harold. *Rifles for Watie*. (A)

Lyon, George Ella. *Cecil's Story*. (P–I)

Meyer, Carolyn. *Where the Broken Heart Still Beats: The Story of Cynthia Ann Parker*. (A)

Monjo, F. N. *The Drinking Gourd*. (P–I)

O'Dell, Scott. *The 290*. (A)

Reeder, Carolyn. *Shades of Gray*. (A)

Shore, Laura Jan. *Sacred Moon Tree*. (I)

Smucker, Barbara. *Runaway to Freedom*. (A)

Steele, William O. *The Perilous Road*. (I–A)

Stowe, Harriet Beecher. *Uncle Tom's Cabin*. (A)

Turner, Ann. *Nettie's Trip South*. (P–I)

Winter, Jeanette. *Follow the Drinking Gourd*. (P–I)

Wisler, G. Clifton. *Thunder on the Tennessee*. (I–A)

Westward Expansion

Aldrich, Bess. *A Lantern in Her Hand*. (A)

Avi. *The True Confessions of Charlotte Doyle*. (I–A)

Blos, Joan. *A Gathering of Days: A New England Girl's Journal, 1830–32*. (I–A)

Brenner, Barbara. *Wagon Wheels*. (P–I)

Brink, Carol Ryrie. *Caddie Woodlawn*. (I–A)

Cather, Willa. *My Antonia*. (A)

Clifford, Eth. *The Year of the Three-Legged Deer*. (A)

Coerr, Eleanor. *The Josefina Story Quilt*. (P)

Conrad, Pam. *Prairie Songs*. (I–A)

Cwiklik, Robert. *Sequoyah and the Cherokee Alphabet*. (A)

Dalgliesh, Alice. *The Courage of Sarah Noble*. (P–I)

Field, Rachel. *Calico Bush*. (I–A)

Fisher, Leonard Everett. *The Oregon Trail*. (I)

Fritz, Jean. *The Cabin Faced West*. (I)

Gerrard, Roy. *Rosie and the Rustlers*. (P)

Goble, Paul. *Death of the Iron Horse*. (P–I)

Harvey, Brett. *Cassie's Journey: Going West in the 1860s*. Illus. Deborah Kogan Ray. (P–I)

———. *My Prairie Year: Based on the Diary of Elenore Plaisted*. Illus. Deborah Kogan Ray. (P–I)

———. *My Prairie Christmas*. (P–I)

Hotze, Sollace. *A Circle Unbroken*. (I)

Howard, Ellen. *The Chickenhouse House*. (P–I)

———. *Sister*. (P–I)

———. *Edith Herself*. (P–I)

Johnston, Tony. *The Quilt Story*. Illus. Tomie de Paola. (P)

---

his family left their home in Sweden and journeyed to America, landing in New York City and going by train and boat to their final destination, Minnesota. The discomfort, fear, hope, and joy of such a journey are captured in these simple stories.

Judy Nagell's ***One Way to Ansonia*** (A) begins with 16-year-old Rose buying a ticket at Grand Central Station in 1899. Her destination is determined by the amount of money she has in her possession; she buys a ticket that takes her as far away

CONTINUED

Keith, Harold. *The Obstinate Land.* (A)

Kroeber, Theodora. *Ishi, Last of His Tribe.* (I–A)

Lydon, Kerry Raines. *A Birthday for Blue.* (P–I)

MacLachlan, Patricia. *Three Names.* (P–I)

———. *Sarah, Plain and Tall.* (I)

Martin, Bill, Jr., and John Archambault. *Knots on a Counting Rope.* (P–I)

McGraw, Eloise Jarvis. *Moccasin Trail.* (A)

Morrow, Honore. *On to Oregon.* (I–A)

Nixon, Joan Lowery. *You Bet Your Britches, Claude.* (P)

O'Dell, Scott. *Carlota.* (I–A)

———. *Sing Down the Moon.* (I–A)

Polacco, Patricia. *The Keeping Quilt.* (P)

Sanders, Scott. *Aurora Means Dawn.* Illus. Jill Kastner. (P–I)

Shub, Elizabeth. *The White Stallion.* Illus. Rachel Isadora.(I)

Speare, Elizabeth George. *Sign of the Beaver.* (I–A)

Turner, Ann. *Dakota Dugout.* Illus. Ronald Himler. (P–I)

———. *Grasshopper Summer.* (I)

———. *Third Girl from the Left.* (I–A)

Van Leeuwen, Jean. *Going West.* Illus. Thomas B. Allen. (P–I)

Walter, Mildred Pitts. *Justin and the Best Biscuits in the World.* (I)

Whelan, Gloria. *Next Spring an Oriole.* (P–I)

Wilder, Laura Ingalls. *Little House in the Big Woods.* Illus. Garth Williams. (P–I)

———. *Little House on the Prairie.* Illus. Garth Williams. (P–I)

from New York as she can afford to go. In flashbacks, we learn to understand why she is anxious to leave the teeming city of New York. Other stories set around the turn of the century are listed in Figure 8-6.

World War I

There is a paucity of books set in World War I, in either picture book or novel form. One excellent novel, however, is Margaret Rostkowski's *After the Dancing Days* (I–A), which is a beautifully told story of a 13-year-old girl's growing awareness that the war is not over for its maimed and crippled veterans. Annie watches for her father, an army doctor, to return to their small town in Kansas at the end of the war. Several badly scarred and injured veterans precede him from the train, and Annie turns away in horror at their appearance. Her father chooses to work at St. John's Hospital, where the soldiers are treated, rather than return to his former position. One day, Annie accompanies him there where she meets Andrew who is so horribly scarred from burns she cannot bear to look at him. Andrew recognizes her revulsion and walks away in shame. Annie's mother believes that everyone should put the war behind them and go on to happier things in life; she forbids Annie to go to St. John's again. The fact that her own brother, Annie's Uncle Paul, was killed in the war is something she would like to suppress. When her mother is away for a month, Annie goes to St. John's each day, knowing it to be against her mother's wishes. She reads to Andrew and others and begins to have a sense that these young men are normal human beings with needs like anyone else. In a traumatic scene, Annie faces her mother about the older woman's insensitivity and gradually helps her to see the young veterans as real people. This is a powerful story of a young girl's growth in humanity.

Set in rural northern Vermont during World War I, Natalie Kinsey-Warnock's *The Night the Bells Rang* (I–A) is the story of young Mason, engaged in his own battles with a local bully as the world is engaged in the war. The emotional journey that Mason takes as he learns to mourn the death of an enemy is both universal and timeless.

Barry Smith tells the simple story of *Minnie and Ginger* (P), two people who lived in England before, during, and after World War I. Smith presents the span of life in a manner that is very understandable to primary-grade readers, and the illustrations are full of rich details about life at that time. Other stories set in this period are listed in Figure 8-6.

The Great Depression

Stories of the Depression years portray America in times of trouble. The beginning of the period is generally recognized as the stock market crash of

The refrain "When I was young in the mountains" echoes through the years as a child recalls going out to the johnny house late at night. Diane Goode's tempera colors show the warmth and love between the grandmother and child. (*When I Was Young in the Mountains* by Cynthia Rylant)

1929. Stories of ruined businessmen jumping from skyscrapers filled the headlines of daily newspapers. Stories for children describe the grim effect of living in poverty. Mildred D. Taylor's books about Cassie Logan and her family, *The Song of the Trees* (I), *Roll of Thunder, Hear My Cry* (I–A), *Let the Circle Be Unbroken* (I–A), *Mississippi Bridge* (A), *The Road to Memphis* (A), and *The Friendship* (I–A) show rural poverty and prevailing racism.

Cynthia Rylant's *When I Was Young in the Mountains* (P–I) conveys feelings and images of the Depression. A personal narrative, this story is a poetic recounting of all the good times of an Appalachian mountain family. The story closes, "I never wanted to go anywhere else in the world, for I was in the mountains. And that was always enough."

New York City during the Depression is the setting for Jackie French Koller's *Nothing to Fear* (A). Told by young Danny, who is in many ways much older than his years, this story depicts the despair and desperation that many people felt during those times. It also depicts the triumph of

will, courage, and kindness that were a part of life in the Depression. Other fine stories are listed in Figure 8-6.

World War II

The years 1933 to 1946 encompassed Adolf Hitler's climb to power in Germany and Japanese military activity in the Pacific. The Second World War brought to vivid awareness the potential of people's inhumanity, particularly to their fellows. The horrors of the period were so unthinkable that it was several decades before the story was told in books for young people. The children who read these books today are reading about the world that their grandparents and great-grandparents lived in; these stories connect with their family histories.

Books About the Holocaust

The admonition that those who do not know the past are condemned to repeat it is adequate cause for attending to the Holocaust tragedy, and the books describing Hitler's reign of terror, with its effects ultimately on all people, are a good place to begin. Many emphasize—some in small ways, some in great ways—that in the midst of inhumanity there can be humaneness. Eric Kimmel, in an article about the importance of writing stories about the Holocaust for juvenile fiction, echoes Santayana: "If the Holocaust remains incomprehensible, it will be forgotten. And if it is forgotten, it is certain to recur" (1977, p. 84).

Despite their grimness, some books are affirmative: Young people work in underground movements, strive against terrible odds, plan escapes, and struggle for survival. Some show heroic resistance, in which characters fight back or live with dignity and hope in the face of a monstrous future. Some teachers will agonize over the place of literature in teaching about the Holocaust. Valid questions for them to consider include the following: Is mass murder a suitable subject for a children's novel? What is the place of an account of it in the school curriculum? What are the possible consequences of not informing young people about one of the most bitter lessons of history?

Holland during World War II is the setting for Shulamith Levey Oppenheim's *The Lily Cupboard* (P), the story of how one Dutch family saved the life of a Jewish child. The context is briefly set at the beginning and end of the story, without a great deal of detail. The story itself is tender, sad, and heartwarming, a vision of the goodness that was

Figure 8-6

Stories of the New Century, World War I, and the Great Depression

New Century: Immigration and Industrial Revolution

Baylor, Byrd. *The Best Town in the World.* (P–I)

Beatty, Patricia. *Sarah and Me and the Lady from the Sea.* (I)

Branson, Karen. *Streets of Gold.* (I)

Cameron, Eleanor. *A Room Made of Windows.* (I)

———. *Julia and the Hand of God.* (I)

———. *That Julia Redfern.* (I)

———. *Julia's Magic.* (I)

———. *The Private Worlds of Julia Redfern.* (I)

Collier, James Lincoln, and Christopher Collier. *The Clock.* (I–A)

Dionetti, Michelle. *Coal Mine Peaches.* (P)

Fleischman, Paul. *The Borning Room.* (A)

Harvey, Brett. *Immigrant Girl: Becky of Eldridge Street.* Illus. Deborah Kogan Ray. (P–I)

Hesse, Karen. *Letters from Rifke.* (I)

Karr, Kathleen. *It Ain't Always Easy.* (I–A)

Kroll, Steven. *The Hokey Pokey Man.* (I)

Leonard, Laura. *Finding Papa.* (I–A)

———. *Saving Damaris.* (I–A)

Levin, Betty. *Brother Moose.* (I–A)

Levinson, Nancy Smiler. *Clara and the Bookwagon.* (I)

Levitin, Sonia. *Journey to America.* (I)

———. *Silver Days.* (I)

McDonald, Megan. *The Potato Man.* (I)

McKissack, Patricia. *Mirandy and Brother Wind.* Illus. Jerry Pinkney. (P)

Mayerson, Evelyn. *The Cat Who Escaped from Steerage.* (I)

Moskin, Marietta. *Waiting for Mama.* (I)

Nagell, Judy. *One Way to Ansonia.* (A)

Oneal, Zibby. *A Long Way to Go.* (I–A)

Paterson, Katherine. *Lyddie.* (I–A)

Posell, Elsa. *Homecoming.* (I)

Sandin, Joan. *The Long Way to a New Land.* (I)

———. *The Long Way Westward.* (I)

Skurzynski, Gloria. *The Tempering.* (A)

World War I

Frank, Rudolph. *No Hero for the Kaiser.* (A)

Houston, Gloria. *The Year of the Perfect Christmas Tree.* Illus. Barbara Cooney. (P)

Kinsey-Warnock, Natalie. *The Night the Bells Rang.* (I)

Rostkowski, Margaret. *After the Dancing Days.* (A)

Smith, Barry. *Minnie and Ginger.* (P)

Voigt, Cynthia. *Tree by Leaf.* (A)

The Great Depression

Hendershot, Judith. *In Coal Country.* (P–I)

Hooks, William. *Circle of Fire.* (A)

Houston, Gloria. *Littlejim.* (I–A)

Kherdian, David. *A Song for Uncle Harry.* (I)

Koller, Jackie French. *Nothing to Fear.* (A)

Levinson, Riki. *DinnieAbbieSister-r-r!* (I)

———. *Watch the Stars Come Out.* Illus. Diane Goode. (P)

———. *We Go to Grandma's House.* (P)

Lyon, George Ella. *Borrowed Children.* (I–A)

Pendergraft, Patricia. *As Far as Mill Springs.* (I–A)

Reeder, Carolyn. *Grandpa's Mountain.* (I–A)

Richard, Adrienne. *Pistol.* (A)

Rylant, Cynthia. *When I Was Young in the Mountains.* Illus. Diane Goode. (P)

Taylor, Mildred. *Let the Circle Be Unbroken.* (I–A)

———. *Mississippi Bridge.* (A)

———. *The Road to Memphis.* (A)

———. *Roll of Thunder, Hear My Cry.* (I–A)

———. *Song of the Trees.* (I–A)

Uchida, Yoshiko. *A Jar of Dreams.* (I)

Yep, Laurence. *The Star Fisher.* (A)

The Dutch family stands staunchly in their wooden shoes ready to take ownership of the forlorn, heartbroken child who gives her father a tenacious embrace before he leaves her with them for safekeeping. (*The Lily Cupboard* by Shulamith Levy Oppenheim, illustrated by Ronald Himler)

present even in the midst of Hitler's madness. Ronald Himler's full-color illustrations add to the emotional drama and the historical setting.

Jane Yolen's **The Devil's Arithmetic** (A), a time-slip fantasy discussed in Chapter 6, is also a moving account of living in the heart of the Nazi persecution as is Lois Lowry's Newbery Award–winning **Number the Stars** (I). Lowry tells the story of how one Danish family saves the lives of their friends, the Rosens. The young daughters of each family are best friends, and initially unaware of the danger in which they are living. The contrast between the implications of Nazi rule for the Jewish Ellen and the Danish Annemarie is striking.

Books about the Holocaust are discussed further in Chapter 11 and are listed in Figure 8-7.

Books About World War II in Europe and Asia

There are many other stories about World War II that are set in the European Theater and focus on the consequences of war, especially for children. **Good Night, Mr. Tom** (A), by Michelle Magorian, won the International Reading Association Children's Book Award for the best book from a promising new writer. In this tender story set during the

bombings in England, Willie, a pale, frightened child, is thrust on old Tom who lives quietly in his English village. It is obvious that Willie has been abused, and Tom patiently nurses Willie back to a shaky health. When Willie returns to London and disappears, Tom goes to find him. Magorian's story keeps readers riveted.

Although American armed forces fought for four years in the Pacific, there are few children's and adolescent novels set in this theater. Stories about the war in Europe and in Asia are listed in Figure 8-7.

Books About World War II in North America

Some stories of the World War II period are set in North America. Many of these are about children who were evacuated from Europe; others chronicle the shameless internment of Japanese Americans; and still others explore the lives of children whose fathers, uncles, and big brothers were fighting in the war abroad. Jane Yolen's picture storybook, **All Those Secrets of the World** (P–I), is a lovely evocation of this time. The text is lyrical, expressing the thoughts of a young girl whose father goes off to war. Leslie Baker's beautiful watercolors are som-

> ### Figure 8-7
>
> ## Stories of World War II and the Holocaust
>
> Bawden, Nina. *Henry.* (I)
>
> Benchley, Nathaniel. *Bright Candles.* (I)
>
> Bergman, Tamar. *Along the Tracks.* (I)
>
> Degens, T. *On the Third Ward.* (A)
>
> ——. *Transport 451—R.* (I–A)
>
> Glassman, Judy. *The Morning Glory War.* (I–A)
>
> Hahn, Mary Downing. *Stepping on the Cracks.* (I–A)
>
> Hartling, Peter. *Crutches.* (I–A)
>
> Hest, Amy. *Love You, Soldier.* (P–I)
>
> Hotze, Sollace. *Summer Endings.* (A)
>
> Innocenti, Robert. *Rose Blanche.* (P–I–A)
>
> Kerr, Judith. *When Hitler Stole Pink Rabbit.* (I–A)
>
> Laird, Christa. *Shadow of the Wall.* (A)
>
> Levitin, Sonia. *Silver Days.* (A)
>
> Lingard, Joan. *Tug of War.* (A)
>
> ——. *Between Two Worlds.* (A)
>
> Lowry, Lois. *Number the Stars.* (I)
>
> Magorian, Michelle. *Good Night, Mr. Tom.* (A)
>
> Maruki, Toshi. *Hiroshima No Pika.* (P–I–A)
>
> McSwigan, Marie. *Snow Treasure.* (I)
>
> Morpurgo, Michael. *Waiting for Anya.* (I–A)
>
> Orlev, Uri. *The Island on Bird Street.* (A)
>
> ——. *The Man from the Other Side.* (A)
>
> Paulsen, Gary. *The Cookcamp.* (I)
>
> Pearson, Kit. *The Sky Is Falling.* (I–A)
>
> Pople, Maureen. *The Other Side of the Family.* (I–A)
>
> Reiss, Johanna. *The Upstairs Room.* (A)
>
> Serraillier, Ian. *Escape from Warsaw.* (A)
>
> Shimin, Margarethe. *The Little Riders.* (I–A)
>
> Tomlinson, Theresa. *Summer Witches.* (I–A)
>
> Vos, Ida. *Hide and Seek.* (I–A)
>
> Westall, Robert. *The Kingdom by the Sea.* (A)
>
> ——. *Echoes of War.* (A)
>
> Wild, Margaret. *Let the Celebrations Begin!* Illus. Julie Vivas. (P)
>
> Yolen, Jane. *The Devil's Arithmetic.* (A)
>
> ——. *All Those Secrets of the World.* (P)

ber extensions of the mood of the story and also provide emotional and physical details about life in America during World War II.

Sollace Hotze's **Summer Endings** (A) tells the story of 12-year-old Christine, a Polish immigrant whose father was trapped in Poland by the Nazi invasion. During the summer of 1945 the Chicago Cubs win the pennant, Christine's sister gets married, Christine gets her first job and her first kiss, the war ends, and Christine's father is found. All of these events are wrapped in a vividly real sense of time and place. Other stories are listed in Figure 8-7.

The Cold War Era

The end of World War II brought with it a change in the social organization of the world and the lifestyles of many people. Peace was not long lasting;

soon the world was disturbed by the Korean, Vietnam, and Cambodian conflicts, as well as other less publicized wars.

Stories set during the conflict in Vietnam and the aftermath in Cambodia are finally becoming more plentiful. Like those about World War II, some of these books are set in the midst of the conflict and consider the lives of children in the war zones. Others are set in North America, Australia, and other countries and deal with issues such as children fleeing war to find a new life, the experiences of children whose grandfathers, uncles, and fathers went to war, the impact of returning veterans on family life, and the deep divisions in America during the Vietnam conflict.

Marc Talbert's **The Purple Heart** (I–A) is a powerful exploration of issues of courage, pride, love, and responsibility. Young Luke's vision of his father as a war hero does not match the man who comes

Flowers and other things have been laid against the wall. There are little flags, an old teddy bear, and letters, weighted with stones so they won't blow away. Someone has left a rose with a droopy head.

A child thoughtfully examines the tokens of remembrance that families leave at the Vietnam Memorial in Washington, DC. His stance and somber expression suggest that he longs for his grandfather whose name appears on the wall. (*The Wall* by Eve Bunting, illustrated by Ronald Himler)

home to recover. As Luke struggles to understand his much changed father, he learns a great deal about himself, and about what constitutes courage. Talbert's treatment of the difficulties that many Vietnam War veterans face is sensitive and even-handed.

A young boy and his father visit the Vietnam Veterans' Memorial to find his grandfather's name in Eve Bunting's picture storybook *The Wall* (P–I). The boy and his father quietly acknowledge their sorrow and their pride as other people pass by them. Ronald Himler's illustrations match the somber mood and underscore the feelings of the little boy as he thinks, "But I'd rather have my grandpa here. . . . "

Allan Baillie's *Little Brother* (A) is set in Cambodia during the conflict there. Young Vithy is separated from his big brother Mang as they try to make their way to the Thai border to escape the Khmer Rouge soldiers. When Vithy finally makes it to a refugee camp, he is befriended by a doctor who helps him search for his brother. Vithy finally agrees to leave Cambodia and return with the doctor to her native Australia. Upon landing, he sees his big brother waiting for him at the gate. The happiness Vithy feels at the end of the story helps relieve the terrible sorrow that precedes it. These and other stories are listed in Figure 8-8.

Today's News, Tomorrow's Historical Fiction

Good books for children about the Vietnam and Cambodian conflicts are just beginning to appear. It takes a while for authors to absorb recent current events and write about them thoughtfully. As our current concerns become history, authors will explore today's people and events as part of the history they inevitably become.

**Figure
8-8**

Cold War Conflicts

Baillie, Allan. *Little Brother.* (A)

Bunting, Eve. *The Wall.* (P–I)

Clark, Ann Nolan. *To Stand Against the Wind.* (I)

Giff, Patricia Reilly. *The War Began at Supper: Letters to Miss Loria.* (I)

Herlihy, Dirlie. *Ludie's Song.* (I–A)

Ho, Ming Fong. *The Clay Marble.* (A)

———. *Rice Without Rain.* (A)

Myers, Walter Dean. *Fallen Angels.* (A)

Nelson, Theresa. *And One for All.* (A)

Paek, Min. *Aekyung's Dream.* (P)

Paterson, Katherine. *Park's Quest.* (I–A)

Rostkowski, Margaret. *The Best of Friends.* (A)

Semel, Nava. *Becoming Gershona.* (A)

Slepian, Jan. *Risk n' Roses.* (I–A)

Talbert, Marc. *The Purple Heart.* (I–A)

Thesman, Jean. *Rachel Chance.* (A)

Watkins, Yoko K. *So Far from the Bamboo Grove.* (A)

TEACHING IDEA 8-5

Trace Family Heritage in Literature

Historical fiction writers frequently tell family stories and relate family origins. Ask students to find books that represent their family's background and activities.

Ask students to consider the following as they talk and write about their heritage:

1. What is your family's history or origin?

2. What kinds of things do you do that make your family special?

3. What holidays do you celebrate?

4. Make a family tree or a family history book. Record major events in your family history.

5. Tell your family story.

6. Read other family books to compare.

Illustrative Books:

Cech, John. *My Grandmother's Journey.* Illus. Sharon McGinley-Nally. (P)

Coerr, Eleanor. *Chang's Paper Pony.* (P–I)

———. *The Josephina Story Quilt.* (P–I)

Fleming, Alice. *The King of Prussia and a Peanut Butter Sandwich.* (P–I)

Hall, Donald. *Ox-Cart Man.* Illus. Barbara Cooney. (P–I)

Johnston, Tony. *The Quilt Story.* (P–I)

———. *Yonder.* (P–I–A)

McCurdy, Michael. *Hannah's Farm: The Seasons on an Early American Homestead.* (P–I)

Polacco, Patricia. *The Keeping Quilt.*

Yarbrough, Camille. *Cornrows.* (P–I)

Patricia Reilly Giff looks at an event in recent history—the Persian Gulf War—through the letters of fictional children in *The War Began at Supper: Letters to Miss Loria* (I). This brief story consists of letters that a group of children write to a former student teacher. The letters reveal the children's personalities and their uncertainties, questions, and fears about the Gulf War. As the children learn more about the war, they also learn about things they can do to help those in the Gulf.

HISTORICAL FICTION IN THE CLASSROOM

Reading historical fiction can help children realize they are players on the historical stage, and that their lives, too, will become part of history. As they read historical fiction they come to realize the hu-

man drama inherent in history as well as the common themes that reach across time and people.

There are several ways to incorporate historical fiction into the curriculum. Middle school teachers can coordinate English language arts and social studies classes, reading historical fiction in both classes that corresponds to the times and places focused on in the social studies curriculum. Elementary-grade teachers who have self-contained classes can easily link their students' reading material with

This black and white photograph emphasizes the starkness of the discord between black and white races during the turbulent days of the 1950s. Here, Rosa Parks sits in the front seat on the day the buses were integrated—December 21, 1956. (*Rosa Parks* by Eloise Greenfield)

the social studies topics they explore. Groups of children can read and discuss books set in a particular period of history, individual children can read independently from a collection of historical fiction, and the teacher can read aloud from a book that explores the time and place the class is studying.

Historical fiction can also be linked to biography, discussed in Chapter 9, and nonfiction, discussed in Chapter 10. All three genres support each other and together enable children to understand history in a way that is not possible through a single textbook.

The first time one teacher tried using historical fiction, biography, and nonfiction instead of the social studies textbook for the study of the American Revolution, she was unsure of the possible outcomes. She asked students to read one novel, one biography, and one informational book on that historical period. In addition, they read an encyclopedia account of one of the events described in the novel. The students then critically examined the presentations in the various sources. The teacher modeled the process, and they worked in collaborative learning groups to discuss their findings. The group concluded no single book could have given them the basis for understanding that they gained from their wide reading. Even more exciting, the children begged their teacher to use the same approach for the next social studies unit.

Another teacher works with her third-grade students to develop a study plan for a unit on early settlers in America. She fills the room with many sources of information, including books, records, films, and pictures. The children spend several days exploring the material and making suggestions about topics that interest them. Their list might include the Pilgrims, Plymouth Rock, the Mayflower, the first Thanksgiving, and witch trials. The group organizes the ideas into reasonably logical categories, and students choose topics they want to pursue, identify sources of information, and begin the research for the study. Examining the past in this way helps students begin to understand human behavior, the ways people and societies interact, the concept of humans as social beings, and the values that make people human.

Presenting Historical Fiction by Theme

Understanding human nature and social patterns can result when we think about themes found in historical fiction and link them to themes in other genres and to our own lives. People have common needs which must be met; these universal needs can be identified as themes that permeate social interactions. For example, the quest for freedom and respect, the struggle between good and evil, love and hate, and the determination to seek a better life are themes as old as time and as current as today. Historical fiction contains the stories of many people caught up in such struggles. Reading a number of books that explore the same theme across different periods of history allows students to understand the similarities of human needs across time; looking at books that explore the same theme in different cultures allows students to understand the similarities of human needs across peoples. They recognize the meaning of universal needs.

Grouping books by theme also encourages students to make connections between historical fiction and other genres. Themes about coming-of-age, learning self-reliance, and fighting for one's beliefs permeate contemporary realism, fantasy, and biography as well as historical fiction. Many books, of course, contain more than one theme. For example, books that explore issues of freedom or tell the story of immigration will likely address prejudice. A sensitive discussion of some of these books illustrates how different cultural groups have struggled to overcome prejudice across the span of history. Illustrative themes that echo throughout historical fiction are listed in Figure 8-9.

Figure
8-9

Themes in Historical Fiction and Biography

Clash of Cultures: Christopher Columbus Explorations

Brenner, Barbara. *If You Were There in 1492.* (I–A)

Conrad, Pam. *Pedro's Journal.* (I)

Dorris, Michael. *Morning Girl.* (I–A)

Foreman, Michael. *The Boy Who Sailed with Columbus.* (I)

Jacobs, Francine. *The Tainos: The People Who Welcomed Columbus.* (I–A)

Liestman, Vicki. *Columbus Day.* (I)

Litowinsky, Olga. *The High Voyage: The Final Crossing of Christopher Columbus.* (I–A)

Meltzer, Milton. *Columbus and the World Around Him.* (I–A)

Sis, Peter. *Follow the Dream: The Story of Christopher Columbus.* (P–I)

Yolen, Jane. *Encounter.* Illus. David Shannon. (P–I–A)

Prejudice

Finkelstein, Norman H. *Captain of Innocence: France and the Dreyfus Affair.* (A)

Kudlinski, Kathleen V. *Pearl Harbor Is Burning: A Story of World War II.* (I)

Parks, Rosa, and Jim Haskins. *Rosa Parks: My Story.* (A)

Siegel, Beatrice. *The Year They Walked: Rosa Parks and the Montgomery Bus Boycott.* (I–A)

Taylor, Mildred D. *Mississippi Bridge.* (I)

Issues found in historical fiction are often the same as those explored in other genres. Prejudice, for example, is also an issue in contemporary realism, fantasy, and biography. Arnold Adoff's biography, *Malcolm X* (I), Eloise Greenfield's *Rosa Parks* (I), and Ruth Franchere's *Cesar Chavez* (I) necessarily explore prejudice when recounting the lives of their subjects as does William Jay Jacobs's *Human Rights* (A), part of the Great Lives series. Nina Bawden's realistic novel *The Witch's Daughter* (I-A) and Bruce Brooks's *The Moves Make the Man* (A) explore issues of prejudice, as does Ursula Le Guin's fantasy, *Tehanu* (A). Reading and discussing books such as these which span the genres can help children understand the powerful emotions that echo throughout human history.

SUMMARY

When teachers put wonderful stories set in the past into children's hands, the past comes alive for them. By reading historical fiction teachers help students see that history was lived by people who, despite their different dress, customs, and habits, were a lot like we are. Whether it's confronting the plague in Europe of the Middle Ages, fleeing from soldiers in the American west, or watching your father go to war, readers of today can experience events of the past. When children are immersed in a compelling story, history becomes alive. It is only then that it becomes real and important for young readers.

9

Biography

MADAME CURIE'S BIOGRAPHY

I wondered what she was like
  at school.
Was she well behaved or bad?
Was she always happy,
Or was she sometimes sad?

Then, when I read a book about her,
I could see she was a lot like me,
And I felt a voice from deep inside . . .
  could it be . . .
Oh, could it really be?

                                    Brod Bagert

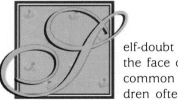

Self-doubt as one's talent begins to emerge, perseverance in the face of failure, and the joy of personal achievement are common elements in the lives of great men and women. Children often see themselves in the lives of such people, and begin to suspect their own potential. Then gradually, in their imaginations, they begin to envision the models from which to shape their own greatness.

A biography tells the story of a person's life and achievements; an autobiography re-creates the story of the author's life. Both are embedded in the time and culture that shaped and was shaped by the subject of the biography. Some biographies are chronological; they recount the events of a subject's life in the order in which they occurred. Some are episodic and highlight only a certain period of a person's life. Other biographies are interpretive, in which "events are selected and arranged so as to bring out a particular aspect of the life or the essence of the personality of the subject. Autobiography, written from an inner perspective, may be particularly revealing of the personal, psychological, or poetic experiences of life" (Herman, 1978, p. 91). Any good biography illuminates the interaction between an individual and historical events, demonstrating how a person's time and culture influence life even as a person influences his or her time and culture. Vivid and accurate portrayals of the *people* of history make history come alive for readers.

BIOGRAPHY IN CHILDREN'S LIVES

Biography used to be regarded as an opportunity for young readers to read about people they might emulate, striving, for example, to be as honest as Abraham Lincoln or as brave as Charles Lindbergh. Biographers in the nineteenth and early twentieth centuries wrote only about the good qualities of their subjects. In a self-conscious effort to provide children with a set of heroes to emulate, they deified America's heroes in a period of intense nationalism (see Chapter 1). They also presented heroes steeped in Victorian morality (Klatt, 1992). Contemporary biographers are more likely to consider their subjects in a less adulatory and more realistic manner. We now view biography not as an opportunity for moral enlightenment, but as a chance for children to learn about themselves as they learn about the lives and times of people who made a significant impact on the world (Herman, 1978).

Biography can help children develop their concepts of historical time; they can discover ideas and empathize with historical characters. Children who read biographies learn that all people have the same basic needs and desires. They begin to see their lives in relation to those of the past, learn a vast amount of social detail about the past, and begin to consider the human problems and relationships of the present in the light of those in the past.

Milton Meltzer hopes that reading well-written biographies will help children learn that they, like the subjects of the biographies, can make a difference in their own lives and the lives of others.

> I want to give young readers vision, hope, energy. I try to do it honestly, without concealing the weaknesses, the false starts, the wrong turns of my heroes and heroines. Even those who try their best not to engage in selfish attempts to outsmart their fellows can make tragic mistakes. Still, I write about them because they share a deep respect for the rights, the dignity, the value of every human being. (1989, p. 157)

Good biographies can enrich young readers' understandings about their history and their potential. Meltzer hopes to "shape a world where every child may grow in the spirit of a community that fulfills the best in us" (1989, p. 157).

CRITERIA FOR SELECTING BIOGRAPHIES

Biographies are stories of people's lives and like all stories can be evaluated in terms of the characterization, the presentation of plot and setting, the style of the writing, the unifying theme, and, in the case of picture books or illustrated books, the quality and contribution of the illustrations. As biographies, they are also subject to special considerations. Biographies need to be (1) stories grounded in source material, (2) portraits of real people rather than paragons, and (3) historically accurate depictions of the time and place in which the subject lived. Good biographies present authentic verifiable facts about a person's life and times in an engaging style. Figure 9-1 presents a brief list of criteria for evaluating biographies.

Accuracy

Although few biographers for children rely solely on primary sources, good biographies are always grounded in research. Some, called biographical fiction, are more fictional than others; they consist entirely of imagined conversations and reconstructed events in the life of an individual. Robert Lawson's **Ben and Me** (P–I), a funny story about Benjamin Franklin narrated by a mouse, is grounded in fact but written in fictional form. Others, called fictionalized biographies, are grounded in research and fact but the dialogue is invented. F. N. Monjo's **Poor Richard in France** (P–I), a fictionalized biography, recounts Franklin's trip to Europe through the eyes of his grandson who travels with him. Still others, called authentic biographies, are well-documented stories about individuals in which even the dialogue is based on some record of what was actually said by particular people at particular times. Jean Fritz's **What's the Big Idea, Ben Franklin?** (I) is an authentic biography of Franklin, with documented evidence woven into an entertaining story. Biographies like this are anchored by primary sources: letters, diaries, collected papers, and photographs.

Biographies need to present both a vivid and an accurate picture of the life and the times of the

---

> ### Figure 9-1
>
> ## Checklist for Selecting Biography
>
> **Accuracy**
>
> ❏ Does the biographer stick to the facts?
>
> (or invent dialogue or the subject's thoughts—when there is no evidence or record?)
>
> ❏ Is the biographer's portrayal supported by the subject's own writings, speeches, essays, letters?
>
> ❏ Are dates, names, and numbers accurate according to reliable reference sources?
>
> **Social Details: Setting and Plot**
>
> ❏ Are facts and story line integrated?
>
> ❏ Are there connections between the social climate and the individual's accomplishments?
>
> ❏ Is the social climate honestly portrayed?
>
> ❏ Does the plot revolve around authentic events?
>
> **Portrayal of the Subject**
>
> ❏ Is the subject's character well developed?
>
> ❏ Are stereotypes avoided?
>
> ❏ Is the person a worthy subject for a biography?
>
> ❏ Does the writer show strengths and weaknesses of subject?
>
> ❏ Are people surrounding the subject developed adequately?
>
> ❏ Is their influence accurately portrayed?
>
> **Style**
>
> ❏ Is the writing style comprehensible and engaging?
>
> ❏ Are complex topics explained adequately without misleading attempts to oversimplify?
>
> **Theme**
>
> ❏ Is there a unifying theme?
>
> ❏ Does the writer characterize the subject's life?
>
> ❏ Does the writer make the subject memorable?
>
> **Illustrations**
>
> ❏ Do the illustrations enrich the interesting details?
>
> ❏ Do illustrations help visualize the time and place?
>
> ❏ Do the illustrations portray authentic scenes?

subject. As is true of historical fiction, accuracy is a complex criterion. Careful biographers do not go beyond the facts as we know them today, but they do interpret these facts through the eyes of the present. For example, the d'Aulaires's biography of **Columbus** (P–I), written in 1955, refers to Native Americans as savages; the biographers seemingly saw no need to consider the humanity of the native people when assessing Columbus's life. Conse-

quently, they present him as he was viewed at the time—as a larger than life benevolent hero—with no mention of his less than admirable behavior (Taxel, 1992). Today's biographers, living in a world in which a respect for all cultures is expected, ought to paint a more accurate picture of Columbus and his journey. Some, like Vicki Liestman's **Columbus Day** (I–A), evaluate Columbus's accomplishments within the context of his time, but also include his flaws and mistakes, such as the abduction of native people. Others, like David Adler's *A Picture Book of Christopher Columbus* (P), are unfortunately more grounded in the legend of Columbus than in the facts of his encounter with the New World (Taxel, 1992).

Judging the accuracy of a biographer's presentation is not easy unless one happens to be an expert on the subject. When evaluating a biography, ask (1) what sources did the author use, (2) are these sources documented, and (3) are unnecessary generalizations about the people of the time or stereotypes of gender, ethnic, or racial groups evident?

Social Details: Setting and Plot

Careful biographers find a balance between telling everything and telling just enough to portray a person's life accurately. Many subjects of biographies for children had lives that were touched with pain, suffering, and hardship; many great achievements were won at great cost. These issues must not be avoided in biographies for children, but must be presented so that children can understand how truly great the subject's accomplishments were. For example, the times and events that shaped Dr. Martin Luther King were not happy ones; he grew up in a country deeply divided by racism. In any biography of King written for young readers, the social climate needs to be portrayed honestly in a way that is understandable to young children without being overwhelming. David Adler does this in *A Picture Book of Martin Luther King, Jr.* (P).

A rich and vivid depiction of the social details of a person's life makes that person's personality and accomplishments more understandable. Children often read for these social details, relishing the minutiae of another person's life. Mary Pope Osborne's *The Many Lives of Benjamin Franklin* (I–A) contains intriguing information about Franklin's life that make him real to readers while also giving them information about life during Franklin's time. Osborne writes:

> When he went into a bakery, he was pleasantly surprised to discover that huge puffy rolls were quite cheap. He bought three of them—stuck two under an arm as he gobbled the third. Continuing on his way up the street, he passed the door of a young woman named Deborah Reed. As Deborah stared at the disheveled young man, she must have thought he looked quite ridiculous. Little did she realize that this grubby boy would someday be her husband.

Look for settings that are (1) clearly and accurately depicted, (2) full of interesting social details, and (3) linked to the development of the subject's character and accomplishments.

The particular events that shaped the subject's life are the basis of the plot. Although some biographies are chronological and present the subject's entire lifetime, plodding through tedious detail about everything that happened in a subject's life makes unwieldy biographies. However, oversimplification often results in an untrue picture of both the individual and the times (Saul, 1986). Biographers have an array of facts available to them; how they select from those facts and craft them into an engaging story is up to them. Certainly whatever events are presented as facts should be accurate. Good authors document their facts and also differentiate between fact and opinion, or fact and legend.

Some biographers for young readers, like David Adler, choose to simplify the facts and present what is in effect an outline of the subject's life. Others, instead of attempting to recount the entire life of an individual, prefer to focus on an episode in a subject's life that illustrates the subject's character or was crucial to the subject's development. One of the best of these episodic biographies is F. N. Monjo's *Letters to Horseface: Young Mozart's Travels in Italy* (I–A). Monjo presents Mozart's thoughts, feelings, and experiences through letters that the young composer could have written to his sister. He bases the content of these letters on standard biographies and the collected letters of Mozart and his family.

Focusing on a brief period allows the biographer to present more details within a manageable length. Some teachers feel that such biographies are more rewarding for young children, since they avoid the problem of oversimplification and include the richness of detail that children enjoy (Carr, 1981).

Selecting key events in a subject's life and presenting them vividly illuminates the subject and keeps a reader's interest. Look for plots that (1) revolve around interesting and authentic events and (2) are told in a fast-moving manner.

Portrayal of the Subject

Jean Fritz's biographies are especially well researched and, at the same time, are quite entertaining. Fritz believes we make history dull by presenting our national heroes as frozen statues immersed in stale facts and images that emasculate our past:

Sometimes it seems to me that we have forced our heroes to play the children's own game of Statues. We have twirled them about, called *time,* and then told them to hold their positions. Whatever stance they happen to assume is the one they must perpetuate. (1976, p. 191)

She believes that these stereotyped impressions carry over into adulthood and rob us of a sense of the full force of a person's character. Her own biographies about Revolutionary War heroes present a refreshing view. They are tinged with humor, one of the most effective ways of bringing a deeper understanding of a person from the past. She presents the foibles as well as the good deeds through character-revealing incidents and anecdotes.

Biographers must consider their subjects as individuals rather than paragons, and individuals are multidimensional. Both foibles and strengths of individuals are presented in excellent biographies. The characters of a biography are unlike the characters of fiction in that they are real people who lived real lives. The biographer has the advantage of working with facts, but chooses how to select, interpret, and present those facts to readers. Exaggerating the good qualities of a subject results in hagiography—the telling of the life of a saint—or the creation of a legend. Biographies are about real people, not legendary figures.

The biographer's point of view and interest in the subject should be apparent, as should the biographer's purpose. Look for subjects that (1) are recognizable human beings, with strengths and weaknesses, and (2) are brought to life through the presentation of vivid details about their lives.

Style

Authors make choices about what they say and how they say it. Even when a story is well grounded in verifiable fact, as in authentic biography, it still represents an author's choice of facts and can still be told in an engaging fashion. The balance between fact and supposition varies across books, but all good biographies weave the facts into an interesting story. Good biographies avoid implying that the greatness of the subject was implicit from birth. They also avoid weaving background knowledge or prescient knowledge of latent talents into unlikely conversations (Herman, 1978).

Further, good biographies incorporate the language and customs of the times. The dialogue should reflect how the subject was likely to have talked, with enough authenticity that readers get a

---

TEACHING IDEA 9-1

Compare Biographies About a Person

Ask your students to:

1. Choose two biographies about the same person.

2. Include one written by Jean Fritz and one by another author.

3. Which biography gives the best idea of what the person was really like?

4. Which tells the most about the person's accomplishments?

5. Compare a biography written before 1970 with one written within the past five years.

6. What differences exist?

7. Do both books idolize the subject of the biography?

8. How are similar events reported?

For example, use the biographies about Christopher Columbus (shown in Figure 9-2) for comparison.

---

true picture but are not overwhelmed by archaic or idiosyncratic speech patterns. Look for (1) authentic language that is not overwhelming and (2) language that rings true to the characters.

Theme

The theme of a biography is the unifying element behind the story. Facts are merely facts until they are subordinated to a theme and a structure that allows them to make a collective statement with universal application and appeal. Fighting against injustice, struggling for independence, or working for human rights happens around the world and in many different ways. Each individual story builds its own theme; combined, they highlight the resilience and courage of human beings. Look for books that (1) blend factual background as subordinate to the story and (2) contain a theme with universal application and appeal.

Illustrations

If the biography is a picture book, the illustrations must also present the setting and the subject in an accurate manner. Illustrations often provide the interesting details that the brief text of many picture book biographies lack. The paintings in *The Glorious Flight: Across the Channel with Louis Bleriot July 25, 1909 (I),* Alice and Martin Provensen's Caldecott Award–winning biography, are full of details about people, places, and airplanes. They ground the textual information in accurate visual detail. Illustrated biographies, like Diane Stanley's *Peter the Great* (I), present a great deal of information

in the text, but rely on the illustrations also to help children visualize the time, place, and people.

Biographers also make use of historic photographs, when they are available, to highlight their subjects' personalities and lives. Russell Freedman's *The Wright Brothers: How They Invented the Airplane (A)* contains black-and-white photographs taken by Wilbur and Orville Wright themselves. This is a carefully constructed biography that presents the story of the first airplane as well as the story of its inventors.

Look for illustrations that (1) include interesting, authentic details appropriate to the setting and (2) illuminate the character of the subject.

A Close Look at *Lincoln: A Photobiography*

Russell Freedman's *Lincoln: A Photobiography* (I–A) won the Newbery Medal in 1988. This distinguished contribution to literature for children exemplifies the qualities of great biography.

Setting and Plot

Freedman chose to tell the story of Lincoln's entire life, from birth to death, but he carefully selected the facts that would build on each other to present an accurate and vivid picture of the man's life. The book begins with a brief chapter presenting the personality and physical characteristics of Lincoln the adult; the chapter is aptly titled "The Mysterious Mr. Lincoln."

Freedman acknowledges that not much is known about Lincoln's early life, but he recounts what is known of his boyhood in just a few pages, telling of the way he lived, the places he lived, and the changes in his family. Accompanying this succinct description of Lincoln's childhood are photographs of Lincoln's father and stepmother, of a replica of the cabin he was born in, and a page from his copybook. Text and illustrations present a picture of a poor, intelligent, hardworking youth—and one who was very tall.

After recounting Lincoln's young adulthood and the experiences that led him to become a lawyer, Freedman concentrates on Lincoln's expertise as a lawyer and his growing fascination with politics. The remainder of the book focuses on Lincoln's years as president, exploring the complex issues of emancipation and the war. As in the earlier chapters, Freedman presents interesting details using text and illustration. In discussing the Lincoln-Douglas debates, Freedman states:

P R O F I L E

RUSSELL FREEDMAN, a master of biographies and nonfiction, worked as a journalist and television publicity writer before he became interested in children's books. He stumbled into the children's book field by chance when he read a newspaper article about a 16-year-old blind boy who had invented a Braille typewriter. On further reading, he discovered that the Braille system itself had been invented by another 16-year-old blind boy, Louis Braille. Freedman was intrigued and began writing a collection of biographies called ***Teenagers Who Made History*** (A).

Freedman did not look favorably upon the "Parson Weems" type of biography that included make believe stories (George Washington saying, "I cannot tell a lie" after cutting down a cherry tree, for example). In addition to the fictionalized parts, early biographies for children had a reverential tone; they avoided controversy and criticism. They were sanitized—idealized stereotypes—that presented a sugarcoated vision of the person.

Freedman's biographies help shape the hero worship of the past into a more realistic picture. He sticks closely to documented evidence about his subject; it is a scholarly approach. He respects today's readers and knows that they prefer the facts. Freedman believes it is healthy for children to know that even the great figures of history shared their same doubts and fears.

Freedman approached writing the biography of Abraham Lincoln with trepidation; so many had already been written. A Lincoln scholar advised him about the best ones but first-hand research helped, too.

Russell Freedman

Freedman says,

Along with my reading, I had a chance to enjoy the pleasures of eyewitness research. I visited Lincoln's log-cabin birthplace in Kentucky, his boyhood home in Indiana, and the reconstructed village of New Salem, Illinois, where he lived as a young man. I went to Springfield, with its wealth of Lincoln historical sites, and to Washington, D. C. for a firsthand look at Ford's Theatre and the rooming house across the street where the assassinated president died. There's something magic about being able to lay your eyes on the real thing—something you can't get from your reading alone. . . . I could picture the scene in my mind's eye, because I had walked down those same dusty lanes, where cattle still graze behind split-rail fences and geese flap about underfoot. When I wrote about Lincoln's morning walk from his house to his law office in downtown Springfield, I knew the route because I had walked it myself. (Excerpt: "Newbery Medal Acceptance." *The Horn Book Magazine.* July/August, 1988. pp. 444–451. Exact quote p. 449.)

Freedman's work helps young readers walk with Abraham Lincoln through some critical historical events.

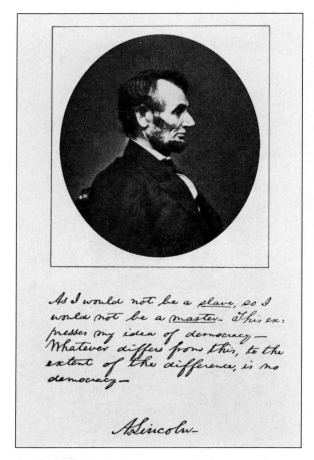

Russell Freedman presents a warm yet provocative picture of Abraham Lincoln's life in a collection of revealing photographs and lucid text. In one touching scene, he describes what was in Mr. Lincoln's pockets the day he was assassinated. (*Lincoln: A Photobiography*)

The striking contrast between Douglas and Lincoln—The Little Giant and Long Abe, as reporters called them—added color and excitement to the contests. Douglas was Lincoln's opposite in every way. Barely five feet four inches tall, he had a huge round head planted on massive shoulders, a booming voice, and an aggressive, self-confident manner. He appeared on the speakers' platform dressed "plantation style"—a navy coat and light trousers, a ruffled shirt, a wide-brimmed felt hat. Lincoln, tall and gangly, seemed plain in his rumpled suit, carrying his notes and speeches in an old carpetbag, sitting on the platform with his bony knees jutting into the air. (pp. 58–59)

This text is accompanied by two photographs side by side that dramatize the vast physical differences in the two men, differences which were mirrored in their opposing views on slavery.

Freedman grapples with the issue of slavery in a straightforward and sensitive fashion. Slavery was a part of life at the time and there were violently opposing views about it. Lincoln's character was shaped by the times in which he lived and the events in his life—and the increasing debate over slavery certainly had a part in shaping his character.

Portrayal of Subject

Perhaps the best example of Freedman's respectful and honest presentation of Lincoln is how he presents Lincoln's views on slavery. Rather than simply labeling Lincoln "The Great Emancipator," Freedman explores the complex issues that Lincoln had to face. He tells us that, although Lincoln was opposed to slavery, he was hopeful that confining it to the southern states would bring about its "natural death." He was not an abolitionist, and it wasn't until the Kansas-Nebraska Act of 1854 that Lincoln entered the political debate. Freedman states:

> Although Lincoln was determined to oppose the spread of slavery, he admitted that he didn't know what to do about those states where slavery was already established. . . . (p. 52)

Lincoln's eventual decision to proclaim emancipation is discussed within the context of the war and his duties as commander-in-chief, with Lincoln's opposition to slavery and his military shrewdness both informing that decision.

Freedman is also careful to separate legend from fact and to portray Lincoln as a real man, warts and all. His moodiness, his penchant for spoiling his children, his uncouth manners, and his reason for growing a beard are all anecdotes that bring life to this historical figure. So, too, are the descriptions of Lincoln's grief over the deaths of two of his sons and his bizarre prescient dream of his own assassination. Freedman's Lincoln is a man to admire *because* he was human, doing the best job of living he could do.

Accuracy and Style

Freedman is always careful to distinguish fact from opinion and truth from legend. This distinction is made in a plain and forthright manner:

> He also fell in love—apparently for the first time in his life. Legend tells us that Lincoln once had a tragic love affair with Ann Rutledge, daughter of the New Salem tavern owner, who died at the age of twenty-two. While this story has become part of American folklore, there

isn't a shred of evidence that Lincoln ever had a romantic attachment with Ann. Historians believe that they were just good friends. (p. 28)

He also presents a significant amount of interesting historical detail. We learn that Lincoln generally bought two suits a year—a significant detail in a time in which most men had one that had to last their lifetime. We learn that Lincoln finished the Gettysburg Address after breakfast on the day he delivered it, writing it out on two pieces of lined paper, and that he felt the speech was a failure.

The text includes many direct quotations from Lincoln, all set off with quotation marks. These quotations, the historical facts, and social details are all taken from sources listed at the end of the book. A sampling of Lincoln's famous quotations, with sources indicated, and the sources for the quotations that begin each chapter immediately follow the text. These are followed by a list and description of historic sites having to do with Lincoln's life, a description of source books about Lincoln, acknowledgments, and a useful five-page index. This end material, and the photographs of historical documents that appear throughout the text, all attest to the integrity and thoroughness of this biography.

Theme

The issue of slavery takes up a large portion of the book and indicates the way in which Freedman views Lincoln and his life. By presenting the events which resulted in Lincoln signing the Emancipation Proclamation, exploring the complex issues that surrounded emancipation, and acknowledging Lincoln's deliberation over the Proclamation, Freedman encourages readers to think about freedom and slavery and to see how divisive the institution of slavery was.

Freedman's **Lincoln** is an outstanding example of the vivid re-creation of the life of a person who profoundly affected history, and thus our lives today.

EXPLORING BIOGRAPHY CHRONOLOGICALLY

Looking at biography in terms of historical period is perhaps the most common way of using biography in the classroom. Like historical fiction, biography can help students envision what life was like in the past. Here we group biographies chronologically as we do historical fiction.

TEACHING IDEA 9-3

Write a Classmate's Biography

Ask your students to:

1. Write a biography about one of their classmates.
2. Draw names to see who (the subject) they write about.
3. Ask the subject for a list of references who can be contacted for information.
4. Interview people about their subject.
5. Write a draft outline of major periods or events in their subject's life.
6. Arrange a conference with their subject to see if additional periods or events need to be included.
7. Collect photographs of their subject at various ages.
8. Revise drafts until they have a satisfactory manuscript.
9. Present their subject to their classmates.
10. Present the final product with photographs to the subject of the biography.
11. Think about what they learned about writing biographies.

From Prehistoric Times to the American Revolution

Biographies from early times are not numerous; there are no historical records to explore to write a biography of a prehistoric person, and less is known about many of those who lived before the eighteenth century than those who lived after. There are, however, several excellent biographies that can support a study of the time periods between prehistoric times and the Revolutionary War period in American history.

The study of the medieval period is enriched by a biography of Eleanor of Aquitaine. **Queen Eleanor: Independent Spirit of the Medieval World** (I–A) by Polly Schoyer Brooks captures the spirit of power, intelligence, and grandeur of a truly remarkable woman. This woman was the wife of two kings, mother of two others, grandmother of an emperor,

Despite a limited palette, Arnold Lobel was able to convey emotions of anger, humor, fear, abandon, and disgust in a portrait of a city in development. (*On the Day Peter Stuyvesant Sailed into Town*)

and great-grandmother of a saint. In addition, Eleanor had strengths other than her dynasty: She led reforms, negotiated with religious and political leaders, and brought an appreciation of the arts into her court. Her influence helped establish the ideals of romantic love. Brooks separates legend from fact in this enchanting life story of a fascinating woman. Children may want to read her book in conjunction with E. L. Konigsburg's *A Proud Taste for Scarlet and Miniver* (A), a stunning work of historical fiction.

Leonard Everett Fisher's story of *Galileo* (I) grounds Galileo's genius in the context of his time. Readers learn about the Church and its weakening role in world affairs as a necessary background to the story of Galileo's forced renunciation of Copernican theory. The succinct text and simple illustrations present a man who invented or discovered many things we take for granted today—such as microscopes and telescopes—as a human being shaped by the time in which he lived. *Leonardo da Vinci: The Artist, Inventor, Scientist in Three-Dimensional Movable Pictures*

(P–I–A) by Alice and Martin Provensen pushes the boundaries of pop-up books to their highest ideals. The Provensens' art and skillful paper engineering combine to provide an artistic look at this inventor's life and work; they include reproductions of some of da Vinci's work, including the *Mona Lisa* as it stood on the easel. This unusual biography calls for repeated viewing.

Christopher Columbus, whose biographies are discussed earlier, was not the only explorer to venture into the unknown. Gian Paolo Ceserani records the adventures of *Marco Polo* (I) in a book beautifully illustrated with exquisite color paintings by Piero Ventura and featuring minute details. The text is informative and straightforward as it describes Polo's explorations and discoveries of new lands. Susan Roth's *Marco Polo: His Notebook* (I) recounts Polo's adventures in journal form.

The early days of America are described in various biographies of people whose impact on life in colonial times has become a part of history. Peter Stuyvesant is one of the more colorful characters among the early settlers. Robert Quackenbush describes him in **Old Silver Leg Takes Over! A Story of Peter Stuyvesant** (P–I), and Arnold Lobel portrays him in **On the Day Peter Stuyvesant Sailed into Town** (P–I). Both books depend heavily on illustration to add significant detail, and both can extend young readers' understanding of the Dutch settlement that became New York. The text in both books is simple but informative, with a touch of humor and hyperbole appropriate for Peter Stuyvesant. Lobel's final drawing shocks the reader with the full-page spread of what the small village of New Amsterdam was to become: New York City with all its glare and bustle.

Some of the most notable biographies of people who lived in these times are listed in Figure 9-2.

The Revolutionary War Period

There are many biographies that present the lives of those who were a part of the American Revolution. In 1976, the bicentennial of the beginning of the Revolution, a number of such biographies were published, including Jean Fritz's series for intermediate-grade readers. Biographies of American heroes continue to be published, the best of which show men and women struggling for freedom in their personal lives and the life of their country. Biographies about the people involved in the American Revolution give a serious view of their beliefs, sometimes a humorous glimpse of their foibles, and, ideally, a feeling that they were real people with blood in their veins.

Jean Fritz's series of biographies about the heroes of the American Revolution include **Why Don't You Get a Horse, Sam Adams?** (I), a humorous look at a colorful hero. Fritz describes Adams in this way: "His clothes were shabby and plain, he refused to get on a horse, and he hated the King of England." Her series of biographies are all authentic, well grounded in documented sources; they are also funny.

George Washington and the Birth of Our Nation (I–A) by Milton Meltzer puts the man in the context of his times, a victim of both ignorance and prejudice. Instead of idealizing a legend, Meltzer paints a realistic picture of George Washington and the world in which he lived. Washington's strength as a leader still shines, although his attitude toward slavery represents the common thought of his day. Meltzer provides documentation in the form of a bibliographic essay, index, reproductions of historic art, manuscript pages, and maps.

Meltzer also captures the spirit of the people involved in the revolution in **The American Revolutionaries: A History in Their Own Words** (I–A).

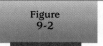

Figure
9-2

Biographies Before the American Revolution

Aliki. *The King's Day.* (P–I)

Brooks, Polly Schoyer. *Queen Eleanor: Independent Spirit of the Medieval World.* (I–A)

Bulla, Clyde Robert. *Squanto: Friend of the Pilgrims.* (I)

Ceserani, Gian Paolo. *Marco Polo.* (I)

d'Aulaire, Ingri, and Edgar Parin d'Aulaire. *Columbus.* (P)

————. *Pocahontas.* (P–I)

Demi. *Chingis Khan.* (P–I)

Fisher, Leonard Everett. *Galileo.* (I)

Fritz, Jean. *The Double Life of Pocahontas.* (I–A)

————. *Where Do You Think You're Going, Christopher Columbus?* (P–I)

————. *Who's That Stepping on Plymouth Rock?* (P–I)

Gleiter, Jan. *Sacagawea.* (I–A)

Hodges, Margaret. *Brother Francis and the Friendly Beasts.* (P)

Konigsburg, Elaine L. *A Proud Taste for Scarlet and Miniver.* (A)

Levinson, Nancy Smiler. *Christopher Columbus.* (P–I)

Lobel, Arnold. *On the Day Peter Stuyvesant Sailed into Town.* (P–I)

Nottridge, Harold. *Joan of Arc.* (I–A)

Provensen, Alice, and Martin Provensen. *Leonardo da Vinci: The Artist, Inventor, Scientist in Three-Dimensional Movable Pictures.* (P–I–A)

Quackenbush, Robert. *Old Silver Leg Takes Over! A Story of Peter Stuyvesant.* (P–I)

Roop, Peter, and Connie Roop. *I, Columbus: My Journal.* (P–I)

Roth, Susan. *Marco Polo: His Notebook.* (I)

Sis, Peter. *Follow the Dream: The Story of Christopher Columbus.* (P–I)

Stanley, Diane, and Peter Vennema. *Good Queen Bess: The Story of Elizabeth I of England.* (P–I–A)

*J*ean Fritz was 5 years old when she announced to her father that she was going to be a writer; she would write about America. At the time, she was living in China, where her parents were missionaries, and spent a good deal of her time defending her country to a neighbor boy who said derogatory things about George Washington.

For her, America represented an ideal, a place where everything was perfect. As an only child, she spent a lot of time with books and "learned early that words could get me where I wanted to go, which was simply some place else but most especially America." As soon as she could write, she composed stories about children doing all the American things she dreamed of doing—exploding fire-crackers on the Fourth of July and going to grandmother's house for Thanksgiving.

After she moved to the United States, she continued to pursue her fascination with America. She says that **The Cabin Faced West,** although ostensibly written about her great-great-grandmother's pioneer girlhood, was really her attempt to establish her roots as an American. She has written about other periods in American history, but her favorite is the Revolutionary era.

Fritz bemoans the dull way in which history is usually taught. She believes that stale facts and images should be replaced with studies that show historical characters as real people and that humorous anecdotes help children re-

Jean Fritz

late to history much better than cold dates. Her series of biographies of Revolutionary-era personalities presents fresh insights into the lives of people too often placed on pedestals, beyond understanding and caring.

Fritz lives in Dobbs Ferry, New York, where she takes an active interest in today's national and international concerns. "I join groups, write letters, make phone calls, and have on occasion demonstrated; in short, my life . . . is caught up in the special agonies of the times." She describes her own childhood in China in **Homesick: My Own Story** (I–A) and her visit as an adult in **China Homecoming** (I–A).

Jean Fritz's deep love for and pride in America enrich yesterday's history and that of tomorrow. Her recent books include: **Bully for You, Teddy Roosevelt, The Great Little Madison,** and a book she co-authored titled **The World in 1492.** (All I).

> Meanwhile, Samuel kept on talking and walking.
> "Why can't you ride a horse like everyone else?" his cousin John asked.
> But Samuel shook his head.

Trina Schart Hyman has a unique ability to use style and line to capture moments of communication. Colonial townsmen taunt Sam Adams when he stubbornly refuses to ride a horse. (*Why Don't You Get a Horse, Sam Adams?* by Jean Fritz)

In this carefully researched book he collects documents from diaries, letters, and other primary sources to show a glimpse of the private lives of people caught up in the American Revolution. Many other biographies set during the American Revolution are listed in Figure 9-3.

The Civil War and Life on the Frontier

It is not surprising that a number of biographies about Abraham Lincoln are available for young readers. There are also biographies of those who, like Harriet Tubman, struggled for freedom and of those who served in the armies that fought the Civil War. The best biographies about this period in history do not present the North as all good and the South as all bad. Rather, they present the individual as a human being, and the setting as a complex one, with heroes and villains on both sides.

Figure 9-3

Biographies of the American Revolution

Adler, David. *A Picture Book of Benjamin Franklin.* (P–I)

———. *A Picture Book of Thomas Jefferson.* (P–I)

Aliki. *The Many Lives of Benjamin Franklin.* (P–I)

d'Aulaire, Ingri, and Edgar Parin d'Aulaire. *George Washington.* (P–I)

Forbes, Esther. *America's Paul Revere.* (I–A)

Fritz, Jean. *And Then What Happened, Paul Revere?* (P–I)

———. *Can't You Make Them Behave, King George?* (P–I)

———. *The Great Little Madison.* (I–A)

———. *Traitor: The Case of Benedict Arnold.* (I–A)

———. *What's the Big Idea, Ben Franklin?* (P–I)

———. *Where Was Patrick Henry on the 29th of May?* (P–I)

———. *Why Don't You Get a Horse, Sam Adams?* (P–I)

———. *Will You Sign Here, John Hancock?* (P–I)

Hilton, Suzanne. *The World of Young Andrew Jackson.* (I)

———. *The World of Young George Washington.* (I)

Jacobs, William Jay. *Washington.* (I–A)

McGovern, Ann. *Secret Soldier, The Story of Deborah Sampson.* (I–A)

Meltzer, Milton. *George Washington and the Birth of Our Nation.* (I–A)

———. *The American Revolutionaries: A History in Their Own Words.* (I–A)

Milton, Joyce. *The Story of Paul Revere.* (I–A)

Monjo, F. N. *Poor Richard in France.* (I–A)

———. *Grand Papa and Ellen Aroon.* (P–I)

The theme of flying, prevalent in African-American folklore and song, is a vivid part of the Harriet Tubman story. (*Aunt Harriet's Underground Railroad in the Sky* by Faith Ringgold)

Julius Lester uses first-person narratives in ***To Be a Slave*** (I–A), edited verbatim transcripts of accounts by blacks who escaped from the antebellum South. Lester also uses interviews, footnotes to history (such as bills of sale for slaves, letters, and marriage registers), and primary sources for six stories about slaves and freedmen in ***Long Journey Home*** (I–A). He tells the stories of minor figures because he feels they are the true movers of history, whereas the famous exist as symbols of their actions. The stories are dramatic, sometimes bitter, always poignant.

Virginia Hamilton's ***Many Thousand Gone: African Americans from Slavery to Freedom*** (I–A) is a well-researched and beautifully written biography that tells 34 brief stories using a great deal of original testimony. The individual stories are brief episodic biographies; the book as a whole becomes a biography of a people journeying from slavery to freedom.

Faith Ringgold combines fantasy, biography, and historical fiction in ***Aunt Harriet's Underground Railroad in the Sky*** (P–I). Young Cassie and her brother Be Be are flying in the sky when they come across the Underground Railroad train with Harriet Tubman as the conductor. They are swept backward through time and join the flight to freedom in Canada. As the children learn about slavery, the Underground Railroad, and Harriet Tubman, readers do too. The end matter contains a brief factual biography of Tubman, suggestions for further reading, and a map of Underground Railroad routes. Other excellent biographies that would enhance a study of the Civil War period are presented in Figure 9-4.

The story of America's past includes the great migration of people toward the western part of America. This migration, like other great events in history, has spawned many stories and many heroes. Recently, these stories and heroes have been reassessed and their place in history examined in light of the terrible destruction of the lives of Native Americans wrought by the westward expansion. While there are not yet enough biographies of Native American figures who lived in these times, heightened awareness of a need for these biographies should result in more becoming available.

Children who enjoy reading Laura Ingalls Wilder's books will want to know more about her life and how her books reflected her life. ***Laura Ingalls Wilder: Growing Up in the Little House*** (I) by Patricia Reilly Giff begins with the 63-year-old Laura deciding to write down the stories her daughter

---

**Figure
9-4**

Civil War and Life on the Frontier

Civil War

Claflin, Edward Beecher. *Sojourner Truth and the Struggle for Freedom.* (I–A)

d'Aulaire, Ingri, and Edgar Parin d'Aulaire. *Abraham Lincoln.* (P–I)

Ferris, Jeri. *Go Free or Die: A Story About Harriet Tubman* (P–I)

Freedman, Russell. *Lincoln: A Photobiography.* (I–A)

Fritz, Jean. *Stonewall.* (I–A)

Gross, Ruth Belov. *True Stories about Abraham Lincoln.* P–I)

Hamilton, Virginia. *Anthony Burns: The Defeat and Triumph of a Fugitive Slave.* (I–A)

Reit, Seymour. *Behind Rebel Lines: The Incredible Story of Emma Edmonds.* (I–A)

Sandburg, Carl. *Abraham Lincoln: The Prairie Years.* (A)

———. *Abe Lincoln Grows Up.* (A)

Turner, Dorothy. *Florence Nightingale.* (A)

Life on the Frontier: Pioneers

Anderson, William. *Laura Ingalls Wilder Country.* (P–I–A)

Conrad, Pam. *Prairie Visions: The Life and Times of Solomon Butcher.* (I–A)

Fritz, Jean. *Make Way for Sam Houston.* (I)

———. *Bully for You, Teddy Roosevelt.* (I–A)

Gleiter, Jan. *Kit Carson.* (I–A)

Harvey, Brett. *My Prairie Year: Based on the Diary of Elenore Plaisted.* (P–I)

Henry, Joanne Landers. *Log Cabin in the Woods: A True Story About a Pioneer Boy.* (I–A)

Jakes, John. *Susanna of the Alamo: A True Story.* (P–I)

Kellogg, Steven. *Johnny Appleseed.* (P–I)

Latham, Jean Lee. *Carry On, Mr. Bowditch.* (I–A)

Lawler, Laurie. *Daniel Boone.* (I–A)

Lindbergh, Reeve. *Johnny Appleseed.* (P–I)

Quackenbush, Robert. *Don't You Dare Shoot That Bear: A Story of Theodore Roosevelt.* (I)

———. *Quit Pulling My Leg! A Story of Davy Crockett.* (I)

Trotman, F. *Davy Crockett.* (I)

**Life on the Frontier—
Native Americans**

Black, Sheila. *Sitting Bull and the Battle of the Little Big Horn.* (I–A)

Ferris, Jeri. *Native American Doctor: The Story of Susan LaFlesche Picotte.* (I)

Freedman, Russell. *An Indian Winter.* (I–A)

———. *Indian Chiefs.* (I–A)

Herman, Viola. *Sitting Bull.* (I)

Rose loved to hear—the stories about Pa and Ma Ingalls in the olden days when Laura was a child. Giff writes lovingly of Laura as she weaves bits from the Little House books themselves into the account of the elderly woman writing them. Other representative biographies are listed in Figure 9-4.

Immigration, World War I, and the Great Depression

Many of those who were part of the westward expansion had another story to tell as well—their immigration to America. As these new immigrants settled in and made new homes, the world was moving closer to the First World War, soon followed by the Depression. The stories of people who lived in these times reflect a courage and determination that enabled them to uproot their lives for another chance in a new world, a world war, or an opportunity for economic survival.

David Kherdian tells a major segment of his mother's life in ***The Road from Home*** and continues it in ***Finding Home*** (both I–A). Veron Dumehjian was born to a prosperous Armenian family living in Turkey. Her childhood was filled with sunlight until the Turkish government in 1915 decided to evict the Armenians. These books tell of her family's deportation, her trip to America as a mail-order bride, and her unhappiness under the constraints of living in a close-knit Armenian family.

A neighbor from Hyde Park speaks earnestly to Governor Franklin Delano Roosevelt during the Great Depression. Russell Freedman's biography of Roosevelt conveys a sense of the man and his times. (*Franklin Delano Roosevelt*)

John Cech chose the story of his wife's mother's life for the topic of his first book, **My Grandmother's Journey** (P). His story begins at bedtime, with grandmother telling granddaughter the story of her life. That story includes life in Russia under the czar, the Russian Revolution and the civil war that followed, capture by the retreating Nazi army and, finally, immigration to America. Sharon McGinley-Nally's bright folk-art illustrations provide colorful details about this remarkable woman's amazing life. Other biographies are listed in Figure 9-5.

Some of the most famous people to live during the Great Depression were Eleanor and Franklin Delano Roosevelt. David Adler's **A Picture Book of Eleanor Roosevelt** covers her life from beginning to end, necessarily omitting a great deal of detail. The book does, however, give readers an idea of who she was, how she lived, and what she stood for as Adler presents her as an important person in her own right, and not just the president's wife.

Russell Freedman's **Franklin Delano Roosevelt** (A) uses archival photographs, the words of Roosevelt and others who lived at the time, popular biographies of Roosevelt, and the collection at the Franklin D. Roosevelt Library to create an accurate, vivid picture of the man and his times. Other biographies set in this period are listed in Figure 9-5.

This well-balanced photograph calls attention to the intense absorption that accompanies a task of writing. The older man wears royal purple and gold to symbolize dignity. The young boy wears yellow as a symbol of happiness and youth. (*Hoang Anh: A Vietnamese–American Boy* by Hoyt-Goldsmith)

World War II and After

The Great Depression ended and World War II began. Those who had been standing in breadlines stood in draft lines or on assembly lines as the world went to war. This war had its heroes, like all wars, but it also had more than its share of villains. Biographies of World War II include notable figures such as Franklin Delano Roosevelt; they also include biographies of Hitler and of those who suffered and died in the Holocaust. While biographies of the stars of the period are interesting and necessary, it is often the biographies of individuals like Anne Frank's *Diary of a Young Girl* (I–A) that really bring home the tragedy of World War II.

Johanna Reiss wrote *The Upstairs Room* (I–A), an autobiographical account of her life during the Nazi occupation, primarily for her own daughters, but readers everywhere learn about persecution from reading it. Ten-year-old Annie and her older sister expect to be hidden in the upstairs room of a Dutch farm home for only a few weeks, but the weeks stretch into more than two years. A sequel, *The Journey Back* (I–A), follows the girls as they make difficult adjustments after the war. Biographies about the famous, infamous, and ordinary people who lived during the war years are listed in Figure 9-6.

Figure 9-5

From Immigration to the Great Depression

Driemen, J. E. *Winston Churchill.* (I–A)

Faber, Doris. *Eleanor Roosevelt: First Lady of the World.* (I–A)

Freedman, Russell. *Franklin Delano Roosevelt.* (I–A)

Greenfield, Eloise. *Mary McLeod Bethune.* (I)

Kherdian, David. *The Road from Home: the Story of an Armenian Girl.* (I–A)

McKissack, Patricia. *Mary McLeod Bethune: A Great American Educator.* (I)

Since the end of the war, America and the world have changed considerably. We have suffered through wars in Korea and in Southeast Asia, watched governments rise and fall and new countries created, and seen a new wave of immigrants

Through his use of color, Michael Foreman conveys messages of peace—blue washes throughout the scene—as the child shows his admiration for the bagpipers. (*War Boy: A Country Childhood*)

---

arrive in America. We have entered the age of the celebrity, with sports and music superstars rocketing to fame almost overnight. All of these events are reflected in the books available for children. America is becoming a more pluralistic society, so more biographies of new immigrants, such as Diane Hoyt-Goldsmith's *Hoang Anh: A Vietnamese-American Boy* (I–A), will be available. A clear text and color photographs by Lawrence Migdale present details in the life of a young adolescent who was a baby when his parents fled with him from Vietnam. The book explores how he is able to keep his Vietnamese traditions alive and be an American kid.

Many artists, musicians, athletes, and politicians who are in today's news are often the subjects of biographies. Some of these biographies, like Patricia C. McKissack's loving portrait of *Jesse Jackson* (A), are carefully researched, well documented, and engagingly written. Others are quickly thrown together accounts of current superstars. Biographies of both the famous and the ordinary reflect life in today's world. Some of the best of these biographies are listed in Figure 9-7.

Figure 9-6

World War II and After

Adler, David. *Martin Luther King, Jr.: Free at Last.* (P–I)

——. *Picture Book of Martin Luther King, Jr.* (P–I)

Darby, Jean. *Dwight D. Eisenhower: A Man Called Ike.* (I)

Davidson, Margaret. *I Have a Dream: The Story of Martin Luther King.* (P–I)

Foreman, Michael. *War Boy: A Country Childhood.* (P–I)

Frank, Anne. *The Diary of a Young Girl.* (I–A)

Hoyt-Goldsmith, Diane. *Hoang Anh: A Vietnamese-American Boy.* (P–I)

Innocenti, Robert. *Rose Blanche.* (P–I–A)

Jakoubek, Robert. *Martin Luther King, Jr.* (A)

Marrin, Albert. *Hitler.* (A)

McMahon, Patricia. *Chi-Hoon: A Korean Girl.* Photos, Michael F. O'Brien. (I)

Reiss, Johanna. *The Upstairs Room.* (I–A)

Schloredt, V. *Martin Luther King, Jr.* (I–A)

Figure 9-7

Current Biographies

Caulkins, Janet. *Picture Life of Mikhail Gorbachev.* (A)

Hoyt-Goldsmith, Diane. *Pueblo Storyteller.* (I)

Jacobs, William Jay. *Mother Teresa: Helping the Poor.* (I)

Keegan, Marcia. *Pueblo Boy: Growing Up in Two Worlds.* (I)

McKissack, Patricia C. *Jesse Jackson: A Biography.* (I–A)

Meltzer, Milton. *Winnie Mandela: The Soul of South Africa.* (A)

White, Ryan, and Ann Marie Cunningham. *Ryan White: My Own Story.* (A)

Winner, David. *Desmond Tutu.* (A)

Biography certainly has a place in today's classroom, and a biography collection is an important part of any classroom or school library.

Building a Biography Collection

Individual biographies are judged according to the criteria explained at the beginning of this chapter. A collection of biographies needs to be assessed in terms of its scope and representativeness. As you gather biographies, be sure to evaluate the breadth of those you have collected in terms of gender and cultural representation. Biography for children has been dominated by the stories of white males. This has changed significantly in the past few decades, and there are now good biographies available of women and people of color. Balancing your collection across gender and race is important, as we discuss further in Chapter 11. If there are biographies of women and minorities related to your subject, be sure to include them in your collection. If there are not, you may want to consider with your students why there are no biographies of, for example, ancient female explorers, and why biographies of modern female explorers are now available. When issues such as these are considered, children can begin to see how the world has changed and how historical and current social conditions influence individual potentials.

BIOGRAPHY IN THE CLASSROOM

Biography can enliven a social studies curriculum; in conjunction with historical fiction and nonfiction, it can illuminate a time and place by telling the story of an individual. It can also support studies in music and art; there are many fine biographies of artists and musicians that explore both their lives and their creative endeavors. An exploration of themes, discussed in Chapter 8, is enriched by biographies.

Biography is the favorite reading material of many children. Intermediate- and advanced-grade children like biographies because they are real, not fictional, and present intriguing details of other people's lives. Children seem to choose biographies according to their interests: Those interested in music will choose biographies of musicians, baseball players will choose biographies of other baseball players (Herman, 1978).

This beautifully crafted illustration provides a strong sense of texture, tone, and emotion. Patterns from the Zulu culture permeate the art. The several textures and Peter Vennema, highlighted are well crafted in this mixed medium. (*Shaka: King of the Zulus* by Diane Stanley illustrated by Diane Stanley)

Robyn Montana Turner gives a close personal glimpse of artists in her series. Georgia O'Keeffe hated it when her teacher touched up her paintings. (*Georgia O'Keeffe*)

Presenting Biography by Theme

Biography, like historical fiction, contains stories of people who explore their world, fight for freedom, revolt against oppression, immigrate, establish new nations, and struggle for survival and human rights. Biographies can be used to complement historical and realistic fiction that explore similar themes; and single themes can be explored primarily through biographies. There are several new collections, such as the Great Lives series, that present brief biographies about various people engaged in similar struggles. Figure 9-8 lists some collective biographies organized around themes.

You can also collect several books that illustrate a particular theme such as geographic exploration or fighting for civil rights, like those cited earlier and those listed in Figure 9-9. By studying the lives of diverse people from around the world and across

Figure 9-8

Collective Biographies

Archer, Jules. *Breaking Barriers: The Feminist Revolution from Susan B. Anthony to Margaret Sanger to Betty Friedan.* (A)

Chang, Ina. *A Separate Battle: Women and the Civil War.* (A)

Faber, Doris, and Harold Faber. *Nature and the Environment.* (I–A)

Faber, Harold. *The Discoverers of America.* (A)

Hancock, Sibyl. *Famous Firsts of Black Americans.* (I)

Igus, Toyomi, Veronica Freeman Ellis, and Diane Patrick. *Great Women in the Struggle: An Introduction for Young Readers.* (I)

Pelz, Ruth. *Black Heroes of the Wild West.* (I)

Zane, Polly and John Zane. *American Women: Four Centuries of Progress.* (A)

Figure 9-9

Explorers and Freedom Fighters

Barnard, Jacqueline. *Journey Toward Freedom.* (A)

Blacknall, Carolyn. *Sally Ride: America's First Woman in Space.* (I–A)

Blumberg, Rhoda. *Commodore Perry in the Land of the Shogun.* (I–A)

————. *The Remarkable Voyages of Captain Cook.* (I)

Burleigh, Robert. *Flight: The Journey of Charles Lindbergh.* (P–I)

Ferris, Jeri. *Arctic Explorer: The Story of Matthew Henson.* (I–A)

Freedman, Russell. *The Wright Brothers: How They Invented the Airplane.* (I–A)

Harrison, Barbara, and Daniel Terris. *A Twilight Struggle: The Life of John Fitzgerald Kennedy.* (I–A)

Jacobs, William Jay. *Mother, Aunt Susan and Me.* (A)

Kendall, Martha E. *Elizabeth Cady Stanton.* (A)

Kerby, Mona. *Amelia Earhart: Courage in the Sky.* (I–A)

Lauber, Patricia. *Lost Star: the Story of Amelia Earhart.* (I–A)

Provensen, Alice, and Martin Provensen. *The Glorious Flight Across the Atlantic Channel with Louis Bleriot.* (P–I)

Stanley, Diane, and Peter Vennema. *Shaka: King of the Zulus.* (P–I)

Stanley, Diane. *Peter the Great.* (P–I)

history, students can come to understand the universal struggles of humankind. What drives human beings to explore their geographic boundaries? Why do people around the world fight for human rights? How are these struggles similar across nations and time? How do they vary according to age and culture? Exploring these kinds of questions can lead to a better understanding of humanity and one's place in it.

The theme of exploration can be widened to include those who explore not geography but science. The people who have made scientific breakthroughs are curious, dedicated individuals, just as many geographic explorers are. Biographies of famous scientists such as Louis Pasteur, Madame Curie, Jonas Salk, and others can enrich students' concepts of what it means to be an explorer. Artists and musicians who break new ground can also be considered explorers. Thus a general theme, like exploration or new frontiers, can be woven from many varying biographies as well as fiction and nonfiction.

Biographies of artists and musicians can support the study of art and music. They can also be compared in terms of the driving force that shaped the lives of these people—what caused them to pursue their talent with such passion and success. Biographies of female artists and musicians might be explored for examples of triumph over discrimination and then related to the general theme of human rights.

Robyn Montana Turner's series, Portraits of Women Artists for Children, presents both the life and the work of famous women artists. The books also explore the effects of living in a discriminatory

---

**Figure
9-10**

Scientists, Artists, and Musicians

Beardsley, John. *Pablo Picasso.* (I)

Blackwood, Alan. *Beethoven.* (I–A)

Brown, John R. *Shakespeare and His Theatre.* (A)

Cobb, Vicki. *Truth on Trial: The Story of Galileo Galilei.* (A)

Cousins, Margaret. *The Story of Thomas Alva Edison.* (A)

Everett, Gwen. *Li'l Sis and Uncle Willie: A Story Based on the Life and Paintings of William H. Johnson.* (P)

Fisher, Leonard Everett. *Galileo.* (I)

Gleiter, Jan. *John James Audubon.* (I)

Harris, Nathaniel. *Leonardo and the Renaissance.* (A)

Hibbard, Howard. *Michelangelo.* (A)

Ipsen, D. C. *Isaac Newton, Reluctant Genius.* (A)

McKissack, Patricia. *Marian Anderson: A Great Singer.* (P–I)

Oneal, Zibby. *Grandma Moses: Painter of Rural America.* (I–A)

Raboff, Ernest. *Albrecht Durer.* (A)

———. *Michelangelo.* (I–A)

———. *Rembrandt.* (I–A)

———. *Leonardo da Vinci.* (I–A)

———. *Raphael.* (I–A)

Rodari, Florian. *A Weekend with Picasso.* (I)

Skira-Venturi, Rosabianca. *A Weekend with Renoir.* (I)

Turner, Robyn Montana. *Georgia O'Keeffe.* (P–I)

———. *Rosa Bonheur.* (P–I)

Wadsworth, Ginger. *Rachel Carson: Voice for the Earth.* (I)

---

society and how each artist fought to pursue her talent. The series includes *Rosa Bonheur* and *Georgia O'Keeffe* (both I). Figure 9-10 contains the titles of some biographies of scientists, artists, and musicians.

There are also a great number of biographies and autobiographies of writers and illustrators of books for children. These biographies can be read in any number of ways. For example, reading about Beatrix Potter's life yields knowledge about her as a writer, but also about the time and place in which she grew up and its effect on her as a human being and especially as a woman. Thus Judy Taylor's ***Beatrix Potter 1866–1943: The Artist and Her Work*** (A) might be included in a study of people pursuing individual dreams despite great obstacles.

The Meet the Author series published by Richard C. Owen Publishers consists of slim picture books about current authors. The simple texts are written by the subjects and accompanied by color photographs that capture the author in his or her daily life and work. These books speak directly to the children who read them; the authors write as if they are talking to their readers. The result is a clear close look at the human being behind the pen. This series includes Cynthia Rylant's ***Best Wishes*** (P–I) and Jane Yolen's ***A Letter from Phoenix Farm*** (P–I). Figure 9-11 contains other titles of biographies and autobiographies of children's writers and illustrators. We discuss using these books to support the study and practice of writing in Chapter 12.

Those who singlemindedly pursue their talents as athletes are not fundamentally different from those who pursue their talents as artists, musicians, or writers. Those, like Arthur Ashe, who used their position as sports heroes to speak out against oppression are linked to others who struggle for human rights. Good sports biographies need not simply be information about personal heroes, but can be a springboard to exploring themes that permeate many other biographies, as well as a great deal of fiction. Figure 9-12 contains the titles of some biographies of contemporary and historical sports figures. Reading these and other biographies can simply end there—with more information about the lives of individual people—or they can be linked to larger themes and studies of the events and people who lived our past.

SUMMARY

Biographies tell the stories of the lives of the people who lived our history. Reading fine biographies helps children understand that people made history, and that these people had strengths and weaknesses, as we all do. Understanding the humanity behind the greatness allows children to dream of their own accomplishments, and to know they are possible.

The photograph draws the viewer's eye to the page proofs and layout that author Jane Yolen and editor Willa Perlman inspect carefully for one of Yolen's books. (*A Letter from Phoenix Farm*)

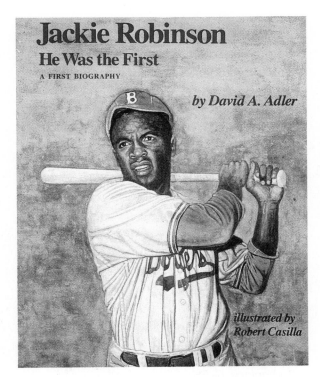

David Adler focuses on sports heroes who were the first to accomplish something of note. *Jackie Robinson: He Was the First* shows his success as the first African American to play in major league baseball. (Illustrated by Robert Casilla)

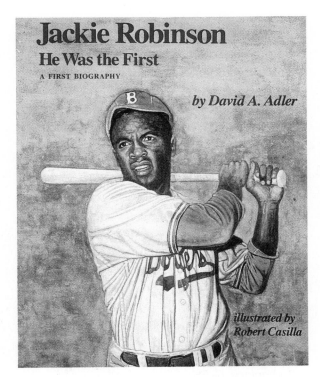

TEACHING IDEA 9-5

Current and Historical Biography

Ask your students to:

1. Find a biography about a contemporary sports star, TV personality, rock star, singer, entertainer, or politician.

2. Compare the biography of the contemporary figure with a biography of a historical figure. How do they differ? What is similar?

3. Decide which they enjoyed reading the most. Why?

4. List ways that biographies of people from the past differ from biographies of contemporary people.

Figure
9-11

Writers, Authors, Poets, Illustrators

Biography (See also Figure 12-3.)

Asher, Sandy. *Where Do You Get Your Ideas? Helping Young Writers Begin.* (I)

Barth, Edna. *I'm Nobody. Who Are You? The Story of Emily Dickinson.* (I–A)

Bassett, L. *Very Truly Yours, Charles L. Dodgson, Alias Lewis Carroll.* (I–A)

Blair, Gwenda. *Laura Ingalls Wilder.* (I)

Bober, Natalie. *A Restless Spirit: The Story of Robert Frost.* (I–A)

Bruce, Harry. *Maud: The Life of L. M. Montgomery.* (I–A)

Campbell, Patricia J. *Presenting Robert Cormier.* (A)

Carpenter, A. S. *Frances Hodgson Burnett: Beyond the Secret Garden.* (I–A)

Collins, D. R. *Country Artist: A Story About Beatrix Potter.* (I–A)

———. *To the Point: A Story About E. B. White.* (I–A)

Daly, Jay. *Presenting S. E. Hinton.* (A)

Giff, Patricia Reilly. *Laura Ingalls Wilder: Growing Up in the Little House.* (I)

Gonzales, Doreen. *Madeleine L'Engle.* (I)

Greene, C. *Hans Christian Andersen: Prince of Storytellers.* (I–A)

Harlan, Judith. *Sounding the Alarm: A Biography of Rachel Carson.* (A)

Hurwitz, Johanna. *Astrid Lindgren: Storyteller to the World.* (I–A)

Kamen, Gloria. *Kipling: Storyteller of East and West.* (I–A)

Kudlinski, Kathleen V. *Rachel Carson.* (A)

Lee, Betsy. *Judy Blume's Story.* (I)

Lyons, Mary E. *Sorrow's Kitchen: The Life and Folklore of Zora Neale Hurston.* (I–A)

Marcus, Leonard S. *Margaret Wise Brown: Awakened by the Moon.* (A)

Meigs, Cornelia. *Invincible Louisa.* (A)

Nilsen, Aileen Pace. *Presenting M. E. Kerr.* (A)

Norris, Jerrie. *Presenting Rosa Guy.* (A)

Quackenbush, Robert. *Mark Twain? What Kind of Name Is That? A Story of Samuel Langhorne Clemens.* (I–A)

———. *Who Said There's No Man on the Moon? Jules Verne.* (A)

Rappaport, Doreen. *American Women: Their Lives in Their Words.* (I–A)

Roginski, Jim. *Behind the Covers.* (A)

Rollock, Barbara. *Black Authors and Illustrators of Children's Books.* (A)

Taylor, Judy. *Beatrix Potter: Artist, Storyteller and Countrywoman.* (A)

———. *Beatrix Potter 1866–1943: The Artist and Her Work.* (A)

Walker, Alice. *Langston Hughes, American Poet.* (A)

Weidt, Maryann N. *Presenting Judy Blume.* (I–A)

Autobiography

Blegvad, Erik. *Self-Portrait: Erik Blegvad.* (P–I)

Bulla, Clyde Robert. *A Grain of Wheat: A Writer Begins.* (I)

Byars, Betsy. *The Moon and I.* (I)

Cleary, Beverly. *A Girl from Yamhill: A Memoir.* (I–A)

Cormier, Robert. *I Have Words to Spend: Reflections of a Small Town Editor.* (A)

Dahl, Roald. *Boy: Tales of Childhood.* (I)

Fox, Mem. *Dear Mem Fox: I Read All Your Books, Even the Pathetic Ones.* (A)

Fritz, Jean. *Homesick: My Own Story.* (I–A)

Henry, Marguerite. *Illustrated Marguerite Henry.* With Wesley Dennis. (I)

Hopkins, Lee Bennett. *The Writing Bug.* (P–I)

Hyman, Trina Schart. *Self-Portrait: Trina Schart Hyman.* (P–I)

Meltzer, Milton. *Starting from Home: A Writer's Beginnings.* (I–A)

Keller, Helen. *The Story of My Life.* (I–A)

Meltzer, Milton. *Starting from Home: A Writer's Beginnings.* (I–A)

CONTINUED

Naylor, Phyllis Reynolds. *How I Came to Be a Writer.* (I)

Nesbit, E. *Long Ago When I Was Young.* (I–A)

Peet, Bill. *Bill Peet: An Autobiography.* (P–I–A)

Potter, Beatrix. *The Journal of Beatrix Potter.* (A)

———. *Beatrix Potter's Americans: Selected Letters.* (A)

Stevenson, James. *When I Was Nine.* (P)

Sutcliff, Rosemary. *Blue Remembered Hills.* (I–A)

Uchida, Yoshiko. *The Invisible Thread: A Memoir by the Author of* The Best Bad Thing. (I–A)

White, E. B. *Essays of E. B. White.* (A)

Yep, Laurence. *The Lost Garden: A Memoir by the Author of* Dragonwings. (I–A)

Zemach, Margot. *Self-Portrait: Margot Zemach.* (P–I)

Figure 9-12

Sports Biographies

Adler, David. *Jackie Robinson: He Was the First.* (P–I)

———. *A Picture Book of Jesse Owens.* (I)

Appel, Marty. *Joe DiMaggio.* (I)

Gilbert, Thomas W. *Lee Trevino.* (A)

Goedecke, Christopher J. *The Wind Warrior: The Training of a Karate Champion.* Photos Rosmarie Hausher. (I)

Goldstein, Margaret J. *Brett Hull: Hockey's Top Gun.* (I)

Grabowski, John. *Sandy Koufax.* (I)

Greenberg, Keith Elliot. *Magic Johnson: Champion with a Cause.* (I)

Hilgers, Laura. *Steffi Graf.* (I)

Kavanagh, Jack. *Walter Johnson.* (I)

Lennon, Adrian. *Jorge Luis Borges.* (A)

Macht, Norman L. *Christy Mathewson.* (I)

———. *Cy Young.* (I)

———. *Satchel Paige.* (I)

Scott, Richard. *Jackie Robinson.* (I)

Tackach, Jim. *Hank Aaron.* (I)

Walker, Paul Robert. *Pride of Puerto Rico: The Life of Roberto Clemente.* (I)

Weissberg, Ted. *Arthur Ashe.* (A)

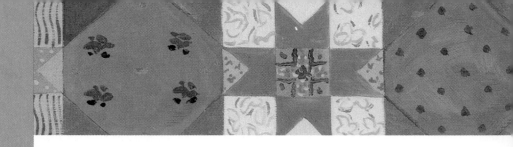

10

onfiction

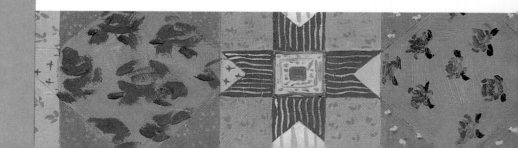

OPEN UP

Some things are pretty tricky.
Did you ever wonder why
The sun gets big and orange
At the bottom of the sky?

What grows hair on Daddy's face?
Who put black in tar?
Where do locusts come from?
How heavy is a star?

Well don't let questions scare you
For you don't have far to look;
The whole world is your crystal ball
When you open up a book.

Brod Bagert

The passion to know is a seed borne in the soul of every human being. For humankind, there is nothing more seductive than the lure of an unanswered question. When children discover that books are a place to find answers, they are infected by the desire *to know* and are thrust into the journey of lifelong learning.

The term *nonfiction* describes books of information and fact. Nonfiction, or informational, books are distinguished from fiction by their emphasis. Both may tell a story and both may include fact. In fiction, however, the story is uppermost, with facts sometimes used to support it; in nonfiction, the facts are uppermost, with storytelling perhaps used as an expressive technique.

Sixty to 70 percent of most library collections in elementary schools and in the children's sections of public libraries are nonfiction—a surprise to most people. In some schools the entire curriculum is taught with informational books rather than textbooks. Nonfiction writers complain, justifiably, that their work—even though numbers are on their side—receives less attention than fiction.

The form of nonfiction now being published has a direct appeal to the young reader. Instead of forbidding, dense texts, we often find spacious pages with color illustrations and brief paragraphs. Writers select topics that interest children rather than those listed in a school curriculum outline. Further, the number of nonfiction books for very young children is increasing tremendously. Nonfiction available today is appealing, attractive, and abundant.

NONFICTION IN CHILDREN'S LIVES

You probably remember only some isolated fragments of information from your elementary school textbooks. You probably remember much more associated with a special project that you may have had to research and develop for a presentation, a science fair, or a demonstration. We learn when our emotions are involved, we learn when we are actively engaged, and we learn when we pursue our own—rather than someone else's—interests. We remember facts when they are integrated into our conception of reality, and we most often learn and retain them when they are part of a meaningful experience. Gardner (1965) stresses the interdependence of our intellectual and emotional life. She states:

> The basis of learning is emotion. . . . There is no intellectual interest which does not spring from the need to satisfy feelings. . . . Not only is learning fostered by the need to satisfy feelings but feelings themselves are relieved and helped by learning. For work to be creative, feeling as well as intellect is involved. Any education must always take into account education of the emotions. (p. 34)

We all learn by fitting new information into a coherent frame, or schema, as we discuss in Chapter 2. Nonfiction makes information available to children in ways that facilitate the creation of meaningful category systems and critical schemata. When children seek out information for themselves, identify what is relevant, and use it for meaningful goals, they become more efficient at storing and retrieving facts. The especially fine informational books published today illuminate their path. Furthermore, trade books on virtually any topic and for almost any level of understanding are readily available. This rich and vast array of materials generates an interest and excitement that encourages students to grow.

The elementary school curriculum is comprised of areas of knowledge divided into specific subjects, such as mathematics, science, and social studies. Children must learn to integrate these disciplines to make sense of the world. Learning, then, is more than the filling in of discrete areas of information; it requires an active response from students, an interpretation or reconstruction of new information in relation to what they already know. Instead of teaching a body of facts for memorization, our goal is to help students learn to think.

Children learn best to think, read, write, speak, and listen when instruction in all curriculum areas is integrated—when, for example, a teacher exploring plant life in a science lesson takes the opportunity to relate the term *phototropism* to other words with the prefix *photo*. This kind of integration in instruction parallels the way children actually learn—not facts in isolation, but rather parts of a meaningful whole.

Teachers fashion learning activities that cut across the curriculum and draw on books of fiction, nonfiction, and poetry in ways that encourage children in an active search for meaning. A winter snowstorm might spark a study of snow that leads children into poems about snow, such as those in Caroline Feller Bauer's ***Snowy Day Stories and Poems*** (P–I). Contemporary stories about snowstorms, such as Marc Harshman's ***Snow Company*** (I), Kathleen Todd's ***Snow*** (P–I), and Cynthia Rylant's ***Henry and Mudge in the Sparkle Days*** (P), along with historical fiction such as E. J. Bird's ***The Blizzard of 1896*** (I), allow children to think about how snow affects people's lives, including their own. Folklore, such as Toni De Gerez's retelling of a portion of a Finnish epic, ***Louhi: Witch of North Farm*** (I), and fantasy, such as Hans Christian Andersen's ***The Snow Queen*** (I), encourage imaginative speculation about snow. Nonfiction such as Betsy Maestro's ***Snow Day*** (P) and Franklyn M. Branley's ***Snow Is Falling*** (P–I) provide factual information about snow and snow removal. All of these reading experiences help children develop a more balanced understanding about snow rather than merely reading about it in a science textbook. We discuss instruction like this in Chapter 12.

Reading for information is related to other language uses; it is part of the scheme of the total language system. Children do read to learn in assigned textbooks, but they read to learn with enthusiasm and excitement in specialized trade books of quality. Compared to a textbook, a trade book can reveal the point of view of the author more directly, focus on an individual or a topic with a sharper light, and present specialized information that often gives readers a fuller understanding. For example, a textbook may mention the eruption of Vesuvius and the subsequent destruction of the city of Pompeii, but a trade book such as Sara C. Bisel's ***The Secrets of Vesuvius*** (I–A) makes the eruption vivid, real, and important to the lives of people. Bisel tells the story of her excavation of Herculaneum, a small town buried by Vesuvius, and simultaneously tells the story of Petronia, a young slave girl who is caught in the flood of lava. Petronia's story is based on evidence that Bisel's work has uncovered. A textbook may say that Vesuvius erupted and many people were killed. A trade book like ***The Secrets of Vesuvius*** can help readers feel what it would be like to flee from the lava, see the consequences for real people, and learn about the processes of archaeology and physical anthropology. Excellent nonfiction provides rich opportunities for learning.

CRITERIA FOR EVALUATING NONFICTION

Each year, committees of subject area specialists and children's literature specialists select the outstanding examples of books in their respective disciplines. The work, coordinated by the Children's Book Council, involves the National Science Teachers Association, the National Council of Social Studies, the International Reading Association, and the National Council of Teachers of English. A list of outstanding books that can enhance teaching and learning in each discipline is published in the professional journals of each organization (cited in Chapter 1 and discussed later in appropriate subject area sections). These lists help teachers select quality trade books for their curriculum.

The science committee, for example, evaluates books using three criteria: The book must be accurate and readable; its format and illustrations must be pleasing; and information must be consistent with current scientific knowledge. In areas where differences occur, a book should present different points of view, and information should not be distorted by personal biases or values. Facts and theories must be clearly distinguished, generalizations supported by facts, and significant facts included. If experiments are a feature of a book, the science committee considers whether they lead to an understanding of basic principles. Moreover, experiments discussed in the books must be appropriate

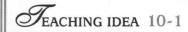

Make an Alphabet Book on Topic of Study

Every discipline, topic, or subject area has a vocabulary of its own. In order to read and comprehend text, students exploring a new area need to become familiar with its vocabulary. One way to develop meaning for vocabulary related to a topic is to create an ABC book. This can be done as an individual or a group project. As a group project, each person is responsible for a different page. For example, if you are studying South America, each person could be responsible for a different country. If you are studying animals, each person could be responsible for one mammal.

1. List all the new words related to topic under study.
2. Create an alphabet book with a letter for each page.
3. List words on appropriate pages using beginning letter.
4. Draw pictures, collect synonyms, write definitions, use the word in language to explain something, build meaningful language around the new word.
5. Write a letter explaining the new word to a friend.
6. Create a book about the topic using the new words.
7. Read the book to peers or younger students.
8. Display the handmade books in the classroom.
9. Have an author's tea to celebrate the publications.

for the reader's age group and be both feasible and safe. The committee eschews anthropomorphized plants and animals. It also rejects books that are racist or sexist, or that extol violence. The following discussion expands on these criteria and those appropriate to books in other disciplines and presents exemplary books in various subject areas. Figure 10-1 contains a checklist of general criteria for evaluating all types of nonfiction.

Figure 10-1

Checklist for Evaluating Nonfiction

INTEGRITY

- ❏ Does the author identify a clear point of view?
- ❏ Does the author care deeply about the subject?
- ❏ Does the author instill a questioning attitude?
- ❏ Does the author reveal sources of research?
- ❏ Do you hear a clear author voice?

Distinguishing Fact From Theory

- ❏ Does the author distinguish fact from theory?
- ❏ Does the author qualify tentative information?

Avoiding Anthropomorphism

- ❏ Does the author avoid anthropomorphism?
- ❏ Do animals act like real animals?

Presenting Balanced Viewpoints

- ❏ Does the author acknowledge other points of view?
- ❏ Does the author discuss strengths/weaknesses of views?

Supporting Generalizations

- ❏ Does the author give facts to support generalizations?
- ❏ Does the author document facts and sources?

Author's Expertise or Sources

- ❏ Does the author have credentials as an authority on the topic?
- ❏ Does the author acknowledge expert advisers?

STYLE

- ❏ Does the tone reveal the significance of the subject?
- ❏ Is there any literary distinction in the writing?
- ❏ Does the author select telling details?
- ❏ Does the author make the reader care about the subject?

PRESENTATION OF CONTENT

- ❏ Is the book well organized?
- ❏ Is it easy to find information?

Organization

- ❏ Are divisions of content easy to follow?
- ❏ Does the book have useful features, for example, index, table of contents, bibliography?
- ❏ Does the book have a clear structure?

Unity

- ❏ Does the book convey ideas in logical progression? Does it present ideas from the simple to complex?

Comprehensibility

- ❏ Can the language be understood by the intended audience?
- ❏ Is information presented in a clear, simple manner?

Layout

- ❏ Does the book have an appealing layout and design?
- ❏ Do photographs, diagrams, and graphics extend information?

Integrity

Nonfiction that demonstrates integrity is written by authors who are honest with their readers. They reveal their point of view and let the reader know how their interest in the topic motivates them. They inculcate a questioning attitude in their readers and reveal the sources of their own research.

Distinguishing Fact From Theory

In excellent nonfiction, facts and theories are clearly distinguished. Highly qualified writers state clearly and succinctly what is known and what is conjectured; they do not mislead by stating as fact what is still a theory or hypothesis. Careful writers use qualifying phrases when they are tentative

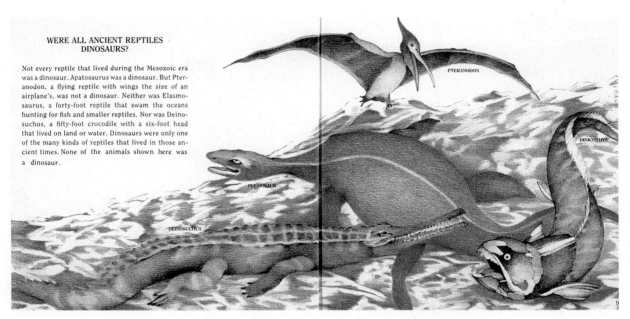

WERE ALL ANCIENT REPTILES DINOSAURS?

Not every reptile that lived during the Mesozoic era was a dinosaur. Apatosaurus was a dinosaur. But Pteranodon, a flying reptile with wings the size of an airplane's, was not a dinosaur. Neither was Elasmosaurus, a forty-foot reptile that swam the oceans hunting for fish and smaller reptiles. Nor was Deinosuchus, a fifty-foot crocodile with a six-foot head that lived on land or water. Dinosaurs were only one of the many kinds of reptiles that lived in those ancient times. None of the animals shown here was a dinosaur.

The panoramic view of prehistoric reptiles shows comparative sizes and modes of travel. Labels help readers identify each species. Seymour Simon's direct question-and-answer format allows readers to find information they want quickly. (*New Questions and Answers About Dinosaurs,* illustrated by Jennifer Dewey)

about the information. For example, some use "many scientists believe," "Dinosaurs probably could not run fast," and "The evidence to date suggests," to indicate that experts in the field are not certain about all things. Good writers also describe the changing status of information about a topic.

Seymour Simon, in ***New Questions and Answers About Dinosaurs*** (P–I), and Philip Whitfield, in ***Why Did the Dinosaurs Disappear?*** (I–A), are both careful to distinguish fact and theory. In answer to the question, How many different dinosaurs have been found?, Simon replies:

> It's difficult to say exactly how many different dinosaurs have been found. Early collectors often named the dinosaurs they found without checking if the skeletons were really different from those already discovered. This meant that the same kind of dinosaur might have been given two different names.
>
> For example, a nineteenth-century collector named a huge dinosaur skeleton he had discovered Brontosaurus, the "thunder lizard." Recently it was found that another collector had already named a different skeleton of the same animal Apatosaurus, the "deceptive lizard." That name is used now because it was given first.

> Today, after scientists combine all the names given to similar dinosaurs, the total is about 350 different kinds. But new ones are found every year.

In this answer Simon carefully states what is known and how that knowledge is changing.

Whitfield presents and evaluates a theory about why the dinosaurs died out:

> Scientists are not really sure what made the last of the species of dinosaurs die out at the end of the Cretaceous Age. But they have several interesting theories about what might have happened 65 million years ago.
>
> One exciting recent idea is that the Earth at that time suffered a collision with a huge asteroid or meteorite. . . .

Whitfield goes on to state two reasons why such a collision might have killed the dinosaurs and discuss the evidence for such a collision. He ends by saying:

> We do not know for sure if this is the correct explanation for the loss of the dinosaurs. Similar effects on the climate might have been produced by greatly increased volcanic activity.

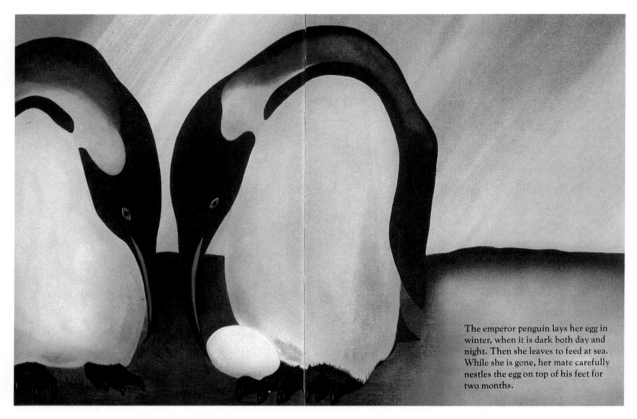

The emperor penguin lays her egg in winter, when it is dark both day and night. Then she leaves to feed at sea. While she is gone, her mate carefully nestles the egg on top of his feet for two months.

The strong use of movement and color lead the eye to the precious egg. The parents send a message of loving care to the egg they protect and shelter. (*Antarctica* by Helen Cowcher)

Avoiding Anthropomorphism

Good nonfiction writers stay away from anthropomorphizing, or attributing human traits to plants or animals, such as "The little bird cried real tears because it was homesick" or "The flower asked the sky for a drink of water." When writers try to disguise information by slipping it into a fictional story the result is often anthropomorphism; they do not clearly distinguish their work as fiction or nonfiction. Talking animals, such as in White's ***Charlotte's Web,*** which are appropriate and integral to fantasy, are not acceptable in nonfiction.

Helen Cowcher's ***Antarctica*** (P) is a fine picture book that avoids anthropomorphism. She depicts Emperor and Adelie penguins as they are disturbed by human intrusions, but she does not ascribe human thoughts to them. For example, the birds panic at the approach of helicopters, but do not *think*, "Oh, how frightened I am."

An interesting reverse of anthropomorphism, Joanne Ryder's ***The Snail's Spell*** (P), invites readers to *become* a snail. The illustrations by Lynne Cherry depict a child shrinking to snail size and doing the things that snails do. The overall effect is an emotional as well as an informational look at snails.

Presenting Balanced Viewpoints

Nonfiction writers with integrity acknowledge other opinions of value; they present different views about their topic. For example, many books about dinosaurs, such as those just discussed, present differing views of the extinction of the dinosaurs. Good writers present various views, discussing their strengths and weaknesses.

In ***Death Is Natural*** (I) Laurence Pringle states,

Although human bodies decay after death, some people believe that there is a soul, or spirit, that lives on afterward. . . . Some people believe there is no life after death. An afterlife is not the sort of idea that scientists can prove or disprove. However, scientists do agree on two facts about death. First, it is inevitable. . . . Second, death is necessary.

*L*AURENCE PRINGLE was born in Rochester, New York and received his Bachelor of Science degree from Cornell University and his Master of Science degree from the University of Massachusetts, majoring in wildlife biology. He also did further graduate work at Syracuse University. He taught science in high school and edited a children's science magazine before beginning his writing career and has served as writer-in-residence at Kean College in New Jersey. He is active in environmental and nature organizations and travels widely, taking photographs and doing research for his books.

Pringle's first book, published in 1968, was **Dinosaurs and Their World.** He endures the hardships of writing to communicate his appreciation and concern for the natural world. He has written over 50 books for young people that convey his concern for the biological and environmental subjects that intrigue him. He has also published articles in numerous magazines, including **Highlights for Children, Ranger Rick,** and **Audubon.**

In 1983, Pringle won the Eva L. Gordon Award for Children's Science Literature from the American Nature Study Society. The award is given to an author whose books exemplify "high standards of accuracy, readability, sensitivity to interrelationships, timeliness and joyousness while they extend either directly or subtly an invitation to the child to become involved." His contributions to the literature of natural history have helped many children discover, enjoy, and understand the world of nature.

When he is doing research, he explains, he is particularly interested in finding out about people who are looking for solutions to problems.

Laurence Pringle

I'm especially looking for real people who are solving, or attempting to solve, real problems. It adds a personal touch. Whenever possible I like to have a name and a face to connect with my story. Once when I was doing some research on a book about dinosaurs, I learned about a woman in Poland, a paleontologist, who had led some important expeditions. It was a treasure to be able to use her in my book, because it helped to destroy the notion that notable scientists are almost always male.

Pringle says of his work:

If there is a single thread that runs through all of my books—including the controversial and gloomy ones like the one on nuclear war—I think it is a thread of hopefulness. It is important to offer children some hope for solving our problems.

The Pringle family resides in the New York Hudson River valley. Laurence Pringle's recent books include: **The Animal Rights Controversy; Global Warming; Living Treasure: Saving Earth's Threatened Biodiversity; Bearman: Exploring the World of Black Bears; Batman: Exploring the World of Bats; Nuclear Energy: Troubled Past, Uncertain Future; Killer Bees;** and **Saving Our Wildlife** (All I).

Supporting Generalizations

Good writers use specific facts to support broad generalizations. Jack Denton Scott, in **The Book of the Pig** (I–A), states: "Young pigs can almost be seen growing right before your eyes." He then goes on to support this generalization with an array of facts:

> It has been scientifically proved that pigs grow more rapidly than any other farm animal: 400 pounds of feed produces 100 pounds of body weight. By the time the piglets are weaned, they have increased their weight more than ten times, to about 35 pounds.

Author's Expertise or Sources

Authors' qualifications to write about a subject are often provided on the book jacket; in other cases, authors acknowledge expert advisers or consultants who reviewed their work prior to publication: For example, Laurence Pringle, in **Living Treasure: Saving Earth's Threatened Biodiversity** (I), notes on the copyright page: "The author thanks Dr. Eric Fajer, Museum of Comparative Zoology, Harvard University, for reading the manuscript of this book and helping to improve its accuracy." As we noted with biographies, many authors list the sources they used at the end of the book; this is often accompanied by a note explaining the author's research process.

Style

A work of nonfiction is also judged by style, or how the information is presented. The tone reveals the significance or the meaningfulness of an author's work and the author's relationship to his or her subject. Even when dealing with facts, graceful language and freshness of vision are important components of excellent literature.

Milton Meltzer, an outstanding biographer and historian, feels that most reviewers do not consider these criteria. He decries the fact that critics look at how much information a book contains and how accurate or up to date it is but rarely compare it with other books on the same subject. Meltzer believes that critics must look at more than mere facts in a work of nonfiction and must ask,

> What literary distinction, if any, does the book have? And here I do not mean the striking choice of word or image but the personal style revealed. I ask whether the writer's personal voice

is heard in the book. In the writer who cares, there is a pressure of feeling which emerges in the rhythm of the sentences, in the choice of details, in the color of the language. Style in this sense is not a trick of rhetoric or a decorative daub; it is a quality of vision. It cannot be separated from the author's character because the tone of voice in which the book is written expresses how a human being thinks and feels. If the writer is indifferent, bored, stupid, or mechanical, it will show in the work. (1976, pp. 21–22)

A nonfiction book's literary value, therefore, depends in large part on how much the author gives of himself or herself. Laurence Pringle acknowledges that his passions enter his work.

> When I'm writing, I write about my values and feelings. Many people ask what nonfiction has to do with feelings. If you want feelings, they would say, turn to fiction. But I don't think that has to be true. In some ways my goals and values are much the same as a teacher's. The majority of teachers are trying to give kids a bigger picture of the world and a better understanding of how it works. In that sense, teaching and good nonfiction writing are the same. (1986, p. 26)

Presentation of the Content

How content is organized and presented affects the overall value of a piece of nonfiction. Ideas and information are not useful unless presented in a way that is compatible with the capabilities of the intended audience.

Organization

Good books are well organized. Looking through a piece of nonfiction will reveal how well a book is arranged. The content should be organized in a way that illuminates concepts and builds understanding. Books that have a great deal of information should have a table of contents to help readers understand how the book is organized; looking at the table of contents can help you make a judgment about the quality of the organization. Some books need additional features such as a glossary, subject and author indexes, a bibliography for further reading, and appendices with further information so readers can easily retrieve information or build on the information presented in the book by going on to further sources.

*T*O FORGET what we know would not be human.

To remember it is to think of what being human means. The Holocaust was a measure of man's dimensions. One can think of the power of evil it demonstrated—and of those people who treated others as less than human, as bacteria. Or of the power of good—and of those people who held out a hand to others.

By nature, man is neither good nor evil. He has both possibilities. And the freedom to realize the one or the other.

Milton Meltzer followed the path to the terror and grief of the Nazi era through eyewitness accounts—letters, diaries, journals, and memoirs in *Never to Forget.* However inadequate words are, he says, language is all we have to reach across barriers to understanding. Letting history speak for itself characterizes all his work and provides accuracy and authenticity normally found only in primary sources. His technique brings a sense of immediacy to the past and recreates a feeling of the time.

Meltzer's more than 85 books reveal his love of the American story and his respect for the struggles of our forebears. He portrays turn-of-the-century working-class life in *Bread and Roses* and the hardships of the Depression in *Brother Can You Spare a Dime?* and in *Poverty in America.*

Milton Meltzer believes that young people are interested in the past and that it is best discovered through letters, memoirs, journals and other documents. He feels it is unnecessary to fabricate stories about historical events

Milton Meltzer

since the truth itself is inherently intriguing. One need only read the letters and poems in *Never to Forget: The Jews of the Holocaust* to recognize the validity of his belief.

The son of hard-working immigrant parents, Milton Meltzer was born in Worcester, Massachusetts, and studied to be a journalist. He and his wife, who have two grown daughters, live in New York City, where he devotes himself to scholarly research and writing. Meltzer tells his own story in *Starting from Home: A Writer's Beginnings,* recalling with affection a teacher who introduced him to the great works of literature. His recent books include *The Bill of Rights: How We Got It and What It Means, Columbus and the World Around Him, Crime in America, Voices from the Civil War: A Documentary History of the Great American Conflict* (all A).

David Macaulay's **Castle** (I–A), for example, has a glossary at the end of the text in which specialized terms are defined. Unfortunately, there is no index. Kathryn Lasky's **Traces of Life: The Origins of Humankind** (A) contains a table of contents, footnotes, a selected bibliography, and an index to help readers retrieve and pursue information presented in the text.

Unity

The unity of a text depicts the relationships among the ideas in the passage. It shows how the author has organized ideas to convey the information. Careful, logical development of concepts is essential. Ideas should flow from the simple to the complex in clear order. The text also needs strong transitions to guide the reader from one idea to the next. Readers find it difficult to follow and to recall texts that jump from one topic to another without logical links.

The first two chapters of William Jay Jacobs's **Ellis Island: New Hope in a New Land** (I) present the story of immigrants entering America from Europe through Ellis Island. Once the human importance of Ellis Island is established, Jacobs goes back in time, telling the story of immigration in America from Native Americans through the establishment of Ellis Island. Chapter 4 chronicles the closing of the immigration center, Chapter 5 the establishment of the museum at Ellis Island. Jacobs makes smooth transitions in his text. Chapter 2 ends: "The newcomers are becoming new people now—free people in a free land. They are becoming 'Americans,' " and on the next page Chapter 3 begins: "The story of America is the story of its newcomers."

Comprehensibility

The information presented in any nonfiction book must be comprehensible to its intended audience. The concepts and vocabulary need to be within a reasonable range of difficulty for the readers. Look for a descriptive style that presents the information in a clear and simple manner. Responsible writers respect their readers and know that children, no matter what their age, can understand important scientific terms and concepts if they are presented clearly and defined in the context.

Lasky's **Traces of Life** (A) and Joanna Cole's **Evolution** (P) discuss the same general idea in very different ways. Cole's simple, clear text is a wonderful introduction to the theory of evolution for young readers. She states:

> More than a hundred years ago, a scientist named Charles Darwin wrote a book that became famous.
>
> The book showed how all plants and animals could have developed from earlier, simpler living things.
>
> This idea is called evolution.

The text is accompanied by simple uncluttered drawings by Aliki that illuminate important concepts.

On the other hand, Lasky's book is a detailed, compelling presentation of the history of hominid research and the paleoanthropologists who do it. Processes and concepts are richly detailed, controversies and frustrations portrayed, and a great deal of information is presented in 144 pages. Cole's book is an excellent resource for primary readers; Lasky's is an excellent resource for older readers interested in the subject.

Layout

Nonfiction books should be as appealing in layout and design as fiction books are. As information is presented it can be supported by photographs, diagrams, maps, sketches, graphs, or other visual support. The illustrations help readers visualize the information contained in the text. Effective layout means that illustrations appear in close proximity to the text they illuminate, headings and subheadings are clearly presented, and the amount of text and illustration on a page does not make the page appear crowded or overwhelming.

Many design variations are available today. The Eyewitness Series, for example, uses clear color photographs, small explanatory notes for each photograph, a brief introduction, and drawings, where appropriate, on each double-page spread devoted to topics within the book. For example, **Butterfly and Moth** (I–A), has sections on "caterpillar to pupa," "the pupa stage," and "an emerging butterfly." Far from being crowded or busy, each page is laid out so that eager readers are drawn to the page, first captivated by the exquisite photographs, then intrigued by the well-written information.

A very different layout marks Marjorie Pillar's **Pizza Man** (P). This informative text is dominated by black-and-white photographs of a pizza maker at work. The photographs, accompanied by a simple text that explains the activities pictured, vary by size and shape; they are grouped on pages according to the information conveyed.

Books of nonfiction are changing in appearance. Whereas they once had few illustrations, they

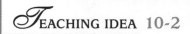

List the Experts

Whole language literature-based programs assume that students become independent learners. Such programs are also based on practices that include students learning collaboratively. Projects involving nonfiction topics and trade books provide an excellent opportunity to implement these practices. The purpose of this teaching idea is to implement collaborative learning and wide reading in trade books, and to develop independent learners.

1. Explore a new topic by reading widely and having your students read widely in nonfiction trade books.

2. Participants select an area within the broader topic in which they would like to specialize. Groups or individuals list questions they would like to answer on the topic.

3. Students begin their research independently.

4. List on a chart each participant's name and the chosen topic of specialization.

5. State "Billy is becoming an expert in _____."

For example, in a study of environmental protection, some students might choose recycling of paper, cans, and bottles. Others might choose pollution of rivers, lakes, and oceans. Others might choose air quality or smoke control. Others might choose to investigate the use of products that destroy the ozone layer. A classroom chart might look like this:

PROTECT THE ENVIRONMENT STUDY

Jorge is becoming an expert in river pollution.

Alison is becoming an expert in effects on the ozone layer.

Erminda is becoming an expert in air quality control.

Jack is becoming an expert in recycling aluminum cans.

When such a list is made public, students can help each other. They watch for resources a classmate might need. They work collaboratively to answer questions. They share information and insights as they work toward group and individual goals. Eventually, the signs may read: "Billy is an expert in _____."

are now profusely illustrated. Award-winning editor James Giblin notes that children today, accustomed to the visual stimulation of television, want graphics—particularly photographs—in their books (1986, p. 14). This has led to a greatly increased number of photo essays. Giblin was the editor for Russell Freedman's **Lincoln: A Photobiography,** winner of the 1988 Newbery Award and discussed in Chapter 9.

NONFICTION ACROSS THE CURRICULUM

So many wonderful books are available today that children can explore almost any topic which interests them using nonfiction trade books. Here we discuss nonfiction, other than biography, that presents information about topics in science, social studies, mathematics, language study, and music and art.

Science

Science, like any other discipline, evolves over time, and books for children reflect the changes in the discipline. Most recently a number of beautifully illustrated books on the solar system have appeared, such as Seymour Simon's series on the planets that includes **Uranus** and **Neptune** (both I–A) and Patricia Lauber's stunning **Seeing Earth from Space** (A). There are also books for young readers, such as Franklyn Branley's **Is There Life in Outer Space?**, that explore the solar system. You can find many other titles by consulting one of the information sources discussed in Chapter 2.

Lauber's **Seeing Earth from Space** (A) uses NASA photographs in conjunction with a very well-written text to explain satellite photography and make a statement about taking care of our earth. The information is accompanied by a table of contents, index, glossary, and a list of further reading.

This European weather satellite makes it obvious why our first astronauts called Earth "a big blue marble." The perspective from outer space helps students realize the interdependence of nations, the need for environmental protection, and the fragility of our planet. (*Seeing Earth from Space* by Patricia Lauber)

The photographs in this book are absolutely essential; no other kind of illustration would suit this topic. Lauber's evocative prose captures the beauty of the visions of earth that space explorations have made possible. It also describes the frightening images that are possible:

> To a person standing on its surface, the earth appears both large and sturdy. From space it seems small and fragile.
>
> These [astronauts] are often concerned by the man-made changes they see on the earth. They look down at the island of Madagascar, where tropical forests are being felled. They see that the ocean around it is red-brown, colored by soil eroding from land without trees and carried to the sea by rivers. . . .

Beneath the text is a satellite photograph of Madagascar that illustrates the terrible erosion.

Lauber concludes her book with a brief poignant plea for concern for the Earth across the globe:

> Space travelers often return with their thinking changed. On Earth we think of boundaries. The view from space is different. Rivers meander or rush from country to country without stopping, on their way to the sea. Forests reach from one country into another.
>
> Sand and dust from the Sahara spread across the Atlantic and blow toward the Americas. Smoke travels hundreds of miles on the winds. . . .
>
> Space travelers see that the earth is one planet, small and fragile, wondrous and lovely. It is the spaceship in which we journey around the sun, and our life-support system is its air and waters and lands. We are all, every person in the world, aboard the same ship. And so we must all, in ways large and small, treasure and protect it.

The magnified photograph brings the intricate detail of the delicate praying mantis into full view. The designs in nature create a sense of wonder. (*Backyard Hunter* by Bianca Lavies)

This book is far more than a presentation of satellite photography; it is a statement about our responsibility for our world.

As concern for our environment has increased, the number of books for children that deal with environmental issues has also increased. Some of these books explore particular habitats or animals; others explore the environmental impact of the modern world on habitats and animals. Some books suggest ways in which children can help to save our environment.

Bianca Lavies and Dwight Kuhn are noted nature photographers who have recently begun to produce picture books for young readers. Lavies's books, such as **Backyard Hunter: The Praying Mantis** (P–I), are especially appealing to primary- and intermediate-grade readers. Her stunning close-up photographs and brief explanatory text present common creatures in an uncommon way,

---

TEACHING IDEA 10-3

Read First, Write Later

Teachers soon discover that students' science and social studies reports sound all too much like the entries in their encyclopedias. This teaching idea will help students write in their own voice, use a variety of resources, and digest information instead of copying it from an encyclopedia. Collect many resources on topics for the classroom library. In any nonfiction study:

1. Ask your students to keep journals as they read.

2. Ask them to write in their journals what they are learning and what they think about what they are learning. See the discussion of double-entry journals in *Language, Literacy and the Child,* (Galda, Cullinan & Strickland, 1993) pages 286–287.

3. At regular intervals, ask students to answer these questions: "What do I know already?" "What do I want to learn?"

4. Ask students to explain to a classmate what they have learned and what they are still trying to find out.

5. Use picture books, concept books, and books of all genres to search for answers to student questions.

6. As they read for a purpose—to find out specific information—ask students to jot down notes about discoveries.

7. When they have read widely, talked about what they are learning, responded in journals about what they are learning and how they feel about what they are learning, then it is time to draft a report. Pair and share. Reports sound like children's voices, not like encyclopedia entries.

---

inviting readers to look closely at their own world and discover its interesting stories.

Dwight Kuhn's beautiful color photographs present portraits of various creatures and plants that coexist in a particular habitat. One book, **The Hidden Life of the Pond** (P–I), begins in the spring,

Figure 10-2

Books for Science: Environmental Issues

Ancona, George. *Riverkeeper.* (P–I)

Arnosky, Jim. *Near the Sea.* (I–A)

———. *Deer at the Brook.* (P–I)

Ashabranner, Brent. *Morning Star, Black Sun: The Northern Cheyenne Indians and America's Energy Crisis.* Photos by Paul Conklin. (I–A)

Bash, Barbara. *Urban Roosts: Where Birds Nest in the City.* (I)

Cherry, Lynne. *The Great Kapok Tree: A Tale of the Amazon Rain Forest.* (P–I)

Clark, Margaret Goff. *The Vanishing Manatee.* (A)

Cobb, Vicki. *Why Doesn't the Sun Burn Out?* (I–A)

Cole, Joanna. *Large as Life Animals.* Illus. Kenneth Lilly. (P)

Darling, Kathy. *Manatee: On Location.* Photos by Tara Darling. (I–A)

Dean, A. *Strange Partners: The Story of Symbiosis.* (I–A)

Dewey, Jennifer Owings. *A Night and Day in the Desert.* (I)

———. *Animal Architecture.* (I–A)

Dorros, Arthur. *Animal Tracks.* (I)

———. *Follow the Water from Brook to Ocean.* (P–I)

Elkington, John, Julia Hailes, Douglas Hill, and Joel Makower. *Going Green: A Kid's Handbook to Saving the Planet.* (I–A)

Fife, Dale H. *The Empty Lot.* Illus. Jim Arnosky. (P)

Gelman, Rita Golden. *Dawn to Dusk in the Galapagos: Flightless Birds, Swimming Lizards, and Other Fascinating Creatures.* Illus. Tui De Roy. (A)

George, Jean. *One Day in the Desert.* (I)

Gibbons, Gail. *The Puffins Are Back!* (P)

Hackwell, W. John. *Desert of Ice: Life and Work in Antarctica.* (I–A)

Hunken, Jorie, and the New England Wildflower Society. *Botany for All Ages: Learning About Nature Through Activities Using Plants.* (I–A)

Lambert, D. *Planet Earth 2000.* (I–A)

Lang, Aubrey. *Eagles.* Illus. Wayne Lynch. (I–A)

Lazo, C. E. *Endangered Species.* (I–A)

---

with the melting snow, and describes the many plants and animals we can see living around a pond, if we just look hard enough.

Some other books about our world are listed in Figure 10-2. A list of outstanding science trade books can be obtained from the Children's Book Council and is also published every March in *Science and Children,* a journal of the National Science Teachers Association for elementary and middle school teachers. Other journals, such as *The Reading Teacher* and *Language Arts,* regularly review books that treat science topics.

Social Studies

Just as in science, social studies evolves as changes in the world result in new configurations of countries and people. New communication technology makes the world seem much smaller than it used to be and increases our interest in other people and places. Children have more books than ever to select from as they pursue their interests in the past and present.

In addition to the fine biographies and excellent historical fiction stories available, many nonfiction texts cover topics such as geography and maps, life in the past, and the social structures and customs of various cultures. Children are quite naturally interested in who they are and where they come from; this natural curiosity and openness to people makes them receptive to books that explore the global community. Edith Baer's **This Is the Way We Go to School** (P) shows children themselves and children from other cultures experiencing a common start to the day. The sparse text is written

CONTINUED

Lowery, Linda. *Earth Day.* Illus. Mary Bergherr. (P)

Mallory, K. *Rescue of the Stranded Whales.* (I–A)

Markle, Sandra. *Earth Alive.* (I–A)

McGovern, Ann, and Eugenie Clark. *The Desert Beneath the Sea.* Illus. Craig Phillips. (I)

Miles, Betty. *Save the Earth: An Action Handbook for Kids.* Illus.. Nelle Davis. (I)

Miller, Christina G., and Louise A. Berry. *Coastal Rescue: Preserving Our Seashores.* (A)

——. *Jungle Rescue: Saving the New World Tropical Rain Forests.* (A)

Norsgaard, E. Jaediker, and Campbell Norsgaard. *Nature's Great Balancing Act: In Your Own Backyard.* (I–A)

Parnall, Peter. *Woodpile.* (P–I)

Patent, Dorothy Hinshaw. *Gray Wolf, Red Wolf.* Illus. William Munoz. (I)

——. *Seals, Sea Lions and Walruses.* (A)

——. *Way of the Grizzly.* (I)

——. *Whooping Crane.* (I)

Phillips, Anne. *The Ocean.* (A)

Pringle, Laurence. *Living Treasure: Saving Earth's Threatened Biodiversity.* Illus. Irene Brady. (I–A)

——. *Saving Our Wildlife.* (I–A)

Rinard, J. E. *Along a Rocky Shore.* (P)

Ryder, Joanne. *When the Woods Hum.* Illus. Catherine Stock. (I)

Simon, Seymour. *Oceans.* (P–I)

Smith, Roland. *Sea Otter Rescue: The Aftermath of an Oil Spill.* (A)

Souza, D. M. *Insects in the Garden.* (P–I)

——. *Insects Around the House.* (P–I)

Viner, Michael, with Pat Hilton. *365 Ways for You and Your Children to Save the Earth One Day at a Time.* (I–A)

White, S. V. *Sterling: The Rescue of a Baby Harbor Seal.* (I–A)

Willow, Diane. *At Home in the Rain Forest.* Illus. Laura Jacques. (P–I)

Winckler, Suzanne. *Our Endangered Planet: Population Growth.* (I–A)

in rhyme and the illustrations by Steve Bjorkman hint at the schoolchildren's nationalities. Hinting rather than telling makes it possible for children to predict the characters' cities and countries. Predictions can be confirmed by checking a list of specific locations and a map at the end of the book.

People and their occupations are also fascinating to children, and several fine books explore a wide variety of occupations. Nancy Price Graff's text in *The Strength of the Hills: A Portrait of a Family Farm* (I–A) with Richard Howard's photographs offer a sympathetic but realistic picture of a way of life that once was the norm and is now increasingly rare. Set in the beautiful hills of Vermont, this moving story of a day on one family's farm offers readers a glimpse of an occupation that is almost timeless.

The past can be brought to life through histori-

cal fiction (discussed in Chapter 8) and biography (discussed in Chapter 9). Nonfiction, as well, can illuminate life in the past in such a way that children of the present will be fascinated. For example, the ancient past of the western United States is depicted in *The Village of Blue Stone* (A), written by Stephen Trimble and illustrated by Jennifer Owings Dewey and Deborah Reade. Trimble imagines a year in an ancient Anasazi village somewhere near the meeting point of Utah, Colorado, New Mexico, and Arizona. Grounded in archeologists' knowledge of this ancient culture, this book also contains an index, glossary, and list of sources.

The span of time is captured in books like Xavier Hernandez and Jordi Ballonga's *Lebek: A City of Northern Europe Through the Ages* (A). Francesco Corni's stunning black-and-white ink drawings illustrate the growth of Lebek, a fictional city

The drum corps was an important part of the communication system for soldiers during the Civil War. When smoke clouded a battlefield, drummers signaled instructions and helped to keep soldiers close together. Photographs show how incredibly young many of the drummers were. (*The Boy's War* by Jim Murphy)

that is a composite of major coastal cities in northern Europe, from the Bronze Age to the present. The social, political, and economic history of the region is clearly and succinctly presented with detailed drawings that illustrate the impact of time and new discoveries.

In Figure 10-3 we list some recent books to indicate the breadth of choice that exists for the social studies curriculum today. Other books that focus on various cultures are discussed in Chapter 11. Further, a list of Notable Trade Books in Social Studies is available from The Children's Book Council and also published in the April/May issue of the journal *Social Education*. You can find lists of other books about particular topics in a number of reference books, such as those listed in Appendix B.

Mathematics

Fewer books support a study of mathematics than either science or social studies, although more are published each year. Mathematics programs today reflect a whole language philosophy in which fiction and nonfiction literature fit naturally. Earlier mathematics instruction involved practicing isolated skills endlessly, calculating answers, memorizing combinations of numerals, and watching for a place to apply memorized routines. Today, we present mathematical problems in context, draw on chil-

dren's background knowledge about possibilities for solving them, and model strategies for different ways to solve problems.

Today, many mathematics lessons begin with a story—a story with a problem that can be solved through a mathematical process. Teachers invite children to propose as many different strategies as possible to try to solve the problem. Together, they apply each strategy, evaluating its accuracy and efficiency. They learn there are different ways to come up with the right answer. Stories structured around numbers and counting, such as Pat Hutchins's **The Doorbell Rang** (P), are especially useful for primary teachers who want to link mathematics and reading.

Other books explain mathematical concepts, such as Bruce McMillan's **Eating Fractions** (P–I). McMillan illustrates fractions with mouth-watering photographs of children sharing—and eating—food. The concept of one-fourth is understandable when it means the difference between a whole pizza and only part of one!

Myriad number books are available for children who are learning to count objects and recognize numbers. As we discuss in Chapter 3, many of these books are stunning works of art as well. The journal *Arithmetic Teacher* reviews books that can be linked to mathematics instruction. Figure 10-4 lists other selected books for mathematics learning.

Figure
10-3

Books for Social Studies

Anderson, Joan. *Pioneer Settlers of New France.* Illus. George Ancona. (I)

Bisel, Sara C. *The Secrets of Vesuvius.* (A)

Black, Wallace B., and Jean Blashfield. *America Prepares for War.* (I–A)

Blumberg, Rhoda. *The Incredible Journey of Lewis and Clark.* (I)

Climo, Shirley. *City! New York.* Illus. George Ancona. (I–A)

Cohen, Daniel. *Ancient Greece.* Illus. James Seward. (I)

Connolly, Peter. *Pompeii.* (A)

Faber, Doris, and Harold Faber. *Birth of a Nation: The Early Years of the United States.* (I–A)

Fisher, Leonard Everett. *The Oregon Trail.* (I–A)

Fradon, Dana. *Harold the Herald: A Book About Heraldry.* (I)

Fritz, Jean. *Shh! We're Writing the Constitution.* Illus. Tomie de Paola. (P–I)

Gibbons, Gail. *Surrounded by Sea: Life on a New England Fishing Island.* (P)

Giblin, James Cross. *The Riddle of the Rosetta Stone: Key to Ancient Egypt.* (I)

Hernandez, X., and P. Comes. *Barmi: A Mediterranean City Through the Ages.* Illus. Jordi Ballonga. Trans. Kathleen Leverich. (A)

Hoig, Stan. *A Capital for the Nation.* (A)

James, Simon. *Ancient Rome.* (A)

Key, Francis Scott. *Star Spangled Banner.* Illus. Peter Spier. (P–I–A)

MacDonald, Fiona. *A Medieval Castle.* Illus. Mark Bergin. (I–A)

———. *A 19th Century Railway Station.* (I–A)

Maestro, Betsy, and Giulio Maestro. *The Discovery of the Americas.* (P–I)

———. *More Perfect Union: The Story of Our Constitution.* (P–I)

Marrin, Alfred. *The Spanish-American War.* (A)

Marzollo, Jean. *In 1492.* Illus. Steve Bjorkman. (P)

Meltzer, Milton. *American Revolutionaries: A History in their own Words—1750–1800.* (I–A)

Morgan, Kate. *The Story of Things.* Illus. Joyce Audy Zarins. (P–I)

Murphy, Jim. *The Boys' War: Confederate and Union Soldiers Talk About the Civil War.* (I–A)

Parker, Nancy Winslow. *The President's Cabinet: And How It Grew.* (I)

Provensen, Alice. *The Buck Stops Here: The Presidents of the United States.* (I)

Rappaport, Doreen. *The Boston Coffee Party.* Illus. Emily Arnold McCully. (P–I)

Ray, Delia. *A Nation Torn: The Story of How the Civil War Began.* (A)

———. *Behind the Blue and Gray: The Soldier's Life in the Civil War.* (A)

Rylant, Cynthia. *Appalachia: The Voices of Sleeping Birds.* Illus. Barry Moser. (I)

St. George, Judith. *The White House: Cornerstone of a Nation.* (I–A)

Waters, Kate. *The Story of the White House.* (P)

Language Study

As writing and language study become a part of an integrated language arts curriculum, the need increases for children's books that explore language. Alphabet books, books about traditional parts of speech, histories of language, and books about writing are becoming more plentiful. Books such as these support the study of language, and, most importantly, support children's explorations of language as they engage in reading and writing.

Ruth Heller is known for her brightly illustrated, eye-catching books about the parts of speech, such as *Up, Up and Away: A Book About Adverbs*

Figure
10-4

Books for Math

Counting

Anno, Mitsumasa. *Anno's Counting Book*. (P)

Bang, Molly. *Ten, Nine, Eight*. (P)

Brown, Marc. *One, Two, Three: An Animal Counting Book*. (P)

Carle, Eric. *The Very Hungry Caterpillar*. (P)

Crews, Donald. *Ten Black Dots*. (P)

Dee, Ruby. *Two Ways to Count to Ten: A Liberian Folktale*. (P)

Ehlert, Lois. *Fish Eyes: A Book You Can Count On*. (N–P)

Feelings, Muriel. *Moja Means One: A Swahili Counting Book*. Illus. Tom Feelings. (N–P)

Garne, S. T. *One White Sail: A Caribbean Counting Book*. Illus. Lisa Etre. (N–P)

Giganti, Paul, Jr. *How Many Snails?* Illus. Donald Crews. (P)

Grossman, Virginia. *Ten Little Rabbits*. Illus. Sylvia Long. (P)

Hoban, Tana. *Count and See*. (P)

Hutchins, Pat. *1 Hunter*. (P)

Jernigan, Gisela. *One Green Mesquite Tree*. Illus. E. Wesley Jernigan. (P)

Kitchen, Bert. *Animal Numbers*. (P–I)

Mahy, Margaret. *The Seven Chinese Brothers*. Illus. Jean Tseng and Mou-Sien Tseng. (P–I)

Ormerod, Jan. *Young Joe*. (N–P)

Rees, Mary. *Ten in a Bed*. (P)

Sendak, Maurice. *One Was Johnny: A Counting Book*. (P)

Tafuri, Nancy. *Who's Counting?* (P)

Thornhill, Jan. *Wildlife 1 2 3: A Nature Counting Book*. (P)

Tudor, Tasha. *1 Is One*. (P–I)

Walsh, Ellen Stoll. *Mouse Count*. (N–P)

Money

Hoban, Tana. *Twenty-Six Letters and Ninety-Nine Cents*. (N–P)

Manes, Stephen. *Make Four Million Dollars by Next Thursday*. (I)

Merrill, Jean. *The Toothpaste Millionaire*. (I)

Schwartz, David. *How Much Is a Million?* Illus. Steven Kellogg. (P–I)

————. *If You Made a Million*. Illus. Steven Kellogg. (P–I)

Viorst, Judith. *Alexander, Who Used to Be Rich Last Sunday*. (P–I)

Time

Anno, Mitsumasa. *All in a Day*. (P–I)

Blackburn, Carol. *Waiting for Sunday*. (P)

Carle, Eric. *The Grouchy Ladybug*. (P–I)

Gibbons, Gail. *Clocks and How They Go*. (P–I)

Hutchins, Pat. *Clocks and More Clocks*. (P)

Rockwell, Anne. *Bear Child's Book of Special Days*. (P)

Weiss, Malcolm E. *Solomon Grundy, Born on One Day: A Finite Arithmetic Puzzle*. Illus. Tomie de Paola. (P–I)

Fractions

McMillan, Bruce. *Eating Fractions*. (P–I)

Pomerantz, Charlotte. *The Half-Birthday Party*. (P–I)

(P–I). The rhyming text is surrounded by double-page illustrations visually depicting the adverbs. Heller's books give concrete and intriguing examples of what many students feel is boringly remote.

Marvin Terban also has a series of fascinating books that explore word play, such as **Guppies in Tuxedos: Funny Eponyms** (I–A). Terban groups the eponyms in nine topically organized chapters. Each word, printed in boldface type, is followed by a brief history of its origin. Funny drawings by Giulio Maestro are interspersed throughout the text. A table of contents and an index help organize the over 100 words that Terban discusses; a brief introduction and a list of other sources are also included.

The study of language can be greatly enhanced by Janet Klausner's **Talk About English: How Words Travel and Change** (A). Klausner makes a very complicated subject quite easy to understand

CONTINUED

Watson, Clyde. *Tom Fox and the Apple Pie.* (P–I–A)

Addition and Subtraction

Aruego, Jose, and Ariane Dewey. *Five Little Ducks.* (P)

Bate, Lucy. *Little Rabbit's Loose Tooth.* (P–I)

Burningham, John. *The Shopping Basket.* (P)

Christelow, Eileen. *Five Little Monkeys Jumping on the Bed.* (N–P)

Gackenbach, Dick. *A Bag Full of Pups.* (P–I)

Peek, Merle. *Roll Over!* (P)

Pomerantz, Charlotte. *One Duck, Another Duck.* (P)

Raffi. *Five Little Ducks.* (N–P)

Russo, Marisabina. *Only Six More Days.* (P)

Tafuri, Nancy. *Have You Seen My Duckling?* (N–P)

Measurement and Size

Blocksma, Mary. *Reading the Numbers, A Survival Guide to the Measurements, Numbers and Sizes Encountered in Everyday Life.* (I–A)

Dahl, Roald. *Esio Trot.* (P–I)

Galdone, Paul. *Three Billy Goats Gruff.* (P)

Kalan, Robert. *Blue Sea.* (P)

Lionni, Leo. *The Biggest House in the World.* (P)

——. *Inch by Inch.* (P–I)

Russo, Marisabina. *The Line Up Book.* (N–P)

Turkle, Brinton. *Deep in the Forest.* (N–P)

Wildsmith, Brian. *Cat on the Mat.* (P)

Multiplication and Division

Aker, Suzanne. *What Comes in 2's, 3's, and 4's?* (I)

Birch, David. *The King's Chessboard.* (I)

Brown, Margaret Wise. *Four Fur Feet.* (P–I)

Hamm, Diane. *How Many Feet in the Bed?* (P–I)

Hulme, Joy. *Sea Squares.* (I)

Hutchins, Pat. *The Doorbell Rang.* (P)

Mathews, Louise. *Bunches and Bunches of Bunnies.* (P–I)

Pittman, Helena. *A Grain of Rice.* (P–I)

Estimation

Clement, Rod. *Counting on Frank.* (I)

Diagram Group. *Comparisons.* (I)

Hennessey, B. G. *The Dinosaur Who Lived in My Backyard.* (I)

Hoban, Tana. *Is It Larger? Is It Smaller?* (N–P)

Hutchins, Pat. *Titch.* (P)

——. *You'll Soon Grow into Them, Titch.* (P)

Reid, Margaret. *The Button Box.* (P–I)

Problem Solving

Anno, Masaichiro, and Mitsumasa Anno. *Anno's Mysterious Multiplying Jar.* Illus. Mitsumasa Anno. (I–A)

Anno, Mitsumasa. *Anno's Hat Trick.* (I–A)

——. *Anno's Math Games.* (I–A)

——. *Anno's Math Games II.* (I–A)

——. *Anno's Math Games III.* (I–A)

NOTE: Teacher Reference: Whitin, David, and Sandra Wilde. ***Read Any Good Math Lately? Children's Books for Mathematical Learning K–6.*** Heinemann, 1992.

without making it simplistic. She narrates a history of the English language in a fresh and exciting style that is appealing to readers. She also discusses root relationships, origins of names, eponyms, and evolving language. The plethora of information she presents is easily retrievable using the table of contents and the index, and interested readers can pursue their interests in the texts cited in suggested readings.

Klausner, like many nonfiction authors, directly addresses the reader, using the pronoun *you.* She begins and ends her book this way, in the imperative mood:

Try to imagine yourself in each of these scenes. . . . You can discover more answers yourself, if you watch and listen . . . and open a dictionary.

"That's one each," said Sam and Victoria.
"They smell as good as your Grandma's," said Joy.
"And look as good," said Simon.

Pat Hutchins uses well-defined acrylics to show anticipation and apprehension in children's faces as they watch for a fair division of cookies. (*The Doorbell Rang*)

Language becomes a plaything for students who like to explore its variations and possibilities. Ruth Heller's books provide interesting options to trigger explorations. (*Many Luscious Lollipops: A Book about Adjectives*)

**Figure
10-5**

Books About Language

Ammer, Christine. *It's Raining Cats and Dogs . . . and Other Beastly Expressions.* (P–I)

Ashton, Christina. *Words Can Tell: A Book About Our Language.* (I)

Butterworth, Nick. *Nice or Nasty: A Book of Opposites.* (I)

Charlip, Remy. *Handtalk: An ABC of Finger Spelling & Sign Language.* With Mary Beth Miller. Illus. George Ancona. (P–I–A)

Edwards, Michelle. *Dora's Book.* (P–I)

Fraser, Betty. *First Things First: An Illustrated Collection of Sayings Useful and Familiar for Children.* (I)

Gross, Ruth Belov. *You Don't Need Words! A Book About Ways People Talk Without Words.* (I–A)

Heller, Ruth. *Cache of Jewels and Other Collective Nouns.* (I)

————. *Many Luscious Lollipops: A Book About Adjectives.* (I)

Hoban, Tana. *All About Where.* (P–I)

————. *Exactly the Opposite.* (N–P)

Kightley, Rosalinda. *Opposites.* (N–P)

Klausner, Janet. *Talk About English: How Words Travel and Change.* (A)

Knowlton, Jack. *Books and Libraries.* (I–A)

Koch, Michelle. *Just One More.* (N–P)

MacCarthy, Patricia. *Herds of Words.* (P–I)

McMillan, Bruce. *Becca Backward, Becca Frontward, A Book of Concept Pairs.* (N–P)

————. *Dry or Wet?* (N–P)

————. *Super, Super, Superwords.* (P)

Suid, Murray. *Demonic Mnemonics: 800 Spelling Tricks for 800 Tricky Words.* (I–A)

Terban, Marvin. *Dove Dove.* (I)

————. *Hey, Hay!: A Wagonful of Funny Homonym Riddles.* (I)

————. *I Think, I Thought and other Tricky Verbs.* (I)

————. *In a Pickle and Other Funny Idioms.* (I)

————. *Mad as a Wet Hen!* (I)

————. *Time to Rhyme: A Rhyming Dictionary.* (I)

————. *Punching the Clock: Funny Action Idioms.* (I)

————. *Your Foot's on My Feet! And other Tricky Nouns.* (I)

Weil, Lisl. *Let's Go to the Library.* (P–I)

Involving readers by directly addressing them highlights the notion that the information contained in the book is personally interesting and important to a reader—as indeed it is.

In Chapter 12 we discuss how literature—both fiction and nonfiction—is a crucial component of a writing program. Here we list in Figure 10-5 a variety of books about language that indicate the breadth of materials available. Other books on this topic can be found by consulting any subject-organized reference source.

Music and Art

In addition to the many fine biographies of musicians and artists listed in Chapter 9, a variety of nonfiction texts explore aspects of music and art.

Just as science, social studies, and language study are enhanced when well-written and beautifully designed books become a part of the curriculum, the study of art and music is made more vivid when accompanied by beautiful books. Several series of books that explore elements of art, such as Philip Yenawine's *Line* (P–I), and books that help readers learn to look at paintings, such as Gladys Blizzard's ***Come Look with Me: Animals in Art*** (I–A), are wonderful resources for those interested in learning more about fine art. Yenawine's book defines line, shows various kinds of lines, explains how they are created, and describes what artists can do with them. Information about line is illustrated by reprints of famous modern paintings and the accompanying text asks readers to look for specific things in the paintings.

Old Grimes

Words adapted from "Old Grimes" by Albert Gorton Greene

Tune: "Auld Lang Syne"   Circa 1873

Pa sang his own version of Greene's song while Ma was making cheese. He thought Old Grimes might have staggered along if his wife hadn't skimmed off every bit of cream. But "She was a mean, tight-fisted woman. Old Grimes got so thin the wind blew him away," Pa said.   LHBW, *page 192*

Music was an integral part of growing up in the little house in the big woods, on the prairie, and other places that Laura Ingalls Wilder lived. Eugenia Garson collected sixty-two songs that Pa played on his fiddle, Ma and the girls sang, and neighbors sang and danced to in *The Laura Ingalls Wilder Songbook.* Garson provides notes on composers, exact references to the book where the song was used, and simple piano arrangements. (Illustrated by Garth Williams)

Blizzard's book also uses a variety of fine paintings and a series of questions to involve readers in discovery. For example, she asks:

> Does this seem like a good place for hummingbirds to have built a nest? Why or why not?
>
> Would you describe the colors in this picture as delicate and subtle, or strong and bold? Why?

Questions like these lead readers into looking at the paintings with certain considerations in mind. The result is a more educated viewing eye. Blizzard also presents interesting biographical material about each artist and painting included.

The Painter's Eye: Learning to Look at Contemporary American Art (A) is a fascinating book that explains complicated concepts in an understandable fashion. Jan Greenberg and Sandra Jordan define and give examples of the elements of art and principles of design that artists use to create paintings. They also present the postwar American artists themselves through conversations, photographs, and brief anecdotes about their childhoods and their work. The text begins with a useful table of contents and includes brief biographies of the artists, a list and description of the paintings discussed, a glossary, bibliography, index, and suggestions for further reading.

A number of books explain different artistic processes and the creation of different products, inviting children to create collages, make paper, or design structures. Others explore objects like bridges and buildings as architectural art. By using nonfiction books about art in conjunction with picture books that contain fine art, teachers can help children become visually literate. Figure 10-6 lists some books about art that will open children's eyes.

Books about music also are becoming increasingly available. Many of these books look at instruments, their development, and how they work; others explore musical groups such as the band or the symphony. The Eyewitness book ***Music*** (I–A) contains a wealth of information about how music is made. Topics range from "seeing sound" to detailed presentations of how specific instruments make music, the evolution of early instruments to today's electric synthesizers. The photographs and sketches that illustrate the various instruments help to clarify some of the complex information. Other books that contain information about music are listed in Figure 10-6.

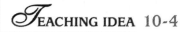

TEACHING IDEA 10-4

Literature Across the Curriculum

Integration Around a Topic: Dinosaurs

Capitalize on your students' interest in dinosaurs to help them discover something about literary genre and how the same topic can be addressed in many different ways. Ask your students to:

1. Read from many of the following books.

2. Compare the kinds of information presented in each one.

3. Discuss the relationship between the types of information presented and the literary genre represented.

4. Ask them what type of book they would search for to answer specific informational questions, to think imaginatively, or to dream poetically?

Poetry:

Hopkins, Lee Bennett (selector). *Dinosaurs*. Illus. Murray Tinkleman. (I)

Yolen, Jane. *Dinosaur Dances*. Illus. Bruce Degen. (I)

Nonfiction:

Aliki. *Fossils Tell of Long Ago*. (P)

Arnold, Caroline. *Dinosaurs Down Under: And Other Fossils from Australia*. Photos Richard Hewett. (I)

Brown, Laura Krasny, and Marc Brown. *Dinosaurs Alive and Well! A Guide to Good Health*. (P)

Lasky, Kathryn. *Dinosaur Dig*. Photos Christopher Knight. (I)

———. *Traces of Life: The Origins of Humankind*. Illus. Whitney Powell. (I–A)

Schlein, Miriam. *Let's Go Dinosaur Tracking!* Illus. Kate Duke. (P)

Simon, Seymour. *New Questions and Answers about Dinosaurs*. Illus. Jennifer Dewey. (P–I)

Taylor, Paul D. *Fossil*. (Eyewitness Series.) (I)

Whitfield, Philip. *Why Did the Dinosaurs Disappear?: Questions about Life in the Past*. (I)

Picture Books:

Barton, Byron. *Bones, Bones, Dinosaur Bones*. (P)

Fleischman, Paul. *Time Train*. Illus. Claire Ewart. (P)

Malam, John. *Dinosaur Skeletons: A Pop-Up Book*. Illus. Bob Cremins. (P)

Pulver, Robin. *Mrs. Toggle and the Dinosaur*. Illus. R. W. Alley. (P)

Whether the subject is science or social studies, language, music, or art, many beautiful children's books present more depth of information than can be contained within the pages of a textbook. The well-written texts of these books not only inform but provide models of good expository prose. The illustrations illuminate concepts and visualize information, bringing life and vitality to the topic under scrutiny. With the many fine nonfiction books available, children can learn many things, including how to be critical consumers of information.

Learning to Read Critically

Critical reading and thinking are basic to learning for a lifetime. The schemata we develop as we learn to read, and read to learn, influence all subsequent knowledge. Thinking readers, called critical read-

ers, evaluate new information in light of what they already know, compare many sources instead of accepting only one point of view, and make judgments about what they read. They can discriminate fact from opinion. If a goal of education is to develop informed, thinking, participating citizens, then helping children learn to read critically is essential.

The skill of reading critically is invaluable. The child who believes that anything found in print is the truth, the whole truth, is at a disadvantage relative to the one who has learned to check sources, compare reports, and evaluate. Children do not question what they read when they are given one textbook that is held up as embodying the final and complete truth on its subject. They do learn to question and evaluate as they read if we encourage them to make comparisons among different sources—often nonfiction trade books.

**Figure
10-6**

Nonfiction: Music and Art

Music

Aliki. *Hush Little Baby: A Folk Lullaby.* (N–P)

Bangs, Edward. *Steven Kellogg's Yankee Doodle.* (N–P)

Beirne, Barbara. *Pianist's Debut: Preparing for the Concert Stage.* (I)

Berger, Melvin. *The Science of Music.* (A)

——. *The Story of Folk Music.* (A)

Britten, Benjamin. *Young Person's Guide to the Orchestra.* (I)

Bryan, Ashley. *All Night, All Day: A Child's First Book of African-American Spirituals.* (P–I–A)

Conover, Chris (reteller, illus.). *Froggie Went A-Courting.* (P)

Delacre, Lulu (selector, illus.). *Arroz Con Leche: Popular Songs and Rhymes from Latin America.* English lyrics by Elena Paz. Musical arrangements by Ana-Maria Rosada. (P–I)

Fox, Dan (editor, music arranger). *Go In and Out the Window: An Illustrated Songbook for Young People.* (P–I–A)

Garson, Eugenia (compiler). *Laura Ingalls Wilder Songbook: Favorite Songs from the "Little House" Books.* (I–A)

Gregory, Cynthia. *Cynthia Gregory Dances Swan Lake.* (A)

Hayes, Ann. *Meet the Orchestra.* Illus. Karmen Thompson. (P–I)

Krementz, Jill. *A Very Young Musician.* (I)

——. *A Very Young Dancer.* (I)

Larrick, Nancy (compiler). *Songs from Mother Goose.* Illus. Robin Spowart. (N–P)

Mayhew, James. *Madame Nightingale Will Sing Tonight.* (P)

Nelson, Esther L. *Great Rounds Songbook.* (P–I–A)

Palmer, H. *Homemade Band: Songs to Sing, Instruments to Make.* (I–A)

Peek, Merle. *Mary Wore Her Red Dress and Henry Wore His Green Sneakers.* Adapted and illus. Merle Peek. (N–P)

——. *Roll Over: A Counting Song.* (N–P)

Price, Leontyne. *Aida.* Illus. Leo and Diane Dillon. (I–A)

Raffi. *Tingalayo.* Illus. Kate Duke. (P)

Rounds, Glen. *I Know an Old Lady Who Swallowed a Fly.* (P)

Sanders, Scott. *Hear the Wind Blow: American Folk Songs Retold.* Illus. Ponder Goembel. (I–A)

Seeger, Pete. *Abiyoyo: Based on a South African Lullaby and Folk Story.* Illus. Michael Hays. (I)

Ventura, Peter. *Great Composers.* (A)

Verdy, Violette. *Of Swans, Sugarplums and Satin Slippers: Ballet Stories for Children.* (P–I–A)

Weiss, Nicki (illus.). *If You're Happy and You Know It: Eighteen Story Songs.* Music arranged by John Krumich. (N–P)

We can engender unquestioning respect for the authority of the textbook by the way we respond to students' questions. Replies such as "Look it up in the book," or "What does the book say?" may inadvertently teach students to pay abject homage to textbooks in general.

Developmental differences in children's ability to think critically are not so much a matter of kind as of degree. Long before they turn to information found in books, very young children can make comparisons: They can consider ideas such as who is taller, which coat is warmer, which cookie is bigger. Listening to stories or looking at books, young children can attend to detail and make comparisons. For example, when looking at the photographs in the portfolios by Jorg Muller, **The Changing City** (P–I–A) and **The Changing Countryside** (P–I–A), they can observe that parts of the landscape such as mountains and rivers may remain the same from one decade to the next, and other parts, such as a

CONTINUED

Zelinsky, Paul. *The Wheels on the Bus.* (N–P–I)

Art

Arnosky, Jim. *Drawing from Nature.* (I)

Brown, Laurene Krasny. *Visiting the Art Museum.* (I–A)

Ehlert, Lois. *Color Farm.* (N–P)

——. *Feathers for Lunch.* (N–P)

Florian, Douglas. *A Carpenter.* (P)

——. *A Potter.* (P)

Glubok, Shirley. *Art and Archaeology.* (I–A)

——. *Olympic Games in Ancient Greece.* (I–A)

Goffstein, M. B. *Artists Album.* (I)

Greenberg, Jan, and Sandra Jordan. *The Painter's Eye: Learning to Look at Contemporary American Art.* (A)

Jonas, Ann. *Color Dance.* (N–P)

Lessac, Frané. *Caribbean Canvas.* (I)

Raboff, Ernest. *Frederic Remington.* (I–A)

——. *Albrecht Dürer.* (I–A)

——. *Paul Klee.* (I–A)

——. *Henri de Toulouse-Lautrec.* (I–A)

——. *Henri Matisse.* (I–A)

——. *Henri Rousseau.* (I–A)

——. *Paul Gauguin.* (I–A)

——. *Pierre-Auguste Renoir.* (I–A)

——. *Leonardo da Vinci.* (I–A)

——. *Marc Chagall.* (I–A)

——. *Michelangelo Buonarroti.* (I–A)

——. *Pablo Picasso.* (I–A)

——. *Raphael Sanzio.* (A)

——. *Diego Rodriguez de Silva y Velasquez.* (I–A)

——. *Rembrandt.* (I–A)

——. *Vincent Van Gogh.* (I–A)

Richardson, Wendy. *Animals: Through the Eyes of Artists.* (I–A)

——. *Families: Through the Eyes of Artists.* (I–A)

——. *Natural World: Through the Eyes of Artists.* (I–A)

Robbins, Ken. *Bridges.* (P–I)

Venezia, M. *Francisco Goya.* (I–A)

——. *Picasso.* (I–A)

——. *Rembrandt.* (I–A)

Ventura, Piero. *Great Painters.* (I–A)

Walsh, Ellen. *Mouse Paint.* (P)

Woolf, F. *Picture This: A First Introduction to Paintings.* (I)

Zhensun, Zheng, and Alice Low. *A Young Painter: The Life and Paintings of Wang Yani.* (I–A)

new highway, are very different. Older children will make many more inferences about what causes the changes in the landscape when a country road becomes a main road with gas stations, shops, restaurants, and motels and later is replaced by a superhighway. Students who are even more mature will draw implications from the scenes about ecology, the quality of life, and the need for planning. Children of all ages can, and do, think critically, especially when encouraged.

Verifying Information

Children of all ages can verify information found in books by checking it against observations made in real life—as, for example, when a forgotten peanut butter sandwich turns up covered with green mold while the class is reading about fungi in Lucia Anderson's *The Smallest Life Around Us* (P–I). Young children can hypothesize about the causes of mold; experiment with different conditions that promote or retard it; see that it grows on bread, lemons, or grass; and learn about useful molds that help make cheese or bread.

Older readers also will evaluate authors' statements in light of their own experiences. They assess an author's qualifications, look at the documentation provided, and critically evaluate the books they read much as we suggest in the evaluation checklist at the beginning of this chapter.

Many books encourage the reader to adopt a critical stance based on observing, collecting, and analyzing data, drawing conclusions, making inferences, and testing hypotheses. In *The Secret Clocks: Time Sense of Living Things* (I), Seymour Simon suggests,

> During the summer or during the warmer months of spring and fall, you can do a simple experiment to demonstrate the time sense of bees. . . .

Books that draw the reader into observation and hypothesis testing help children develop an observant critical stance that spills over from books into daily life.

Comparing Sources

Children can also compare one book with others and decide which they prefer—and why. During a study of plants, primary-grade children in Georgia compared and evaluated two books about popcorn—*The Popcorn Book* (P), by Tomie de Paola, and *Popcorn* (P), by Millicent E. Selsam. Both books tell about varieties of corn and where and when popcorn was discovered. They differ markedly, however, in style of presentation, illustrations, and amount and kind of information given. Selsam's book contains striking color and black-and-white photographs, whereas de Paola's book is illustrated with humorous and whimsical cartoonlike drawings. Selsam devotes a major part of her discussion to germinating seeds, planting and growing corn, the properties of corn plants, and pollenization. Tomie de Paola devotes more of his book to the popping process; he has one character read from an encyclopedia some interesting facts about popcorn: how much is eaten each year, which cities are the top popcorn-eating cities, and funny stories about popcorn (such as the popcorn blizzard in the Midwest). After the books had been read aloud, children in one group said, "*The Popcorn Book* is more fun but the other one tells you more stuff"; "If you want to know about growing popcorn, you should read *Popcorn* because it tells you what to do."

The children also found a discrepancy between the two books concerning when popcorn was first found. Tomie de Paola says, "In a bat cave in New Mexico, archeologists found some popped corn that was 5,600 years old." Selsam says, "Scientists do know that people who lived in caves in New Mexico 2,000 years ago did pop corn, because popped kernels of that age were found there in a cave named Bat Cave." Tomie de Paola also states, "and 1,000-year-old popcorn kernels were found in Peru that could still be popped." Selsam adds, "There were also unpopped kernels in the cave [in New Mexico], and the scientists studying the corn were able to pop some of these 2,000-year-old kernels." When the children discussed which was right, one said, "Well, I think she's [Selsam] right because we have a lot of other books by both of them and hers are all science books and his are mostly funny books." In further evaluation one child said, "Hers is more like a real science book but his tells you real stuff in a funnier way."

The remarks of children show how natural it is for them to make comparisons. They also illustrate the usefulness of informational books in the curriculum to foster growth in critical reading and thinking.

Students in advanced grades deal with topics, compare sources, and use more complex skills than younger students. Sixth-grade students in Iowa were learning all they could about what the world was like when Columbus sailed to America. They consulted many books—including encyclopedias and biographies of Columbus—to find the information they needed. One of the first books they read was Betsy and Giulio Maestro's *The Discovery of the Americas* (I–A), which provides information about the early inhabitants of America and how they might have traveled there; it also includes the stories of other famous explorers, many the students had never heard of. Armed with some astonishing new information, the students read Piero Ventura's *1492: The Year of the New World* (I), an overview of the world in Europe and America. Many students went on to read *The World in 1492* (A) with sections by Jean Fritz, Katherine Paterson, Patricia McKissack, Margaret Mahy, and Jamake Highwater. This book presents a great deal of information about Europe, Asia, Africa, Australia, and the Americas, including photographs of varied artifacts from around the world. It is much more comprehensive than the Ventura or the Maestro book, and students quickly began to compare earlier information with what they found in *The World in 1492,* using it as their definitive source. They discussed the footnotes and detailed bibliography that are included as reasons for trusting the information they were discovering.

SUMMARY

When children are given excellent nonfiction books to explore topics of interest, they learn a great deal about those topics. They learn more because the intriguing formats of nonfiction make them intrinsically more interesting to read and because trade books contain more detailed information than textbooks or encyclopedias. When reading nonfiction, children also have the opportunity to experience well-written and organized expository prose that can then serve as a model for their own informational writing. Further, reading several nonfiction books provides a perfect opportunity to think critically, evaluating and verifying information by making comparisons with experience and with other books. Children who learn to look in multiple sources for the information they need are less likely to believe everything they see in print, developing instead a healthy attitude of critical judgment.

**Part
Three**

The
Threads
That Bind
Children
and Books

11

Multicultural Literature

OUR COUNTRY'S QUILT

All we had was a bunch of rags
Tattered torn and stuffed in bags,
With nothing else to keep us warm
Against the coming winter storm.

There was gabardine,
Some faded silk,
Beaded buckskin and a cotton shawl,
Calico and old wool pants,
And a lace mantilla from a formal
    ball.
There was lots more cloth from
    which to choose
But each piece was too small to use.

So we gathered what we had,
While remaining very calm,
And we cut each patch in a special
    shape
To reveal its special charm.
Then we snipped and sewed and
    stitched,
And we all danced, arm in arm,
To celebrate the country quilt
We made to keep us warm.

Brod Bagert

ust as we learn to value variety in the patterns and patches of fabric, we can learn to cherish our racial, ethnic, cultural, and religious differences. When we read literature that reflects those differences, we see the world through another's eyes. As we learn more about each other, we appreciate variety in the patterns of the patchwork quilt of our international family.

DEFINITION OF CULTURALLY DIVERSE LITERATURE

Culturally diverse literature portrays what is unique to an individual culture and universal to all cultures. It accurately portrays the nuances and variety of day-to-day living in the culture depicted. It does not distort or misrepresent the culture it reflects (Sims Bishop, 1992, p. 41).

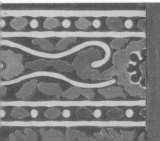

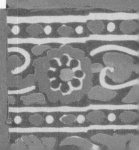

The term *culturally diverse* differs in emphasis from both *cross cultural* and *multicultural.* Cross cultural means an international exchange from one country to another. Multicultural refers to a mix of cultures within one country. Culturally diverse literature accurately portrays both unique and universal qualities. We discuss all three types of cultural exchanges in this chapter.

The image of a patchwork quilt replaces the melting pot once used to characterize the population of the United States. Supposedly early (twentieth-century) immigrants were homogenized into Americans when they tried to remove all traces of their former culture, but that stance no longer represents the distinctive cultural groups that are proud of their heritage now living in the United States. Contrary to popular belief, people in the United States are not homogenized into a melting pot. We share common experiences, but diverse groups retain their distinctive cultural traditions. We are a culturally diverse society (Sims Bishop, 1982). We believe the patterns, colors, and designs of a patchwork quilt with threads that bind us all together is a fitting and vivid metaphor to describe our culturally diverse society. It also describes the literature appropriate for children.

America has always been a culturally diverse society since its beginnings; it is becoming more diverse. The U.S. population of 230 million, of whom 30 million are foreign born, constitutes an enormous group who read and speak English as well as many others who speak, read, write, and study other languages. Immigration accounts for 25 percent of U.S. population growth with estimates that three-quarters of these are from Latin America. This figure does not include Puerto Ricans, who are U.S. citizens, not immigrants (Giniger, 1989).

By the year 2000, one-third of the students entering school will be of African-American, Asian-American, or Latino backgrounds. In California, European Americans will be in the minority in the state's school population (Heath, 1993).

We can no longer talk about immigrants as minorities; groups that were once a minority are now a majority. Even though they blend in with the larger patterns of American culture, the groups do not want to lose their cultural distinctiveness. The image of a patchwork quilt is an apt metaphor for our population. Each patch represents a unique tradition that enhances the beauty of the overall pattern. Other images—a box of jewels, a kaleidoscope, a rainbow—can be used to describe varied groups living together. Each group blends with the larger society, when such is demanded for the common good, but preserves its own cultural traditions

in the home and community in the culturally diverse society we live in today. Society is richer because of the varied contributions.

CRITERIA FOR SELECTING CULTURALLY DIVERSE LITERATURE

A culturally diverse society requires a culturally authentic literature, but how do we choose it? First, look at the work done by people involved in the process for a long time—librarians in El Paso, Texas, a border city to Mexico, who developed criteria for selecting material for Hispanic children. Their guidelines can be applied to selecting materials for other cultural groups. Look for books with the following characteristics:

1. Language reflects the standards set by local usage. The quality of translations is evaluated; they must be accurate and poetic, lyrical, or straightforward expository prose.

2. Characterization and illustrations portray positive images of the cultural group. The book is nonsexist and nonracist. A child from that group can relate to the book positively.

3. The value system incorporates the cultural groups' values. For example, books on sex education, treatment of the elderly, and social etiquette must reflect the group's beliefs.

4. Culturally authentic literature avoids stereotypes—those commonly held views, often simplified and rigid—of the characteristics of a group. Stereotypes portray members of a group without individuality—a "you've seen one, you've seen them all" view—or "they're all alike" statements. Books must represent the diversity and range among members of a group.

5. Literature is good when it broadens the reader's horizon, validates his or her experiences, invites reflection, and awakens an aesthetic sense. (Ada, 1990)

Books representing culturally diverse groups must represent them accurately. Look for books that (1) avoid stereotypes, (2) portray the values and the cultural group in an authentic way, (3) use language which reflects standards set by local usage, (4) validate children's experience, (5) broaden our vision, and (6) invite reflection.

A study of children's picture books that present pluralistic, balanced racial and ethnic images of children shows that book publication figures seldom

> **Figure 11-1**
>
> ### Checklist for Evaluating Culturally Diverse Literature
>
> ❑ Are characters from different cultures portrayed as individuals without stereotyping?
>
> ❑ Does the work qualify as good literature in its own right?
>
> ❑ Is the culture accurately portrayed from the point of view of someone inside the cultural group?
>
> ❑ Are issues presented in their true complexity as an integral part of the story—not just a focus on problems or social concerns?
>
> ❑ Does the dialogue maintain the natural melodies of the native language or dialect without making it difficult to read?
>
> ❑ Do the books show the diversity within as well as across human cultures?
>
> ❑ Do the illustrations contain accurate, authentic representations of people and scenes from different cultural groups?
>
> ❑ Do people of color lead as well as follow? Do they solve their own problems or do they depend on white benefactors?

parallel census figures. Although immigrant, racial, and ethnic groups increased dramatically in number, few books representing those groups were published during the 1960s, 1970s, and 1980s. Edmonds (1986) compared two samples of picture books by mainstream publishers between 1928 and 1974 and between 1980 and 1984, taking into account the race of major characters and the positive or negative treatment of various racial groups. In the 1928 to 1974 grouping, 57 percent of the books featured major characters who were white; 27 percent presented a racial mix of main characters; 7 percent were African American; 5 percent, Asian; 2 percent, Native American; and 2 percent, Latino. In the later sample (1980 to 1984), Edmonds found that books about Native Americans were being published at about the same level, but there were fewer books published about other groups. A later study, *Our Family, Our Friends, Our World* by Miller-Lachmann (1992), shows an impressive increase in the publication of multicultural books; however, given the rapid growth of immigrant, racial, and ethnic groups, much more needs to be done.

CULTURALLY DIVERSE LITERATURE IN CHILDREN'S LIVES

Readers shape their view of the world and of themselves partially through the books they read. If children never see themselves in books, then their absence subtly tells them "You are not important enough to appear in books." Missing, negative, and stereotyped images of an ethnic group are harmful not only to the children of that group but to others who get a distorted view. Culturally diverse literature informs us about ourselves and helps us to know each other.

African Americans are presented more frequently with more variety and less stereotyping than other cultural groups although the ratio to all books published is small. For example, in 1990 of the 5,000 children's books published, only 51 of these were written and/or illustrated by African Americans (Harris, 1992, p. 68). There are still few strong images of Asian characters or cultures other than Chinese and Japanese, and Latinos continue to receive extremely meager coverage in children's books.

African-American Literature

Nancy Larrick's article, "The All-White World of Children's Books," September 11, 1965, *Saturday Review,* proclaimed the absence of people of color in children's literature. Larrick decried the hurtful effects on black children who never see themselves in books, but she also said that the impact on white children is even worse. When the only images children see are white ones, she said, "There seems little chance of developing the humility so urgently

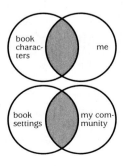
needed for world cooperation, instead of world conflict, as long as our children are brought up on gentle doses of racism through their books." During the 1970s, there was an increase in the number of books with black characters, but the 1980s saw a steady decline. Rudine Sims Bishop assessed the situation in 1985:

> Since the mid-70's, the number of available children's books dealing with Black life has declined steadily. *The Black Experience in Children's Books*, a comprehensive bibliography published about every five years that lists in-print children's books about Blacks, reflects some dramatic statistics: the 1974 edition listed approximately 950 titles, but the 1984 edition cites only about 450 books. Approximately 100 of the books in this latest edition are titles newly published between 1979 and 1984, and only 80 of the new books published between 1980 and 1983—an average of 20 per year—focus on American Blacks. If publishers release approximately 2,000 new children's books each year, as the bibliography's compiler, Barbara Rollock, notes, only about 1 percent of the children's books published in the first half of the 80's focused on Black experience in the United States. (Sims Bishop, 1985)

Estimates for the 1990s differ some, but not a great deal. Currently about 5,000 children's books are published annually, but only about 2 percent (about 100 books) contain people of color. Even though the percentages are small, there are more books that reflect African-American heritage than any other cultural group. The folklore, poetry, fiction (including picture books and novels), informational books, and biographies help children from all racial and ethnic groups to appreciate the contributions of African Americans.

Charles Sullivan's book, ***Children of Promise: African American Literature and Art for Young People*** (I–A), contains selections from many of the genre categories listed here. This outstanding anthology presents prose, poetry, and paintings that let us see images and hear voices which speak to the heart. For example, W. E. B. Du Bois's "The Schoolhouse Was a Log Hut," Frances E. W. Harper's poem, "Learning to Read," Arna Bontemps's "Southern Mansion," Sonia Sanchez's, "poem at thirty," and Langston Hughes's "Laughers" are outstanding examples of art and literature portraying the life of African Americans.

Folklore

Folktales provide a window on the collective experiences, dreams, and values of a cultural group.

Called a "mirror of a people," they reflect the beliefs, rituals, and songs of a group's heritage. African-American folklore with its roots in Africa and the Caribbean reflect those origins.

Verna Aardema retells African folktales in colorful, lilting language that retains the sound of drumbeats and the rhythm of native dances. She echoes the storyteller's voice by representing the sounds with unusual words. For example, she describes an animal moving through the grass with words such as "wasawusu, wasawusu, wasawusu," "mek, mek, mek," or "krik, krik, krik" in **Why Mosquitoes Buzz in People's Ears** (P). In another, she captures the melody and rhyme in a cumulative tale, **Bringing the Rain to Kapiti Plain** (P). A repetitive refrain describes the starving cattle on the barren Kapiti Plain, which is suffering a drought.

> These are the cows,
> all hungry and dry,
> Who mooed for the rain
> to fall from the sky;
> To green-up the grass,
> all brown and dead,
> That needed the rain
> from the cloud overhead—
> The big, black cloud,
> all heavy with rain,
> That shadowed the ground
> on Kapiti Plain.

Aardema

The plain grows verdant green after Ki-pat pierces a rain cloud with an eagle feather to bring down the rain to Kapiti Plain. Aardema's retelling sings with the rhythm and cadence of a West African storyteller's voice.

Award-winning author Virginia Hamilton has shaped several collections of African-American tales, such as the creation tales in **In the Beginning,** tales of the spirit world in **The Dark Way,** and slave narratives in **Thousands Gone Before** (all I–A). In one, **The People Could Fly** (I–A), illustrated by Leo and Diane Dillon, she includes animal tales, fanciful tales, tales of the supernatural, and tales of freedom. In the introduction, Hamilton explains:

> Folktales take us back to the very beginnings of people's lives, to their hopes and their defeats. American black folktales originated with peoples, most of whom long ago were brought from Africa to this country against their will. These peoples were torn from their individual cultures as they left the past, their families and their social groups, and their languages and customs behind. (Hamilton, 1985)

SET MY TONGUE ON FIRE

Vaudeville, Jacob Lawrence, 1951
In the old days, some people were afraid to say
what they really thought and felt.

LAUGHERS
LANGSTON HUGHES

Dream singers,
Story tellers,
Dancers,
Loud laughers in the hands of Fate—
 My people.
Dish-washers,
Elevator-boys,
Ladies' maids,
Crap-shooters,
Cooks,
Waiters,
Jazzers,
Nurses of babies,
Loaders of ships,
Rounders,
Number writers,
Comedians in vaudeville
And band-men in circuses—
Dream-singers all,—
 My people.
Story-tellers all,—
 My people.
Dancers—
God! What dancers!
 Singers—
God! What singers!
Singers and dancers.
Dancers and laughers.
 Laughers?
Yes, laughers...laughers...laughers—
Loud-mouthed laughers in the hands
 Of Fate.

112

Jacob Lawrence expresses the essence of vaudeville in harlequin shapes and bold black tuxedos. Do tears drop from the performer's eye? (**Children of Promise** by Charles Sullivan) Copyright © Jacob Lawrence/VAGA, New York 1993

African slaves brought the art of storytelling with them and created in America even more subtle tales to counter racial oppression. The storytellers created towering beings as well as animal figures who personified their experiences of defeat, triumph, and hope. The familiar theme of the weak overpowering the strong through wit and humor, universally appealing, shows up in many stories. Hamilton reminds us that the folktales were once a creative way for an oppressed people to express their fears and hopes to one another.

Poetry

The major poets writing African-American and Caribbean poetry include Ashley Bryan, Gwendolyn Brooks, Lucille Clifton, Maya Angelou, and Eloise Greenfield.

Ashley Bryan says that reading aloud from poems of African-American poets greatly influences the poetry and prose of stories he writes. When he tells African tales to an audience, he reads aloud first from African-American poets to demonstrate the vocal language play he carries over into the stories. Once you've heard him speak, you can never again read his work in the same way—you hear the sound of his voice in your ear. His books are listed in Figure 11-2.

Gwendolyn Brooks, notable African-American poet, received the Pulitzer Prize for poetry in 1950 for **Annie Allen** (I–A), a collection of poems about black life in Chicago. She is best known in the children's book world for **Bronzeville Boys and Girls** (I–A), which contains poems such as "Cynthia in the Snow" and "Rudolph Is Tired of the City." For Cynthia, the snow "Sushes, it hushes" and "whitely whirs away,/To be/Some otherwhere."

Lucille Clifton, poet laureate of Maryland, writes both stories and poetry for children and adults. She introduced a lovable child in the Everett Anderson series. Clifton says, "Interestingly enough, I don't think of 'Everett Anderson' as poetry, because it doesn't take as much out of me [to write it]. I think it's very good verse, and I think it's useful. It's a way to get kids into poetry, to head them towards poetry. But I don't think it's poetry" (Clifton, in Sims Bishop, 1982a). Despite Clifton's distinction between poetry and lyrical prose, her work has much to offer as a positive image of African Americans. Her books are listed in Figure 11-2.

Maya Angelou, 1993 presidential poet, spoke eloquently about the rock, the tree, and the river in "Good Morning." Her poetry, primarily for adults, includes **I Know Why the Caged Bird Sings** (A) and **Now Sheba Sings the Song** (A). She has written some works that young adults enjoy in **Poems** (A) and **I Shall Not Be Moved.** (A).

Eloise Greenfield's work reached a new high in **Honey, I Love and Other Love Poems** (P–I–A). The melodies and rhythms of her language ring forth true to the child narrator's voice in each poem. Greenfield has also written beautifully in **Nathaniel Talking** (P–I) and **Neighborhood Street** (P–I).

Fiction

Picture Books. Prior to the 1960s, most books for children totally ignored racial and ethnic minorities. Even those that did include any minorities often did so through blatant stereotyping and exaggerated dialect. Different racial groups were rarely shown interacting in any way.

Marguerite De Angeli was one of the first white writers to integrate characters and to explore racial

John Steptoe carefully researched the setting for **Mufaro's Beautiful Daughters.** His illustrations were inspired by the ruins of an ancient city found in Zimbabwe and the flora and fauna of the region. His paintings glow with the beauty, family love, and internal vision of the land and peoples of Africa.

prejudice and discrimination openly. In **Bright April** (I) the character April confronts discrimination in a member of her Brownie Scout troop. Although considered inadequate by today's standards, this book does focus—for the first time—on a black child's difficulties in a white society.

Eloise Greenfield, poet and prose writer, has written more than a dozen picture books, as well as many collections of poetry. Greenfield, according to Rudine Sims Bishop, tries

through her books, to sustain children by (1) giving them a love of the arts, (2) encouraging them to hold positive attitudes towards themselves, (3) presenting them with alternative methods for coping with the negative aspects of their lives, (4) giving them an appreciation for the contributions of their elders, (5) providing true knowledge of Black (African and American) heritage, (6) allowing them to fall in love with Black heroes, (7) reflecting and reinforcing positive aspects of their lives, and (8) sharing her own love of words. (Sims Bishop, 1982b)

Greenfield and her mother wrote **Childtimes: A Three-Generation Memoir** (P–I), an autobiography. In a foreword in **Childtimes,** the authors state,

James Ransome captures the feelings of warmth and loving humor in Elizabeth Fitzgerald Howard's story about two girls who like to visit Aunt Flossie. Part of the fun comes from trying on the hats and listening to stories Aunt Flossie tells about them. [*Aunt Flossie's Hats (and Crab Cakes Later)*]

This book is about family. Kinsfolk touching across the centuries, walking with one hand clasping the hands of those who have gone before, the other hand reaching back for those who will come after. This book, most of all, is about black people struggling, not just to stay alive, but to live, to give their talents, whether too many or too few. Through all of their pain and grief, and even their mistakes, black people have kept on going, had some good times, given a lot of love to one another, and never stopped trying to help their children get on board the freedom train. (Greenfield, 1979)

The authentic portrayal of African-American culture helps us to achieve multicultural understanding.

Novels. Virginia Hamilton, one of the most distinguished and talented writers in the field today, was the first African American to win the John Newbery Award and the international Hans Christian Andersen Award. Her numerous honors include the National Book Award, the Coretta Scott King Award, the Boston Globe-Horn Book Award, and the International Board on Books for Young People (IBBY) Honor List, among others. Her writing includes fantasy, mystery, folklore, realistic fiction, historical fiction, and biographical works. Hamilton's vivid writing describes the real world, the folkloric world, and the fanciful world with equal clarity and force.

Jesse Jackson, the first black writer to write openly about discrimination, tells the story of the only black child in a white school where he is tolerated but not welcomed in ***Call Me Charley*** (I). Charley is bitterly disappointed when he is excluded from the class play but he patiently accepts his lot. Charley's meek acceptance of his treatment would not be acceptable by today's standards but the book was groundbreaking in 1945.

**Figure
11-2**

African-American Literature

Folklore

Aardema, Verna. *Bimwili and the Zimwi.* (P)

——. *Bringing the Rain to Kapiti Plain.* (P)

——. *Oh, Kojo! How Could You!* (I)

——. *Traveling to Tondo: A Tale of the Nkundo of Zaire.* (I)

——. *What's So Funny, Ketu? A Nuer Tale.* (I)

——. *Who's in Rabbit's House?* (P)

——. *Why Mosquitoes Buzz in People's Ears.* (P–I)

Bryan, Ashley. *All Night, All Day: A Child's First Book of African American Spirituals.* (P–I–A)

——. *Beat the Story Drum, Pum-Pum.* (P–I–A)

——. *The Cat's Purr.* (I)

——. *The Dancing Granny.* (I)

——. *Lion and the Ostrich Chicks and Other African Folk Tales.* (I)

——. *Turtle Knows Your Name.* (P–I)

——. *What a Morning! The Christmas Story in Black Spirituals.* (P–I)

Courlander, Harold, and George Herzog. *The Cow-Tail Switch and Other West African Stories.* (P–I)

Grifalconi, Ann. *The Village of Round and Square Houses.* (P)

Guy, Rosa. *Mother Crocodile.* Illus. John Steptoe. (P)

Haley, Gail. *A Story, a Story.* (P)

Hamilton, Virginia. *The People Could Fly.* Illus. Leo and Diane Dillon. (I)

Harris, Joel. *Jump: The Adventures of Brer Rabbit.* Illus. Barry Moser. (P–I)

——. *Jump Again! More Adventures of Brer Rabbit.* Illus. Barry Moser. (P–I)

Hooks, William H. (reteller). *The Ballad of Belle Dorcas.* Illus. Brian Pinkney. (P–I)

Jaquith, Priscilla. *Bo Rabbit Smart for True: Folktales from the Gullah.* Illus. Ed Young. (P–I)

Keats, Ezra Jack. *John Henry.* (I)

Lester, Julius. *How Many Spots Does a Leopard Have?* (I)

——. *The Tales of Uncle Remus: The Adventures of Brer Rabbit.* (P–I)

Lyons, Mary E. (selector). *Raw Head, Bloody Bones: African American Tales of the Supernatural.* (I)

McDermott, Gerald. **Anansi the Spider.** (P)

Mollel, Tololwa. *A Promise to the Sun.* Illus. Beatriz Vidal. (P)

San Souci, Robert D. *Sukey and the Mermaid.* Illus. Brian Pinkney. (P–I)

Steptoe, John. *Mufaro's Beautiful Daughters.* (P)

Tadjo, Veronique (reteller/illus.). *Lord of the Dance: An African Retelling.* (I)

Poetry

Adoff, Arnold. *All the Colors of the Race.* (I)

——. *Black Is Brown Is Tan.* (P)

——. *Eats.* (P–I)

——. *In for Winter, Out for Spring.* (P–I)

——. *My Black Me: A Beginning Book of Black Poetry.* (P)

——. *Sports Pages.* (I)

Brooks, Gwendolyn. *Bronzeville Boys and Girls.* (P–I)

Bryan, Ashley. *Sing to the Sun.* (P–I)

Clifton, Lucille. *Some of the Days of Everett Anderson.* (P)

——. *Everett Anderson's Goodbye.* (P)

——. *Everett Anderson's Nine Month Long.* (P)

Giovanni, Nikki. *Spin a Soft Black Song.* (P–I)

Greenfield, Eloise. *Honey, I Love and Other Love Poems.* (P–I–A)

——. *Night on Neighborhood Street.* Illus. Jan Spivey Gilchrist. (P)

Price, Leontyne. *Aïda.* Illus. Leo and Diane Dillon. (A)

CONTINUED

Picture Books

Adoff, Arnold. *Hard to Be Six.* Illus. Cheryl Hanna. (P)

Anderson, Joy. *Juma and the Magic Jinn.* Illus. Charles Mikolaycak. (P)

Clifton, Lucille. *Boy Who Didn't Believe in Spring.* (P)

————. *Everett Anderson's Christmas Coming.* (P)

————. *Three Wishes.* Illus. Michael Hays. (P)

Crews, Donald. *Bigmama's.* (P)

Daly, Niki. *Not So Fast Songololo.* (P)

Greenfield, Eloise. *Grandpa's Face.* (P)

————. *Me and Neesie.* (P–I)

————. *She Come Bringing Me That Little Baby Girl.* (P)

————. *Sister.* (I)

Grifalconi, Ann. *Darkness and the Butterfly.* (P)

————. *Osa's Pride.* (P)

Hamilton, Virginia. *Drylongso.* Illus. Jerry Pinkney. (I)

Haskins, Francine. *I Remember "121."* (I)

Hoffman, Mary. *Amazing Grace.* Illus. Caroline Binch. (P)

Howard, Elizabeth Fitzgerald. *Aunt Flossie's Hats (and Crab Cakes Later).* Illus. James Ransome. (P)

Johnson, Angela. *One of Three.* Illus. David Soman. (P)

————. *Tell Me a Story, Mama.* Illus. David Soman. (P)

Mathis, Sharon Bell. *The Hundred Penny Box.* (P–I)

McKissack, Patricia C. *Flossie and the Fox.* (P)

————. *Mirandy and Brother Wind.* Illus. Jerry Pinkney. (P–I)

————. *Nettie Jo's Friends.* Illus. Scott Cook. (P)

Pinkney, Gloria Jean. *Back Home.* Illus. Jerry Pinkney. (P)

Polacco, Patricia. *Chicken Sunday.* (P)

————. *Mrs. Katz and Tush.* (P–I)

Ringgold, Faith. *Tar Beach.* (P–I)

Schroeder, Alan. *Ragtime Tumpie.* Illus. Bernie Fuchs. (P–I)

Smalls-Hector, Irene. *Irene and the Big, Fine Nickel.* Illus. Tyrone Geter. (P)

Steptoe, John. *Stevie.* (P)

Stolz, Mary. *Go Fish.* Illus. Pat Cummings. (P–I)

Williams, Sherley Anne. *Working Cotton.* Illus. Carole Byard. (P)

Wilson, Beth P. *Jenny.* Illus. Dolores Johnson. (P)

Novels

Davis, Ossie. *Just Like Martin.* (I)

Greenfield, Eloise. *Koya Delaney and the Good Girl Blues.* (I)

Hamilton, Virginia. *Cousins.* (I)

————. *House of Dies Drear.* (I)

————. *M. C. Higgins, the Great.* (I–A)

————. *Mystery of Drear House.* (I–A)

————. *Planet of Junior Brown.* (I–A)

————. *Willie Bea and the Time the Martians Landed.* (I–A)

————. *Zeely.* (I)

Herlihy, Dirlie. *Ludie's Song.* (I)

Moore, Yvette. *Freedom Songs.* (I)

Myers, Walter Dean. *Fast Sam, Cool Clyde, and Stuff.* (I–A)

————. *The Young Landlords.* (A)

————. *Hoops.* (A)

————. *Motown and Didi.* (A)

————. *Somewhere in the Darkness.* (A)

————. *Won't Know Till I Get There.* (A)

Smothers, Ethel Footman. *Down in the Piney Woods.* (I–A)

Taylor, Mildred. *The Road to Memphis.* (A)

Taylor, Theodore. *The Cay.* (I–A)

CONTINUED

Nonfiction

Golenbock, Peter. *Teammates.* Illus. Paul Bacon. (I)

Haskins, James. *Black Theater in America.* (A)

———. *Street Gangs, Yesterday and Today.* (A)

Katz, William Loren. *Breaking the Chains: African-American Slave Resistance.* (I–A)

McKissack, Patricia, and Frederick McKissack. *A Long Hard Journey: The Story of the Pullman Porter.* (I)

Myers, Walter Dean. *Now Is Your Time!: The African-American Struggle for Freedom.* (I–A)

Rosenberg, Maxine B. *Brothers and Sisters.* Photos by George Ancona. (P–I)

Biography

Freedman, Florence B. *Two Tickets to Freedom: The True Story of Ellen and William Craft, Fugitive Slaves.* (I–A)

Hamilton, Virginia. *Anthony Burns: The Defeat and Triumph of a Fugitive Slave.* (I–A)

Haskins, James. *Bill Cosby: America's Most Famous Father.* (I)

———. *Diana Ross, Star Supreme.* (I)

Lester, Julius. *To Be a Slave.* (A)

———. *Long Journey Home.* (A)

Lyons, Mary E. *Sorrow's Kitchen: The Life and Folklore of Zora Neale Hurston.* (A)

Meltzer, Milton. *The Black Americans: A History in Their Own Words.* (A)

Nonfiction and Biography

Julius Lester comments in the opening pages of ***To Be a Slave*** (I–A) that one of the greatest overlooked sources for information concerning slavery has been the words of those who were slaves. During the first half of the nineteenth century, abolitionists took down the stories of thousands of African Americans who escaped from the South; narratives of ex-slaves became a literary genre unto itself before the Civil War. After the Civil War, however, interest in slave narratives dwindled and was not revived until the 1930s when workers on the Federal Writers' Project (a part of the Works Progress Administration or WPA) interviewed the ex-slaves still alive. Lester selected material from both the nineteenth-century narratives and the oral history recorded by the WPA workers to convey, in their own words, how it feels to be a slave. In one excerpt, an ex-slave describes the slave auction:

> My brothers and sisters were bid off first, and one by one, while my mother, paralyzed with grief, held me by the hand. Her turn came and she was bought by Isaac Riley of Montgomery County. Then I was offered. . . . My mother, half distracted with the thought of parting forever from all her children, pushed through the crowd while the bidding for me was going on, to the spot where Riley was standing. She fell at his feet, and clung to his knees, entreating him in tones that a mother could only command, to buy her baby as well as herself, and spare to her one, at least, of her little ones. . . . This man disengage[ed] himself from her with . . . violent blows and kicks. . . . I must have been then between five and six years old. (Lester, 1968)

Lester extends oral history in ***Long Journey Home*** (I–A) by recording stories of ordinary people—stories based on historical fact. Lester believes the essence of black history lies in the lives of common people who need to have their stories told along with those of the heroes. That is what he has done.

The number of high-quality books featuring Asian Americans is increasing. Most of the existing books focus on China and Japan, but some other Asian countries are slowly being recognized. Excellent retellings of folklore and the works of outstanding writers are changing the situation rapidly (Aoki, 1981). See Figure 11-3.

Folklore

Variants of the same folktale appear in many different countries, causing scholars to believe that similar human needs gave rise to them. The Cinderella story, for example, has over 450 variants; some are from Asian cultures. One variant from China, ***Yeh-Shen*** (P), dates back to the T'ang Dynasty (A.D. 618–907). Yoshiko Uchida retold many Japanese folktales in her early work.

The Crane Wife (P–I), one of Japan's most beloved folktales, tells of a woman who could weave beautiful fabrics but unbeknownst to her husband she transformed herself into a crane to do the finest and most intricate work. When her husband pressured her to make more and more delicate textures, she worked even harder, but one day she disappeared, flying off with a flock of cranes. Every year thousands of Japanese see some version of this story as a play, movie, or opera in addition to reading it aloud to their children. It is a treasured bit of cultural heritage.

Zang Xiu Shi, adapter of ***Monkey and the White Bone Demon*** (P–I), translated by Ye Pin Kue and revised by Jill Marius, shows the monkey character that permeates Asian folklore. Similar to the Anansi character from African folklore, the monkey plays clever tricks and is valued for his wit.

Poetry

The brief nonrhyming haiku of Issa and Basho, among the best known Japanese poets, popularized a form that has traveled worldwide. Haiku, written in just 17 syllables, whisper about marvels of nature, laughs at incongruity, or shouts about the excitement of beauty. For example, in a collection by Demi, ***In the Eyes of the Cat,*** (P–I)

> TRAVELER
>
> *Where can he be going*
> *In the rain,*
> *This snail?*
>
> *Issa 1763–1827*

According to Virginia Olsen Baron, collector and adapter of ***Sunset in a Spider Web: Sijo Poetry of Ancient Korea*** (I–A), the sijo is one of the most popular and earliest poetic forms found in Korean literature. The sijo is written in three lines with approximately 44 syllables, but because they are awkwardly long in English, they are presented in six lines instead of the traditional three. The first line usually states the theme, the second elaborates on it, and the third line is a twist on the theme or a resolution, sometimes called an antitheme. The

Ed Young reflects cultural patterns and images in his illustrations of folklore. He paints in the tradition of Chinese panel art for Ai-Ling Louie's retelling of the Chinese variant of the Cinderella story, ***Yeh-Shen,*** and portrays the fairy godmother as a fish.

following example is found in ***Sunset in a Spider Web:***

> *When a shadow appeared on the water,*
> *I looked up to see a monk crossing the bridge.*
> *Stay, I said, so I could ask*
> *Where he was going.*
>
> *But, pointing at white clouds, he moved on,*
> *Answering without words.*
>
> *Anonymous*

Fiction

Picture Books. One of the best picture books portraying an Asian American is among the oldest: ***Crow Boy*** (P) by Taro Yashima. It remains unparalleled in capturing the image of a lonely child from the mountains who attends the village school. Chibi's greatest school achievement is perfect attendance, although he travels miles to get there. His biggest talent is imitating the voices of crows—an accomplishment he displays at a school performance. Yashima's colored pencil drawings extend the story in an outstanding manner.

Diane Snyder tells about Taro, the lazy son of a hardworking seamstress, in ***Boy of the Three-Year Nap*** (P) illustrated by Allen Say. In a story based on a folktale and illustrated in traditional Japanese black-bordered paintings, Taro plays a trick on a rich merchant and marries his daughter. His trick backfires, however, because he must work very hard for his money. Fortunately, Taro is also very happy.

Jeanne M. Lee tells a Vietnamese story in **Ba-Nam** (P). A young girl is frightened by the custom of visiting a relative's grave when she sees the old woman who cares for the graves. Traditional visits to graves are practiced in many cultures.

Novels. Laurence Yep explores his own Chinese-American family history in a fictionalized biography, **The Star Fisher** (I–A). The narrator, Joan Lee, is 15 years old when her family moves, in 1927, from Ohio to a small West Virginia town. Joan, her parents and younger brother and sister—

$\mathcal{Y}$OSHIKO UCHIDA was born in Alameda, California, and grew up in Berkeley. Her parents were first-generation immigrants from Japan (called Issei). Her father came first to work in the United States; her mother joined him a few years later. She said of her parents,

My mother came from Japan to marry my father, a man with whom she had only corresponded. Their marriage was a successful one. I remember them both as strong, sensitive, and loving people. Rinko's parents [in **A Jar of Dreams**] had the same kind of marriage arranged by a go-between which was the accepted tradition of that time.

Uchida valued her Japanese and American cultural heritage. As a college student, she was forced to go to a relocation camp with her family. As a result, she explained, "I received my college diploma from the mailman in Tanforan. My sister and I volunteered to teach the children at the camp. We had practically no supplies but we had eager, enthusiastic children who wanted to learn."

All of Yoshiko Uchida's books are about Japan and its children or about Japanese Americans because, as she said, "I felt I could make the best contribution in this area." Her early books

Yoshiko Uchida

are Japanese folktales, such as **The Dancing Kettle, The Magic Listening Cap,** and **Samurai of Gold Hill** (all P–I).

Yoshiko Uchida received the University of Oregon's Distinguished Service Award for "having made a significant contribution to the cultural development of society . . . and . . . [helping] to bring about a greater understanding of the Japanese American culture." She also received the California Commonwealth Club Medal for **Samurai of Gold Hill** (1972) and **A Jar of Dreams** (1982).

Uchida described her feelings of alienation growing up and expressed how such feelings seem universal: "I

characters based on Laurence Yep's family—face many changes in their lives. Since they are the first Chinese-American family to live in the West Virginia town they are considered oddities—different—by the provincial townspeople. They are welcomed warmly, however, by some residents and stared at openly or disparaged by others. Joan's papa moves the family into a converted schoolhouse and attempts to run a new laundry business there. No

one comes as a customer but someone comes to paint warnings on the front fence. Joan battles discrimination at school and traditional Chinese versus American values at home. She was born an American and she intends to act like one despite her parents' wishes to retain their Chinese traditions. Joan learns to follow her dreams and to "fish for stars" in this coming-of-age novel that is true although not every word is factual.

CONTINUED

know that any child can feel alienated, not just Asian Americans. Through Rinko [in *A Jar of Dreams*], I help children link up with the feelings of one child in a minority group. I had Rinko express how she felt about speaking up in class," Rinko says:

I don't know why I can't speak up in class. I certainly can make myself heard when I'm at home. And when I'm having conversations with people inside my head, I'm always speaking up, telling them exactly what I think in a loud, firm voice. But at school it's different. If you feel like a big nothing and don't like who you are, naturally you don't speak up in a loud, firm voice. You don't talk to other people either, unless they talk to you first.

Yoshiko Uchida also wrote *Journey to Topaz* and *Journey Home* (both I–A), both of which reveal the story of Yuki Sakane and her family as they are uprooted from their California home and sent to a desert concentration camp (or relocation camp) during World War II. Uchida describes the tragic herding of innocent people with a sorrowful sense of injustice yet does not become bitter. During World War II, Uchida and her family were placed in a relocation camp because they were Japanese American. She said,

On the day that Pearl Harbor was bombed by Japan, I was studying for my final exams in the library at the University of California. When I returned home, FBI men were in the living room watching everything my family did. My father, along with other leaders of the Japanese community, had been taken for questioning and was being held at the Immigration Detention Quarters. He was later sent to an Army Prisoner of War camp in Montana. My mother, my older sister, and I had ten days to pack in preparation for our "removal" from Berkeley. We were forced to sell most of our possessions at a tremendous loss. We were taken, along with thousands of other Japanese Americans, to a temporary "relocation camp" at Tanforan, an abandoned racetrack. My father was eventually released from the camp in Montana and joined us in Tanforan, where we lived in a 10' by 20' horse stall. Later we were all transferred to Topaz, a square mile area in the middle of the Utah desert, which housed eight thousand internees.

The Invisible Thread, a later autobiography, describes her childhood as a Nisei (a person of Japanese descent whose parents were immigrants from Japan) and her preparation for a writing career. The memoir includes the chapters in her life when she was detained in the Japanese prison camp at Topaz. Yoshiko Uchida died in 1992.

Figure 11-3

Asian-American Literature

Folklore

Birdseye, Tom (adapter). *A Song of Stars.* Illus. Ju-Hong Chen. (P)

Demi (author/illus.). *The Empty Pot.* (P)

Johnston, Tony. *The Badger and the Magic Fan.* Illus. Tomie de Paola. (P)

Louie, Ai-Ling. *Yeh-Shen: A Cinderella Story from China.* Illus. Ed Young. (P–I)

Mahy, Margaret (reteller). *The Seven Chinese Brothers.* Illus. Jean and Mou-sien Tseng. (P–I)

Mosel, Arlene. *The Funny Little Woman.* Illus. Blair Lent. (P)

Yacowitz, Caryn (adapter). *The Jade Stone: A Chinese Folktale.* Illus. Ju-Hong Chen. (I)

Yagawa, Sumiko (reteller). *The Crane Wife.* Trans. Katherine Paterson. Illus. Suekichi Akaba. (P–I)

Yep, Laurence. (reteller). *Tongues of Jade.* Illus. David Wiesner. (I)

——. *The Rainbow People.* (I)

Poetry

Baron, Virginia Olsen. *Sunset in a Spider Web: Sijo Poetry of Ancient Korea.* (I–A)

Behn, Harry. *Cricket Songs.* (I–A)

——. *More Cricket Songs.* (I–A)

Demi. *In the Eyes of the Cat: Japanese Poetry for All Seasons.* Tze-si Huang. (P–I–A)

Lewis, Richard. *In a Spring Garden.* illus. Ezra Jack Keats. (I–A)

Picture Books

Baker, Keith. *The Magic Fan.* (P)

Breckler, Rosemary. *Hoang Breaks the Lucky Teapot.* Illus. Adrian Frankel. (P)

Friedman, Ina. *How My Parents Learned to Eat.* (P)

Kalman, Maira. *Sayonara, Mrs. Kackleman.* (P)

Lee, Jeanne M. *Silent Lotus.* (P–I)

McCunn, Ruthanne Lum. *Pie-Biter.* Illus. You-shan Tang. (P)

Rappaport, Doreen. *The Journey of Meng.* Illus. Yang Ming-Yi. (P–I)

Say, Allen. *Bicycle Man.* (P)

——. *El Chino.* (P–I)

——. *Tree of Cranes.* (P–I)

Tejima. *Ho-limlim: A Rabbit Tale from Japan.* (P–I)

Turner, Ann. *Through Moon and Stars and Night Skies.* Illus. James Graham Hale. (P–I)

Wisniewski, David. *The Warrior and the Wise Man.* (P–I)

Yashima, Taro. *Crow Boy.* (P–I)

——. *Umbrella.* (P)

——. *Youngest One.* (P)

——. *Momo's Kitten.* (P)

Novels and Short Stories

Baillie, Allan. *Little Brother.* (I–A)

Choi, Sook Nyul. *Year of Impossible Goodbyes.* (A)

Haugaard, Erik Christian. *The Boy and the Samurai.* (A)

Ho, Minfong. *The Clay Marble.* (A).

——. *Rice Without Rain.* (A)

Nonfiction and Biography

Nonfiction is seldom selected as a literary prizewinner, but **Commodore Perry in the Land of the Shogun** (I–A) received a Newbery Honor Book Award for its distinguished literary quality. Rhoda Blumberg vividly describes the engaging story of Matthew Perry's expedition to open Japan to American trade. The significance of the diplomatic achievement is foreshadowed in text and illustra-tions that were selected from museum collections. The opening paragraphs herald the storytelling flavor of the informational report.

If monsters had descended upon Japan the effect could not have been more terrifying.

People in the fishing village of Shimoda were the first to spot four huge hulks, two

CONTINUED

Kidd, Diana. *Onion Tears.* (A)

Merrill, Jean. *The Girl Who Loved Caterpillars.* Illus. Floyd Cooper. (I)

Namioka, Lensey. *Yang the Youngest and His Terrible Ear.* (I)

Staples, Suzanne Fisher. *Shabanu.* (A)

Soto, Gary. *Pacific Crossing.* (A)

Uchida, Yoshiko. *A Jar of Dreams.* (I)

———. *The Best Bad Thing.* (I)

———. *The Happiest Ending.* (I)

Watkins, Yoko Kawashima. *So Far from the Bamboo Grove.* (I–A)

Whelan, Gloria. *Goodbye Vietnam.* (A)

Yee, Paul. *Tales from Gold Mountain: Stories of the Chinese in the New World.* (I–A)

Yep, Laurence. *Dragonwings.* (A)

———. *Sea Glass.* (I–A)

———. *Child of the Owl.* (A)

———. *Mountain Light.* (A)

———. *The Serpent's Children.* (I–A)

Nonfiction

Banish, Roslyn (author/photographer). *A Forever Family.* (I)

Blumberg, Rhoda. *Commodore Perry in the Land of the Shogun.* (I–A)

Brown, Tricia. *Lee Ann.* Photos by Ted Thai. (I)

Davis, Daniel S. *Behind Barbed Wire: The Imprisonment of Japanese Americans During World War II.* (A)

Hoyt-Goldsmith, Diane. *Hoang Anh: A Vietnamese-American Boy.* Photos by Lawrence Migdale. (I)

McMahon, Patricia. *Chi-Hoon: A Korean Girl.* (P–I)

Meltzer, Milton. *The Chinese Americans.* (A)

Schlein, Miriam. *The Year of the Panda.* Illus. Kam Mak. (P–I)

Waters, Kate, and Madeline Slovenz-Low. *Lion Dancer: Ernie Wan's Chinese New Year.* (P–I)

Wolf, Bernard. *In the Year of the Tiger.* (I)

Biography

Fritz, Jean. *Homesick: My Own Story.* (I–A)

———. *China Homecoming.* (I–A)

Huynh, Quang Nhuong. *The Land I Lost: Adventures of a Boy in Vietnam.* (I)

Lord, Bette Bao. *In the Year of the Boar and Jackie Robinson.* (I)

Morey, Janet Nomura, and Wendy Dunn. *Famous Asian Americans.* (I–A)

Tobias, T. *Isamuo Noguchi: The Life of a Sculptor.* (I–A)

streaming smoke, on the ocean's surface approaching the shore. "Giant dragons puffing smoke," cried some. "Alien ships of fire," cried others. According to a folktale, smoke above water was made by the breath of clams. Only a child would believe that. Perhaps enemies knew how to push erupting volcanoes toward the Japanese homeland. Surely something horrible was happening on this day, Friday, July 8, 1853. (Blumberg, 1985)

Blumberg's work is an example of good informational sources that describe Asian-American relations historically.

Laurence Yep, well-known Asian-American writer, describes growing up in San Francisco in ***The Lost Garden*** (I–A). Yep's autobiography, illustrated with photographs, tells how he came to use his writing to celebrate his family and ethnic heritage. His fictionalized biography of his mother's family,

A Japanese artist illustrates a Japanese folktale in a traditional mood, using line and wash on textured paper. Good literature presents authentic cultural images in text and illustrations. (*The Crane Wife* retold by Katherine Paterson, illustrated by Suekichi Akaba)

The Star Fisher (I–A), is discussed earlier. Many of Yep's other books celebrate his Asian heritage.

Biographies about famous Asian Americans are limited in number, but those that do exist contain well-written, engaging stories. For example, one set in Vietnam by Quang Nhuong Huynh speaks lovingly of **The Land I Lost: Adventures of a Boy in Vietnam** (I). The collection of biographical essays features scenes from his childhood in the central highlands. The author describes his life in the small hamlet of 50 bamboo houses. The village, surrounded by a jungle on one side and a river on the other, was in close proximity to many animals, some life threatening, others friendly. His father, like most of the villagers, was a farmer and a hunter, depending on the season. But he also had a college education, so in the evenings he helped to teach other children in the hamlet. Huynh recalls,

> I went to the lowlands to study for a while because I wanted to follow my father as a teacher when I grew up. I always planned to return to my hamlet to live the rest of my life there. But war disrupted my dreams. The land I love was lost to me forever. These stories are my memories. (Huynh, p. xi)

Some of his fondest memories center on the family's water buffalo, Tank, so named because when he hit another male during a fight, he struck as heavily as a tank. Tank does collide head on with other young bulls who trespass on his territory or challenge his authority, but he also is gentle enough to allow children to ride astride his broad back. Tank overpowers a vicious tiger, helps catch eels and a huge white catfish, and continually serves as the village protector. The final essay is called "Sorrow," because Tank is hit by a stray bullet and killed.

Latino Literature

According to the U.S. Census Bureau, over 20 million Spanish-speaking people live in America today with the Latino population growing more rapidly than any other cultural group. The census prediction is that Latinos will replace African Americans as the country's largest cultural group. By the year 2000, the Latino population will have increased 60 percent, more than double the 29 percent increase expected for African Americans. Among the Latinos, Mexicans outnumber all others: Of the 20 million, about 12 million are Mexican; 4 million are Puerto Rican; about 1 million, Cuban; and 3 million, other origins, including Caribbean and Central and South American (specifically Dominican and Nicaraguan). The Latino population is concentrated in specific geographic areas, namely California, Texas, New York, Florida, Illinois, Arizona, New Jersey, New Mexico, and Colorado. More than half of the total Latino population lives in California and Texas.

Milton Meltzer, in **The Hispanic Americans** (A), reminds us that this ethnic group is quite diverse. He says that although they have much in common in the Spanish language, Latinos differ in many ways. To lump all Latinos together and suggest they are alike would be foolish. Each group has its own identity and each person feels the importance of the differences between groups. A Puerto Rican does not like to be mistaken for a Cuban, just as someone from the South does not like to be called a Yankee (Meltzer, 1982).

The number of books for children potraying Latino characters stands in stark contrast to the numbers of Latinos in the population. According to the study conducted by Edmonds, only 2 percent of all children's books published represent the Latino culture. Compared to the numbers of Latino children who need to see themselves represented in books, there is a dearth of books available. The situation is changing slowly as mainstream publishers add Latino authors and illustrators to their lists and small presses increase the quantity and quality of their publications.

Barbara Cooney uses a folk art style to convey Mexican scenes. Her primary colors and strong lines capture the clay-washed tones of a Mexican kitchen. (***Tortillitas para Mama***)

Folklore

The Latino tradition contains folktales and nursery rhymes crafted over centuries into easily remembered verbal patterns. Like other cultures, the unique style of rendering folktales and nursery rhymes is apparent in the retelling. Collected from the Spanish community in the Americas, ***Tortillitas Para Mama*** (P) retains the melodies of its Latin American origins. This book contains 13 well-known nursery rhymes in both Spanish and English that are passed along from one generation to the next. "Little Frog Tail" ("Colita de Rana"), "The Chicks" ("Los Pollitos"), and "Lullaby" ("Arrullo") are among the favorite lilting rhymes. Despite the authenticity of the text, members inside the cultural group criticize the illustrations for inaccuracies and stereotypes (Allen, 1992).

Poetry

Latino poetry has a new voice in Gary Soto's work. His poems in ***Neighborhood Odes*** (I–A) center on growing up in Fresno, California. The 21 poems, all odes, celebrate things he valued as a child, such as "La Tortilla," "The Sprinkler," "Pablo's Tennis Shoes," and "The Library."

ODE TO LA TORTILLA

They are flutes
When rolled, butter
Dripping down my
    elbow
As I stand on the
Front lawn, just eating,
Just watching a
    sparrow
Hop on the lawn,

His breakfast of worms
Beneath the green,
    green lawn,
Worms and a rip of
Tortilla I throw
At his thorny feet.
I eat my tortilla,
breathe in, breathe out,
And return inside,

Wiping my oily hands
On my knee-scrubbed
    jeans.
The tortillas are still
    warm
In a dish towel,
Warm as gloves just
Taken off, finger by
    finger.
Mamá is rolling
Them out. The radio
On the window sings.
El cielo es azul . . .
I look in the black pan:
The face of the tortilla
With a bubble of air
Rising. Mamá
Tells me to turn
It over, and when
I do, carefully,
It's blistered brown.
I count to ten,
Uno, dos, tres . . .
And then snap it out

Of the pan. The tortilla
Dances in my hands
As I carry it
To the drainboard,
Where I smear it
With butter,
The yellow ribbon of
    butter
That will drip
Slowly down my arm
When I eat on the front
    lawn.
The sparrow will drop
Like fruit
From the tree
To stare at me
With his glassy eyes.
I will rip a piece
For him. He will jump
On his food
And gargle it down,
Chirp once and fly
Back into the wintry
    tree.

                            Gary Soto

Gary Soto has also written excellent collections in **A Fire in My Hands** (cited in Chapter 4), **Black Hair, Who Will Know Us?,** and **Home Course in Religion** (all I–A).

Fiction

Picture Books. Carmen Lomas Garza is the author/illustrator of **Family Pictures: Cuadros de Familia** (P–I), a bilingual book. Rosalma Zubizarreta wrote the Spanish version. A young girl reminisces about her life growing up in a Mexican-American family in South Texas. Bright primitive folk-art illustrations convey authentic details of the culture.

In **Yagua Days** (P) by Martel Cruz, Adan, a Puerto Rican child born in New York, thinks that rainy days are boring. When he goes with his parents to Puerto Rico he discovers what children there do on rainy days. He had heard about "yagua days," and in Puerto Rico Adan finds out what that means. When the grass is slick with rain, he uses a yagua (pronounced yag·wa), a large palm leaf, to slide down the grassy hills, over a ledge, and into the river. This book, chosen as a Notable Trade Book in the Field of Social Studies, a Reading Rainbow Review Book, and a runner-up for the Council on Interracial Books for Children Award, holds great appeal.

Novels and Short Stories. Gary Soto's novel, **Taking Sides** (A), has a central character named Lincoln

Mendoza, the only Latino child on the basketball team. Lincoln not only has to cope with his feelings about that but also must deal with a racist coach. When his new suburban school team plays against the team from his old barrio school, he has conflicting loyalties. Soto's writing is poetic. He includes Spanish words with English translations to maintain more of the cultural flavor. Soto's work includes **A Summer Life** (I–A).

The House on Mango Street (A) by Sandra Cisneros is a collection of graceful vignettes that captures glimpses of Esperanza Cordero's life growing up in a Latino quarter of Chicago. Esperanza says that in English her name means hope but in Spanish it is a muddy color which reminds her of Mexican songs that sound like sobbing. Cisneros' evocative vignettes describe Esperanza's life on the street with rundown tenements where she meets an abused wife, girlfriends, and boyfriends. The vignettes show how Esperanza creates for herself a quiet space in the midst of oppressive surroundings.

Nonfiction and Biography

When authors write about a person who lived long ago, they must sometimes infer what happened in between the known facts. Elizabeth Borten de Treviño had to fill in around the few facts that are known about the seventeenth-century painter, Velázquez, and his talented black assistant in **I, Juan de Pareja** (A). In an afterword, de Treviño explains,

> Whenever one tells a story about personages who actually lived, it becomes necessary to hang many invented incidents, characters, and events upon the thin thread of truth which has come down to us. The threads of the lives of Velázquez and Pareja are weak and broken; very little, for certain, is known about them. (de Treviño, 1965)

Treviño knew that Velázquez, the Spanish court painter in the first half of the seventeenth century, had a black slave standing by his side handing him brushes and grinding his colors. There is evidence, too, that Velázquez had inherited the slave, Juan de Pareja, from relatives in Seville and had later granted Pareja his freedom. She also knew that Pareja became an accomplished artist in his own right because his canvases hang in several European galleries. While it is true that slaves were not allowed to practice the arts in Spain, Treviño hypothesizes how it might have come about that Juan de Pareja learned to paint and became a close companion and friend to Velázquez. The story of the two men who began as slave and master and ended as equals and friends is a fascinating one. De Tre-viño writes about a family member in **El Guero** (I). Her husband's father became a leader in Mexican government and political arenas.

In an attempt to provide more multicultural literature, some publishing houses produce a series. One such series by Chelsea features Hispanics of Achievement. As is often true with series, the quality of the books vary. **Lee Trevino** (A) by Thomas W. Gilbert and **Jorge Luis Borges** (A) by Adrian Lennon, however, are quite well-written biographies.

Native American Literature

The Native American experience has been interpreted in literature for children by members of various tribal groups, anthropologists, folklorists, and others who have lived among Native Americans. Their literature is a link in the chain of universal understanding and, when it is filled with accurate details, it rings true to its culture. Joseph Bruchac is recognized as an authentic reteller of Native-American folklore. See Figure 11–5.

Folklore

When asked about the myths and legends that provide the basis for **Anpao** (A), Jamake Highwater said; "That is something I would like to discuss but you're using the *wrong words*. They are *not* myths and legends, they are an alternate way of viewing reality." He further explains his point in the storyteller's farewell in **Anpao:**

> You may have noticed that I am disinclined to refer to "myths" and "legends" when I talk about *Anpao*. This is because these words express the dominant society's disregard for the beliefs of other peoples, just as I would be expressing a nonchalant superiority were I to speak to Christians of their "Jesus myths." *Anpao* is not concerned with myths but with a reality which seems to have escaped the experience of non-Indians.

Highwater's perspective comes from a Black-foot-Cherokee heritage and his study of cultural anthropology, comparative literature, and music. The old tales are neither curiosities nor naive fiction; they are alternate visions of the world and reveal an alternate process of history. Indeed, he says the stories

> exist as the river of memory of a people, surging with their images and their rich meanings from

Literature and art provide avenues of learning about a culture. The artist's use of a filmy transparent veil could symbolize the veil of fiction, the unwillingness of people to reveal their true nature, or the inability of one person to be able to see into another's life. It may suggest the distance humans keep between themselves. Readers can experience how three young women face the harsh realities of their lives screened by the veil of fiction. (**The House on Mango Street** by Sandra Cisneros)

> one *place* to another, from one generation to the next—the tellers and the told so intermingled in time and space that no one can separate them.

Highwater contributes to the river of memory of Native Americans through his own work and by calling attention to the work of others in his lectures and book and music reviews.

Tales, chants, poetry, and song serve as a bridge to understanding Native American cultures. John Bierhorst, a folklorist, compiled several volumes showing how, in their lore, Native Americans pay tribute to the beauty of nature, the power of spirits, and the role of the supernatural. Bierhorst's major works include **Doctor Coyote: A Native American Aesop's Fables** (P), **Naked Bear: Folktales of the Iroquois** (I), and **Sacred Paths: Spells,**

Figure 11-4

Latino Literature

Folklore

Aardema, Verna. *Borreguita and the Coyote.* Illus. Petra Mathers. (Mexico) (P–I)

———. *Pedro and the Padre: A Tale from Jalisco, Mexico.* Illus. Friso Henstra. (P–I)

———. *The Riddle of the Drum: A Tale from Tizapan, Mexico.* (P–I)

Alexander, Ellen. *Llama and the Great Flood.* (Quechua story from Peru) (I)

Belpre, Pura. *Once in Puerto Rico.* (I)

———. *The Rainbow-Colored Horse.* (Puerto Rico) (P–I)

Bierhorst, John. *The Monkey's Haircut and Other Stories Told by the Maya.* Illus. Robert Andrew Parker. (Guatemala and Southeastern Mexico) (I)

Blackmore, Vivien. *Why Corn Is Golden: Stories About Plants.* Illus. Susana Martinez-Ostos. (Mexico) (P–I)

Cruz-Martinez, Alejandro. *The Woman who Outshone the Sun/La Mujer Que Brillaba Aun Mas Que el Sol.* Adapted by Rosalma Zubizarreta, Harriet Rohmer, and David Shecter. (P)

de Paola, Tomie. *The Lady of Guadalupe.* (Mexico) (P–I)

de Sauza, James. *Brother Anansi and the Cattle Ranch.* (Nicaragua) (P)

Finger, Charles J. (editor). *Tales from Silver Lands.* Woodcuts by Paul Honore. (I)

Flora. *Feathers Like a Rainbow: An Amazon Indian Tale.* (Amazon) (P)

Griego, Margot C., et al. *Tortillitas para Mama and Other Nursery Rhymes: Spanish and English.* Illus. Barbara Cooney. (N–P)

Joseph, Lynn. *A Wave in Her Pocket: Stories from Trinidad.* Illus. Brian Pinkney. (I)

Kurtycz, Marcos. *Tigers and Opossums: Animal Legends.* (Mexico) (I)

Rohmer, Harriet. *The Invisible Hunters.* (Nicaragua Miskito Indian) (P–I)

———. *Uncle Nacho's Hat: A Folktale from Nicaragua.* (P–I)

———. *Atariba & Niguayona: A Story from the Taino People of Puerto Rico.* (P–I)

Schon, Isabel. *Doña Blanca and Other Hispanic Nursery Rhymes and Games.* (P–I)

Vidal, Beatriz. *The Legend of El Dorado.* Adapted by Nancy Van Laan. (Colombia) (P–I)

Wolkstein, Diane. *Banza: A Haitian Story.* Illus. Marc Tolon Brown. (P)

Poetry

de Gerez, Toni (adapter). *My Song Is a Piece of Jade: Poems of Ancient Mexico in English and Spanish.* (I–A)

Delacre, Lulu. *Arroz Con Leche: Popular Songs and Rhymes from Latin America.* (P–I)

Holguin, Jiminez, et al. *Para Chiquitines.* (P–I)

Soto, Gary. *A Fire in My Hands.* Illus. James M. Cardillo. (I)

———. *Neighborhood Odes.* Illus. David Diaz. (I)

Picture Books

Belpre, Pura. *Santiago.* Illus. Symeon Shimin. (P)

Cruz, Martel. *Yagua Days.* (P)

Czernicki, Stefan, and Timothy Rhodes. *The Sleeping Bread.* (P)

Dorros, Arthur. *Abuela.* Illus. Elisa Kleven. (P)

Ets, Marie Hall, and Aurora Latastida. *Nine Days to Christmas, a Story of Mexico.* (P)

Prayers and Power Songs of the American Indians (I). In 1899, Edward Curtis, a photohistorian who realized the Indian culture might soon disappear, saved remnants of a vanishing race through photographs and transcriptions. Nine of the tales Curtis preserved appear in **The Girl Who Married a Ghost** (I–A) edited by John Bierhorst.

Within recent decades we have developed a new consciousness about Native Americans and about the differences between their concepts and view of the world and those of the early settlers. The Native Americans believed, for example, that the land belonged to everyone, whereas the European settlers brought with them the idea of individ-

CONTINUED

Garne, S. T. *One White Sail.* Illus. Lisa Etre. (Caribbean) (P)

Garza, Carmen Lomas. *Family Pictures. Cuadros de Familia.* (P–I)

Havill, Juanita. *Treasure Nap.* Illus. Elivia Savadier. (Mexico) (P)

James, Betsy. *The Dream Stair.* (P)

Keller, Holly. *Island Baby.* (P)

Linden, Ann Marie. *One Smiling Grandma.* Illus. Lynne Russell. (Caribbean counting book) (P)

Politi, Leo. *Pedro, the Angel of Olvera Street.* (P)

Roe, Eileen. *Con Mi Hermano: With My Brother.* (P)

Tompert, Ann. *The Silver Whistle.* Illus. Beth Peck. (P)

Wisniewski, David. *Rain Player.* (Mayan) (P–I)

Novels and Short Stories

Brenner, Barbara. *Mystery of the Plumed Serpent.* (I)

Cameron, Ann. *The Most Beautiful Place in the World.* Illus. Thomas B. Allen. (P–I)

Carlson, Lori M., and Cynthia L. Ventura (editors). *Where Angels Glide at Dawn: New Stories from Latin America.* Illus. José Ortega. (I)

Mohr, Nicholasa. *Felita.* (I)

————. *Going Home.* (I–A)

Soto, Gary. *Baseball in April and Other Stories.* (I)

————. *Taking Sides.* (I–A)

Nonfiction

Ancona, George. *Bananas: From Manolo to Margie.* (P–I)

Anderson, Joan. *Spanish Pioneers of the Southwest.* (P–I)

Brown, Tricia. *Hello, Amigos!* Photos by Fran Ortiz. (P–I)

Brusca, Maria Christina. *On the Pampas.* (I)

Emberley, Rebecca. *My House: A Book in Two Languages/Mi Casa: Un Libro en Dos Lenguas.* (I)

————. *Taking a Walk: A Book in Two Languages/Caminando: Un Libro en Dos Lenguas.* (I)

McDonald's Hispanic Heritage Art Contest. *Our Hispanic Heritage.* (P)

Meltzer, Milton. *The Hispanic Americans.* (A)

Perl, Lila. *Pinatas and Paper Flowers, Holidays of the Americas in English and Spanish.* (I–A)

Shalant, Phyllis. *Look What We've Brought You from Mexico.* (I)

Stanek, M. *I Speak English for My Mom.* Illus. Judith Friedman. (P)

Zak, Monica. *Save My Rainforest.* Illus. Bengt-Arne Runnerstrom. Trans. Nancy Schimmel. (I)

Biography

Codye, C. *Luis W. Alvarez.* (I–A)

de Treviño, Elizabeth Borten. *I, Juan de Pareja.* (A)

————. *Juarez, Man of Law.* (A)

————. *El Guero.* (I–A)

Gleiter, Jan. *David Farragut.* (A)

————. *Diego Rivera.* (A)

Shorto, R. *David Farragut and the Great Naval Blockade.* (A)

---

ual ownership. Staking claims to lands that the Native American had roamed freely for hundreds of years set the stage for conflict—from grisly battles, in which hundreds were killed, to inner conflicts, in which individuals who had come to know each other as friends had to choose between friendship and loyalty to the violently opposed groups.

The folklore of Native Americans is voluminous; it is as varied as the languages and lifestyles of many tribal groups, but like all folklore, the tales share commonalities. Many stories explain the how and why of natural phenomena and stress the close association between people and nature; others are creation myths, transformation tales, trickster tales,

*J*OSEPH BRUCHAC's heritage reflects the multicultural nature of our world; his interests are those of a concerned student of ecology. Bruchac's ancestry includes Abenaki, English, and Slovak parentage. His grandfather was an Abenaki Indian and he draws upon his Abenaki heritage to retell stories such as *Thirteen Moons on Turtle's Back: A Native American Year of Moons* (I). He draws upon his heritage and his scholarship to write nonfiction such as *Keepers of the Earth: Native American Stories and Environmental Activities for Children* (A).

Bruchac is deeply concerned about the environmental health of our world, and he puts strong emphasis in his writing on the importance of spiritual balance. He links the telling of Native-American stories and the study of native cultures with positive social and environmental activities. Bruchac approaches environmental ethics and issues in human and environmental interrelationships by placing the study in the context of Native-American cultures, past and present.

Bruchac shows how stories arose from various Native-American groups and how they can be used to teach, to entertain, and to worship. He explains how various cultures came to be here on this continent and describes the nature of their religious practices and spirituality.

Joseph Bruchac received his Bachelor of Arts from Cornell University, his Master of Arts degree from Syracuse University, and his Ph.D. from Union Graduate School. While studying at Cornell, he took a writing class. He

Joseph Bruchac

says, "I always loved to write, even though I was in the school of agriculture at Cornell, majoring in wildlife conservation. Three weeks into my class, my instructor said, 'Give it up. You'll never write a good poem.' From that point on, I literally ate, slept and dreamt poetry." He switched his major to English a year later.

Joseph Bruchac has had poems and stories published in over 400 magazines and anthologies. He has published two novels, 14 collections of poetry, and two books of nonfiction. He is the recipient of an NEA Creative Writing Fellowship, the American Book Award, a CCLM Editors Fellowship, a Rockefeller Foundation Humanities Fellowship, a PEN Syndicated Fiction Award, and the Cherokee Nation Prose Award.

Joseph Bruchac lives with his wife and two sons in the foothills of the Adirondacks, in the town of Greenfield Center. The family resides in the same house where he was raised by his maternal grandparents.

John Bierhorst retells traditional Aesop's fables as the Aztecs recast them in the sixteenth century. Coyote was clever and compassionate but sometimes foolish, according to the Aztecs. Wendy Watson uses a cartoon style to portray segments of the fable in which Coyote outsmarts Goat. (***Doctor Coyote: A Native American Aesop's Fables***)

and sacred legends. Ravens, eagles, wolves, bears, and buffalo often appear in the tales. Storytelling is deeply rooted in the culture and ceremonial life of the Native American; they hold storytellers in high regard.

Elizabeth Cleaver tells an Inuit Indian transformation tale in ***The Enchanted Caribou*** (P–I). Tyya, a young woman, is lost in a dense fog and Etosack, a young Inuit, rescues her and takes her to the tent he and his two brothers share. When the three brothers go off to hunt caribou they warn Tyya not to let anyone in, but she forgets and allows an old woman, a shaman, to enter. The old woman turns Tyya into a white caribou who trots across the tundra to join the herd. Heartbroken, Etosack dreams of his dead grandmother who had also been a shaman. She speaks to him:

Do what I tell you and you will have her back.
In the morning take a feather, the bone and

TEACHING IDEA 11-2

Distinguish Between Native American and European Beliefs

Have your students read books that reveal Native American views. For example, Jamake Highwater's *Anpao: An American Indian Odyssey* (A).

1. To recapture the spirit of Indian lore, share parts of *Anpao* through dramatic reading or storytelling.

2. Trace variants of the tales in the folklore of other tribes and cultures. For example, look at *The Angry Moon* by William Sleator, *The Girl Who Loved Wild Horses* by Paul Goble, and *The Naked Bear: Folktales of the Iroquois* by John Bierhorst.

3. Discuss how the views of Native Americans and early settlers differed on these issues:

   a. the wholeness of experience,

   b. the interdependence of people and nature,

   c. the importance of the quest for love, and

   d. the search for one's destiny.

4. Discuss how basic concepts of settlers and Native Americans made conflict inevitable during the westward expansion. Discuss meanings of these concepts:

   a. the concept of time,

   b. the concept of space,

   c. a "contrary" (a person who does and says everything in reverse—like Oapna in *Anpao*),

   d. the river of stars,

   e. the relationship with one's horse,

   f. the ownership of land, and

   g. the meaning of fences.

sinew of a caribou, a stone, and the doll that Tyya made. Then go out and look for the white caribou. When you find it, throw these things on its back and you will see what happens.

Etosack does as his grandmother bids: When he sees the white caribou he tosses the magical objects onto its back. Instantly the caribou changes back into Tyya and they live together happily. "And ever since," the story concludes, "when hunters meet a white caribou they treat it kindly and do not kill it, for it might be enchanted." Transformation tales appear in many cultures.

The Story of Jumping Mouse (P–I), retold and illustrated by John Steptoe, is from the Great Plains Indians. The story contains animals native to the region and portrays the values the Plains Indians held dear.

Teri Sloat lived and worked in Yupik Eskimo villages in Alaska before she retold *The Eye of the Needle* (P). The story she tells is about Amik who is sent out by his grandmother to bring back food for both of them, but he is too hungry to share. Amik swallows everything in sight, including a whale. Grandmother uses a magic needle to draw forth the food from Amik's stomach to share with all the villagers. Sloat's retelling is both humorous and poignant.

Poetry

Ritual occasions—such as daybreak, hunts, festivals, and times of initiation—have their special sounds and rhythms. In *The Trees Stand Shining: Poetry of the North American Indians* (P–I), Hettie Jones explains that the songs show the Native Americans' view of their world, their land, and their lives. The song-poems include prayers, stories, lullabies, and war chants.

Ann Nolan Clark, who lived and worked among Native American children, wrote down stories and poems they created. These were published as a collection called *In My Mother's House* (P), a book that was reissued. The collection, specifically from the Tewa of Tesuque Pueblo, near Santa Fe, provides insight into the views and writings of Native American children. In one fourth-grade classroom, students read from Ann Nolan Clark's book plus many other types of Native American poetry. They tried to write in the same vein. Here is an example of one child's response.

THE DESERT

The sound of a coyote
howling breaks the stillness

ᐱᓯᒡᐸᐊᑦ

ᐅᐃᖕᖑᖕᑯᑦ ᐊᒡᓗ ᐊᐅᖕᒥᒃ ᐃᓄᐃᑦ ᐃᖓᐊᖕᑍᔅᑐᖕᑎᑦ,
ᐱᓯᒡᐸᐊᖕᒪᐅᖕᒪᑦ ᓂᖕᓴᔾᒡᑏᖕᔅᑎᑦ. ᐅᐱᐅᖕᒡ
ᒡᒐᑲᖕᒪᐅᖕᒪᑦ ᒡᒡᒡᔾᖕᑎᒡᔅᒡᖕᑎᖕ
ᐱᖕᑎᒡᑕᐃᑎᐅᑯᑦᐃᖕᖑᖕᑎᖕ ᐊᓄᖕᒪᑦ, ᐊᒡᖕᒡᓂᒡ ᐊᒡᓗ
ᑎᑎᒡᑳᒡᖕᑎᖕ.

ᒪᐊᖓᐅᖕᔾᐱ ᐅᐅᖕᐱᖕ ᒐᑯᐊᖕᖑ ᐊᓄᖕᒡ ᖕᖑᐅᖕᒡ
ᐅᓂᖕᑑᖕᖕᔾᔅᒡᑰᖕ ᐃᓄᖕᒡ. ᐃᖕᒡᔾᐊᑦ ᐃᖕᑎᖕᖕᔾᔅᒡᑰᖕ
ᐃᐅᑐᒡ ᐊᓄᖕ ᑭᖕᐊᓄ ᖕᑕᒐᖕᔅᑦ.

Hanging Fish

After the fish have been caught, the people have to hang them up to dry and to freeze. They cannot leave the fish under the snow, or the polar bear or wolf or fox could find the fish and eat it.

Here the snowy owl sees the polar bear coming and warns the people. They take the fish with them inside the iglus and wait for the bear to go away. Then they will hang the fish up again.

Okpik watches over his people and makes sure that their food is safe.

Inuit Normee Ekoomiak uses the native art of felt appliqué stitching and acrylic paintings to show scenes from his Eskimo childhood. He recalls the fishing and hunting aspects of his life and records them in the Inuktitut language and English. (*Arctic Memories*)

of the night in the desert. . . .
Pitter . . . Patter . . .
But what's that?
Pit . . . Pat . . . Pit . . . Pat . . .
Oh, yes. It's my good friend
the rain.

Daniel Poler

Fiction

Picture Books. Our insistence on having books written or at least evaluated by members inside the culture continues to be a valid position. The same criterion applies to the illustrator as well. Edith Tony, teacher at the Chuska Boarding School on a Navajo reservation in Tohatchie, New Mexico, discussed **Knots on a Counting Rope** (P) by Bill Martin, Jr., and John Archambault and illustrated by Ted Rand. She said, "The story is wonderful and, yes, it is a Navajo story. But the illustrator ruined it. He put Plains Indians in the pictures! They should be Navajos. Everybody knows that Plains Indians are dead—and we're not dead." The art must be culturally authentic, too.

Novels. ***Morning Girl*** (I–A) by Michael Dorris is told in first-person voices in alternating chapters by 12-year-old Morning Girl and her slightly younger brother, Star Boy. They are Taino Indians who live on a Bahamian island in 1492. Morning Girl and Star Boy see things differently and are mostly at odds with each other, but they eventually achieve an understanding between themselves and their wider community. An ominous ending closes the story—Morning Girl sees an odd-looking canoe filled with strangers coming toward their island. She predicts they will invite the strangers to join them in a meal and it will be a memorable day. The epilogue contains the entry Columbus wrote in

Figure 11-5

Native American Literature

Folklore

Bierhorst, John (editor). *The Girl Who Married a Ghost and Other Tales from the North American Indian.* (I–A)

———. *The Mythology of North America.* (A)

———. *The Ring in the Prairie: A Shawnee Legend.* (I)

———. *A Cry from the Earth: Music of the North American Indians.* (I–A)

———. *Doctor Coyote.* (I)

———. *The Sacred Path: Spells, Prayers, and Power Songs of the American Indians.* (I–A)

de Paola, Tomie. *The Legend of the Indian Paintbrush.* (P–I)

Dixon, Ann. *How Raven Brought Light to People.* Illus. James Watts. (P–I)

Goble, Paul. *Crow Chief: A Plains Indian Story.* (I)

———. *Death of the Iron Horse.* (P–I)

———. *Her Seven Brothers.* (P–I)

———. *Iktomi and the Boulder: A Plains Indian Story.* (P–I)

———. *Iktomi and the Berries: A Plains Indian Story.* (P–I)

———. *Iktomi and the Ducks: A Plains Indian Story.* (P–I)

———. *Iktomi and the Buffalo Skull: A Plains Indian Story.* (P–I)

Harris, Christie. *Once Upon a Totem.* (I–A)

———. *Once More Upon a Totem.* (I–A)

———. *Mouse Woman and the Vanished Princesses.* (I–A)

———. *The Trouble with Princesses.* (I–A)

Highwater, Jamake. *Anpao: An American Indian Odyssey.* (I–A)

MacGill-Callahan, Sheila. *And Still the Turtle Watched.* Illus. Barry Moser. (P)

Martin, Rafe. *The Rough-Face Girl.* Illus. David Shannon. (P–I)

Monroe, Jean Guard, and Ray A. Williamson. *They Dance in the Sky.* illus. Edgar Stewart. (I–A)

Osofsky, Audrey. *Dream-catcher.* (Ojibway) (P–I)

Oughton, Jerrie. *How the Stars Fell into the Sky.* Illus. Lisa Desimini. (P–I)

Rodanas, Kristina (reteller/illus.) *Dragonfly's Tale.* (P–I)

Siberell, Anne (reteller and illus.) *The Whale in the Sky.* (P–I)

Taylor, C. J. *How Two-Feather Was Saved from Loneliness.* (P–I)

Poetry

Baylor, Byrd. *The Other Way to Listen.* (P–I)

Bierhorst, John. *A Cry from the Earth: Music of the North American Indians.* (P–I–A)

Bruchac, Joseph, and Jonathan London. *Thirteen Moons on Turtle's Back: A Native American Year of Moons.* Illus. Thomas Locker. (P–I–A)

Clark, Ann Nolan. *In My Mother's House.* Illus. Velino Herrera. (P–I)

---

his diary that day—these "were a people poor in everything." The bitter irony of his comment stings.

In a novel by David Carkeet, **Quiver River** (A), Ricky works at a summer resort in the Sierra mountains. He becomes involved in helping the ghost of a Miwok Indian boy reach manhood through his initiation rites. Ricky has his own struggles with reaching manhood and his efforts lead to humorous situations.

Nonfiction and Biography

Two photo essays by Diane Hoyt-Goldsmith contain information about Native Americans. One book with photographs by Lawrence Migdale is about a popular subject—**Totem Pole** (P). The story is told by David, a half white, half Indian boy (white mother), whose father is carving the totem pole. David is proud of his heritage and the tradition of his Tsimshian tribe, part of the Pacific Northwest

CONTINUED

Ferris, Susan. *Children of the Great Muskeg.* (Ontario) (I)

Hirschfelder, Arlene, and Beverly Singer. *Rising Voices: Writings of Young Native Americans.* (I–A)

Jones, Hettie. *The Trees Stand Shining: Poetry of the North American Indians.* Illus. Robert Andrew Parker. (P–I)

Van Laan, Nancy. *Rainbow Crow: A Lenape Tale.* Illus. Beatriz Vidal. (P–I)

Wood, Nancy. *Many Winters.* (I–A)

Picture Books

Baker, Olaf. *Where the Buffaloes Begin.* Illus. Stephen Gammell. (P)

Buchanan, Ken. *This House Is Made of Mud.* Illus. Libba Tracy. (P–I)

Yolen, Jane. *Sky Dogs.* Illus. Barry Moser. (P)

Novels

Hill, Kirkpatrick. *Toughboy and Sister.* (A)

Hobbs, Will. *Bearstone.* (A)

Hudson, Jan. *Dawn Rider.* (A)

———. *Sweetgrass.* (I–A)

O'Dell, Scott, and Elizabeth Hall. *Thunder Rolling in the Mountains.* (A)

Rohmer, Harriet, Octavia Chow and Morris Vidaure. *The Invisible Hunters.* Illus. Joe Sam. (I–A)

Spinka, Penina Keen. *Mother's Blessing.* (I)

Wosmek, Frances. *A Brown Bird Singing.* (I)

Nonfiction

Freedman, Russell. *Children of the Wild West.* (I–A)

———. *Buffalo Hunt.* (I–A)

———. *Cowboys of the Wild West.* (I–A)

———. *An Indian Winter.* (I–A)

Hoyt-Goldsmith, Diane. *Pueblo Storyteller.* Photos Lawrence Migdale. (I)

Jacobs, Francine. *The Tainos.* (I–A)

Keegan, Marcia (author/photographer). *Pueblo Boy: Growing Up in Two Worlds.* (P–I)

Kendall, Russ. *Eskimo Boy: Life in an Inupiaq Eskimo Village.* (I)

King, J. C. H. *Arctic Hunters.* (I–A)

Peters, Russell. *Clambake: A Wampanoag Tradition.* Photos by John Madama. (I–A)

Regguinti, Gordon. *The Sacred Harvest: Ojibway Wild Rice Gathering.* Photos by Dale Kakkak. (I–A)

Shemie, Bonnie. *Houses of Bark.* (I)

Yolen, Jane. *Encounter.* (P–I–A)

Biography

Ekoomiak, Normee. *Arctic Memories.* (Inuit in Arctic Quebec) (I)

Freedman, Russell. *Indian Chiefs.* (I–A)

Sufrin, M. *George Catlin: Painter of the Indian West.* (I–A)

Coast Indians who had distinctive meanings for each image on the totem pole. The other book, **Pueblo Storyteller** (P), is about a young Cochiti Indian girl. April, the girl, celebrates her family heritage made visible through Cochiti pottery and storytelling. The book concludes with a telling of a Pueblo legend.

Another informational book by Richard Red Hawk combines an opportunity for children to learn the alphabet with learning about American Indian culture in **A, B, C's: The American Indian Way** (P–I). The book features people, places, and objects from Native American culture organized according to the alphabet.

Russell Freedman wrote about six western **Indian Chiefs** (A), namely Sitting Bull of the Hunkpapa Sioux, Red Cloud of the Oglala Sioux, Joseph of the Nez Percé, Quanah Parker of the Comanche,

---

TEACHING IDEA 11-3

Common Folkloric Elements Across Cultures

Ask your students to read the folklore of several cultural groups. Discuss some of the following points:

1. What parallel characters appear? Who are the tricksters, the noodle-heads, the one who sacrifices for another?

2. What kind of animals appear? Which folklore includes ravens, eagles, wolves, bears, rabbits, terrapins?

3. Some cultures include magical objects in their stories. Discuss the kinds of objects and the powers they have: a rose, a ring, a spindle, an amulet, a bone and sinew of a caribou, a stone, a doll. See if the magical objects differ within and across cultural groups.

4. Make a patchwork quilt of the folklore studied. Find common threads and unique patterns. Put symbols from the cultural groups and their folktales into the patches. Bind the patches together with threads holding all the patches together. Make a border with symbols common to many groups.

Satanta of the Kiowa, and Washakie of the Shoshoni. The story of the courageous Native Americans who led the resistance to whites taking over their western lands is a tragic one. They had roamed the country freely and did not understand why that should change. For example, Sitting Bull insisted that his people should be able to live freely in the Black Hills and the Powder River country, as promised by the Treaty of Fort Laramie. He said, "The Great Spirit made me an Indian, but not a reservation Indian, and I don't intend to become one!" Freedman lightens the story of broken treaties and deadly battles with touches of humor. For example, while fleeing from the army in 1877, the Nez Percé paced themselves to stay two days ahead of General Howard; they began to call him "General Day-After-Tomorrow."

The Native American way of life ended as a result of encroachments, reprisals, and broken treaties, but the legendary heroes leave a rich heritage. Freedman's human interest approach to his subjects gives us a better understanding of the Indian chiefs as real people. He includes excellent photographs from numerous university and national archival collections.

Scott O'Dell contributes immensely to our understanding of Native Americans through many carefully researched historical fiction stories and biographies. His last book before his death, also about Joseph of the Nez Percé—**Thunder Rolling in the Mountains** (A)—is discussed in Chapter 8.

LITERATURE OF RELIGIOUS AND REGIONAL CULTURAL GROUPS

There are a number of factors that draw people together as a community—sometimes it is shared religion, a cultural heritage, geographic proximity, or a mix of several factors. In this section we look at the literature about groups based on religious, cultural, and geographic identity. These examples illustrate some of the many ways to look at culture through literature and to look at literature through a cultural lens.

Jewish-American Literature

Looking for books with Jewish characters is not so much a problem as finding ones that truly embody Jewish traditions. Teachers and librarians untrained in Jewish values, customs, and rituals sometimes identify books they believe to be appropriate, but on examination find the books contain only a superficial reflection of Jewish values. Some books that do reflect Jewish values may be of poor literary quality or may be intended primarily for religious instruction. Such books have limited appeal for the average reader. The most effective books for the general public use a subtle approach in which the values permeate the entire story and theme. Marcia Posner, leading authority in Jewish children's literature, points out that there are different readerships for even the most didactic books.

> In the world of Jewish books there is more than one marketplace—which is as it should be, because the book that fits one type of marketplace may not be right for another. Traditional Jews have their own standards for the books they will allow into their homes, schools, and libraries; and libraries in Reform synagogues will usually not want books suitable for traditional Jews.

Children's books for the Traditional (Orthodox) Jewish marketplace (from right-wing Orthodox to Modern Orthodox) must represent their beliefs. . . . On the other hand, because the books frequently deal with subjects not found elsewhere, and because of their increasing attractiveness, the books are often purchased and/or read by those outside the Orthodox community.

Posner, who conducts extensive research on identifying Jewish values and assessing their presence in children's literature, has written a number of useful guides: *Jewish Children's Books: How to Choose Them—How to Use Them,* and *Selected Jewish Children's Books.* The following are some of the criteria Posner uses to select books:

1. Is Jewish ritual behavior displayed? (everyday, on holidays, for life cycle events—in the home and in the synagogue)

2. Is involvement in Jewish education evident? Is respect for education per se, including secular education evident?

3. Is the responsibility of one Jew for another demonstrated?

4. Is the sense of "peoplehood," that of belonging to one family, shown?

5. Are the religious and secular roles of Israel recognized?

6. Are the effects of Jewish ethical teachings shown?

7. Do the characters care for the poor, the sick, the elderly?

8. Do they shown concern for social justice?

Posner cites a number of other ways Jewish identity can be displayed in books. A librarian by training and inclination, she makes it clear that Jewish content alone does not necessarily make a good book; it must first of all meet the accepted standards of good literature in general.

Folklore

Jewish folklore echoes the wry humor of Eastern European storytellers who can laugh at themselves and make jokes about their own foibles—or those of the arrogantly proud whether of riches or scholarship. Humility, a prime virtue in Jewish folklore derived from Eastern Europe, augurs against excessive pride. Some of the most poignant humor is ironic and, like black humor, is a defense against otherwise unbearable civil, religious, and political restrictions. Other folklore revolves around religious holidays and Jewish values. See Figure 11–6.

Donna Diamond's art looks so realistic that it could be a photograph. Nine-year-old Joshua spends each Friday night and Saturday with his grandmother, and each week they sort through memories from her remembering box. Here, grandmother and grandson focus on Sabbath candles that pull the viewer's attention upward toward the worshipper's faces and create the intensity of worship. (*The Remembering Box* by Eth Clifford)

Never before have so many collections of Jewish folklore been published. Among recent award-winning books: ***The Diamond Tree*** (I) by Howard Schwartz and Barbara Rush (Association of Jewish Libraries Sydney Taylor Award for Best Older Children's Book in 1992); ***My Grandmother's Stories*** (I) by Adele Geras (National Jewish Book Award for Children's Literature in 1990); and Eric Kimmel's ***Hershel and the Hanukkah Goblins*** (P), illustrated by Trina Schart Hyman (1991 Caldecott Honor Book).

Recognized as an eloquent and beloved spokesman who captures both Jewish and universal values

Figure 11-6

Jewish-American Literature

Folklore

Geras, Adele. *My Grand-mother's Stories: A Collection of Jewish Folk Tales.* Illus. Jael Jordan. (P–I)

Hirsch, Marilyn (adapter). *Joseph Who Loved the Sabbath.* Illus. Devis Grebu. (P–I)

Kimmel, Eric (adapter). *Days of Awe: Stories for Rosh Hashanah and Yom Kippur.* Illus. Erika Weihs. (I)

Schwartz, Howard, and Barbara Rush (retellers). *The Diamond Tree: Jewish Tales from around the World.* Illus. Uri Shulevitz. (I)

Singer, Isaac Bashevis. *Zlateh the Goat and Other Stories.* Illus. Maurice Sendak. (I)

———. *Stories for Children.* (I–A)

Poetry

Hirsh, Marilyn. *One Little Goat: A Passover Song.* (P)

Livingston, Myra Cohn. *Poems for Jewish Holidays.* (P–I–A)

Children in Theresienstadt Concentration Camp. *I Never Saw Another Butterfly.* (I)

Picture Books

Cech, John. *My Grandmother's Journey.* Illus. Sharon McGinley-Nally. (P)

Cohen, Barbara. *Gooseberries to Oranges.* (P–I)

———. *Molly's Pilgrim.* (P–I)

Edwards, Michelle. *Chicken Man.* (P)

Levine, Arthur A. *All the Lights in the Night.* Illus. James E. Ransome. (P)

Oppenheim, Shulamith Levey. *The Lily Cupboard.* Illus. Ronald Himler. (P)

Polacco, Patricia. *The Keeping Quilt.* (P)

———. *Mrs. Katz and Tush.* (P)

Rosen, Michael J. *Elijah's Angel: A Story for Chanukah and Christmas.* Illus. Aminah Brenda Lynn Robinson. (P)

Schwartz, Amy. *Mrs. Moskowitz and the Sabbath Candlesticks.* (P)

Treseder, Terry Walton. *Hear O Israel: A Story of the Warsaw Ghetto.* Illus. Lloyd Bloom. (A)

Novels

Clifford, Eth. *The Remembering Box.* (P–I)

Hahn, Mary Downing. *Stepping on the Cracks.* (I–A)

Kushner, Arlene. *Falasha No More: An Ethiopian Jewish Child Comes Home.* (A)

Laird, C. *Shadow of the Wall.* (A)

Lasky, Kathryn. *The Night Journey.* (I–A)

Levitin, Sonia. *The Return.* (A)

Moskin, Marietta. *I Am Rosemarie.* (A)

Orlev, Uri. *The Island on Bird Street.* (A)

———. *The Man from the Other Side.* (A)

Richter, H. P. *Friedrich.* (I)

Roth-Hano, R. *Touch Wood: A Girlhood in Occupied France.* (A)

Segal, Jerry. *The Place Where Nobody Stopped.* Illus. Dav Pilkey. (A)

Sherman, Eileen Bluestone. *Monday in Odessa.* (A)

Nonfiction

Burstein, Chaya. *The Jewish Kid's Catalog.* (I–A)

---

in his work, Isaac Bashevis Singer's stories represent the best available to children today. See the profile in Chapter 5 for a discussion of his books.

Poetry

Contemporary poets write about cultural traditions in poetry and prose, for example, Myra Cohn Livingston's **Poems for Jewish Holidays** (P–I), and Jean Little's collection **Hey World! Here I Am!** (P–I),

which combines both prose and poetry. In one selection, "Feeling Jewish," Little describes how Kate and Emily feel like the other person after reading what they have written.

Fiction

Picture Books. Many excellent writers in the Jewish tradition draw on their heritage for picture storybooks. Folklore has proven to be not only a rich

CONTINUED

Chaikin, Miriam. *Light Another Candle: The Story and Meaning of Hanukkah.* (P–I)

———. *Make Noise, Make Merry: The Story and Meaning of Purim.* (P–I)

———. *Shake a Palm Branch: The Story and Meaning of Sukkot.* (P–I)

———. *Ask Me Another Question: The Story and Meaning of Passover.* (P–I)

———. *Sound the Shofar: The Story and Meaning of Rosh Hashanah.* (P–I)

Drucker, Malka. *Celebrating Life: Jewish Rites of Passage.* (I–A)

Meltzer, Milton. *Remember the Days.* (A)

———. *World of Our Fathers.* (A)

———. *Taking Root: Jewish Immigrants in America.* (A)

———. *The Jewish Americans: A History in Their Own Words, 1650–1950.* (A)

———. *Never to Forget: The Jews of the Holocaust.* (A)

Shamir, Ilana, and Shlomo Shavit (editors). *The Young Reader's Encyclopedia of Jewish History.* (I–A)

Biography

Atkinson, Linda. *In Kindling Flame: The Story of Hannah Senesh, 1921–1944.* (A)

Bernheim, M. *Father of the Orphans: The Story of Janusz Korczak.* (A)

Bober, Natalie. *Breaking Tradition: The Story of Louise Nevelson.* (A)

Cowen, Ida, and Irene Gunther. *A Spy for Freedom: The Story of Sarah Aaronsohn.* (A)

Frank, Anne. *The Diary of a Young Girl.* (I–A)

Gross, David. *Justice Felix Frankfurter: A Justice for All the People.* (A)

Isaacman, C. *Clara's Story, as Told to Joan Adess Grossman.* (I–A)

Krantz, Hazel. *Daughter of My People: Henrietta Szold and Hadassah.* (A)

Kresh, Paul. *Isaac Bashevis Singer: The Story of a Storyteller.* (I–A)

———. *An American Rhapsody: The Story of George Gershwin.* (A)

Levinson, Nancy Smiler. *I Lift My Lamp: Emma Lazarus and the Statue of Liberty.* (I)

Schur, Maxine. *Hannah Szenes: A Song of Light.* (A)

Siegal, Aranka. *Upon the Head of a Goat: A Childhood in Hungary 1939–1944.* (A)

———. *Grace in the Wilderness: After the Liberation, 1945–1948.* (A)

lode for picture storybook adaptations but also an inspiration for original tales with a folk flavor that embody similar values. Eric Kimmel and Barbara Diamond Goldin, both established writers, have published wonderful picture books that draw on Jewish legends, for example, Barbara Diamond Goldin's *Just Enough Is Plenty: A Hanukkah Tale* (P), illustrated by Seymour Chwast, and Eric Kimmel's *The Chanukkah Guest* (P), illustrated by Giora Carmi. These picture books are outstanding.

Novels. Eth Clifford's *The Remembering Box* (P–I) is a tender story about 9-year-old Joshua who spends every Friday night with his grandmother. Joshua and his grandmother observe their Jewish traditions from lighting the Sabbath candles to reading from the Torah. Her love stays with Joshua after her death.

Uri Orlev's gripping novel, *The Man from the Other Side* (A), is for more mature students. Marek, a Polish boy, begins taking food and weapons to

James Ransome's glowing oil paintings reflect the lantern light in the boys' faces as they kneel in a prayerful mood. (*All the Lights in the Night* by Arthur A. Levine)

people in the Warsaw Ghetto during World War II. Eventually he helps his stepfather smuggle Jews through the dangerous sewers, out of the ghetto, and to "the other side." The other side is the free side of the wall surrounding the Warsaw Ghetto, and the tension mounts each time Marek returns. The story conveys Marek's deep convictions and the courage he draws from to act on them. Another powerful Orlev book, *Island on Bird Street* (A), is also set in the Warsaw Ghetto.

Nonfiction and Biography

Never to Forget (A) is one of Milton Meltzer's most poignant books. Instead of chronicling the bitter facts of the Holocaust, Meltzer provides eyewitness accounts through the letters, diaries, journals, and memoirs of those who experienced the terror and grief. Meltzer asks,

> How could it have happened?
> It did not occur in a vacuum. It was the logical outcome of certain conditions of life. Given the antihuman nature of Nazi beliefs,

the crime of the Holocaust could be expected. We see that now. That it happened once, unbelievable as it seems, means it could happen again. Hitler made it a possibility for anyone. Neither the Jews nor any other group on earth can feel safe from that crime in the future.

That is the reason underlying Meltzer's title: We must never forget, lest it should happen again.

Mark Bernheim wrote *Father of the Orphans: The Story of Janusz Korczak* (A), a biography about a doctor who behaved nobly in the face of tyranny during World War II. Janusz Korczak believed and demonstrated that any child could be molded into a productive adult through love and understanding. When his Polish-Jewish orphans were captured by Hitler's troops, he followed them into the ovens of Treblinka. Janusz Korczak also appears in Christa Laird's novel, *Shadow of the Wall* (A). This story is told from the point of view of 14-year-old Misha who lives in the Orphans' Home founded by Dr. Korczak. Misha joins the Resistance to fight Nazi oppression.

Regional Literature: Southeastern United States

Every region has its natural beauty, cultural traditions, folklore, dialect, traditional foods, and unique manners or mannerisms. The culture of the southeastern United States is particularly colorful and charming. See books listed in Figure 11–7.

Folklore

Richard Chase is one of the major folklorists who has collected Appalachian stories. In *Grandfather Tales: American English Folk Tales* (P–I), Chase tells how "Bobtail beat the devil" and other stories heard in North Carolina and Virginia. In *Jack Tales: Set Down from These Sources and Edited by Richard Chase* (I), he tells of Jack's adventures with giants before and after Jack climbs the bean tree. Gail Haley retells the story in *Jack and the Bean Tree* (I), couched in lilting mountain folk speech patterns and rhythms. William Hooks retells an Appalachian version of *Three Little Pigs and the Fox* (P–I). Hooks says that Rooter and Oinky were too busy to mind their mother when she warned them to "Watch out for the mean, tricky old drooly-mouth fox; build a safe, strong house, and come home every Sunday." Their sister, Hamlet, gets along better out in the world than they do.

Poetry

In an introductory note to a lively collection, Gerald Milnes explains how he came to hear the rhymes in ***Granny Will Your Dog Bite and Other Mountain Rhymes*** (P–I–A). The rhymes, part of the culture of the Southern Appalachian region, are recorded on audiotape available with the book.

Cynthia Rylant's work adds to the poetry and prose of the southeastern region. In a poetry collection, a small town ***Soda Jerk*** (A) views his customers in insightful ways. In ***Waiting to Waltz: A Childhood*** (I–A) Rylant allows us to look inside a childhood journal to share the feelings of a girl growing up in a small Appalachian town. Her crystal clear images convey poignant moments of childhood.

Fiction

Picture Books. Cynthia Rylant repeats the phrase ***"When I Was Young in the Mountains"*** (P) as she recounts her memories of growing up. The memories include going to an outside johnny house, draping a dead snake across her shoulders, eating okra, being baptized, and sitting on the porch swing shelling beans. Rylant's prose sounds like poetry. Diane Goode's illustration merited the book a Caldecott Honor Award.

Gloria Houston's ***Year of the Perfect Christmas Tree*** (P–I), illustrated by Barbara Cooney, is the story of a child in 1918 whose father must go off to war. While he is gone she and her mother carry out his promise to bring the perfect Christmas tree he had found into the village church. In a heartwarming scene, the father returns on Christmas Eve as the tree is lighted.

Novels. Cynthia Rylant, one of our finest writers, received the 1993 Newbery Medal for ***Missing May*** (I). Twelve-year-old Summer was orphaned when she was 6, but Aunt May and Uncle Ob raise her with all the love and devotion an elderly West Virginia couple who had hoped for, but never believed they'd be blessed with, a child hold in store. Their boundless, unconditional love supports and sustains Summer in ways she has never known. But Aunt May dies and, although Summer is grief stricken, it is Uncle Ob who seems unable to go on without May. Uncle Ob gives up even trying to find a reason to live. Cletus Underwood, Summer's classmate, helps Uncle Ob find some new resolve—much to Summer's surprise and chagrin. In fact, Cletus, Uncle Ob, and Summer drive to another county to search for a spiritualist preacher who claims to be able to get in touch with people who

Barbara Cooney's art leads the viewer up the mountainside to its very peak, following Gloria Houston's heartwarming story of family love. The young girl ties a bright red ribbon to mark the tree that symbolizes a forthcoming family celebration. (***Year of the Perfect Christmas Tree***)

have "passed on." Uncle Ob hopes to talk with Aunt May. When they learn the preacher herself has died, it appears that Uncle Ob will allow his sorrow to engulf him. As they are driving mournfully homeward, Uncle Ob suddenly "turns that buggy around" and heads toward the state capitol building with its gold dome—a place Cletus had dreamed of exploring. The turnaround goes far deeper than a route change, and the three strange companions find consolation in their memories and in each other. Rylant captures the feeling and mood of West Virginia mountain people; she tells the story in language that catches the sounds and expressions of mountain people. She gives substance to the concept of love and defines the process of grieving in heartrending terms.

Carol Saller describes the quiet strength of a mountain family in ***The Bridge Dancers*** (I). The story focuses on 11-year-old Maisie who helps her mother collect herbs to use in healing the sick. When her sister Callie injures herself, Maisie uses her knowledge of herbal medicines to deal with Callie's emergency. On one level the story is about accepting differences in others; on another it is

Figure 11-7

Regional Books: Southeastern United States

Folklore

Harris, Joel Chandler. *Jump: The Adventures of Brer Rabbit.* (P–I)

Peek, Merle. *Mary Wore Her Red Dress and Henry Wore His Green Sneakers.* (P)

Sanders, S. R. *Hear the Wind Blow: American Folk Songs Retold.* (P–I–A)

Zemach, Margot, *Mommy Buy Me a China Doll.* (P)

Poetry

Lindbergh, Reeve. *Legend of Johnny Appleseed: A Poem.* (P–I)

Picture Books

Houston, Gloria. *Year of the Perfect Christmas Tree.* Illus. Barbara Cooney. (P)

O'Kelley, Mattie Lou. *A Winter Place.* (P–I)

———. *The Hills of Georgia.* (P–I)

Rylant, Cynthia. *Miss Maggie.* Illus. Thomas DiGrazia. (P–I)

———. *The Relatives Came.* Illus. Stephen Gammell. (P)

———. *When I Was Young in the Mountains.* Illus. Diane Goode. (P)

Novels and Short Stories

Caudill, Rebecca. *Did You Carry the Flag Today, Charley?* (P–I)

Cleaver, Vera. *Kissimmee Kid.* (Florida) (I)

———. *Trial Valley.* (Appalachian mountains) (A)

———. *Where the Lilies Bloom.* (Appalachian mountains) (I–A)

Griffiths, Helen V. *Foxy.* (Florida Keys) (I)

Houston, Gloria. *Littlejim.* (North Carolina) (A)

Lawson, John. *You Better Come Home With Me.* (mountains) (I–A)

Marino, Jan. *The Day That Elvis Came to Town.* (Georgia) (A)

Paterson, Katherine. *Jacob Have I Loved.* (Chesapeake Bay) (A)

Rawlings, Marjorie. *Yearling.* (I–A)

Ross, Rhea Beth. *Hillbilly Choir.* (Arkansas) (A)

Rylant, Cynthia. *Missing May.* (West Virginia) (I)

Smith, Doris Buchanan. *Return to Bitter Creek.* (I)

Taylor, Mildred. *Mississippi Bridge.* (A)

Tilly, Nancy. *Golden Girl.* (A)

Wilkinson, Brenda. *Ludell.* (A)

Nonfiction and Biography

Anderson, J. *From Map to Museum.* (A)

———. *Pioneer Children of Appalachia.* (I)

Bial, Raymond (author/photographer). *County Fair.* (I)

Ewald, W. *Portraits and Dreams: Photographs and Stories by Children of the Appalachians.* (I)

Fradin, D. B. *Georgia Colony.* (I–A)

Kent, Z. *Georgia.* (I)

Rylant, Cynthia. *Appalachia: The Voices of Sleeping Birds.* Illus. Barry Moser. (I)

Thompson, Kathleen. *Pedro Menendez de Aviles.* (Florida) (I–A)

---

about finding courage and recognizing talents—and on still another it is about using nature to heal ourselves.

Nonfiction and Biography

When Leslie Schulten of Atlanta, Georgia, began a peace project, she had no idea it would culminate in a family trip to the Soviet Republic of Georgia, but that is exactly what happened. The trip, described in *Georgia to Georgia: Making Friends in the U.S.S.R.* (P–I) by Laurie Dolphin, is told from the perspective of Leslie's son. The pictorial record is provided through photographs by E. Alan McGee.

Mattie Lou O'Kelley, a primitive painter in the style of Grandma Moses, describes her life in rural Georgia during the first half of the twentieth century in *From the Hills of Georgia: An Autobiography*

I REMEMBER Mama talking about when I was born, March 30, 1908. There were three brothers and three sisters waiting for me: Willie, Lillie, Gertrude, Ruth, Tom, and Ben. Mama had a doctor for the first time. I don't know how many women friends were there to help, but I did survive the name they gave me—Emily Mattie Lou.

EMILY MATTIE ARRIVES

Mattie Lou O'Kelley's primitive style appropriately portrays the hooked rugs and antique detail of this turn-of-the-century childhood home of the author artist. (*From the Hills of Georgia*)

in Paintings (P–I). Her scenes are filled with details of a birthing room, remodeling the house, family dinners, celebrations, and climbing the mountains. It is an unusual and colorful autobiography.

EXCHANGE AMONG CULTURES

International Literature: Stories of the Present

In the previous sections of this chapter, we discussed culturally diverse books—those dealing with four specific cultural groups (African, Asian, Latino, Native American) and two dealing with religious and regional groups (Jewish and the southeastern United States). In the first section here, we discuss multicultural books that deal with intermingling cultures within one country. In the second section, we discuss books that describe exchanges between

TEACHING IDEA 11-4

History Makers From All Cultural Groups

Increase your students' cultural awareness of how various groups contribute to the patchwork quilt of America. Have them select and read biographies of people who have made significant contributions to the United States. Contributions may come through the arts, music, dance, politics, sports, writing, or inventions. Plan a "Living Picture" presentation in which they present their subject and tell about that person's life. Choose from books in figures in this chapter or biographies listed in Chapter 9.

Bouncing braids, bare feet, and vivid colors speak volumes about the joy of playing hopscotch in Peru. (*Hopscotch Around the World,* by Mary D. Lankford, illustrated by Karen Milone)

cultures in the past—unfortunately, most often, war. Finally, we discuss cross-cultural books—those that come from one country to another in an international exchange. These books were first published in another country and brought to the United States later or co-published simultaneously.

The goal of creating a more equitable society requires that people from many backgrounds learn to live together peaceably. If we understand people of other cultures and other nations, it is difficult to view them as being on a different side in times of conflict.

Children can begin to know people of other lands through literature; they can recognize similarities between themselves and others. They can understand universal qualities of humankind. Although we do not *use* literature to teach lessons of tolerance, developing understanding of others is a natural outgrowth of reading it.

Teachers, librarians, parents, writers, and publishers are aware that we need to understand each other and to develop a multicultural literature. As a result, there are more multicultural books published today than ever before. Galda (1993) in "One World, One Family" states that publishing multicultural books has reached an all-time high. She attributes the growth to the demand from teachers, librarians, and parents.

Multicultural books show interaction between one or more cultural groups within one country. They portray kindness between African Americans and Jewish Americans, for example, Michael J. Rosen's *Elijah's Angel: A Story for Chanukah and Christmas* (P), Robert Lehrman's *The Store That Mama Built* (I–A), Jill Pinkwater's *Tails of the Bronx: A Tale of the Bronx* (I), Patricia Polacco's *Chicken Sunday* (P) and *Mrs. Katz and Tush* (P), and Barbara Ann Porte's *Harry Gets an Uncle* (P–I).

Other international multicultural books show that children do the same things the world around. For example, Mary Lankford presents 19 different versions of *Hopscotch Around the World* (P). Jane Yolen shares *Street Rhymes Around the World* (P) in both English and the native language. The illustrations were painted by artists native to the country of origin of each street rhyme.

Norah Dooley's nonfiction picture book, *Everybody Cooks Rice* (P), illustrates an integrated multicultural view. Carrie finds that everybody is cooking some sort of rice when she wanders about her multicultural neighborhood looking for her little brother. Her neighbors come from Haiti, China, Vietnam, and elsewhere, all with favorite rice recipes, some of which are included.

Other books show us how much we are alike through travel and friendship as in Claire Murphy's

Friendship Across Arctic Waters (I). This documentary shows 11 Alaskan Cub Scouts visiting the Soviet Union. Ken Heyman's photographs and Ann Morris's text work together to present a variety of cultures in ***Houses and Homes*** (P). The stories of the present convey an easy interaction among varied cultural groups.

International Literature: Stories of the Past

It may seem incongruous to tell children about past wars in the hope of assuring peace, but we know it is necessary. Children understand tragedies best by hearing about them in narratives. Stories of the past must be told over and over again to each new generation of children. One group states:

> [Children] have to be told the lessons of maturity long before they are mature. But slogans can't be relied upon to spread the meaning of the maturity a peaceful mankind will require. The poetry and drama of individual experience, the fragile wonder of individual discovery, the mysterious resolve of those willing and able to stand alone—all this has to be continually renewed, or even born for the first time, in the young.

Literature is a compelling way to hand down the poetry and drama of individual experience. The fragile wonder of discovery cast in first-person accounts by authors who write with passion becomes a plea to make the world a safe place for children.

International stories of the past are overshadowed by the enormity of the inhumanity of the Holocaust, the Nazi extermination of six million Jews during World War II. The tragedy is difficult to fathom but the facts stand stark and clear. ***The Diary of a Young Girl*** (I–A), one of the first pieces of literature to appear after the war, contains the actual words that a 13-year-old Jewish girl, Anne Frank, wrote during the two years she and her family were hiding in an old Amsterdam warehouse. The innocent and honest introspection of a young girl caught up in survival has moments of pathos and shows the abiding sweetness of a loving child.

A number of books tell the heartbreaking story of what happened to Anne when she and her family were captured. The process of documenting the authenticity of Anne's handwriting is described in some; others contain photographs of Anne and excerpts from her other writings. Some are listed in Figure 11-8. There are also books that show cooper-

The torn photograph, the scattered grains of rice, the barbed wire, and the symbolic red cross suggest images of the character's Asian-American background and the unavoidable heartache. (***Year of Impossible Goodbyes*** by Sook Nyul Choi)

ation between Gentiles and Jews, like ***Rescue*** (A) by Milton Meltzer.

Multicultural books that relate stories from the past are discussed throughout this text. See, for example, ***So Far from the Bamboo Grove*** (A) by Yoko Kawashima Watkins, ***The Road from Home: The Story of an Armenian Girl*** (A) by David Kherdian, and ***Year of Impossible Goodbyes*** (A) by Sook Nyul Choi.

International Literature: Cross-Cultural Understanding

When Neil Armstrong was hurtling around the world in a space capsule in outer space, he said that looking back at Earth was like looking at a big blue marble. His comment made us aware that our "marble" is not a very big one and that what happens in one part of it affects every other part. The telephone company slogan reminds us—we're

**Figure
11-8**

Books About Other Countries

Stories of the Present

Ashabranner, Brent. *The Arab-American Minority.* (Middle East) (I–A)

Buss, Fran Leeper, and Daisy Cubias. *Journey of the Sparrows.* (A)

Case, Dianne. *Love, David.* (Cape Flats of South Africa) (I)

Castaneda, Omar S. *Among the Volcanoes.* (Mayan family, Guatemala) (I)

Dorros, Arthur. *This Is My House.* (P–I)

Fox, Paula. *Lily and the Lost Boy.* (Greek Islands) (A)

Gordon, Sheila. *The Middle of Somewhere: A Story of South Africa.* (A)

————. *Waiting for the Rain: A Novel of South Africa.* (A)

Heide, Florence Parry, and Judith Heide Gilliland. *The Day of Ahmed's Secret.* Illus. Ted Lewin. (Cairo, Egypt) (P–I)

Hicyilmaz, Gaye. *Against the Storm.* (Turkey) (I–A)

Hirst, Robin, and Sally Hirst. *My Place in Space.* Illus. Roland Harvey. With Joe Levine. (Gumbridge, Australia) (P)

Isadora, Rachel. *Over the Green Hills.* (P)

Jenness, Aylette. *In Two Worlds: A Yup'ik Eskimo Family.* (P–I)

Knight, Margy Burns. *Talking Walls.* Illus. Anne Sibley O'Brien. (P)

Kuklin, Susan. *How My Family Lives in America.* (P–I)

Lankford, Mary. *Hopscotch Around the World.* Illus. Karen Milone. (P–I)

Maartens, Maretha. *Paper Bird.* (South Africa) (A)

Mennen, Ingrid, and Niki Daly. *Somewhere in Africa.* Illus. Nicolas Maritz. (Cape Town, South Africa). (A)

Morris, Ann. *Houses and Homes.* Photos by Ken Heyman. (P–I)

Murphy, Claire. *Friendship Across Arctic Waters.* Photos by Charles Mason. (I–A)

Naidoo, Beverley. *Chain of Fire.* (South Africa) (A)

————. *Journey to Jo'burg.* (South Africa) (A)

Rudolph, Marguerita. Adapted from Konstantin Ushinsky. *How a Shirt Grew in the Field.* Illus. Erika Weihs. (I)

Schermbrucker, Reviva. *Charlie's House.* Illus. Niki Daly. (South Africa) (P)

Stock, Catherine (author/illus.). *Armien's Fishing Trip.* (South Africa) (P)

Williams, Karen Lynn. *Galimoto.* Illus. Catherine Stock. (Malawi, Africa. South Africa) (P)

Zheleznikov, Vladimir. *Scarecrow.* Transl. Antonina W. Bouis. (I)

Stories of the Past

Abells, Chana Byers. *The Children We Remember.* (P–I–A)

Adler, David A. *We Remember the Holocaust.* (I–A)

Bernbaum, Israel. *My Brother's Keeper: The Holocaust Through the Eyes of an Artist.* (I–A)

Chaikin, Miriam. *Nightmare in History: The Holocaust, 1933–1945.* (I–A)

Frank, Anne. *The Diary of a Young Girl.* (I–A)

Innocenti, Roberto. *Rose Blanche.* (P–I–A)

Marrin, Albert. *Hitler.* (A)

Meltzer, Milton. *Never to Forget: The Jews of the Holocaust.* (A)

————. *Rescue: The Story of How Gentiles Saved Jews in the Holocaust.* (A)

Rogasky, Barbara. *Smoke and Ashes: The Story of the Holocaust.* (A)

Schnabel, Ernest. *Anne Frank: A Portrait of Courage.* (A)

Schur, M. *Hannah Szenes; A Song of Light.* (A)

Siegal, A. *Grace in the Wilderness; After the Liberation 1945–48.* (A)

Steenmeijer, Anna. *A Tribute to Anne Frank.* (I–A)

𝒯EACHING IDEA 11-5

Exploring Social Issues in a Global Village

To expand your students' understanding of national and international social issues, have them do one or more of the following projects:

1. Read some of the books listed here. Write in their journal to reflect on what the books are saying. Discuss some of the shared meanings before choosing from the projects described.

2. Write to ecology agencies or the Environmental Protection Agency. Ask for free literature. Greenpeace, USA (2007 R Street, NW. Washington, DC 20009 (202) 462-1177) is an international organization focused on ecology. It has four main campaigns: wildlife conservation, ocean ecology, toxic waste, and disarmament.

3. During the Clinton-Gore campaign, Clinton said, "We don't want to come off sounding like some Greenpeace warriors." Gore replied, "Who is We, kemo sabe?" Discuss this interchange and what it means for governmental policy about the environment.

4. Become well informed about issues that relate to ecology. Start a scrapbook of articles in the news related to ecology. Make an ecology quilt. Design the quilt and work on sections with embroidery, fabric crayons, or other techniques. Display the quilt at the library or school. Raffle the quilt off and donate profits to a charity for the homeless or an environmental project.

Berck, Judith. *No Place to Be: Voices of Homeless Children.* (I) Of all the homeless children in the United States, one-half of them are in New York City. These are their poems and prose.

Brown, Laurie Krasny, and Marc Brown. *Dinosaurs to the Rescue!: A Guide to Protecting Our Planet.* (P–I) Dinosaurs show us how to change our habits and protect the earth. Slobosaurus finally follows the rules: Reduce, reuse, recycle.

Cone, Molly. *Come Back, Salmon.* Illus. Sidnee Wheelwright. (I) Jackson Elementary School in Everett, Washington, in conjunction with Adopt-a-Stream Foundation, adopted Pigeon Creek and brought it back to life.

Gibbons, Gail. *Recycle!: A Handbook for Kids.* (P–I) The growing garbage problem can be reduced by recycling, reusing, and avoiding some products. Organize cleanup crews.

all connected. Viewing our world as a global village makes it clear that children's literature should reflect the interdependence of nations and people around the world. See Figures 11–8, 11–9.

Living in a global village is an appropriate focus for a chapter on culturally diverse literature. Advanced communication technology and air travel make the world very small. The U.N. General Assembly regularly proclaims an International Year of Peace with goals about the need for people to practice tolerance and to live together amicably. During the Gulf War we were once again reminded of global interdependence.

Our goal is to work toward a world where all people can exercise their human rights and fundamental freedoms—a world where discrimination and apartheid are eliminated. Safeguarding the world and protecting the rights of humankind are one and the same. Most of the present and continuing conflicts in the world today revolve around peo-

ple who are denied their civil rights or their human rights. Nationalistic fervor and civil wars show that ethnic groups want recognition; they do not want to be swallowed up by an imposed authority. They want to retain their language, their customs, their traditions—in other words, their culture. They do not want to be homogenized. They want to retain their cultural identity.

The exchange of books among nations is widespread due to the ease of international travel and modern technology. Moreover, many authors and illustrators of children's books published in the United States live in England, Australia, Japan, Africa, and other parts of the world. Publishers from all over the world meet at book fairs in Israel, Italy, Germany, Spain, Mexico, Argentina, Brazil, Colombia, and elsewhere to buy manuscripts and arrange for co-publication of the same book in several languages. Thus children in many countries may read the very same book written in their native language.

Children's literature has become truly international.

In all countries there are many literatures shaped by many influences. In the United States, the countries that shaped the cultural groups have an increasing impact on the literature. People from all over the world discuss children's books through their work in professional organizations, namely the International Board on Books for Young People (IBBY), the United States Board on Books for Young People (USBBY), the American Library Association (ALA), the American Booksellers Association (ABA), the Modern Language Association (MLA), and the International Reading Association (IRA), among others. More than 50 countries were represented at the 23rd IBBY Congress in Berlin, Germany, in 1992. The prestigious Hans Christian Andersen Award, presented at the IBBY Congress, is given for the entire body of an author's and an illustrator's work. Nominees from all over the world are eligible. Winners are listed in Appendix A. The International Youth Library, located at Blutenburg Castle on the outskirts of Munich, Germany, is devoted to the collection, study, and propagation of international children's literature. An Associated Project of UNESCO since 1953, the International Youth Library was founded by Jella Lepman in 1948. The IBBY magazine, *Bookbird,* provides current information about children's literature from around the world. A community of friends from many countries has grown up around children's books.

When books present authentic images from another country, children learn a very important lesson. They recognize that although all cultures are distinct and different, all people share universal needs for love, belonging, and acceptance. They learn that all people share the need for family, friends, and neighbors; they all share the need for food, clothing, and shelter.

The books discussed in this section are primarily cross cultural—they come from countries outside the United States. They are set in countries around the world and, most often, were first published elsewhere. They were originally written in a language other than English and translated. They portray the universal republic of childhood—principles, values, and needs of children everywhere.

The Mildred L. Batchelder Award is given in the United States annually to the publisher of the most outstanding book of the year, first published in another country, and published in translation in the United States. Batchelder Award winners are found in *Children's Books of International Understanding,* cited in Appendix B. It is a source for good books from other countries. Figure 11-9 illustrates the kinds of books that come from other countries; it is not a comprehensive list.

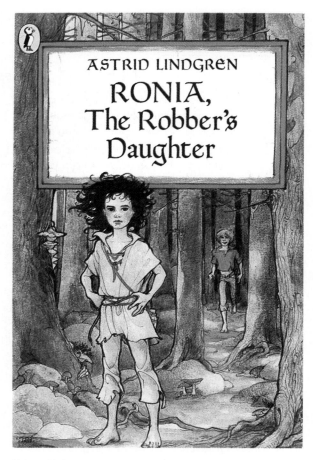

Trina Schart Hyman establishes the forest scene for Astrid Lindgren's story of a robber's daughter. Ronia, the daughter, stands courageously undaunted by her father's orders and restrictions. (*Ronia, the Robber's Daughter*)

Choosing only one book to examine closely is difficult when we would like to talk about them all. We were tempted to choose **Pippi Longstocking** (I), since it was one of the first and most successful books to begin the international exchange but because it is widely known, we chose another of Astrid Lindgren's books, **Ronia, The Robber's Daughter** (I–A), dust jacket illustration by Trina Schart Hyman.

The night Ronia is born a thunderstorm rages through Matt's Forest but in Matt's Castle among his band of robbers, there is wild celebration. Matt is overjoyed to have a daughter and is determined that Ronia will take her place as the new robber chieftain when he is ready to step down. He adores his black-haired daughter and allows not a single disapproving word said against her. The setting and the problem are quickly established; characterization develops rapidly.

Ronia is a spirited child given free rein of the robber kingdom, forest, and castle. Ronia feels

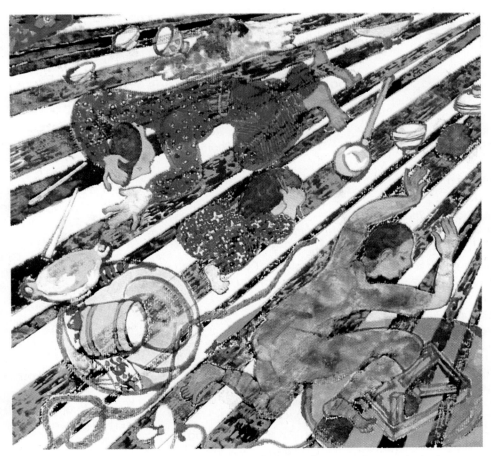

Toshi Maruki's art and diagonal lines convey the force and overwhelming chaos of the blast of the atomic bomb on Hiroshima. (***Hiroshima No Pika***)

most at home in Matt's Woods where she likes to spend endless hours alone. One day in the forest Ronia meets Birk, son of Borka, Matt's rival robber chieftain. The two children become friends and meet in the forest despite their fathers' warlike tactics.

The friendship between Ronia and Birk creates numerous problems for the rival chieftains, but Astrid Lindgren resolves the conflict in a believable and satisfying way. The theme can be interpreted differently by many readers but one reasonable meaning is that we can resolve conflicts when we truly know each other. Another is that children should not inherit their father's enemies.

Although the story is a fantasy, Lindgren clearly shares Swedish values: Ronia is a strong liberated female, she assumes a leadership position, she does her own bidding—not her father's, and she lives happily in Bear's Cave with Birk as she shapes her own future.

SUMMARY

The origins of children's literature are culturally mixed where many contribute and many receive. The tangled roots of all literature, certainly, lie in folklore, the ancient stories told since humans first learned to speak. According to Thackeray, many of the stories have been retold, almost in their present form, for thousands of years: "The very same tale has been heard by the Northmen Vikings, as they lay on their shields on deck; and by the Arabs, couched under the stars in the Syrian plains, when the flocks were gathered in, and the mares were picketed by the tents." Children's literature has international roots.

Children's books, however, are a recent development in the history of humankind. We explored the origins of early American children's books in Chapter 1. "The Story of Children's Literature." Here we discussed books that represent people

**Figure
11-9**

Books From Other Countries

France

Bemelmans, Ludwig. *Madeline.* (P)

Bjork, Christina. *Linnea in Monet's Garden.* Illus. Lena Anderson. (P–I)

Clement, Claude. *The Voice of the Wood.* Illus. Frederic Clement. (I)

Fatio, Louise. *The Happy Lion.* Illus. Roger Duvoisin. (P)

Solotareff, Gregoire. *Don't Call Me Little Bunny.* (P)

————. *Noel's Christmas Secret.* (P)

Titus, Eve. *Anatole.* (P)

Ungerer, Tomi. *Crictor.* (P–I)

Germany

Baumann, Hans. *In the Land of Ur.* Trans. Stella Humphries. (I–A)

Frank, Rudolf. *No Hero for the Kaiser.* Trans. Patricia Crampton. (I–A)

Hartling, Peter. *Crutches.* Trans. Elizabeth D. Crawford. (I–A)

Hurlimann, Ruth. *The Cat and Mouse Who Shared a House.* Trans. Anthea Bell. Illus. by author. (P–I)

Kastner, Erich. *The Little Man.* Trans. James Kirkup. Illus. Rick Schreiter. (I)

Nostlinger, Christine. *Konrad.* Illus. Carol Nicklaus. (I–A)

Richter, Hans Peter. *Friedrich.* Trans. Edite Kroll. (I)

Steiner, Jorg. *Rabbit Island.* Transl. Ann Conrad Lammers. Illus. Jorg Muller. (P–I)

Scandinavia

Aamundsen, Nina Ring. *Two Long and One Short.* (I)

Bjork, Christina. *Linnea's Almanac.* Illus. Lena Anderson. (P–I)

————. *Linnea's Windowsill Garden.* Illus. Lena Anderson. (P–I)

Lagercrantz, Rose, and Samuel Lagercrantz. *Is It Magic?* Illus. Eva Erikson. (P)

Lindgren, Astrid. *I Don't Want to Go to Bed.* Illus. Ilon Wikland. (P)

————. *I Want a Brother or Sister.* Illus. Ilon Wikland. (P)

————. *Lotta's Bike.* Illus. Ilon Wikland. (P–I)

————. *Pippi Longstocking.* (I)

————. *Ronia, the Robber's Daughter.* (I–A)

Nygren, Tord. *The Red Thread.* (P–I)

Reuter, Bjarne. *Buster's World.* Trans. Anthea Bell. (I)

Svedberg, Ulf. *Nicky the Nature Detective.* Illus. Lena Anderson. (P)

Widerberg, Siv. *The Big Sister.* Illus. Cecilia Torudd. (P)

Italy

Eco, Umberto. *The Bomb and the General.* Illus. Eugenio Carmi. Trans. William Weaver. (P)

————. *the Three Astronauts.* Illus. Eugenio Carmi. Trans. William Weaver. (P)

Innocenti, Roberto, and Christophe Gallaz. *Rose Blanche.* Trans. Martha Coventry and Richard Graglia. (I)

Japan

Fukami, Haruo. *An Orange for a Bellybutton.* Trans. Cathy Hirano. (P)

Funakoshi, Canna. *One Evening.* Illus. Yohji Izawa. (I–A)

Isami, Iksuyo. *The Fox's Egg.* Trans. Cathy Hirano. (P)

Kaizuki, Kiyonori. *A Calf Is Born.* Trans. Cathy Hirano. (P)

Maruki, Toshi. *Hiroshima No Pika.* (I–A)

Sato, Satoru. *I Wish I Had a Big, Big Tree.* Illus. Tsutomu Murakami. (P)

Sri Lanka

Wettasinghe, Sybil. *The Umbrella Thief.* (P)

South America

Bojunga-Nunes, Lygia. *The Companions.* Trans. Ellen Watson. Illus. Larry Wilkes (I)

Gutierrez, Douglas. *The Night of the Stars.* Trans. Carmen Diana Dearden. Illus. Maria Fernanda Oliver. (P)

Russia

Marshak, Samuel. *The Pup Grew Up.* Trans. Richard Pevear. Illus. Vladimir Radunsky. (P)

Rudolph, Marguerita. *Gray Neck.* Adapted from D. N. Mamin-Sibiryak. Illus. Leslie Shuman Kronz. (P–I)

from four large groups in the United States with discernible cultural traditions: African Americans, Asian Americans, Latinos, and Native Americans. Next we discussed books that portray religious and regional cultural traditions and lifestyles. Finally, we discussed international books with a multicultural thrust of the present and the past, and cross-cultural books to illustrate the growth in international literature for children.

Paul Hazard, renowned French literary critic of the early 1900s, described the international exchange of literature in *Books, Children and Men*. He describes his experiences through reading: Through books, he traveled with Don Quixote and Sancho across the plains of Castile, white hot in the sun, with dusty roads and inns full of adventure. He also lived in *Uncle Tom's Cabin* and cultivated sugarcane with slaves as companions. He states:

Yes, children's books keep alive a sense of nationality; but they also keep alive a sense of humanity. They describe their native land lovingly, but they also describe faraway lands where unknown brothers live. They understand the essential quality of their own race; but each of them is a messenger that goes beyond mountains and rivers, beyond the seas, to the very ends of the world in search of new friendships. Every country gives and every country receives—innumerable are the exchanges—and so it comes about that in our first impressionable years the universal republic of childhood is born. (Hazard, 1967)

The world is enriched by the universal republic of childhood and the international exchange of children's books. Through the international exchange we can increase world understanding.

12

Planning a Literature Curriculum

FIRST STEPS

Young poets imitate.
Mature poets steal.

T.S. Eliot

I read my first poem
And I felt like frowning;
It sounded too much
Like Elizabeth Browning.

Then in my next poem
I noticed a change,
I was Emily Dickinson —
Quiet and strange.

Now it's happened again,
Please don't think I'm weird,
But today I'm Walt Whitman,
Without the long beard.

When I read all my writing
I discover a rule:
I write like whomever
We're reading at school.

Brod Bagert

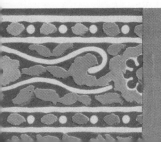

oung writers unconsciously imitate the styles of the authors they read. Thus, as with all things, a good model produces good results.

Everywhere you look in Betty Shockley's first-grade classroom you can see children and books. Piles of children are on the floor in the book corner where the most books can be found and where many are displayed with the covers facing outward, inviting children in. Other children are sitting on the edge of a raised area (the stage), looking at the books that are in boxes on the stage. Here are the alphabet books they have been exploring over the past few weeks, and a box of books by Donald Crews, the author they are currently studying. During writing time many children have books with them. Some use them to find words to copy, some use them to copy entire pages or stories, and some write original stories based on the patterns they find in the books. During center time, too, children have books in their hands as they reenact favorite

stories. Betty reads a lot to the whole class, doing choral reading with big books, introducing new books into the classroom collection, singing songs that are in book form, and discussing patterns, word choice, illustration style, and many other issues with her first-grade students. Literature permeates the day in this classroom, and these children know that literature is fundamental to their lives as readers and writers.

Betty's classroom is a literature-based classroom, one in which learning about literature and learning through literature are essential to every school day. The linguist M. A. K. Halliday has remarked that people *learn* language, *learn about* language, and *learn through* language. We can apply this model to literature as well. Readers certainly learn language—the language of story, poem, and well-crafted nonfiction. Readers also learn about language—how language can be crafted to suit different purposes, how varied genres are structured, and the effect and power of particular stylistic choices. And of course readers learn through language, as reading about other places, people, and ideas broadens knowledge and understanding. Beyond this, readers who are engaged with books learn about themselves by considering the virtual experiences they have through story and by constructing their own value systems.

When readers and books meet, they create a fragile and complex experience. Reader response theory and research, as well as the many teacher reports of children reading in classrooms, attest to the unpredictability, complexity, and power of the act of reading. As they read, readers turn texts into stories, poems, or meaningful information, creating meaning for themselves. That meaning varies across readers and readings. Because of this complexity and variability, planning an effective literature curriculum involves careful consideration and flexible construction.

A LITERATURE-BASED CURRICULUM

Implementing a literature-based curriculum means that teachers seek to increase their knowledge of the books available for today's children. Teachers faced with the need to incorporate literature into the curriculum but not given the time or training to implement change often ask for books on topics, books that can teach children some reading skill, books that can teach children something. And when those books are in the classroom, they become the means for learning whatever topic or skill is being studied; the books themselves get lost in the curriculum. Even worse, the children who are reading those books are not necessarily becoming joyful readers. They may be learning about the topic, and they may even be learning how to read, but they are learning in an atmosphere that militates against reading for the joy of it. In this kind of atmosphere, literature is used in the service of learning about topics, and the books and the readers themselves are forgotten.

Children will, of course, learn many things through literature. They can learn to read, learn about many topics, and learn to be better writers, among other skills. They can learn all this, and more, in an atmosphere that has not lost sight of the fact that good books are important in and of themselves, and don't need to "teach" anyone anything. The challenge is to teach with literature in a manner that preserves its integrity as well as the integrity of children's responses to it. It is not easy to keep the focus on children and their responses to the books they read. Indeed, children and books can easily get lost in a maze of goals, work sheets, and assessments when a literature-based curriculum is implemented without careful planning.

Natalie Babbitt (1990) speaks eloquently about some very real dangers inherent in a poorly planned literature-based curriculum. One danger that she sees is what Rosenblatt (1978, 1991) calls *basalizing literature*. Babbitt writes:

> I know that there is a movement underway to stop using texts for the teaching of reading and to start using works of fiction. In the beginning that seemed to me to be a good idea. But now I'm not so sure. The texts had related workbooks with sentences to complete, quizzes, questions to think about, and all kinds of suggested projects. The feeling has been, as I understand it, that these texts and workbooks were making a dry and tedious thing out of learning to read at the very time when concern about literacy levels was growing more and more serious. So it seemed sensible to try using real stories in the classroom—stories that could grab the children's fancies and show them what the joy of reading is all about. But what I see happening now is that these real stories are being used in the same way that the old texts were used. . . . I worry that this will make a dry and tedious thing out of fiction. (1990, pp. 696–697)

If teachers use trade books in the curriculum to interest children and help them become literate in the full sense of the word, then it is crucial we let the books be as interesting as they can be. It is crucial that we not ruin the power of trade books by turning them into material for exercises. In Chapter 2 we discussed the differences between reading *efferently* (to gain information) and *aesthetically* (to live for a while in the spell of a good book, have a vicarious experience, feel pleasure in the words and rhythm of the text and the images and emotions we evoke as we read). Because of this difference in how we read, and the different purposes that nonfiction and fiction and poetry serve, it is inappropriate to read a work of fiction or poetry primarily for information, for facts. Workbook-like exercises and predetermined questions and projects that force readers into an efferent mode (asking for recall of details, for example), work against the goal of providing children with pleasurable experiences with literature. This literature-workbook-quiz-project cycle may, in fact, be worse than the basals because it destroys the potential of the trade books themselves.

Another concern centers around the individuality of emotional response. Stories and poems are about feelings, about meanings and significances, about questions rather than answers. Most authors do not write stories to teach lessons. Certainly, stories deal with values, with morality, but teaching object lessons is not what they are about. Babbitt voices this concern in response to a discussion of the moral lessons in **Tuck Everlasting** when she says,

> I don't think any [young readers of *Tuck*] are coming away with a heightened sense of social responsibility. They could be made to, of course. You can come away from any book with that, if it's thrust upon you. But how sad for the book! . . . What children take away with them when they've finished a book will depend on each child's personal needs and personal quirks. (1990, p. 701)

Katherine Paterson, Marion Dane Bauer, and many other authors say the same thing: Their books aren't meant to teach children morals, but rather meant to engage readers, to allow children to discover, explore, and build their own values.

A Response-Centered Literature Curriculum

What, then, is the purpose of a literature-based curriculum? We might better describe this curriculum as a response-centered literature curriculum, since the primary goal is to engage readers in the act of reading responsively. The focus is not on the works of literature, nor on the topics or skills, but on the response of individual readers (Purves &

Soter, 1990). The goals of a response-centered curriculum are listed in Figure 12-1. A response-centered curriculum recognizes and encourages diversity among readers, recognizes and encourages connections among readers, and "recognizes that response is joyous" (Purves & Soter, 1990, p. 56). In this curriculum, the teacher provides a variety of books, time to read and explore those books, time to talk and write, and time to draw and dramatize those books. In addition, teachers provide opportunities for the collaborative company of peers with whom to explore similarities and differences in responses. The teacher also helps students find the language with which to articulate their responses, and challenges them to "understand why they respond as they do" (Purves & Soter, 1990, p. 56). We discuss some ways of responding in Chapter 2 and later in this chapter.

A second goal is to build on the engagement that a response-centered curriculum makes possible and develop children's awareness of "the family of stories" (Moss & Stott, 1986) and of how words work (Benton, 1984) in literature. This goal focuses on helping children learn of and about language and its use in literature through reading.

A third goal is to give children the opportunity to learn about themselves and their world through books, to learn *through* language. The vicarious experiences that are possible with fiction, the emotional expansion that is possible with poetry, the exposure to information about the child's world that is possible with nonfiction all increase children's knowledge of themselves and their worlds. And this increased knowledge widens children's horizons and makes even more learning possible.

We advocate a response-centered literature curriculum because it is through such a curriculum that we as teachers can best help our students realize their potential as learners, as language users, and as readers. Research has documented what teachers have known for years: Reading literature helps children learn to like to read, and this means they read more, and in the process become better readers and better language users (Anderson, Hiebert, Scott, & Wilkinson, 1985; Fielding, Wilson, & Anderson, 1984). Other research points out that

> the dearth of literature in the elementary school may go far toward explaining some of the problems encountered by secondary-school teachers, who complain that children don't like to read, don't read well, and can't apply what they read to their own lives. . . . [They] know how, but not why or what. They have been miseducated; they have been taught to read without learning to love reading. (Ravitch, 1985, pp. 78–79)

**Figure
12-1**

Goals of a Response-Centered Curriculum

A response-centered curriculum should help students:

feel secure in their own responses to literature

trust their own feelings

explore why they respond as they do

make connections between literature and life

see connections among texts—intertextuality—and make connections among books

respect the responses of others

recognize commonalities among their own and others' responses

develop a lasting (deep and abiding) love of reading

establish the lifelong habit of reading

see variations of meaning in stories and poems

recognize different purposes for reading
—aesthetic (read to savor experience)
—efferent (read to remember)

recognize different types of reading material: informational/expository, narrative, poetic

learn about language and how it is used
—understand how words work
—appreciate beauty of things well said
—grasp subtleties of language

Ways to achieve these goals are to:

encourage students to interact with books
—provide time to read and explore
—give time to (talk, write, draw, and dramatize)
—provide time to collaborate with peers
—plan time to explore similarity/difference in responses

accept/encourage diversity among readers
—give choice of material to read
—provide choice of ways to respond (talk, write, draw, and dramatize)

provide ways to respond joyously

provide a variety of books

present motivation to read through:
—book talks, contagious enthusiasm
—integrating reading with other areas
—creating a rich literacy environment

help students find language to express responses

give children the opportunity to learn language

help students realize their potential as learners, as language users, and as readers

help students to understand why they respond as they do

give children the opportunity to learn about themselves and their world—learn through language

---

In the Teaching Ideas throughout this text we have presented a variety of activities designed to lead children deeper into their own responses and to help children explore how literature works. Because children's literature is so rich and varied, it certainly can be used to enhance every area of the curriculum. More important, though, are those experiences that keep literature central. Activities surrounding reading should bring readers back to books and guide them to others. Connie and Harold Rosen state the case well:

It is as though there is a deep lack of confidence in the power of literature to do its work and a profound conviction that unless literature can be converted into the hard currency of familiar school learning it has not earned its keep. What will take children more deeply into the experience of the book? This is the question we should be asking rather than, by what means can I use this book as a launching-pad into any one of a dozen endeavors which leave the book further and further behind, at best a distant sound, at worst forgotten entirely. (1973, p. 195)

In an integrated response-centered literature curriculum, books and readers are at the center of many types of learning. Each time you read a story aloud, children learn to enjoy literature, to listen, to reason, and to respond to oral presentations. They are also observing models for their own writing. When children retell a story, they are learning speaking skills, organization, sequence, and dramatic presentation. When they read on their own, children are learning to become fluent readers, to enjoy literature, and to build a storehouse of language and story possibilities. And when they write their own stories, they are becoming more proficient writers, selecting significant details, organizing thoughts, and expressing the thoughts with clarity. All of this is important, but children should also learn something about their literature in the process. Many of the teaching ideas presented throughout this text suggest ideas for involving children in exploring how literature works. These ideas can all be adapted to suit the particular needs of you and your students as you develop your own literature curriculum.

LITERATURE IN THE CLASSROOM

There are many ways to organize a literature curriculum. In a study of how literature-based reading programs look in various classrooms, Hiebert and Colt (1989) discovered that these programs varied along two dimensions: the instructional format and the selection of literature; these variations were linked to the amount of teacher control in each dimension. Their scheme for representing these variations appears in Figure 12-2.

Some programs are marked by a high degree of teacher control; teachers select the materials and lead the instruction. Other programs are marked by student selection of materials and student direction of their own learning with little or no teacher intervention. There are all sorts of variations and combinations of student independence and teacher direction that are possible, represented in this scheme by the midpoint of teacher- and student-shared responsibility for instruction and material selection.

A print-rich environment has many books, inviting students to read and write. In this classroom, books are not only accessible, they are unavoidable! (Joanne Payne Lionetti's third grade class)

Although Hiebert and Colt were looking specifically at literature-based reading programs, their scheme can be applied to literature programs in general. In some cases, you will want to select materials that will help students construct new knowledge. Later we discuss two ways of doing this: a unit designed to learn about literature and a unit designed to learn about a topic through literature. In other cases, you and your students will negotiate what is to be explored, how it will be explored, and the materials with which to do so. And often, students will be independently selecting books and deciding what to do with them. For more information on this kind of curriculum see Galda, Cullinan, and Strickland (1993), *Language, Literacy, and the Child.*

Learning About Literature

Experiencing literature and studying literature are *not* the same, yet both have a place in the curriculum. Even before learning to read independently, children have rich literary experiences. For the youngest child, literature attracts for the pure pleasure it brings. Even while listening for pure pleasure, however, children unconsciously internalize a sense of the total form of a literary work.

*T*EACHING IDEA 12-1

Ten Ways to Explore Literature

A straightforward literary approach helps you and others to explore literature. First, steep yourself and your students in as much literature as possible; responses, then, are based on true experiences with literature and a growing awareness of its power. These activities are part of a literature curriculum.

1. Read aloud. This models what good reading is and exposes students to the high-quality literature you choose.

2. Retell stories and poems. Retelling makes stories and poems a natural part of talk, like friendly gossip or "did you hear this?" Students retell stories and poems to younger children and to their peers.

3. Create a picture story. Tell a story in pictures as a sequence of drawings, comic strip style, collage, stylized frieze, or a map inset with small pictures. This technique helps students recognize literary elements, such as setting, sequence, plot development, dialogue, and denouement.

4. Talk about books. Make talking about books a natural part of every day. Enthusiasm is contagious; start an epidemic. Share enthusiasm for books.

5. Recast old tales. Take the underlying situation or conflict of an old tale, list the elements, ask students to write their own stories in a modern setting around these elements, for example, Anthony Browne, *Hansel & Gretel* (P), or Jon Scieszka, *The Stinky Cheese Man* (P–I). Create a chart on which you compare elements of various stories and make

generalizations. This helps students realize that situations from literature are retold and recast endlessly.

6. Dramatize scenes. Role-play characters confronting each other, working their way out of dilemmas. Improvisation makes literature memorable and helps students own it.

7. Keep diaries or reading logs. Keeping a diary or reading log gives students a means of recording the sequence of events and thus understanding a story's structure better. Keeping a diary or log takes readers inside a character and a situation to look at events imaginatively from a different point of view.

8. Identify themes. Ask students to search for books with similar themes. Recognizing that themes are developed in various ways helps students make connections among books and see patterns in literature.

9. Organize the classroom library. Ask students to consider alternate ways to organize books. Discuss pros and cons of each way. As a group decide which method works best for you. Choosing various ways to order books puts students in charge of the classroom library and helps them know books.

10. Plot story structures. Stories proceed in cyclical ways, along a straight line with rising action, in flashbacks, or interrelated sequences of events. Graphing memorable events makes story frameworks understandable.

The *study* of literature or of any topic related to the literature does not begin until *after* the literature is experienced: Someone tells, reads, or dramatizes a story, and a fortunate child just enjoys it. When the time comes for children to look at literature analytically and to make abstractions about its

forms, structures, archetypes, and patterns, they have joyful experiences on which to draw.

Even with older children, enjoyment is still uppermost, and the study of literature is sensitively introduced only as it adds to their appreciation and insight. The study of literature does *not* replace the

Figure 12-2

Two Dimensions of Effective Literacy Programs

INSTRUCTIONAL FORMAT

Teacher-led instruction	Teacher- and student-led interaction	Independent application
Teacher-selected material	Teacher- and student-selected materials	Student-selected material

LITERATURE SELECTION

original literary experience; neither does study always need to follow the experience. There is a time and a place for both. As Northrop Frye explains,

> In all of our literary experience there are two kinds of response. There is the direct experience of the work itself, while we're reading a book, . . . especially for the first time. This experience is uncritical, or rather precritical. . . . Then there is the conscious, critical response we make after we've finished reading . . . where we compare what we've experienced with other things of the same kind, and form a judgment of value and proportion on it. This critical response, with practice, gradually makes our precritical responses more sensitive and accurate. . . . But behind our responses to individual works, there's a bigger response to our literary experience as a whole, as a total possession. (1970, pp. 104–105)

As children read and listen to stories they begin to build their own personal literary storehouse of understanding. They begin to recognize thematic connections across stories, similarities in plot structures and characterization, and distinctive styles in text and illustration. Teachers can encourage these kinds of understanding by planning a literature curriculum that contains books selected specifically to help students make connections among texts, connections which result in a deeper understanding of what literature is and how it works. This kind of curriculum, which Stott (1981) calls a "spiraled curriculum," helps children develop an understanding of the unity of all literature.

While connections between life and text are still at the core of children's experience with literature, connections among books are important as well. If several pieces of folklore are read across the span

of a few days, children begin to recognize patterns that transcend individual stories. Recognizing the motifs and patterns in folklore builds a base for understanding other literature in terms of mythic archetypes. In Chapter 5 we discuss motifs in folklore and present Teaching Ideas you can adapt to help children develop a knowledge of folkloric archetypes. This knowledge will make them stronger readers as they read books of other genres that rely on these archetypes.

Talking about characters enables children to make comparisons among characters from various stories. These comparisons can lead to generalizations about character types that children will meet as they read widely. Mischievous Peter in Beatrix Potter's **Peter Rabbit** (P), who gets into trouble in MacGregor's garden, is very much like Ramona Quimby in Beverly Cleary's **Ramona** (I) series. They both are recognizable in other mischievous characters such as Julia Redfern in Eleanor Cameron's series, which includes **The Private Worlds of Julia Redfern** (I), and Aldo in Johanna Hurwitz's series, including **Aldo Peanut Butter** (I).

Discussing plot results in identification of various kinds of plots and understandings about archetypal plots like the quest story in which a character begins at home, leaves in search of something important (an object, a person, self-knowledge), and returns home changed in some way. Books such as Barbara Cooney's **Island Boy** (P), Barbara Holland's **Prisoners at the Kitchen Table** (I), Candice Ransom's **Millicent the Magnificent** (I), Hila Colman's **Rich and Famous Like My Mom** (A), Katherine Paterson's **Lyddie** (A), and Cynthia Voigt's **Dicey's Song** (A) have characters who are struggling to find their own identity. When students read and discuss these books, identifying the problems the characters must solve and the strengths they exhibit, they

---

Teaching Idea 12-2

Discovering and Comparing Story Structures

Story Structure and Sequence

Choose two or more well-known folktales: Jack and the Beanstalk and Rapunzel, for example.

Read aloud the folktales several times.

Talk about the stories until students know them well.

Invite students to retell the stories verbally and in writing.

Discuss ways to divide the stories into three or four events. Model ways to divide the stories.

Ask students to choose their own significant events.

Fold drawing paper into equal sections.

Ask students to draw events for the story sequence. Show examples in photographs: sequencing story events.

Comparing Stories

Review the stories.

Draw a Venn diagram (two overlapping circles).

Relate comparison to the same process used in math.

Ask students to talk about the two stories.

Write students' observations on strips of paper.

If a statement applies to one story only, place it in the circle for that story.

If the statement applies to both stories place it in the overlapping section of the circles.

Illustrative comments children made

Jack and the Beanstalk   Same   *Rapunzel*

Jack is about a boy   Rapunzel is about a girl

A long time ago   Once upon a time

                                    Jack has a vine to climb

                                    The witch climbs Rapunzel's hair

Jack doesn't get locked up   The mother cuts the beanstalk   Rapunzel gets locked up

There is not a father   The witch cuts Rapunzel's hair   There's a mother and father

                                    Jack has magic beans

                                    Rapunzel has magic tears

                                    There's a wicked person in both stories

                                    Both start out poor and end up rich

                                    Both had castles in their stories

                                    Both lived happily ever after

Based on a teaching idea developed by Diane Potente, first-grade teacher, Munsey Park School, Manhasset, New York

---

can discover similarities and differences in each character's quest and thus build their understanding of quest tales. This understanding can also be linked to the quest stories of folklore (discussed in Chapter 5) and fantasy (discussed in Chapter 6).

Finding similarities and differences in the underlying conflicts of stories also helps children make connections among books. Some books, like Jean George's ***Julie of the Wolves*** (A), revolve around

several conflicts: person versus self, person versus person, person versus society, and person versus nature. Others have only one or two central conflicts. Discussing these conflicts, or problems, helps children notice their presence in stories and gives them another dimension along which to connect stories with each other.

A consideration of themes often brings about an important recognition of the various ways that

This first-grade class compared two folk tales with the use of a Venn diagram. Braided yellow hair forms the circle for Rapunzel's story while a green beanstalk becomes the circle for Jack and the Beanstalk. In the parts that overlap, the students listed things about the stories that were the same. (Diane Potente's first grade class)

different authors treat the same general theme. Readers read the same story about growing up and becoming independent in many different books. In Chapter 3 we discuss some general themes that appear in picture storybooks; in Chapter 7 we discuss some general themes that appear in contemporary realistic fiction. Teachers who want to help their students make thematic connections across books select books according to similarity of theme.

Moss and Stott (1986) suggest exploring books in terms of linear and circular journey patterns, conflicts, genres, and identity quest stories. Explorations of this kind lead to comparisons and generalizations that help children build knowledge about the "family of stories" (Moss & Stott, 1986) as they note similarities and differences across various stories and genres.

Children who do this also learn to look at books as works of art crafted by a writer. They explore the language that the writer uses and learn to appreciate the nuances that distinguish Katherine Paterson from Judy Blume. These children also use their knowledge about literature in their own writing, incorporating patterns, structures, themes, character types, and language that they have read. Books

build on books, and children become knowledgeable readers and writers.

However, none of this happens unless children experience delight in books. The delight must come first. Then it becomes natural to talk about books in such a way that literary understanding and appreciation develops. Early (1960) describes how readers develop by moving from unconscious enjoyment to self-conscious appreciation to conscious delight. This kind of growth is not possible without a firm foundation in the joy of books. Through carefully planned encounters with particular books, teachers build on this foundation of joy as they help their students delight in the artistry and interconnections in literature.

Learning Through Literature

We also can structure a literature curriculum around topics other than literature. Literature can support any area of concentration, whether it be reading or writing, mathematics, science, social studies, language study, art, or music, as discussed in Chapters 8, 9, and 10. Here we present examples of how

Dicey needs to shoulder more responsibility than any child should be required to bear. At times, the stretch of sand and sea beckon the lonely teenager who tries to refurbish an old boat as a means of escape to solitude. (*Dicey's Song* by Cynthia Voigt)

literature can enhance children's writing development, looking at books that illustrate what good writers do, books that explore authors' lives and their practice of the craft of writing, and nonfiction that explores how books are made.

Thematic Unit: Writing

Where can we locate the finest models for children's writing? Naturally they appear in the literature written for children themselves. Teachers show children what good writers do by showing them high-quality books and discussing them. When they read on their own, children build a storehouse of language and story possibilities. The stories they read and hear are written by some of the most skilled writers of all times. These well-written sto-

ries and poems serve as models for children in their own writing.

When children write, they draw on the stories they know as they select significant details, organize their thoughts, and express them with clarity. Notice the echoes of literature present in the beginning of this story written by a third-grade North American child.

Karry Kangaroo

Chapter 1

G'Day

> It was a hot day in the bush. Many animals went to the bilabong more than once that day. Karry and her son, Joey, went to the outback to visit some old friends. Joey took an apple to eat on the ride. All of a sudden, Karry stopped and yelled, "KOOEEE, KOOEEE."

Not only did this young writer learn a lot about Australia through the books she read, she also learned a lot about story language.

Children who write read differently from those who do not write. They say things like, "Now I read like a writer—you know, I pay attention to how the guy is writing." Children who read are better writers than those who don't read. Tway (1970) and Calder (1984) used recognized criteria to evaluate students' writing and found that those who had read widely wrote richer compositions. When students are learning the craft of writing, they are sensitive to what other writers do and adopt some of the strategies as their own.

Hearing and reading good stories develops vocabularies, sharpens a sensitivity to language, and fine-tunes a sense of writing styles. We draw on our prior verbal experience when we write (Moffett, 1983). If that experience has been rich with good literature, the storehouse will be fuller. Frank Smith (1982) says that the only source of knowledge sufficiently rich and reliable for learning about written language is the writing already done by others. We learn to write by reading what others have written; we enrich our repertoire of language possibilities by reading what others have said.

Nick Aversa, teacher at Great Neck South Middle School, talks about how his students' reading influences their writing:

> We read *My Life and Hard Times* by James Thurber and then I saw aspects of Thurber's style cropping up in students' writing the rest of the year. The literature we read is actually a demonstration of good writing; students try on other writers' style in the process of creating their own. (personal communication, Nov. 13, 1986)

TEACHING IDEA 12-3

Using Literature to Help Students Become Independent Readers

The kinds of books we select for beginning readers assist them in becoming confident and competent independent readers. Books that present strong language patterns, clear illustrations, and familiar experiences support children in learning to read independently.

Books written in predictable language patterns that are easy for children to hear help them to read words on their own. Rhythmic language patterns ring in children's ears as they see the words on the page and match up what they say with what they see. The following are good examples:

Carlstrom, Nancy White. *Jesse Bear, What Will You Wear?* Illus. Bruce Degen. (N–P)

Guarino, Deborah. *Is Your Mama a Llama?* Illus. Steven Kellogg. (N–P)

Hennessy, B. G. *Jake Baked the Cake.* Illus. Mary Morgan. (N–P)

Hutchins, Pat. *What Game Shall We Play?* (N–P)

Martin, Bill, Jr. *Brown Bear, Brown Bear, What Do You See?* Illus. Eric Carle. (N–P)

———. *Polar Bear, Polar Bear, What Do You Hear?* Illus. Eric Carle. (N–P)

Clear illustrations also assist children in independent reading. Illustrations supply the context and give the child clues for decoding new words. They help a child anticipate what is coming. They also confirm the story. The following are good examples:

Browne, Anthony. *I Like Books.* (P)

———. *Things I Like.* (P)

Lobel, Arnold. *Days with Frog and Toad.* (P)

———. *Frog and Toad All Year.* (P)

———. *Frog and Toad Are Friends.* (P)

———. *Frog and Toad Together.* (P)

Books written about experiences that are common to children are important. The background knowledge helps the child anticipate new reading words and confirms his or her understanding of the story. The following are good examples:

Katz, Michael Jay. *Ten Potatoes in a Pot: And Other Counting Rhymes.* Illus. June Otani. (P)

Kovalski, Maryann. *The Wheels on the Bus.* (N–P)

Martin, Bill, Jr., and John Archambault. *Chicka Chicka Boom Boom.* Illus. Lois Ehlert. (N–P)

Marzollo, Jean. *Pretend You're a Cat.* Illus. Jerry Pinkney. (P)

Rylant, Cynthia. *Henry and Mudge in Puddle Trouble.* Illus. Sucie Stevenson. (P)

Zelinsky, Paul. *The Wheels on the Bus.* (N–P)

Young writers learn about writing by reading widely and examining their literature closely. They observe the writing of the authors they read and experiment with some of their techniques. When they read well-crafted stories, they intuitively develop a sense of beginnings, middles, and endings. They also observe how changing the point of view alters a story, how an author develops characterization, how the setting influences events, and how the same story can be told in a variety of ways. All of these experiences enrich the store of possibilities on which they draw as they mature as writers themselves.

There are many ways to explore children's books when the focus is on writing. Style is always an option, of course, as students consider the words and the arrangements of those words in favorite stories, poems, and nonfiction texts. Structure can be explored in this way as well, with young readers experimenting with the forms they find in the books they read.

The lead, or the opening sentence or paragraph in a piece of writing, must immediately grab the reader's interest. Reading the first sentence must make us want to read the second one. Young writers naturally want to make their own pieces interesting and often enjoy studying the leads in books for children. Kevin Henkes's *Chrysanthemum* begins: "The day she was born was the happiest day in her parents' lives. 'She's perfect,' said her mother. 'Absolutely,' said her father. And she was. She was absolutely perfect." Evaline Ness, in *Sam, Bangs, & Moonshine,* begins: "On a small island, near a large harbor, there once lived a fisherman's little daughter (named Samantha, but always called Sam), who had the reckless habit of lying." E. B.

*G*ARY SOTO is currently associate professor of Chicano studies and English at the University of California at Berkeley. His poems have appeared in many magazines, including the *New Yorker* and *Poetry*. He has written **Baseball in April** (I–A), **A Summer Life** (I–A) and **Taking Sides** (A) for children and young adults. **A Fire in My Hands** (I–A) is a collection of poetry in which Soto discusses how he began writing poetry and how he chooses his topics:

When I first studied poetry, I was single-minded. I woke to poetry and went to bed with poetry. I memorized poems, read English poets. . . . But I was most taken by Spanish and Latin American poets, particularly Pablo Neruda. My favorites of his were the odes—long, short-lined poems celebrating common things like tomatoes, socks, scissors, and artichokes. I felt joyful when I read these odes; and when I began to write my own poems, I tried to remain faithful to the common things of my childhood—dogs, alleys, my baseball mitt, curbs, and the fruit of the valley, especially the orange. I wanted to give these things life, to write so well that my poems would express their simple beauty. (pp. 5–6)

Soto's most autobiographical book, **Living Up the Street,** is a warm, human account of growing up in the barrio. The following excerpt is taken from **Living Up the Street** (I–A).

We were terrible kids, I think. My brother, sister, and I felt a general meanness begin to surface from our tiny souls while living on Braly Street, which was in the middle of industrial Fresno [CA]. Across the street was Coleman Pickles, while on the right of us was a junkyard that dealt in metals—aluminum, iron, sheet metal, and copper stripped from refrigerators. Down the street was Sun-Maid Raisin, where a concrete tower rose above the scraggly sycamores that lined Braly Street. . . .

Gary Soto

This was 1957. My brother Rick was six, I was five, and Debra was four. Although we looked healthy, clean in the morning, and polite as only Mexicans can be polite, we had a streak of orneriness that we imagined to be normal play. That summer—and the summer previous—we played with the Molinas who lived down the alley from us right across from the broom factory and its brutal "whack" of straw being tied into brooms. There were eight children on the block that year, ranging from twelve down to one, so there was much to do: Wrestle, eat raw bacon, jump from the couch, sword fight with rolled-up newspapers, steal from neighbors, kick chickens, throw rocks at passing cars. . . .

What we learned from the Molinas was how to have fun, and what we taught them was how to fight. It seemed that the Sotos were inherently violent. . . . (pages 1 and 2).

Gary Soto's vignettes about growing up in the barrio, attending parochial school, church, and public summer school, and his attempts to court his first girl friend are filled with absorbing detail and touched with humor. He relates the fascinating minutiae of his life in an engaging manner; his work deserves to be read in the original.

Then one day Gregory waited for Charlie with a gift. He had brought for Charlie an easel of his own, and new brushes, and new paints, and clean canvases.

Peter Catalanotto shows the world through an artist's eyes and Cynthia Rylant's story inspires all to see anew. (*All I See*)

White's **Charlotte's Web** begins: "Where's Papa going with that ax?" and Madeleine L'Engle begins **A Wrinkle in Time** with "It was a dark and stormy night." Once leads are pointed out, young readers will notice them everywhere and will use them in their own writing.

Topic choice is another concern of young writers. Writers choose very unusual topics for their writing; at first glance some of them may sound uninteresting. It seems that good writers, however, can choose an apparently insignificant or ordinary topic and make it interesting to us. Who would think, for example, that bugs would lead to a fascinating collection of poems? Yet they do in Aileen Fisher's **When it Comes to Bugs** and in Paul Fleischman's **Joyful Noise.** Authors capture small moments of their lives and make them memorable by the way they write about them. When readers discuss the topic choices that authors make, they learn about the kinds of topics they can write about themselves. Reading and discussing Julie Brinckloe's **Fireflies,** Judith Hendershot's **In Coal Country,** Lynn Joseph's **A Coconut Kind of Day,**

and Cynthia Rylant's **All I See,** or any number of other fine books, can help young readers think about topics in a new way.

Literature provides a rich resource to use in any writing program. It can be used as a model for writing, as examples of interesting language used well, and as an illustration of topics to write about. There are books that illustrate unique formats: journals, letters, postcards, diaries, and autobiographies. There are books that parody other literature, books that tell stories from different points of view, and books that illustrate unique story patterns. No matter what point you want to illustrate about writing, there are books to help you make it clear.

Most writers have a dimension to their lives that differs from people who are not writers. For example, they reflect on their experiences and think about how those experiences can feed into material they write. We say they lead a "writerly sort of life." Many books illustrate what it means to lead a writerly sort of life, some of which are listed in Figure 12-3. Some of these books are autobiography, some biography, some memoir, some

TEACHING IDEA 12-4

Studying an Author or Illustrator

Knowing the works of an author or illustrator enriches the study of children's literature. Have your students conduct an individual study of an author/illustrator or conduct one with a group of elementary school students.

1. Choose a person whose work they like a great deal.

2. Read as many of this person's books as possible.

3. Write responses to the works in a log or journal.

4. Locate biographical information in *Something About the Author,* magazines, or other sources. Birthdays are listed in Appendix D.

5. Draw some generalizations about the person's work.

6. Compare across books: for example, characters, events, dialogue, artistic style.

7. Share findings with others.

Third-grade students enjoy reading a big book they wrote, a biography of Tomie de Paola. As a part of an author study, the students learned a lot about de Paola and wrote their own book. It is the profile about Tomie de Paola that appears in this chapter. (Teacher Joanne Payne Lionetti, Marion Street School, Lynbrook, NY)

Joanne Lionetti made a special box to hold all the Tomie de Paola books the students brought in to read about their favorite author.

journals, some fiction, and some letters. Use them to explore what writers do. Children can choose a favorite author, learn about that author's life as a writer, and then track down all of the books that author has written. Or children can read widely, developing understandings about authors in general. A calendar of authors' birthdays appears in Appendix D.

Children who write are also interested in how writing happens in the real world—how books get made. Several books look at the process of creating a book that can answer children's questions and give them ideas about their own writing. Some of these books are listed in Figures 9-11 and 12-3.

Thematic Unit: Animals

Many teachers weave literature into everything they do in a classroom. Using selection guides such as those discussed in Chapter 2 and working with their school media specialists, teachers gather books to support the units their classes are exploring. A primary-grade class might focus on zoo animals, for example.

Children learn from firsthand experiences, such as a trip to a zoo, but they also learn from books. Examining books on zoo animals both before and after a trip to a zoo yields vast results. Book exploration not only introduces new information, it solidifies ephemeral information and puts into context—or organizes—information children already know. Figure 12-4 lists some fiction and nonfiction books that can enrich a study of zoo animals.

Thematic units, such as zoo animals, often incorporate science, reading, writing, mathematics, and social studies, connecting all with and through literature. Four first-grade teachers from Munsey

---

Figure 12-3

Books About Writers and Writing

Books About Writers (See also Figure 9–11)

Aardema, Verna. *A Bookworm Who Hatched.* (P–I)

Byars, Betsy. *The Moon and I.* (I)

Conford, Ellen. *Jenny Archer, Author.* Illus. Diane Palmisciano. (I)

Fritz, Jean. *Surprising Myself.* (P–I)

Gherman, Beverly. *E. B. White: Some Writer!* (I-A)

Greenfield, Eloise, and Lessie Jones Little. *Childtimes: A Three-Generation Memoir.* (I–A)

Little, Jean. *Little by Little: A Writer's Education.* (I–A)

———. *The Stars Come Out Within.* (I-A)

Martin, Rafe. *A Storyteller's Story.* Photos by Jill Krementz. (P–I)

Meltzer, Milton. *Starting from Home: A Writer's Beginnings.* (I)

Peck, Richard. *Anonymously Yours: A Memoir.* (A)

Rylant, Cynthia. *Best Wishes.* Photos by Carol Ontal. (P–I)

———. *But I'll Be Back Again: An Album.* (I)

———. *Waiting to Waltz: A Childhood.* Illus. Stephen Gammell. (I)

Yolen, Jane. *A Letter from Phoenix Farm.* Photos by Jason Stemple. (P-I)

Books About Writing

Aliki. *How a Book Is Made.* (P)

Asher, Sandy. *Where Do You Get Your Ideas?* Illus. Susan Hellard. (I)

Cassedy, Sylvia. *In Your Own Words: A Beginner's Guide to Writing.* Rev. ed. (I-A)

Cobb, Vicki. *Writing It Down.* Illus. Marylin Hafner. (I)

Gibbons, Gail. *Deadline! From News to Newspaper.* (P–I)

Goffstein, M. B. *A Writer.* (I)

Greenfeld, Howard. *Books: From Writer to Reader.* (I–A)

James, Elizabeth, and Carol Barkin. *How to Write a Great School Report.* (I)

———. *How to Write Your Best Book Report.* (I)

Kehoe, Michael. *Puzzle of Books.* (I)

Nixon, Joan Lowery. *If You Were a Writer.* Illus. Bruce Degen. (P–I)

Sears, Peter. *Gonna Bake Me a Rainbow Poem: A Student Guide to Writing Poetry.* (I–A)

Tchudi, Susan, and Stephen Tchudi. *The Young Writer's Handbook: A Practical Guide for the Beginner Who Is Serious About Writing.* (I–A)

Park School, Manhasset, New York, pursued many directions with their students as they explored the zoo.

All four first grades went to the zoo, but each group interpreted its experience differently. First-grade teachers Betts Carpenter, Elaine Hinton, Ronnie Brooks, and Diane Potente provided many literacy experiences that were based on the trip. Before the trip they and their students planned what to look for, read books to build background knowledge, and made plans for personal safety. After the trip they and their students drew geographic maps, maps of the zoo, and traced where they walked. They created semantic maps about the zoo, organizing them around (1) animals (mammals, amphibians, fish,

reptiles, birds), (2) buildings, (3) jobs, and (4) types of animals (wild, domesticated, tame, farm). They categorized the vertebrate animals they saw as mammals, reptiles, amphibians, and birds, and drew pictures to place on the chart in the correct category. They also listed animals that live in Africa, Asia, South America, North America, Europe, and Australia.

They also used the story pattern of Bill Martin, Jr.'s **Brown Bear, Brown Bear** to report what they saw using the same order as their list. For example, using African animals they wrote the following:

Bronx Zoo, Bronx Zoo, what do you see?
I see giraffes looking at me.

Giraffes, giraffes, what do you see?
I see elephants looking at me. . . .

The children and their teachers read and wrote poetry about animals, such as Eve Merriam's "If You Were an Animal Inside the Zoo." They wrote and illustrated individual reports about the zoo—about the animals they saw and how they felt about them. An environmental protection theme ran throughout their work. They tied themes of self-respect, and caring for oneself and our world, into a theme of caring for animals—all creatures of our world.

These children read books about zoo animals, created mobiles of animal families, labeled with correct terms, and created bulletin boards to display their work. They discussed types of figurative language based on animals, like monkeys having "a barrel of fun," and used these ideas on the bulletin boards. They created murals about the continents, painting the backgrounds and placing pictures of animals they had drawn in the appropriate scenes.

PROFILE

This essay, "The Art of the Heart Man: Tomie de Paola," was written by the third grade students in Joanne Payne Lionetti's classroom, Marion Street School, Lynbrook, New York, after they completed a lengthy study of Tomie de Paola.

Tomie de Paola

Tomie de Paola was born in 1934 in Meriden, Connecticut. He grew up in the country. His parents were good to him. He had a happy life.

His mother was a housewife. His mother always bought books when people came to the house. She bought all kinds of encyclopedias. Tomie learned how to look up things in the encyclopedias.

His father was a barber. When Tomie drew, his father would hang the pictures up in his barber shop.

There were four children in Tomie's family. He had two brothers and one sister. He was second to the oldest.

Tomie also had grandparents who were good to him. His grandfather worked in a grocery store. His grandfather told him make believe stories but Tomie thought they were real.

He had two grandmothers. One was Irish and the other was Italian. His Italian grandmother lived 3 hours away in Fall River, Massachusetts. Tomie liked his Italian grandmother's chicken soup.

He also had a great grandmother who was 94 years old. Since no one would talk to either of them, Tomie and his great grandmother would talk to each other.

When Tomie was a little boy, he liked to tap dance, roller skate, and make up stories. He started to draw when he was four years old.

Tomie's favorite times were when his mother invited company over and the noise would wake Tomie up. This gave him an excuse to join the party. Another favorite time was Christmas, because he would always get art supplies.

They shared all of their experiences with others through displays in hallways, newsletters, and talk. One focus became the catalyst for a lot of learning, and this learning was based on a hands-on experience and on books.

A fifth-grade class in Georgia studied wildlife and wildlife management using the same approach. They read a number of books on wildlife, many of which are listed in Figure 12-5. They invited a local wildlife management expert to speak to their class, discussing and preparing the questions they would ask. After the presentation they decided to focus on endangered species. They identified endangered species and selected one to focus on, gathered information about their habitats, mating, and life patterns, and found out what has been done to protect the species. They turned this information into posters calling attention to these animals and suggesting ways to help protect them. During this time their teacher was reading aloud from Jean George's ***Who Really Killed Cock Robin?: An Ecological Mystery*** (A).

CONTINUED

Tomie drew on anything that he could find instead of paper. He drew on the walls, sheets, and his math book.

Tomie was good at spelling, reading and science. He had a good memory. He was a good artist, tap dancer, and roller skater. He liked to see shows in New York City and he enjoyed the Natural History Museum. Tomie was not good at math. He was also not good at sports and everybody called him a sissy.

Rose Milligan was Tomie's fifth grade teacher who read to them the most and always left off at the good parts. His favorite storyteller was his grandfather.

Tomie went to art school. He became a teacher. He made his first book in 1964. The book was a science book.

Tomie used to be very short. When he was in high school, he was 4'11". When he was 21, he was 5'2". Now he's 5'9" inc. He was glad he grew.

He has curly gray hair. He wears glasses. He has a nice smile and a wrinkly face and a fat chin.

Tomie likes to put himself in books to tell things that happened to him when he was a little boy. Some books that tell about him are *Oliver Button is a Sissy, Nana Upstairs, Nana Downstairs,* and *The Art Lesson.* He dedicates his books to his friends and people who helped him.

He lives and works in a 100 year old house that used to be a barn. He lives in New Hampshire. He writes and illustrates books. Margaret Frith is his editor. She comes from New York and helps him.

His books are fun to read. Some books have pictures from other books in them. He puts a lot of hearts in his books. He's a very good author. We should know because we read 23 of his magnificent books!

About the Authors:

The authors go to Marion Street School. They are in the 3rd grade. They like to read, put poems in their pockets and write. They wrote this book in Reader's Workshop.

They read 23 Tomie de Paola books. All the books were exciting. The authors fell in love with Tomie's illustrations and stories.

They wrote this book to share what they know about the wonderful heart man.

[The authors signed their work:]

Rashad Lemonier	Joey Morreale
Jason Paul	Omar Montalvo
Michael Gillis	Michael Winn
Mike Russo	Maurizio Fuduli
Melissa Scheiner	Joanne Payne
Susan Brush	Lionetti
Krystal Bloom	Matt Papol
Justin Spigonardo	Janet Fingeret
Marie Schimenti	Sara Haass
Robert McCurdy	

I named Berlioz the bear after a French composer, Hector Berlioz. If you want to hear some music that he wrote, my favorite is "The Hungarian March". This is how to pronounce his name: **BEAR-LEE-OZE** (the last part rhymes with toes)

Just remember, there is a "bear" in Berlioz.

Creating the character of Berlioz was easy. I just took my husband, Joe, and lengthened his nose. When it was long enough I added a black bear nose tip. Then I moved his ears up and rounded them. Last of all, I covered him with thick fur.

I exaggerated Joe's personality for my book. He's enthusiastic and he tries hard to make things go well. I made Berlioz even more so. When everything goes wrong, Berlioz struggles to control himself. He tugs his ears.

People may use body language to express themselves. Watching people skip with lightheartedness, gnash their teeth because they're frustrated, or pop their eyes with surprise gives me ideas for my animal characters.

I wanted each member of Berlioz's band to look different. I asked five members of the Boston Symphony Orchestra to help me.

Author-artist Jan Brett sends a newsletter to students who are interested in the way she creates a character. Here, she discusses Berlioz the Bear.

These students also identified the geographic location of the habitats of endangered species. They then wrote letters to the National Wildlife Federation, the International Wildlife Society, the Audubon Society, the Sierra Club, the Wilderness Society, and other organizations to request materials to display and suggestions for projects that could help endangered species in Georgia. Some of these projects continued for the rest of the school year.

In both of these units students were reading, writing, talking, planning, learning about science and geography, and reading good books. The books sparked an interest in and were resources for finding out about a particular topic. Reading about endangered animals made the issue important to these students; the books helped the children to personalize an abstract idea.

Essentials of a Literature Curriculum

Whatever you decide to focus on and however you structure your literature program, make sure you have the time, materials, and spatial arrangements necessary for a successful literature-based curriculum. This includes many opportunities for students

---

Figure 12-4

Books About Zoo Animals

Arnold, Caroline. *Cheetah.* Photos by Richard Hewett. (P–I)

——. *Giraffe.* Photos by Richard Hewett. (P–I)

——. *Zebra.* Photos by Richard Hewett. (P–I)

——. *Hippo.* Photos by Richard Hewett. (P–I)

——. *Llama.* Photos by Richard Hewett. (P–I)

——. *Penguin.* Photos by Richard Hewett. (P–I)

——. *Koala.* Photos by Richard Hewett. (P–I)

Bare, Colleen Stanley. *Never Kiss an Alligator!*

Lauber, Patricia. *Snakes Are Hunters.* Illus. Holly Keller. (I)

Martin, Bill, Jr. *Brown Bear, Brown Bear, What Do You See?* Illus. Eric Carle. (P)

Martin, Bill, Jr. *Polar Bear, Polar Bear, What Do You Hear?* Illus. Eric Carle. (P)

Matthews, Downs. *Polar Bear Cubs.* Photos by Dan Guravich. (P–I)

Powzyk, Joyce. *Tracking Wild Chimpanzees in Kibira National Park.* (I)

Sattler, Helen Roney. *Giraffes, the Sentinels of the Savannas.* Illus. Christopher Santoro. (I)

Scott, Jack Denton. *Swans.* Photos by Ozzie Sweet. (I)

Yoshida, Toshi. *Young Lions.* (P–I)

---

to read and talk with others and to explore their responses to the books they read.

Time to Read

Time to read is crucial. You need time to read aloud, no matter what grade you are teaching, time for students to read independently and with peers, and time for students to explore their responses to what they read. One of the teacher's most important roles—and one of the most exciting—is sharing good literature with children. Children show their excitement eagerly and enthusiastically as they respond to literature they hear and see and turn to books themselves as a source of pleasure. They beg you to read a story again and to keep on reading. They begin to recognize authors and illustrators and ask for those people's books. They share their own enthusiasm for reading with their classmates by eagerly talking about books.

Teachers and librarians who surround children with books and poetry will observe these natural responses and, with careful planning, can stimulate even more. Students will begin to compare different versions of a folktale or contrast the print and media versions of a story. They will find poetry that goes with a book or topic. When teachers give book talks, share media presentations and read aloud good books and poetry, they are showing children that reading is worth the effort.

In Chapter 2 we discuss reading aloud and sustained silent reading. There are other ways of reading that involve collaboration among students, such as literature circles and shared reading. Plenty of time is key to the success of any literature program. If you want children to read you must give them time to read and respond. Spending time with books shows that you value books and gives your students the opportunity to value them as well.

Eric Carle's collage art presents children's faces as the ultimate answer to the repeated question: "What do you see?" Bill Martin, Jr.'s story has served as a pattern for children to use to predict words and to write their own stories. (***Brown Bear, Brown Bear, What Do You See?***)

An integrated literature-based program involves science, social studies, math, and language arts. These students categorized the animals they saw at the zoo; made maps of the zoo; studied vertebrate and invertebrate species; made graphs of miles, amounts, and quantities; and wrote patterned stories about the animals.

Children care about the earth and its creatures. They work to make certain the world they inherit is worth having.

Books

In addition to plenty of time, a response-centered literature curriculum requires plenty of books. Classroom libraries and central (school or public) libraries differ markedly in size, organization, and purpose. Classroom libraries contain focused, mostly temporary, and continuously changing collections whereas central libraries contain comprehensive, permanent, and continually growing collections.

What books you have in your classroom will vary according to the interests, needs, and abilities of your students. Your own knowledge of children's literature, resources such as the book lists provided in this text, book award lists, the reference tools discussed in Chapter 1, and your school librarian will inform the selections you make. Whatever specific titles you decide to include in your classroom library, you will want to have a variety of authors, genres, topics, themes, and reading levels in your core collection. The core of your classroom library should be constant—available throughout the year. The core collection represents books that can be returned to over and over again; a revolving collection changes according to specific needs. Each preceding chapter in this text lists outstanding examples of books in different genres; select from those lists as you begin to develop your library.

Figure 12-5

Books and Magazines About Wildlife

Ancona, George. *Turtle Watch.* (I)

Arnold, Caroline. *Orangutan.* (P)

———. *Kangaroo.* (P)

———. *Snakes.* (P)

———. *Saving the Peregrine Falcon.* (P–I)

———. *Wild Goats.* (P)

Bishop, Gerald. *Ranger Rick National Wildlife Federation.* (P–I)

Cajacob, Thomas, and Theresa Burton. *Close to the Wild: Siberian Tigers in a Zoo.* (I)

Cristini, Ermanno, and Luigi Puricelli. *In the Woods.* (P)

———. *In My Garden.* (P)

———. *In the Pond.* (P)

Lazo, Caroline E. *Endangered Species.* (I–A)

Malnig, Anita. *Where the Waves Break: Life at the Edge of the Sea.* (I)

Morris, Rick. *Mysteries and Marvels of Ocean Life.* (I)

Patent, Dorothy Hinshaw. *Gray Wolf, Red Wolf.* Photos William Munoz. (I–A)

———. *Way of the Grizzly.* (I–A)

Peters, Lisa Westberg. *Condor.* (I)

Pringle, Laurence. *Saving Our Wildlife.* (A)

Rinard, Judith E. *Wildlife, Making a Comeback: How Humans Are Helping.* (I–A)

Schorsch, Nancy T. *Saving the Condor.* (I–A)

You will also want to have revolving collections, books that represent the interests you and your class explore across the year. Whether you are involved in a study of the Middle Ages, or are focusing on particular genres, structures, or themes, you will want to gather as many books as you can that will support your study. These books, from your own collection, children's collections, the school or public library, or any other source, will remain in your

**Figure
12-6**

Classroom Libraries

Classroom libraries: focused, continuously changing.

Central libraries: comprehensive, permanent, growing.

Classroom libraries provide easy access to books, magazines, print materials

    on curriculum topics being studied
    related to current literature focus
    for recreational reading
    organized in a simple manner
    routinely changed

  story props
    flannel boards, feltboards
    taped and VCR stories with headsets
    roller movies, puppets
    posters, bulletin boards, dust jackets

  comfortable quiet space
    to read privately, to sit and relax
    removed from vigorous activity
    with appealing display of books
    with book covers, not spines, visible

Research Facts: When there's a classroom library, students read 50 percent more books. Students use a classroom library more when the teacher reads aloud, tells stories, uses storytelling props (feltboard stories, puppets, filmstrips, tapes), gets children to discuss literal and critical issues in stories. (Lesley Mandel Morrow, *Reading Teacher,* Nov. 1984)

classroom for as long as you explore the topic. In many of the chapters in this text we present lists organized according to topics; you will develop your own lists as you discover the interests of your students. If you are engaged in an author study, then books by and about the focal author will become the material for the revolving collection. Sometimes books from a revolving collection become so popular that they become part of the core collection. Figure 12-6 lists some guidelines for classroom libraries.

Space

We know that excitement about literature is indeed contagious. Children are inherently motivated when their teacher is enthusiastic. Enthusiasm for books is primary and can be reflected in the physi-

cal environment of the room. The books in your classroom should be easily accessible to students and attractively displayed, with many covers facing outward. Children should help devise a simple scheme to organize the books. Comfortable places to sit and relax with a book and attractive displays such as posters and book jackets make the reading area inviting. This area should be on the edge of the classroom, removed from vigorous activity, but arranged so it is the focal point of the room.

Opportunities to Read and Talk With Others

The way you arrange your classroom can promote social interaction around books. Having room for children to talk quietly about favorite stories promotes deeper thought about what they have read and helps them learn about themselves and each other as readers. Room for spontaneous dramatic activity also promotes a closer connection with books and with each other. A general sharing area with an author's chair, often in the book corner, promotes group discussions of books.

While a lot of reading might take the form of individual encounters with books, many children find it rewarding to read with peers. Paired reading involves two children reading a book together. They might share one copy of the book or each have a copy. They might decide to read alternate pages, read in chorus, or have one person read more than the other.

Another way of reading with others is to form literature circles. Literature circles involve small groups of readers either reading and discussing one book they are reading in common or several books that revolve around a central topic or focus. In literature circles children work together to understand what they are reading and explore their own responses (Galda, Cullinan, & Strickland, 1993; Short & Pierce, 1990).

Even if a book has been read individually, readers often want to share and compare their responses. Spontaneous sharing of opinions and responses gives children ideas about books to read, and helps them realize that responses vary across individual readers. It also helps children learn to be tolerant about diverse responses and offers opportunities for reconsidering, reformulating, and enlarging their own responses.

These spontaneous opportunities for sharing talk about books are vital to the life of a classroom, but you will also want to plan some structured activities, such as those we discuss in Chapter 2 and present in Teaching Ideas throughout the text, that

Students lean against the wall and use the floor for writing and reading. Low shelves keep additional books handy—at arm's length.

Student authors celebrate their own writing as they display it to illustrate the various steps of the writing process.

encourage students to share responses. The structured activities that students engage in will provide them with models for response options that they can select individually. Writing, storytelling, choral speaking, discussing, dramatic activities, art, and song are some ways of responding that allow chil-

dren to live a little longer in the spell of a good book. One powerful way that you help your students learn about possibilities for response is the questions you ask. If you ask interesting questions about the books you read, your students will soon internalize those questions and ask them of themselves and each other. Peterson and Eeds (1990) suggest that teachers prepare for book discussions by asking themselves about the structure, the characters, the setting (place and time), the point of view, the mood, and any symbols or metaphors central to the story. The evaluative checklists that appear in each genre chapter in this text can help you formulate some questions to keep in mind as you read. Thinking about the literary qualities of the books you read prepares you to help your students understand how literature works. If you have thought carefully about what you read and if you listen carefully to what your students say as they discuss books, you will be ready to build on your students' responses, providing them with the opportunity to discover what they know and expand their literary understanding.

Media Materials

Media materials, like structured activities, should connect readers with books. Media materials that are used to present literature to children are not substitutes for books; they create a totally different literary experience. A group of nursery school children giggled as they watched *Rosie's Walk* (Weston Woods), a film based on Pat Hutchins's picture book. They saw the fox sneak up behind Rosie the hen, jump to pounce on her, land on a garden rake, and get smacked on the nose with the rake handle. The background country music enlivens Rosie's perky walk, the slyness of the crafty fox, and the trauma of each boomeranging blow. After watching the film, the children immediately ran for the book so they could relive the excitement of the story, and they continued to reread it for weeks.

Today's children, born to television, respond naturally to media presentations of literature. They are as close as fingers in a mitten to characters from their favorite TV shows and quickly identify story characters from their favorite books in a visual interpretation. Fortunately, we have a wealth of media products because of technical advances and tremendous growth in the film industry.

Films should illuminate books and yet leave room for the imaginative participation of the audience. Many filmmakers, conscientious about the work they produce, take great pains to remain faithful to the original story. Films based on picture books require extra caution. Because the filmmaker needs a great deal more art than appears in most picture books, the original artwork is often painstakingly re-created in a style that suits the graphic requirements of the film medium, while embodying the styles of the original artist; in some cases, the original artist creates the drawings for the film productions, and in some cases the film production consists of an interpretive reading against a still shot of the original book illustrations. An informative film about the intricate and imaginative process of animation is *Gene Deitch: The Picture Book Animated* (Weston Woods).

Unfortunately, some adaptations of literature insult the audience and sensationalize the work. Some of the most offensive are media presentations of folklore with cartoonlike illustrations, simplified plot retellings, and unadorned moralistic preachments. Full-length novels condensed into filmstrips often degenerate into a series of inconsequential pictures that rob children of the joy of creating their own mental images. Rather than inviting participation in creating images, some films spell out details unequivocally, undermining the subtle essence of characterization and expressive language and diminishing the emotional power of the work. Evocative prose is reduced to a full-color slide show that requires a passive sponge instead of an active participant. The child's imagination, experience, and emotions are deadened.

Media presentations and interpretations, therefore, are an asset to a literature program as long as they complement the books and draw children back to literature. Evaluate media materials for use in a literature program in the following manner.

1. Consider the literary value of the work; a good film cannot improve a bad book. Criteria for evaluating literature appear in each of the genre chapters in this text.

2. Consider if the treatment is appropriate to the literary work. Does it enrich and expand the book's original purpose without sensationalizing it into something beyond the author's intent? A good example is Robert McCloskey's *Time of Wonder* (P) (Weston Woods), which is presented with his original illustrations and appropriate music to capture the book's sensitive tribute to nature. Or look at Gerald McDermott's *Arrow to the Sun* (I), a marvelous film version of the picture book which adds dimensions of sound and movement that are not possible in the book.

3. Decide if the work is appropriate to the audience. Diluting a work of art to make it accessible to a younger audience changes the author's purpose and deceives children. A particularly conspicuous example of this is the Walt Disney Productions treatment of A. A. Milne's *Winnie the Pooh* (P–I). The film replaces Ernest Shepard's original winsome illustrations

---

**Figure
12-7**

Checklist for Media Adaptations of Literature

❏　Is the adaptation based on high-quality literature?

❏　Does the presentation encourage students to return to the book?

❏　Does the adaptation enrich or extend the original material?

❏　Is the presentation a different experience from that of the book?

❏　Does the presentation invite students' imaginative participation?

❏　Does the presentation remain true to authentic versions of the story, poem, or information? Does it maintain the integrity of the original work?

❏　Does the media producer give credit to the author of the original piece?

❏　Does the presentation respect the original literary art form?

❏　Does the presentation retain the flavor of the language of the book?

❏　Is the presentation geared to an appropriate age group?

❏　Is the adaptation technically excellent: clear sound and sight quality reproduction?

❏　Does the presentation avoid moralistic messages—or add-ons?

---

with cartoons, reduces Milne's poetic language to stilted dialogue, and adds an unnecessary character, a groundhog, who repeats "I'm not in the book." Unless they are introduced to the original work at an appropriate age, children who see these films have been robbed of the joy of really knowing these lovable characters.

4.　In addition to maintaining the integrity of the original work, media materials should be technically excellent; clear sound and visual reproduction are vital. They should also be durable enough to hold up to repeated use.

Selection, then, may be even more critical for media materials than for books. The teacher's job is to select without compromise; the same standards for excellence apply to all presentations of literature. Figure 12-7 provides a list of criteria to keep in mind as you are selecting media material.

The greatest advantage of audiovisual presentations is their flexibility: Many more children can share a literary experience at the same time than with a book. This is especially true in the case of small books, such as those of Beatrix Potter, which are simply not suitable for sharing with a large group of children.

Tape-recorded versions of favorite stories are also available for classroom use. Both commercial and homemade tapes of clear dramatic readings of stories are important materials to have in a litera-

ture-rich classroom. Busy teachers do not have as much time to share books as they or the children would like. Sound filmstrip viewers and video players set up for individuals or small groups allow many children to use them at any time. Tape-recorded versions of favorite books allow individuals or groups of children to hear a book being read over and over again.

Media presentations do not, of course, replace oral reading by teachers. They can, however, supplement a strong read-aloud program. Children return to the media presentations of stories time and again for pleasure and reinforcement. Further, students with certain learning disabilities often learn best when they hear and see the words at the same time. This provides important practice in fusing the printed letters and words into comprehensible language patterns. Some high-quality media adaptations, films, audiotapes and videotapes, are listed in Figure 12-8.

Many media presentations also focus on the creation of books and illustrations. These can be exciting additions to any study of individual authors or the craft of writing. Some of the best of these presentations also are listed in Figure 12-8.

While media presentations cannot replace the books themselves, the wise selection and use of media can certainly enrich a strong literature program, helping students enjoy and learn about literature.

Media Resources to Enhance Literature Programs

Wonderworks series
Ramona series
The Little House on the Prairie series
Aladdin
Roger Rabbit
Hallmark series: *Sarah, Plain and Tall,
Skylark*
Children's Television Workshop
Ghost Writer series
Reading Rainbow series
WGBH Boston *Long Ago and Far Away*
series
After School Specials
Weston Woods productions

Media Presentations on Authors and Illustrators

Karla Kuskin, Gerald McDermott, Weston
Woods
Lois Lowry, Houghton Mifflin
Series on 30 or more authors from Philadel-
phia Free Library.
Kellogg, Steven. *How a Picture Book Is
Made: The Island of the Skog.* Weston
Woods. Sound filmstrip. Teachers guide.

Steven Kellogg tells how he grew up
to be an author and how *The Island of
the Skog* was written, illustrated, edited,
and published.

Assessment

When literature abounds in classrooms there is less time for traditional assessment procedures than when children are busy working on "gradeable" products. There is, however, more opportunity for authentic assessment. Authentic assessment involves observing children as they are reading and responding to literature, examining the work they produce as part of their reading and responding, and talking with them about what they are doing. It also involves assessing yourself as a teacher, looking critically at your planning, at the daily life of your classroom, and at your students' literacy development to determine what is and is not effective practice. In authentic assessment the focus is on what children *can* do, not on how far behind an adult model they are, and on what they actually are doing.

Successful teachers assess their literature programs by keeping records and collecting children's work, observing their behavior, and listening to their talk. You will certainly want to *keep records* of what your students are reading. Many teachers ask students to keep a journal to record what they are reading and their response to it. Other teachers, especially those working with beginning readers and writers, ask students to keep a record of the titles of the books they read. Still others, knowing that the act of copying the title is a time-consuming act for some young children, jot down what they see their students reading each day.

If your students do keep *journals,* then you also have a record of the breadth and depth of their reading. You can determine what genres of books they are reading, and their favorite authors and genres. This information can help you determine if they need to be introduced to particular books, authors, or genres.

A *journal* also allows you to keep track of your students' developing understandings about literature. Reading student journals allows you to assess what they say about what they read, discovering if they read for plot or identify with the characters. Journals allow you to see how and what connections they make between their own lives and the stories they read; you can also see how they connect books with other books. When students begin to recognize authors' distinctive styles and to read like writers, paying attention to structure, word choice, and syntax, their journals will reflect this ability.

You will also want to *observe your students* as they select books and as they read and respond to books. Watch to see if your students select a book they can read and are likely to enjoy. If they are not yet reading fluently, can they retell the story through the pictures? Determine what reading strategies they rely on as they read; do they focus on meaning or do they get bogged down in the words themselves? Find out how your students are selecting books and whom they ask for suggestions. Discover whom they read with and where they like to read.

Keep track of how your students respond to the books they read and examine the kinds of things they do. Notice the kinds of writing they do in response, how often they choose art or dramatic activities as response options. Examine these activities closely, looking for demonstrations of your students' engagement with and understanding of the books they read.

As you observe your students, jot down brief anecdotes about what they are doing. If you use

*T*EACHING IDEA 12-5

Building a Portfolio of Literature Learning

Historically, tests have dictated curriculum—what is tested must be taught. Therefore, because tidbits of information could be tested easily, they became the literature curriculum. Authentic assessment reflects what students learn in a literature program in a more accurate way.

Assessment procedures help students assess what they are learning. The following activities help students build portfolios that accurately reflect their learning.

1. Ask students to keep samples of student work in portfolios. Date them. Periodically review samples with the student and together decide which ones to keep for parent information reports or for the year's collection. Talk with students about what they are learning and what would best reflect their learning. Ask what else they feel they need to learn. State your assessment of what they do well and what they need to learn or work toward.

2. Have students discuss in small groups what they are learning.

3. Ask students to keep a log of what they read. Ask them to keep records of what they read.

4. Ask students to keep journals about their reading.

5. Keep samples of a variety of ways students respond to what they read.

Some records are valuable for your own assessment of your literature program. The following activities help you decide when to revamp the curriculum.

1. Summarize the genres that students read.

2. Summarize the list of favorite authors that students read.

3. Examine what your students discuss about the books they read: plot, character, language, theme.

4. Notice how your students relate what they are reading to things they have read previously.

5. Observe how students select books: Do they select ones they can read? Ones that provide information they need?

---

mailing labels to write on, you can affix each label to a sheet of paper in each child's record. As you keep adding anecdotes you build a picture of each child's behavior.

Listening to children discuss books is another way of assessing their development as readers. Note the kinds of things they talk about, whether they attend to others' ideas, and whether others' ideas enrich their own reading and responding. *Listen to yourself* (on a tape recording) as you discuss books with children. Assess your questioning behavior, noting the kinds of questions you ask and if they are open questions that really request children's opinions and ideas. Determine if you ask questions that stretch their understandings about the stories they are reading.

As you read to and with your students, and as you watch them read to and with each other, you will begin to see the power that good books hold to open our eyes to other worlds, other ideas, and new concepts. You will be able to see children learning about the written word and how it works—its complexities and its power—as they are engaged in reading. The reading you will see will be real—reading for meaning and for joy. When a knowledgeable and sensitive teacher puts good books in the hands of children, magic happens.

ISSUES IN SELECTION: CENSORSHIP

Sometimes the books that teachers and librarians choose to use in classrooms provoke adverse reactions from parents or other members of the community. Often a parent will simply request that his or her child not read a particular book, and we make provisions for that. Sometimes, however, an individual parent, school board member, or member of the larger community will request that no child be allowed to read a particular book; this is a bigger problem.

Suppressing reading material is *censorship*—a remedy that causes more problems than it solves. Selecting reading material that does not offend our taste, however, is *selection*—not censorship. Censorship is the attempt to deny others the right to read something the censor thinks is offensive. Selection is the process of choosing appropriate material for readers according to literary and educational judgments.

The National Council of Teachers of English (1983) differentiates between professional guidelines for selection and censorship along five dimensions. (1) Censorship excludes specific materials; selection includes specific materials to give breadth to collections. (2) Censorship is negative; selection is affirmative. (3) Censorship is intended to control the reading of others; selection is intended to advise the reading of others. (4) Censorship seeks to indoctrinate and "limit access to ideas and information," whereas selection seeks to educate and "increase access to ideas and information." (5) Censorship looks at specific aspects and parts of a work in isolation, whereas selection examines the "relationship of parts to each other and to a work as a whole" (p. 18).

The controversies surrounding many books is rooted in a blatant attempt to impose censorship, to limit student access to materials, and to impose the religious and political views of a small segment of society on those whose views may be different. The International Reading Association, the National Council of Teachers of English, and the American Library Association condemn attempts by self-appointed censors to restrict students' access to quality reading materials and programs. These associations and most school districts have procedures in place for dealing with attempted censor-

ship. The school media specialist or the principal will have a standard process that teachers follow if a book is challenged.

Appendix F contains the National Council of Teachers of English statement of Students' Right to Read and their suggestions for procedures to follow if challenged. These procedures follow these general steps:

1. Establish book selection procedures *before* the censors come. Make your procedures public.

2. Involve professional librarians, teachers, parents, administrators, and lay community members in the book selection process.

3. When complaints are registered, have them put in writing.

4. Ask that the person who makes the complaint read the entire book and put the incident or language in question in context.

5. Meet with the person who makes the complaint to discuss alternatives.

If you select wisely, you lessen the chances of an unpleasant experience.

SUMMARY

In a literature-based curriculum students read and respond to literature in an atmosphere that allows them choice about what they read, who they read with, and how they respond to their reading. A literature-based curriculum requires plenty of books and plenty of time to read and respond to them. Reading trade books can be a springboard to learning about literature and also a way of learning about other topics of interest. As students read and respond to literature they build a lifelong love of reading and a storehouse of language experiences that enriches their own language use; they also experience the pleasure and excitement of being engaged with wonderful books.

Appendix A

Children's Book Awards

The John Newbery Medal

The John Newbery Medal, named for an eighteenth-century British publisher and bookseller, the first to publish books for children, is given annually for the most distinguished contribution to literature for children published in the United States in the year preceding the award.

Selection of the award winner is made by a committee of the Association for Library Services for Children of the American Library Association.

The following list gives the title, author, and publisher of winners and of runners-up (honor books) since the inception of the award in 1922.

1922
The Story of Mankind by Hendrik Willem van Loon, Liveright

Honor Books: *The Great Quest* by Charles Hawes, Little, Brown; *Cedric the Forester* by Bernard Marshall, Appleton; *The Old Tobacco Shop* by William Bowen, Macmillan; *The Golden Fleece and the Heroes Who Lived Before Achilles* by Padraic Colum, Macmillan; *Windy Hill* by Cornelia Meigs, Macmillan

1923
The Voyages of Doctor Doolittle by Hugh Lofting, HarperCollins

Honor Books: No Record

1924
The Dark Frigate by Charles Hawes, Little, Brown, Atlantic

Honor Books: No record

1925
Tales from Silver Lands by Charles Finger, Doubleday

Honor Books: *Nicholas* by Anne Carroll Moore, Putnam's; *Dream Coach* by Anne Parrish, Macmillan

1926
Shen of the Sea by Arthur Bowie Chrisman, Dutton

Honor Book: *Voyagers* by Padraic Colum, Macmillan

1927
Smoky, The Cowhorse by Will James, Scribner's

Honor Books: No record

1928
Gayneck, The Story of a Pigeon by Dhan Gopal Mukerji, Dutton

Honor Books: *The Wonder Smith and His Son* by Ella Young, Longmans; *Downright Dencey* by Caroline Snedeker, Doubleday

1929
The Trumpeter of Krakow by Eric P. Kelly, Macmillan

Honor Books: *Pigtail of Ah Lee Ben Loo* by John Benett, Longmans; *Millions of Cats* by Wanda Gág, Coward-McCann; *The Boy Who Was* by Grace Hallock, Dutton; *Clearing Weather* by Cornelia Meigs, Little, Brown; *Runaway Papoose* by Grace Moon, Doubleday; *Tod of the Fens* by Elinor Whitney, Macmillan

1930
Hitty, Her First Hundred Years by Rachel Field, Macmillan

Honor Books: *Daughter of the Seine* by Jeanette Eaton, HarperCollins; *Pran of Albania* by Elizabeth Miller, Doubleday; *Jumping-Off Place* by Marian Hurd McNeely, Longmans; *Tangle-Coated Horse and Other Tales* by Ella Young, Longmans; *Vaino* by Julia Davis Adams, Dutton; *Little Black-nose* by Hildegarde Swift, Harcourt Brace

1931

The Cat Who Went to Heaven by Elizabeth Coatsworth, Macmillan

Honor Books: *Floating Island* by Anne Parrish, HarperCollins; *The Dark Star of Itza* by Alida Malkus, Harcourt Brace; *Queer Person* by Ralph Hubbard, Doubleday; *Mountains Are Free* by Julia Davis Adams, Dutton; *Spice and the Devil's Cave* by Agnes Hewes, Knopf; *Meggy Macintosh* by Elizabeth Janet Gray, Doubleday; *Garram the Hunter* by Herbert Best, Doubleday; *Ood-Le-Uk the Wanderer* by Alice Lide and Margaret Johansen, Little, Brown

1932

Waterless Mountain by Laura Adams Armer, Longmans

Honor Books: *The Fairy Circus* by Dorothy P. Lathrop, Macmillan; *Calico Bush* by Rachel Field, Macmillan; *Boy of the South Seas* by Eunice Tietjens, Coward-McCann; *Out of the Flame* by Eloise Lownsbery, Longmans; *Jane's Island* by Marjorie Allee, Houghton-Mifflin; *Truce of the Wolf and Other Tales of Old Italy* by Mary Gould Davis, Harcourt Brace

1933

Young Fu of the Upper Yangtze by Elizabeth Foreman Lewis, Winston

Honor Books: *Swift Rivers* by Cornelia Meigs, Little, Brown; *The Railroad to Freedom* by Hildegarde Swift, Harcourt Brace; *Children of the Soil* by Nora Burglon, Doubleday

1934

Invincible Louisa by Cornelia Meigs, Little, Brown

Honor Books: *The Forgotten Daughter* by Caroline Snedeker, Doubleday; *Swords of Steel* by Elsie Singmaster, Houghton Mifflin; *ABC Bunny* by Wanda Gág, Coward-McCann; *Winged Girl of Knossos* by Erik Berry, Appleton; *New Land* by Sarah Schmidt, McBride; *Big Tree of Bunlahy* by Padraic Colum, Macmillan; *Glory of the Seas* by Agnes Hewes, Knopf; *Apprentice of Florence* by Ann Kyle, Houghton Mifflin

1935

Dobry by Monica Shannon, Viking

Honor Books: *Pageant of Chinese History* by Elizabeth Seeger, Longmans; *Davy Crockett* by Constance Rourke, Harcourt Brace; *Day on Skates* by Hilda Van Stockum, HarperCollins

1936

Caddie Woodlawn by Carol Ryrie Brink, Macmillan

Honor Books: *Honk, the Moose* by Phil Stong, Dodd, Mead; *The Good Master* by Kate Seredy, Viking; *Young Walter Scott* by Elizabeth Janet Gray, Viking; *All Sail Set* by Armstrong Sperry, Winston

1937

Roller Skates by Ruth Sawyer, Viking

Honor Books: *Phoebe Fairchild: Her Book* by Lois Lenski, Stokes; *Whistler's Van* by Idwal Jones, Viking; *Golden Basket* by Ludwig Bemelmans, Viking; *Winterbound* by Margery Bianco, Viking; *Audubon* by Constance Rourke, Harcourt Brace; *The Codfish Musket* by Agnes Hewes, Doubleday

1938

The White Stag by Kate Seredy, Viking

Honor Books: *Pecos Bill* by James Cloyd Bowman, Little, Brown; *Bright Island* by Mabel Robinson, Random House; *On the Banks of Plum Creek* by Laura Ingalls Wilder, HarperCollins

1939

Thimble Summer by Elizabeth Enright, Rinehart

Honor Books: *Nino* by Valenti Angelo, Viking; *Mr. Popper's Penguins* by Richard and Florence Atwater, Little, Brown; *"Hello the Boat!"* by Phyllis Crawford, Holt; *Leader by Destiny: George Washington, Man and Patriot* by Jeanette Eaton, Harcourt Brace; *Penn* by Elizabeth Janet Gray, Viking

1940

Daniel Boone by James Daugherty, Viking

Honor Books: *The Singing Tree* by Kate Seredy, Viking; *Runner of the Mountain Tops* by Mabel Robinson, Random House; *By the Shores of Silver Lake* by Laura Ingalls Wilder, *Boy with a Pack* by Stephen W. Meader, Harcourt Brace

1941

Call It Courage by Armstrong Sperry, Macmillan

Honor Books: *Blue Willow* by Doris Gates, Viking; *Young Mac of Fort Vancouver* by Mary Jane Carr, HarperCollins; *The Long Winter* by Laura Ingalls Wilder, HarperCollins; *Nansen* by Anna Gertrude Hall, Viking

1942

The Matchlock Gun by Walter D. Edmonds, Dodd

Honor Books: *Little Town on the Prairie* by Laura Ingalls Wilder, HarperCollins; *George Washington's World* by Genevieve Foster, Scribner's; *Indian Captive: The Story of Mary Jemison* by Lois Lenski, HarperCollins; *Down Ryton Water* by Eva Roe Gaggin, Viking

1943

Adam of the Road by Elizabeth Janet Gray, Viking

Honor Books: *The Middle Moffat* by Eleanor Estes, Harcourt Brace; *Have You Seen Tom Thumb?* by Mabel Leigh Hunt, HarperCollins

1944

Johnny Tremain by Esther Forbes, Houghton Mifflin

Honor Books: *These Happy Golden Years* by Laura Ingalls Wilder, HarperCollins; *Fog Magic* by Julia Sauer, Viking; *Rufus M.* by Eleanor Estes, Harcourt Brace; *Mountain Born* by Elizabeth Yates, Coward-McCann

1945

Rabbit Hill by Robert Lawson, Viking

Honor Books: *The Hundred Dresses* by Eleanor Estes, Harcourt Brace; *The Silver Pencil* by Alice Dalgliesh, Scribner's; *Abraham Lincoln's World* by Genevieve Foster, Scribner's; *Lone Journey: The Life of Roger Williams* by Jeanette Eaton, Harcourt Brace

1946

Strawberry Girl by Lois Lenski, HarperCollins

Honor Books: *Justin Morgan Had a Horse* by Marguerite Henry, Rand; *The Moved-Outers* by Florence Crannel Means, Houghton Mifflin; *Bhimsa, the Dancing Bear* by Christine Weston, Scribner's; *New Found World* by Katherine Shippen, Viking

1947

Miss Hickory by Carolyn Sherwin Bailey, Viking

Honor Books: *Wonderful Year* by Nancy Barnes, Messner; *Big Tree* by Mary and Conrad Buff, Viking; *The Heavenly Tenants* by William Maxwell, HarperCollins; *The Avion My Uncle Flew* by Cyrus Fisher, Appleton; *The Hidden Treasure of Glaston* by Eleanore Jewett, Viking

1948

The Twenty-One Balloons by William Pène du Bois, Viking

Honor Books: *Pancakes-Paris* by Claire Huchet Bishop, Viking; *Li Lun, Lad of Courage* by Carolyn Treffinger, Abingdon; *The Quaint and Curious Quest of Johnny Longfoot* by Catherine Besterman, Bobbs; *The Cow-Tail Switch, and Other West African Stories* by Harold Courlander, Holt; *Misty of Chincoteague* by Marguerite Henry, Rand

1949

King of the Wind by Marguerite Henry, Rand

Honor Books: *Seabird* by Holling C. Holling, Houghton Mifflin; *Daughter of the Mountains* by Louise Rankin, Viking; *My Father's Dragon* by Ruth S. Gannett, Random House; *Story of the Negro* by Arna Bontemps, Knopf

1950

The Door in the Wall by Marguerite de Angeli, Doubleday

Honor Books: *Tree of Freedom* by Rebecca Caudill, Viking; *The Blue Cat of Castle Town* by Catherine Coblentz, Longmans; *Kildee House* by Rutherford Montgomery, Doubleday; *George Washington* by Genevieve Foster, Scribner's; *Song of the Pines* by Walter and Marion Havighurst, Winston

1951

Amos Fortune, Free Man by Elizabeth Yates, Aladdin

Honor Books: *Better Known as Johnny Appleseed* by Mabel Leigh Hunt, HarperCollins; *Gandhi; Fighter Without a Sword* by Jeanette Eaton, Morrow; *Abraham Lincoln, Friend of the People* by Clara Ingram Judson, Follett; *The Story of Appleby Capple* by Anne Parrish, HarperCollins

1952

Ginger Pye by Eleanor Estes, Harcourt Brace

Honor Books: *Americans Before Columbus* by Elizabeth Baity, Viking; *Minn of the Mississippi* by Holling C. Holling, Houghton Mifflin; *The Defender* by Nicholas Kalashnikoff, Scribner's; *The Light at Tern Rock* by Julia Sauer, Viking; *The Apple and the Arrow* by Mary and Conrad Buff, Houghton Mifflin

1953

Secret of the Andes by Ann Nolan Clark, Viking

Honor Books: *Charlotte's Web* by E. B. White, HarperCollins; *Moccasin Trail* by Eloise McGraw, Coward-McCann; *Red Sails to Capri* by Ann Weil, Viking; *The Bears on Hemlock Mountain* by Alice Dalgliesh, Scribner's; *Birthdays of Freedom,* Vol. 1, by Genevieve Foster, Scribner's

1954

. . . and now Miguel by Joseph Krumgold, HarperCollins

Honor Books: *All Alone* by Claire Huchet Bishop, Viking; *Shadrach* by Meindert DeJong, HarperCollins; *Hurry Home, Candy* by Meindert DeJong, HarperCollins; *Theodore Roosevelt, Fighting Patriot* by Clara Ingram Judson, Follett; *Magic Maize* by Mary and Conrad Buff, Houghton Mifflin

1955

The Wheel on the School by Meindert DeJong, HarperCollins

Honor Books: *The Courage of Sarah Noble* by Alice Dalgliesh, Scribner's; *Banner in the Sky* by James Ullman, HarperCollins

1956

Carry on, Mr. Bowditch by Jean Lee Latham, Houghton Mifflin

Honor Books: *The Secret River* by Marjorie Kinnan Rawlings, Scribner's; *The Golden Name Day* by Jennie Linquist, HarperCollins; *Men, Microscopes, and Living Things* by Katherine Shippen, Viking

1957

Miracles on Maple Hill by Virginia Sorensen, Harcourt Brace

Honor Books: *Old Yeller* by Fred Gipson, HarperCollins; *The House of Sixty Fathers* by Meindert DeJong, HarperCollins; *Mr. Justice Holmes* by Clara Ingram Judson, Follett; *The Corn Grows Ripe* by Dorothy Rhoads; Viking; *Black Fox of Lorne* by Marguerite de Angeli, Doubleday

1958

Rifles for Watie by Harold Keith, Crowell

Honor Books: *The Horsecatcher* by Mari Sandoz, Westminster; *Gone-Away Lake* by Elizabeth Enright, Harcourt Brace; *The Great Wheel* by Robert Lawson, Viking; *Tom Paine, Freedom's Apostle* by Leo Gurko, HarperCollins

1959

The Witch of Blackbird Pond by Elizabeth George Speare, Houghton Mifflin

Honor Books: *The Family Under the Bridge* by Natalie Savage Carlson, HarperCollins; *Along Came a Dog* by Meindert DeJong, HarperCollins; *Chucaro: Wild Pony of the Pampa* by Francis Kalnay, Harcourt Brace; *The Perilous Road* by William O. Steele, Harcourt Brace

1960

Onion John by Joseph Krumgold, HarperCollins

Honor Books: *My Side of the Mountain* by Jean George, Dutton: *America Is Born* by Gerald W. Johnson, Morrow; *The Gammage Cup* by Carol Kendall, Harcourt Brace

1961

Island of the Blue Dolphins by Scott O'Dell, Houghton Mifflin

Honor Books: *America Moves Forward* by Gerald W. Johnson, Morrow; *Old Ramon* by Jack Schaefer, Houghton Mifflin; *The Cricket in Times Square* by George Selden, Farrar, Straus & Giroux

1962

The Bronze Bow by Elizabeth George Speare, Houghton Mifflin

Honor Books: *Frontier Living* by Edwin Tunis, World; *The Golden Goblet* by Eloise McGraw, Coward-McCann; *Belling the Tiger* by Mary Stolz, HarperCollins

1963

A Wrinkle in Time by Madeleine L'Engle, Farrar, Straus & Giroux

Honor Books: *Thistle and Thyme* by Sorche Nic Leodhas, Holt; *Men of Athens* by Olivia Coolidge, Houghton Mifflin

1964

It's Like This, Cat by Emily Cheney Neville, HarperCollins

Honor Books: *Rascal* by Sterling North, Dutton; *The Loner* by Ester Wier, McKay

1965

Shadow of a Bull by Maia Wojciechowska, Atheneum

Honor Book: *Across Five Aprils* by Irene Hunt, Follett

1966

I, Juan de Pareja by Elizabeth Borten de Treviño, Farrar, Straus & Giroux

Honor Books: *The Black Cauldron* by Lloyd Alexander, Holt; *The Animal Family* by Randall Jarrell, Pantheon; *The Noonday Friends* by Mary Stolz, HarperCollins

1967

Up a Road Slowly by Irene Hunt, Follett

Honor Books: *The King's Fifth* by Scott O'Dell, Houghton Mifflin; *Zlateh the Goat and Other Stories* by Isaac Bashevis Singer, HarperCollins; *The Jazz Man* by Mary H. Weik, Atheneum

1968

From the Mixed-Up Files of Mrs. Basil E. Frankweiler by E. L. Konigsburg, Atheneum

Honor Books: *Jennifer, Hecate, Macbeth, William McKinley, and Me, Elizabeth* by E. L. Konigsburg, Atheneum; *The Black Pearl* by Scott O'Dell, Houghton Mifflin; *The Fearsome Inn* by Isaac Bashevis Singer, Scribner's *The Egypt Game* by Zilpha Keatley Snyder, Atheneum

1969

The High King by Lloyd Alexander, Holt

Honor Books: *To Be a Slave* by Julius Lester, Dial; *When Shlemiel Went to Warsaw and Other Stories* by Isaac Bashevis Singer, Farrar, Straus & Giroux

1970

Sounder by William H. Armstrong, HarperCollins

Honor Books: *Our Eddie* by Sulamith Ish-Kishor, Pantheon; *The Many Ways of Seeing: An Introduction to the Pleasures of Art* by Janet Gaylord Moore, World; *Journey Outside* by Mary Q. Steele, Viking

1971

Summer of the Swans by Betsy Byars, Viking

Honor Books: *Kneeknock Rise* by Natalie Babbitt, Farrar Straus & Giroux; *Enchantress from the Stars* by Sylvia Louise Engdahl, Atheneum; *Sing Down the Moon* by Scott O'Dell, Houghton Mifflin

1972

Mrs. Frisby and the Rats of NIMH by Robert C. O'Brien, Atheneum

Honor Books: *Incident at Hawk's Hill* by Allan W. Eckert, Little, Brown; *The Planet of Junior Brown* by Virginia Hamilton, Macmillan; *The Tombs of Atuan* by Ursula K. Le Guin, Atheneum; *Annie and the Old One* by Miska Miles, Little, Atlantic; *The Headless Cupid* by Zilpha Keatley Snyder, Atheneum

1973

Julie of the Wolves by Jean Craighead George, HarperCollins

Honor Books: *Frog and Toad Together* by Arnold Lobel, HarperCollins; *The Upstairs Room* by Johanna Reiss, HarperCollins; *The Witches of Worm* by Zilpha Keatley Snyder, Atheneum

1974

The Slave Dancer by Paula Fox, Bradbury

Honor Books: *The Dark Is Rising* by Susan Cooper, Atheneum, McElderry

1975

M. C. Higgins, The Great by Virginia Hamilton, Macmillan

Honor Books: *Figgs & Phantoms* by Ellen Raskin, Dutton; *My Brother Sam Is Dead* by James Lincoln Collier & Christopher Collier, Four Winds; *The Perilous Gard* by Elizabeth Marie Pope, Houghton Mifflin; *Philip Hall Likes Me. I Reckon Maybe* by Bette Greene, Dial

1976

The Grey King by Susan Cooper, Atheneum, McElderry

Honor Books: *The Hundred Penny Box* by Sharon Bell Mathis, Viking; *Dragonwings* by Laurence Yep, HarperCollins

1977

Roll of Thunder, Hear My Cry by Mildred D. Taylor, Dial

Honor Books: *Abel's Island* by William Steig, Farrar Straus & Giroux; *A String in the Harp* by Nancy Bond, McElderry

1978

Bridge to Terabithia by Katherine Paterson, HarperCollins

Honor Books: *Ramona and Her Father* by Beverly Cleary, Morrow; *Anpao: An American Indian Odyssey* by Jamake Highwater, HarperCollins

1979

The Westing Game by Ellen Raskin, Dutton

Honor Books: *The Great Gilly Hopkins* by Katherine Paterson, HarperCollins

1980

A Gathering of Days: A New England Girl's Journal, 1830–32 by Joan Blos, Scribner's

Honor Book: *The Great Gilly Hopkins* by Katherine Paterson, HarperCollins

1981

Jacob Have I Loved by Katherine Paterson, HarperCollins

Honor Books: *The Fledgling* by Jane Langton, HarperCollins; *A Ring of Endless Light* by Madeleine L'Engle, Farrar, Straus & Giroux

1982

A Visit to William Blake's Inn: Poems for Innocent and Experienced Travelers by Nancy Willard, Harcourt Brace

Honor Books: *Ramona Quimby, Age 8* by Beverly Cleary, Morrow; *Upon the Head of the Goat: A Childhood in Hungary, 1939–1944* by Aranka Siegel, Farrar, Straus & Giroux

1983

Dicey's Song by Cynthia Voigt, Atheneum

Honor Books: *The Blue Sword* by Robin McKinley, Greenwillow; *Dr. De Soto* by William Steig, Farrar, Straus & Giroux; *Graven Images* by Paul Fleischman, HarperCollins; *Homesick: My Own Story* by Jean Fritz, Putnam's; *Sweet Whispers, Brother Rush* by Virginia Hamilton, Philomel

1984

Dear Mr. Henshaw by Beverly Cleary, Morrow

Honor Books: *The Wish Giver: Three Tales of Coven Tree* by Bill Brittain, HarperCollins; *A Solitary Blue* by Cynthia Voigt, Atheneum; *The Sign of the Beaver* by Elizabeth George Speare, Houghton Mifflin; *Sugaring Time* by Kathryn Lasky, Macmillan

1985

The Hero and the Crown by Robin McKinley, Greenwillow

Honor Books: *The Moves Make the Man* by Bruce Brooks, HarperCollins; *One-Eyed Cat* by Paula Fox, Bradbury; *Like Jake and Me* by Mavis Jukes, Knopf

1986

Sarah, Plain and Tall by Patricia MacLachlan, HarperCollins

Honor Books: *Commodore Perry in the Land of Shogun* by Rhoda Blumberg, Lothrop, Lee & Shepard; *Dogsong* by Gary Paulsen, Bradbury

1987

The Whipping Boy by Sid Fleischman, Greenwillow

Honor Books: *On My Honor* by Marion Dane Bauer, Clarion; *A Fine White Dust* by Cynthia Rylant, Bradbury; *Volcano* by Patricia Lauber, Bradbury.

1988

Lincoln: A Photobiography by Russell Freedman, Clarion

Honor Books: *Hatchet* by Gary Paulsen, Bradbury; *After the Rain* by Norma Fox Mazer, Morrow

1989

Joyful Noise: Poems for Two Voices by Paul Fleischman, HarperCollins

Honor Books: *In the Beginning: Creation Stories from Around the World* by Virginia Hamilton, Harcourt Brace; *Scorpions* by Walter Dean Myers, HarperCollins

1990

Number the Stars by Lois Lowry, Houghton

Honor Books: *Afternoon of the Elves* by Janet Taylor Lisle, Orchard; *Shabanu: Daughter of the Wind* by Suzanne Fisher Staples, Knopf; *The Winter Room* by Gary Paulsen, Orchard

1991

Maniac Magee by Jerry Spinelli, Little, Brown

Honor Book: *The True Confessions of Charlotte Doyle* by Avi, Orchard

1992

Shiloh by Phyllis Reynolds Naylor, Athenuem

Honor Books: *Nothing But the Truth: A Documentary Novel* by Avi, Orchard; *The Wright Brothers: How They Invented the Airplane* by Russell Freedman, Holiday

1993

Missing May by Cynthia Rylant, Orchard

Honor Books: *What Hearts* by Bruce Brooks, HarperCollins; *The Dark Thirty: Southern Tales of the Supernatural* by Patricia C. McKissack, Knopf; *Somewhere in the Darkness* by Walter Dean Myers, Scholastic

The Randolph Caldecott Medal

The Randolph Caldecott Medal, named for a nineteenth-century British illustrator of books for children, is given annually for the most distinguished picture book for children published in the United States in the year preceding the award.

Selection of the award winner is made by a committee of the Association for Library Services for Children of the American Library Association.

The following list gives the title, illustrator, author, and publisher of winners and runners-up (honor books) since inception of the award in 1938. Where two names are given, the illustrator is listed first, followed by the text's author in parentheses. Where only one name is given, the book was written and illustrated by the same person.

1938

Animals of the Bible by Dorothy P. Lathrop (Helen Dean Fish), HarperCollins

Honor Books: *Seven Simeons* by Boris Artzybasheff, Viking; *Four and Twenty Blackbirds* by Robert Lawson (Helen Dean Fish), HarperCollins

1939

Mei Li by Thomas Handforth, Doubleday

Honor Books: *The Forest Pool* by Laura Adams Armer, Longmans; *Wee Gillis* by Robert Lawson (Munro Leaf), Viking; *Snow White and the Seven Dwarfs* by Wanda Gág, Coward; *Barkis* by Clare Newberry, HarperCollins; *Andy and the Lion* by James Daugherty, Viking

1940

Abraham Lincoln by Ingri and Edgar Parin d'Aulaire, Doubleday

Honor Books: *Cock-a-Doodle Doo . . .* by Berta and Elmer Hader, Macmillan; *Madeline* by Ludwig Bemelmans, Viking; *The Ageless Story,* by Lauren Ford, Dodd, Mead

1941

They Were Strong and Good by Robert Lawson, Viking

Honor Books: *April's Kittens* by Clare Newberry, HarperCollins

1942

Make Way for Ducklings by Robert McCloskey, Viking

Honor Books: *An American ABC* by Maud and Miska Petersham, Macmillan; *In My Mother's House* by Velino Herrera (Ann Nolan Clark), Viking; *Paddle-to-the-Sea* by Holling C. Holling, Houghton Mifflin; *Nothing at All* by Wanda Gág, Coward-McCann

1943

The Little House by Virginia Lee Burton, Houghton Mifflin

Honor Books: *Dash and Dart* by Mary and Conrad Buff, Viking; *Marshmallow* by Clare Newberry, HarperCollins

1944

Many Moons by Louis Slobodkin (James Thurber), Harcourt Brace

Honor Books: *Small Rain: Verses from the Bible* by Elizabeth Orton Jones (selected by Jessie Orton Jones), Viking; *Pierre Pigeon* by Arnold E. Bare (Lee Kingman), Houghton Mifflin; *The Mighty Hunter* by Berta and Elmer Hader, Macmillan; *A Child's Good Night Book* by Jean Charlot (Margaret Wise Brown), Scott, Foresman; *Good Luck Horse* by Plao Chan (Chin-Yi Chan), Whittlesey

1945

Prayer for a Child by Elizabeth Orton Jones (Rachel Field), Macmillan

Honor Books: *Mother Goose* by Tasha Tudor, Walck; *In the Forest* by Marie Hall Ets, Viking; *Yonie Wondernose* by Marguerite de Angeli, Doubleday; *The Christmas Anna Angel* by Kate Seredy (Ruth Sawyer), Viking

1946

The Rooster Crows . . . (traditional Mother Goose) by Maud and Miska Petersham, Macmillan

Honor Books: *Little Lost Lamb* by Leonard Weisgard (Golden MacDonald), Doubleday; *Sing Mother Goose* by Marjorie Torrey (Opal Wheeler), Dutton; *My Mother Is the Most Beautiful Woman in the World* by Ruth Gannett (Becky Reyher), Lothrop, Lee & Shepard; *You Can Write Chinese* by Kurt Wiese, Viking

1947

The Little Island by Leonard Weisgard (Golden MacDonald), Doubleday

Honor Books: *Rain Drop Splash* by Leonard Weisgard (Alvin Tresselt), Lothrop, Lee & Shepard; *Boats on the River* by Jay Hyde Barnum (Marjorie Flack), Viking; *Timothy Turtle* by Tony Palazzo (Al Graham), Viking; *Pedro, the Angel of Olvera Street* by Leo Politi, Scribner's; *Sing in Praise: A Collection of the Best Loved Hymns* by Marjorie Torrey (Opal Wheeler), Dutton

1948

White Snow, Bright Snow by Roger Duvoisin (Alvin Tresselt), Lothrop, Lee & Shepard

Honor Books: *Stone Soup* by Marcia Brown, Scribner's; *McElligot's Pool* by Dr. Seuss, Random House; *Bambino the Clown* by George Schreiber, Viking; *Roger and the Fox* by Hildegard Woodward (Lavinia Davis), Doubleday; *Song of Robin Hood* by Virginia Lee Burton (edited by Anne Malcolmson), Houghton Mifflin

1949

The Big Snow by Berta and Elmer Hader, Macmillan

Honor Books: *Blueberries for Sal* by Robert McCloskey, Viking; *All Around the Town* by Helen Stone (Phyllis McGinley), HarperCollins; *Juanita* by Leo Politi, Scribner's; *Fish in the Air* by Kurt Wiese, Viking

1950

Song of the Swallows by Leo Politi, Scribner's

Honor Books: *America's Ethan Allen* by Lynd Ward (Stewart Holbrook), Houghton Mifflin; *The Wild Birthday Cake* by Hildegard Woodward (Lavinia Davis), Doubleday; *The Happy Day* by Marc Simont (Ruth Krauss), HarperCollins; *Bartholomew and the Oobleck* by Dr. Seuss, Random House; *Henry Fisherman* by Marcia Brown, Scribner's

1951

The Egg Tree by Katherine Milhous, Scribner's

Honor Books: *Dick Whittington and His Cat* by Marcia Brown, Scribner's; *The Two Reds* by Nicholas Mordvinoff (William Lipkind), Harcourt Brace; *If I Ran the Zoo* by Dr. Seuss, Random House; *The Most Wonderful Doll in the World* by Helen Stone (Phyllis McGinley), HarperCollins; *T-Bone, the Baby Sitter* by Clare Newberry, HarperCollins

1952

Finders Keepers by Nicholas Mordvinoff (William Lipkind), Harcourt Brace

Honor Books: *Mr. T. W. Anthony Woo* by Marie Hall Ets, Viking; *Skipper John's Cook* by Marcia Brown, Scribner's; *All Falling Down* by Margaret Bloy Graham (Gene Zion), HarperCollins; *Bear Party* by William Pène du Bois, Viking; *Feather Mountain* by Elizabeth Olds, Houghton Mifflin

1953

The Biggest Bear by Lynd Ward, Houghton Mifflin

Honor Books: *Puss in Boots* retold and illustrated by Marcia Brown (Charles Perrault), Scribner's; *One Morning in Maine* by Robert McCloskey, Viking; *Ape in a Cape* by Fritz Eichenberg, Harcourt

Brace; *The Storm Book* by Margaret Bloy Graham (Charlotte Zolotow), HarperCollins; *Five Little Monkeys* by Juliet Kepes, Houghton Mifflin

1954

Madeline's Rescue by Ludwig Bemelmans, Viking

Honor Books: *Journey Cake, Ho!* by Robert McCloskey (Ruth Sawyer), Viking; *When Will the World Be Mine?* by Jean Charlot (Miriam Schlein), Scott, Foresman; *The Steadfast Tin Soldier* by Marcia Brown (Hans Christian Andersen), Scribner's; *A Very Special House* by Maurice Sendak (Ruth Krauss), HarperCollins; *Green Eyes* by A. Birnbaum, Capitol

1955

Cinderella, or the Little Glass Slipper retold and illustrated by Marcia Brown (Charles Perrault), Scribner's

Honor Books: *Book of Nursery and Mother Goose Rhymes* by Marguerite de Angeli, Doubleday; *Wheel on the Chimney* by Tibor Gergely (Margaret Wise Brown), HarperCollins; *The Thanksgiving Story* by Helen Sewell (Alice Dalgliesh), Scribner's

1956

Frog Went A-Courtin' by Feodor Rojankovsky (John Langstaff), Harcourt Brace

Honor Books: *Play with Me* by Marie Hall Ets, Viking; *Crow Boy* by Taro Yashima, Viking

1957

A Tree Is Nice by Marc Simont (Janice May Udry), HarperCollins

Honor Books: *Mr. Penny's Race Horse* by Marie Hall Ets, Viking; *1 Is One* by Tasha Tudor, Walck; *Anatole* by Paul Galdone (Eve Titus), McGraw-Hill; *Gillespie and the Guards* by James Daugherty (Benjamin Elkin), Viking; *Lion* by William Péne du Bois, Viking

1958

Time of Wonder by Robert McCloskey, Viking

Honor Books: *Fly High, Fly Low* by Don Freeman, Viking; *Anatole and the Cat* by Paul Galdone (Eve Titus), McGraw-Hill

1959

Chanticleer and the Fox adapted and illustrated by Barbara Cooney, HarperCollins

Honor Books: *The House That Jack Built* by Antonio Frasconi, Harcourt Brace; *What Do You Say, Dear?* by Maurice Sendak (Sesyle Joslin), Scott, Foresman; *Umbrella* by Taro Yashima, Viking

1960

Nine Days to Christmas by Marie Hall Ets (Aurora Labastida, Marie Hall Ets), Viking

Honor Books: *Houses from the Sea* by Adrienne Adams (Alice E. Goudey), Scribner's; *The Moon Jumpers* by Maurice Sendak (Janice May Udry), HarperCollins

1961

Baboushka and the Three Kings by Nicholas Sidjakov (Ruth Robbins), Parnassus

Honor Books: *Inch by Inch* by Leo Lionni, Obolensky

1962

Once a Mouse . . . by Marcia Brown, Scribner's

Honor Books: *Fox Went Out on a Chilly Night* by Peter Spier, Doubleday; *Little Bear's Visit* by Maurice Sendak (Else Holmelund Minarik), HarperCollins; *The Day We Saw the Sun Come Up* by Adrienne Adams (Alice E. Goudey), Scribner's

1963

The Snowy Day by Ezra Jack Keats, Viking

Honor Books: *The Sun Is a Golden Earring* by Bernarda Bryson (Natalia M. Belting), Holt; *Mr. Rabbit and the Lovely Present* by Maurice Sendak (Charlotte Zolotow), HarperCollins

1964

Where the Wild Things Are by Maurice Sendak, HarperCollins

Honor Books: *Swimmy* by Leo Lionni, Pantheon; *All in the Morning Early* by Evaline Ness (Sorche Nic Leodhas), Holt; *Mother Goose and Nursery Rhymes* by Philip Reed, Atheneum

1965

May I Bring a Friend? by Beni Montresor (Beatrice Schenk De Regniers), Atheneum

Honor Books: *Rain Makes Applesauce* by Marvin Bileck (Julian Scheer), Holiday House; *The Wave* by Blair Lent (Margaret Hodges), Houghton Mifflin; *A Pocketful of Cricket* by Evaline Ness (Rebecca Caudill), Holt

1966

Always Room for One More by Nonny Hogrogian (Sorche Nic Leodhas), Holt

Honor Books: *Hide and Seek Fog* by Roger Duvoisin (Alvin Tresselt), Lothrop, Lee & Shepard; *Just Me* by Marie Hall Ets, Viking; *Tom Tit Tot* by Evaline Ness, Scribner's

1967

Sam, Bangs and Moonshine by Evaline Ness, Holt

Honor Book: *One Wide River to Cross* by Ed Emberley (Barbara Emberley), Prentice-Hall

1968

Drummer Hoff by Ed Emberley (Barbara Emberley), Prentice-Hall

Honor Books: *Frederick* by Leo Lionni, Pantheon; *Seashore Story* by Taro Yashima, Viking; *The Emperor and the Kite* by Ed Young (Jane Yolen), World

1969

The Fool of the World and the Flying Ship by Uri Shulevitz (Arthur Ransome), Farrar, Straus & Giroux

Honor Book: *Why the Sun and the Moon Live in the Sky* by Blair Lent (Elphinstone Dayrell), Houghton Mifflin

1970

Sylvester and the Magic Pebble by William Steig, Windmill

Honor Books: *Goggles!* by Ezra Jack Keats, Macmillan; *Alexander and the Wind-Up Mouse* by Leo Lionni, Pantheon; *Pop Corn and Ma Goodness* by Robert Andrew Parker (Edna Mitchell Preston), Viking; *Thy Friend, Obadiah* by Brinton Turkle, Viking; *The Judge* by Margot Zemach (Harve Zemach), Farar, Straus & Giroux

1971

A Story—A Story by Gail E. Haley, Atheneum

Honor Books: *The Angry Moon* by Blair Lent (William Sleator), Little, Atlantic; *Frog and Toad Are Friends* by Arnold Lobel, HarperCollins; *In the Night Kitchen* by Maurice Sendak, HarperCollins

1972

One Fine Day by Nonny Hogrogian, Macmillan

Honor Books: *If All the Seas Were One Sea,* by Janina Domanska, Macmillan; *Moja Means One: Swahili Counting Book* by Tom Feelings (Muriel Feelings), Dial; *Hildilid's Night* by Arnold Lobel (Cheli Durán Ryan), Macmillan

1973

The Funny Little Woman by Blair Lent (retold by Arlene Mosel), Dutton

Honor Books: *Anansi the Spider* adapted and illustrated by Gerald McDermott, Holt; *Hosie's Alphabet* by Leonard Baskin (Hosea, Tobias and Lisa Baskin), Viking; *Snow White and the Seven Dwarfs* by Nancy Ekholm Burkert (translated by Randall Jarrell), Farrar, Straus & Giroux; *When Clay Sings* by Tom Bahti (Byrd Baylor), Scribner's

1974

Duffy and the Devil by Margot Zemach (Harve Zemach), Farrar, Straus & Giroux

Honor Books: *Three Jovial Huntsmen* by Susan Jeffers, Bradbury; *Cathedral: The Story of Its Construction* by David Macaulay, Houghton Mifflin

1975

Arrow to the Sun retold and illustrated by Gerald McDermott, Viking

Honor Book: *Jambo Means Hello* by Tom Feelings (Muriel Feelings), Dial

1976

Why Mosquitoes Buzz in People's Ears by Leo and Diane Dillon (retold by Verna Aardema), Dial

Honor Books: *The Desert Is Theirs* by Peter Parnall (Byrd Baylor), Scribner's; *Strega Nona* retold and illustrated by Tomie dePaola, Prentice-Hall

1977

Ashanti to Zulu: African Traditions by Leo and Diane Dillon (Margaret Musgrove), Dial

Honor Books: *The Amazing Bone* by William Steig, Farrar, Straus & Giroux; *The Contest* retold and illustrated by Nonny Hogrogian, Greenwillow; *Fish for Supper* by M. B. Goffstein, Dial; *The Golem* by Beverly Brodsky McDermott, HarperCollins; *Hawk, I'm Your Brother* by Peter Parnall (Byrd Baylor), Scribner's

1978

Noah's Ark by Peter Spier, Doubleday

Honor Books: *Castle* by David Macaulay, Houghton Mifflin; *It Could Always Be Worse* by Margot Zemach, Farrar, Straus & Giroux

1979

The Girl Who Loved Wild Horses by Paul Goble, Bradbury

Honor Books: *Freight Train* by Donald Crews, Greenwillow; *The Way to Start a Day* by Peter Parnall (Byrd Baylor), Scribner's

1980

Ox-Cart Man by Barbara Cooney (Donald Hall), Viking

Honor Books: *Ben's Trumpet* by Rachel Isadora, Greenwillow; *The Treasure* by Uri Shulevitz, Farrar, Straus & Giroux; *The Garden of Abdul Gasazi* by Chris Van Allsburg, Houghton Mifflin

1981

Fables by Arnold Lobel, HarperCollins

Honor Books: *The Bremen-Town Musicians* by Ilse Plume, Doubleday; *The Grey Land and the Strawberry Snatcher* by Molly Bang, Four Winds; *Mice Twice* by Joseph Low, McElderry; *Truck* by Donald Crews, Greenwillow

1982

Jumanji by Chris Van Allsburg, Houghton Mifflin

Honor Books: *On Market Street* by Anita Lobel (Arnold Lobel), Greenwillow, *Outside Over There* by Maurice Sendak, HarperCollins; *A Visit to William Blake's Inn: Poems for Innocent and Experienced Travelers* by Alice and Martin Provensen (Nancy Willard), Harcourt Brace; *Where the Buffaloes Begin* by Stephen Gammell (Olaf Baker), Warne

1983

Shadow by Marcia Brown (Blaise Cendrars), Scribner's

Honor Books: *A Chair for My Mother* by Vera B. Williams, Greenwillow; *When I was Young in the Mountains* by Diane Goode (Cynthia Rylant), Dutton

1984

The Glorious Flight: Across the Channel with Louis Blériot by Alice and Martin Provensen, Viking

Honor Books: *Little Red Riding Hood* retold and illustrated by Trina Schart Hyman, Holiday House; *Ten, Nine, Eight* by Molly Bang, Greenwillow

1985

Saint George and the Dragon by Trina Schart Hyman (retold by Margaret Hodges), Little, Brown

Honor Books: *Hansel and Gretel* by Paul O. Zelinsky (retold by Rika Lesser), Dodd, Mead; *Have You Seen My Duckling?* by Nancy Tafuri, Greenwillow; *The Story of Jumping Mouse* retold and illustrated by John Steptoe, Lothrop, Lee & Shepard

1986

The Polar Express by Chris Van Allsburg, Houghton Mifflin

Honor Books: *The Relatives Came* by Stephen Gammell (Cynthia Rylant), Bradbury; *King Bidgood's in the Bathtub* by Don Wood (Audrey Wood), Harcourt Brace

1987

Hey, Al by Richard Egielski (Arthur Yorinks), Farrar, Straus & Giroux

Honor Books: *The Village of Round and Square Houses* by Ann Grifalconi, Little, Brown; *Alphabatics* by Suse MacDonald, Bradbury; *Rumpelstiltskin* by Paul O. Zelinsky, Dutton

1988

Owl Moon by John Schoenherr (Jane Yolen), Philomel

Honor Books: *Mufaro's Beautiful Daughters* by John Steptoe, Lothrop, Lee & Shepard

1989

Song and Dance Man by Stephen Gammell (Karen Ackerman), Knopf

Honor Books: *The Boy of the Three-Year Nap* by Allen Say (Dianne Snyder), Houghton Mifflin; *Free Fall* by David Wiesner, Lothrop; *Goldilocks and the Three Bears* by James Marshall, Dial; *Mirandy and Brother Wind* by Jerry Pinkney (Patricia C. McKissack), Knopf

1990

Lon Po Po: A Red Riding Hood Story from China by Ed Young, Philomel

Honor Books: *Bill Peet: An Autobiography* by Bill Peet, Houghton Mifflin; *Color Zoo* by Lois Ehlert, HarperCollins; *Hershel and the Hanukkah Goblins* by Trina Schart Hyman (Eric Kimmel), Holiday; *The Talking Eggs* by Jerry Pinkney (Robert D. San Souci), Dial

1991

Black and White by David Macaulay, Houghton Mifflin

Honor Books: *"More More More," Said the Baby: 3 Love Stories* by Vera B. Williams, Greenwillow; *Puss in Boots* by Fred Marcellino (Charles Perrault, translated by Malcolm Arthur), Farrar, Straus & Giroux

1992

Tuesday by David Wiesner, Clarion

Honor Book: *Tar Beach* by Faith Ringgold, Crown

1993

Mirette on the High Wire by Emily Arnold McCully, Putnam

Honor Books: *The Stinky Cheese Man* by Lane Smith (Jon Scieszka), Viking; *Working Cotton* by Carole Byard (Sherley Anne Williams), Harcourt Brace; *Seven Blind Mice* by Ed Young, Philomel

Boston Globe-Horn Book Awards

This award has been presented annually in the fall since 1967 by *The Boston Globe* and *The Horn Book Magazine.* Through 1975, two awards were given, one for outstanding text and one for outstanding illustration; in 1976, the award categories were changed to outstanding fiction or poetry, outstanding nonfiction, and outstanding illustration. A monetary gift is awarded to the winner in each category.

1967

Text: *The Little Fishes* by Erik Christian Haugaard, Houghton Mifflin
Illustration: *London Bridge Is Falling Down!* illustrated by Peter Spier, Doubleday

1968

Text: *The Spring Rider* by John Lawson, HarperCollins
Illustration: *Tikki Tikki Tembo* by Arlene Mosel, illustrated by Blair Lent, Holt

1969

Text: *A Wizard of Earthsea* by Ursula K. Le Guin, Houghton Mifflin, Parnassus

Illustration: *The Adventures of Paddy Pork* by John S. Goodall, Harcourt Brace

1970

Text: *The Intruder* by John Rowe Townsend, HarperCollins

Illustration: *Hi, Cat!* by Ezra Jack Keats, Macmillan

1971

Text: *A Room Made of Windows* by Eleanor Cameron, Little, Brown, Atlantic

Illustration: *If I Built a Village* by Kazue Mizumura, HarperCollins

1972

Text: *Tristan and Iseult* by Rosemary Sutcliff, Dutton

Illustration: *Mr. Gumpy's Outing* by John Burningham, Holt

1973

Text: *The Dark Is Rising* by Susan Cooper, Atheneum, McElderry

Illustration: *King Stork* by Trina Schart Hyman, Little, Brown

1974

Text: *M. C. Higgins, the Great* by Virginia Hamilton, Macmillan

Illustration: *Jambo Means Hello* by Muriel Feelings, illustrated by Tom Feelings, Dial

1975

Text: *Transport 7-41-R* by T. Degens, Viking

Illustration: *Anno's Alphabet* by Mitsumasa Anno, HarperCollins

1976

Fiction: *Unleaving* by Jill Paton Walsh, Farrar, Straus & Giroux

Nonfiction: *Voyaging to Cathay: Americans in the China Trade* by Alfred Tamarin and Shirley Glubok, Viking

Illustration: *Thirteen* by Remy Charlip and Jerry Joyner, Four Winds

1977

Fiction: *Child of the Owl* by Laurence Yep, HarperCollins

Nonfiction: *Chance, Luck and Destiny* by Peter Dickinson, Little, Brown, Atlantic

Illustration: *Granfa' Grig Had a Pig and Other Rhymes Without Reason from Mother Goose* by Wallace Tripp, Little, Brown

1978

Fiction: *The Westing Game* by Ellen Raskin, Dutton

Nonfiction: *Mischling, Second Degree: My Childhood in Nazi Germany* by Ilse Koehn, Greenwillow

Illustration: *Anno's Journey* by Mitsumasa Anno, Philomel

1979

Fiction: *Humbug Mountain* by Sid Fleischman, Little, Brown, Atlantic

Nonfiction: *The Road from Home: The Story of an Armenian Girl* by David Kherdian, Greenwillow

Illustration: *The Snowman* by Raymond Briggs, Random House

1980

Fiction: *Conrad's War* by Andrew Davies, Crown

Nonfiction: *Building: The Fight Against Gravity* by Mario Salvadori, McElderry

Illustration: *The Garden of Abdul Gasazi* by Chris Van Allsburg, Houghton Mifflin

1981

Fiction: *The Leaving* by Lynn Hall, Scribner's

Nonfiction: *The Weaver's Gift* by Kathryn Lasky, Warne

Illustration: *Outside Over There* by Maurice Sendak, HarperCollins

1982

Fiction: *Playing Beatie Bow* by Ruth Park, Atheneum

Nonfiction: *Upon the Head of the Goat: A Childhood in Hungary 1939–1944* by Aranka Siegal, Farrar, Straus & Giroux

Illustration: *A Visit to William Blake's Inn: Poems for Innocent and Experienced Travelers* by Nancy Willard, illustrated by Alice and Martin Provensen, Harcourt Brace

1983

Fiction: *Sweet Whisper, Brother Rush* by Virginia Hamilton, Philomel

Nonfiction: *Behind Barbed Wire: The Imprisonment of Japanese Americans During World War II* by Daniel S. Davis, Dutton

Illustration: *A Chair for My Mother* by Vera B. Williams, Greenwillow

1984

Fiction: *A Little Fear* by Patricia Wrightson, Atheneum, McElderry

Nonfiction: *The Double Life of Pocahontas* by Jean Fritz, Putnam

Illustration: *Jonah and the Great Fish* retold and illustrated by Warwick Hutton, McElderry

1985

Fiction: *The Moves Make the Man* by Bruce Brooks, HarperCollins

Nonfiction: *Commodore Perry in the Land of the Shogun* by Rhoda Blumberg, Lothrop, Lee & Shepard

Illustration: *Mama Don't Allow* by Thacher Hurd, HarperCollins

Special Award: *1, 2, 3,* by Tana Hoban, Greenwillow

1986
Fiction: *In Summer Light* by Zibby Oneal, Viking

Nonfiction: *Auks, Rocks and the Odd Dinosaur: Inside Stories from the Smithsonian's Museum of Natural History* by Peggy Thomsen, HarperCollins

Illustration: *The Paper Crane* by Molly Bang, Greenwillow

1987
Fiction: *Rabble Starkey* by Lois Lowry, Houghton Mifflin

Nonfiction: *The Pilgrims of Plimoth* by Marcia Sewall, Atheneum

Illustration: *Mufaro's Beautiful Daughters* by John Steptoe, Lothrop, Lee & Shepard

1988
Fiction: *The Friendship* by MIldred Taylor, Dial

Nonfiction: *Anthony Burns: The Defeat and Triumph of a Fugitive Slave* by Virginia Hamilton, Knopf

Illustration: *The Boy of the Three-Year Nap* by Diane Snyder, Houghton Mifflin

1989
Fiction: *The Village by the Sea* by Paula Fox, Orchard

Nonfiction: *The Way Things Work* by David Macaulay, Houghton Mifflin

Illustration: *Shy Charles* by Rosemary Wells, Dial

1990
Fiction: *Maniac Magee* by Jerry Spinelli, Little, Brown

Nonfiction: *The Great Little Madison* by Jean Fritz, Putnam

Illustration: *Lon Po Po: A Red-Riding Hood Story from China* by Ed Young, Philomel

Special Award: *Valentine and Orson* by Nancy Ekholm Burkert, Farrar, Straus & Giroux

1991
Fiction: *The True Confessions of Charlotte Doyle* by Avi, Orchard

Nonfiction: *Appalachia: The Voices of Sleeping Birds* by Cynthia Rylant, Harcourt Brace

Illustration: *The Tale of the Mandarin Ducks* by Katherine Paterson, Lodestar

1992
Fiction: *Missing May* by Cynthia Rylant, Orchard

Nonfiction: *Talking with Artists* by Pat Cummings, Bradbury

Illustration: *Seven Blind Mice* by Ed Young, Philomel

Coretta Scott King Awards

Administered by the Social Responsibilities Round Table, with the cooperation of the American Library Association, these awards annually recognize an outstanding African-American author and illustrator. The award "commemorate[s] and foster[s] the life, work, and dreams" of Dr. Martin Luther King, Jr., and honors Coretta Scott King's "courage and determination to continue the work for peace and world brotherhood."

1970
Lillie Patterson, *Martin Luther King, Jr.: Man of Peace,* Garrard

1971
Charlemae Rollins, *Black Troubador: Langston Hughes,* Rand McNally

1972
Elston C. Fax, *17 Black Artists,* Dodd

1973
Jackie Robinson (as told to Alfred Duckett), *I Never Had It Made,* Putnam

1974
Author: Sharon Bell Mathis, *Ray Charles,* HarperCollins

Illustrator: George Ford, *Ray Charles* by Sharon Bell Mathis, HarperCollins

1975
Author: Dorothy Robinson, *The Legend of Africana,* Johnson

Illustrator: Herbert Temple, *The Legend of Africana* by Dorothy Robinson, Johnson

1976
Author: Pearl Bailey, *Duey's Tale,* Harcourt Brace

Illustrator: no award

1977
Author: James Haskins, *The Story of Stevie Wonder,* Lothrop

Illustrator: no award

1978
Author: Eloise Greenfield, *Africa Dream,* Day/HarperCollins

Illustrator: Carole Byard, *Africa Dream* by Eloise Greenfield, Day/HarperCollins

1979
Author: Ossie Davis, *Escape to Freedom*, Viking
Illustrator: Tom Feelings, *Something on My Mind* by Nikki Grimes, Dial

1980
Author: Walter Dean Myers, *The Young Landlords*, Viking
Illustrator: Carole Bayard, *Cornrows* by Camille Yarbrough, Coward

1981
Author: Sidney Poitier, *This Life*, Knopf
Illustrator: Ashley Bryan, *Beat the Story-Drum, Pum-Pum*, Atheneum

1982
Author: Mildred D. Taylor, *Let the Circle Be Unbroken*, Dial
Illustrator: John Steptoe, *Mother Crocodile: An Uncle Amadou Tale from Senegal* adapted by Rosa Guy, Delacorte

1983
Author: Virginia Hamilton, *Sweet Whispers, Brother Rush*, Philomel
Illustrator: Peter Mugabane, *Black Child*, Knopf

1984
Author: Lucille Clifton, *Everett Anderson's Good-Bye*, Holt
Illustrator: Pat Cummings, *My Mama Needs Me* by Mildred Pitts Walter, Lothrop

1985
Author: Walter Dean Myers, *Motown and Didi*, Viking
Illustrator: no award

1986
Author: Virginia Hamilton, *The People Could Fly: American Black Folktales*, Knopf
Illustrator: Jerry Pinkney, *The Patchwork Quilt* by Valerie Flournoy, Dial

1987
Author: Mildred Pitts Walter, *Justin and the Best Biscuits in the World*, Lothrop
Illustrator: Jerry Pinkney, *Half a Moon and One Whole Star* by Crescent Dragonwagon, Macmillan

1988
Author: Mildred D. Taylor, *The Friendship*, Dial
Illustrator: John Steptoe, *Mufaro's Beautiful Daughters: An African Tale*, Lothrop

1989
Author: Walter Dean Myers, *Fallen Angels*, Scholastic

Illustrator: Jerry Pinkney, *Mirandy and Brother Wind* by Patricia McKissack, Knopf

1990
Author: Patricia and Frederick McKissack, *A Long Hard Journey: The Story of the Pullman Porter*, Walker
Illustrator: Jan Spivey Gilchrist, *Nathaniel Talking* by Eloise Greenfield, Black Butterfly

1991
Author: Mildred D. Taylor, *The Road to Memphis*, Dial
Illustrator: Leo and Diane Dillon, *Aïda* told by Leontyne Price, Gulliver/Harcourt Brace

1992
Author: Walter Dean Myers, *Now Is Your Time!: The African American Struggle for Freedom*, HarperCollins
Illustrator: Faith Ringgold, *Tar Beach*, Crown

1993
Author: Patricia C. McKissack, *The Dark-Thirty: Southern Tales of the Supernatural*, Knopf
Illustrator: Katherine Atkins Wilson, *The Origin of Life on Earth: An African Myth* retold by David A. Anderson/SANKOFA, Sight Productions

The Laura Ingalls Wilder Award

The Laura Ingalls Wilder Award, named for its first winner, the author of the Little House books, is given to an author or illustrator whose books, published in the United States, have made a substantial and lasting contribution to literature for children. Until 1980, the award was given every five years; now it is awarded every three years. Selection of the award winner is made by the Association for Library Services for Children of the American Library Association. The winners since inception of the award in 1954 are as follows:

1954
Laura Ingalls Wilder

1960
Clara Ingram Judson

1965
Ruth Sawyer

1970
E. B. White

1975
Beverly Cleary

1980
Theodor S. Geisel (Dr. Seuss)

1983
Maurice Sendak

1986
Jean Fritz

1989
Elizabeth George Speare

1992
Marcia Brown

The National Council of Teachers of English Award for Excellence in Poetry for Children

Sponsored by the National Council of Teachers of English, the award was given annually from 1977 to 1982 to a living American poet in recognition of an aggregate body of work for children ages 3–13. Currently, the award is presented every three years. A citation is given to the poet and a medallion design of the seal is available for use on the dust jacket of all the poet's books.

1977
David McCord

1978
Aileen Fisher

1979
Karla Kuskin

1980
Myra Cohn Livingston

1981
Eve Merriam

1982
John Ciardi

1985
Lilian Moore

1988
Arnold Adoff

1991
Valerie Worth

The Hans Christian Andersen Award

This award has been given biennially since 1956 by the International Board on Books for Young People to one author and one illustrator (since 1966) in recognition of his or her entire body of work. A medal is presented to the recipient.

1956
Eleanor Farjeon (Great Britain)

1958
Astrid Lindgren (Sweden)

1960
Erich Kästner (Germany)

1962
Meindert DeJong (U.S.A.)

1964
René Guillot (France)

1966
Author: Tove Jansson (Finland)
Illustrator: Alois Carigiet (Switzerland)

1968
Authors: James Krüss (Germany)
José Maria Sanchez-Silva (Spain)
Illustrator: Jiri Trnka (Czechoslovakia)

1970
Author: Gianni Rodari (Italy)
Illustrator: Maurice Sendak (U.S.A.)

1972
Author: Scott O'Dell (U.S.A.)
Illustrator: Ib Spang Olsen (Denmark)

1974
Author: Maria Gripe (Sweden)
Illustrator: Farshid Mesghali (Iran)

1976
Author: Cecil Bødker (Denmark)
Illustrator: Tatjana Mawrina (U.S.S.R.)

1978
Author: Paula Fox (U.S.A.)
Illustrator: Svend Otto S. (Denmark)

1980
Author: Bohumil Říha (Czechoslovakia)
Illustrator: Suekichi Akaba (Japan)

1982
Author: Lygia Bojunga Nunes (Brazil)
Illustrator: Zbigniew Rychlicki (Poland)

1984
Author: Christine Nöstlinger (Austria)
Illustrator: Mitsumasa Anno (Japan)

1986
Author: Patricia Wrightson (Australia)
Illustrator: Robert Ingpen (Australia)

1988
Author: Annie M. G. Schmidt (Holland)
Illustrator: Dusan Kallay (Czechoslovakia)

1990
Author: Tormod Haugen (Norway)
Illustrator: Lisbeth Zwerger (Austria)

1992
Author: Virginia Hamilton (U.S.A.)
Illustrator: Kveta Pacovská (Czechoslovakia)

International Reading Association (IRA) Children's Book Award

The IRA award, sponsored by the Institute for Reading Research and administered by the IRA, is presented annually for a children's book (published in the year preceding the award) by an author who shows unusual promise. Books originating in any country are eligible. For a book written in a language other than English, the IRA first determines if the book warrants an English translation and, if so, then extends to it an additional year of eligibility.

The following list gives title, author, and publisher of winners since inception of the award in 1975. Since 1987, the award has been presented for both picture books and novels.

1975
Transport 7-41-R by T. Degens, Viking

1976
Dragonwings by Lawrence Yep, HarperCollins

1977
A String in the Harp by Nancy Bond, Atheneum

1978
A Summer to Die by Lois Lowry, Houghton Mifflin

1979
Reserved for Mark Anthony Crowder by Alison Smith, Dutton

1980
Words by Heart by Ouida Sebestyen, Little, Brown

1981
My Own Private Sky by Delores Beckman, Dutton

1982
Goodnight Mr. Tom by Michelle Magorian, Kestrel, Great Britain; HarperCollins, U.S.A.

1983
The Darkangel by Meredith Pierce, Little, Brown, Atlantic

1984
Ratha's Creature by Clare Bell, Atheneum, McElderry

1985
Badger on the Barge by Janni Howker, MacRae, Great Britain; Greenwillow, U.S.A./Harper-Collins

1986
Prairie Songs by Pam Conrad, HarperCollins

1987
Picture Book: *The Line Up Book* by Marisabina Russo, Greenwillow
Novel: *After the Dancing Days* by Margaret I. Rostkowski, HarperCollins

1988
Picture Book: *The Third-Story Cat* by Leslie Baker, Little, Brown
Novel: *The Ruby in the Smoke* by Philip Pullman, Knopf

1989
Picture Book: *Rechenka's Eggs* by Patricia Polacco, Philomel
Novel: *Probably Still Nick Swansen* by Virginia Euwer Wolff, Holt

1990
Picture Book: *No Star Nights* by Anna Egan Smucker, Knopf
Novel: *Children of the River* by Linda Crew, Delacorte

1991
Picture Book: *Is This a House for Hermit Crab?* by Megan McDonald, Orchard
Novel: *Under the Hawthorn Tree* by Marita Conlon-McKenna, O'Brien Press

1992
Picture Book: *Ten Little Rabbits* by Virginia Grossman, Chronicle
Novel: *Rescue Josh McGuire* by Ben Mikaelsen, Hyperion

1993
Picture Book: *Old Turtle* by Douglas Wood, Pfeiffer-Hamilton
Novel: *Letters from Rifke* by Karen Hesse, Holt

The Ezra Jack Keats New Writer Award

This award, first presented in 1985 and 1986, is given biennially to a promising new writer. It honors work done in the tradition of Ezra Jack Keats: appeal to young children, storytelling quality, relation between text and illustration, positive reflection of families, and the multicultural nature of the world. The award is presented at the Early Childhood Resource and Information Center of the New York Public Library. Funded by the Ezra Jack Keats Foundation, the recipient receives a monetary award and a medallion.

1985
Valerie Flournoy, *The Patchwork Quilt,* illustrated by Jerry Pinkney, Dial

1987
Juanita Havill, *Jamaica's Find,* illustrated by Anne Sibley O'Brien, Houghton Mifflin

1988
Yoriko Tsutsui, *Anna's Special Present,* illustrated by Akiko Hayashi, Viking

1990
Angela Johnson, *Tell Me a Story, Mama,* illustrated by David Soman, Orchard

1993
Faith Ringgold, *Tar Beach,* Crown

Other Awards

There are approximately 125 different awards given for children's books, each with its own unique selection process and criteria. Some are chosen by adults and some by children; some are international, some state or regional. A comprehensive listing of the various award winners is provided in *Children's Books: Awards and Prizes,* published by the Children's Book Council. This publication is updated periodically.

Appendix B

Resources

Book Selection Aids

A to Zoo: Subject Guide to Children's Picture Books, 4th ed., compiled by Carolyn Lima, Bowker, 1993. 900 pages. Approximately 10,000 picture books grouped by topic, author, and title under subject headings.

Adventuring with Books: A Booklist for Pre-K–Grade 6, National Council of Teachers of English. A comprehensive list of books selected for their merit and potential use in the classroom. Approximately 2,000 new books are annotated and several hundred from previous editions are listed by genre. New editions are prepared periodically.

Best Books for Children: Preschool Through the Middle Grades, 3rd ed., edited by John T. Gillespie and Christine B. Gilbert, Bowker, 1985. 595 pages. A listing of 11,000 books arranged alphabetically by author under 500 subject headings.

Best Science and Technology Reference Books for Young People, edited by H. Robert Malinowsky, Oryx, 1991. Reviews content and recommends grade levels for sci-tech reference books.

The Best in Children's Books: The University of Chicago Guide to Children's Literature: 1979–1984, edited by Zena Sutherland, University of Chicago Press, 1986. 522 pages. Selected reviews from the Bulletin of the Center for Children's Books listed alphabetically by author. Previous editions cover 1966 to 1972 and 1973 to 1978. Indexes include title, developmental values, curricular use, reading level, type of literature, and subject.

Beyond Fact: Nonfiction for Children and Young People, edited by Jo Carr, American Library Association, 1982. 236 pages. Articles on qualities of good nonfiction and lists of titles.

Beyond Picture Books: A Guide to First Readers by Barbara Barstow and Judith Riggle, Bowker, 1989. 336 pages. Lists 1,600 easy-to-read books with corresponding reading levels and annotations.

Bibliography of Books for Children, rev. ed., edited by Sylvia Sunderlin, Association for Childhood Education International, 1983. Criteria for selecting books for children and annotated list of books that qualify.

The Black Experience in Children's Books, rev. ed., compiled by Barbara Rollock, New York Public Library, 1984. Annotated bibliography of books about black life in America, Africa, the Caribbean, and England.

The Bookfinder: A Guide to Children's Literature About the Needs and Problems of Youth Aged 2 and Up, edited by Sharon Spredemann Dreyer, American Guidance Service, Vol. 1, 1977; Vol. 2, 1981; Vol. 3, 1985. Reviews of children's and adolescent books that identify the problem or need touched upon. A subject index with headings, such as courage, death, and friendship, lists relevant titles. The cumulative index in Volume 3 includes the earlier volumes.

Books, Children and Men by Paul Hazard, translated by Marguerite Mitchell, Horn Book, 1944 (5th rev. ed., 1985). An enlightened discussion of children's literature among the literatures of the world. Hazard, a distinguished French scholar, establishes basic criteria that underlie quality literature for children.

Books for You: A Booklist for Senior High Students, National Council of Teachers of English. Lively annotations of young adult books grouped by categories, such as careers and jobs, computers, robots and microprocessors, ethnic experiences, and drama and theater. New editions are produced periodically.

Books to Help Children Cope with Separation and Loss, 2nd ed., compiled by Joanne E. Bernstein, Bowker, 1983. 439 pages. Vol. 3, 1989 by Joanne E. Bernstein and Masha Rudman. Discussions of bibliotherapy and annotated lists of books grouped by categories, such as adoption, divorce, and disabilities.

Building a Children's Literature Collection: A Suggested Basic Reference Collection for Academic Libraries and a Suggested Basic Collection of Children's Books, 3rd ed., by Harriet B. Quimby and Margaret Mary Kimmel, *Choice* Magazine, 1986. 45 pages. Materials to support the study of children's literature at all levels including reference and children's books.

Children's Books: Awards and Prizes, compiled and edited by the Children's Book Council, 1992. 404 pages. A comprehensive list of honors awarded to children's books. Awards chosen by adults and children are grouped by state, national, and international designations.

Children's Books in Print, Bowker, Annual. A comprehensive index of all children's books in print at time of publication. Author, title, and illustrator indexes give pertinent publishing information. A directory of publishers and addresses is included.

Children's Catalog, Wilson, annual. A comprehensive catalog classified by Dewey Decimal system with nonfiction, fiction, short stories, and easy books. Five-year cumulations and annual supplements available.

Children's Literature Review, Gale Research. Since 1976, new volumes added periodically. Articles about authors and topics of interest with excerpts from reviews of the works of each author.

Choosing Books for Children by Betsy Hearne, Delacorte, 1981. An excellent guide for choosing books.

A Comprehensive Guide to Children's Literature with a Jewish Theme by Enid Davis, Schocken, 1981. Fiction and nonfiction related to Judaism arranged in subject categories.

Eye Openers! How to Choose and Use Children's Books About Real People, Places, and Things, by Beverly Kobrin, Viking, 1988. Subject categories with annotated booklists, index.

Elementary School Library Collection, 19th ed., edited by Lauren K. Lee, Bro-Dart Co., 1994 Comprehensive bibliography of print and nonprint materials for school media collections. Dewey Decimal subject classification, age level, and brief annotations.

The Family Story-Telling Handbook by Anne Pellowski, illustrated by Lynn Sweat, Macmillan, 1987. 150 pages. A guide to using stories, anecdotes, rhymes, handkerchiefs, paper, and other objects to enrich family traditions. Line drawings appear alongside scripts for the storyteller to make it clear how objects and stories relate.

For Reading Out Loud! by Margaret Mary Kimmel and Elizabeth Segel, Delacorte, 1983. A guide to selecting books for sharing with young people and techniques for sharing them. Subject, title, author index.

Handbook for the Newbery Medal and Honor Books, 1980–1989, by Bette D. Ammon and Gale W. Sherman, Alleyside Press, 1991. Booktalk material and related books chosen by Knowledgeable guides.

Her Way: A Guide to Biographies of Women for Young People, 2nd ed., by Mary Ellen Siegal, American Library Association, 1984. 430 pages. Single and collective biographies of 1,000 notable women in history.

Hey! Listen to This: Stories to Read Aloud, edited by Jim Trelease, Penguin, 1992. Selections from literature to read to primary grade children. Trelease adds intriguing background information about each excerpt.

Jewish Children's Books: How to Choose Them, How to Use Them by Marcia Posner, Hadassah, 1986. 48 pages. Summaries, themes, discussion guides, questions and activities, and further resources are given for more than 30 books.

Let's Read About . . . Finding Books They'll Love to Read by Bernice E. Cullinan, Scholastic, 1993. Lists books by topic and age-level interests.

Library Services for Hispanic Children: A Guide for Public and School Librarians, edited by Adela Artola Allen, Oryx Press, 1987. 201 pages. Articles on professional issues related to library service for Hispanic children. Annotated bibliographies of children's books in English about Hispanics, recent noteworthy children's books in Spanish, computer software, and resources about Hispanic culture for librarians.

Michele Landsberg's Guide to Children's Books: With a Treasury of More Than 350 Great Children's Books by Michele Landsberg, Penguin, 1985. 272 pages. A book-loving Canadian's journey through children's literature with commentary on reasons for loving and/or detesting specific books. Annotated list and chapters about various genres.

More Notes from a Different Drummer: A Guide to Juvenile Fiction Portraying the Disabled by Barbara H. Baskin and Karen H. Harris, Bowker, 1984. 495 pages. Extends *Notes from a Different Drummer*. Discusses criteria for selection of 450 books about the disabled and provides a comprehensive annotated guide of fiction for a readership ranging from infants to adolescents.

The New Read-Aloud Handbook, 4th ed., by Jim Trelease, Penguin, 1990. An enthusiastic argument for why we should read to children, techniques for reading aloud, and a treasury of over 300 books that worked well as read alouds.

Newbery and Caldecott Medalists and Honor Book

Winners: Bibliographies and Resource Material Through 1977 by James W. Roginski, Libraries Unlimited, 1982. A comprehensive listing of source material on Newbery and Caldecott medalists and honor book winners.

Notes from a Different Drummer: A Guide to Juvenile Fiction Portraying the Handicapped by Barbara H. Baskin and Karen H. Harris, Bowker, 1977. Criteria for selection of books about the disabled with critical reviews of 400 plus books with disabled characters.

Pass the Poetry, Please by Lee Bennett Hopkins, HarperCollins, 1987. Hopkins introduces outstanding poets and suggests ways to use their work.

Read to Me: Raising Kids Who Love to Read by Bernice E. Cullinan, Scholastic, 1992. A book for parents containing suggestions for turning children into readers.

Storytelling: Art and Technique, 2nd ed., by Augusta Baker and Ellin Greene, Bowker, 1987. Two masters of storytelling give practical advice on how to select, prepare, and tell stories. Recommended stories are included.

Selected Jewish Children's Books, compiled by Marcia Posner, Jewish Book Council, 1991. Annotated list of books containing Jewish content and values categorized by topic and age levels.

Selecting Materials for and About Hispanic and East Asian Children and Young People by Patricia F. Beilke and Frank J. Sciara, Library Professional Publications, 1986. 178 pages. Chapters on selection of materials, staff development, backgrounds of Hispanic and East Asian children and young people in the United States and guidelines for selecting culturally relevant materials. Some children's book titles are discussed in the text.

The Story Vine by Anne Pellowski, illustrated by Lynn Sweat, Macmillan, 1984. A source book of unusual and easy-to-tell stories from around the world. An internationally known storyteller shares some of her secrets about telling stories, some with string, objects, and musical or visual effects.

Subject Guide to Children's Books in Print, Bowker, Annual. Over 60,000 titles grouped under 6,630 subject categories. An indispensable reference for finding picture books, fiction, and nonfiction on specific topics. Books are available from 4,528 United States publishers and distributors.

Subject Index to Poetry for Children and Young People, compiled by Violet Sell, Core Collection Books, 1982. 1,035 pages. An index of poetry organized by subject with a code for title and author.

With Women's Eyes: Visitors to the New World, 1775–1918, edited by Marion Tinling, Shoe String Press, 1993. 204 pages. Twenty-seven European women who visited America between 1775 and 1918 tell about their experiences.

Your Reading: A Booklist for Junior High and Middle School Students, National Council of Teachers of English. An annotated list of over 3,000 fiction and nonfiction books recommended for junior high and middle school students, arranged by subject. Author and title indexes. New editions are produced periodically.

Books About Authors and Illustrators

The Art of Leo and Diane Dillon, edited by Byron Preiss, Ballantine Books, 1981. Introductory critical essay with 120 illustrations, including 8 color plates of the Dillons' art. The Dillons comment on the meaning, context, and techniques used in each painting.

The Art of Nancy Ekholm Burkert, edited by David Larkin, HarperCollins, 1977. 50 pages. Full-page color spreads of 40 Burkert paintings with an interpretive essay by Michael Danoff.

Authors of Books for Young People, 2nd ed., edited by Martha E. Ward and Dorothy Marquant, Scarecrow Press, 1971. 579 pages. (Supplement to the 2nd ed., 1979. 308 pages.) Biographical information about authors including publications.

Books Are by People: Interviews with 104 Authors and Illustrators of Books for Young Children by Lee Bennett Hopkins, Citation Press, 1969. (Companion volume: *More Books by More People*, Citation Press, 1974.) Conversations between Hopkins and his talented friends.

Boy: Tales of Childhood by Roald Dahl, Puffin, Viking, 1984. 176 pages. An autobiography that describes the origins of one author's ideas.

Carl Larsson by the Brooklyn Museum and the National Museum in Stockholm with the support of the Swedish Institute in Stockholm, the Brooklyn Museum, 1982. 96 pages. A catalog of Carl Larsson's paintings with commentary by Sarah Faunce, Gorel Cavalli-Bjorkman, Ulf Hard af Segerstad, and Madeleine von Heland. Chronology and selected bibliography.

Caldecott Medal Books: 1938–1957 by Bertha Mahony Miller and Elinor Whitney Field, Hewn Book, 1958. Artists' acceptance speeches and biographical articles of the Caldecott Medal winners.

Celebrating Children's Books, edited by Betsy Hearne and Marilyn Kaye, Lothrop, Lee & Shepard, 1981. Writings about their craft by some of the foremost authors writing for children today. The essays appear in this collection in honor of Zena Sutherland.

From Writers to Students: The Pleasures and Pains of Writing, edited by Jerry Weiss, International Reading Association, 1979. 113 pages. Interviews about their work with 19 top-notch authors who reveal the inside story on their writing. Includes Judy Blume, Mollie Hunter, Milton Meltzer, Mary Rodgers, Laurence Yep, and others.

Horn Book Reflections, edited by Elinor Whitney Field, Horn Book, 1969. Essays, selected from 18 years of the *Horn Book* Magazine, 1949–1966, represent the reflections of authors and illustrators as they comment on their craft.

Illustrators of Books for Young People, 2nd ed., edited by Martha E. Ward and Dorothy A. Marquant, Scarecrow Press, 1975. 223 pages. Biographical information about illustrators. Bibliographies and references to further sources are included.

Illustrators of Children's Books, 1744–1945, edited by Bertha E. Mahony, Louise Payson Latimer, and Beulah Folmsbee, Horn Book, 1947. 527 pages.

Illustrators of Children's Books, 1946–1956, edited by Bertha Mahony Miller, Ruth Hill Viguers, and Marcia Dalphin, Horn Book, 1958. 229 pages.

Illustrators of Children's Books, 1957–1966, edited by Lee Kingman, Joanna Foster, and Ruth Giles Lontoft, Horn Book, 1968. 295 pages. *Illustrators of Children's Books, 1967–1976*, edited by Lee Kingman, Grace Allen Hogarth, and Harriet Quimby, Horn Book, 1978. 290 pages. *Illustrators of Children's Books, 1977–1986*, edited by Lee Kingman, Horn Book, 1987. All volumes contain biographical sketches of illustrators during the period covered by each volume. The artists' techniques and point of view, trends in illustration, and bibliographies are included.

Little by Little: A Writer's Education by Jean Little, Viking, 1987. 233 pages. Jean Little's life story.

Meet the Authors and Illustrators by Deborah Kovacs and James Preller, Scholastic, 1991. Sixty creators of favorite children's books talk about their work.

Newbery and Caldecott Medal Books: 1956–1965, edited by Lee Kingman, Horn Book, 1965. 300 pages. Acceptance papers, biographical notes, and evaluative essays by Elizabeth H. Gross, Carolyn Horovitz, and Norma R. Fryatt.

Newbery and Caldecott Medal Books: 1966–1975, edited by Lee Kingman, Horn Book, 1975. Acceptance papers, biographies of the award winners, and evaluative essays by John Rowe Townsend, Barbara Bader, and Elizabeth Johnson.

Newbery and Caldecott Medal Books, 1976–1985, edited by Lee Kingman, Horn Book, 1987. Compiles the winning speeches, biographies, and book notes. Essays by Barbara Bader, Ethel L. Heins, and Zena Sutherland.

Newbery Medal Books: 1922–1955, edited by Bertha Mahony Miller and Elinor Whitney Field, Horn Book, 1955. Acceptance papers and biographical sketches, plus notes on and excerpts from Newbery Award-winning books.

Oxford Companion to Children's Literature, compiled by Humphrey Carpenter and Mari Prichard, Oxford University Press, 1984. Included are nearly 2,000 entries, more than 900 of which are biographical sketches of authors, illustrators, printers, and publishers. Other entries cover traditional materials such as fairy tales and folklore; characters from books, cartoons, comic strips, radio, and television; and genres such as school stories, dime novels, and science fiction. Plot summaries for major works of fiction and their publishing history are given.

Pipers at the Gates of Dawn: The Wisdom of Children's Literature by Jonathan Cott, Random House, 1983. 327 pages. A noted historian and critic of children's literature reflects on his encounters with six extraordinary creators of children's literature—Dr. Seuss, Maurice Sendak, William Steig, Astrid Lindgren, Chinua Achebe, P. L. Travers—and with Iona and Peter Opie, scholars of children's lore, games, and language.

Secret Gardens by Humphrey Carpenter, Houghton Mifflin, 1985. A book about the authors who wrote during the so-called golden age of children's literature in the late nineteenth and early twentieth centuries.

Self-Portrait: Erik Blegvad, written and illustrated by Erik Blegvad, Addison-Wesley, 1979. 32 pages. Blegvad discusses himself, his life, and his work.

Self-Portrait: Trina Schart Hyman, written and illustrated by Trina Schart Hyman, Addison-Wesley, 1981. 32 pages. Hyman describes her life, friends, and family and their reflections in her painting.

Self-Portrait: Margot Zemach, written and illustrated by Margot Zemach, Addison-Wesley, 1978. 32 pages. Zemach talks about her life, her family, and her work.

A Sense of Story: Essays on Contemporary Writers for Children by John Rowe Townsend, Horn Book, 1973. 216 pages. Critical essays on 19 notable authors and their works, including Joan Aiken, L. M. Boston, H. F. Brinsmead, John Christopher, Helen Cresswell, Meindert DeJong, Eleanor Estes, Madeleine L'Engle, Andre Norton, Scott O'Dell, Philippa Pearce, and Rosemary Sutcliff. Seven others are included in *A Sounding of Storytellers*.

Something About the Author, edited by Anne Commire, Gale Research. 50 volumes in print with periodic additions. Biographical information, photographs, publication records, honors and awards received, and quotations from and about thousands of authors and illustrators of children's books.

A Sounding of Storytellers: New and Revised Essays on Contemporary Writers for Children by John Rowe Townsend, HarperCollins, 1979. 218 pages. 14 essays about contemporary writers; seven are about writers who were not in *A Sense of Story*: Nina Bawden, Vera and Bill Cleaver, Peter Dickinson, Virginia Hamilton, E. L. Konigsberg, Penelope Lively, and Jill Paton Walsh. The other seven, included in the earlier book, are Paula Fox, Leon Garfield, Alan Garner, William Mayne, K. M. Patton, Ivan Southall, and Patricia Wrightson.

Starting from Home: A Writer's Beginnings by Milton Meltzer, Viking, 1988. Meltzer's life story.

Talking with Artists, edited by Pat Cummings, Bradbury, 1992. Fourteen children's book illustrators talk about their work.

Twentieth-Century Children's Writers, 2nd ed., edited by Daniel Kirkpatrick, St. Martin's Press, 1983. 1,500 pages. More than 700 entries, critical essays, and bibliographies of contemporary writers and illustrators, including William Steig, Maurice Sendak, Nikki Giovanni, and Isaac Bashevis Singer.

Ways of the Illustrator: Visual Communication in Children's Literature by Joseph H. Schwarz, American Library Association, 1982. 202 pages. An informed presentation of the role of illustration in communicating meaning in picture books. The relationship between the text and illustration, the use of style and technique, and the effect on the child's aesthetic experience are discussed and illustrated with examples.

Written for Children: An Outline of English-Language Children's Literature, 3rd rev. ed., by John Rowe Townsend, HarperCollins, 1987. 364 pages. An account of the development of children's books in the United States, England, Canada, and Australia.

Periodicals About Children's Literature

Bookbird: International Periodical on Literature for Children and Young People. Published quarterly by Forlaget ARNIS, Postboks 130, Toendervej 197, DK–6200 Aabenraa, Denmark. An international forum for the exchange of experience and information among contractors and readers in about 50 nations. Essays about outstanding authors and illustrators from many countries.

Booklist. Barbara Elleman, children's books editor. American Library Association, published biweekly. Reviews of children's and adults' books and nonprint materials. Periodic bibliographies on a specific subject, reference tools, and commentary on issues are invaluable.

Bulletin of the Center for Children's Books. Betsy Hearne, editor; Zena Sutherland, associate editor. University of Illinois Press, published monthly except August. Critical reviews of books rated as * (books of special distinction), R (recommended), Ad (additional), M (marginal), NR (not recommended), SpC (special collection), SpR (special reader). Curricular use and developmental values are assigned when appropriate.

CBC Features. Children's Book Council, published semiannually. A newsletter about current issues and events, free and inexpensive materials, materials for Children's Book Week, topical bibliographies, and essays by publishers and authors or illustrators.

Children's Literature Association Quarterly. Children's Literature Association. Book reviews and articles on British and American children's literature, research, teaching children's literature, theater, and conference proceedings. Special sections on current topics of interest, poetry, censorship, awards and announcements.

Children's Literature in Education. Anita Moss, editor. Agathon Press, published quarterly. Essays on children's books, including critical reviews, research reviews, biographical studies, creators' views of their craft, and discussions of poetry and prose.

The Horn Book Magazine. Anita Silvey, editor. Horn Book, published bimonthly. Enlightened commentary by the editor, articles by creators of children's books, publishers, critics, teachers, and librarians. Starred reviews for outstanding books, comprehensive reviews of recommended books. Newbery and Caldecott acceptance speeches, biographical sketches of winners, *Boston Globe*–Horn Book Award winners, and other notable awards. Announcements of children's literature conferences and events. Cumulative index in *Horn Book Guide.*

Journal of Youth Services in Libraries (formerly *Top of the News*). Association of Library Services to Children and Young Adult Services Division. American Library Association, published quarterly. Articles of interest to teachers and librarians on current issues, specialized bibliographies, acceptance speeches by the Newbery and Caldecott Award winners, conference proceedings, and organizational news.

Language Arts. National Council of Teachers of English, published September through May. Book review column reviews current recommended books for children. Profiles on authors and illustrators, articles on using books in the classroom, response to literature, and writing as an outgrowth of reading literature.

The Lion and the Unicorn. Department of English, Brooklyn College. Articles on literary criticism, current issues, and themes in children's literature.

The New Advocate. Joel Taxel, editor; Christopher Gordon, publisher. Norwood, MA. A lively journal that addresses current issues and topics of interest in the children's book world.

The New York Times Book Review. Weekly column of reviews, written by other authors, plus a spring and fall special section devoted to children's books. Annual list of 10 best illustrated books of the year.

Phaedrus: An International Journal of Children's Literature Research. James Fraser, editor. Fairleigh Dickinson University, published semiannually. Essays on cross-cultural aspects of children's literature, research reviews, biographical studies of authors and illustrators, and international reports. For the serious student of children's literature.

Publisher's Weekly. Bowker, published weekly with a spring and fall special edition on children's books. Both positive and negative reviews of books and news articles of interest to publishers, teachers, librarians, and authors.

The Reading Teacher. International Reading Association, published nine times a year. Monthly column of reviews of children's books. Articles on the use of books in the classroom, special bibliographies, cross-cultural studies, and research using children's books in reading programs.

School Library Journal. Lillian Gerhardt, editor. Bowker, 11 issues per year. Reviews of children's books, written by practicing school and public librarians, often include comparisons with other books on the same topic. Articles on current issues, conferences, library services, and special features. An annual "Best Books of the Year" column. Cumulative index of starred reviews in *Star Track.*

School Library Media Quarterly. American Association of School Librarians. American Library Association, published quarterly. Articles on censorship, using books in the classroom, research, library services, and current issues.

Science and Children. National Science Teachers Association, published eight times per year. Monthly column of reviews of informational books on science topics, plus an annual list of recommended books chosen by NSTA/Children's Book Council Liaison Committee.

The Web: Wonderfully Exciting Books. Ohio State University, published quarterly. Reviews of current books plus a "web of possibilities" for activities and related readings on a theme, topic, author, or illustrator.

Wilson Library Bulletin. Wilson, published monthly September to June. A monthly column of book reviews, articles on authors and illustrators, current issues, and news of interest to professionals. The October issue is devoted to children's books.

Appendix C

Publishers of Children's Books

Below are the most frequently cited publishers. For less well known publishers, please see *Literary Market Place* (LMP) or *Children's Books in Print*. Because publishers' addresses or names may change, consult these two sources for complete and up-to-date information.

Abrams
100 Fifth Avenue
New York, NY 10010

Addison-Wesley
1 Jacob Way
Reading, MA 01867

Aladdin Books
866 Third Avenue
New York, NY 10022

Arcade Publishing
141 Fifth Avenue
New York, NY 10010

Astor Honor
48 East 43rd Street
New York, NY 10017

Atheneum Publishers
866 Third Avenue
New York, NY 10022

Atlantic Monthly Press
19 Union Square West
New York, NY 10003

Avon Books
1350 Avenue of the Americas
New York, NY 10017

Bantam Books
666 Fifth Avenue
New York, NY 10103

Boyds Mills Press
815 Church Street
Honesdale, PA 18431;
distributed by St. Martin's
Press

Bradbury Press
866 Third Avenue
New York, NY 10022

Camelot
1350 Avenue of the Americas
New York, NY 10017

Candlewick Press
2067 Massachusetts Avenue
Cambridge, MA 02140

Carolrhoda Books, Inc.
241 First Avenue North
Minneapolis, MN 55401

Children's Book Press
1461 Ninth Avenue
San Francisco, CA 94122

Clarion Books
215 Park Avenue
New York, NY 10003

Cobblehill Books
375 Hudson Street
New York, NY 10014

Collier
866 Third Avenue
New York, NY 10022

Crestwood House
866 Third Avenue
New York, NY 10022

Crown Publishers
225 Park Avenue South
New York, NY 10003

Delacorte Press
666 Fifth Avenue
New York, NY 10103

Dell Publishing
666 Fifth Avenue
New York, NY 10103

Dial
375 Hudson Street
New York, NY 10014

Disney Publications
114 Fifth Avenue
New York, NY 10011

Doubleday
666 Fifth Avenue
New York, NY 10103

Dover Publications, Inc.
180 Varick Street
New York, NY 10014

Dutton Children's Books
375 Hudson Street
New York, NY 10014

Farrar, Straus, & Giroux, Inc.
19 Union Square West
New York, NY 10003

Four Winds Press
866 Third Avenue
New York, NY 10022

David R. Godine
Publishers, Inc.
300 Massachusetts Avenue
Boston, MA 02115

Green Tiger Press
15 Columbus Circle
New York, NY 10023

Greenwillow Books
1350 Avenue of the Americas
New York, NY 10019

Grosset & Dunlap, Inc.
200 Madison Avenue
New York, NY 10016

Gulliver Books
1250 Sixth Avenue
San Diego, CA 92101

Harcourt Brace & Company
Children's Books
1250 Sixth Avenue
San Diego, CA 92101

HarperCollins Children's Books
10 East 53rd Street
New York, NY 10022
includes discontinued imprints
Crowell, Lippincott, Harper &
Row

Harper Trophy Paperbacks
10 East 53rd Street
New York, NY 10022

Henry Holt and Company, Inc.
115 West 18th Street
New York, NY 10011

Holiday House
425 Madison Avenue
New York, NY 10017

Houghton Mifflin
2 Park Street
Boston, MA 02108

Hyperion Books for Children
114 Fifth Avenue
New York, NY 10011

The Jewish Publication Society
2112 Broadway
New York, NY 10023

Joy Street Books
34 Beacon Street
Boston, MA 02108

Just Us Books
301 Main Street, Suite 22–24
Orange NJ 07050

Alfred A. Knopf
225 Park Avenue South
New York, NY 10003

Lerner Publications Company
241 First Avenue North
Minneapolis, MN 55401

Little, Brown & Co.
34 Beacon Street
Boston, MA 02108

Lodestar Books
375 Hudson Street
New York, NY 10014

Lothrop, Lee & Shepard Books
1350 Avenue of the Americas
New York, NY 10019

Margaret K. McElderry Books
866 Third Avenue
New York, NY 10022

Macmillan Publishing Co.
866 Third Avenue
New York, NY 10022

Julian Messner
15 Columbus Circle
New York, NY 10023

Morrow Junior Books
1350 Avenue of the Americas
New York, NY 10019

Mulberry Books
1350 Avenue of the Americas
New York, NY 10019

North-South Books
1133 Broadway, Suite 1016
New York, NY 10010

Orchard Books
387 Park Avenue South
New York, NY 10016

Oxford University Press
200 Madison Avenue
New York, NY 10016

Penguin USA
375 Hudson Street
New York, NY 10014

Philomel Books
200 Madison Avenue
New York, NY 10016

Picture Book Studio
10 Central Street
Saxonville, MA 01701
distributed by Simon &
Schuster

Pleasant Company
8400 Fairway Place
P. O. Box 998
Middleton, WI 53562

Puffin Books
375 Hudson Street
New York, NY 10014

G. P. Putnam's Sons
200 Madison Avenue
New York, NY 10016

Random House
225 Park Avenue South
New York, NY 10003

Scholastic Inc.
730 Broadway
New York, NY 10003

Charles Scribner's Sons
866 Third Avenue
New York, NY 10022

Simon and Schuster Books for
Young Readers
15 Columbus Circle
New York, NY 10023

St. Martin's Press
175 Fifth Avenue
New York, NY 10010

Tambourine Books
1350 Avenue of the Americas
New York, NY 10019

Viking
375 Hudson Street
New York, NY 10014

Walker & Co.
720 Fifth Avenue
New York, NY 10019

Frederick Warne & Co., Inc.
375 Hudson Street
New York, NY 10014

Franklin Watts, Inc.
387 Park Avenue South
New York, NY 10016

Paperback Book Club Addresses

The Trumpet Book Clubs
Bantam, Doubleday, or Dell
666 Fifth Avenue
New York, NY 10103

The Scholastic Book Clubs
Scholastic, Inc.
730 Broadway
New York, NY 10003
(Firefly: Preschool–K; See Saw:
K–1; Lucky: Grade 2–3)

Weekly Reader
245 Long Hill Road
Middletown, CT 06457

Professional Associations

American Library Association
50 East Huron Street
Chicago, IL 60611

Children's Book Council
568 Broadway
New York, NY 10012

International Reading
Association
800 Barksdale Road
Newark, DE 19714

National Council of Teachers of
English
1111 Kenyon Road
Urbana, IL 61801

Appendix D

Birthdays of Selected Authors and Illustrators

January
2   Isaac Asimov, Crosby Bonsall, Jean Little
3   Carolyn Haywood, J. R. R. Tolkien
4   Jacob Grimm
6   Carl Sandburg, Vera Cleaver
7   Kay Chorao
9   Clyde Robert Bulla
10 Remy Charlip
11 Robert C. O'Brien
12 Charles Perrault, Jack London
13 Michael Bond
14 Hugh Lofting
18 A. A. Milne, Raymond Briggs
19 Edgar Allen Poe
22 Blair Lent, Brian Wildsmith
25 James Flora
26 Mary Mapes Dodge
27 Lewis Carroll, Jean Merrill
28 Ann Jonas
29 Bill Peet
30 Lloyd Alexander

February
1   Langston Hughes
2   Rebecca Caudill
4   Russell Hoban
5   Patricia Lauber
7   Laura Ingalls Wilder
8   Jules Verne
9   Hilda Van Stockum
10 Elaine Konigsburg
11 Jane Yolen
12 Judy Blume

15 Norman Bridwell, Doris Orgel
16 Nancy Ekholm Burkert, Mary O'Neill
19 Louis Slobodkin
24 Wilhelm Grimm
25 Frank Bonham, Cynthia Voigt
27 Henry Wadsworth Longfellow, Uri Shulevitz
28 Sir John Tenniel

March
2   Dr. Seuss, Leo Dillon
4   Meindert DeJong
5   Errol Le Cain
8   Kenneth Grahame
11 Wanda Gág, Ezra Jack Keats
12 Virginia Hamilton, Leo Lionni
13 Ellen Raskin, Dorothy Aldis, Diane Dillon
14 Marguerite de Angeli, Lee Galda
16 Sid Fleischman
17 Kate Greenaway
20 Ellen Conford, Mitsumasa Anno, Lois Lowry
22 Randolph Caldecott
23 Eleanor Cameron
24 Mary Stolz, Bill Cleaver
26 Robert Frost
27 Dick King-Smith

April
2   Hans Christian Andersen
3   Washington Irving
8   Trina Schart Hyman
9   Joseph Krumgold
10 David Adler
12 Hardie Gramatky

13   Marguerite Henry, Genevieve Foster, Lee Bennett Hopkins

19   Jean Lee Latham

22   William Jay Smith

23   William Shakespeare

24   Evaline Ness

25   Walter De la Mare

26   Patricia Reilly Giff

27   Ludwig Bemelmans, John Burningham

29   Jill Paton Walsh

30   Dorothy Hinshaw Patent

May

7   **Nonny Hogrogian**

8   **Milton Meltzer**

9   **Eleanor Estes, Sir James Barrie, William Pène du Bois, Keith Robertson**

10   John Rowe Townsend, Margaret Wise Brown

11   Zilpha Keatley Snyder

12   Edward Lear

14   George Selden

15   L. Frank Baum

17   Eloise Greenfield

18   Lillian Hoban, Irene Hunt

21   Virginia Haviland

22   Arnold Lobel

23   Scott O'Dell, Susan Cooper

25   Martha Alexander

30   Millicent Selsam

31   Jay Williams, Elizabeth Coatsworth, Walt Whitman

June

1   James Daugherty

2   Norton Juster, Paul Galdone, Helen Oxenbury

3   Anita Lobel

5   Franklyn M. Branley

6   Peter Spier, Verna Aardema

7   Gwendolyn Brooks, John Goodall

10   Maurice Sendak

12   James Houston

14   Penelope Farmer, Laurence Yep

18   Pat Hutchins, Chris Van Allsburg

24   John Ciardi, Leonard Everett Fisher

25   Eric Carle

26   Charlotte Zolotow, Lynd Ward, Robert Burch, Wallace Tripp, Walter Farley

27   Lucille Clifton, Helen Keller

30   Mollie Hunter

July

2   Jean Craighead George

4   Nathaniel Hawthorne

6   Beatrix Potter

11   E. B. White, Helen Cresswell

12   Johanna Spyri, Herbert S. Zim

13   Marcia Brown

14   Isaac Bashevis Singer, Peggy Parish

15   Walter Edmonds

16   Arnold Adoff, Richard Egielski

17   Karla Kuskin

19   Eve Merriam, John Newbery

23   Robert Quackenbush

27   Scott Corbett, Hilaire Belloc

28   Natalie Babbitt

August

1   Gail Gibbons

6   Matt Christopher, Barbara Cooney

7   Betsy Byars

8   Jan Pienkowski

9   José Aruego, Seymour Simon

10   Margot Tomes

11   Don Freeman, Joanna Cole

12   Mary Ann Hoberman

15   Walter Crane, Brinton Turkle

17   Myra Cohn Livingston, Ariane Dewey

19   Ogden Nash

21   Arthur Yorinks

26   Patricia Beatty

28   Phyllis Krasilovsky, Roger Duvoisin, Tasha Tudor

30   Virginia Lee Burton, Donald Crews

September

2   Eugene Field

3   Aliki

4   Syd Hoff, Joan Aiken

8   Jack Prelutsky

9   Aileen Fisher

11   Alfred Slote

13   Roald Dahl, Else Minarik

14   William Armstrong

15   Robert McCloskey, Tomie dePaola

16   H. A. Rey

19   Arthur Rackham, Rachel Field, James Haskins

20   Donald Hall

23   Jan Ormerod

24   Harry Behn, Leslie Brooke, Jane Curry, Felice Holman

27	Bernard Waber, Paul Goble
28	Kate Douglas Wiggin
30	Alvin Tresselt

October
3	Natalie Savage Carlson, Molly Cone
4	Julia Cunningham, Robert Lawson, Donald Sobol
5	Louise Fitzhugh
6	Steven Kellogg
7	James Whitcomb Riley, Alice Dalgliesh, Susan Jeffers
10	James Marshall
11	Russell Freedman
12	Bernice Cullinan
13	Katherine Paterson
14	Lois Lenski
19	Ed Emberley
21	Ursula Le Guin
23	Marjorie Flack
24	Bruno Munari
27	Constance Greene

November
1	Symeon Shimin
7	Armstrong Sperry
12	Marjorie Weinman Sharmat
13	Robert Louis Stevenson
14	Astrid Lindgren, William Steig
15	David McCord, Manus Pinkwater
16	Jean Fritz
18	Mickey Mouse
20	William Cole
21	Elizabeth George Speare, Leo Politi
24	C. Collodi, Sylvia Engdahl, Frances Hodgson Burnett, Yoshiko Uchida
26	Doris Gates, Laurence Pringle
28	Tomi Ungerer
29	Louisa May Alcott, Madeleine L'Engle, C. S. Lewis
30	Mark Twain, Margot Zemach

December
2	David Macaulay
5	Christina Rossetti, Harve Zemach
6	Elizabeth Yates
8	Padraic Colum, Edwin Tunis
9	Joel Chandler Harris, Joan Blos
10	Emily Dickinson, Rumer Godden, Ernest Shepard
12	Barbara Emberley
13	Leonard Weisgard
16	Marie Hall Ets, Arthur C. Clarke
18	Marilyn Sachs
19	Eve Bunting
22	William O. Steele
24	Feodor Rojankovsky, Margaret J. Anderson
28	Carol Ryrie Brink
30	Rudyard Kipling, Mercer Mayer

Appendix E

Children's Magazines and Newspapers

Boy's Life — Age range: 8–18. For boys, especially those involved in scouting. Boy's Life, 1325 Walnut Hill Lane, Irving, TX 75038-3096

Chickadee — Age range: 4–9. Teaches children about the environment through interesting articles and outstanding illustrations. Chickadee, The Young Naturalist Foundation, 59 Front Street E, Toronto, Ontario, Canada M5E 1B3

Cobblestone — Age range: 8–14. The history magazine for young people. Cobblestone, 30 Grove Street, Peterborough, NH 03458

Cricket — Age range: 6–12. Contains quality literature and illustration for children. Cricket, Box 51144, Boulder, CO 80321

Current Events — Age range: 11–16. For students in social studies classes in the middle, junior, and early senior high school (grades 5–10). Current Events, 245 Long Hill Road, Middletown, CT 06457

Current Science — Age range: 11–16. For students in science classes in the middle, junior, and early senior high school (grades 5–10). Current Science, 245 Long Hill Road, Middletown, CT 06457

The Electric Company — Age range: 6–10. Contains general interest reading. The Electric Company, 200 Watt Street, P.O. Box 2923, Boulder, CO 80322

Faces — Age range: 8–14. Written and published in cooperation with the American Museum of Natural History of New York City about people from all over the world. Faces, 30 Grove Street, Peterborough, NH 03458

Highlights for Children — Age range: 2–12. Has "Fun with a Purpose" recreational yet educational features; an all-purpose magazine for children. Highlights for Children, P.O. Box 269, Columbus, OH 43272-0002

Junior Scholastic — Age range: 6–12. Contains features that pertain to social studies. Scholastic Inc., 730 Broadway, New York, NY 10003

Ladybug — Age range: 4–9. Stories, games, and activities intended to create a love of reading.

The Mini Page — Age range: 5–12. Offers general interest reading. Universal Press Syndicate, 4400 Johnson Drive, Kansas City, KS 66205

National Geographic World — Age range: 8–13. Outstanding illustrations and content in this nature and science magazine. National Geographic World, Department 01085, 17th and M Streets, NW, Box 2330, Washington, DC 20036

Odyssey — Age range: 8–14. For children with an interest in astronomy and space science; contains quality photography and illustration. Cobblestone Publishing, Inc., 30 Grove Street, Peterborough, NH 03458

Owl — Age range: 8–14. Teaches children about the environment through quality articles and outstanding photography. The Young Naturalist Foundation, 59 Front Street E, Toronto, Ontario, Canada M5E 1B3

Penny Power — Age range: 8–14. Youthful version of *Consumer Reports*. Penny Power Magazine, P.O. Box 2878, Boulder, CO 80322

Pennywhistle Press — Age range: 5–13. Contains general interest features. Pennywhistle Press, Box 500-P, Washington, DC 20044

Ranger Rick — Age range: 6–12. Well-illustrated and reliable nature magazine. Ranger Rick, The National Wildlife Federation, 8925 Leesburg Pike, Vienna, VA 22184

Science World — Age range: 7–10. Offers diverse features in the field of science. Science World, 730 Broadway, New York, NY 10003

Sesame Street — Age range: 2–6. Preschool prereading publication. Sesame Street, P.O. Box 2896, Boulder, CO 80322

Sports Illustrated for Kids — Age range: 8–13. Sports-oriented subjects. Time Inc., P.O. Box 830607, Birmingham, AL 35283–0607

Stone Soup — Age range: 6–13. Literary magazine written by children. Stone Soup, P.O. Box 83, Santa Cruz, CA 95063

3-2-1 Contact — Age range: 8–14. Offers interesting articles and activities in the fields of science and technology. 3-2-1 Contact, Box 53051, Boulder, CO 80322

*U*S* Kids* — Age range: 8–13. Stories, articles, and activities to interest children in their world and themselves. Field Publications, 245 Long Hill Road, Middletown, CT 06457

Your Big Backyard — Age range: 8–12. Outstanding photography and illustration in this nature magazine. Your Big Backyard, The National Wildlife Federation, 1412 16th Street, NW, Washington, DC 20036

Zillions — Age range: 7–12. Consumer education for children. Consumers Union, 256 Washington Street, Mount Vernon, NY 10553

Excerpts from *The Students' Right to Read*

The National Council of Teachers of English, 1982

For many years, American schools have been pressured to restrict or deny students access to books or periodicals deemed objectionable by some individual or group on moral, political, religious, ethnic, racial, or philosophical grounds. These pressures have mounted in recent years, and English teachers have no reason to believe they will diminish. The fight against censorship is a continuing series of skirmishes, not a pitched battle leading to a final victory over censorship.

We can safely make two statements about censorship: first, any work is potentially open to attack by someone, somewhere, sometime, for some reason; second, censorship is often arbitrary and irrational.

The immediate results of demands to censor books or periodicals vary. At times, school boards and administrators have supported and defended their teachers, their use of materials under fire, and the students' right of access to the materials. At other times, however, special committees have been formed to cull out "objectionable works" or "modern trash" or "controversial literature." Some teachers have been summarily reprimanded for assigning certain works, even to mature students. Others have been able to retain their positions only after initiating court action.

Not as sensational, but perhaps more important, are the long-range results. Schools have removed from libraries and classrooms and English teachers have avoided using or recommending works which might make members of the community angry. Many students are consequently "educated" in a school atmosphere hostile to free inquiry. And many teachers learn to emphasize their own safety rather than their students' needs.

Program of Action

Teachers, librarians, and school administrators can best serve students, literature, and the profession today if they prepare now to face pressures sensibly, demonstrating on the one hand a willingness to consider the merits of any complaint and on the other the courage to defend their literature program with intelligence and vigor. The Council therefore recommends that every school undertake the following two-step program to protect the students' right to read:

- the establishment of a representative committee to consider book selection procedures and to screen complaints; and

- a vigorous campaign to establish a community atmosphere in which local citizens may be enlisted to support the freedom to read.

To respond to complaints about books, every school should have a committee of teachers (and possibly students, parents, and other representatives from the community) organized to:

- inform the community about book selection procedures

- enlist the support of citizens, possibly by explaining the place of literature in the educational process or by discussing at meetings of parents and other community groups the books used at that school

- consider any complaints against any work.

No community is so small that it lacks concerned people who care about their children and the educational program of the schools. No community is so small that it lacks readers who will support teachers in defending books when complaints are received.

Despite the care taken to select worthwhile books for student reading and the qualifications of teachers selecting and recommending books, occasional objections to a work will undoubtedly be made. All books are potentially open to criticism in one or more general areas: the treatment of ideologies, of minorities, of love and sex; the use of language not acceptable to some people; the type of illustrations; the private life or political affiliations of the author or, in a few cases, the illustrator.

If some attacks are made by groups or individuals frankly hostile to free inquiry and open discussion, others are made by misinformed or misguided people who, acting on emotion or rumor, simply do not understand how the books are to be used. Others are made by well-intentioned and conscientious people who fear that harm will come to some segment of the community if a particular book is read or recommended.

What should be done upon receipt of a complaint?

- If the complainant telephones, listen courteously and refer him or her to the teacher involved. That teacher should be the first person to discuss the book with the person objecting to its use.

- If the complainant is not satisfied, invite him or her to file the complaint in writing, but make no commitments, admissions of guilt, or threats.

- If the complainant writes, contact the teacher involved and let that teacher call the complainant.

Sometimes the problem seems less serious and more easily resolved through personal contact over the phone. If the complainant is not satisfied, invite him or her to file the complaint in writing on a form prepared for this purpose (see sample).

At first, except for politely acknowledging the complaint and explaining the established procedures, the teacher should do nothing. The success of much censorship depends upon frightening an unprepared school or English department into some precipitous action. A standardized procedure will take the sting from the first outburst of criticism. When the responsible objector learns that he or she will be given a fair hearing through following the proper channels, he or she is more likely to be satisfied. The idle censor, on the other hand, may well be discouraged from taking further action. A number of advantages will be provided by the form, which will

- formalize the complaint

- indicate specifically the work in question

- identify the complainant

- suggest how many others support the complaint

- require the complainant to think through objections in order to make an intelligent statement on work (1, 2, and 3)

- cause the complainant to evaluate the work for other groups than merely the one he or she first had in mind (4)

- establish his or her familiarity with the work (5)

Citizen's Request for Reconsideration of a Work

Paperback _____
Hardcover _____

Author _____

Title _____

Publisher (if known) _____

Request initiated by _____

Telephone _____ Address _____

City _____ Zip Code _____

Complainant represents

_____ Himself/Herself

_____ (Name organization) _____

_____ (Identify other group) _____

1. Have you been able to discuss this work with the teacher or librarian who ordered it or who used it?

        Yes _____ No _____

2. What do you understand to be the general purpose for using this work?

    a. Provide support for a unit in the curriculum?

        Yes _____ No _____

    b. Provide a learning experience for the reader in one kind of literature?

        Yes _____ No _____

    c. Other _____

_____

3. Did the general purpose for the use of the work, as described by the teacher or librarian, seem a suitable one to you?

Yes _____ No _____

If not, please explain. _____

_____

4. What do you think is the general purpose of the author in this book? _____

_____

5. In what ways do you think a work of this nature is not suitable for the use the teacher or librarian wishes to carry out? _____

_____

6. Have you been able to learn what is the students' response to this work?

Yes _____ No _____

7. What response did the students make? _____

_____

8. Have you been able to learn from your school library what book reviewers or other students of literature have written about this work?

Yes _____ No _____

9. Would you like the teacher or librarian to give you a written summary of what book reviewers and other students have written about this book or film?

Yes _____ No _____

10. Do you have negative reviews of the book?

Yes _____ No _____

11. Where were they published? _____

12. Would you be willing to provide summaries of the reviews you have collected?

Yes _____ No _____

13. What would you like your library/school to do about this work?

_____ Do not assign/lend it to my child.

_____ Return it to the staff selection committee/department for reevaluation.

_____ Other—Please explain. _____

14. In its place, what work would you recommend that would convey as valuable a picture and perspective of the subject treated? _____

_____

Signature _____

Date _____

- give the complainant an opportunity to consider the criticism about the work and the teacher's purpose in using the work (6, 7, and 8) and

- give the complainant an opportunity to suggest alternative actions to be taken on the work (9 and 10)

The committee reviewing complaints should be available on short notice to consider the completed "Citizen's Request for Reconsideration of a Work" and to call in the complainant and the teacher involved for a conference. Members of the committee should have reevaluated the work in advance of the meeting, and the group should be prepared to explain its findings. Membership of the committee should ordinarily include an administrator, the English department chair, and at least two classroom teachers of English. But the department might consider the advisability of including members from the community and the local or state NCTE affiliate. As a matter of course, recommendations from the committee would be forwarded to the superintendent, who would in turn submit them to the board of education, the legally constituted authority in the school.

Teachers and administrators should recognize that the responsibility for selecting works for class study lies with classroom teachers and that the responsibility for reevaluating any work begins with the review committee. Both teachers and administrators should refrain from discussing the objection with the complainant, the press, or community groups. Once the complaint has been filed, the authority for handling the situation must ultimately rest with the administration and school board.

Freedom of inquiry is essential to education in a democracy. To establish conditions essential for freedom, teachers and administrators need to follow procedures similar to those recommended here. Where schools resist unreasonable pressures, the cases are seldom publicized and students continue to read works as they wish. The community that entrusts students to the care of an English teacher should also trust that teacher to exercise professional judgment in selecting or recommending books. The English teacher can be free to teach literature, and students can be free to read whatever they wish only if informed and vigilant groups, within the profession and without, unite in resisting unfair pressures.

Resources

Special materials to assist teachers and administrators are available from the National Council of Teachers of English, 1111 Kenyon Road, Urbana, IL 61801.

"The Open Letter Taken from *The Students' Right to Read*." Additional copies of this statement are available from the National Council of Teachers of English.

Censors in the Classroom: The Mind Benders. Edward B. Jenkinson. Southern Illinois University Press, 1979.

"Censorship Game and How to Play It." Benjamin C. Cox. The National Council for the Social Studies Bulletin, No. 50. Washington, DC, 1977.

Dealing with Censorship. Ed. James E. Davis. National Council of Teachers of English, 1979.

"Lobbying for Freedom: A Citizen's Guide to Fighting Censorship at the State Level." St. Martin's Press, 1975.

Students' Right to Know. Eds. Lee Burress and Edward B. Jenkinson. National Council of Teachers of English, 1982.

Valuable material is also available from the American Library Association, 50 East Huron Street, Chicago, IL 60611, particularly the Library Bill of Rights and the Newsletter on Intellectual Freedom, the latter a bimonthly publication available by subscription.

Glossary of Literary Terms

Alliteration	Repetition of initial consonant.
Antagonist	Character directly opposed to protagonist or hero.
Anthropomorphism	Gives human qualities to animals or objects.
Character	A personality in literature.
Characterization	Means by which an author establishes credibility of person or creature created by words, for example, physical description, or character's actions, words, thoughts, and feelings.
Chronological order	Events related in order of happening.
Classic	Literary work from past generation that retains popularity over time.
Cliché	Expression used so often it loses its freshness and clarity. Overused term that loses meaning.
Cliffhanger	Suspenseful plot structure.
Climax	Peak of action that brings about resolution of conflict.
Conflict	Central problem or struggle; person against self, person against person, person against society, person against nature.
Connotation	Emotional meaning of a word.
Convention	Formulas and elements taken from folklore.
Denotation	Dictionary meaning of a word.
Denouement	Closing action after climax and resolution.
Didactic	Preachy, moralistic.
End papers	Insides of front and back covers.
Episodic plot	Independent chapters.
Folklore	Myths, legends, proverbs, nursery rhymes, stories handed down by word of mouth from generations past.
Folksong	Song of unknown authorship preserved and transmitted by oral tradition.
Folktale	Short narrative handed down through oral tradition.
Format	Physical makeup of a book including page size, typeface, margins, paper, and binding.
Flashback	Earlier scene out of sequence.
Foreshadowing	Hints of things to come.
Genre	Category of literature.
Hyperbole	Exaggeration and overstatement.
Imagery	Words that appeal to senses.
Jacket	Dust jacket. Paper cover on hardbound book.
Language style	Choice and arrangement of words to tell a story or poem that express the individuality, the ideas, and the intent of the author.
Metaphor	Implied comparison.
Motif	Recurring element in literature; a conventional situation, device, or incident; prevailing idea or design.

Omniscient narrator	All-knowing narrator tells story in third person.	Resolution	Action following climax; solution of the central problem.
Onomatopoeia	Words sound like their meaning: boom!	Rhythm	Recurring flow of strong and weak beats in the language of prose or poetry.
Parody	Composition designed to ridicule in humorous fashion another piece of work or its author. Burlesque or humorous imitation of a work.	Setting	Time and place of the story events.
		Simile	Stated comparison.
Pattern	Repeated structure or device, for example, use of three.	Symbol	Element with figurative and literal meaning.
Personification	Gives human traits to inanimate objects.	Tall tale	Humorous tale on American frontier that recounts extravagantly impossible happenings.
Plot	Sequence and relationship of events.	Theme	Central or dominating idea. In nonfiction, it may be the topic. In poetry, fiction, drama, it is an abstract concept that is made vivid through character, plot, and image.
Plot structure	Way a story is organized, the arrangements of the incidents, the ordering of events, the sequence, the story pattern. Types of plots: episodic, cumulative, flashbacks, chronological, cyclical.	Unity	Coordination of text and illustration.
Point of view	Perspective from which an author tells a story or a poet speaks: first person, third person, omniscient narrator. Vantage point the author chooses.	Variant	Different version of the same folktale.
		Verisimilitude	Appearance or semblance of truth.
Protagonist	Central character; hero.	Verse	Unit of poetry; a metrical composition.

Professional References

Ada, A. F. (1990). *A magical encounter: Spanish language children's literature in the classroom.* San Francisco: Santillana.

Alexander, L. (1970). Identifications and identities. *Wilson Library Bulletin, 45* (2), 144–148.

Alexander, L. (1981). The grammar of story. In B. Hearne & M. Kaye (Eds.), *Celebrating children's books* (pp. 3–13). New York: Lothrop, Lee & Shepard.

Allington, R. L. (1984). Oral reading. In P. D. Pearson (Ed.), *Handbook of reading research* (pp. 829–864). New York: Longman.

Anderson, R. C., Hiebert, E. H., Scott, J. A., & Wilkinson, I. A. G. (1985). *Becoming a nation of readers: The report of the commission on reading.* Washington, DC: National Institute of Education.

Anzul, M. (1988). *Exploring literature with children within a transactional framework. Dissertation Abstracts International, 49,* 08, 2132A.

Aoki, E. M. (1981). Are you Chinese? Are you Japanese? Or are you just a mixed-up kid? *The Reading Teacher, 34*(4), 382–385.

Applebee, A. N. (1978). *The child's concept of story.* Chicago: University of Chicago Press.

Applebee, A. N. (1979). Children and stories: Learning the rules of the game. *Language Arts 56,* 645.

Babbitt, N. (1990). Protecting children's literature. *The Horn Book Magazine, 66,* 696–703.

Baumann, J. F., & Kameenui, E. J. (1991). Research on vocabulary instruction: Ode to Voltaire. In J. Flood, J. M. Jensen, D. Lapp, & J. R. Squire (Eds.), *Handbook on teaching the English language arts* (pp. 604–632). New York: Macmillan.

Benton, M. (1984). The methodology vacuum in teaching literature. *Language Arts, 61,* 265–275.

Blos, J. (1992). Perspectives on historical fiction. In R. Ammon & M. Tunnell (Eds.), *The story of ourselves: Teaching history through children's literature* (pp. 11–17). Portsmouth, NH: Heinemann.

Blumberg, R. (1985). *Commodore Perry in the land of the shogun.* New York: Lothrop, Lee & Shepard.

Botkin, B. A. (1944). *A treasury of American folklore.* New York: Crown.

Brewton, J. E., Blackburn, M., & Blackburn, L. A. (1978). *Index to poetry for children and young people.* New York: H. W. Wilson.

Britton, J. (1970). *Language and learning.* London: Penguin.

Bromley, K. D. (1991). *Webbing with literature: Creating story maps with children's books.* Boston: Allyn & Bacon.

Bruner, J. S. (1987). *Actual minds, possible worlds.* Cambridge, MA: Harvard University Press.

Calder, J. W. (1984). *The effects of story structure instruction on third-graders' concept of story, reading comprehension, response to literature, and written composition. Dissertation Abstracts International, 46,* 02, 387A.

Cameron, E. (1969). *The green and burning tree.* New York: Atlantic, Little, Brown.

Carr, J. (1981). What do we do about bad biographies? *School Library Journal, 27*(9), 19–21.

Cianciolo, P. J. (1990). *Picture books for children* (3rd ed.). Chicago: American Library Association.

Cianciolo, P. J. (1976). *Illustrations in children's books.* Dubuque, IA: William C. Brown.

Cianciolo, P. J., & Quirk, B. A. (1993). *Teaching and learning critical aesthetic response to literature: An instructional improvement study in grades K-5.* East Lansing, MI: The Center for the Learning and Teaching of Elementary Subjects, Institute for Research on Teaching, Michigan State University.

Clark, M. M. (1976). *Young fluent readers*. London: Heinemann.

Cochran-Smith, M. (1984). *The making of a reader*. Norwood, NJ: Ablex.

Cole, J. (1982). *Best-loved folktales of the world*. New York: Doubleday.

Commager, H. S. (1969). Introduction to the first edition. In C. Meigs, A. T. Eaton, E. Nesbitt, & R. H. Viguers (Eds.), *A critical history of children's literature* (pp. xvi–xvii). New York: Macmillan.

Cooper, S. (1981). Escaping into ourselves. In B. Hearne & M. Kaye (Eds.), *Celebrating children's books* (pp. 14–23). New York: Lothrop.

Corso, G. (1983). Comment. In P. Janeczko (Ed.), *Poetspeak* (p. 11). New York: Bradbury.

Cox, M. R. (1893). *Cinderella: Three hundred and forty-five variants*. New York: David Nutt/The Folklore Society.

Cullinan, B. E. (Ed.). (1989). *Children's literature in the reading program*. Newark, DE: International Reading Association.

Cullinan, B. E. (Ed.). (1992). *Invitation to read*. Newark, DE: International Reading Association.

Cullinan, B. E., Harwood, K., & Galda, L. (1983). The reader and the story: Comprehension and response. *Journal of Research and Development in Education, 16* (3), 29–38.

Darton, F. J. H. (1982). *Children's books in England* (3rd ed.). London: Cambridge University Press.

de la Mare, W. (1942). *Peacock pie*. London: Faber & Faber.

de la Mare, W. (1962). Cited in W. S. Baring-Gould & C. Baring-Gould, *The annotated Mother Goose*. New York: Bramhall.

de Trevino, E. B. (1965). *I, Juan de Pareja*. New York: Farrar, Straus & Giroux.

Demers, P., & Moyles, C. (1982). *From instruction to delight: An anthology of children's literature to 1850*. Toronto: Oxford University Press.

Donaldson, M. (1978). *Children's minds*. New York: Norton.

Durkin, D. (1966). *Children who read early*. New York: Teachers College Press.

Early, M. J. (1960). Stages of growth in literary appreciation. *English Journal, 49,* 161–167.

Edmiston, B., Enciso, P., & King, M. L. (1987). Empowering readers and writers through drama: Narrative theater. *Language Arts, 64,* 219–229.

Edmonds, L. (1986). The treatment of race in picture books for young children. *Book Research Quarterly, 2*(3), 30–41.

Eeds, M., & Peterson, R. (1991). Teacher as curator: Learning to talk about literature. *The Reading Teacher, 45,* 118–126.

Eeds, M., & Wells, D. (1989). Grand conversations: An exploration of meaning construction in literature study groups. *Research in the Teaching of English, 23,* 4–29.

Egoff, S. A. (1981). *Thursday's child: Trends and patterns in contemporary children's literature*. Chicago: American Library Association.

Farmer, P. (1979). *Beginnings: Creation myths of the world*. New York: Atheneum.

Favat, F. A. (1977). *Child and tale: The origins of interest*. Urbana, IL: National Council of Teachers of English.

Feitelsen, D., Kita, B., & Goldstein, Z. (1986). Effects of listening to series stories on first graders' comprehension and use of language. *Research in the Teaching of English, 20,* 339–356.

Fielding, L., Wilson, P. T., & Anderson, R. (1984). A new focus on free reading: The role of trade books in reading instruction. In T. E. Raphael & R. E. Reynolds (Eds.), *The contexts of school-based literacy* (pp. 149–160). New York: Random House.

Fisher, C. J., & Natarella, M. (1982). Young children's preferences in poetry: A national survey of first, second and third graders. *Research in the Teaching of English, 16*(4), 339–354.

Fitzgerald, F. (1979). *America revised: History schoolbooks in the twentieth century*. Boston: Little, Brown.

Fritz, J. (1976). George Washington, my father, and Walt Disney. *Horn Book Magazine, 52*(2), 191–198.

Frye, N. (1963). *The well-tempered critic*. Bloomington: Indiana University Press.

Frye, N. (1970). *The educated imagination*. Bloomington: Indiana University Press.

Galda, L. (1982). Assuming the spectator stance: An examination of the responses of three young readers. *Research in the Teaching of English, 16,* 1–20.

Galda, L. (1988). Readers, texts, and contexts: A response-based view of literature. *The New Advocate, 1,* 92–102.

Galda, L. (1990). A longitudinal study of the spectator stance as a function of age and genre. *Research in the Teaching of English, 24,* 261–278.

Galda, L. (1992). Evaluation as a spectator: Changes across time and genre. In J. Many & C. Cox (Eds.), *Reader stance and literary understanding: Exploring the theories, research, and practice* (pp. 127–142). Norwood, NJ: Ablex.

Galda, L. (1993). How preferences and expectations influence evaluative responses to literature. In K. E. Holland, R. Hungerford, & S. Ernst (Eds.), *Journeying: Children responding to literature* (pp. 302–315). Portsmouth, NH: Heinemann.

Galda, L., & Cullinan, B. (1991). Literature for literacy: What research says about the benefits of using trade books in the classroom. In J. Flood, J. M. Jensen, D. Lapp, & J. R. Squire (Eds.), *Handbook of research on teaching the English language arts* (pp. 529–535). New York: Macmillan.

Galda, L., Cullinan, B. E., & Strickland, D. (1993). *Language, literacy and the child.* Fort Worth: Harcourt Brace Jovanovich.

Gardner, D. (1965). Emotions: A basis for learning. *Feelings and learning.* Washington, DC: Association for Childhood Education International.

Giblin, J. C. (1986, July). *Children's literature in the eighties.* Second Annual Highlights Foundation Writer's Workshop, Chautauqua, NY, p. 14.

Giblin, J. C. (1991, July). *Trends in children's publishing.* Words and pictures of the Highlights Foundation Writers Workshop, Chautauqua, NY, p. 9.

Giniger, K. S. (1989). *The distribution and sale of foreign language books in the United States.* Alexandria, VA: *International Publishing Newsletter.*

Goldstone, B. P. (1984). *Lessons to be learned: A study of eighteenth-century English didactic children's literature (American University Studies Series),* New York: Peter Lang, XIV, Vol. 1.

Goodman, K. S. (1985). Transactional psycholinguistics model: Unity in reading. In H. Singer & R. B. Ruddell (Eds.), *Theoretical models and processes of reading* (3rd ed.) (pp. 813–840). Newark, DE: International Reading Association.

Grimal, P. (1965). *Larousse world mythology.* Secaucus, NJ: Chartwell.

Hall, S. (1990). *Using picture storybooks to teach literary devices: Recommended books for children and young adults.* Phoenix: Oryx Press.

Hardy, B. (1978). Towards a poetics of fiction: An approach through narrative. In M. Meek, A. Warlow, & G. Barton (Eds.), *The cool web* (pp. 12–23). New York: Atheneum.

Harris, V. (Ed.). (1992). *Teaching multicultural literature in grades K–8.* Norwood, MA: Christopher-Gordon.

Harste, J. C., Short, K. C., & Burke, C. (1988). *Creating classrooms for authors: The reading-writing connection.* Portsmouth, NH: Heinemann.

Hazard, P. (1967). *Books, children and men.* Boston: Horn Book.

Heath, S. B. (1982). What no bedtime story means: Narrative skills at home and school. *Language and Society, 11,* 49–75.

Heath, S. B. (1983). *Ways with words: Language, life, and work in communities and classrooms.* Cambridge, MA: Cambridge University Press.

Heath, S. B. (1993). Report to the English Standards Board. Chicago, IL: CSR, NCTE, IRA Standards Project.

Heinlein, R. A. (1953). Ray guns and rocket ships. *Library Journal, 78* (July), 1188.

Hepler, S. I., & Hickman, J. (1982). The book was okay, I love you—Social aspects of response to literature. *Theory into Practice, 21,* 278–283.

Herman, G. B. (1978). "Footprints in the sands of time": Biography for children. *Children's Literature in Education, 9*(2), 85–94.

Hickman, J. (1981). A new perspective on response to literature: Research in an elementary school setting. *Research in the Teaching of English, 15,* 343–354.

Hiebert, E. H., & Colt, J. (1989). Patterns of literature-based reading instruction. *The Reading Teacher, 43,* 14–20.

Hodges, M., & Steinfirst, S. (1980). *Elva S. Smith's the history of children's literature.* Chicago: American Library Association.

Holland, R. (1970). *Mill child: The story of child labor in America.* New York: Macmillan.

Hunter, M. (1976). *Talent is not enough: Mollie Hunter on writing for children.* New York: HarperCollins.

Hynds, S. (1992). Challenging questions in the teaching of literature. In J. A. Langer (Ed.), *Literature instruction: A focus on student response* (pp. 78–100). Urbana, IL: National Council of Teachers of English.

Ingham, J. (1981). *Books and reading development.* London: Heinemann.

Jackson, J. (1992). Paper presented at the Holmes-Hunter Lecture. University of Georgia, Athens.

Jordan, A. (1983). *From Rollo to Tom Sawyer, and other papers.* Boston: Horn Book.

Kiefer, B. Z. (1986). The child and the picture book: Creating live circuits. *Children's Literature Association Quarterly, 11,* 63–68.

Kimmel, E. A. (1977). Confronting the ovens: The Holocaust and juvenile fiction. *Horn Book Magazine, 53*(1).

Kimmel, M. M., & Segel, E. (1988). *For reading out loud: A guide to sharing books with children.* New York: Delacorte.

Kuskin, K. (1980). Introduction. *Dogs and dragons, trees and dreams.* New York: HarperCollins.

Langer, J. A. (1990). The process of understanding: Reading for literary and informative purposes. *Research in the Teaching of English, 24,* 229–260.

Larrick, N. (1965). The all-white world of children's books. *Saturday Review* (September 11), 63–65.

Leinhardt, G., Zigmond, N., & Cooley, W. W. (1981). Reading instruction and its effects. *American Educational Research Journal, 18,* 343–361.

Lehr, S. S. (1991). *The child's developing sense of theme: Responses to literature.* New York: Teacher's College Press.

Luthi, M. (1970). *Once upon a time: On the nature of fairy tales.* New York: Ungar.

May, J. (1984). Editorial: Judy Blume as Archie

Bunker. *Children's Literature Association Quarterly, 9* (1), 2.

Marcus, Leonard S. (1991). *Margaret Wise Brown: Awakened by the moon.* Boston: Beacon Press.

McClure, A. (1990). *Sunrises and songs: Reading and writing poetry in an elementary classroom.* Portsmouth, NH: Heinemann.

Meigs, C., Eaton, A. T., Nesbitt, E., & Viguers, R. H. (1969). *A critical history of children's literature.* New York: Macmillan.

Meltzer, M. (1976). Where do all the prizes go? The case for nonfiction. *Horn Book Magazine, 52*(1), 21–22.

Meltzer, M. (1982). *The Hispanic Americans.* New York: Crowell.

Meltzer, M. (1989). The social responsibility of the writer. *The New Advocate, 2*(3), 155–157.

Merriam, E. (1981). Acceptance speech, National Council of Teachers of English Award for Excellence in Poetry for Children.

Miller-Lachman, L. (1992). *Our family, our friends, our world.* New Providence, NJ: R. R. Bowker.

Moffett, J. (1983). *Teaching the universe of discourse.* Boston: Houghton Mifflin.

Monson, D. L., & Sebesta, S. L. (1991). Reading preferences. In J. Flood, J. M. Jensen, D. Lapp, & J. R. Squire (Eds.), *Handbook of research on teaching the English language arts* (pp. 664–673). New York: Macmillan.

Moss, A., & Stott, J. C. (1986). *The family of stories: An anthology of children's literature.* New York: Holt, Rinehart, and Winston.

National Council of Teachers of English. (1983). Statement on censorship and professional guidelines. *The Bulletin, 9* (1–2), 17–18.

Nodelman, P. (1988). *Words about pictures.* Athens: University of Georgia Press.

O'Neill, C. (1989). Dialogue and drama: The transformation of events, ideas, and teachers. *Language Arts, 66*, 147–158.

Opie, I., & Opie, P. (1951). *The Oxford dictionary of nursery rhymes.* London: Oxford University Press.

Opie, I., & Opie P. (1974). *Classic fairy tales.* London: Oxford University Press.

Perkinson, H. J. (1978). American textbooks and educational change. In National Institute of Education, *Early American Textbooks 1775–1900* (pp. 21–57). Washington, DC: Alvina Treut Burrows Institute.

Piaget, J. (1964). *The language and thought of the child* (2nd ed.). (M. Gabain, Trans.). London: Routledge & Kegan Paul. (Original work published 1926)

Pillar, A. M. (1983). Aspects of moral judgment in response to fables. *Journal of Research and Development in Education, 16* (3), 37–46.

Posner, M. (1987). The broad range of Jewish children's books. *A. B. Bookman's Weekly, 79*, 1225–1233.

Pringle, L. (1986, July). *Science writing.* Second Annual Highlights Foundation Writer's Workshop, Chautauqua, NY, p. 26.

Purves, A. C., Rogers, T., & Soter, A. D. (1990). *How porcupines make love II: Teaching a response-centered literature curriculum.* New York: Longman.

Ravitch, D. (1985). *The schools we deserve: Reflections on the educational crises of our times.* New York: Basic.

Rollock, Barbara. (1988). *Black authors and illustrators of children's books.* New York: Garland.

Rosen, C., & Rosen, H. (1973). *The language of primary school children.* London: Penguin.

Rosenbach, A. S. W. (1966). *Early American children's books.* Millwood, NY: Kraus Reprint (Original work published 1933)

Rosenblatt, L. M. (1976). *Literature as exploration.* New York: Noble & Noble. (Original work published 1938)

Rosenblatt, L. M. (1978). *The reader, the text, the poem: The transactional theory of the literary work.* Carbondale, IL: Southern Illinois University Press.

Rosenblatt, L. M. (1991). Literature—S.O.S.! *Language Arts, 68*, 444–448.

Rosenshine, B., & Stevens, R. (1984). Classroom instruction in reading. In P. D. Pearson (Ed.), *Handbook of reading research* (pp. 745–798). New York: Longman.

Roser, N., & Frith, M. (1983). *Children's choices: Teaching with books children like.* Newark, DE: International Reading Association.

Saul, W. (1986). Living proof: Children's biographies of Marie Curie. *School Library Journal, 33* (October), 103–108.

Sawyer, R. (1962). *The way of the storyteller.* New York: Viking.

Schlager, N. (1978). Predicting children's choices in literature: A developmental approach. *Children's Literature in Education, 9*, 136–142.

Short, K. G., & Pierce, K. M. (1990). *Talking about books: Creating literate communities.* Portsmouth, NH: Heinemann.

Sims Bishop, R. (1982a). Profile: Lucille Clifton. *Language Arts, 59*(2), 160–167.

Sims Bishop, R. (1982b). *Shadow and substance: Afro-American experience in contemporary children's fiction.* Urbana, IL: National Council of Teachers of English.

Sims Bishop, R. (1985). Children's books about blacks: A mid-eighties status report. *Children's Literature Review, 8*, 9–14. Detroit: Gale Research.

Sims Bishop, R. (1987). Extending multicultural understanding through children's books. In B. E. Cullinan (Ed.), *Children's literature in the reading program* (pp. 60–67). Newark, DE: International Reading Association.

Sims Bishop, R. (1992). Multicultural literature for

Children's Books References

Aamundsen, Nina Ring. (1990). *Two long and one short.* Boston: Houghton.

Aardema, Verna. (1975). *Why mosquitoes buzz in people's ears: A West African tale.* Illus. Leo & Diane Dillon. New York: Dial.

Aardema, Verna. (1979; o.p.). *The riddle of the drum: A tale from Tizapan, Mexico.* Illus. Tony Chen. New York: Four Winds.

Aardema, Verna. (1979). *Who's in rabbit's house?* Illus. Leo & Diane Dillon. New York: Dial.

Aardema, Verna. (1981). *Bringing the rain to Kapiti Plain.* Illus. Beatriz Vidal. New York: Dial.

Aardema, Verna. (1988). *Bimwilli and the Zimwi.* Illus. Susan Meddaugh. New York: Dial.

Aardema, Verna. (1988). *Oh, Kojo! How could you!* Illus. Marc Brown. New York: Dial.

Aardema, Verna. (1991). *Borreguita and the coyote: A tale from Ayutila, Mexico.* Illus. Petra Mathers. New York: Knopf.

Aardema, Verna. (1991). *Pedro and the padre: A tale from Jalisco, Mexico.* Illus. Friso Henstra. New York: Dial.

Aardema, Verna. (1992). *Traveling to Tondo: A tale of the Nkundo of Zaire.* Illus. Will Hillenbrand. New York: Knopf.

Aardema, Verna. (1993). *A bookworm who hatched.* Katonah, NY: Richard C. Owen.

Aardema, Verna (reteller). (1988). *Princess Gorilla and a new kind of water.* Illus. Victoria Chess. New York: Dial.

Aardema, Verna (reteller). (1989). *Rabbit makes a monkey of lion: A Swahili tale.* Illus. Jerry Pinkney. New York: Dial.

Abbott, Jacob. (1834). *Rollo learning to talk.* Boston: Reynolds.

Abbott, Jacob. (1854). *Rollo in Paris.* Boston: Reynolds.

Abbott, Jacob. (1858). *Rollo's tour of Europe.* Boston: Reynolds.

Abells, Chana Byers. (1986). *The children we remember.* New York: Greenwillow.

Abercrombie, Barbara. (1990). *Charlie Anderson.* Illus. Mark Graham. New York: McElderry.

Ackerman, Karen. (1988). *Song and dance man.* Illus. Stephen Gammell. New York: Knopf.

Adams, Ken. (1991). *When I was your age.* Illus. Val Biro. New York: Barron.

Adams, Richard. (1974). *Watership down.* New York: Macmillan.

Adler, David A. (1981). *Cam Jansen & the mystery of the dinosaur bones.* New York: Viking.

Adler, David A. (1982). *A picture book of Hanukkah.* Illus. Linda Heller. New York: Holiday.

Adler, David A. (1986). *Martin Luther King, Jr.: Free at last.* New York: Holiday.

Adler, David A. (1989). *Jackie Robinson: He was the first.* New York: Holiday.

Adler, David A. (1989). *A picture book of Martin Luther King, Jr.* New York: Holiday.

Adler, David A. (1989). *We remember the Holocaust.* New York: Holt.

Adler, David A. (1990). *A picture book of Benjamin Franklin.* New York: Holiday.

Adler, David A. (1990). *A picture book of Thomas Jefferson.* New York: Holiday.

Adler, David A. (1991). *A picture book of Christopher Columbus.* New York: Holiday.

Adler, David A. (1991). *A Picture Book of Eleanor Roosevelt.* Illus. Robert Casilla. New York: Holiday.

Adoff, Arnold. (1973). *Black is brown is tan.* Illus. Emily A. McCully. New York: HarperCollins.

Adoff, Arnold. (1979). *Eats: Poems.* Illus. Susan Russo. New York: Lothrop.

Adoff, Arnold. (1982). *All the colors of the race.* Illus. John Steptoe. New York: Lothrop.

Adoff, Arnold. (1985). *Malcolm X.* New York: HarperCollins.

Adoff, Arnold. (1986). *Sports pages.* Illus. Steve Kuzma. New York: HarperCollins.

Adoff, Arnold. (1989). *Chocolate dreams.* Illus. Turi MacCombie. New York: Lothrop.

Adoff, Arnold. (1990). *Hard to be six.* New York: Lothrop.

Adoff, Arnold. (1991). *In for winter, out for spring.* Illus. Jerry Pinkney. San Diego: Harcourt.

Adoff, Arnold (ed.). (1974) *My black me: A beginning book of black poetry.* New York: Dutton.

Aesop. (1991). *Androcles and the lion.* Adapter & illus. Janet Stevens. New York: Holiday.

Afanasyev, Alexander Nikolayevich. (1990). Retold by Lenny Hort. *The fool and the fish.* Illus. Gennady Spirin. New York: Dial.

Agee, Jon. (1988). *The incredible painting of Felix Clousseau.* New York: Farrar, Straus & Giroux.

Ahlberg, Allan. (1989). *Ten in a bed.* Illus. Andre Amstutz. New York: Viking.

Ahlberg, Janet, & Ahlberg, Allan. (1979). *Each peach pear plum.* New York: Viking.

Ahlberg, Janet, & Ahlberg, Allan. (1981). *Peek-a-boo.* New York: Viking.

Aker, Suzanne. (1990). *What comes in 2's, 3's, and 4's?* New York: Simon & Schuster.

Alcock, Vivien. (1987). *Ghostly companions.* New York: Delacorte.

Alcock, Vivien. (1988). *Monster garden.* New York: Delacorte.

Alcott, Louisa May. (1868; 1968 reissue). *Little women.* Illus. Jessie Willcox Smith. Boston: Little, Brown.

Alcott, Louisa May. (1869; 1971 reissue). *An old fashioned girl.* New York: Grosset.

Alcott, Louisa May. (1886; 1971 reissue). *Jo's boys.* New York: Grosset.

Alcott, Louisa May. (1870; 1977 reissue). *Eight cousins.* New York: Webster, Golden Press.

Alderson, Brian. (1978; o.p.). *Popular folk tales: The brothers Grimm.* Illus. Michael Foreman. New York: Doubleday.

Alderson, Sue Ann. (1988). *Ida and the wool smugglers.* Illus. Ann Blades. New York: McElderry.

Aldrich, Bess. (1928; o.p.). *A lantern in her hand.* New York: D. Appleton.

Aldrich, Thomas Bailey. (1870; 1976 reissue). *The story of a bad boy.* New York: Garland.

Alexander, Ellen. (1989). *Llama and the great flood.* New York: HarperCollins.

Alexander, Lloyd. (1964). *The book of three.* New York: Holt.

Alexander, Lloyd. (1965). *The black cauldron.* New York: Holt.

Alexander, Lloyd. (1966). *The castle of Llyr.* New York: Holt.

Alexander, Lloyd. (1967). *Taran wanderer.* New York: Holt.

Alexander, Lloyd. (1968). *The high king.* New York: Holt.

Alexander, Lloyd. (1988). *The Drackenburg adventure.* New York: Dutton.

Alger, Horatio. (1868). *Ragged Dick.* Boston: Loring.

Aliki. (1968). *Hush little baby: A folk lullaby.* New York: Simon & Schuster.

Aliki. (1979). *The two of them.* New York: Greenwillow.

Aliki. (1981). *Digging up dinosaurs.* New York: HarperCollins.

Aliki. (1982). *We are best friends.* New York: Greenwillow.

Aliki. (1983). *A medieval feast.* New York: HarperCollins.

Aliki. (1985). *Dinosaurs are different.* New York: HarperCollins.

Aliki. (1985). *My visit to the dinosaurs* (rev. ed.). New York: HarperCollins.

Aliki. (1986). *Go tell Aunt Rhody.* New York: Macmillan.

Aliki. (1986). *How a book is made.* New York: HarperCollins.

Aliki. (1989). *The king's day.* New York: HarperCollins.

Aliki. (1989). *Many lives of Benjamin Franklin.* New York: Simon & Schuster.

Aliki. (1972, 1990). *Fossils tell of long ago.* New York: HarperCollins.

Allard, Harry. (1977). *Miss Nelson is missing.* Illus. James Marshall. Boston: Houghton.

Allard, Harry. (1982). *Miss Nelson is back.* Illus. James Marshall. Boston: Houghton.

Allard, Harry. (1985). *Miss Nelson has a field day.* Illus. James Marshall. Boston: Houghton.

Allen, Thomas B. (1989). *On Grandaddy's farm.* New York: Knopf.

Allingham, William. (1870). *In fairyland.* Illus. Richard Doyle. London: Longmans, Green.

American boy magazine. 1929–1941.

Ammer, Christine. (1989). *It's raining cats and dogs . . . and other beastly expressions.* New York: Paragon House.

Ancona, George. (1982). *Bananas: From Manolo to Margie.* Boston: Houghton.

Ancona, George. (1987). *Turtle watch.* New York: Macmillan.

Ancona, George. (1990). *Riverkeeper.* New York: Macmillan.

Andersen, Hans Christian. (1979). *The princess and the pea.* Illus. Paul Galdone. New York: Clarion.

Andersen, Hans Christian. (1979). *The steadfast tin soldier.* Illus. Paul Galdone. New York: Clarion.

Andersen, Hans Christian. (1979). *Thumbelina.* Illus. Susan Jeffers. New York: Dial.

Andersen, Hans Christian. (1981). *The ugly duckling.* Retold by Marianna Mayer. New York: Macmillan.

Andersen, Hans Christian. (1982). *The emperor's*

new clothes. Reteller & Illus. Anne Rockwell. New York: HarperCollins.

Andersen, Hans Christian. (1982). *The snow queen.* Illus. Susan Jeffers. New York: Dial.

Andersen, Hans Christian. (1984). *The little mermaid.* Illus. Chihiro Iwasaki. Saxonville, MA: Picture Book.

Anderson, Joan. (1984). *The first Thanksgiving feast.* Photos by George Ancona. New York: Clarion.

Anderson, Joan. (1986). *Pioneer children of Appalachia.* New York: Clarion.

Anderson, Joan. (1988). *From map to museum.* New York: Morrow.

Anderson, Joan. (1989). *Spanish pioneers of the Southwest.* New York: Dutton.

Anderson, Joan. (1990). *Pioneer settlers of New France.* Illus. George Ancona. New York: Dutton.

Anderson, Joy. (1986). *Juma and the magic Jinn.* Illus. Charles Mikolaycak. New York: Lothrop.

Anderson, Lena. (1989). *Stina.* New York: Greenwillow.

Anderson, Lena. (1991). *Stina's visit.* New York: Greenwillow.

Anderson, Lucia. (1987). *The smallest life around us.* Illus. Leigh Grant. New York: Crown.

Anderson, William. (1989). *The people and places in Laura Ingalls Wilder's life and books.* New York: HarperCollins.

Anderson, William, & Kelly, Leslie. (1989). *Little house country: A full-color photo guide to the homesites of Laura Ingalls Wilder.* New York: HarperCollins.

Angell, Judie. (1985). *One-way to Ansonia.* New York: Bradbury.

Angelou, Maya. (1987). *Now Sheba sings the song.* New York: Dutton.

Anholt, Catherine, & Anholt, Laurence. (1992). *All about you.* New York: Viking.

Anno, Mitsumasa. (1975). *Anno's alphabet.* New York: HarperCollins.

Anno, Mitsumasa. (1977). *Anno's counting book.* New York: HarperCollins.

Anno, Mitsumasa. (1978). *Anno's journey.* New York: Philomel.

Anno, Mitsumasa. (1982). *Anno's Britain.* New York: Philomel.

Anno, Mitsumasa. (1983). *Anno's mysterious multiplying jar.* New York: Philomel.

Anno, Mitsumasa. (1987). *Anno's math games.* New York: Philomel.

Anno, Mitsumasa. (1989). *Anno's Aesop: A book of fables by Aesop and Mr. Fox.* New York: Orchard.

Anno, Mitsumasa. (1989). *Anno's math games II.* New York: Philomel.

Anno, Mitsumasa. (1989). *Topsy turvies.* New York: Philomel.

Anno, Mitsumasa. (1990). *All in a day.* New York: Philomel.

Anno, Mitsumasa. (1991). *Anno's math games III.* New York: Philomel.

Anno, Mitsumasa, & Nozaki, Akihiro. (1985). *Anno's hat trick.* New York: Philomel.

Appel, Marty. (1992). *Joe DiMaggio.* New York: Chelsea.

Appleton, Victor. (1910; 1977 reissue). *Tom Swift* series. New York: Grosset.

Aragon, Jane Chelsea. (1989). *Winter harvest.* Illus. Leslie Baker. Boston: Little, Brown.

Archer, Jules. (1991). *Breaking barriers: The feminist revolution from Susan B. Anthony to Margaret Sanger to Betty Friedan.* New York: Viking.

Ardley, Neil. (1989). *Music.* New York: Knopf.

Arnold, Caroline. (1985). *Saving the peregrine falcon.* Minneapolis: Carolrhoda.

Arnold, Caroline. (1987). *Giraffe.* Photos by Richard Hewett. New York: Morrow.

Arnold, Caroline. (1987). *Kangaroo.* New York: Morrow.

Arnold, Caroline. (1987). *Koala.* Photos by Richard Hewett. New York: Morrow.

Arnold, Caroline. (1987). *Zebra.* Photos by Richard Hewett. New York: Morrow.

Arnold, Caroline. (1988). *Llama.* Photos by Richard Hewett. New York: Morrow.

Arnold, Caroline. (1988). *Penguin.* Photos by Richard Hewett. New York: Morrow.

Arnold, Caroline. (1989). *Cheetah.* Photos by Richard Hewett. New York: Morrow.

Arnold, Caroline. (1989). *Hippo.* Photos by Richard Hewett. New York: Morrow.

Arnold, Caroline. (1989). *The terrible Hodag.* Illus. Lambert Davis. San Diego: Harcourt.

Arnold, Caroline. (1990). *Dinosaurs down under: And other fossils from Australia.* Photos by Richard Hewett. Boston: Houghton.

Arnold, Caroline. (1990). *Orangutan.* New York: Morrow.

Arnold, Caroline. (1990). *Wild goat.* New York: Morrow.

Arnold, Caroline. (1991). *Snake.* New York: Morrow.

Arnosky, Jim. (1983). *Secrets of a wildlife watcher.* New York: Lothrop.

Arnosky, Jim. (1986). *Deer at the brook.* New York: Lothrop.

Arnosky, Jim. (1987). *Drawing from nature.* New York: Lothrop.

Arnosky, Jim. (1990). *Near the sea.* New York: Lothrop.

Arter, Jim. (1991). *Gruel and unusual punishment.* New York: Delacorte.

Aruego, Jose. (1988). *Look what I can do.* New York: Macmillan.

Asbjørnsen, Peter Christian, & Moe, Jorgen E. (1963; o.p.). *East o' the sun and west o' the moon.* New York: Macmillan.

Asbjørnsen, Peter Christian, & Moe, Jorgen E. (1972). *Three billy goats gruff.* Illus. Marcia Brown. San Diego: Harcourt.

Ashabranner, Brent. (1982). *Morning star, black sun: The northern Cheyenne Indians and America's energy crisis.* Photos by Paul Conklin. New York: Putnam.

Ashabranner, Brent. (1991.). *An ancient heritage: The Arab-American minority.* New York: HarperCollins.

Asher, Sandy. (1987). *Where do you get your ideas? Helping young writers.* Illus. Susan Hellard. New York: Walker.

Ashton, Christina. (1989). *Words can tell: A book about our language.* New York: Messner.

Asimov, Isaac. (1966). *Fantastic voyage: A novel.* Boston: Houghton.

Asimov, Isaac. (1983). *Norby the mixed-up robot.* New York: Walker.

Asimov, Isaac, Greenberg, Martin, & Waugh, Charles (eds.). (1984). *Time warp.* Milwaukee: Raintree.

Atkinson, Linda. (1985). *In kindling flame: The story of Hannah Senesh, 1921–1944.* New York: Lothrop.

Atwater, Richard. (1938). *Mr. Popper's penguins.* Illus. Richard & Florence Atwater. Boston: Little, Brown.

Atwood, Ann. (1971; o.p.). *Fly with the wind, flow with the water.* New York: Scribner's.

Atwood, Ann. (1973; o.p.). *My own rhythm: An approach to haiku.* New York: Scribner's.

Atwood, Ann. (1977; o.p.). *Haiku vision: In poetry and photographs.* New York: Scribner's.

Atwood, Ann. (1979). *Haiku: The mood of earth.* Illus. Ann Atwood. New York: Scribner's.

Avi. (1984). *The fighting ground.* New York: HarperCollins.

Avi. (1990). *The true confessions of Charlotte Doyle.* New York: Orchard.

Avi. (1991). *Nothing but the truth: A documentary novel.* New York: Orchard, Watts.

Avi. (1991). *Windcatcher.* New York: Macmillan.

Axelrod, Alan. (1991). *Songs of the wild west.* Arrangements by Dan Fox. New York: Simon & Schuster.

Aylesworth, Jim. (1985). *Shenandoah Noah.* New York: Holt.

Aylesworth, Jim. (1992). *The folks in the valley: A Pennsylvania Dutch ABC.* Illus. Stefano Vitale. New York: HarperCollins.

Aylesworth, Jim. (1992). *Old black fly.* Illus. Stephen Gammell. New York: Holt.

Babbitt, Natalie. (1975). *Tuck everlasting.* New York: Farrar, Straus & Giroux.

Bach, Alice, & Exum, J. Cheryl. (1989). *Moses's ark: Stories from the Bible.* Illus. Leo & Diane Dillon. New York: Delacorte.

Bach, Alice, & Exum, J. Cheryl. (1991). *Miriam's well: Stories about women in the Bible.* Illus. Leo & Diane Dillon. New York: Delacorte.

Baer, Edith. (1990). *This is the way we go to school.* New York: Scholastic.

Baer, Gene. (1989). *Thump, thump, rat-a-tat-tat.* Illus. Lois Ehlert. New York: HarperCollins.

Bagert, Brod. (1992). *Let me be . . . the boss.* Illus. G. L. Smith. Honesdale, PA: Boyds Mills.

Bagnold, Enid. (1985). *National velvet.* Illus. Ted Lewin. New York: Morrow.

Baillie, Allan. (1992). *Little brother.* New York: Viking.

Baker, Jeannie. (1987). *Where the forest meets the sea.* New York: Greenwillow.

Baker, Jeannie. (1991). *Window.* New York: Greenwillow.

Baker, Keith. (1989). *The magic fan.* San Diego: Harcourt.

Baker, Leslie. (1987). *The third story cat.* Boston: Little, Brown.

Baker, Leslie. (1992). *The antique store cat.* Boston: Little, Brown.

Baker, Olaf. (1989). *Where the buffaloes begin.* Illus. Stephen Gammell. New York: Viking.

Bang, Molly. (1976). *Wiley and the hairy man.* New York: Macmillan.

Bang, Molly. (1983). *Ten, nine, eight.* New York: Greenwillow.

Bangs, Edward. (1984). *Steven Kellogg's Yankee Doodle.* New York: Macmillan.

Banish, Roslyn (author/photographer). (1992). *A forever family.* New York: HarperCollins.

Banks, Lynne Reid. (1980). *Indian in the cupboard.* New York: Doubleday.

Barbauld, Mrs. Anna. (c. 1786). *Easy lessons for children.* London: Longmans.

Bare, Colleen Stanley. (1989) *Never kiss an alligator!* New York: Cobblehill, Dutton.

Barnard, Jacqueline. (1967; o.p.). *Journey toward freedom.* New York: Norton.

Baron, Virginia Olsen. (1974; o.p.). *Sunset in a spider web: Sijo poetry of ancient Korea.* New York: Holt.

Barrie, James M. (1988). *Peter Pan.* Illus. Jan Ormerod. New York: Viking.

Barth, Edna. (1979). *Balder and the mistletoe: A story for the winter holidays.* New York: Clarion.

Barth, Edna. (1979). *Cupid and Psyche: A love story.* New York: Clarion.

Barth, Edna. (1979). *I'm nobody. Who are you? The story of Emily Dickinson.* Boston: Houghton.

Barton, Byron. (1988). *I want to be an astronaut.* New York: HarperCollins.

Barton, Byron. (1990). *Bones, bones, dinosaur bones.* New York: HarperCollins.

Base, Graeme. (1987). *Animalia.* New York: Abrams.

Bash, Barbara. (1990). *Urban roosts: Where birds nest in the city*. Boston: Little, Brown.

Bassett, Lisa. (1987). *Very truly yours, Charles L. Dodgson, alias Lewis Carroll*. New York: Lothrop.

Bate, Lucy. (1988). *Little rabbit's loose tooth*. New York: Crown.

Bauer, Caroline Feller (ed). (1986). *Snowy day: Stories and poems*. Illus. Margot Tomes. New York: HarperCollins.

Bauer, Marion Dane. (1985). *Like mother, like daughter*. New York: Clarion.

Bauer, Marion Dane. (1986). *On my honor*. New York: Clarion.

Bauer, Marion Dane. (1991). *Face to face*. New York: Clarion.

Bauer, Marion Dane. (1992). *Ghost eye*. New York: Scholastic.

Baum, L. Frank. (1900; 1970 reissue). *The wizard of Oz*. Illus. W. W. Denslow. New York: Macmillan.

Baumann, Hans. (1969; o.p.). *In the land of Ur*. Trans. Stella Humphries. New York: Pantheon.

Bawden, Nina. (1978). *Rebel on a rock*. New York: HarperCollins.

Bawden, Nina. (1979). *Robbers*. New York: Lothrop.

Bawden, Nina. (1988). *Henry*. New York: Lothrop.

Bawden, Nina. (1989). *Outside child*. New York: Lothrop.

Bawden, Nina. (1991). *A handful of thieves*. New York: Clarion.

Bawden, Nina. (1991). *The witch's daughter*. New York: Clarion.

Bawden, Nina. (1992). *The house of secrets*. New York: Clarion.

Baylis-White, Mary. (1991). *Sheltering Rebecca*. New York: Dutton.

Baylor, Byrd. (1975, 1986). *The desert is theirs*. Illus. Peter Parnall. New York: Scribner's, Aladdin.

Baylor, Byrd. (1976). *Hawk, I'm your brother*. Illus. Peter Parnall. New York: Scribner's.

Baylor, Byrd. (1978). *The other way to listen*. Illus. Peter Parnall. New York: Scribner's.

Baylor, Byrd. (1978). *The way to start a day*. Illus. Peter Parnall. New York: Scribner's.

Baylor, Byrd. (1983). *The best town in the world*. Illus. Ronald Himler. New York: Scribner's.

Baylor, Byrd. (1986). *I'm in charge of celebrations*. Illus. Peter Parnall. New York: Scribner's.

Baylor, Byrd. (1976; o.p.). *And it is still that way: Legends told by Arizona Indian children*. New York: Scribner's.

Baynes, Pauline. (1988). *Noah and the ark*. New York: Holt.

Beardsley, John. (1991). *Pablo Picasso*. New York: Abrams.

Beatty, John, & Beatty, Patricia. (o.p.). *Master Rosalind*. New York: Morrow.

Beatty, Patricia. (1984). *Turn homeward, Hannalee*. New York: Morrow.

Beatty, Patricia. (1987). *Charlie Skedaddle*. New York: Morrow.

Beatty, Patricia. (1989). *Sarah and me and the lady from the sea*. New York: Morrow.

Beatty, Patricia. (1990). *Wait for me, watch for me, Eula Bea*. New York: Morrow.

Beatty, Patricia. (1991). *Jayhawker*. New York: Morrow.

Beatty, Patricia. (1992). *Who comes with cannons?* New York: Morrow.

Bechard, Margaret. (1990). *My sister, my science report*. New York: Viking.

Behn, Harry. (1964; o.p.). *Cricket songs*. San Diego: Harcourt.

Behn, Harry. (1971; o.p.). *More cricket songs*. San Diego: Harcourt.

Beirne, Barbara. (1990). *Pianist's debut: Preparing for the concert stage*. Minneapolis: Carolrhoda.

Bell, Claire. (1987). *Ratha's creature*. New York: Dell.

Bellairs, John. (1983). *The curse of the blue figurine*. New York: Dial.

Belpre, Pura. (1969; o.p.). *Santiago*. Illus. Symeon Shimin. New York: Warne.

Belpre, Pura. (1973; o.p.). *Once in Puerto Rico*. New York: Warne.

Belpre, Pura. (1978; o.p.). *The rainbow colored horse*. New York: Warne.

Bemelmans, Ludwig. (1939, 1962). *Madeline*. New York: Viking.

Benchley, Nathaniel. (1974). *Bright candles*. New York: HarperCollins.

Bennett, Jill. (1989). *Spooky poems*. Illus. Mary Rees. Boston: Little, Brown, Joy Street.

Berck, Judith. (1992). *No place to be: Voices of homeless children*. Foreword by Robert Coles. Boston: Houghton.

Berger, Melvin. (1976). *The story of folk music*. Chatham, New York: S.G. Phillips.

Berger, Melvin. (1989). *The science of music*. New York: HarperCollins.

Bergman, Tamar. (1988). *Boy from over there*. Boston: Houghton.

Bergman, Tamar. (1991). *Along the tracks*. Boston: Houghton.

Bernbaum, Israel. (1985). *My brother's keeper: The Holocaust through the eyes of an artist*. New York: Putnam.

Bernheim, M. (1989). *Father of the orphans: The story of Janusz Korczak*. New York: Dutton.

Bernos de Gasztold, Carmen. (1992). *Prayers from the ark: Selected poems*. Trans. Rumer Godden. Illus. Barry Moser. New York: Viking.

Bernotas, Bob. (1991). *Sitting Bull: Chief of the Sioux*. New York: Chelsea.

Berry, James. (1991). *When I dance*. Illus. Karen Barbour. San Diego: Harcourt.

Bial, Raymond (author/photographer). (1992). *County fair*. Boston: Houghton.

Bible. (1988). *The nativity*. Illus. Julie Vivas. San Diego: Harcourt.

Bider, Djemma. (1989). *A drop of honey*. Illus. Armen Kojoyian. New York: Simon & Schuster.

Bierhorst, John. (1970; o.p.). *The ring in the prairie: A Shawnee legend*. New York: Dial.

Bierhorst, John. (1983). *The sacred path: Spells, prayers, and power songs of the American Indians*. New York: Morrow.

Bierhorst, John. (1986). *The monkey's haircut and other stories told by the Maya*. Illus. Robert Andrew Parker. New York: Morrow.

Bierhorst, John. (1987). *Doctor Coyote*. Illus. Wendy Watson. New York: Macmillan.

Bierhorst, John. (1987). *The naked bear: Folktales of the Iroquois*. Illus. Dirk Zimmer. New York: Morrow.

Bierhorst, John. (1988). *The mythology of South America*. New York: Morrow.

Bierhorst, John. (1990). *Spirit child: A story of the nativity*. Illus. Barbara Cooney. New York: Morrow.

Bierhorst, John. (1992). *A cry from the earth: Music of the North American Indians*. Santa Fe: Ancient City Press.

Bierhorst, John (ed.). (1984). *The girl who married a ghost and other tales from the North American Indian*. New York: Four Winds.

Birch, David (1988). *The king's chessboard*. Illus. Devis Grebu. New York: Dial.

Birdseye, Tom. (1988). *Air mail to the moon*. Illus. Stephen Gammell. New York: Holiday.

Birdseye, Tom (adapter). (1990). *A song of stars*. Illus. Ju-Hong Chen. New York: Holiday.

Bisel, S. C. (1990). *The secrets of Vesuvius: Exploring the mysteries of an ancient buried city*. New York: Scholastic.

Bishop, Gerald. (1993). *Ranger Rick*. Washington, DC: National Wildlife Federation.

Bjork, Christina. (1987). *Linnea in Monet's garden*. Illus. Lena Anderson. Trans. Joan Sandin. New York: Farrar, Straus & Giroux.

Bjork, Christina. (1988). *Linnea's windowsill garden*. Illus. Lena Anderson. Trans. Joan Sandin. New York: Farrar, Straus & Giroux.

Bjork, Christina. (1989). *Linnea's almanac*. Illus. Lena Anderson. Trans. Joan Sandin. New York: Farrar, Straus & Giroux.

Black, Sheila. (1989). *Sitting Bull and the battle of the Little Big Horn*. New York: Silver Burdett.

Black, Wallace B., & Blashfield Jean. (1991). *America prepares for war*. New York: Macmillan.

Blackmore, Vivien. (1984). *Why corn is golden: Stories about plants*. Illus. Susana Martinez-Ostos. Boston: Little, Brown.

Blacknall, Carolyn. (1984). *Sally Ride: America's first woman in space*. New York: Macmillan.

Blackwood, Alan. (1987). *Beethoven*. New York: Watts.

Blackwood, Gary. (1991). *Beyond the door*. New York: Atheneum.

Blades, Ann. (1971). *Mary of mile 18*. Plattsburgh, New York: Tundra.

Blaine, Marge. (1975). *The terrible thing that happened at our house*. Illus. John Wallner. New York: Four Winds.

Blair, Gwenda. (1981). *Laura Ingalls Wilder*. New York: Putnam.

Blair, Walter. (1987). *Tall tale America: A legendary history of our humorous heroes*. Illus. Glen Rounds. Chicago: University of Chicago Press.

Blake, William. (1789; 1966 reissue). *Songs of innocence*. Illus. Ellen Raskin. New York: Doubleday.

Blake, William. (1794; 1927 reissue). *Songs of experience*. London: E. Beun.

Blegvad, Erik. (1979). *Self-Portrait: Erik Blegvad*. Reading, MA: Addison-Wesley.

Blizzard, Gladys S. (1992). *Come look with me: Animals in art*. Charlottesville, VA: Thomasson-Grant.

Blos, Joan. (1979). *A gathering of days: A New England girl's journal, 1830–32*. New York: Macmillan.

Blumberg, Rhoda. (1985). *Commodore Perry in the land of the shogun*. New York: Lothrop.

Blumberg, Rhoda. (1987). *The incredible journey of Lewis and Clark*. New York: Lothrop.

Blumberg, Rhoda. (1991). *The remarkable voyages of Captain Cook*. New York: Bradbury.

Blume, Judy. (1970). *Are you there God? It's me, Margaret*. New York: Bradbury.

Blume, Judy. (1971). *Then again, maybe I won't*. New York: Bradbury.

Blume, Judy. (1972). *Tales of a fourth grade nothing*. New York: Dutton.

Blume, Judy. (1973). *Deenie*. New York: Bradbury.

Blume, Judy. (1974). *Blubber*. New York: Bradbury.

Blume, Judy. (1980). *Superfudge*. New York: Dutton.

Blume, Judy. (1981). *The one in the middle is the green kangaroo*. New York: Bradbury.

Blume, Judy. (1984). *The pain and the great one*. New York: Bradbury.

Blume, Judy. (1987). *Just as long as we're together*. New York: Orchard.

Blume, Judy. (1990). *Fudge-a-mania*. New York: Dutton.

Bober, Natalie. (1984; o.p.). *Breaking tradition; The story of Louise Nevelson*. New York: Atheneum.

Bober, Natalie. (1986). *Let's pretend: Poems of flight and fancy*. Illus. Bill Bell. New York: Viking.

Bober, Natalie. (1991). *A restless spirit: The story of Robert Frost*. New York: Holt.

Bodecker, N. M. (1991). *Water pennies: And other poems*. Illus. Erik Blegvad. New York: McElderry.

Bojunga-Nunes, Lygia. (1989; o.p.). *The companions*. Trans. Ellen Watson. Illus. Larry Wilkes. New York: Farrar Straus & Giroux.

Bonsall, Crosby. (1963). *The case of the hungry stranger*. New York: HarperCollins.

Bonsall, Crosby. (1965). *The case of the cat's meow*. New York: HarperCollins.

Bosse, Malcolm. (1980). *Cave beyond time*. New York: HarperCollins.

Boston, Lucy. (1961). *A stranger at Green Knowe*. San Diego: Harcourt.

Botkin, B. A. (1944; o.p.). *Treasury of American folklore*. New York: Crown.

Bowen, Betsy. (1991; o.p.). *Antler, bear, canoe: A northwoods alphabet year*. Boston: Little, Brown.

Brady, Esther Wood. (1988). *Toliver's secret*. New York: Crown.

Branley, Franklyn M. (1984). *Is there life in outer space?* Illus. Don Madden. New York: HarperCollins.

Branley, Franklyn M. (1963, 1986). *Snow is falling*. Illus. Holly Keller. New York: HarperCollins.

Branley, Franklyn. (1991). *What happened to the dinosaurs?* Illus. Marc Simont. New York: HarperCollins.

Branson, Karen. (1981; o.p.). *Streets of gold*. New York: Putnam.

Breckler, Rosemary. (1992). *Hoang breaks the lucky teapot*. Illus. Adrian Frankel. Boston: Houghton.

Brenner, Barbara. (1978). *Wagon wheels*. New York: HarperCollins.

Brenner, Barbara. (1981). *Mystery of the plumed serpent*. New York: Knopf.

Brenner, Barbara. (1991). *If you were there in 1492*. New York: Bradbury.

Brett, Jan. (1985). *Annie and the wild animals*. Boston: Houghton.

Brett, Jan. (1987). *Goldilocks and the three bears*. New York: Putnam.

Brett, Jan. (1989). *Beauty and the beast*. New York: Clarion.

Brett, Jan. (1990). *The mitten: A Ukranian folktale*. New York: Putnam.

Briggs, Raymond. (1978). *The snowman*. New York: Random.

Briggs, Raymond. (1989). *Jim and the beanstalk*. New York: Putnam.

Brinckloe, Julie. (1985). *Fireflies*. New York: Macmillan.

Brink, Carol Ryrie. (1973). *Caddie Woodlawn*. New York: Macmillan.

Brittain, Bill. (1989). *My buddy, the king*. New York: HarperCollins.

Britten, Benjamin. (1990; o.p.). *Young person's guide to the orchestra*. New York: Lothrop.

Brooke, L. Leslie. (1903; 1986 reprint). *Johnny Crow's garden*. New York: Warne.

Brooke, L. Leslie. (1905; 1977 reprint). *The golden goose book*. New York: Warne.

Brooke, William J. (1990). *A telling of the tales: Five stories*. Illus. Richard Egielski. New York: HarperCollins.

Brooks, Bruce. (1984). *The moves make the man*. New York: HarperCollins.

Brooks, Bruce. (1986). *Midnight hour encores*. New York: HarperCollins.

Brooks, Bruce. (1989). *No kidding*. New York: HarperCollins.

Brooks, Bruce. (1990). *Everywhere*. New York: HarperCollins.

Brooks, Bruce. (1991). *Nature by design*. New York: Farrar, Straus & Giroux.

Brooks, Bruce. (1992). *What hearts*. New York: HarperCollins.

Brooks, Gwendolyn. (1967). *Bronzeville boys and girls*. New York: HarperCollins.

Brooks, Polly Schoyer. (1983). *Queen Eleanor: Independent spirit of the medieval world*. New York: HarperCollins.

Brown, Drollene P. (1985). *Sybil rides for independence*. Morton Grove, II: Whitman.

Brown, John R. (1982). *Shakespeare and his theatre*. New York: Lothrop.

Brown, Laurie Krasny, & Brown, Marc. *Dinosaurs alive and well! A guide to good health*. Boston: Little, Brown.

Brown, Laurie Krasny, & Brown, Marc. (1990). *Visiting the art museum*. New York: Dutton.

Brown, Laurie Krasny, & Brown, Marc. (1992). *Dinosaurs to the rescue!: A guide to protecting our planet*. Boston: Little, Brown.

Brown, Marc. (1987). *Arthur's baby*. Boston: Little, Brown.

Brown, Marc. (1987). *Play rhymes*. New York: Dutton.

Brown, Marcia. (1954). *Cinderella*. New York: Scribner's.

Brown, Marcia. (1957). *Three billy goats gruff*. San Diego: Harcourt.

Brown, Marcia. (1961). *Once a mouse*. New York: Scribner's.

Brown, Marcia. (1982, 1986). *Shadow*. New York: Macmillan, Aladdin.

Brown, Margaret Wise. (1947). *Goodnight moon*. Illus. Clement Hurd. New York: HarperCollins.

Brown, Margaret Wise. (1961, 1989). *Four fur feet*. Illus. Remy Charlip. Wichita, KS: Watermark.

Brown, Margaret Wise. (1990). *The important*

book. Illus. Leonard Weisgard. New York: HarperCollins.

Brown, Margaret Wise. (1992). *Red light, green light*. Illus. Leonard Weisgard. New York: Scholastic.

Brown, Mary Barrett. (1992). *Wings along the waterway*. New York: Orchard.

Brown, Tricia. (1986). *Hello, amigos*. Photos by Fran Ortiz. New York: Holt.

Brown, Tricia. (1991). *Lee Ann: The story of a Vietnamese-American girl*. Photos by Ted Thai. New York: Putnam.

Browne, Anthony. (1986). *Piggybook*. New York: Knopf.

Browne, Anthony. (1989). *I like books*. New York: Knopf.

Browne, Anthony. (1989). *Things I like*. New York: Knopf.

Browne, Anthony. (1990). *The tunnel*. New York: Knopf.

Browne, Anthony. (1991). *Changes*. New York: Knopf.

Browning, Robert. (1988). *The pied piper*. Illus. Terry Small. San Diego: Harcourt.

Bruce, Harry. (1992). *Maud: The life of L.M. Montgomery*. New York: Bantam.

Bruchac, Joseph, & London, Jonathan. (1992). *Thirteen moons on turtle's back: A Native American year of moons*. Illus. Thomas Locker. New York: Philomel.

Bruchac, Joseph, & Caduto, Michael. (1989). *Keepers of the earth: Native American stories and environmental activities for children*. Illus. John Kahionhes Fadden & Carol Wood. Golden, Fulcrum.

Brusca, Maria Christina. (1991). *On the pampas*. New York: Holt.

Bryan, Ashley. (1980). *Beat the story drum, pumpum*. New York: Atheneum.

Bryan, Ashley. (1985). *The cat's purr*. New York: Atheneum.

Bryan, Ashley. (1986). *Lion and the ostrich chicks and other African folk tales*. New York: Atheneum.

Bryan, Ashley. (1987). *The dancing granny*. New York: Atheneum.

Bryan, Ashley. (1989). *Turtle knows your name*. New York: Atheneum.

Bryan, Ashley (1991). *All night, all day: A child's first book of African-American spirituals*. New York: Atheneum.

Bryan, Ashley. (1992). *Sing to the sun*. New York: McElderry.

Buchanan, Ken. (1991). *This house is made of mud*. Illus. Libba Tracy. Northland, Arizona:

Bucknall, Caroline. (1987). *Three little pigs*. New York: Dial.

Buffet, Jimmy & Buffett, Savannah Jane. (1988). *The jolly mon*. Illus. Lambert Davis. San Diego: Harcourt.

Bulla, Clyde Robert. (1963; o.p.). *Viking adventure*. New York: HarperCollins.

Bulla, Clyde Robert. (1971). *Squanto: Friend of the Pilgrims*. New York: Scholastic.

Bulla, Clyde Robert. (1981). *A lion to guard us*. New York: HarperCollins.

Bulla, Clyde Robert. (1985). *A grain of wheat*. Boston: Godine.

Bulla, Clyde Robert. (1956; o.p.). *John Billington: Friend of Squanto*. New York: HarperCollins.

Bunting, Eve. (1986). *The Mother's Day mice*. Illus. Jan Brett. New York: Clarion.

Bunting, Eve. (1987). *Ghost's hour, spook's hour*. Illus. Donald Carrick. New York: Clarion.

Bunting, Eve. (1988). *Is anybody there?* New York: HarperCollins.

Bunting, Eve. (1990). *The wall*. Illus. Ronald Himler. New York: Houghton, Clarion.

Bunting, Eve. (1991). *Fly away home*. Illus. Ronald Himler. New York: Clarion.

Bunting, Eve. (1991). *Sharing Susan*. New York: HarperCollins.

Bunyan, John. (1678; 1979 reprint). *Pilgrim's progress*. New York: Dodd, Mead.

Burch, Robert. (1980). *Ida Early comes over the mountain*. New York: Viking.

Burch, Robert. (1983). *Christmas with Ida Early*. New York: Viking.

Burch, Robert. (1986). *King Kong and other poets*. New York: Viking.

Burkert, Nancy Ekholm. (1989). *Valentine & Orson*. New York: Farrar, Straus & Giroux.

Burleigh, Robert, & Wimmer, Mike. (1991). *Flight: The journey of Charles Lindbergh*. New York: Philomel.

Burnett, Frances Hodgson. (1886; 1976 reissue). *Little Lord Fauntleroy*. New York: Garland.

Burnett, Frances Hodgson. (1888; 1963 revised). *Sara Crewe*. Revised as *The little princess*. New York: HarperCollins.

Burnett, Frances Hodgson. (1911; 1988 reissue). *The secret garden*. Illus. Tasha Tudor. New York: Viking.

Burnford, Sheila. (1961). *The incredible journey*. Illus. Carl Burger. Boston: Little, Brown.

Burningham, John. (1971). *Mr. Gumpy's outing*. New York: Holt.

Burningham, John. (1977). *Come away from the water, Shirley*. New York: HarperCollins.

Burningham, John. (1978). *Time to get out of the bath, Shirley*. New York: HarperCollins.

Burningham, John. (1980). *The shopping basket*. New York: HarperCollins.

Burroughs, Margaret Taylor. (1969; o.p.). *Did you feed my cow? Rhymes and games from city streets and country lanes*. Illus. Joe DeVelasco. Chicago: Follett.

Burstein, Chaya. (1983). *The Jewish kid's catalogue*. Philadelphia: Jewish Publication Society.

Burton, Virginia Lee. (1939). *Mike Mulligan and his steam shovel*. Boston: Houghton.

Burton, Virginia Lee. (1942). *The little house*. Boston: Houghton.

Buss, Fran L. (1991). *Journey of the sparrows*. New York: Dutton.

Butterworth, Nick, & Inkpen, Mick. (1987). *Nice or nasty: A book of opposites*. Boston: Little, Brown.

Byars, Betsy. (1970). *Summer of the swans*. New York: Viking.

Byars, Betsy. (1975). *The midnight fox*. Illus. Ann Grifalconi. New York: Avon.

Byars, Betsy. (1977). *The pinballs*. New York: HarperCollins.

Byars, Betsy. (1981). *The Cybil war*. Illus. Gail Owens. New York: Viking.

Byars, Betsy. (1982). *A Blossom promise*. New York: Delacorte.

Byars, Betsy. (1983). *The glory girl*. New York: Viking.

Byars, Betsy. (1985). *Cracker Jackson*. New York: Viking, Kestrel.

Byars, Betsy. (1986). *Blossoms meet the Vulture Lady*. New York: Delacorte.

Byars, Betsy. (1986, 1989). *The Golly sisters go west*. New York: HarperCollins.

Byars, Betsy. (1986). *The not-just-anybody family*. Illus. Jacqueline Rogers. New York: Delacorte.

Byars, Betsy. (1987). *Blossoms and the Green Phantom*. New York: Delacorte.

Byars, Betsy. (1987). *The pinballs*. New York: HarperCollins.

Byars, Betsy. (1988). *The burning questions of Bingo Brown*. New York: Viking.

Byars, Betsy. (1989). *Bingo Brown and the language of love*. New York: Viking.

Byars, Betsy. (1990). *Bingo Brown, gypsy lover*. New York: Viking.

Byars, Betsy. (1991). *The moon and I*. Englewood Cliffs, New Jersey: Simon & Schuster, Messner.

Cajacob, Thomas, & Burton, Theresa. (1986). *Close to the wild: Siberian tigers in a zoo*. Minneapolis: Carolrhoda.

Caldecott, Randolph. (1878; 1978 reissue). *The diverting history of John Gilpin*. Available as *Randolph Caldecott's John Gilpin and other stories*. New York: Warne.

Caldecott, Randolph. (1888). *An elegy on the glory of her sex, Mrs. Mary Blaize*. London: Warne.

Cameron, Ann. (1981). *Stories Julian tells*. New York: Pantheon.

Cameron, Ann. (1986). *More stories Julian tells*. New York: Pantheon.

Cameron, Ann. (1987). *Julian's glorious summer*. New York: Pantheon.

Cameron, Ann. (1988). *The most beautiful place in the world*. Illus. Thomas B. Allen. New York: Knopf.

Cameron, Ann. (1990). *Julian, dream doctor*. New York: Pantheon.

Cameron, Eleanor. (1954; 1988). *Wonderful flight to the mushroom planet*. Boston: Little, Brown.

Cameron, Eleanor. (1971). *A room made of windows*. Boston: Little, Brown.

Cameron, Eleanor. (1977). *Julia and the hand of God*. New York: Dutton.

Cameron, Eleanor. (1982). *That Julia Redfern*. New York: Dutton.

Cameron, Eleanor. (1984). *Julia's magic*. New York: Dutton.

Cameron, Eleanor. (1988). *The private worlds of Julia Redfern*. New York: Dutton.

Campbell, Elizabeth. (1974). *Jamestown: The beginning*. Boston: Little, Brown.

Campbell, Patricia J. (1989). *Presenting Robert Cormier*. Boston: G. K. Hall.

Caraker, Mary. (1991). *Faces of Ceti*. Boston: Houghton.

Carkeet, David. (1991). *Quiver river*. New York: HarperCollins.

Carle, Eric. (1969). *The very hungry caterpillar*. New York: Philomel.

Carle, Eric. (1988). *A house for hermit crab*. Saxonville, MA: Picture Book.

Carle, Eric. (1989). *The very busy spider*. New York: Philomel.

Carle, Eric. (1991). *Dragons and other creatures that never were*. Compiled by Laura Whipple. New York: Philomel.

Carlson, Lori M., & Ventura, Cynthia L. (eds). (1990). *Where angels glide at dawn: New stories from Latin America*. Illus. Jose Ortega. New York: HarperCollins.

Carlstrom, Nancy White. (1986). *Jesse Bear, what will you wear?* Illus. Bruce Degen. New York: Macmillan.

Carlstrom, Nancy White. (1988). *Better not get wet, Jesse Bear*. Illus. Bruce Degen. New York: Macmillan.

Carpenter, Angelica S. (1990). *Frances Hodgson Burnett: Beyond the Secret Garden*. Minneapolis: Lerner.

Carrick, Carol. (1976). *The accident*. Illus. Donald Carrick. New York: Clarion.

Carrick, Carol. (1982). *Sleep out*. Illus. Donald Carrick. New York: Clarion.

Carrick, Carol. (1983). *Patrick's dinosaurs*. Illus. Donald Carrick. New York: Clarion.

Carrick, Carol. (1984). *Dark and full of secrets*. Illus. Donald Carrick. New York: Clarion.

Carrick, Carol. (1986). *What happened to Patrick's dinosaurs?* Illus. Donald Carrick. New York: Clarion.

Carrick, Carol. (1987). *Lost in the storm*. Illus. Donald Carrick. New York: Clarion.

Carrick, Carol. (1988). *Left behind*. Illus. Donald Carrick. New York: Clarion.

Carroll, Lewis. (1865; 1977 reissue). *Through the looking glass*. Illus. John Tenniel. New York: St. Martin's.

Carroll, Lewis. (1865; 1989 reissue). *Alice's adventures in wonderland*. Illus. John Tenniel. New York: Philomel.

Carter, Ann (compiler). (1991). *Birds, beasts, and fishes: A selection of animal poems*. Illus. Reg. Cartwright. New York: Macmillan.

Carter, Dorothy. (1987). *His majesty, queen Hatshepsut*. New York: HarperCollins.

Carter, Peter. (1990; o.p.). *Borderlands*. New York: Farrar.

Case, Dianne. (1991). *Love, David*. New York: Dutton.

Caseley, Judith. (1991). *Harry and Willy and Carrothead*. New York: Greenwillow.

Cassedy, Sylvia. (1983). *Behind the attic wall*. New York: HarperCollins.

Cassedy, Syliva. (1987). *M. E. and Morton*. New York: HarperCollins.

Cassedy, Sylvia. (1987). *Roomrimes*. Illus. Michele Chessare. New York: HarperCollins.

Cassedy, Sylvia. (1989). *Lucie Babbidge's house*. New York: HarperCollins.

Cassedy, Sylvia. (1990). *In your own words: A beginner's guide to writing* (rev. ed.). New York: HarperCollins.

Castaneda, Omar S. (1991). *Among the volcanoes*. New York: Dutton.

Cather, Willa. (1949 reprint). *My Àntonia*. New York: Random.

Catholic Youth's Magazine. 1857–1861.

Caudill, Rebecca. (1966). *Did you carry the flag today, Charley?* New York: Holt.

Caudill, Rebecca. (1988). *Tree of freedom*. New York: Viking, Puffin.

Cauley, Lorinda Bryan. (1984). *The town mouse and the country mouse*. New York: Putnam.

Cauley, Lorinda Bryan (reteller/illus.). (1988). *The pancake boy: An old Norwegian folk tale*. New York: Putnam.

Caulkins, Janet. (1989). *The picture life of Mikhail Gorbachev*. New York: Watts.

Cazet, Denys. (1987). *A fish in his pocket*. New York: Orchard.

Cech, John. (1991). *My grandmother's journey*. Illus. Sharon McGinley-Nally. New York: Macmillan, Bradbury.

Ceserani, Gian Paolo. (1982). *Marco Polo*. New York: Putnam.

Chaikin, Miriam. (1981). *Light another candle: The story and meaning of Hanukkah*. New York: Clarion.

Chaikin, Miriam. (1986). *Ask me another question: The story and meaning of Passover*. New York: Clarion.

Chaikin, Miriam. (1986). *Shake a palm branch: The story and meaning of Sukkot*. New York: Clarion.

Chaikin, Miriam. (1986). *Sound the shofar: The story and meaning of Rosh Hashanah*. New York: Clarion.

Chaikin, Miriam. (1986). *Make noise, make merry: The story and meaning of Purim*. New York: Clarion.

Chaikin, Miriam. (1987). *Nightmare in history: The Holocaust, 1933–1945*. New York: Clarion.

Chang, Ina. (1991). *A separate battle: Women and the Civil War*. New York: Dutton.

Charlip, Remy. (1985). *Thirteen*. New York: Four Winds, Macmillan.

Charlip, Remy. (1987). *Handtalk: An ABC of finger spelling & sign language*. With Mary Beth Miller. Illus. George Ancona. New York: Macmillan.

Chase, Richard. (1943). *Jack tales*. Boston: Houghton.

Chase, Richard. (1973). *Grandfather tales*. Boston: Houghton.

Chaucer, Geoffrey. (1988). *Canterbury tales*. Trans. Barbara Cohen. Illus. Trina Schart Hyman. New York: Lothrop

Cherry, Lynne. (1990). *The great Kapok tree: A tale of the Amazon rain forest*. San Diego: Harcourt.

Cherry, Lynne. (1992). *A river ran wild*. New York: Dutton.

Child, Lydia Marie. (1989). *Over the river and through the wood*. Illus. Iris Van Rynback. Boston: Little, Brown.

Children in the Theresienstadt Concentration Camp (World War II). (1964; 1993). *I never saw another butterfly*. New York: McGraw-Hill.

The Children's Magazine. 1911–1914.

Childress, Alice. (1973). *A hero ain't nuthin but a sandwich*. New York: Putnam.

Choi, Sook Nyul. (1991). *Year of impossible goodbyes*. Boston: Houghton.

Christelow, Eileen. (1990). *Five little monkeys jumping on the bed*. New York: Clarion.

Christopher, John. (1967). *The city of gold and lead*. New York: Macmillan.

Christopher, John. (1970). *The pool of fire*. New York: Macmillan.

Christopher, John. (1970). *The white mountains*. New York: Macmillan.

Christopher, John. (1978). *Empty world*. New York: Dutton.

Christopher, John. (1988). *When the Tripods came*. New York: Dutton.

Christopher, Matt. (1964). *Catcher with a glass arm*. Illus. Foster Caddell. Boston: Little, Brown.

Christopher, Matt. (1969). *Catch that pass!* Illus. Harvey Kidder. Boston: Little, Brown.

Christopher, Matt. (1979). *Dirt bike racer*. Illus. Barry Bomzer. Boston: Little, Brown.

Christopher, Matt. (1984). *Great quarterback switch*. Illus. Eric Jon Nones. Boston: Little, Brown.

Ciardi, John. (1985). *Doodle soup*. Illus. Merle Nacht. Boston: Houghton.

Cardi, John. (1989). *The hopeful trout and other limericks*. Illus. Susan Meddaugh. Boston: Houghton.

Ciardi, John. (1991). *The monster den*. Illus. Edward Gorey. Honesdale, PA: Boyds Mills.

Ciardi, John. (1991). *You know who*. Illus. Edward Gorey. Honesdale, PA: Boyds Mills.

Ciardi, John. (1993). *Someone could win a polar bear*. Illus. Edward Gorey. Honesdale, PA: Boyds Mills.

Cisneros, Sandra. (1988). *The house on Mango Street*. Houston: Arte Publico.

Clafin, Edward Beecher. (1987). *Sojourner Truth and the struggle for freedom*. New York: Barron.

Clapp, Patricia. (1987). *The witch's children*. New York: Puffin.

Clark, Ann Nolan. (1991). *In my mother's house*. Illus. Velino Herrera. New York: Viking.

Clark, Ann Nolan. (1978; o.p.). *To stand against the wind*. New York: Viking.

Clark, Margaret (reteller). (1990). *The best of Aesop's fables*. Illus. Charlotte Voake. Boston: Little, Brown.

Clark, Margaret Goff. (1990). *The vanishing manatee*. New York: Dutton.

Cleary, Beverly. (1950). *Henry Huggins*. New York: Morrow.

Cleary, Beverly. (1952). *Henry and Beezus*. New York: Morrow.

Cleary, Beverly. (1954). *Henry and the paper route*. New York: Morrow.

Cleary, Beverly. (1955). *Beezus and Ramona*. Illus. Louis Darling. New York: Morrow.

Cleary, Beverly. (1957). *Henry and Ribsy*. New York: Morrow.

Cleary, Beverly. (1964). *Ribsy*. New York: Morrow.

Cleary, Beverly. (1975). *Ramona the brave*. New York: Morrow.

Cleary, Beverly. (1977). *Ramona and her father*. New York: Morrow.

Cleary, Beverly. (1979). *Ramona and her mother*. New York: Morrow.

Cleary, Beverly. (1981). *Ramona Quimby, age 8*. New York: Morrow.

Cleary, Beverly. (1983). *Dear Mr. Henshaw*. Illus. Paul O. Zelinsky. New York: Morrow.

Cleary, Beverly. (1988). *A girl from Yamhill*. New York: Morrow.

Cleary, Beverly. (1990). *Muggie Maggie*. Illus. Kay Life. New York: Morrow.

Cleary, Beverly. (1991). *Strider*. New York: Morrow.

Cleaver, Elizabeth. (1985). *The enchanted caribou*. New York: Atheneum.

Cleaver, Vera. (1969). *Where the lilies bloom*. New York: HarperCollins.

Cleaver, Vera. (1977). *Trial valley*. New York: HarperCollins.

Cleaver, Vera. (1981). *Kissimmee kid*. New York: Lothrop.

Cleaver, Vera. (1988). *Belle Pruitt*. New York: HarperCollins.

Clement, Claude. (1989). *The voice of the wood*. Illus. Frederic Clement. New York: Dial.

Clement, Claude. (1990). *The painter and the wild swans*. Illus. Frederic Clement. New York: Dial.

Clement, Rod. (1991). *Counting on Frank*. Milwaukee: Gareth Stevens.

Clifford, Eth. (1971; o.p.). *The year of the three-legged deer*. Boston: Houghton.

Clifford, Eth. (1985). *The remembering box*. Boston: Houghton.

Clifton, Lucille. (1970). *Some of the days of Everett Anderson*. Illus. Evaline Ness. New York: Holt.

Clifton, Lucille. (1973). *The boy who didn't believe in spring*. Illus. Brinton Turkle. New York: Dutton.

Clifton, Lucille. (1978). *Everett Anderson's nine month long*. Illus. Ann Grifalconi. New York: Holt.

Clifton, Lucille. (1980). *My friend Jacob*. Illus. Thomas Di Grazia. New York: Dutton.

Clifton, Lucille. (1983). *Everett Anderson's goodbye*. Illus. Ann Grifalconi. New York: Holt.

Clifton, Lucille. (1991). *Everett Anderson's Christmas is coming*. Illus. Jan Gilchrist. New York: Holt.

Clifton, Lucille. (1992). *Three wishes*. New York: Doubleday.

Climo, Shirley. (1989). *The Egyptian Cinderella*. Illus. Ruth Heller. New York: HarperCollins.

Climo, Shirley. (1990). *City! New York*. Photos by George Ancona. New York: Macmillan.

Cobb, Vicki. (1989). *Writing it down*. Illus. Marylin Hafner. New York: HarperCollins.

Cobb, Vicki. (1990). *Why doesn't the sun burn out?* New York: Dutton.

Cobb, Vicki. (1979; o.p.). *Truth on trial: The story of Galileo Galilei*. New York: Coward, McCann & Geoghegan.

Cobblestone: The History Magazine for Young People. 20 Grove Street, Peterborough, NH 03458. 1980–present.

Codye, Corinn. (1990). *Luis W. Alvarez*. Milwaukee: Raintree.

Coerr, Eleanor. (1986). *The Josefina story quilt*. New York: HarperCollins.

Coerr, Eleanor. (1988). *Chang's paper pony*. New York: HarperCollins.

Coffin, Charles C. (1876). *Boys of '76*. New York: Harper Brothers.

Cohen, Barbara. (1980). *The donkey's story: A Bible story*. Illus. Susan Jeanne Cohen. New York: Lothrop.

Cohen, Barbara. (1982; o.p.). *Gooseberries to oranges*. Illus. Beverly Brodsky. New York: Lothrop.

Cohen, Barbara. (1983). *Molly's Pilgrim*. New York: Lothrop.

Cohen, Barbara. (1988). *Thank you, Jackie Robinson*. New York: Lothrop.

Cohen, Barbara. (1988). *Unicorns in the rain*. New York: Macmillan.

Cohen, Barbara. (1991). *213 Valentines*. New York: Holt.

Cohen, Daniel. (1990). *Ancient Greece*. Illus. James Seward. New York: Doubleday.

Cohen, Miriam. (1967). *Will I have a friend?* Illus. Lillian Hoban. New York: Macmillan.

Cohen, Miriam. (1988). *It's George!* Illus. Lillian Hoban. New York: Greenwillow.

Cohen, Miriam. (1989). *See you in second grade!* Illus. Lillian Hoban. New York: Greenwillow.

Cole, Brock. (1989). *Celine*. New York: Farrar, Straus & Giroux.

Cole, Joanna. (1986). *Magic school bus at the water works*. Illus. Bruce Degen. New York: Scholastic.

Cole, Joanna. (1987). *Evolution*. Illus. Aliki. New York: HarperCollins.

Cole, Joanna. (1989). *A gift from Saint Francis: The first creche*. Illus. Michele Lemieux. New York: Morrow.

Cole, Joanna. (1990). *Large as life animals*. Illus. Kenneth Lilly. New York: Knopf.

Cole, William. (1977). *Beastly boys and ghastly girls*. New York: Dell.

Cole, William. (1990). *Oh, how silly!* Illus. Tomi Ungerer. New York: Puffin.

Cole, William. (1990). *Oh, what nonsense!* Illus. Tomi Ungerer. New York: Puffin.

Cole, William (ed.). (1978). *An arkful of animals: Poems for the very young*. Illus. Lynn Munsinger. Boston: Houghton.

Cole, William (ed.). (1978). *Oh, such foolishness!* Illus. Tomie de Paola. New York: HarperCollins.

Cole, William (ed). (1981). *Poem stew*. Illus. Karen Weinhaus. New York: HarperCollins.

Cole, William (selector). (1988). *Oh, that's ridiculous!* Illus. Tomi Ungerer. New York: Puffin.

Coleridge, Samuel Taylor. (1992). *The rime of the ancient mariner*. Illus. Ed Young. New York: Atheneum.

Collier, James Lincoln, & Collier, Christopher. (1974). *My brother Sam is dead*. New York: Macmillan.

Collier, James Lincoln, & Collier, Christopher. (1977). *The bloody country*. New York: Macmillan.

Collier, James Lincoln, & Collier, Christopher. (1983). *War comes to Willy Freeman*. New York: Delacorte.

Collier, James Lincoln, & Collier, Christopher. (1992). *The clock*. New York: Doubleday.

Collins, David R. (1989). *Country artist: A story about Beatrix Potter*. Minneapolis: Carolrhoda.

Collins, David R. (1989). *To the point: A story about E. B. White*. Minneapolis: Carolrhoda.

Colman, Benjamin. (1714). *A devout contemplation on the meaning of divine providence, in the early death of pious and lovely children. Preached upon the sudden and lamented death of Mrs. Elizabeth Wainwright, who departed this life, April the 8th, 1714. Having just compleated the fourteenth year of her age*. Boston: John Allen.

Colman, Hila. (1988). *Rich & famous like my mom*. New York: Crown.

Colum, Padraic. (1983). *Golden Fleece and heroes who lived before Achilles*. New York: Macmillan.

Colum, Padraic. (1984). *Children of Odin: The book of northern myths*. New York: Macmillan.

Comenius, Johann Amos. (1659; 1970 reissue). *Orbis sensualium pictus*. Menston, England: Scolar.

Cone, Molly. (1992). *Come back, Salmon*. Illus. Sidnee Wheelwright. Boston: Houghton.

Conford, Ellen. (1983). *If this is love, I'll take spaghetti*. New York: Four Winds.

Conford, Ellen. (1989). *Jenny Archer, author*. Boston: Little, Brown.

Connolly, James E (collector). (1985). *Why the possum's tail is bare and other North American Indian nature tales*. Illus. Adrienne Adams. Owings Mills, MD: Stemmer.

Connolly, Peter. (1990). *Pompeii*. New York: Oxford University Press.

Conover Chris (reteller, illus.). (1986). *Froggie went a-courting*. New York: Farrar, Straus & Giroux.

Conover, Chris (reteller/illus.). (1989). *Mother Goose and the sly fox*. New York: Farrar, Straus & Giroux.

Conrad, Pam. (1986). *Prairie songs*. New York: HarperCollins.

Conrad, Pam. (1989). *My Daniel*. New York: HarperCollins.

Conrad, Pam. (1989). *The tub people*. Illus. Richard Egielski. New York: HarperCollins.

Conrad, Pam. (1990). *Stonewords*. New York: HarperCollins.

Conrad, Pam. (1991). *Pedro's journal: A voyage with Christopher Columbus, August 3, 1492–February 14, 1493*. Illus. Peter Koeppen. Honesdale, PA: Boyds Mills.

Conrad, Pam. (1991). *Prairie Visions: The life and times of Solomon Butcher*. New York: HarperCollins.

Coolidge, Susan. (1872; 1977 reprint). *What Katy did*. New York: Dent.

Cooney, Barbara (adapter and illus.). (1958). *Chanticleer and the fox*. New York: HarperCollins.

Cooney, Barbara. (1982). *Miss Rumphius*. New York: Viking.

Cooney, Barbara. (1988). *Island boy*. New York: Viking, Kestrel.

Cooney, Barbara. (1990). *Hattie and the wild waves*. New York: Viking, Penguin.

Cooper, Susan. (1966). *Over sea, under stone*. San Diego: Harcourt.

Cooper, Susan. (1973). *The dark is rising*. Illus. Alan E. Cober. New York: Atheneum.

Cooper, Susan. (1973). *Greenwitch*. New York: McElderry.

Cooper, Susan. (1974). *The grey king*. New York: McElderry.

Cooper, Susan. (1977). *Silver on the tree*. New York: McElderry.

Cooper, Susan. (1986). *The selkie girl*. New York: McElderry.

Cooper, Susan (reteller). (1991). *Tam Lin*. Illus. Warwick Hutton. New York: McElderry.

Corbett, Scott. (1981). *Deadly hoax*. New York: Dutton.

Corcoran, Barbara. (1986). *A horse named sky*. New York: Macmillan.

Corcoran, Barbara. (1989). *The potato kid*. New York: Atheneum.

Corcoran, Barbara. (1991). *Stay tuned*. New York: Atheneum.

Cormier, Robert. (1986). *The chocolate war*. New York: Dell.

Cormier, Robert. (1991). *I have words to spend: Reflections of a small town editor*. New York: Doubleday.

Courlander, Harold, & Herzog, George. (1988). *The cow-tail switch and other West African stories*. New York: Holt.

Cousins, Margaret. (1965, 1981). *The story of Thomas Alva Edison*. New York: Random.

Coville, Bruce. (1991). *Jeremy Thatcher, dragon hatcher*. San Diego: Harcourt.

Covington, Dennis. (1991). *Lizard*. New York: Delacorte.

Cowcher, Helen. (1990). *Antarctica*. New York: Farrar, Straus & Giroux.

Cowen, Ida, & Gunther, Irene. (1984). *A spy for freedom: The story of Sarah Aaronsohn*. New York: Dutton.

Cox, Clinton. (1991). *The undying glory*. New York: Scholastic.

Craig, Helen. (1993). *I see the moon, and the moon sees me*. New York: HarperCollins.

Craig, M. Jean. (1986). *The three wishes*. New York: Scholastic.

Crane, Walter. (1865). *Dame Trot and her comical cat*. London: Warne.

Crane, Walter. (1865). *The house that Jack built*. London: Warne.

Crane, Walter. (1866). *The history of Cock Robin and Jenny Wren*. London: Warne.

Crane, Walter. (1867). *Sing a song of sixpence*. London: Warne.

Cresswell, Helen. (1984). *Bagthorpes abroad*. New York: Macmillan.

Cresswell, Helen. (1985). *Bagthorpes haunted*. New York: Macmillan.

Cresswell, Helen. (1987). *Absolute zero*. New York: Penguin.

Cresswell, Helen. (1989). *Bagthorpes liberated: Being the seventh part of the Bagthorpe saga*. New York: Macmillan.

Crews, Donald. (1980). *Truck*. New York: Greenwillow.

Crews, Donald. (1982). *Carousel*. New York: Greenwillow.

Crews, Donald. (1986). *Flying*. New York: Greenwillow.

Crews, Donald (1992). *Bigmama's*. New York: Greenwillow.

Crews, Donald (1992). *Shortcut*. New York: Greenwillow.

Cricket Magazine. 1973–present. P.O. Box 2670, Boulder, CO 80321.

Cristini, Ermano & Puricelli, Luigi. (1985). *In my garden*. Saxonville, MA: Picture Book.

Cristini, Ermano, & Puricelli, Luigi. (1985). *In the woods*. Saxonville, MA: Picture Book.

Cristini, Ermano, & Puricelli, Luigi. (1985). *In the pond*. Saxonville, MA: Picture Book.

Croll, Carolyn (adapter/illus). (1991). *The three brothers*. New York: Putnam.

Cross, Gillian. (1989). *A map of nowhere*. New York: Holiday.

Cross, Gillian. (1991). *Wolf*. New York: Holiday.

Crossley-Holland, Kevin. (1985). *Axe age, wolf age: A selection for children from the Norse myths*. North Pomfret, VT: Trafalgar.

Crossley-Holland, Kevin. (1988). *Beowulf*. Illus. Charles Keeping. New York: Oxford University Press.

Cruikshank, George. (1853–1854). *George Cruikshank's fairy library*. 4 volumes. London: David Bogue.

Cruz, Martel. (1987; o.p.). *Yagua days*. Illus. Jerry Pinkney. New York: Dial.

Cruz-Martinez, Alejandro. (1991). *The woman who outshone the sun/La mujer que brillaba aun más que el sol*. Adapted by Rosalma Zubizarreta, Harriet Rohmer, & David Shecter. San Francisco: Children's Book Press.

Cummings, Pat (ed.). (1992). *Talking with artists*. New York: Bradbury.

Cwiklik, Robert. (1989). *Sequoyah and the Cherokee alphabet*. Englewood Cliffs, NJ: Silver Burdett.

Czernicki, Stefan, & Rhodes, Timothy. (1992). *The sleeping bread*. New York: Walt Disney.

Dahl, Roald. (1961). *James and the giant peach*. Illus. Nancy Ekholm Burkert. New York: Knopf.

Dahl, Roald. (1964). *Charlie and the chocolate

factory. Illus. Joseph Schindelman. New York: Knopf.

Dahl, Roald. (1984). *Boy: Tales of childhood*. New York: Farrar, Straus & Giroux.

Dahl, Roald. (1990). *Esio Trot*. Illus. Quentin Blake. New York: Viking.

Dakos, Kalli. (1990). *If you're not here, please raise your hand: Poems about school*. Illus. G. Brian Karas. New York: Four Winds.

Dale, Mitzi. (1991). *Round the bend*. New York: Doubleday.

Dalgliesh, Alice. (1950). *The Thanksgiving story*. New York: Macmillan.

Dalgliesh, Alice. (1954, 1987). *The courage of Sarah Noble*. New York: Macmillan.

Daly, John. (1989). *Presenting S. E. Hinton*. New York: Dell.

Daly, Niki. (1986). *Not so fast Songololo*. New York: Macmillan.

Darby, Jean. (1989). *Dwight D. Eisenhower: A man called Ike*. Minneapolis: Lerner.

Darling, Kathy. (1991). *Manatee: On location*. Photos by Tara Darling. New York: Lothrop.

Davis, Jenny. (1991). *Checking on the moon*. New York: Orchard.

Davis, Ossie. (1992). *Just like Martin*. New York: Simon & Schuster.

Day, Thomas. (1783; 1977 reprint). *The history of Sandford and Merton*. New York: Garland.

Day, Thomas. (1788). *The history of little Jack*. Boston: Lee & Shepard.

De Angeli, Marguerite. (1954). *Book of nursery & Mother Goose rhymes*. Illus. Marguerite De Angeli. New York: Doubleday.

De Angeli, Marguerite. (1989). *The door in the wall*. New York: Doubleday.

De Angeli, Marguerite. (1946). *Bright April*. New York: Doubleday.

D'Aulaire, Ingri. (1972; o.p.). *East o' the sun and west o' the moon*. New York: Doubleday.

D'Aulaire, Ingri. (1986). *Norse gods and giants*. New York: Doubleday.

d'Aulaire, Ingri, & d'Aulaire, Edgar Parin. (1936). *George Washington*. New York: Doubleday.

d'Aulaire, Ingri, & d'Aulaire, Edgar Parin. (1957). *Abraham Lincoln*. New York: Doubleday.

d'Aulaire, Ingri, & d'Aulaire, Edgar Parin. (1985). *Pochahontas*. New York: Doubleday.

d'Aulaire, Ingri, & d'Aulaire, Edgar Parin. (1987). *Columbus*. New York: Doubleday.

d'Aulaire, Ingri, & d'Aulaire, Edgar Parin. (1980). *Ingri and Edgar Parin d'Aulaire's book of Greek myths*. New York: Zephyr, Doubleday.

Davidson, Margaret. (1986). *I have a dream: The story of Martin Luther King*. New York: Scholastic.

Davis, Daniel S. (1982). *Behind barbed wire: The imprisonment of Japanese Americans during World War II*. New York: Dutton.

Dayrell, Elphinstone. (1990). *Why the sun and the moon live in the sky: An African folktale*. Boston: Houghton.

Dean, Anabel. (1976). *Strange partners: The story of symbiosis*. Minneapolis: Lerner.

De Armond, Dale (adapter). (1988). *The seal oil lamp*. Boston: Little, Brown.

De Brunhoff, Jean. (1967). *Story of Babar, the little elephant*. New York: Random.

DeClements, Barthe. (1989). *Five finger discount*. New York: Delacorte.

DeClements, Barthe. (1990). *Monkey see. Monkey do*. New York: Delacorte.

DeClements, Barthe. (1991). *Breaking out*. New York: Delacorte.

Dee, Ruby. (1988). *Two ways to count to ten: A Liberian folktale*. New York: Holt.

Defoe, Daniel. (1719; 1920 reprint). *Robinson Crusoe*. Illus. N. C. Wyeth. New York: Scribner's.

Degens, T. (1990). *On the third ward*. New York: HarperCollins.

Degens, T. (1979, 1991). *Transport 41-R*. New York: Viking, Puffin.

De Gerez, Toni. (1986). *Louhi, witch of North Farm*. Illus. Barbara Cooney. New York: Viking, Kestrel.

Delacre, Lulu (selector, illus). (1989). *Arroz con leche: Popular songs and rhymes from Latin America*. English lyrics by Elena Paz. Musical arrangements by Ana-Maria Rosada. New York: Scholastic.

de la Mare, Walter. (1947). *Rhymes and verses: Collected poems for children*. Illus. Ellinore Blaisdell. New York: Henry Holt.

de la Mare, Walter. (1989). *Peacock pie*. Illus. Louise Brierly. New York: Henry Holt.

Demarest, Chris. (1992). *My little red car*. Honesdale, PA: Boyds Mills.

Demi. (1990). *The empty pot*. New York: Henry Holt.

Demi. (1990). *The magic boat*. New York: Henry Holt.

Demi. (1991). *Chingis Khan*. New York: Holt.

Demi. (1992). *In the eyes of the cat: Japanese poetry for all seasons*. Trans. Tze-si Huang. New York: Holt.

Denzel, Justin. (1988). *The boy of the painted cave*. New York: Philomel.

de Paola, Tomie (1973, 1987). *Nana upstairs & Nana downstairs*. New York: Putnam.

de Paola, Tomie. (1974). *Watch out for the chicken feet in your soup*. Englewood Cliffs, NJ: Prentice Hall.

de Paola, Tomie. (1975). *Strega Nona*. New York: Simon & Schuster.

de Paola, Tomie. (1977; 1984). *The quicksand book*. New York: Holiday.

de Paola, Tomie. (1978). *Pancakes for breakfast*. San Diego: Harcourt.

de Paola, Tomie. (1978). *The popcorn book*. New York: Holiday.

de Paola, Tomie. (1979). *Big Anthony and the magic ring*. San Diego: Harcourt.

de Paola, Tomie. (1980). *The lady of Guadalupe*. New York: Holiday.

de Paola, Tomie. (1981). *Now one foot, now the other*. New York: Putnam,

de Paola, Tomie. (1983). *The legend of the bluebonnet: A tale of old Texas*. New York: Putnam.

de Paola, Tomie. (1985). *Tomie de Paola's Mother Goose*. New York: Putnam.

de Paola, Tomie. (1986). *Tomie de Paola's favorite nursery tales*. New York: Putnam.

de Paola, Tomie. (1987). *Tomie de Paola's book of Christmas carols*. New York: Putnam

de Paola, Tomie. (1988). *Tomie de Paola's book of poems*. New York: Putnam.

de Paola, Tomie. (1989). *The art lesson*. New York: Putnam.

de Paola, Tomie. (1989). *Tony's bread*. New York: Putnam.

de Paola, Tomie. (1990). *Francis: The poor man of Assisi*. New York: Holiday.

de Paola, Tomie. (1992). *Bonjour, Mr. Satie*. New York: Putnam.

de Paola, Tomie (reteller). (1988). *The legend of the Indian paintbrush*. New York: Putnam.

de Regniers, Beatrice Schenk. (1964). *May I bring a friend?* Illus. Beni Montressor. New York: Atheneum.

de Regniers, Beatrice Schenk. (1985). *So many cats!* Illus. Ellen Weiss. New York: Clarion.

de Regniers, Beatrice Schenk. (1988). *The way I feel . . . sometimes*. Illus. Susan Meddaugh. New York: Clarion.

de Regniers, Beatrice Schenk. (1990). *Red Riding Hood*. Illus. Edward Gorey. New York: Aladdin, Macmillan.

de Regniers, Beatrice Schenk. (1983; o.p.). *Keep a poem in your pocket*. In J. Prelutsky (ed.), *The Random House Book of Poetry*. New York: Random House.

de Regniers, Beatrice Schenk (compiler). (1988). *Sing a song of popcorn: Every child's book of poems*. New York: Scholastic.

de Sauza, James (1989). *Brother Anansi and the cattle ranch*. San Francisco: Children's Book Press.

de Trevino, Elizabeth Borten. (1974; o.p.). *Juarez, man of law*. New York: Farrar, Straus & Giroux.

de Trevino, Elizabeth Borten. (1987). *I, Juan de Pareja*. New York: Farrar, Straus & Giroux.

de Trevino, Elizabeth Borten. (1989). *El Guero*. New York: Farrar, Straus & Giroux.

Dewey, Ariane. (1983). *Pecos Bill*. New York: Greenwillow.

Dewey, Ariane. (1987). *Gib Morgan, oilman*. New York: Greenwillow.

Dewey, Jennifer Owings. (1991). *Animal architecture*. New York: Orchard.

Dewey, Jennifer Owings. (1991). *Night and day in the desert*. Boston: Little, Brown.

Diagram Group. (1980). *Comparisons*. New York: St. Martin's Press.

Dillon, Eilis. (1986). *The seekers*. New York: Scribner's.

Dionetti, Michelle. (1991). *Coal mine peaches*. Illus. Anita Riggio. New York: Orchard.

DiSalvo-Ryan, DyAnne. (1991). *Uncle Willie and the soup kitchen*. New York: Morrow.

Dixon, Ann. (1992). *How raven brought light to people*. Illus. James Watts. New York: McElderry.

Dixon, Franklin W. *Hardy boys* series. New York: Grosset.

Dodge, Mary Mapes. (1865; 1975 reprint). *Hans Brinker; Or, the silver skates*. Illus. Hilda Van Stockum. Philadelphia: Collins.

Doherty, Berlie. (1990). *White peak farm*. New York: Orchard, Watts.

Dolphin, Laurie. (1991). *Georgia to Georgia: Making friends in the USSR*. New York: Tambourine.

Domanska, Janina. (1971). *If all the seas were one sea*. New York: Macmillan.

Dooley, Norah. (1991). *Everybody cooks rice*. Minneapolis: Carolrhoda.

Dorris, Michael. (1992). *Morning girl*. New York: Hyperion.

Dorros, Arthur. (1991). *Abuela*. Illus. Elisa Kleven. New York: Dutton.

Dorros, Arthur. (1991). Animal tracks. New York: Scholastic.

Dorros, Arthur. (1991). *Follow the water from brook to ocean*. New York: HarperCollins.

Dorros, Arthur. (1991). *Tonight is carnaval*. New York: Dutton.

Dorros, Arthur. (1992). *This is my house*. New York: Scholastic.

Dragonwagon, Crescent. (1990). *Home place*. Illus. Jerry Pinkney. New York: Macmillan.

Drieman, J. E. (1990). *An unbreakable spirit: A biography of Winston Churchill*. New York: Macmillan.

Drucker, Malka. (1984; o.p.). *Celebrating life: Jewish rites of passage*. New York: Holiday.

Duder, Tessa. (1986). *Jellybean*. New York: Viking, Kestrel.

Duder, Tessa. (1989). *In lane three, Alex Archer*. Boston: Houghton.

Dugan, Barbara. (1992). *Loop the loop*. Illus. James Stevenson. New York: Greenwillow.

Dumbleton, Mike. (1991). *Dial-a-croc*. Illus. Ann James. New York: Orchard.

Duncan, Lois. (1974). *Down a dark hall*. Boston: Little, Brown.

Duncan, Lois. (1981). *Stranger with my face*. Boston: Little, Brown.

Duncan, Lois. (1984). *Third eye*. Boston: Little, Brown.

Dunning, Stephen (compiler). (1966). *Reflections on a gift of watermelon pickle & other modern verse*. New York: Lothrop.

Dunrea, Olivier. (1986). *Skara Brae: The story of a prehistoric village*. New York: Holiday.

Durell, Ann (compiler). (1989). *The Diane Goode book of American folk tales and songs*. Illus. Diane Goode. New York: Dutton.

Dyer, T. A. (1990). *A way of his own*. Boston: Houghton.

Dygard, Thomas J. (1982). *Quarterback walk-on*. New York: Morrow.

Dygard, Thomas J. (1989). *Forward pass*. New York: Morrow.

Eastman, P. D. (1986). *Are you my mother?* New York: Random.

Eckert, Allan. (1971). *Incident at Hawk's Hill*. Illus. John Schoenherr. Boston: Little, Brown.

Eco, Umberto. (1989). *The bomb and the general*. Illus. Eugenio Carmi. Trans. William Weaver. San Diego: Harcourt.

Eco, Umberto. (1989). *The three astronauts*. Illus. Eugenio Carmi. Trans. William Weaver. San Diego: Harcourt.

Edens, Cooper (selector). (1988). *The glorious Mother Goose*. Illus. with reproductions. New York: Atheneum.

Edgeworth, Maria. (1796). *The parent's assistant*. New York: Macmillan.

Edgeworth, Maria. (1801). *Moral tales*. New York: W.B. Gilley.

Edgeworth, Maria. (1801). *Early lessons*. London: Routledge.

Edmonds, Walter. (1937; o.p.). *Drums along the Mohawk*. Boston: Little, Brown.

Edwards, Michelle. (1990). *Dora's book*. Minneapolis: Carolrhoda.

Edwards, Michelle. (1991). *Chicken man*. New York: Lothrop.

Ehlert, Lois. (1989). *Color zoo*. New York: HarperCollins.

Ehlert, Lois. (1989). *Eating the alphabet*. San Diego: Harcourt.

Ehlert, Lois. (1990). *Color farm*. New York: HarperCollins.

Ehlert, Lois. (1990). *Feathers for lunch*. San Diego: Harcourt.

Ehlert, Lois. (1990). *Fish eyes: A book you can count on*. San Diego: Harcourt.

Ehlert, Lois. (1992). *Circus*. New York: HarperCollins.

Ekoomiak, Normee. (1988). *Arctic memories*. New York: Henry Holt.

The Electric Company magazine. 1974–present.

Eliot, George. (1907; o.p.). *Romola*. New York: Dutton.

Elkington, John; Hailes, Julia; Hill, Douglas & Makower, Joel. (1990). *Going green: A kid's handbook to saving the planet*. New York: Viking.

Elledge, Scott (ed.). (1990). *Wider than the sky: Poems to grow up with*. New York: HarperCollins.

Emberley, Barbara. (1967). *Drummer Hoff*. Illus. Ed Emberley. Englewood Cliffs, NJ: Prentice Hall.

Emberley, Rebecca. (1990). *My house: A book in two languages/ Mi casa: Un libro en dos lenguas*. Boston: Little, Brown.

Emberley, Rebecca. (1990). *Taking a walk: A book in two languages/ Caminando: Un libro en dos lenguas*. Boston: Little, Brown.

The Encourager magazine. 1866–1946.

Engdahl, Sylvia. (1970). *Enchantress from the stars*. New York: Atheneum.

Engdahl, Sylvia. (1974). *Beyond the tomorrow mountains*. New York: Antheneum.

Enright, Elizabeth. (1941; 1987 reissue). *Saturdays*. New York: Dell.

Enright, Elizabeth. (1987). *Four story mistake*. New York: Dell.

Enright, Elizabeth. (1987). *Spiderweb for two*. New York: Dell.

Esbensen, Barbara. (1988). *The star maiden: An Ojibway tale*. Illus. Helen K. Davie. Boston: Little, Brown.

Esbensen, Barbara Juster. (1986). *Words with wrinkled knees: Animal poems*. Illus. John Stadler. New York: HarperCollins.

Esbensen, Barbara Juster (reteller). (1989). *Ladder to the sky: How the gift of healing came to the Ojibway nation*. Boston: Little, Brown.

Esbensen, Barbara Juster. (1992). *Who shrank my grandmother's house?* Illus. Eric Beddows. New York: HarperCollins.

Esbensen, Barbara Juster. (1990). *Great northern diver: The loon*. Boston: Little, Brown.

Espeland, Pamela. (1980). *Story of Cadmus*. Minneapolis: Carolrhoda.

Estes, Eleanor. (1941). *The Moffats*. San Diego: Harcourt.

Estes, Eleanor. (1943, 1970). *Rufus M.* San Diego: Harcourt.

Estes, Eleanor. (1983). *Moffat museum*. San Diego: Harcourt.

Ets, Marie Hall. (1955). *Play with me*. New York: Viking.

Ets, Marie Hall. (1965). *Just Me*. New York: Viking.

Ets, Marie Hall, & Labastida, Aurora. (1959). *Nine days to Christmas, a story of Mexico*. New York: Viking.

Everett, Gwen. (1992). *Li'l Sis and Uncle Willie: A story based on the life and paintings of William H. Johnson*. New York: Rizzoli.

Evslin, Bernard. (1984). *Hercules*. New York: Morrow.

Evslin, Bernard. (1989). *Scylla and Charybdis*. New York: Chelsea.

Evslin, Bernard. (1988). *Heroes and Monsters of Greek Myth*. New York: Scholastic.

Ewald, Wendy (1985; o.p.). *Portraits and dreams:*

Photographs and stories by children of the Appalachians. New York: Writers & Readers.

Faber, Doris. (1985). *Eleanor Roosevelt: First lady of the world*. New York: Viking.

Faber, Doris, & Faber, Harold. (1989). *Birth of a nation: The early years of the United States*. New York: Scribner's.

Faber, Doris, & Faber, Harold. (1991). *Great lives: Nature and the environment*. New York: Scribner's.

Faber, Harold. (1992). *The discoveries of America*. New York: Scribner's.

Fahrmann, Willi. (1985; o.p.). *The long journey of Lucas B*. New York: Bradbury.

Farber, Norma. (1979). *How does it feel to be old?* Illus. Trina Schart Hyman. New York: Dutton.

Farjeon, Eleanor. (1984). *Eleanor Farjeon's poems for children*. New York: HarperCollins.

Farley, Walter. (1941). *The black stallion*. Illus. Keith Ward. New York: Random

Fassler, Joan. (1975). *Howie helps himself*. Niles, IL: Whitman.

Fast, Howard. (1983). *April morning*. New York: Bantam.

Fatio, Louise. (1986). *The happy lion*. Illus. Roger Duvoisin. New York: Scholastic.

Feelings, Muriel. (1974). *Jambo means hello*. Illus. Tom Feelings. New York: Dial.

Feelings, Muriel. (1975). *Moja means one: A Swahili counting book*. Illus. Tom Feelings. New York: Dial.

Fenner, Carol. (1991). *Randall's wall*. New York: McElderry.

Ferguson, Alane. (1990). *Cricket and the crackerbox kid*. New York: Bradbury.

Ferris, Jeri. (1988). *Go free or die: A story about Harriet Tubman*. Minneapolis: Carolrhoda.

Ferris, Jeri. (1989). *Arctic explorer: The story of Matthew Henson*. Minneapolis: Carolrhoda.

Ferris, Jeri. (1991). *Native American doctor: The story of Susan LaFlesche Picotte*. Minneapolis: Carolrhoda.

Ferris, Sean. (1991). *Children of the great muskeg*. Windsor, Ontario: Black Moss Press, Firefly.

Field, Rachel. (1987 reissue). *Calico bush*. New York: Macmillan.

Field, Rachel. (1988). *General store*. Illus. Nancy Winslow Parker. New York: Greenwillow.

Field, Rachel. (1990). *A road might lead to anywhere*. Illus. Giles Laroche. Boston: Little, Brown.

Fields, Julia. (1988). *Green lion of Zion Street*. Illus. Jerry Pinkney. New York: McElderry.

Fife, Dale H. (1991). *The empty lot*. Illus. Jim Arnosky. Boston: Little, Brown.

Finger, Charles (ed.). (1965). *Tales from silver lands*. New York: Doubleday.

Finkelstein, Norman. (1991). *Captain of innocence: France and the Dreyfus affair*. New York: Putnam.

Finley, Martha. (1867; 1981 reissue). *Elsie Dins-more*. Edited by Alison Lurie & Justin G. Schiller. New York: Garland.

Fisher, Aileen. (1964). *Listen, rabbit!* New York: HarperCollins.

Fisher, Aileen. (1991). *Always wondering*. Illus. Joan Sandin. New York: HarperCollins.

Fisher, Aileen. (1960; o.p.). *Going barefoot*. Illus. Adrienne Adams. New York: HarperCollins.

Fisher, Aileen. (1962; o.p.). *Like nothing at all*. Illus. Leonard Weisgard. New York: HarperCollins.

Fisher, Aileen. (1965; o.p.). *In the middle of the night*. Illus. Adrienne Adams. New York: HarperCollins.

Fisher, Aileen. (1969; o.p.). *Sing little mouse*. Illus. Symeon Shimin. New York: HarperCollins.

Fisher, Aileen. (1980; o.p.). *Anybody home?* Illus. Susan Bonners. New York: HarperCollins.

Fisher, Leonard Everett. (1984). *Olympians: Great gods and goddesses of ancient Greece*. New York: Holiday.

Fisher, Leonard Everett. (1989). *The wailing wall*. New York: Macmillan.

Fisher, Leonard Everett (1990). *The Oregon trail*. New York: Holiday.

Fisher, Leonard Everett. (1991). *The ABC exhibit*. New York: Macmillan.

Fisher, Leonard Everett (1992). *Galileo*. New York: Macmillan.

Fisher, Leonard Everett. (1988; o.p.). *Across the sea from Galway*. New York: Holiday.

Fisher, Leonard Everett. (1981 o.p.). *The seven days of creation*. New York: Holiday.

Fitzhugh, Louise. (1964). *Harriet, the spy*. New York: HarperCollins.

Flack, Marjorie. (1933). *The story about Ping*. Illus. Kurt Wiese. New York: Viking.

Flack, Marjorie. (1991 reprint). *The boats on the river*. New York: Viking.

Fleischman, Paul. (1986). *I am Phoenix: Poems for two voices*. Illus. Ken Nutt (Eric Beddows). New York: HarperCollins.

Fleischman, Paul. (1986). *Rear-view mirrors*. New York: HarperCollins.

Fleischman, Paul. (1988). *Joyful noise: Poems for two voices*. Illus. Eric Beddows. New York: HarperCollins.

Fleischman, Paul. (1991). *The borning room*. New York: HarperCollins.

Fleischman, Paul. (1991). *Time train*. Illus. Claire Ewart. New York: HarperCollins.

Fleischman, Sid. (1987). *Scarebird*. Illus. Peter Sis. New York: Greenwillow.

Fleming, Alice. (1988). *The King of Prussia and a peanut butter sandwich*. New York: Scribner's.

Fleming, Denise. (1991). *In the tall, tall grass*. New York: Holt.

Fleming, Ian. (1952, 1964, 1989). *Chitty, chitty, bang, bang: The magical car*. Illus. John Burningham. New York: Knopf.

Flora. (1989). *Feathers like a rainbow: An Amazon Indian tale*. New York: HarperCollins.

Florian, Douglas. (1991). *A carpenter*. New York: Greenwillow.

Florian, Douglas. (1991). *A potter*. New York: Greenwillow

Flournoy, Valerie. (1985). *The patchwork quilt*. Illus. Jerry Pinkney. New York: Dial.

Forbes, Esther. (1946, 1991). *America's Paul Revere*. Boston: Houghton.

Forbes, Esther. (1969). *Johnny Tremain*. Illus. Lynd Ward. New York: Dell.

Foreman, Michael. (1990). *War boy: A country childhood*. New York: Arcade.

Foreman, Michael. (1992). *The boy who sailed with Columbus*. New York: Arcade.

Forest, Heather. (1988). *The baker's dozen: A colonial American tale*. Illus. Susan Gaber. San Diego: Harcourt.

Forman, James. (1969; o.p.). *The Cow Neck rebels*. New York: Farrar, Straus, & Giroux.

Fox, Dan (editor/arranger). (1987; o.p.). *Go in and out the window: An illustrated songbook for young people*. New York: Metropolitan Museum of Art.

Fox, Dan (arranger). (1989; o.p.). *We wish you a merry Christmas: Songs of the season for young people*. New York: Metropolitan Museum of Art.

Fox, Mem. (1985). *Wilfrid Gordon McDonald Partridge*. Illus. Julie Vivas. Brooklyn: Kane Miller.

Fox, Mem. (1987, 1990). *Possum magic*. Illus. Julie Vivas. Abingdon (1987); San Diego: Harcourt (1990).

Fox, Mem. (1988). *Hattie and the fox*. Illus. Patricia Mullins. New York: Bradbury.

Fox, Mem. (1990). *Guess what?* Illus. Vivienne Goodman. San Diego: Harcourt, Gulliver.

Fox, Mem. (1991). *Night noises*. Illus. Terry Denton. San Diego: Harcourt.

Fox, Mem. (1992, 1990). *Dear Mem Fox. I have read all your books even the pathetic ones* San Diego: Harcourt.

Fox, Paula. (1970). *Blowfish live in the sea*. New York: Bradbury.

Fox, Paula. (1980). *A place apart*. New York: Farrar, Straus & Giroux.

Fox, Paula. (1982). *The slave dancer*. New York: Bradbury.

Fox, Paula. (1984). *One-eyed cat*. New York: Bradbury.

Fox, Paula. (1985). *Portrait of Ivan*. New York: Bradbury.

Fox, Paula. (1986). *The moonlight man*. New York: Bradbury.

Fox, Paula. (1987). *Lily and the lost boy*. New York: Orchard.

Fox, Paula. (1991). *Monkey island*. New York: Orchard, Watts.

Fradin, Dennis B. (1989). *Georgia colony*. San Francisco: Children's Book Press.

Fradon, Dana. (1990). *Harold the herald: A book about heraldry*. New York: Dutton.

Franchere, Ruth. (1986). *Cesar Chavez*. New York: HarperCollins.

Frank, Anne. (1967). *The diary of a young girl*. New York: Doubleday.

Frank, Josette (selector). (1990). *Snow toward evening, a year in river valley*. Illus. Thomas Locker. New York: Dial.

Frank Leslie's Chatterbox magazine. 1879–1886.

Frank, Rudolf. (1931, 1986). *No hero for the Kaiser*. Trans. Patricia Crampton. New York: Lothrop.

Fraser, Betty. (1990). *First things first: An illustrated collection of sayings useful and familiar for children*. New York: HarperCollins.

Freedman, Florence B. (1989). *Two tickets to freedom: The true story of Ellen and William Craft, fugitive slaves*. New York: Peter Bedrick.

Freedman, Russell. (1983). *Children of the wild west*. New York: Clarion.

Freedman, Russell. (1985). *Cowboys of the wild west*. New York: Clarion.

Freedman, Russell. (1987). *Indian chiefs*. New York: Holiday.

Freedman, Russell. (1988). *Buffalo hunt*. New York: Holiday.

Freedman, Russell. (1989). *Lincoln: A photobiography*. New York: Clarion.

Freedman, Russell. (1990). *Franklin Delano Roosevelt*. New York: Houghton, Clarion.

Freedman, Russell. (1991). *The Wright brothers: How they invented the airplane*. Illus. Wilbur & Orville Wright. New York: Holiday.

Freedman, Russell. (1992). *An Indian winter*. Illus. Karl Bodmer. New York: Holiday.

Freeman, Don. (1968). *Corduroy*. New York: Viking, Penguin.

Friedman, Ina. (1984). *How my parents learned to eat*. Boston: Houghton.

Friend, David. (1990). *Baseball, football, Daddy and me*. Illus. Rick Brown. New York: Viking.

Fritz, Jean. (1958). *The cabin faced west*. Illus. Feodor Rojankovsky. New York: Putnam.

Fritz, Jean. (1960). *Brady*. New York: Putnam.

Fritz, Jean. (1967). *Early thunder*. New York: Putnam.

Fritz, Jean. (1973). *And then what happened, Paul Revere?* Illus. Margot Tomes. New York: Putnam.

Fritz, Jean. (1974). *Why don't you get a horse, Sam Adams?* Illus. Trina Schart Hyman. New York: Putnam.

Fritz, Jean. (1975). *Who's that stepping on Plymouth Rock?* Illus. J. B. Handelsman. New York: Putnam.

Fritz, Jean. (1976). *What's the big idea, Ben*

Franklin? Illus. Margot Tomes. New York: Putnam.

Fritz, Jean. (1976). *Will you sign here, John Hancock?* Illus. Trina Schart Hyman. New York: Putnam.

Fritz, Jean. (1979). *Stonewall*. Illus. Stephen Gammell. New York: Putnam.

Fritz, Jean. (1981). *Traitor: The case of Benedict Arnold*. New York: Putnam.

Fritz, Jean. (1981). *Where do you think you're going, Christopher Columbus?* Illus. Margot Tomes. New York: Putnam.

Fritz, Jean. (1982). *Can't you make them behave, King George?* Illus. Tomie de Paola. New York: Putnam.

Fritz, Jean. (1982). *Homesick: My own story*. New York: Putnam.

Fritz, Jean. (1983). *The double life of Pocahontas*. New York: Putnam.

Fritz, Jean. (1985). *China homecoming*. New York: Putnam.

Fritz, Jean. (1986). *Make way for Sam Houston*. New York: Putnam.

Fritz, Jean. (1987). *Shh! We're writing the constitution*. Illus. Tomie de Paola. New York: Putnam.

Fritz, Jean. (1989). *The great little Madison*. New York: Putnam.

Fritz, Jean. (1991). *Bully for you, Teddy Roosevelt*. New York: Putnam.

Fritz, Jean. (1993). *Surprising myself*. Katonah, NY: Richard C. Owens.

Fritz, Jean; Paterson, Katherine; McKissack, F.; Mahy, Margaret & Highwater, Jamake. (1992). *The world in 1492*. Illus. Stefano Vitale. New York: Henry Holt.

Froman, Robert. (1974). *Seeing things*. New York: HarperCollins.

Frost, Robert. (1959). *You come too: Favorite poems for young readers*. New York: Holt.

Frost, Robert. (1978). *Stopping by woods*. Illus. Susan Jeffers. New York: Dutton.

Frost, Robert. (1988). *Birches*. Illus. Ed Young. New York: Holt.

Fukami, Haruo. (1990). *An orange for a bellybutton*. Trans. Cathy Hirano. Minneapolis: Carolrhoda.

Fukuda, Hanako. (1970 o.p.). *Wind in my hand: The story of Issa*. San Carlos, CA.: Golden Gate.

Funakoshi, Canna. (1988). *One evening*. Illus. Yohji Izawa. Saxonville, MA: Picture Book.

Gackenbach, Dick. (1983). *A bag full of pups*. New York: Clarion.

Gág, Wanda. (1928). *Millions of cats*. New York: Coward McCann, Putnam.

Gág, Wanda, (1936; o.p.). *Tales from Grimm*. New York: Coward-McCann.

Galdone, Paul. (1960). *The old woman and her pig*. New York: McGraw-Hill.

Galdone, Paul. (1975). *The gingerbread boy*. New York: Clarion.

Galdone, Paul. (1979). *Henny penny*. New York: Clarion.

Galdone, Paul. (1979). *Little red hen*. New York: Clarion.

Galdone, Paul. (1988). *Three little kittens*. New York: Clarion.

Garcia, Ann O'Neal. (1982; o.p.). *Spirit on the wall*. New York: Holiday.

Garelick, May. (1990). *Just my size*. Illus. William Pène Du Bois. New York: HarperCollins.

Garne, S. T. (1992). *One white sail: A Caribbean counting book*. Illus. Lisa Etre. New York: Simon & Schuster.

Garson, Eugenia (compiler). (1968). *Laura Ingalls Wilder songbook: Favorite songs from the "Little House" books*. New York: HarperCollins

Garza, Carmen Lomas. (1990). *Family pictures: Cuadros de familia*. Spanish version by Rosalma Zubizarreta. Edited by Harriet Rohmer. San Francisco: Children's Book Press.

Gates, Doris. (1982). *Lord of the sky: Zeus*. New York: Penguin.

Gates, Doris. (1983). *Two queens of heaven: Aphrodite and Demeter*. Illus. Trina Schart Hyman. New York: Penguin, Puffin.

Gauch, Patricia Lee. (1974, 1992). *This time, Tempe Wick?* New York: Putnam.

Geisert, Arthur. (1991). *Oink*. Boston: Houghton.

Geisert, Arthur. (1992). *Pigs from 1 to 10*. Boston: Houghton.

Gelman, Rita Golden. (1991). *Dawn to dusk in the Galapagos: Flightless birds, swimming lizards, and other fascinating creatures*. Illus. Tui De Roy. Boston: Little, Brown.

George, Jean Craighead. (1959). *My side of the mountain*. New York: Dutton.

George, Jean Craighead. (1971, 1991). *Who really killed Cock Robin?: An ecological mystery*. New York: HarperCollins.

George, Jean Craighead. (1972). *Julie of the wolves*. Illus. John Schoenherr. New York: HarperCollins.

George, Jean Craighead. (1980). *The cry of the crow*. New York: HarperCollins.

George, Jean Craighead. (1983). *One day in the desert*. New York: HarperCollins.

George, Jean Craighead. (1989). *Shark beneath the reef*. New York: HarperCollins.

Geras, Adele. (1990). *My grandmother's stories: A collection of Jewish folk tales*. Illus. Jael Jordan. New York: Knopf.

Geras, Adele. (1991). *Happy endings*. San Diego: Harcourt.

Geringer, Laura. (1991). *Silverpoint*. New York: HarperCollins.

Gerrard, Roy. (1989). *Rosie and the rustlers*. New York: Farrar, Straus & Giroux.

Gerson, Mary-Joan (reteller). (1992; o.p.). *Why the*

sky is far away. Illus. Carla Golembe. Boston: Joy Street.

Gherman, Beverly. (1992). *E. B. White: Some writer*. New York: Atheneum.

Gibbons, Gail. (1979). *Clocks and how they go*. New York: HarperCollins.

Gibbons, Gail. (1981). *Trucks*. New York: HarperCollins.

Gibbons, Gail. (1987). *Deadline! From news to newspaper*. New York: HarperCollins.

Gibbons, Gail. (1987). *Dinosaurs*. New York: Holiday.

Gibbons, Gail. (1987). *Zoo*. New York: HarperCollins.

Gibbons, Gail. (1988). *Farming*. New York: Holiday.

Gibbons, Gail. (1991). *The puffins are back!* New York: HarperCollins.

Gibbons, Gail. (1991). *Surrounded by sea: Life on a New England fishing island*. Boston: Little, Brown.

Gibbons, Gail. (1992; o.p.). *Recycle! A handbook for kids*. Boston: Little, Brown.

Giblin, James Cross. (1990). *The riddle of the Rosetta Stone: Key to ancient Egypt*. New York: HarperCollins.

Giff, Patricia Reilly. (1987). *Laura Ingalls Wilder: Growing up in the little house*. New York: Viking.

Giff, Patricia Reilly. (1991). *The war began at supper: Letters to Miss Loria*. Illus. Betsy Lewin. New York: Dell.

Giganti, Paul, Jr. (1988). *How many snails? A counting book*. Illus. Donald Crews. New York: Greenwillow.

Gilbert, Thomas W. (1992). *Lee Trevino*. New York: Chelsea.

Gilson, Jamie. (1987). *Hobie Hanson, you're weird*. Illus. Elise Primavera. New York: Lothrop.

Ginsburg, Mirra. (1980). *Good morning, chick*. Adapted from story by Kornei Chukovsky. Illus. Byron Barton. New York: Greenwillow.

Ginsburg, Mirra. (adapter). (1988). *The Chinese mirror*. San Diego: Harcourt, Gulliver.

Ginsburg, Mirra. (1992). *Asleep, asleep*. Illus. Nancy Tafuri. New York: Greenwillow.

Giovanni, Nikki. (1987). *Spin a soft black song*. New York: Farrar, Straus & Giroux.

Girling, Brough. (1990). *I know an old lady*. Illus. Glen Rounds. New York: Holiday.

Glassman, Judy. (1990). *The morning glory war*. New York: Dutton.

Glazer, Tom. (1973, 1978). *Eye winker, Tom Tinker, chin chopper: Fifty musical fingerplays*. Illus. Ronald Himler. New York: Doubleday.

Gleiter, Jan. (1984). *Paul Bunyan and Babe the blue ox*. Milwaukee: Raintree.

Gleiter, Jan. (1987). *John James Audubon*. Milwaukee: Raintree.

Gleiter, Jan. (1987). *Kit Carson*. Milwaukee: Raintree.

Gleiter, Jan. (1987). *Sacagawea*. Milwaukee: Raintree.

Gleitzman, Morris. (1991). *Two weeks with the queen*. New York: Putnam.

Glenn, Mel. (1986). *Class dismissed: High school poems*. New York: Clarion.

Glenn, Mel. (1989). *My friend's got this problem, Mr. Candler: High school poems*. New York: Clarion.

Glubok, Shirley. (1965; o.p.). *Art and archaeology*. New York: HarperCollins.

Glubok, Shirley. (1976). *Olympic games in ancient Greece*. New York: HarperCollins.

Goble, Paul. (1982). *The girl who loved wild horses*. New York: Macmillan.

Goble, Paul. (1982). *Star boy*. New York: Bradbury.

Goble, Paul. (1984). *Buffalo woman*. New York: Bradbury.

Goble, Paul. (1987). *Death of the iron horse*. New York: Bradbury.

Goble, Paul. (1988). *Her seven brothers*. New York: Bradbury.

Goble, Paul. (1988). *Iktomi and the boulder: A Plains Indian story*. New York: Orchard.

Goble, Paul. (1989). *Beyond the ridge*. New York: Bradbury.

Goble, Paul. (1989). *Iktomi and the berries: A Plains Indian story*. New York: Orchard.

Goble, Paul. (1990). *Dream wolf*. New York: Bradbury.

Goble, Paul. (1991). *Iktomi and the buffalo skull: A Plains Indian story*. New York: Orchard.

Goble, Paul. (1992). *Crow chief: A Plains Indian story*. New York: Orchard.

Goble, Paul. (1992). *Iktomi and the ducks: A Plains Indian story*. New York: Orchard.

Goedecke, Christopher J. (1992). *The wind warrior: The training of a karate champion*. Photos by Rosmarie Hausher. New York: Four Winds.

Goennel, Heidi. (1989). *My dog*. New York: Orchard.

Goennel, Heidi. (1992). *The circus*. New York: Morrow.

Goffstein, M. B. (1984). *A writer*. New York: HarperCollins.

Goffstein, M. B. (1985). *Artists album*. New York: HarperCollins.

Goldin, Barbara Diamond. (1988). *Just enough is plenty: A Hanukkah tale*. Illus. Seymour Chwast. New York: Viking.

Goldsmith, Oliver. (1765; 1924 reissue). *The renowned history of Little Goody Two Shoes*. Illus. Alice Woodward. New York: Macmillan.

Goldstein, Bobbye S. (selector). (1992). *Inner Chimes: Poems on poetry*. Illus. Jane Breskin Zalben. Honesdale, PA: Boyds Mills, Wordsong.

Goldstein, Margaret J. (1992). *Brett Hull: Hockey's top gun*. Minneapolis: Lerner.

Goldenbock, Peter. (1990). *Teammates*. Illus. Paul Bacon. San Diego: Harcourt.

Gonzales, Doreen. (1991). *Madeleine L'Engle: Author of A Wrinkle in Time*. New York: Dillon.

Goodall, John. (1979). *The story of an English village*. New York: Macmillan.

Goodall, John. (1985). *Naughty Nancy goes to school*. New York: McElderry.

Goodall, John. (1988). *Little red riding hood*. New York: McElderry.

Goodrich, Samuel G. (1822). *Peter Parley's history of the United States of America*. New York: Garland.

Goodrich, Samuel G., & Goodrich, Charles. (1827; 1976 reissue). *Tales of Peter Parley about America*. New York: Garland.

Gordon, Gaelyn. (1992). *Duckat*. Illus. Chris Gaskin. New York: Scholastic.

Gordon, Jeffie Ross. (1992). *Six sleepy sheep*. Illus. John O'Brien. Honesdale, PA: Boyds Mills.

Gordon, Ruth. (1991). *Time is the longest distance*. New York: HarperCollins, Zolotow.

Gordon, Sheila. (1987). *Waiting for the rain: A novel of South Africa*. New York: Orchard.

Gordon, Sheila. (1990). *The middle of somewhere: A story of South Africa*. New York: Orchard.

Gould, Deborah. (1987). *Grandpa's slide show*. Illus. Cheryl Harness. New York: Lothrop.

Grabowski, John. (1992). *Sandy Koufax*. New York: Chelsea.

Graff, Nancy Price. (1989). *The strength of the hills: A portrait of a family farm*. Boston: Little, Brown.

Graham, Bob. (1988). *Crusher is coming*. New York: Viking, Kestrel.

Graham, Bob. (1989). *Has anyone here seen William?* Boston: Little, Brown.

Grahame, Kenneth. (1908, 1940, 1961). *Wind in the willows*. New York: Scribner's.

Gramatky, Hardie. (1939). *Little Toot*. New York: Putnam.

Grant, Joan. (1987). *The monster that grew small*. Illus. Jill Karla Schwarz. New York: Lothrop.

Gray, Elizabeth Vining. (1942, 1987). *Adam of the road*. New York: Viking.

Greeley, Valerie. (1990). *Animals*. New York: Peter Bedrick.

Greenaway, Kate. (1878). *Under the window*. London: Warne.

Greenberg, David. (1989). *The great school lunch rebellion*. Illus. Maxie Chambliss. New York: Bantam.

Greenberg, Jan, & Jordan, Sandra. (1991). *The painter's eye: Learning to look at contemporary American art*. New York: Delacorte.

Greenberg, Keith Elliot. (1992). *Magic Johnson: Champion with a cause*. Minneapolis: Lerner.

Greene, Bette. (1974). *Philip Hall likes me. I reckon maybe*. New York: Dial.

Greene, Carol. (1991). *Hans Christian Andersen: Prince of storytellers*. San Francisco Children's Book Press.

Greene, Constance. (1969). *A girl called Al*. New York: Viking.

Greene, Constance. (1975). *I know you, Al*. New York: Viking.

Greene, Constance. (1979). *Beat the turtle drum*. New York: Dell.

Greene, Constance. (1979). *Your old pal Al*. New York: Viking.

Greene, Constance. (1992). *Al(exandra) the great*. New York: Viking.

Greene, Constance. (1986). *Just plain Al*. New York: Viking.

Greenfeld, Howard. (1989). *Books: From writer to reader*. New York: Crown.

Greenfield, Eloise. (1973). *Rosa Parks*. New York: HarperCollins.

Greenfield, Eloise. (1974). *Sister*. New York: HarperCollins.

Greenfield, Eloise. (1975). *Me and Neesie*. New York: HarperCollins.

Greenfield, Eloise. (1977). *Mary McLeod Bethune*. New York: HarperCollins.

Greenfield, Eloise. (1978). *Honey, I love and other love poems*. Illus. Leo & Diane Dillon. New York: HarperCollins.

Greenfield, Eloise. (1988). *Nathaniel talking*. New York: Writers and Readers.

Greenfield, Eloise. (1988). *Under the Sunday Tree*. Illus. Amos Ferguson. New York: HarperCollins.

Greenfield, Eloise. (1990). *She come bringing me that little baby girl*. Illus. John Steptoe. New York: HarperCollins.

Greenfield, Eloise. (1991). *Grandpa's face*. Illus. Floyd Cooper. New York: Putnam.

Greenfield, Eloise. (1991). *Night on neighborhood street*. Illus. Jan Spivey Gilchrist. New York: Dial.

Greenfield, Eloise. (1992). *Koya Delaney and the good girl blues*. New York: Scholastic.

Greenfield, Eloise, & Little, Lessie Jones. (1979). *Childtimes: A three-generation memoir*. New York: HarperCollins.

Greenwald, Sheila. (1980). *It all began with Jane Eyre*. Boston: Little, Brown.

Greenwald, Sheila. (1981). *Give us a great big smile, Rosy Cole*. Boston: Little, Brown.

Greenwald, Sheila. (1984). *Valentine Rosy*. Boston: Little, Brown.

Greenwald, Sheila. (1987). *Alvin Webster's sure-fire plan for success (and how it failed)*. Boston: Little, Brown.

Greenwald, Sheila. (1989). *Rosy's romance*. Boston: Little, Brown.

Greenwald, Sheila. (1989). *Secret in Miranda's closet*. New York: Dell.

Greenwald, Sheila. (1991). *Here's Hermione: A Rosy Cole production*. Boston: Little, Brown.

Gregory, Cynthia. (1990). *Cynthia Gregory dances Swan Lake*. New York: Simon & Schuster.

Gretchen, Sylvia (adapter). (1990). *Hero of the land of snow*. Illus. Julia Weaver. Berkeley, CA: Dharma.

Griego, Margot C., et al. (1981). *Tortillitas para Mama and other nursery rhymes: Spanish and English*. Illus. Barbara Cooney. New York: Holt.

Grifalconi, Ann. (1986). *The village of round and square houses*. Boston: Little, Brown.

Grifalconi, Ann. (1987). *Darkness and the butterfly*. Boston: Little, Brown.

Grifalconi, Ann. (1990). *Osa's pride*. Boston: Little, Brown.

Griffith, Helen V. (1984). *Foxy*. New York: Greenwillow.

Griffith, Helen V. (1987). *Grandaddy's place*. Illus. James Stevenson. New York: Greenwillow.

Grimal, Pierre (ed.). (1965). *Larousse World Mythology*. Secaucus, NJ: Chartwell.

Grimm, Jacob. (1983). *Little Red Cap*. Trans. Elizabeth Crawford. Illus. Lizbeth Zwerger. New York: Morrow.

Grimm, Jacob. (1986). *Rumpelstiltskin*. Reteller & Illus. Paul O. Zelinsky. New York: Dutton.

Grimm, Jacob, & Grimm, Wilhelm. (1977; 1823 reprint). *Grimm's fairy tales*. Illus. George Cruikshank. San Diego: Green Tiger.

Grimm, Jacob, & Grimm, Wilhelm. (1977; 1886 reissue). *Household stories of the Brothers Grimm*. New York: Dover.

Grimm, Jacob, & Grimm, Wilhelm. (1973). *The Juniper tree and other tales from Grimm*. 2 vols. Trans. Lore Segal & Randall Jarrell. Illus. Maurice Sendak. New York: Farrar, Straus & Giroux.

Grimm, Jacob, & Grimm, Wilhelm. (1983). *Little Red Riding Hood*. Reteller & Illus. Trina Schart Hyman. New York: Holiday.

Grimm, Jacob, & Grimm, Wilhelm. (1988). *Hansel and Gretel*. Illus. Anthony Browne. New York: Knopf.

Grimm, Jacob, & Grimm, Wilhelm. (1991). *Rumpelstiltskin*. New York: Dial.

Grindley, Sally. (1986). *Knock, knock! Who's there?* Illus. Anthony Browne. New York: Knopf.

Grinnell, George. (1900). *Jack among the Indians*. Boston: Stokes.

Gross, David. (1993). *Justice Felix Frankfurter: A justice for all the people*. New York: Chelsea.

Gross, Ruth Belov. (1988). *True stories about Abraham Lincoln*. New York: Scholastic.

Gross, Ruth Belov. (1991). *You don't need words! A book about ways people talk without words*. New York: Scholastic.

Grossman, Virginia. (1991). *Ten little rabbits*. Illus. Sylvia Long. San Francisco: Chronicle.

Guarino, Deborah. (1989). *Is your mama a llama?* Illus. Steven Kellogg. New York: Scholastic.

Gunning, Monica. (1993). *Not a copper penny in me house*. Illus. Frané Lessac. Honesdale, PA: Boyds Mills.

Gutierrez, Douglas. (1988). *The night of the stars*. Trans. Carmen Diana Dearden. Illus. Maria Fernanda Oliver. Brooklyn: Kane Miller.

Guy, Rosa. (1982). *Mother crocodile: An Uncle Amadou tale from Senegal*. Illus. John Steptoe. New York: Delacorte.

Hackwell, W. John. (1991). *Desert of ice: Life and work in Antarctica*. New York: Scribner's.

Hadithi, Mwenye. (1987). *Crafty chameleon*. Illus. Adrienne Kennaway. Boston: Little, Brown.

Hahn, Mary Downing. (1991). *Dead man in Indian Creek*. New York: Avon.

Hahn, Mary Downing. (1991). *Stepping on the cracks*. Boston: Houghton.

Hale, Irina. (1983). *Brown bear in a brown chair*. New York: Atheneum.

Hale, Lucretia. (1880; 1960 reprint). *The Peterkin Papers*. Boston: Houghton.

Hale, Lucretia. (1989). *The lady who put salt in her coffee*. Adapter & Illus. Amy Schwartz. San Diego: Harcourt.

Hale, Sara Josepha. (1830). "Mary's lamb." *Juvenile Miscellany*.

Haley, Gail. (1973; o.p.). *Jack Jouett's ride*. New York: Viking.

Haley, Gail. (1970). *A story, a story*. New York: Atheneum.

Haley, Gail. (1986). *Jack and the bean tree*. New York: Crown.

Hall, Donald. (1979). *Ox-cart man*. Illus. Barbara Cooney. New York: Viking, Penguin.

Hall, Donald (ed.). (1990). *The Oxford book of children's verse in America*. New York: Oxford University Press.

Hall, Lynn. (1989). *Dagmar Schultz and the powers of darkness*. New York: Macmillan.

Hall, Lynn. (1991). *Dagmar Schultz and the green-eyed monster*. New York: Macmillan.

Hamilton, Virginia. (1967). *Zeely*. Illus. Symeon Shimin. New York: Macmillan.

Hamilton, Virginia. (1971). *Planet of Junior Brown*. New York: Macmillan.

Hamilton, Virginia. (1974). *M. C. Higgins, the great*. New York: Macmillan.

Hamilton, Virginia. (1983). *The magical adventures of Pretty Pearl*. New York: HarperCollins.

Hamilton, Virginia. (1983). *Willie Bea and the time the Martians landed*. New York: Greenwillow.

Hamilton, Virginia. (1984). *House of Dies Drear*. New York: Macmillan.

Hamilton, Virginia. (1984). *A little love*. New York: Philomel.

Hamilton, Virginia. (1985). *The people could fly: American black folk tales*. Illus. Leo & Diane Dillon. New York: Knopf.

Hamilton, Virginia. (1987). *Mystery of Drear House*. New York: Greenwillow.

Hamilton, Virginia. (1988). *Anthony Burns: The defeat and triumph of a fugitive slave*. New York: Knopf.

Hamilton, Virginia. (1988). *In the beginning: Creation stories from around the world*. Illus. Barry Moser. San Diego: Harcourt.

Hamilton, Virginia. (1990). *The dark way: Stories from the spirit world*. Illus. Lambert Davis. San Diego: Harcourt.

Hamilton, Virginia. (1990). *Cousins*. New York: Putnam.

Hamilton, Virginia. (1992). *Drylongso*. Illus. Jerry Pinkney. San Diego: Harcourt.

Hamilton, Virginia. (1993). *Many thousand gone: African Americans from slavery to freedom*. Illus. Leo & Diane Dillon. New York: Knopf.

Hamm, Diane. (1991). *How many feet in the bed?* New York: Simon & Schuster.

Hammerstein, Oscar II. (1992). *A real nice clambake*. Illus. Nadine Bernard Westcott. Boston: Little, Brown, Joy Street.

Hancock, Sibyl. (1983). *Famous first of black Americans*. Gretna, LA: Pelican.

Hanft, P. (1991). *Never fear, Flip the Dip is here*. Illus. Thomas B. Allen. New York: Dial.

Harlan, Judith. (1989). *Sounding the alarm: A biography of Rachel Carson*. New York: Macmillan.

Harris, Benjamin. (1679). *The protestant tutor*. London: Benjamin Harris.

Harris, Benjamin. (1689). *The New England primer*. Boston: Benjamin Harris.

Harris, Christie. (1963; o.p.). *Once upon a totem*. New York: Atheneum.

Harris, Christie. (1973; o.p.). *Once more upon a totem*. New York: Atheneum.

Harris, Christie (1976; o.p.). *Mouse woman and the vanished princesses*. New York: Atheneum.

Harris, Christie. (1980). *The trouble with princesses*. New York: Atheneum.

Harris, Joel Chandler. (1986). *Jump: The adventures of Brer Rabbit*. Edited by Van Dyke Parks & Malcolm Jones. Illus. Barry Moser. San Diego: Harcourt.

Harris, Joel Chandler. (1987). *Jump again!: More adventures of Brer Rabbit*. Illus. Barry Moser. San Diego: Harcourt.

Harris, Joel Chandler. (1989). *Jump on over!: The adventures of Brer Rabbit and his family*. Adapter Van Dyke Parks. Illus. Barry Moser. San Diego: Harcourt.

Harris, Nathaniel. (1987). *Leonardo and the Renaissance*. New York: Watts.

Harrison, Barbara, & Terris, Daniel. (1992). *A twilight struggle: The life of John Fitzgerald Kennedy*. New York: Lothrop.

Harrison, David. (1992). *Somebody catch my homework*. Illus. Betsy Lewin. Honesdale, PA: Boyds Mills.

Harrison, David. (1993). *Never talk to plants*. Illus. Betsy Lewin. Honesdale, PA: Boyds Mills.

Harshman, Marco. (1990). *Snow company*. Illus. Leslie W. Bowman. New York: Dutton, Cobblehill.

Hart, Jane (compiler). (1982). *Singing bee: A collection of children's songs*. Illus. Anita Lobel. New York: Lothrop.

Hartling, Peter. (1988). *Crutches*. Trans. Elizabeth D. Crawford. New York: Lothrop.

Hartling, Peter. (1990). *Old John*. Trans. Elizabeth Crawford. New York: Lothrop.

Harvey, Brett. (1986). *My prairie year: Based on the diary of Elenore Plaisted*. Illus. Deborah Kogan Ray. New York: Holiday.

Harvey, Brett. (1987). *Cassie's journey: Going west in the 1860s*. Illus. Deborah Kogan Ray. New York: Holiday.

Harvey, Brett. (1987). *Immigrant girl: Becky of Eldridge Street*. Illus. Deborah Kogan Ray. New York: Holiday.

Harvey, Brett. (1990). *My prairie Christmas*. New York: Holiday.

Haseley, Dennis. (1991). *Shadows*. New York: Farrar, Straus & Giroux.

Haskins, Francine. (1991). *I remember "121."* San Francisco: Children's Book Press.

Haskins, James. (1977). *Street gangs, yesterday and today*. Mamaroneck, New York: Hastings.

Haskins, James. (1982). *Black theater in America*. New York: HarperCollins.

Haskins, James. (1986). *Diana Ross, star supreme*. New York: Viking, Puffin.

Haskins, James. (1988). *Bill Cosby: America's most famous father*. New York: Walker.

Hastings, Selina. (1991). *Reynard the fox*. Illus. Graham Percy. New York: Tambourine.

Hathorn, Libby. (1991). *Thunderwith*. Boston: Little, Brown.

Haugaard, Erik Christian. (1963; o.p.). *Hakon of Rogen's saga*. Boston: Houghton.

Haugaard, Erik Christian. (1968; o.p.). *The rider and his horse*. Boston: Houghton.

Haugaard, Erik Christian. (1984). *The samurai's tale*. Boston: Houghton.

Haugaard, Erik Christian. (1990). *Cromwell's boy*. Boston: Houghton.

Haugaard, Erik Christian. (1991). *The boy and the samurai*. Boston: Houghton.

Havill, Juanita. (1992). *Treasure nap*. Illus. Elivia Savadier. Boston: Houghton.

Hawthorne, Nathaniel. (1959). *The golden touch.* New York: McGraw-Hill

Hayes, Ann. (1991). *Meet the orchestra.* Illus. Karmen Thompson. San Diego: Harcourt.

Hayes, Sara. (1989). *This is the bear.* Illus. Helen Craig. Boston: Little, Brown.

Haywood, Carolyn. (1939). *"B" is for Betsy.* San Diego: Harcourt.

Haywood, Carolyn. (1941, 1988). *Betsy and Billy.* San Diego: Harcourt.

Haywood, Carolyn. (1945). *Betsy and the boys.* San Diego: Harcourt.

Haywood, Carolyn. (1949). *Eddie and the fire engine.* New York: Morrow.

Haywood, Carolyn. (1962). *Snowbound with Betsy.* New York: Dell.

Haywood, Carolyn. (1975). *Eddie's valuable property.* New York: Morrow.

Haywood, Carolyn. (1978). *Eddie's menagerie.* New York: Morrow.

Heard, Georgia. (1992). *Creatures of earth, sea, and sky.* Illus. Jennifer Owings Dewey. Honesdale, PA: Boyds Mills.

Hearne, Betsy. (1991). *Polaroid and other poems of view.* New York: Macmillan.

Heide, Florence Parry & Gilliland, Judith Heide. (1990). *The day of Ahmed's secret.* Illus. Ted Lewin. New York: Lothrop.

Heller, Ruth. (1989). *Cache of jewels and other collective nouns.* New York: Putnam.

Heller, Ruth. (1989). *Many luscious lollipops: A book about adjectives.* New York: Putnam.

Heller, Ruth. (1991). *Up, up and away: A book about adverbs.* New York: Putnam.

Hendershot, Judith. (1987). *In coal country.* Illus. Thomas B. Allen. New York: Knopf.

Henkes, Kevin. (1986). *Grandpa and Bo.* New York: Greenwillow.

Henkes, Kevin. (1987). *Sheila Rae, the brave.* New York: Greenwillow.

Henkes, Kevin. (1988). *Chester's way.* New York: Greenwillow.

Henkes, Kevin. (1989). *Jessica.* New York: Greenwillow.

Henkes, Kevin. (1990). *Julius, the baby of the world.* New York: Greenwillow.

Henkes, Kevin. (1991). *Chrysanthemum.* New York: Greenwillow.

Henkes, Kevin. (1992). *Words of stone.* New York: Greenwillow.

Hennessey, B. G. (1988). *The dinosaur who lived in my backyard.* New York: Viking.

Hennessy, B. G. (1990). *Jake baked the cake.* Illus. Mary Morgan. New York: Viking, Kestrel.

Henry, Joanne Landers. (1988). *Log cabin in the woods: A true story about a pioneer boy.* Macmillan, Four Winds.

Henry, Marguerite. (1947). *Misty of Chincoteague.* Illus. Wesley Dennis. New York: Macmillan.

Henry, Marguerite. (1948). *King of the wind.* Illus. Wesley Dennis. New York: Macmillan.

Henry, Marguerite. (1963). *Stormy, Misty's foal.* Illus. Wesley Dennis. New York: Macmillan.

Henry, Marguerite. (1980; o.p.). *Illustrated Marguerite Henry.* Illus. Wesley Dennis. Chicago: Rand McNally.

Henty, George. (1880). *The young buglers.* New York: Dutton.

Henty, George. (1903). *With Kitchener in the Soudan: A story of Atbara and Omdurman.* London: Blackie.

Herlihy, Dirlie. (1988). *Ludie's song.* New York: Dial.

Hermes, Patricia. (1991). *Mama, let's dance.* Boston: Little, Brown.

Hernandez, Xavier, & Ballonga, Jordi. (1991). *Lebek: A town of northern Europe through the ages.* Illus. Francesco Corni. Trans. Kathleen Leverich. Boston: Houghton.

Hernandez, Xavier, & Comes, Pilar. (1990). *Barmi: A Mediterranean city through the ages.* Illus. Jordi Ballonga. Trans. Kathleen Leverich. Boston: Houghton.

Herzig, Alison C., & Mali, Jane Lawrence. (1990). *Sam and the moon queen.* New York: Clarion.

Hesse, Karen. (1992). *Letters from Rifke.* New York: Holt.

Hest, Amy. (1991). *Love you, soldier.* New York: Macmillan.

Heyer, Marilee (reteller/illus.). (1986). *Weaving of a dream: A Chinese folktale.* New York: Viking, Kestrel.

Hibbard, Howard. (1974). *Michelangelo.* New York: HarperCollins.

Hicyilmaz, Gaye. (1992). *Against the storm.* Boston: Joy Street.

Hieatt, Constance. (1988). *Arthurian legends.* New York: Bantam.

Highlights for Children magazine. 1946–present. P.O. Box 269, Columbus, OH 43272-0002.

Highwater, Jamake. (1977). *Anpao: An American Indian odyssey.* New York: HarperCollins.

Hildick, E. W. (1984). *Ghost squad breaks through.* New York: Dutton.

Hilgartner, Beth. (1986). *A murder for her majesty.* Boston: Houghton.

Hill, Elizabeth Starr. (1967, 1991). *Evan's corner.* Illus. Sandra Speidel. New York: Viking, Penguin.

Hill, Eric. (1980). *Where's Spot?* New York: Putnam.

Hill, Eric. (1982). *My pets.* London: Heinemann.

Hill, Eric. (1984). *Spot goes splash!* New York: Putnam.

Hill, Kirkpatrick. (1990). *Toughboy and sister.* New York: McElderry.

Hilton, Suzanne. (1987). *The world of young George Washington.* New York: Walker.

Hilton, Suzanne. (1988). *The world of young Andrew Jackson.* New York: Walker.

Hines, Anna Grosnickle. (1987). *It's just me, Emily.* New York: Clarion.

Hirschfelder, Arlene, & Singer, Beverly. (1992). *Rising voices: Writings of young Native Americans.* New York: Scribner's.

Hirschi, Ron. (1990). *Spring.* Illus. Thomas D. Mangelsen. New York: Cobblehill.

Hirsh, Marilyn. (1979; o.p.). *One little goat: A Passover song.* New York: Holiday.

Hirsh, Marilyn (adapter). (1986). *Joseph who loved the sabbath.* Illus. Devis Grebu. New York: Viking.

Hirst, Robin, & Hirst, Sally. (1990). *My place in space.* Illus. Roland Harvey with Joe Levine. New York: Orchard.

Hitchcock, Alfred. (1983). *Alfred Hitchcock's supernatural tales of terror and suspense.* New York: Random.

Ho, Minfong. (1990). *Rice without rain.* New York: Lothrop.

Ho, Minfong. (1991). *The clay marble.* New York: Farrar, Straus & Giroux.

Hoban, Russell. (1967). *The mouse and his child.* New York: HarperCollins.

Hoban, Russell. (1960). *Bedtime for Frances.* Illus. Lillian Hoban. New York: HarperCollins.

Hoban, Russell. (1964, 1986). *Bread and jam for Frances.* Illus. Lillian Hoban. New York: HarperCollins.

Hoban, Tana. (1985). *Is it larger? Is it smaller?* New York: Greenwillow.

Hoban, Tana. (1987). *Dots, spots, speckles, and stripes.* New York: Greenwillow.

Hoban, Tana. (1989). *Of colors and things.* New York: Greenwillow.

Hoban, Tana. (1987). *Twenty-six letters and ninety-nine cents.* New York: Greenwillow.

Hoban, Tana. (1988). *Look! look! look!* New York: Greenwillow.

Hoban, Tana. (1990). *Exactly the opposite.* New York: Greenwillow.

Hoban, Tana. (1991). *All about where.* New York: Greenwillow.

Hoberman, Mary Ann. (1978, 1982). *A house is a house for me.* Illus. Betty Frasier. New York: Viking.

Hoberman, Mary Ann. (1991). *Fathers, mothers, sisters, brothers.* Illus. Marylin Hafner. Boston: Little, Brown.

Hoberman, Mary Ann. (1991). *A fine fat pig and other animal poems.* Illus. Malcah Zeldis. New York: HarperCollins.

Hodges, Margaret. (1957). *The wave.* Illus. Blair Lent. Boston: Houghton.

Hodges, Margaret. (1980). *The little humpbacked horse: A Russian tale retold.* Illus. Chris Conover. New York: Farrar, Straus & Giroux.

Hodges, Margaret. (1989). *Arrow and the lamp.* Boston: Little, Brown.

Hodges, Margaret. (1990). *The kitchen knight: A tale of King Arthur.* Illus. Trina Schart Hyman. New York: Holiday.

Hodges, Margaret. (1990). *Saint George and the dragon.* Illus. Trina Schart Hyman. Boston: Little, Brown.

Hodges, Margaret. (1991). *Brother Francis and the friendly beasts.* Illus. Ted Lewin. New York: Scribner's.

Hodges, Margaret. (1991). *St. Jerome and the lion.* Illus. Barry Moser. New York: Orchard.

Hoffman, Mary. (1991). *Amazing Grace.* Illus. Caroline Binch. New York: Dial.

Hogrogian, Nonny. (1965). *Always room for one more.* New York: Holt.

Hogrogian, Nonny. (1976). *The contest.* New York: Greenwillow.

Hogrogian, Nonny. (1986). *Noah's ark.* New York: Knopf.

Hoig, Stan. (1990). *A capitol for the nation.* New York: Dutton.

Holabird, Katharine. (1984). *Angelina and Alice.* Illus. Helen Craig. New York: Potter.

Holabird, Katharine. (1989). *Angelina's birthday surprise.* Illus. Helen Craig. New York: Potter.

Holder, Heide. (1981). *Aesop's fables.* Illus. Heide Holder. New York: Viking.

Holguin, Jiminez, Puncel, Emma Morales, & Puncel, Conchita Morales. (1969; o.p.). *Para chiquitines.* New York: Bowker.

Holland, Barbara. (1979). *Prisoners at the kitchen table.* Boston: Houghton.

Holman, Felice. (1974). *Slake's limbo.* New York: Scribner's.

Honeycutt, Natalie. (1991). *Ask me something easy.* New York: Orchard.

Hooks, William H. (1982). *Circle of fire.* New York: McElderry.

Hooks, William H. (1987). *Moss gown.* Illus. Donald Carrick. New York: Clarion.

Hooks, William H. (reteller). (1989). *The three little pigs and the fox.* Illus. S. D. Schindler. New York: Macmillan.

Hooks, William H. (reteller). (1990). *The ballad of Belle Dorcas.* Illus. Brian Pinkney. New York: Knopf.

Hoover, H. M. (1977; o.p.). *The delikon.* New York: Viking.

Hoover, H. M. (1984). *The shepherd moon.* New York: Viking.

Hoover, H. M. (1987). *Orvis.* New York: Viking, Penguin.

Hope, Laura Lee. (1904–present). *The Bobbsey twins* series. New York: Grosset.

Hopkins, Lee Bennett. (1986). *Surprises.* Illus. Megan Lloyd. New York: HarperCollins.

Hopkins, Lee Bennett. (1987). *Dinosaurs: Poems.* Illus. Murray Tinkelman. San Diego: Harcourt.

Hopkins, Lee Bennett. (1990). *Good books, good times.* Illus. Harvey Stevenson. New York: HarperCollins.

Hopkins, Lee Bennett. (1993 reissue). *Easter buds are springing.* Illus. Tomie de Paola. Honesdale, PA: Boyds Mills.

Hopkins, Lee Bennett. (1993 reissue). *Good morning to you, Valentine.* Illus. Tomie de Paola. Honesdale, PA: Boyds Mills.

Hopkins, Lee Bennett. (1993). *The writing bug.* Katonah, NY: Richard C. Owens.

Hopkins, Lee Bennett (ed.). (1987). *Click, rumble roar: Poems about machines.* New York: HarperCollins.

Hopkins, Lee Bennett (compiler). (1987). *More surprises.* Illus. Megan Lloyd. New York: HarperCollins.

Hopkins, Lee Bennett (selector). (1989). *Still as a star: A book of nighttime poems.* Illus. Karen Milone. Boston: Little, Brown.

Hopkins, Lee Bennett (selector). (1988; o.p.). *Voyages: Poems by Walt Whitman.* San Diego: Harcourt.

Hopkinson, Deborah. (1993). *Sweet Clara and the freedom quilt.* Illus. James Ransome. New York: Knopf.

Hotze, Sollace. (1988). *A circle unbroken.* New York: Clarion.

Hotze, Sollace. (1991). *Summer endings.* New York: Clarion.

Houston, Gloria. (1988). *The year of the perfect Christmas tree.* Illus. Barbara Cooney. New York: Dial.

Houston, Gloria. (1990). *Littlejim.* Illus. Thomas B. Allen. New York: Philomel.

Houston, Gloria. (1992). *My great aunt Arizona.* New York: HarperCollins.

Houston, James. (1977). *Frozen fire.* New York: McElderry.

Howard, Elizabeth F. (1991). *Aunt Flossie's hats (and crab cakes later).* Illus. James Ransome. New York: Clarion.

Howard, Ellen. (1987). *Edith herself.* New York: Atheneum.

Howard, Ellen. (1990). *Sister.* New York: Atheneum.

Howard, Ellen. (1991). *The chickenhouse house.* New York: Atheneum.

Howe, James. (1991). *Dew drop dead.* New York: Avon.

Howitt, Mary. (1839). *Hymns and fireside verses.* London: Darton.

Hoyt-Goldsmith, Diane. (1990). *Totem Pole.* Photos by Lawrence Migdale. New York: Holiday.

Hoyt-Goldsmith, Diane, & Migdale, Lawrence. (1991). *Pueblo storyteller.* New York: Holiday.

Hoyt-Goldsmith, Diane. (1992). *Hoang Anh: A Vietnamese-American boy.* Photos by Lawrence Migdale. New York: Holiday.

Huck, Charlotte. (1989). *Princess Furball.* Illus. Anita Lobel. New York: Greenwillow.

Huck, Charlotte. (1993). *Secret places.* Illus. Lindsay George. New York: Greenwillow.

Hudson, Jan. (1989). *Sweetgrass.* New York: Philomel.

Hudson, Jan. (1990). *Dawn rider.* New York: Philomel.

Hughes, Langston. (1962). *Dreamkeeper and other poems.* New York: Knopf.

Hughes, Shirley. (1988). *Alfie gives a hand.* New York: Lothrop.

Hughes, Shirley. (1990). *The snow lady.* New York: Lothrop.

Hughes, Shirley. (1991). *Wheels.* New York: Lothrop.

Hulme, Joy. (1991). *Sea squares.* Illus. Carol Schwartz. New York: Hyperion, Walt Disney.

Hulme, Joy. (1993). *What if? Poems of the imagination.* Illus. Valerie Gorbachev. Honesdale, PA: Boyds Mills.

Hunken, Jorie. (1989). *Botany for all ages: Learning about nature through activities using plants.* Chester, CT: Globe Pequot.

Hunken, Jorie. (1992). *Birdwatching for all ages: An activity book for children and adults.* Chester, CT: Globe Pequot.

Hunt, Irene. (1964). *Across five Aprils.* Chicago: Follett.

Hunt, Irene. (1988). *Up a road slowly.* New York: Scholastic.

Hunt, Jonathan. (1989). *Illuminations.* New York: Bradbury.

Hunter, Mollie. (1972; o.p.). *Sound of chariots.* New York: HarperCollins.

Hunter, Mollie. (1988). *The mermaid summer.* New York: HarperCollins.

Hunter, Mollie. (1975, 1977). *A stranger came ashore.* New York: HarperCollins.

Hurd, Thacher. (1992). *The quiet evening.* New York: Greenwillow.

Hurlimann, Ruth. (1973; o.p.). *The cat and mouse who shared a house.* Trans. Anthea Bell. New York: H. Z. Walck.

Hurmence, Belinda. (1984). *Tancy.* New York: Clarion.

Hurwitz, Johanna. (1978, 1989). *Much ado about Aldo.* New York: Morrow.

Hurwitz, Johanna. (1979). *Aldo Applesauce.* Illus. John Wallner. New York: Morrow.

Hurwitz, Johanna. (1980). *Once I was a plum tree.* New York: Morrow.

Hurwitz, Johanna. (1981). *Aldo ice cream.* New York: Morrow.

Hurwitz, Johanna. (1983). *Rip-roaring Russell.* New York: Morrow.

Hurwitz, Johanna. (1985). *Russell rides again.* New York: Morrow.

Hurwitz, Johanna. (1987). *The adventures of Ali Baba Bernstein.* Illus. Gail Owens. New York: Scholastic.

Hurwitz, Johanna. (1987). *Russell sprouts.* Illus. Lillian Hoban. New York: Morrow.

Hurwitz, Johanna. (1988). *Class clown.* New York: Scholastic.

Hurwitz, Johanna. (1989). *Astrid Lindgren: Storyteller to the world.* New York: Viking, Puffin.

Hurwitz, Johanna. (1989). *Russell and Elisa.* Illus. Lillian Hoban. New York: Morrow.

Hurwitz, Johanna. (1990). *Aldo peanut butter.* New York: Morrow.

Hurwitz, Johanna (1992). *School's out.* New York: Morrow.

Hutchins, Pat. (1971). *Changes, changes.* New York: Macmillan.

Hutchins, Pat. (1971). *Titch.* New York: Greenwillow.

Hutchins, Pat. (1978). *Happy birthday, Sam.* New York: Greenwillow.

Hutchins, Pat. (1983). *You'll soon grow into them, Titch.* New York: Greenwillow.

Hutchins, Pat. (1985). *Very worst monster.* New York: Greenwillow.

Hutchins, Pat. (1986). *The doorbell rang.* New York: Greenwillow.

Hutchins, Pat. (1988). *Where's the baby?* New York: Greenwillow.

Hutchins, Pat. (1990). *What game shall we play?* New York: Greenwillow.

Hutchins, Pat. (1970). *Clocks and more clocks.* New York: Macmillan.

Hutton, Warwick (adapter). (1987). *Adam and Eve: The Bible story.* New York: McElderry.

Hutton, Warwick. (1990). *Theseus and the minotaur.* New York: Macmillan.

Huynh, Quang Nhuong. (1986). *The land I lost: Adventures of a boy in Vietnam.* New York: HarperCollins.

Hyman, Trina Schart. (1979). *Self-portrait: Trina Schart Hyman.* Reading, MA: Addison-Wesley.

Igus, Toyomi, et al. (1991). *Book of black heroes, Vol. 2: Great women in the struggle: An introduction for young readers.* Orange, NJ: Just Us Books.

Innocenti, Robert, & Gallaz, Christophe. (1986). *Rose Blanche.* Trans. Richard Graglia & Martha Coventry. Mankato, MN: Creative Education.

Ipsen, David. (1985). *Isaac Newton, reluctant genius.* Hillside, NJ: Enslow.

Isaacman, Clara, & Grossman, Joan. (1984). *Clara's story, as told to Joan Adess Grossman.* Philadelphia: Jewish Publication Society.

Isadora, Rachel. (1985). *I see. I hear. I touch.* New York: Greenwillow. [Set]

Isadora, Rachel. (1989). *The princess and the frog.* New York: Greenwillow.

Isadora, Rachel. (1990). *Babies.* New York: Greenwillow.

Isadora, Rachel. (1990). *Friends.* New York: Greenwillow.

Isadora, Rachel. (1992). *Over the green hills.* New York: Greenwillow.

Isami, Ikuyo. (1989). *The fox's egg.* Trans. Cathy Hirano. Minneapolis: Carolrhoda.

Ishii, Momoko (reteller). (1987). *The tongue-cut sparrow.* Trans. Katherine Paterson. Illus. Suekichi Akaba. New York: Lodestar.

Issa. (1969; o.p.). *Don't tell the scarecrow.* New York: Four Winds.

Jackson, Jesse. (1945). *Call me Charley.* New York: HarperCollins.

Jacobs, Francine. (1992). *The Tainos: The people who welcomed Columbus.* New York: Putnam.

Jacobs, Joseph (reteller). (1989). *Tattercoats.* Illus. Margot Tomes. New York: Putnam.

Jacobs, Joseph. (1990). *Ardizonne's English fairy tales.* New York: Viking, Puffin.

Jacobs, William J. (1979). *Mother, Aunt Susan and me.* New York: Coward.

Jacobs, William J. (1990). *Ellis Island: New hope in a new land.* New York: Macmillan, Scribner's.

Jacobs, William J. (1990). *Great lives: Human rights.* New York: Scribner's.

Jacobs, William J. (1991). *Mother Teresa: Helping the poor.* New York: Millbrook.

Jacobs, William J. (1991). *Washington.* New York: Scribner's.

Jacques, Brian (1986). *Redwall.* New York: Philomel.

Jaffrey, Madhur (adapter). (1985). *Seasons of splendour: Tales, myths, and legends of India.* Illus. Michael Foreman. New York: Atheneum.

Jagendorf, M. A. (1957; o.p.). *Noodlehead stories from around the world.* New York: Vanguard.

Jakes, John. (1986). *Susanna of the Alamo: A true story.* San Diego: Harcourt.

Jakoubek, Robert. (1990). *Martin Luther King, Jr.* New York: Chelsea.

James, Betsy. (1990). *The dream stair.* New York: HarperCollins.

James, Elizabeth, & Barkin, Carol. (1991). *How to write a great school report.* New York: Morrow.

James, Elizabeth, & Barkin, Carol. (1991). *How to write your best book report.* New York: Morrow.

James, Simon. (1987). *Rome.* New York: Watts.

Jameson, Cynthia. (1973; o.p.). *The clay pot boy.* Illus. Arnold Lobel. New York: Coward.

Janeczko, Paul. (1985). *Pocket poems.* New York: Macmillan.

Janeczko, Paul. (1989). *Brickyard summer.* Illus. Ken Rush. New York: Orchard.

Janeczko, Paul B. (1990). *The place my words are*

looking for: What poets say about and through their work. New York: Bradbury.

Janeczko, Paul B. (selector). (1991). *Preposterous: Poems of youth.* New York: Orchard, Watts.

Janeway, James. (1672; 1976 reprint). *A token for children: Being an exact account of the conversation, holy and exemplary lives, and joyful deaths of several young children.* New York: Garland.

Jansson, Tove. (1964). *Tales from Moominvalley.* New York: Walck.

Jeffers, Susan. (1991). *Brother eagle, sister sky: A message from Chief Seattle.* New York: Dial.

Jenness, Aylette. (1989). *In two worlds: A Yup'ik Eskimo family.* Boston: Houghton.

Jernigan, Gisela. (1989). *One green mesquite tree.* Tucson: Harpinger House.

Johnson, Angela. (1989). *Tell me a story, Mama.* Illus. David Soman. New York: Orchard.

Johnson, Angela. (1990). *When I am old with you.* Illus. David Soman. New York: Orchard.

Johnson, Angela. (1991). *One of three.* Illus. David Soman. New York: Orchard.

Johnston, Tony. (1985). *The quilt story.* Illus. Tomie de Paola. New York: Putnam.

Johnston, Tony. (1988). *Yonder.* Illus. Lloyd Bloom. New York: Dial.

Johnston, Tony (adapter). (1990). *The badger and the magic fan.* Illus. Tomie de Paola. New York: Putnam.

Jonas, Ann. (1989). *Color dance.* New York: Greenwillow.

Jonas, Ann. (1990). *Aardvarks, disembark!* New York: Greenwillow.

Jones, Hettie (ed.). (1971). *The trees stand shining: Poetry of the North American Indians.* Illus. Robert Andrew Parker. New York: Dial.

Jones, Rebecca. (1991). *Matthew and Tilly.* New York: Dutton.

Joosse, Barbara. (1991). *Mama, do you love me?* Illus. Barbara Lavallee. San Francisco: Chronicle.

Josephs, Anna. (1985). *Mountain boy.* Illus. Bill Ersland. Milwaukee: Raintree.

Joyce, William. (1985, 1987). *George shrinks.* New York: HarperCollins.

Joyce, William. (1988). *Dinosaur Bob & his adventures with the Family Lazardo.* New York: HarperCollins.

Joyce, William. (1992). *Bentley and egg.* New York: HarperCollins.

The Juvenile Instructor magazine. (1866–?)

Juvenile Miscellany magazine. (1826–1834).

Kaizuki, Kiyonori. (1990). *A calf is born.* Trans. Cathy Hirano. New York: Orchard.

Kalman, Maira. (1989). *Sayonara, Mrs. Kackleman.* New York: Viking.

Kamen, Gloria. (1985). *Kipling: Storyteller of east and west.* New York: Atheneum.

Kandoian, Ellen. (1989). *Is anybody up?* New York: Putnam.

Karr, Kathleen. (1990). *It ain't always easy.* New York: Farrar, Straus & Giroux.

Katz, Michael Jay. (1990). *Ten potatoes in a pot: And other counting rhymes.* Illus. June Otani. New York: HarperCollins.

Katz, William Loren. (1990). *Breaking the chains: African-American slave resistance.* New York: Atheneum.

Kavanagh, Jack. (1992). *Walter Johnson.* New York: Chelsea.

Kaye, M. M. (1989). *The ordinary princess.* New York: Archway.

Keats, Ezra Jack. (1962). *The snowy day.* New York: Viking.

Keats, Ezra Jack. (1964). *Whistle for Willie.* New York: Viking.

Keats, Ezra Jack. (1967). *Peter's chair.* New York: HarperCollins.

Keats, Ezra Jack. (1984). *Kitten for a day.* New York: Four Winds.

Keats, Ezra Jack. (1987). *John Henry.* New York: Knopf.

Keegan, Marcia. (1991). *Pueblo boy: Growing up in two worlds.* New York: Dutton.

Kehoe, Michael. (1982). *The puzzle of books.* Minneapolis: Carolrhoda.

Keith, Harold. (1957). *Rifles for Watie.* New York: HarperCollins.

Keith, Harold. (1956; o.p.). *The obstinate land.* New York: HarperCollins.

Keller, Helen. (1954). *The story of my life.* New York: Doubleday.

Keller, Holly. (1991). *Horace.* New York: Greenwillow.

Keller, Holly. (1992). *Island baby.* New York: Greenwillow.

Kellogg, Steven. (1979). *Pinkerton behave.* New York: Dial.

Kellogg, Steven. (1984). *Paul Bunyan, a tall tale.* New York: Morrow.

Kellogg, Steven. (1986). *Best friends.* New York: Dial.

Kellogg, Steven. (1987). *Aster Aardvark's alphabet adventures.* New York: Morrow.

Kellogg, Steven. (1987). *Prehistoric Pinkerton.* New York: Dial.

Kellogg, Steven. (1988). *Johnny Appleseed.* New York: Morrow.

Kellogg, Steven. (1991). *Jack and the beanstalk.* New York: Morrow.

Kelly, Eric. (1973). *The trumpeter of Krakow.* New York: Macmillan.

Kendall, Carol. (1959, 1986, 1990). *The Gammage cup.* San Diego: Harcourt.

Kendall, Carol. (1986). *Whisper of Glocken.* San Diego: Harcourt.

Kendall, Martha E. (n.d.). *Elizabeth Cady Stanton.* Edina, MN: Highland.

Kendall, Russ. (1992). *Eskimo boy: Life in an Inupiaq Eskimo village.* New York: Scholastic.

Kennedy, X. J. (1985). *The forgetful wishing well: Poems for young people.* New York: McElderry.

Kennedy, X. J. (1989). *Ghastlies, goops & pincushions: Nonsense verse.* Illus. Ron Barrett. New York: McElderry.

Kennedy, X. J. (1990). *Fresh brats.* Illus. James Watts. New York: McElderry.

Kennedy, X. J., & Kennedy, Dorothy. (1985). *Knock at a star: A child's introduction to poetry.* Boston: Little, Brown.

Kennedy, X. J., & Kennedy, Dorothy. (1992). *Talking like the rain: A first book of poems.* Illus. Jane Dyer. Boston: Little, Brown.

Kent, Zachary. (1988). *Georgia.* San Francisco: Children's Book Press.

Kerby, Mona. (1990). *Amelia Earhart: Courage in the sky.* New York: Viking.

Kerr, Judith. (1972). *When Hitler stole pink rabbit.* New York: Putnam.

Kessler, Leonard. (1965). *Here comes the strikeout.* New York: HarperCollins.

Kessler, Leonard. (1969). *Last one in is a rotten egg.* New York: HarperCollins.

Key, Alexander. (1968). *Escape to Witch Mountain.* Philadelphia: Westminster, John Knox.

Key, Francis Scott. (1973). *Star spangled banner.* Illus. Peter Spier. New York: Doubleday.

Khalsa, Dayal Kaur. (1989). *How pizza came to Queens.* New York: Potter.

Kherdian, David. (1979). *The road from home: The story of an Armenian girl.* New York: Greenwillow.

Kherdian, David. (1981; o.p.). *Finding home.* New York: Greenwillow.

Kherdian, David. (1989). *A song for Uncle Harry.* Illus. Nonny Hogrogian. New York: Philomel.

Kidd, Diana. (1991). *Onion tears.* New York: Orchard.

Kightley, Rosalinda. (1986). *Opposites.* Boston: Little, Brown.

Killien, Christi. (1992). *The daffodils.* New York: Scholastic.

Kimmel, Eric. (1985). *Hershel and the Hanukkah goblins.* Illus. Trina Schart Hyman. New York: Holiday.

Kimmel, Eric. (1988). *Anansi and the moss-covered rock.* Illus. Janet Stevens. New York: Holiday.

Kimmel, Eric (adapter). (1991). *Days of awe: Stories for Rosh Hashanah and Yom Kippur.* Illus. Erika Weihs. New York: Viking.

Kimmel, Eric. (1993). *Anansi goes fishing.* Illus. Janet Stevens. New York: Holiday.

King, J. C. H. (1990). *Arctic hunters.* Vancouver: Firefly.

King-Smith, Dick. (1985). *Babe: The gallant pig.* New York: Crown.

King-Smith, Dick. (1988). *Martin's mice.* New York: Crown.

King-Smith, Dick. (1989). *Sophie's snail.* New York: Delacorte.

King-Smith, Dick. (1990). *Ace: The very important pig.* New York: Crown.

Kingsley, Charles. (1968 reissue). *Westward ho!* Airmont.

Kinsey-Warnock, Natalie. (1991). *The night the bells rang.* New York: Dutton.

Kipling, Rudyard. (1894; 1964 reissue). *The jungle book.* Illus. Robert Shore. New York: Macmillan.

Kipling, Rudyard. (1983). *The elephant's child.* San Diego: Harcourt.

Kipling, Rudyard. (1987). *The just-so stories.* Illus. Safaya Salter. New York: Holt.

Kismaric, Carole (adapter). (1988). *The rumor of Pavel Paali: A Ukranian folktale.* Illus. Charles Mikolaycak. New York: HarperCollins.

Kitamura, Satoshi. (1992). *From acorn to zoo: And everything in between in alphabetical order.* New York: Farrar, Straus & Giroux.

Kitchen, Bert. (1984). *Animal alphabet.* New York: Dial.

Klagsbrun, Francine. (1984, 1989). *Too young to die: Suicide and youth* (rev. ed). New York: Pocket.

Klausner, Janet. (1990). *Talk about English: How words travel and change.* Illus. Nancy Doniger. New York: HarperCollins.

Kline, Suzy. (1987). *Herbie Jones and the class gift.* Illus. Richard Williams. New York: Putnam.

Kline, Suzy. (1988). *Herbie Jones and the monster ball.* New York: Putnam.

Kline, Suzy. (1991). *Horrible Harry and the green slime.* Illus. Frank Remkiewicz. New York: Viking, Puffin.

Knight, Eric. (1978 reprint). *Lassie come home.* New York: Holt.

Knight, Margy Burns. (1992). *Talking walls.* Illus. Anne Sibley O'Brien. Gardner, ME: Tilbury.

Knowlton, Jack. (1991). *Books and libraries.* New York: HarperCollins.

Knudson, R. R. (1986). *Zanballer.* New York: Viking, Puffin.

Knudson, R. R. (1977). *Zanbanger.* New York: HarperCollins.

Knudson, R. R. (1978). *Zanboomer.* New York: HarperCollins.

Knudson, R. R., & Swenson, May. (1988). *American sports poems.* New York: Orchard, Watts.

Knutson, Barbara. (1987). *Why the crab has no head.* Minneapolis: Carolrhoda.

Koch, Michelle. (1989). *Just one more.* New York: Greenwillow.

Koertge, Ron. (1991). *Mariposa blues.* Boston: Little, Brown.

Koller, Jackie French. (1991). *Nothing to fear.* San Diego: Harcourt.

Konigsburg, Elaine. (1967). *From the mixed-up files of Mrs. Basil E. Frankweiler.* New York: Macmillan, Atheneum.

Konigsburg, Elaine. (1973). *A proud taste for Scarlet and Miniver.* New York: Atheneum.

Koren, Edward (1972; o.p.). *Behind the wheel.* New York: Holt.

Korman, Gordon. (1984). *I want to go home!* New York: Scholastic.

Korman, Gordon. (1985). *No coins, please.* New York: Scholastic.

Korman, Gordon. (1988). *The zucchini warriors.* New York: Scholastic.

Korman, Gordon. (1992). *The twinkle squad.* New York: Scholastic.

Kovalski, Maryann. (1987). *The wheels on the bus.* Boston: Little, Brown, Joy Street.

Krantz, Hazel. (1992). *Daughter of my people: Henrietta Szold and Hadassah.* New York: Dutton.

Krasilovsky, Phyllis. (1950). *The man who didn't wash his dishes.* Illus. Barbara Cooney. New York: Doubleday.

Kraus, Robert. (1986). *Whose mouse are you?* Illus. Jose Aruego. New York: Macmillan.

Krauss, Ruth. (1953). *A very special house.* Illus. Maurice Sendak. New York: HarperCollins.

Krementz, Jill. (1986). *A very young dancer.* New York: Dell.

Krementz, Jill. (1991). *A very young musician.* New York: Simon & Schuster.

Kresh, Paul. (1984). *Isaac Bashevis Singer: The story of a storyteller.* New York: Dutton.

Kresh, Paul. (1988). *An American rhapsody: The story of George Gershwin.* New York: Dutton.

Kroeber, Theodora. (1964; o.p.). *Ishi, last of his tribe.* Berkeley: Parnassus.

Kroll, Steven. (1989). *The hokey pokey man.* Illus. Deborah Kogan Ray. New York: Holiday.

Krull, Kathleen. (1992). *Gonna sing my head off!* Illus. Allen Garns. New York: Knopf.

Kudlinski, Kathleen V. (1988). *Rachel Carson: Pioneer of ecology.* Illus. Ted Lewin. New York: Viking.

Kudlinski, Kathleen V. (1991). *Pearl Harbor is burning: A story of World War II.* New York: Viking.

Kuhn, Dwight. (1988). *The hidden life of the pond.* New York: Crown.

Kuklin, Susan. (1992). *How my family lives in America.* New York: Bradbury.

Kunhardt, Dorothy. (1940). *Pat the bunny.* Racine, WI: Western.

Kunhardt, Edith. (1990). *Which pig would you choose?* New York: Greenwillow.

Kurtycz, Marcos. (1984). *Tigers and opossums: Animal legends.* Boston: Little, Brown.

Kushner, Arlene. (1986). *Falasha no more: An Ethiopian Jewish child comes home.* New York: Shapolsky.

Kuskin, Karla. (1956, 1991). *Roar and more.* New York: HarperCollins.

Kuskin, Karla. (1959). *Just like everyone else.* New York: HarperCollins.

Kuskin, Karla. (1980). *Dogs and dragons, trees and dreams.* New York: HarperCollins.

Kuskin, Karla. (1985). *Something's sleeping in the hall.* New York: HarperCollins.

Kuskin, Karla. (1987). *Jerusalem, shining still.* Illus. David Frampton. New York: HarperCollins.

Kuskin, Karla. (1992). *Soap soup.* New York: HarperCollins.

La Fontaine, J. D. (1987). *The hare and the tortoise.* New York: Oxford University Press.

La Fontaine, J. D. (1987). *The lion and the rat.* New York: Oxford University Press.

La Fontaine, J. D. (1987). *The north wind and the sun.* New York: Oxford University Press.

La Fontaine, J. D. (1965; o.p.). *The rich man and the shoemaker.* Illus. Brian Wildsmith. New York: Watts.

Lagercrantz, Rose, & Lagercrantz, Samuel. (1990). *Is it magic?* Illus. Eva Eriksson. New York: Farrar, Straus & Giroux.

Laird, Christa. (1990). *Shadow of the wall.* New York: Greenwillow.

Laird, Elizabeth. (1987). *The road to Bethlehem: An Ethiopian nativity.* New York: Holt.

Lambert, David. (1986). *Planet Earth 2000.* San Francisco: Facts on File.

Lang, Andrew. (1988 reprint). *The blue fairy book.* New York: Puffin, Viking.

Lang, Aubrey. (1990). *Eagles.* Illus, Wayne Lynch. Boston: Little, Brown.

Langstaff, John. (1987). *What a morning! The Christmas story in black spirituals.* Illus. Ashley Bryan. New York: McElderry.

Langstaff, John. (1991). *Climbing Jacob's ladder: Heroes of the Bible in African-American spirituals.* Illus. Ashley Bryan. Music arranged by John Andrew Ross. New York: McElderry.

Lankford, Mary. (1992). *Hopscotch around the world.* Illus. Karen Milone. New York: Morrow.

Larrick, Nancy. (1970; o.p.). *I heard a scream in the street.* New York: M. Evans.

Larrick, Nancy. (1988). *Bring me all of your dreams.* New York: M. Evans.

Larrick, Nancy (compiler). (1988). *Cats are cats.* Illus. Ed Young. New York: Philomel.

Larrick, Nancy (compiler). (1989). *Songs from Mother Goose.* Illus. Robin Spowart. New York: HarperCollins.

Larrick, Nancy. (1990). *Mice are nice.* Illus. Ed Young. New York: Philomel.

Lasker, Joe. (1974). *He's my brother.* Niles, IL: Whitman.

Lasker, Joe. (1978). *Merry ever after: The story of*

two medieval weddings. New York: Viking, Penguin.

Lasker, Joe. (1986). *A tournament of knights.* New York: HarperCollins.

Lasky, Kathryn. (1986). *The night journey.* Illus. Trina Schart Hyman. New York: Viking.

Lasky, Kathryn. (1989). *Traces of life: The origins of humankind.* Illus. Whitney Powell. New York: Morrow.

Lasky, Kathryn. (1990). *Dinosaur dig.* Photos by Christopher Knight. New York: Morrow.

Latham, Jean Lee. (1957; o.p.). *This dear-bought land.* New York: HarperCollin.

Latham, Jean Lee. (1973). *Carry on, Mr. Bowditch.* Boston: Houghton.

Latham, Jean Lee. (1991). *David Glasgow Farragut: Our first admiral.* New York: Chelsea.

Lattimore, Deborah Nourse. (1988). *The prince and the golden ax.* New York: HarperCollins.

Lattimore, Deborah Nourse. (1989). *Why there is no arguing in heaven: A Mayan myth.* New York: HarperCollins.

Lattimore, Deborah Nourse. (1990). *The dragon's robe.* New York: HarperCollins.

Lattimore, Deborah Nourse. (1991). *The sailor who captured the sea: A story of the Book of Kells.* New York: HarperCollins.

Lauber, Patricia. (1987). *Get ready for robots.* Illus. True Kelley. New York: HarperCollins.

Lauber, Patricia. (1988). *Lost star: The story of Amelia Earhart.* New York: Scholastic.

Lauber, Patricia. (1988). *Snakes are hunters.* Illus. Holly Keller. New York: HarperCollins.

Lauber, Patricia. (1990). *Seeing earth from space.* New York: Orchard.

Lavies, Bianca. (1990). *Backyard hunter: The praying mantis.* New York: Dutton.

Lawlor, Laurie. (1989). *Daniel Boone.* Niles, IL: A. Whitman.

Lawrence, Louise. (1978). *Star lord.* New York: HarperCollins.

Lawrence, Louise. (1985). *Children of the dust.* New York: HarperCollins.

Lawson, John. (1990 reissue). *You better come home with me.* New York: HarperCollins.

Lawson, Robert. (1939). *Ben and me: A new and astonishing life of Benjamin Franklin as written by his good mouse Amos.* Boston: Little, Brown.

Lawson, Robert. (1944). *Rabbit hill.* New York: Viking.

Lawson, Robert. (1953). *Mr. Revere and I.* Boston: Little, Brown.

Lazo, Caroline E. (1990). *Endangered species.* New York: Macmillan.

Lear, Edward. (1846; 1976 reprint). *A book of nonsense.* New York: Garland.

Lear, Edward. (1987). *Owl and the pussycat.* Illus. Paul Galdone. New York: Houghton, Clarion.

Lear, Edward. (1992). *The complete nonsense of Edward Lear.* New York: Knopf.

Lee, Betsy. (1981). *Judy Blume's story.* New York: Dillon.

Lee, Dennis. (1977). *Garbage delight.* Boston: Houghton.

Lee, Dennis. (1979). *Alligator pie.* Boston: Houghton.

Lee, Jeanne. (1987). *Ba-nam.* New York: Holt.

Lee, Jeanne. (1991). *Silent lotus.* New York: Farrar, Straus & Giroux.

Le Guin, Ursula. (1968). *Wizard of earthsea.* Illus. Ruth Robbins. Boston: Houghton.

Le Guin, Ursula. (1971). *The tombs of Atuan.* New York: Atheneum.

Le Guin, Ursula. (1972). *The farthest shore.* New York: Atheneum.

Le Guin, Ursula. (1990). *Tehanu: The last book of Earthsea.* New York: Atheneum.

Lehrman, Robert. (1992). *The store that Mama built.* New York: Macmillan.

L'Engle, Madeleine. (1965). *The arm of the starfish.* New York: Farrar, Straus & Giroux.

L'Engle, Madeleine. (1962). *A wrinkle in time.* New York: Farrar, Straus & Giroux.

L'Engle, Madeleine. (1973). *A wind in the door.* New York: Farrar, Straus & Giroux.

L'Engle, Madeleine. (1978). *A swiftly tilting planet.* New York: Farrar, Straus & Giroux.

L'Engle, Madeleine. (1986). *Many waters.* New York: Farrar, Straus & Giroux.

Lennon, Adrian. (1992; o.p.). *Jorge Luis Borges.* New York: Chelsea.

Lenski, Lois. (1987). *Sing a song of people.* Illus. Giles Laroche. Boston: Little, Brown.

Leonard, Laura. (1989). *Saving Damaris.* New York: Atheneum.

Leonard, Laura. (1991). *Finding papa.* New York: Atheneum.

Lessac, Frané. (1989). *Caribbean canvas.* New York: HarperCollins.

Lester, Julius. (1968). *To be a slave.* Illus. Tom Feelings. New York: Dial.

Lester, Julius. (1972). *Long journey home: Stories from black history.* New York: Dial.

Lester, Julius. (1987). *The tales of Uncle Remus: The adventures of Brer Rabbit.* Illus. Jerry Pinkney. New York: Dial.

Lester, Julius. (1988). *More tales of Uncle Remus: Further adventures of Brer Rabbit, his friends, enemies, and others.* Illus. Jerry Pinkney. New York: Dial.

Lester, Julius. (1989). *How many spots does a leopard have?* Illus. David Shannon. New York: Scholastic.

Lester, Julius. (1990). *Further tales of Uncle Remus: The misadventures of Brer Rabbit, Brer Fox, Brer Wolf, the Doodang, and other creatures.* Illus. Jerry Pinkney. New York: Dial.

Levin, Betty. (1990). *Brother Moose.* New York: Greenwillow.

Levine, Arthur A. (1991). *All the lights in the night.* Illus. James Ransome. New York: Morrow.

Levinson, Nancy Smiler. (1986). *I lift my lamp: Emma Lazarus and the Statue of Liberty.* New York: Dutton.

Levinson, Nancy Smiler. (1988). *Clara and the bookwagon.* New York: HarperCollins.

Levinson, Nancy Smiler. (1990). *Christopher Columbus.* New York: Dutton.

Levinson, Riki. (1985). *Watch the stars come out.* Illus. Diane Goode. New York: Dutton.

Levinson, Riki. (1987). *DinnieAbbieSister-r-r!* New York: Bradbury.

Levinson, Riki. (1990). *I go with my family to Grandma's.* Illus. Diane Goode. New York: Dutton.

Levitin, Sonia. (1973; o.p.). *Roanoke: A novel of the lost colony.* New York: Atheneum.

Levitin, Sonia. (1987). *Journey to America.* New York: Macmillan.

Levitin, Sonia. (1987). *The mark of Conte.* New York: Macmillan.

Levitin, Sonia. (1987). *The return.* New York: Atheneum.

Levitin, Sonia. (1989). *Silver days.* New York: Macmillan.

Levy, Elizabeth. (1982). *Something queer is going on (a mystery).* New York: Dell.

Levy, Elizabeth. (1983). *The shadow nose.* New York: Morrow.

Lewis, Claudia. (1987). *Long ago in Oregon.* Illus. Joel Fontaine. New York: HarperCollins.

Lewis, Claudia. (1991). *Up in the mountains and other poems of long ago.* Illus. Joel Fontaine. New York: HarperCollins, Zolotow.

Lewis, C. S. (1950). *The lion, the witch, and the wardrobe.* Illus. Pauline Baynes. New York: Macmillan.

Lewis, C. S. (1955). *The magician's nephew.* Illus. Pauline Baynes. New York: Macmillan.

Lewis, C. S. (1950–1955). *Narnia* series. New York: Macmillan.

Lewis, J. Patrick. (1990). *A hippopotamusn't: And other animal verses.* Illus. Victoria Chess. New York: Dial.

Lewis, Richard. (1965; 1989 reprint). *In a spring garden.* Illus. Ezra Jack Keats. New York: Dial.

Lewis, Richard. (1991). *All of you was singing.* Illus. Ed Young. New York: Atheneum.

Lewison, Wendy C. (1992). *Going to sleep on the farm.* Illus. Juan Wijngaard. New York: Dial.

Liestman, Vicki. (1991). *Columbus Day.* Minneapolis: Carolrhoda.

Lindbergh, Anne. (1992). *Travel far, pay no fare.* New York: HarperCollins.

Lindbergh, Reeve. (1990). *Johnny Appleseed; a poem.* Illus. Kathy Jacobsen. Boston: Little, Brown.

Linden, Ann Marie. (1992). *One smiling grandma.* Illus. Lynne Russell. New York: Dial.

Lindgren, Astrid. (1950). *Pippi Longstocking.* New York: Viking.

Lindgren, Astrid. (1985). *Ronia, the robber's daughter.* New York: Viking, Puffin.

Lindgren, Astrid. (1988). *I don't want to go to bed.* Illus. Ilon Wikland. Trans. Barbara Lucas. New York: Farrar, Straus & Giroux.

Lindgren, Astrid. (1988). *I want a brother or sister.* Illus. Ilon Wikland. Trans. Eric Bibb. New York: Farrar, Straus & Giroux.

Lindgren, Astrid. (1991). *Lotta on Troublemaker Street.* Illus. Julie Brinckloe. New York: Macmillan.

Lingard, Joan. (1991). *Between two worlds.* New York: Dutton.

Lingard, Joan. (1990). *Tug of war.* New York: Dutton.

Lionni, Leo. (1959). *Little blue and little yellow.* New York: Astor.

Lionni, Leo. (1962). *Inch by inch.* New York: Astor.

Lionni, Leo. (1963). *Swimmy.* New York: Knopf.

Lionni, Leo. (1970; 1987). *Fish is fish.* New York: Knopf.

Lionni, Leo. (1975). *Pezzetino.* New York: Pantheon.

Lipsyte, Robert. (1967). *The contender.* New York: HarperCollins.

Lipsyte, Robert. (1991). *The brave.* New York: HarperCollins.

Lisle, Janet Taylor. (1989). *Afternoon of the elves.* New York: Orchard, Watts.

Litowinsky, Olga. (1991). *The high voyage: The final crossing of Christopher Columbus.* New York: Delacorte.

Littke, Lael. (1991). *Blue skye.* New York: Scholastic.

Little, Jean. (1962). *Mine for keeps.* Boston: Little, Brown.

Little, Jean. (1965). *Home from far.* Boston: Little, Brown.

Little, Jean. (1972). *From Anna.* New York: HarperCollins.

Little, Jean. (1977, 1991). *Listen for the singing.* New York: HarperCollins.

Little, Jean (1985). *Mama's going to buy you a mockingbird.* New York: Viking, Kestrel.

Little, Jean. (1987). *Different dragons.* New York: Viking.

Little, Jean. (1987). *Little by little: A writer's education.* New York: Viking, Kestrel.

Little, Jean. (1989). *Hey world, here I am.* New York: HarperCollins.

Little, Jean. (1992). *Jess was the brave one.* New York: Viking.

Little, Jean. (1992). *Stars come out within.* New York: Viking.

Livingston, Myra Cohn. (1979). *O sliver of liver.* Illus. Iris Van Rynbach. New York: Atheneum.

Livingston, Myra Cohn. (1982). *Why am I grown so cold? Poems of the unknowable.* New York: Macmillan.

Livingston, Myra Cohn. (1984). *Sky songs.* Illus. Leonard Everett Fisher. New York: Holiday.

Livingston, Myra Cohn. (1986). *Higgledy piggledy: Verses and pictures.* New York: Macmillan.

Livingston, Myra Cohn. (1986). *Sea songs.* Illus. Leonard Everett Fisher. New York: Holiday.

Livingston, Myra Cohn. (1987). *Cat poems.* Illus. Trina Schart Hyman. New York: Holiday.

Livingston, Myra Cohn. (1987). *I like you, if you like me.* New York: Macmillan.

Livingston, Myra Cohn. (1988). *Poems for mothers.* Illus. Deborah Kogan Ray. New York: Holiday.

Livingston, Myra Cohn. (1988). *Space songs.* Illus. Leonard Everett Fisher. New York: Holiday.

Livingston, Myra Cohn. (1988). *There was a place and other poems.* New York: McElderry.

Livingston, Myra Cohn. (1989). *Halloween poems.* Illus. Stephen Gammell. New York: Holiday.

Livingston, Myra Cohn. (1990). *Dog poems.* Illus. Leslie Morrill. New York: Holiday.

Livingston, Myra Cohn. (1991). *Poem making.* New York: HarperCollins.

Livingston, Myra Cohn (selector). (1986). *Poems for Jewish Holidays.* Illus. Lloyd Bloom. New York: Holiday.

Lobel, Anita. (1991). *The dwarf giant.* New York: Holiday.

Lobel, Arnold. (1970). *Frog and Toad are friends.* New York: HarperCollins.

Lobel, Arnold. (1971). *On the day Peter Stuyvesant sailed into town.* New York: HarperCollins.

Lobel, Arnold. (1972). *Frog and Toad together.* New York: HarperCollins.

Lobel, Arnold. (1976). *Frog and Toad all year.* New York: HarperCollins.

Lobel, Arnold. (1979). *Days with Frog and Toad.* New York: HarperCollins.

Lobel, Arnold. (1980). *Fables.* New York: HarperCollins.

Lobel, Arnold. (1981). *On Market Street.* Illus. Anita Lobel. New York: Greenwillow.

Lobel, Arnold. (1985). *Whiskers and rhymes.* New York: Greenwillow.

Lobel, Arnold. (1986). *The Random House book of Mother Goose.* New York: Random.

Lobel, Arnold. (1988). *The book of pigericks.* New York: HarperCollins.

Locker, Thomas. (1984). *Where the river begins.* New York: Dial.

Locker, Thomas. (1985). *Mare on the hill.* New York: Dial.

Locker, Thomas. (1987). *The boy who held back the sea.* New York: Dial.

Locker, Thomas. (1988). *Family farm.* New York: Dial.

Loh, Morag. (1987). *Tucking mommy in.* Illus. Donna Rawlins. New York: Orchard.

London, Jack. (1970). *Call of the wild.* New York: Macmillan.

Longfellow, Henry Wadsworth. (1983). *Hiawatha.* Illus. Susan Jeffers. New York: Dial.

Longfellow, Henry Wadsworth. (1984). *Hiawatha's childhood.* Illus. Errol Le Cain. New York: Farrar, Straus & Giroux.

Longfellow, Henry Wadsworth. (1985). *Paul Revere's ride.* Illus. Nancy Winslow Parker. New York: Greenwillow.

Longfellow, Henry Wadsworth. (1990). *Paul Revere's ride.* Illus. Ted Rand. New York: Dutton.

Lord, Bette Bao. (1984). *In the year of the boar and Jackie Robinson.* New York: HarperCollins.

Lord, Bette Bao. (1982; o.p.). *Spring moon.* New York: Avon.

Louie, Ai-Ling. (1990). *Yeh-Shen: A Cinderella story from China.* Illus. Ed Young. New York: Philomel.

Lourie, Peter. (1991). *Amazon: A young reader's look at the last frontier.* Photos by Marcos Santilli. Honesdale, PA: Boyds Mills.

Lourie, Peter. (1992). *Hudson River.* Honesdale, PA: Boyds Mills.

Lowery, Linda. (1991). *Earth Day.* Minneapolis: Carolrhoda.

Lowry, Lois. (1977). *A summer to die.* Boston: Houghton.

Lowry, Lois. (1979). *Anastasia Krupnik.* Boston: Houghton.

Lowry, Lois. (1980). *Autumn Street.* Boston: Houghton.

Lowry, Lois. (1982). *Anastasia at your service.* Boston: Houghton.

Lowry, Lois. (1985). *Anastasia has the answers.* Boston: Houghton.

Lowry, Lois. (1985). *Anastasia on her own.* Boston: Houghton.

Lowry, Lois. (1987). *Anastasia's chosen career.* Boston: Houghton.

Lowry, Lois. (1987). *Rabble Starkey.* Boston: Houghton.

Lowry, Lois. (1988). *All about Sam.* Illus. Diane deGroat. Boston: Houghton.

Lowry, Lois. (1989). *Number the stars.* Boston: Houghton.

Ludwig, Warren. (1991). *Old Noah's elephants.* New York: Whitebird, Putnam.

Lunn, Janet. (1983). *The root cellar.* New York: Scribner's.

Lydon, Kerry Raines. (1989). *A birthday for Blue.* Niles, IL: A. Whitman.

Lyon, George Ella. (1988). *Borrowed children.* New York: Orchard.

Lyon, George Ella. (1989). *Red rover, red rover.* New York: Orchard.

Lyon, George Ella. (1989). *Together.* Illus. Vera Rosenberry. New York: Orchard.

Lyon, George Ella. (1990). *Come a tide.* Illus. Stephen Gammell. New York: Orchard.

Lyon, George Ella. (1991). *Cecil's story.* Illus. Peter Catalanotto. New York: Orchard.

Lyons, Mary E. (1990). *Sorrow's kitchen: The life and folklore of Zora Neale Hurston.* New York: Scribner's.

Lyons, Mary. (1991). *Raw head, bloody bones: African American tales of the supernatural.* New York: Scribner's.

Lyttle, Richard. (1989). *Pablo Picasso: The man and his image.* New York: Atheneum.

Maartens, Maretha. (1991). *Paper bird.* Boston: Houghton.

MacCarthy, Patricia. (1991). *Herds of words.* New York: Dial.

Macaulay, David. (1973). *Cathedral: The story of its construction.* Boston: Houghton.

Macaulay, David. (1975). *Pyramid.* Boston: Houghton.

Macaulay, David. (1977). *Castle.* Boston: Houghton.

Macaulay, David. (1983). *City: A story of Roman planning and construction.* Boston: Houghton.

Macaulay, David. (1987). *Why the chicken crossed the road.* Boston: Houghton.

Macaulay, David. (1988). *The way things work.* Boston: Houghton.

Macaulay, David. (1990). *Black and white.* Boston: Houghton.

MacDonald, Amy. (1990). *Rachel Fister's blister.* Illus. Marjorie Priceman. Boston: Houghton.

MacDonald, Caroline. (1989). *The lake at the end of the world.* New York: Dial.

MacDonald, Fiona. (1990). *A medieval castle.* Illus. Mark Bergin. New York: P. Bedrick.

MacDonald, Fiona. (1990). *A 19th century railway station.* Illus. John James. New York: P. Bedrick.

MacDonald, Suse. (1986). *Alphabatics.* New York: Bradbury.

MacDonald, Suse. (1990). *Once upon another: The tortoise and the hare—the lion and the mouse.* Reteller & Illus. Suse MacDonald & Bill Oakes. New York: Doubleday.

MacGill-Callahan, Sheila. (1991). *And still the turtle watched.* Illus. Barry Moser. New York: Dial.

Macht, Norman L. (1991). *Christy Mathewson.* New York: Chelsea.

Macht, Norman L. (1991). *Satchel Paige.* New York: Chelsea.

Macht, Norman L. (1992). *Cy Young.* New York: Chelsea.

McKay, David. (1969). *A flock of words: An anthology of poetry for children and others.* Illus. Margery Gill. San Diego: Harcourt.

MacKinnon, Bernie. (1991). *Song for a shadow.* Boston: Houghton.

MacLachlan, Patricia. (1980). *Arthur, for the very first time.* New York: HarperCollins.

MacLachlan, Patricia. (1983). *Seven kisses in a row.* Illus. Maria Pia Marrella. New York: HarperCollins.

MacLachlan, Patricia. (1984). *Unclaimed treasures.* New York: HarperCollins.

MacLachlan, Patricia. (1985). *Sarah, plain and tall.* New York: HarperCollins.

MacLachlan, Patricia. (1988). *The facts and fictions of Minna Pratt.* New York: HarperCollins.

MacLachlan, Patricia. (1991). *Journey.* New York: Delacorte.

MacLachlan, Patricia. (1991). *Three names.* New York: HarperCollins.

Maestro, Betsy. (1989). *Snow day.* Illus. Giulio Maestro. New York: Scholastic.

Maestro, Betsy, & Maestro, Giulio. (1987). *More perfect union: The story of our constitution.* New York: Lothrop.

Maestro, Betsy & Maestro, Giulio. (1991). *The discovery of the Americas.* New York: Lothrop.

Magorian, Michelle. (1982). *Good Night Mr. Tom.* New York: HarperCollins.

Mahy, Margaret. (1986). *Aliens in the family.* New York: Scholastic.

Mahy, Margaret. (1987). *17 kings and 42 elephants.* Illus. Patricia MacCarthy. New York: Dial.

Mahy, Margaret. (1988). *Memory.* New York: Macmillan, McElderry.

Mahy, Margaret. (1989). *The great white man-eating shark: A cautionary tale.* Illus. Jonathan Allen. New York: Dial.

Mahy, Margaret. (1990). *The seven Chinese brothers.* Illus. Jean Tseng and Mou-Sien Tseng. New York: Scholastic.

Mahy, Margaret. (1992). *The horrendous hullabaloo.* Illus. Patricia MacCarthy. New York: Viking.

Malam, John (1991). *Pop-up dinosaurs.* Illus. Andy Eveeret-Stewart and Dudley Moseley. New York: Random.

Mallory, K. (1989). *Rescue of the stranded whales.* New York: Simon & Schuster.

Malnig, Anita. (1985). *Where the waves break: Life at the edge of the sea.* Minneapolis: Carolrhoda.

Malory, Sir Thomas. (1988). *Le morte d'Arthur.* New York: Crown.

Manes, Stephen. (1991). *Make four million dollars by next Thursday.* New York: Bantam.

Manniche, Lise. (1982). *The prince who knew his fate.* New York: Philomel.

Marcus, Leonard, & Schwartz, Amy. (1990). *Mother Goose's little misfortunes.* Illus. Amy Schwartz. New York: Bradbury.

Margolis, Richard. (1984). *Secrets of a small*

brother. Illus. Donald Carrick. New York: Macmillan.

Marino, Jan. (1991). *The day that Elvis came to town.* Boston: Little, Brown.

Markle, Sandra. (1991). *Earth alive.* New York: Lothrop.

Marrin, Albert. (1987). *Hitler.* New York: Viking.

Marrin, Albert. (1991). *The Spanish-American war.* New York: Atheneum.

Marsden, John (1989). *So much to tell you.* Boston: Little, Brown, Joy Street.

Marshak, Samuel. (1989). *The pup grew up.* Trans. Richard Pevear. Illus. Vladimir Radunsky. New York: Holt.

Marshall, Edward. (1982). *Space case.* New York: Dial.

Marshall, James. (1979). *James Marshall's Mother Goose.* New York: Farrar, Straus & Giroux.

Marshall, James. (1988). *Goldilocks and the three bears.* New York: Dial.

Marshall, James. (1991). *Old Mother Hubbard and her wonderful dog.* New York: Farrar, Straus & Giroux.

Marshall, James. (1992). *The cut-ups crack up.* Viking.

Martin, Bill, Jr. (1964, 1992). *Brown bear, brown bear, what do you see?* Illus. Eric Carle. New York: Henry Holt.

Martin, Bill, Jr. (1991). *Polar bear, polar bear, what do you hear?* Illus. Eric Carle. New York: Henry Holt.

Martin, Bill, Jr., & Archambault, John. (1985). *The ghost eye tree.* Illus. Ted Rand. New York: Holt.

Martin, Bill, Jr., & Archambault, John. (1987). *Here are my hands.* Illus. Ted Rand. New York: Holt.

Martin, Bill, Jr., & Archambault, John. (1987). *Knots on a counting rope.* New York: Henry Holt.

Martin, Bill, Jr., & Archambault, John. (1988). *Up and down on the merry-go-round.* Illus. Ted Rand. New York: Holt.

Martin, Bill, Jr., & Archambault, John. (1989). *Chicka chicka boom boom.* Illus. Lois Ehlert. New York: Simon & Schuster.

Martin, C. L. G. (1988). *The dragon nanny.* Illus. Robert Rayevsky. New York: Macmillan.

Martin, Jacqueline Briggs. (1992). *Good times on grandfather mountain.* Illus. Susan Gaber. New York: Orchard.

Martin, Rafe. (1989). *Will's mammoth.* Illus. Stephen Gammell. New York: Putnam.

Martin, Rafe. (1992). *The rough-face girl.* Illus. David Shannon. New York: Putnam.

Martin, Rafe. (1992). *A storyteller's story.* Photos by Jill Krementz. Katonah, NY: Richard C. Owens.

Maruki, Toshi. (1982). *Hiroshima, no pika.* New York: Lothrop.

Marzollo, Jean (1984). *Ruthie's rude friends.* New York: Dial.

Marzollo, Jean. (1989). *Jed and the space bandits.* New York: Dial.

Marzollo, Jean. (1990). *Pretend you're a cat.* Illus. Jerry Pinkney. New York: Dial.

Marzollo, Jean. (1991). *In 1492.* Illus. Steve Bjorkman. New York: Scholastic.

Marzollo, Jean, & Marzollo, Claudio. (1982). *Jed's junior space patrol.* Illus. David Rose. New York: Dial.

Mather, Cotton. (1749). *A token for the children of New England, or some examples of children in whom the fear of God was remarkably budding before they died.* Philadelphia: Franklin & Hall.

Mathers, Petra. (1991). *Sophie and Lou.* New York: HarperCollins.

Mathews, Louise. (1991). *Bunches and bunches of bunnies.* New York: Scholastic.

Mathis, Sharon Bell. (1975). *The hundred penny box.* Illus. Leo & Diane Dillon. New York: Viking.

Matthews, Downs. (1989). *Polar bear cubs.* Photos by Dan Guravich. New York: Simon & Schuster.

Mayer, Marianna. (1988). *Iduna and the magic apples.* Illus. Laszlo Gal. New York: Macmillan.

Mayer, Marianna. (1989). *The prince and the princess: A Bohemian fairy tale.* Illus. Jacqueline Rogers. New York: Skylark/Bantam.

Mayer, Mercer. (1967). *A boy, a dog, and a frog.* New York: Dial.

Mayer, Mercer. (1974). *Frog goes to dinner.* New York: Dial.

Mayer, Mercer. (1976). *Hiccup.* New York: Dial.

Mayerson, Evelyn. (1990). *The cat who escaped from steerage.* New York: Scribner's.

Mayhew, James. (1991). *Madame Nightingale will sing tonight.* New York: Bantam.

Mazer, Norma Fox. (1973). *A figure of speech.* New York: Dell.

Mazer, Norma Fox. (1983). *Taking Terri Mueller.* New York: Morrow.

Mazer, Norma Fox. (1987). *After the rain.* New York: Morrow.

McAfee, Annalena. (1985). *The visitors who came to stay.* Illus. Anthony Browne. New York: Viking.

McCaffrey, Anne. (1976). *Dragonsong.* New York: Atheneum.

McCloskey, Robert. (1941). *Make way for ducklings.* New York: Viking.

McCloskey, Robert. (1943). *Homer Price.* New York: Viking.

McCloskey, Robert. (1948). *Blueberries for Sal.* New York: Viking.

McCloskey, Robert. (1952). *One morning in Maine.* New York: Viking.

McCloskey, Robert. (1957). *Time of wonder.* New York: Viking.

McCord, David. (1977; 1986 reissue). *One at a time.* Boston: Little, Brown.

McCully, Emily Arnold. (1984). *Picnic.* New York: HarperCollins.

McCully, Emily Arnold. (1987). *School.* New York: HarperCollins.

McCully, Emily Arnold. (1988). *New baby.* New York: HarperCollins.

McCully, Emily Arnold. (1992). *Mirette on the high wire.* New York: Putnam.

McCunn, Ruthanne Lum. (1983; o.p.). *Pie biter.* Illus. You-shan Tang. San Francisco: Design Enterprises.

McCurdy, Michael. (1988). *Hannah's farm: The seasons on an early American homestead.* New York: Holiday.

McDermott, Gerald (reteller). (1972). *Anansi the spider: A tale from the Ashanti.* New York: Holt.

McDermott, Gerald. (1974). *Arrow to the sun.* New York: Viking.

McDermott, Gerald. (1978). *The stonecutter: A Japanese folktale.* New York: Penguin, Puffin.

McDermott, Gerald. (1984). *Daughter of the Earth: A Roman myth.* New York: Delacorte.

McDermott, Gerald. (1990). *Tim O'Toole and the wee folk.* New York: Viking, Kestrel.

McDonald, Megan. (1990). *Is this a house for hermit crab?* Illus. S. D. Schindler. New York: Orchard.

McDonald, Megan. (1991). *The potato man.* Illus. Ted Lewin. New York: Orchard.

McDonald's Hispanic Heritage Art Contest. (1989). *Our Hispanic heritage.* Milwaukee: Raintree.

McDonnell, Christine. (1982). *Toad food and measle soup.* New York: Penguin.

McDonnell, Christine. (1984). *Lucky charms and birthday wishes.* New York: Penguin.

McDonnell, Christine. (1990). *Friends first.* New York: Viking.

McGovern, Ann. (1987). *Secret soldier: The story of Deborah Sampson.* New York: Four Winds, Macmillan.

McGovern, Ann, & Clark, Eugenie. (1991). *The desert beneath the sea.* Illus. Craig Phillips. New York: Scholastic.

McGraw, Eloise. (1985). *Mara, daughter of the Nile.* New York: Viking, Puffin.

McGraw, Eloise. (1986). *Moccasin trail.* New York: Viking, Puffin.

McGraw, Eloise. (1991). *The striped ships.* New York: McElderry, Macmillan.

McGuffey, William H. (1837; reprint 1982). *McGuffey's eclectic readers.* Milford, MI: Mott.

McHugh, Elisabet. (1983; o.p.). *Karen's sister.* New York: Greenwillow.

McHugh, Elisabet. (1983; o.p.). *Raising a mother isn't easy.* New York: Greenwillow.

McHugh, Elisabet. (1984; o.p.). *Karen and Vicki.* New York: Greenwillow.

McKinley, Robin. (1978). *Beauty: A retelling of the story of Beauty and the Beast.* New York: HarperCollins.

McKinley, Robin. (1982). *The blue sword.* New York: Greenwillow.

McKinley, Robin. (1984). *The hero and the crown.* New York: Greenwillow.

McKinley, Robin (adapter). (1988). *The outlaws of Sherwood.* New York: Greenwillow.

McKissack, Patricia C. (1986). *Flossie and the fox.* Illus. Rachel Isadora. New York: Dial.

McKissack, Patricia C. (1988). *Mirandy and Brother Wind.* Illus. Jerry Pinkney. New York: Knopf.

McKissack, Patricia C. (1989). *Jesse Jackson: A biography.* New York: Scholastic.

McKissack, Patricia C. (1989). *Nettie Jo's friends.* Illus. Scott Cook. New York: Knopf.

McKissack, Patricia C. (1991). *Marian Anderson: A great singer.* Illus. Ned Ostendorf. Hillside, NJ: Enslow.

McKissack, Patricia C. (1991). *Mary McLeod Bethune: A great teacher.* Illus. Ned Ostendorf. Hillside, NJ: Enslow.

McKissack, Patricia, & McKissack, Frederick. (1990). *A long hard journey: The story of the Pullman porter.* New York: Walker.

McLerran, Alice. (1991). *Roxaboxen.* Illus. Barbara Cooney. New York: Lothrop.

McMahon, Patricia. (1992). *Chi-Hoon: A Korean girl.* Photos by Michael F. O'Brien. Honesdale, PA: Boyds Mills.

McMillan, Bruce. (1986). *Becca backward, Becca frontward, a book of concept pairs.* New York: Lothrop.

McMillan, Bruce. (1987). *Step by step.* New York: Lothrop.

McMillan, Bruce. (1988). *Dry or wet?* New York: Lothrop.

McMillan, Bruce. (1989). *Super, super superwords.* New York: Lothrop.

McMillan, Bruce. (1991). *Eating fractions.* New York: Scholastic.

McMillan, Bruce (author/photographer). (1991). *Play day: A book of terse verse.* New York: Holiday.

McMillan, Bruce. (1992). *Beach ball—left, right.* New York: Holiday.

McPhail, David. (1984). *Fix-it.* New York: Dutton.

McPhail, David. (1985). *Emma's pet.* New York: Dutton.

McPhail, David. (1987). *Emma's vacation.* New York: Dutton.

McPhail, David. (1990). *Lost!* Boston: Little, Brown, Joy Street.

McPhail, David. (1990). *Pig Pig gets a job.* New York: Dutton.

McPhail, David (1992). *Farm boy's year.* New York: Atheneum.

McSwigan, Marie. (1986). *Snow treasure.* New York: Scholastic.

McVitty, Walter (reteller). (1988). *Ali Baba and the forty thieves.* Illus. Margaret Early. New York: Abrams.

Medaris, Angela Shelf. (1991). *Dancing with the Indians.* Illus. Samuel Byrd. New York: Holiday.

Meigs, Cornelia. (1968). *Invincible Louisa.* Boston: Little, Brown.

Meltzer, Milton. (1974; o.p.). *Remember the days.* New York: Doubleday.

Meltzer, Milton. (1974; o.p.). *World of our fathers.* New York: Farrar, Straus & Giroux.

Meltzer, Milton. (1976). *Never to forget: The Jews of the Holocaust.* New York: HarperCollins.

Meltzer, Milton. (1976; o.p.). *Taking root: Jewish immigrants in America.* New York: Farrar, Straus & Giroux.

Meltzer, Milton. (1980). *The Chinese Americans.* New York: HarperCollins.

Meltzer, Milton. (1982). *The Hispanic Americans.* New York: HarperCollins.

Meltzer, Milton. (1982). *The Jewish Americans: A history in their own words, 1650–1950.* New York: HarperCollins.

Meltzer, Milton. (1984). *The black Americans: A history in their own words.* New York: HarperCollins.

Meltzer, Milton. (1986). *George Washington and the birth of our nation.* New York: Watts.

Meltzer, Milton. (1986). *Winnie Mandela: The soul of South Africa.* New York: Viking.

Meltzer, Milton. (1987). *The American revolutionaries: A history in their own words.* New York: HarperCollins.

Meltzer, Milton. (1988). *Rescue: The story of how Gentiles saved Jews in the Holocaust.* New York: HarperCollins.

Meltzer, Milton. (1988). *Starting from home: A writer's beginnings.* New York: Viking.

Meltzer, Milton. (1989). *Voices from the Civil War: A documentary history of the great American conflict.* New York: HarperCollins.

Meltzer, Milton. (1990). *The Bill of Rights: How we got it and what it means.* New York: HarperCollins.

Meltzer, Milton. (1990). *Bread and roses: The struggle of American labor, 1865–1915.* New York: Facts on File.

Meltzer, Milton. (1990). *Brother, can you spare a dime?* New York: Facts on File.

Meltzer, Milton. (1990). *Columbus and the world around him.* New York: Watts.

Meltzer, Milton. (1990). *Crime in America.* New York: Morrow.

Mennen, Ingrid, & Daly, Niki. (1991). *Somewhere in Africa.* Illus. Nicolaas Maritz. New York: Dutton.

Merriam, Eve. (1964; o.p.). *It doesn't always have to rhyme.* Illus. Malcolm Spooner. New York: Atheneum.

Merriam, Eve. (1973; o.p.). *Out loud.* Illus. Harriet Sherman. New York: Atheneum.

Merriam, Eve. (1985). *Blackberry ink.* New York: Morrow.

Merriam, Eve. (1986). *Fresh paint.* Illus. David Frampton. New York: Macmillan.

Merriam, Eve. (1987). *Halloween ABC.* Illus. Lane Smith. New York: Macmillan.

Merriam, Eve. (1989). *Chortles: New and selected wordplay poems.* Illus. Sheila Hamanaka. New York: Morrow.

Merriam, Eve. (1989). *A poem for a pickle: Funnybone verses.* Illus. Sheila Hamanaka. New York: Morrow.

Merrill, Jean. (1974). *The toothpaste millionaire.* Boston: Houghton.

Merrill, Jean. (1992). *The girl who loved caterpillars.* Illus. Floyd Cooper. New York: Putnam.

Metropolitan Museum of Art. (1987). *Go in and out the window: An illustrated songbook for young people.* Music arranged by Dan Fox. Commentary by Claude Marks. New York: Holt.

Meyer, Carolyn. (1992). *Where the broken heart still beats: The story of Cynthia Ann Parker.* San Diego: Harcourt.

Michl, Reinhard. (1986). *A day on the river.* Hauppauge, NY: Barron.

Miles, Betty. (1991). *Save the earth: An action handbook for kids.* Illus. Nelle Davis. New York: Knopf.

Miles, Miska. (1985). *Annie and the old one.* Illus. Peter Parnall. Boston: Little, Brown.

Miller, Christina G., & Berry, Louise A. (1989). *Coastal rescue: Preserving our seashores.* New York: Atheneum.

Miller, Christina G., & Berry, Louise A. (1991). *Jungle rescue: Saving the new world tropical rain forests.* New York: Atheneum.

Miller, Margaret. (1988). *Whose hat?* New York: Greenwillow.

Miller, Margaret. (1990). *Who uses this?* New York: Greenwillow.

Miller, Margaret. (1991). *Whose shoe?* New York: Greenwillow.

Milne, A. A. (1924). *When we were very young.* Illus. E. H. Shepard. New York: Dutton.

Milne, A. A. (1926). *Winnie the pooh.* Illus. E. H. Shepard. New York: Dutton.

Milne, A. A. (1927). *Now we are six.* Illus. E. H. Shepard. New York: Dutton.

Milnes, Gerald. (1990). *Granny will your dog bite and other mountain rhymes.* New York: Knopf.

Milton, Joyce. (1990). *The story of Paul Revere.* Illus. Tom La Padula. New York: Dell.

Minarik, Else. (1959). *Father Bear comes home.* Illus. Maurice Sendak. New York: HarperCollins.

Mohr, Nicholasa. (1979). *Felita.* New York: Dial.

Mohr, Nicholasa. (1986). *Going home.* New York: Dial.

Mollel, Tololwa M. (1990). *The orphan boy: A Maasai story.* Illus. Paul Morin. New York: Clarion.

Monjo, F. N. (1970). *The drinking gourd.* Illus. Fred Brenner. New York: HarperCollins.

Monjo, F. N. (1973). *Poor Richard in France.* Illus. Brinton Turkle. New York: Dell.

Monjo, F. N. (1975). *Letters to Horseface: Young Mozart's travels in Italy.* Illus. Don Bolognese & Elaine Raphael. New York: Puffin.

Monjo, F. N. (1990). *Grand Papa and Ellen Aroon.* New York: Dell.

Monjo, F. N. (1991). *The house on Stink Alley.* New York: Dell.

Monroe, Jean Guard, & Williamson, Ray A. (1987). *They dance in the sky.* Illus. Edgar Stewart. Boston: Houghton.

Montgomery, Lucy M. (1976). *Anne of Avonlea.* New York: Bantam.

Montgomery, Lucy M. (1908; 1983 reprint). *Anne of Green Gables.* New York: Grosset.

Moore, Clement Clarke. (1823; 1971 reprint). *A visit from St. Nicholas.* Illus. T. C. Boyd. New York: Simon & Schuster.

Moore, Clement C. (1991). *The night before Christmas.* Illus. James Marshall. New York: Scholastic.

Moore, Lilian. (1976). *I feel the same way.* Illus. Robert Quackenbush. New York: Macmillan.

Moore, Lilian. (1982). *Something new begins.* New York: Macmillan.

Moore, Yvette. (1991). *Freedom songs.* New York: Orchard.

Morey, Janet Nomura, & Dunn, Wendy. (1992). *Famous Asian Americans.* New York: Dutton.

Morimoto, Junko. (1990). *My Hiroshima.* New York: Viking.

Morgan, Kate. (1991). *The story of things.* Illus. Joyce Audy Zarins. New York: Walker.

Morpurgo, Michael. (1991). *Waiting for Anya.* New York: Viking.

Morris, Ann. (1992). *Houses and homes.* Photos by Ken Heyman. Edited by Susan Pearson. New York: Lothrop.

Morris, Rick. (1983). *Ocean life.* Tulsa, OK: Usborne-Haynes.

Morris, Winifred. (1987). *The magic leaf.* Illus. Ju-Hong Chen. New York: Atheneum.

Morrison, Lillian. (1977; o.p.). *Sidewalk racer and other poems of sports and motion.* New York: Lothrop.

Morrison, Lillian. (1989). *Best wishes, amen: Autograph verse.* New York: HarperCollins.

Morrison, Lillian. (1992). *Whistling the morning in.* Illus. Joel Cook. Honesdale, PA: Boyds Mills.

Morrow, Honore. (1926, 1946). *On to Oregon.* New York: Morrow.

Mosel, Arlene. (1972). *The funny little woman.* Illus. Blair Lent. New York: Dutton.

Moskin, Marietta. (1975; o.p.). *Waiting for Mama.* New York: Coward.

Moskin, Marietta. (1987). *I am Rosemarie.* New York: Dell.

Moss, Jeff. (1989). *The butterfly jar.* Illus. Chris Demarest. New York: Bantam.

Mother Goose. (1987). *The real Mother Goose.* Illus. Blanche Fisher Wright. New York: Macmillan. Reproduction of 1916 edition, Checkerboard Press.

Mott, Michael. (1986). *Master Entrick.* New York: Dell.

Mowat, Farley. (1962). *Owls in the family.* Boston: Little, Brown.

Muller, Jorg. (1977). *The changing city.* New York: Macmillan.

Muller, Jorg. (1977; o.p.). *The changing countryside.* New York: Atheneum.

Murphy, Claire. (1991). *Friendship across Arctic waters.* Photos by Charles Mason. New York: Dutton.

Murphy, Jim. (1990). *The boy's war: Confederate and Union soldiers talk about the Civil War.* Boston: Houghton.

Musgrove, Margaret. (1976). *Ashanti to Zulu.* Illus. Leo & Diane Dillon. New York: Dial.

Myers, Walter Dean. (1975). *Fast Sam, Cool Clyde, and Stuff.* New York: Viking.

Myers, Walter Dean. (1985). *It ain't all for nothin'.* New York: Avon.

Myers, Walter Dean. (1981). *Hoops.* New York: Delacorte.

Myers, Walter Dean. (1982). *Won't know till I get there.* New York: Viking.

Myers, Walter Dean. (1984). *Motown and Didi.* New York: Viking.

Myers, Walter Dean. (1988). *Fallen angels.* New York: Scholastic.

Myers, Walter Dean. (1989). *The young landlords.* New York: Viking, Puffin.

Myers, Walter Dean. (1990). *The mouse rap.* New York: HarperCollins.

Myers, Walter Dean. (1991). *Now is your time!: The African-American struggle for freedom.* New York: HarperCollins.

Myers, Walter Dean. (1992). *Somewhere in the darkness.* New York: Scholastic.

Nabb, Magdalen. (1989). *Josie Smith at school.* New York: McElderry.

Nabwire, Constance, & Montgomery, Bertha. (1990). *Cooking the African way.* Minneapolis: Lerner.

Naidoo, Beverley. (1988). *Journey to Jo'burg.* New York: HarperCollins.

Naidoo, Beverley. (1990). *Chain of fire.* New York: HarperCollins.

Namioka, Lensey. (1992). *Yang the youngest and his terrible ear.* Boston: Little, Brown.

Nash, Ogden. (1991). *The adventures of Isabel.*

Illus. James Marshall. Boston: Little, Brown, Joy Street.

Nash, Ogden. (1973). *Custard the dragon.* Boston: Little, Brown.

National Geographic World magazine. 1975–present.

Naylor, Phyllis Reynolds. (1985). *The agony of Alice.* New York: Atheneum.

Naylor, Phyllis Reynolds. (1986). *The keeper.* New York: Atheneum.

Naylor, Phyllis Reynolds. (1987). *How I came to be a writer.* New York: Macmillan.

Naylor, Phyllis Reynolds. (1989). *Alice in rapture, sort of.* New York: Atheneum.

Naylor, Phyllis Reynolds. (1991). *Reluctantly Alice.* New York: Atheneum.

Naylor, Phyllis Reynolds. (1991). *Shiloh.* New York: Atheneum.

Neitzel, Shirley. (1989). *The jacket I wear in the snow.* Illus. Nancy Winslow Parker. New York: Greenwillow.

Nelson, Esther. (1985). *The great rounds songbook.* Illus. Joyce Behr. New York: Sterling.

Nelson, Theresa. (1989). *And one for all.* New York: Orchard.

Nesbit, E. (1899; 1986 reissue). *The story of the treasure seekers.* New York: Penguin.

Nesbit, E. (1902; 1959 reissue). *Five children and it.* New York: Random.

Nesbit, E. (1988). *Long ago when I was young.* New York: Dial.

Ness, Evaline. (1965; o.p.). *Tom tit tot.* New York: Scribner's.

Ness, Evaline. (1966). *Sam, Bangs and moonshine.* New York: Holt.

Newbery, John. (1744; 1967 reissue). *A little pretty pocket book: Intended for instruction and amusement of Little Master Tommy and Pretty Miss Polly.* San Diego: Harcourt.

Newlands, Anne. (1988). *Meet Edgar Degas.* New York: HarperCollins.

Newton, Suzanne. (1991). *Where are you when I need you?* New York: Viking.

Nicholson, William. (1926, 1927). *Clever Bill.* London, Heinemann; New York: Doubleday.

Nilsen, Aileen Pace. (1990). *Presenting M. E. Kerr.* New York: Dell.

Nims, Bonnie Larkin. (1992). *Just beyond reach and other riddle poems.* Photos by George Ancona. New York: Scholastic.

Nixon, Joan Lowery. (1983). *Deadly game of magic.* San Diego: Harcourt.

Nixon, Joan Lowery. (1988). *If you were a writer.* Illus. Bruce Degen. New York: Four Winds, Macmillan.

Nixon, Joan Lowery. (1989). *You bet your britches, Claude.* Illus. Tracey Campbell Pearson. New York: Viking.

Noble, Trina Hakes. (1980). *The day Jimmy's boa ate the wash.* Illus. Steven Kellogg. New York: Dial.

Noll, Sally. (1990). *Watch where you go.* New York: Greenwillow.

Norman, Charles. (1988). *The hornbeam tree and other poems.* Illus. Ted Rand. New York: Henry Holt.

Norris, Jerrie. (1990). *Presenting Rosa Guy.* New York: Dell.

Norsgaard, E. Jaediker, & Norsgaard, Campbell. (1990). *Nature's great balancing act: In your own backyard.* New York: Dutton.

North, Sterling. (1990). *Rascal.* Illus. John Schoenherr. New York: Viking.

Norton, Mary. (1953). *The borrowers.* Illus. Beth & Joe Krush. San Diego: Harcourt.

Nostlinger, Christine. (1991). *Conrad: The factory made boy.* Illus. Carol Nicklaus. Boston: G. K. Hall.

Nottridge, Harold. (1988; o.p.). *Joan of Arc.* New York: Watts.

Noyes, Alfred. (1983). *The highwayman.* Illus. Charles Mikolaycak. New York: Lothrop.

Nygren, Tord. (1988). *The red thread.* New York: Farrar, Straus & Giroux.

O'Brien, Robert C. (1975). *Z for Zachariah.* New York: Atheneum.

O'Brien, Robert C. (1971). *Mrs. Frisby and the rats of NIMH.* New York: Atheneum.

O'Connor, Jim. (1989). *Jackie Robinson and the story of all-black baseball.* New York: Random.

O'Dell, Scott. (1960). *Island of the blue dolphin.* Boston: Houghton.

O'Dell, Scott. (1970). *Sing down the moon.* Boston: Houghton.

O'Dell, Scott. (1976). *The 290.* (The two hundred ninety) Boston: Houghton.

O'Dell, Scott. (1977). *Carlota.* Boston: Houghton.

O'Dell, Scott. (1980). *Sarah Bishop.* Boston: Houghton.

O'Dell, Scott. (1985). *The road to Damietta.* Boston: Houghton.

O'Dell, Scott. (1988). *Black star, bright dawn.* Boston: Houghton.

O'Dell, Scott, & Hall, E. (1992). *Thunder rolling in the mountains.* Boston: Houghton.

O'Kelley, Mattie Lou. (1983). *From the hills of Georgia: An autobiography in paintings.* Boston: Little, Brown.

O'Kelley, Mattie Lou. (1991). *Moving to town.* Boston: Little, Brown.

Okimoto, Jean Davies. (1990). *Take a chance, Gramps!* Boston: Little, Brown.

Olson, Arielle. (1992). *Noah's cats and the devil's fire.* Illus. Barry Moser. New York: Orchard.

Oneal, Zibby. (1980). *The language of goldfish.* New York: Viking.

Oneal, Zibby. (1985). *In summer light.* New York: Viking, Kestrel.

Oneal, Zibby. (1986). *Grandma Moses: Painter of rural America.* New York: Viking.

Oneal, Zibby. (1990). *A long way to go.* New York: Viking.

O'Neill, Mary. (1973, 1989). *Hailstones and halibut bones.* Illus. John Wallner. New York: Doubleday.

Opie, Iona, & Opie, Peter. (1951). *The Oxford dictionary of nursery rhymes.* New York: Oxford University Press.

Opie, Iona, & Opie, Peter. (1955). *The Oxford nursery rhyme book.* New York: Oxford University Press.

Opie, Iona, & Opie, Peter (compilers). (1988). *Tail feathers from Mother Goose: The Opie rhyme books.* Illus. various artists. Boston: Houghton.

Opie, Iona, & Opie, Peter. (1992). *I saw Esau.* Illus. Maurice Sendak. Cambridge, MA: Candlewick.

Oppenheim, Joanne. (1986). *You can't catch me.* Boston: Houghton.

Oppenheim, Levey. (1992). *The lily cupboard.* Illus. Ronald Himler. New York: HarperCollins.

Orgel, Doris. (1991). *Nobodies and somebodies.* New York: Viking.

Orlev, Uri. (1984). *The island on Bird Street.* Boston: Houghton.

Orlev, Uri. (1991). *The man from the other side.* Boston: Houghton.

Ormerod, Jan. (1981). *Moonlight.* New York: Lothrop.

Ormerod, Jan. (1981). *Sunshine.* New York: Lothrop.

Ormerod, Jan. (1985). *Young Joe.* New York: Lothrop.

Ormerod, Jan, & Lloyd, David (retellers). (1990). *The frog prince.* Illus. Jan Ormerod. New York: Lothrop.

Ormondroyd, Edward. (1963). *Time at the top.* Boston: Parnassus.

Osborne, M. P. (1990). *The many lives of Benjamin Franklin.* New York: Dial.

Osofsky, Audrey. (1992). *Dreamcatcher.* New York: Orchard.

Oughton, Jerrie. (1992). *How the stars fell into the sky: A Navajo tale.* Illus. Lisa Desimini. Boston: Houghton.

Owens, Mary Beth. (1990). *A caribou alphabet.* New York: Farrar, Straus & Giroux.

Oxenbury, Helen. (1983). *Helen Oxenbury's ABC of things.* New York: Delacorte.

Oxenbury, Helen. (1986). *I can. I hear. I see. I touch.* New York: Random. [Boxed set]

Oxenbury, Helen. (1991). *Mother's helper.* New York: Dial.

Oxenbury, Helen. (1991). *Shopping trip.* New York: Dial.

Oxenbury, Helen (1992). *Good night, good morning.* New York: Dial.

Paik, Min. (1988). *Aekyung's dream.* San Francisco: Children's Book Press.

Palmer, Hap. (1990). *Homemade band: Songs to sing, instruments to make.* New York: Crown.

Parish, Peggy. (1977). *Teach us, Amelia Bedelia.* Illus. Lynn Sweat. New York: Greenwillow.

Parish, Peggy. (1986). *Ghosts of Cougar Island.* New York: Dell.

Parish, Peggy. (1988). *Scruffy.* Illus. Kelly Oechsli. New York: HarperCollins.

Park, Barbara. (1981). *The kid in the red jacket.* New York: Knopf.

Park, Barbara. (1982). *Skinnybones.* New York: Knopf.

Park, Ruth. (1982). *Playing Beatie Bow.* New York: Atheneum.

Parker, Nancy Winslow. (1991). *The president's cabinet: And how it grew.* New York: HarperCollins.

Parks, Rosa, with Jim Haskins. (1992). *Rosa Parks: Mother to a movement.* New York: Dial.

Parnall, Peter. (1991). *Marsh cat.* New York: Macmillan.

Parnall, Peter. (1991). *The rock.* New York: Macmillan.

Parnall, Peter. (1990). *Woodpile.* New York: Macmillan.

Parnall, Peter. (1984; o.p.). *The daywatchers.* New York: Macmillan.

Pascal, Francine. *Sweet Valley High* series. New York: Bantam.

Pascal, Francine. *Sweet Valley Twins* series. New York: Bantam.

Patent, Dorothy Hinshaw. (1988). *Whooping crane: A comeback story.* Photos by William Munoz. New York: Clarion.

Patent, Dorothy Hinshaw. (1990). *Gray wolf, red wolf.* Illus. William Munoz. Boston: Houghton.

Patent, Dorothy Hinshaw. (1990). *Seals, sea lions and walruses.* New York: Holiday.

Patent, Dorothy Hinshaw. (1991). *Way of the grizzly.* New York: Clarion.

Paterson, Katherine. (1976). *Bridge to Terabithia.* Illus. Donna Diamond. New York: HarperCollins.

Paterson, Katherine. (1976). *The sign of the chrysanthemum.* New York: HarperCollins.

Paterson, Katherine. (1978). *The great Gilly Hopkins.* New York: HarperCollins.

Paterson, Katherine. (1980). *Jacob have I loved.* New York: HarperCollins.

Paterson, Katherine. (1985). *Come sing, Jimmy Jo.* New York: Lodestar, Dutton.

Paterson, Katherine. (1988). *Park's quest.* New York: Lodestar.

Paterson, Katherine. (1991). *Lyddie.* New York: Dutton, Lodestar.

Paton Walsh, Jill. (1978). *Chance child.* New York: Farrar, Straus & Giroux.

Paton, Walsh, Jill. (1978; o.p.). *Children of the fox.* New York: Farrar, Straus & Giroux.

Paton Walsh, Jill. (1982). *The green book.* New York: Farrar, Straus & Giroux.

Patrick, Denise Lewis. (1992). *Red dancing shoes.*

Illus. James Ransome. New York: Tambourine, Morrow.

Paul, Ann Whitford. (1991). *Eight hands round: A patchwork alphabet.* Illus. Jeanette Winter. New York: HarperCollins.

Paulsen, Gary. (1985). *Dogsong.* New York: Bradbury.

Paulsen, Gary. (1987). *Hatchet.* New York: Macmillan, Bradbury.

Paulsen, Gary. (1989). *The voyage of the Frog.* New York: Orchard.

Paulsen, Gary. (1990). *The boy who owned the school.* New York: Orchard.

Paulsen, Gary. (1991). *The cookcamp.* New York: Orchard.

Paulsen, Gary. (1991). *The winter room.* New York: Orchard, Watts.

Paulsen, Gary. (1990). *Woodsong.* New York: Bradbury.

Pausacker, Jenny. (1991). *Fast forward.* New York: Lothrop.

Paxton, Tom (reteller). (1988). *Aesop's fables.* New York: Morrow.

Paxton, Tom (reteller). (1990). *Belling the cat: And other Aesop's fables.* Illus. Robert Rayevsky. New York: Morrow.

Pearce, Philippa. (1958, 1984). *Tom's midnight garden.* New York: HarperCollins.

Pearce, Philippa. (1981). *Who's afraid? And other strange stories.* New York: Greenwillow.

Pearce, Philippa. (1985). *The way to Sattin Shore.* New York: Viking, Puffin.

Pearce, Philippa. (1987). *Emily's own elephant.* Illus. John Lawrence. New York: Greenwillow.

Pearson, Kit. (1990). *The sky is falling.* New York: Viking.

Peck, Richard. (1975). *The ghost belonged to me.* New York: Viking.

Peck, Richard. (1976). *Are you in the house alone?* New York: Viking.

Peck, Richard. (1978). *Father figure.* New York: Viking.

Peck, Richard. (1991). *Anonymously yours: A memoir.* Englewood Cliffs, NJ: Simon & Schuster, Messner.

Peek, Merle. (1981). *Roll over!: A counting song.* New York: Clarion.

Peek, Merle. (1988). *Mary wore her red dress and Henry wore his green sneakers.* Adapted by Merle Peek. New York: Clarion.

Peet, Bill. (1989). *Bill Peet: An autobiography.* Boston: Houghton.

Pelz, Ruth. (1989; o.p.). *Black heroes of the wild west.* Seattle: Open Hand.

Pendergraft, Patricia. (1991). *As far as Mill Springs.* New York: Philomel.

Perl, Lila, & Ada, Alma Flor. (1985). *Pinatas and paper flowers, holidays of the Americas in English and Spanish.* New York: Clarion.

Perrault, Charles. (1794). *Contes de ma Mère L'Oye (Tales of Mother Goose).* Haverhill, MA: Peter Edes.

Perrault, Charles. (1697; 1925). *Histoires ou contes du temps passé avec moralités (Stories of long ago with morals).* London: Nonesuch.

Perrault, Charles. (1954). *Cinderella.* Illus. Marcia Brown. New York: Scribner's.

Perrault, Charles. (1965). *Little red riding hood.* Illus. Beni Montresor. New York: Knopf.

Peters, Lisa Westberg. (1990). *Good morning, river.* Illus. Deborah Kogan Ray. New York: Arcade.

Peters, Russell. (1992). *Clambake: A Wampanoag tradition.* Photos by John Madama. Minneapolis: Lerner.

Petry, Ann. (1988). *Tituba of Salem Village.* New York: HarperCollins.

Pfanner, Louise. (1990). *Louise builds a boat.* New York: Orchard.

Philip, Neil. (1991). *Fairy tales from eastern Europe.* Illus. Larry Wilkes. New York: Clarion.

Phillips, Anne W. (1990). *The ocean.* New York: Macmillan.

Picard, Barbara. (1966; o.p.). *One is one.* New York: Holt.

Pierce, Meredith Ann. (1985). *A gathering of gargoyles.* New York: Tor.

Pillar, Marjorie. (1990). *Pizza man.* New York: HarperCollins.

Pillar, Marjorie. (1992). *Join the band!* New York: HarperCollins.

Pinkney, Gloria Jean. (1992). *Back home.* Illus. Jerry Pinkney. New York: Dial.

Pinkwater, Daniel. (1978). *Alan Mendelsohn, the boy from Mars.* New York: Dutton.

Pinkwater, Jill. (1991). *Tails of the Bronx: A tale of the Bronx.* New York: Macmillan.

Pittman, Helena. (1986). *A grain of rice.* Mamaroneck, NY: Hastings.

Plotz, Helen (compiler). (1976). *As I walked out one evening: A book of ballads.* New York: Greenwillow.

Plotz, Helen (compiler). (1979). *This powerful rhyme: A book of sonnets.* New York: Greenwillow.

Plotz, Helen (ed.). (1988). *Week of lullabies.* Illus. Marisabina Russo. New York: Greenwillow.

Polacco, Patricia. (1988). *The keeping quilt.* New York: Simon & Schuster.

Polacco, Patricia. (1990). *Thunder cake.* New York: Philomel.

Polacco, Patricia. (1992). *Chicken Sunday.* New York: Philomel.

Polacco, Patricia. (1992). *Mrs. Katz and Tush.* New York: Bantam.

Politi, Leo. (1946; o.p.). *Pedro, the angel of Olvera Street.* New York: Scribner's.

Pomerantz, Charlotte. (1974). *The piggy in the puddle.* Illus. James Marshall. New York: Macmillan.

Pomerantz, Charlotte. (1984). *The half-birthday party.* Illus. DyAnne DiSalvo-Ryan. New York: Clarion.

Pomerantz, Charlotte. (1989). *The chalk doll.* Illus. Frané Lessac. New York: HarperCollins.

Pomerantz, Charlotte. (1989). *Flap your wings and try.* Illus. Nancy Tafuri. New York: Greenwillow.

Pomerantz, Charlotte. (1993). *The tamarindo puppy and other poems.* Illus. Byron Barton. New York: Greenwillow.

Pomerantz, Charlotte. (1982; o.p.). *If I had a paka: Poems in eleven languages.* New York: Greenwillow.

Pople, Maureen. (1988). *The other side of the family.* New York: Holt.

Porte, Barbara. (1989). *Harry in trouble.* Illus. Yossi Abolafia. New York: Greenwillow.

Porte, Barbara. (1989). *Ruthann and her pig.* New York: Orchard.

Porte, Barbara. (1991). *Fat Fanny, Beanpole Bertha, and the boys.* New York: Orchard.

Porte, Barbara. (1991). *Harry gets an uncle.* Illus. Yossi Abolafia. New York: Greenwillow.

Porter, Eleanor. (1912). *Pollyanna.* Boston: Parnassus.

Posell, Elsa. (1987). *Homecoming.* San Diego: Harcourt.

Potter, Beatrix. (1902). *The tale of Peter Rabbit.* New York: Warne.

Potter, Beatrix. (1982). *Beatrix Potter's Americans: Selected letters.* Boston: Horn Book.

Potter, Beatrix. (1989). *The journal of Beatrix Potter: 1881–1897.* New York: Warne.

Powell, Pamela. (1992). *The turtle watchers.* New York: Viking.

Powzyk, Joyce. (1988). *Tracking wild chimpanzees in Kibira National Park.* New York: Lothrop.

Powzyk, Joyce. (1990). *Animal camouflage: A closer look.* New York: Bradbury.

Prater, John. (1986). *The gift.* New York: Viking, Penguin.

Prelutsky, Jack. (1976). *Nightmares: Poems to trouble your sleep.* Illus. Arnold Lobel. New York: Greenwillow.

Prelutsky, Jack. (1978). *The mean old mean hyena.* Illus. Arnold Lobel. New York: Greenwillow.

Prelutsky, Jack. (1980). *Rolling Harvey down the hill.* Illus. Victoria Chess. New York: Greenwillow.

Prelutsky, Jack. (1984). *The new kid on the block.* Illus. James Stevenson. New York: Greenwillow.

Prelutsky, Jack. (1986). *Ride a purple pelican.* Illus. Garth Williams. New York: Greenwillow.

Prelutsky, Jack. (1988). *Tyrannosaurus was a beast.* New York: Greenwillow.

Prelutsky, Jack. (1989). *The baby uggs are hatching.* New York: Greenwillow.

Prelutsky, Jack. (1989). *Circus.* Illus. Arnold Lobel. New York: Macmillan.

Prelutsky, Jack. (1990). *Beneath a blue umbrella.* Illus. Garth Williams. New York: Greenwillow.

Prelutsky, Jack. (1990). *Something big has been here.* Illus. James Stevenson. New York: Greenwillow.

Prelutsky, Jack (selector). (1983). *Random House book of poetry.* Illus. Arnold Lobel. New York: Random.

Prelutsky, Jack (compiler). (1986). *Read-aloud rhymes for the very young.* Illus. Marc Brown. New York: Knopf.

Prelutsky, Jack (selector). (1989). *Poems of A. Nonny Mouse.* Illus. Henrik Drescher. New York: Knopf.

Prelutsky, Jack (selector). (1991). *For laughing out loud: Poems to tickle your funnybone.* Illus. Marjorie Priceman. New York: Knopf.

Price, Leontyne. (1990). *Aïda.* Illus. Leo & Diane Dillon. San Diego: Harcourt.

Pringle, Laurence. (1989). *The animal rights controversy.* San Diego: Harcourt.

Pringle, Laurence. (1989). *Bearman: Exploring the world of black bears.* New York: Scribner's.

Pringle, Laurence. (1989). *Nuclear energy: Troubled past, uncertain future.* New York: Macmillan.

Pringle, Laurence. (1990). *Global warming: Assessing the greenhouse threat.* Boston: Arcade.

Pringle, Laurence. (1990). *Killer bees.* New York: Morrow.

Pringle, Laurence. (1990). *Saving our wildlife.* Hillside, NJ: Enslow.

Pringle, Laurence. (1991). *Batman: Exploring the world of bats.* New York: Scribner's.

Pringle, Laurence. (1991). *Death is natural.* New York: Morrow.

Pringle, Laurence. (1991). *Living treasure: Saving earth's threatened biodiversity.* Illus. Irene Brady. New York: Morrow.

Proddow, Penelope. (1979; o.p.). *Art tells a story: Greek and Roman myths.* New York: Doubleday.

Provensen, Alice. (1990). *The buck stops here: The presidents of the United States.* New York: HarperCollins.

Provensen, Alice, & Provensen, Martin. (1976 reissue). *The Mother Goose book.* New York: Random.

Provensen, Alice, & Provensen, Martin. (1983). *The glorious flight: Across the channel with Louis Bleriot, July 25, 1909.* New York: Viking.

Provensen, Alice, & Provensen, Martin. (1984). *Leonardo da Vinci: The artist, inventor, scientist in three-dimensional movable pictures.* New York: Viking.

Provensen, Alice, & Provensen, Martin. (1987). *Shaker Lane.* New York: Viking, Kestrel.

Pryor, Bonnie. (1988). *Seth of the lion people.* New York: Morrow.

Pullman, Philip. (1992). *The broken bridge.* New York: Knopf.

Pulver, Robin. (1991). *Mrs. Toggle and the dinosaur.* Illus. Amy Schwartz. New York: Four Winds, Macmillan.

Pyle, Howard. (1913, 1968). *The merry adventures of Robin Hood of great renown in Nottinghamshire.* New York: Scribner's.

Pyle, Howard. (1903, 1968). *The story of King Arthur and his knights.* Illus. N. C. Wyeth. New York: Scribner's.

Quackenbush, Robert. (1984). *Mark Twain? What kind of name is that? A story of Samuel Langhorne Clemens.* New York: Simon & Schuster.

Quackenbush, Robert. (1986). *Who said there's no man on the moon? A story of Jules Verne.* New York: Simon & Schuster.

Quackenbush, Robert. (1986). *Old Silver Leg takes over: A story of Peter Stuyvesant.* Englewood Cliffs, NJ: Prentice Hall.

Quackenbush, Robert. (1990). *Don't you dare shoot that bear: A story of Theodore Roosevelt.* New York: Simon & Schuster.

Quackenbush, Robert. (1990; o.p.). *Quit pulling my leg: A story of Davy Crockett.* New York: Simon & Schuster.

Quayle, Eric (reteller). (1989). *The shining princess and other Japanese legends.* Boston: Arcade.

Raboff, Ernest. (1987). *Leonardo da Vinci.* New York: HarperCollins.

Raboff, Ernest. (1987). *Pablo Picasso.* New York: HarperCollins.

Raboff, Ernest. (1987). *Pierre-Auguste Renoir.* New York: HarperCollins.

Raboff, Ernest. (1987). *Rembrandt.* New York: HarperCollins.

Raboff, Ernest. (1988). *Albrecht Dürer.* New York: HarperCollins.

Raboff, Ernest. (1988). *Diego Rodriguez de Silva y Velasquez.* New York: HarperCollins.

Raboff, Ernest. (1988). *Frederic Remington.* New York: HarperCollins.

Raboff, Ernest. (1988). *Henri de Toulouse-Lautrec.* New York: HarperCollins.

Raboff, Ernest. (1988). *Henri Matisse.* New York: HarperCollins.

Raboff, Ernest. (1988). *Henri Rousseau.* New York: HarperCollins.

Raboff, Ernest. (1988). *Marc Chagall.* New York: HarperCollins.

Raboff, Ernest. (1988). *Michelangelo Buonarroti.* New York: HarperCollins.

Raboff, Ernest. (1988). *Paul Gauguin.* New York: HarperCollins.

Raboff, Ernest. (1988). *Paul Klee.* New York: HarperCollins.

Raboff, Ernest. (1988). *Raphael Sanzio.* New York: HarperCollins.

Raboff, Ernest. (1988). *Vincent Van Gogh.* New York: HarperCollins.

Radin, Ruth Yaffe. (1982). *A winter place.* Illus. Mattie Lou O'Kelley. Boston: Little, Brown.

Radin, Ruth Yaffee. (1989). *High in the mountains.* Illus. Ed Young. New York: Macmillan.

Raffi. (1992). *Five little ducks.* Illus. Jose Aruego & Ariane Dewey. New York: Crown.

Raffi. (1989). *Everything grows.* Illus. Bruce McMillan. New York: Crown.

Ranger Rick's Nature Magazine. 1967–present. Washington, DC: National Wildlife Foundation.

Rankin, Laura. (1991). *The handmade alphabet.* New York: Dial.

Ransome, Arthur (reteller). (1968). *The fool of the world and the flying ship: A Russian tale.* Illus. Uri Shulevitz. New York: Farrar, Straus & Giroux.

Rappaport, Doreen. (1988). *The Boston coffee party.* Illus. Emily Arnold McCully. New York: HarperCollins.

Rappaport, Doreen (ed.). (1990). *American women: Their lives in their words.* New York: HarperCollins.

Rappaport, Doreen. (1991). *The journey of Meng.* Illus. Yang Ming-yi. New York: Dial.

Raskin, Ellen. (1978). *The westing game.* New York: Dutton.

Rawlings, Marjorie Kinnan. (1938, 1967). *The yearling.* Illus. N. C. Wyeth. New York: Scribner's.

Rawls, Wilson. (1961). *Where the red fern grows: The story of two dogs and a boy.* New York: Doubleday.

Ray, Deborah Kogan. (1990). *My daddy was a soldier.* New York: Holt.

Ray, Delia. (1990). *A nation torn: The story of how the Civil War began.* New York: Dutton.

Ray, Delia. (1991). *Behind the blue and gray: The soldier's life in the Civil War.* New York: Dutton.

Ray, Jane. (1990). *Noah's ark: Words from the book of Genesis.* New York: Dutton.

Rayevsky, Inna (reteller). (1990). *The talking tree: An old Italian tale.* Illus. Robert Rayevsky. New York: Putnam.

Rayner, Mary. (1987). *Mrs. Pig gets cross: And other stories.* New York: Atheneum.

Red Hawk, Richard. (1988). *ABCs: The American Indian way.* Newcastle, CA: Sierra Oaks.

Reeder, Carolyn. (1989). *Shades of gray.* New York: Macmillan.

Reeder, Carolyn. (1991). *Grandpa's mountain.* New York: Macmillan.

Rees, Mary. (1988). *Ten in a bed.* Boston: Little, Brown.

Regguinti, Gordon. (1992). *The sacred harvest: Ojibway wild rice gathering.* Minneapolis: Lerner.

Reid, Margarette. (1990). *The button box.* New York: Dutton.

Reiss, Johanna. (1987). *The upstairs room.* New York: HarperCollins.

Reit, Seymour. (1989). *Behind rebel lines: The incredible story of Emma Edmonds, Civil War spy.* San Diego: Harcourt.

Reuter, Bjarne. (1989). *Buster's world.* Trans. Anthea Bell. New York: Dutton.

Rey, H. A. (1941). *Curious George.* Boston: Houghton.

Richard, Adrienne. (1989). *Pistol.* Boston: Little, Brown.

Richardson, Wendy. (1991). *Animals: Through the eyes of artists.* San Francisco: Children's Book Press.

Richardson, Wendy. (1991). *Families: Through the eyes of artists.* San Francisco: Children's Book Press.

Richardson, Wendy. (1991). *Natural world: Through the eyes of artists.* San Francisco: Children's Book Press.

Richmond, Robin. (1992). *Introducing Michelangelo.* Boston: Little, Brown.

Richter, H. P. (1970). *Friedrich.* Trans. Edite Kroll. New York: Holt.

Rinard, Judith, E. (1990). *Along a rocky shore.* Washington, DC: National Geographic.

Rinard, Judith E. (1987). *Wildlife, making a comeback: How humans are helping.* Washington, DC: National Geographic.

Ringgold, Faith. (1991). *Tar beach.* New York: Crown.

Ringgold, Faith. (1992). *Aunt Harriet's underground railroad in the sky.* New York: Crown.

Robart, Rose. (1987). *The cake that Mack ate.* Illus. Maryann Kovalski. Boston: Little, Brown, Joy Street.

Robbins, Ken. (1991). *Bridges.* New York: Dial.

Roberts, Willo Davis. (1975). *The view from the cherry tree.* New York: Atheneum.

Roberts, Willo Davis. (1989). *What could go wrong?* New York: Atheneum.

Roberts, Willo Davis. (1990). *To grandmother's house we go.* New York: Atheneum.

Robertson, Keith. (1958). *Henry Reed, Inc.* New York: Viking.

Robertson, Keith. (1963). *Henry Reed's journey.* New York: Viking.

Robertson, Keith. (1966). *Henry Reed's babysitting service.* New York: Viking.

Robertson, Keith. (1970). *Henry Reed's big show.* New York: Viking.

Robertson, Keith. (1986). *Henry Reed's think tank.* New York: Viking.

Robins, Joan. (1985). *Addie meets Max.* Illus. Sue Truesdell. New York: HarperCollins.

Rockwell, Anne. (1973). *My doctor.* New York: Macmillan.

Rockwell, Anne. (1987). *Bikes.* New York: Dutton.

Rockwell, Anne. (1989). *Bear child's book of special days.* New York: Dutton.

Rockwell, Thomas. (1973). *How to eat fried worms.* New York: Watts.

Rodanas, K. (1991). *Dragonfly's Tale.* New York: Clarion.

Rodari, Florian. (1992). *A weekend with Picasso.* New York: Rizzoli.

Rodgers, Mary. (1972). *Freaky friday.* New York: HarperCollins.

Roe, Eileen. (1991). *Con mi hermano: With my brother.* New York: Bradbury.

Rogasky, Barbara. (1988). *Smoke and ashes: The story of the Holocaust.* New York: Holiday.

Rogers, Jean. (1988). *Runaway mittens.* Illus. Rie Munoz. New York: Greenwillow.

Roginski, Jim. (1985). *Behind the covers.* Littleton, CO: Libraries Unlimited.

Rohmer, Harriet. (1989; o.p.). *The invisible hunters.* Illus. Joe Sam. San Francisco: Children's Book Press.

Rohmer, Harriet. (1990). *Uncle Nacho's hat: A folktale from Nicaragua.* San Francisco: Children's Book Press.

Rohmer, Harriet. (1988). *Atariba & Niguayona: A story from the Taino people of Puerto Rico.* San Francisco: Children's Book Press.

Roop, Peter, & Roop, Connie. (1986). *Buttons for General Washington.* Minneapolis: Carolrhoda.

Roop, Peter, & Roop, Connie. (1990). *I. Columbus: My journal—1492.* New York: Walker.

Roscoe, William. (1807). *The butterfly's ball.* London: J. Harris.

Rosen, Michael. (1989). *We're going on a bear hunt.* New York: Macmillan, McElderry.

Rosen, Michael J. (1992). *Elijah's angel: A story for Chanukah and Christmas.* Illus. Aminah Brenda Lynn Robinson. San Diego: Harcourt.

Rosen, Michael J. (1992). *Home: A collaboration of thirty distinguished authors and illustrators of children's books to aid the homeless.* New York: HarperCollins, Zolotow.

Rosenberg, Maxine B. (1991). *Brothers and sisters.* Photos by George Ancona. Boston: Houghton.

Ross, Rhea Beth. (1991). *Hillbilly choir.* Boston: Houghton.

Rostkowski, Margaret. (1986). *After the dancing days.* New York: HarperCollins.

Rostkowski, Margaret. (1989). *The best of friends.* New York: HarperCollins.

Roth, Susan. (1990). *Marco Polo: His notebook.* New York: Doubleday.

Roth-Hano, Renee. (1988). *Touch wood: A girl-*

hood in occupied France. New York: Macmillan.

Rounds, Glen. (1984). *The morning the sun refused to rise: An original Paul Bunyan tale.* New York: Holiday.

Rounds, Glen. (1990). *I know an old lady who swallowed a fly.* New York: Holiday.

Royds, Caroline (ed.). (1986; o.p.). *Poems for young children.* Illus. Inga Moore. New York: Doubleday.

Rubenstein, G. (1988). *Space demons.* New York: Dial.

Rudolph, Marguerita. (1992). Adapted from Konstantin Ushinsky. *How a shirt grew in the field.* Illus. Erika Weih. New York: Clarion.

Rudolph, Marguerita. (1988). *Gray neck.* Adapted from D. N. Mamin-Sibiryak. Illus. Leslie Shuman Kronz. Owings Mills, MD: Stemmer.

Russell, William F. (1989). *Classic myths to read aloud.* New York: Crown.

Russo, Marisabina. (1986). *The line up book.* New York: Greenwillow.

Russo, Marisabina. (1988). *Only six more days.* New York: Greenwillow.

Ryan, Mary. (1991). *Me two.* Illus. Rob Sauber. Boston: Little, Brown.

Ryder, Joanne. (1982). *The snail's spell.* Illus. Lynne Cherry. New York: Warne.

Ryder, Joanne. (1992). *Dancers in the garden.* San Francisco: Sierra Club.

Ryder, Joanne. (1991). *When the woods hum.* Illus. Catherine Stock. New York: Morrow.

Rylant, Cynthia. (1982). *When I was young in the mountains.* Illus. Diane Goode. New York: Dutton.

Rylant, Cynthia. (1983). *Miss Maggie.* Illus. Thomas DiGrazia. New York: Dutton.

Rylant, Cynthia. (1984). *Waiting to waltz: A childhood.* Illus. Stephen Gammell. New York: Bradbury.

Rylant, Cynthia. (1985). *Every living thing.* Illus. S. D. Schindler. New York: Bradbury.

Rylant, Cynthia. (1985). *The relatives came.* Illus. Stephen Gammell. New York: Bradbury.

Rylant, Cynthia. (1986). *A fine white dust.* New York: Bradbury.

Rylant, Cynthia. (1987). *Henry and Mudge in the green time.* New York: Bradbury.

Rylant, Cynthia. (1987). *Henry and Mudge in puddle trouble.* Illus. Sucie Stevenson. New York: Bradbury.

Rylant, Cynthia. (1987). *Henry and Mudge: The first book.* Illus. Sucie Stevenson. New York: Bradbury.

Rylant, Cynthia. (1987). *Henry and Mudge under the yellow moon.* New York: Bradbury.

Rylant, Cynthia. (1988). *All I see.* Illus. Peter Catalanotto. New York: Orchard.

Rylant, Cynthia. (1988). *Henry and Mudge in the sparkle days.* Illus. Sucie Stevenson. New York: Bradbury.

Rylant, Cynthia. (1989). *But I'll be back again: An album.* New York: Orchard.

Rylant, Cynthia. (1989). *Henry and Mudge and the forever sea.* Illus. Sucie Stevenson. New York: Bradbury.

Rylant, Cynthia. (1989). *Henry and Mudge get the cold shivers.* Illus. Sucie Stevenson. New York: Bradbury.

Rylant, Cynthia. (1990). *Henry and Mudge and the happy cat.* Illus. Sucie Stevenson. New York: Bradbury.

Rylant, Cynthia. (1990). *Soda jerk.* Illus. Peter Catalanotto. New York: Orchard.

Rylant, Cynthia. (1991). *Appalachia: The voices of sleeping birds.* Illus. Barry Moser. San Diego: Harcourt.

Rylant, Cynthia. (1991). *Henry and Mudge and the bedtime thumps.* Illus. Sucie Stevenson. New York: Bradbury.

Rylant, Cynthia. (1991). *Henry and Mudge take the big test.* Illus. Sucie Stevenson. New York: Bradbury.

Rylant, Cynthia. (1992). *Best wishes.* Illus. Carlo Ontal. Katonah, NY: Richard C. Owen.

Rylant, Cynthia. (1992). *Henry and Mudge and the long weekend.* Illus. Sucie Stevenson. New York: Bradbury.

Rylant, Cynthia. (1992). *Missing May.* New York: Orchard.

Sachs, Marilyn. (1983). *Fourteen.* New York: Dutton.

Sachs, Marilyn. (1987). *Almost fifteen.* New York: Dutton.

Sachs, Marilyn. (1987). *Bear's house.* New York: Dutton.

Sachs, Marilyn. (1987). *Fran Ellen's house.* New York: Dutton.

Sachs, Marilyn. (1989). *Just like a friend.* New York: Dutton.

Sachs, Marilyn. (1992). *Circles.* New York: Dutton.

Sage, Alison (reteller). (1991). *Rumpelstiltskin.* Illus. Gennady Spirin. New York: Dial.

St. George, Judith. (1990). *The White House: Cornerstone of a nation.* New York: Putnam.

St. Nicholas magazine. 1873–1943.

Saller, Carol. (1991). *The bridge dancers.* Minneapolis: Carolrhoda.

Sandburg, Carl. (1975). *Abe Lincoln grows up.* San Diego: Harcourt.

Sandburg, Carl. (1975). *Abraham Lincoln: The prairie years.* San Diego: Harcourt.

Sanders, Scott. (1985). *Hear the wind blow: American folk songs retold.* Illus. Ponder Goembel. New York: Bradbury.

Sanders, Scott. (1989). *Aurora means dawn.* Illus. Jill Kastner. New York: Bradbury.

Sandin, Joan. (1981). *The long way to a new land.* New York: HarperCollins.

Sandin, Joan. (1989). *The long way westward.* New York: HarperCollins.

San Souci, Robert. (1990). *The talking eggs: A folktale from the American South.* Illus. Jerry Pinkney. New York: Dial.

San Souci, Robert. (1991). *N. C. Wyeth's pilgrims.* San Francisco: Chronicle.

San Souci, Robert. (1992). *Sukey and the mermaid.* Illus. Brian Pinkney. New York: Four Winds, Macmillan.

Sara. (1991). *Across town.* New York: Orchard.

Sargent, Sara. (1986). *Watermusic.* New York: Clarion.

Sato, Satoru. (1989). *I wish I had a big, big tree.* Illus. Tsutomu Nurakami. New York: Lothrop.

Sattler, Helen Roney. (1990). *Giraffes, the sentinels of the Savannas.* Illus. Christopher Santoro. New York: Lothrop.

Say, Allen. (1982). *Bicycle man.* Boston: Houghton.

Say, Allen. (1990). *El chino.* Boston: Houghton.

Say, Allen. (1991). *Tree of cranes.* Boston: Houghton.

Scheer, Julian. (1964). *Rain makes applesauce.* Illus. Marvin Bileck. New York: Holiday.

Schermbrucker, Reviva. (1991). *Charlie's house.* Illus. Niki Daly. New York: Viking.

Schick, Eleanor. (1992). *I have another language: The language is dance.* New York: Macmillan.

Schlein, Miriam. (1990). *The year of the Panda.* Illus. Kam Mak. New York: HarperCollins.

Schlein, Miriam. (1991). *Let's go dinosaur tracking!* Illus. Kate Duke. New York: HarperCollins.

Schloredt, Valeri. (1990). *Martin Luther King, Jr.* Milwaukee: Gareth Stevens.

Schnabel, Ernst. (1959). *Anne Frank: A portrait of courage.* London: Longmans Green.

Schon, Isabel. (1983). *Dona Blanca and other Hispanic nursery rhymes and games.* Minneapolis: Denison.

Schorsch, Nancy T. (1991). *Saving the condor.* New York: Watts.

Schroeder, Alan. (1989). *Ragtime Tumpie.* Illus. Bernie Fuchs. Boston: Little, Brown.

Schur, Maxine. (1986). *Hannah Szenes: A song of light.* Philadelphia: Jewish Publication Society.

Schwartz, Alvin. (1973). *Witcracks: Jokes and jests from American folklore.* Illus. John O'Brien. New York: HarperCollins.

Schwartz, Alvin. (1975, 1990). *Whoppers: Tall tales and other lies.* New York: HarperCollins.

Schwartz, Alvin. (1980). *Flapdoodle: Pure nonsense from American folklore.* New York: HarperCollins.

Schwartz, Alvin. (1989). *I saw you in the bathtub and other folk rhymes.* Illus. Syd Hoff. New York: HarperCollins.

Schwartz, Alvin. (1992). *And the green grass grew all around.* Illus. Sue Truesdell. New York: HarperCollins.

Schwartz, Amy. (1983). *Mrs. Moskowitz and the sabbath candlesticks.* Philadelphia: Jewish Publication Society.

Schwartz, Amy. (1988). *Annabelle Swift, kindergartner.* New York: Orchard.

Schwartz, D. M. (1988). *The hidden life of the pond.* Illus. Dwight Kuhn. New York: Crown.

Schwartz, David. (1985). *How much is a million?* Illus. Steven Kellogg. New York: Lothrop.

Schwartz, David. (1989). *If you made a million.* Illus. Steven Kellogg. New York: Lothrop.

Schwartz, Howard, & Rush, Barbara (retellers). (1991). *The diamond tree: Jewish tales from around the world.* Illus. Uri Shulevitz. New York: HarperCollins.

Scieszka, Jon. (1989). *The true story of the Three Little Pigs.* Illus. Lane Smith. New York: Viking.

Scieszka, Jon. (1991). *The Frog Prince continued.* Illus. Steve Johnson. New York: Viking, Kestrel.

Scieszka, Jon. (1992). *The stinky cheese man: And other fairly stupid tales.* Illus. Lane Smith. New York: Viking.

Scott, Ann Herbert. (1967). *Sam.* Illus. Symeon Shimin. New York: McGraw-Hill.

Scott, Ann Herbert. (1992). *On mother's lap.* Illus. Glo Coalson. New York: Clarion.

Scott, Jack Denton. (1988). *Swans.* Photos by Ozzie Sweet. New York: Putnam.

Scott, Richard. (1987). *Jackie Robinson.* New York: Chelsea.

Sears, Peter. (1990). *Gonna bake me a rainbow: A student guide to writing poetry.* New York: Scholastic.

Sebestyen, Ouida. (1979). *Words by heart.* Boston: Little, Brown.

Sebestyen, Ouida. (1982). *IOU's.* Boston: Little, Brown.

Seeger, Pete. (1986). *Abiyoyo: Based on a South African lullaby and folk story.* Illus. Michael Hays. New York: Macmillan.

Segal, Jerry. (1991). *The place where nobody stopped.* Illus. Dav Pilkey. New York: Orchard.

Segal, Lore. (1970). *Tell me a Mitzi.* Illus. Harriet Pincus. New York: Farrar, Straus & Giroux.

Segal, Lore. (1977). *Tell me a Trudy.* Illus. Rosemary Wells. New York: Farrar, Straus & Giroux.

Segal, Lore. (1987). *The book of Adam to Moses.* Illus. Leonard Baskin. New York: Schocken.

Selden, George. (1960). *Cricket in Times Square.* New York: Farrar, Straus & Giroux.

Semel, Nava. (1990). *Becoming Gershona.* New York: Viking.

Sendak, Maurice. (1962). *Chicken soup with rice: A book of months.* New York: HarperCollins.

Sendak, Maurice. (1962). *One was Johnny: A counting book.* New York: HarperCollins.

Sendak, Maurice. (1962). *Pierre: A cautionary tale in five chapters and a prologue.* New York: HarperCollins.

Sendak, Maurice. (1963). *Where the wild things are.* New York: HarperCollins.

Sendak, Maurice. (1970). *In the night kitchen.* New York: HarperCollins.

Sendak, Maurice. (1981). *Outside over there.* New York: HarperCollins.

Sendak, Maurice. (1988). *Dear Mili.* From Grimm. New York: Farrar, Straus & Giroux.

Sendak, Maurice, & Margolis, Matthew. (1976). *Some swell pup or are you sure you want a dog.* New York: Farrar, Straus & Giroux.

Serfozo, Mary. (1988). *Who said red?* Illus. Keiko Narashashi. New York: McElderry.

Service, Pamela. (1988). *Stinker from space.* New York: Scribner's.

Service, Robert. (1987). *The cremation of Sam McGee.* Illus. Ted Harrison. New York: Greenwillow.

Service, Robert. (1988). *The shooting of Dan McGrew.* Illus. Ted Harrison. Boston: Godine.

Sesame Street magazine. 1971–present. New York: Children's Television Workshop.

Seuss, Dr. (1958). *Yertle the turtle.* New York: Random.

Seuss, Dr. (1961). *Sneetches and other stories.* New York: Random.

Seuss, Dr. (1966). *The cat in the hat.* New York: Random.

Seuss, Dr. (1971). *The lorax.* New York: Random.

Seuss, Dr. (1990). *Oh, the places you'll go!* New York: Random.

Sewall, Marcia. (1986). *The Pilgrims of Plimoth.* New York: Atheneum.

Sewall, Marcia. (1990). *People of the breaking day.* New York: Atheneum.

Sewell, Anna. (1945). *Black Beauty: The autobiography of a horse.* New York: Putnam.

Serraillier, Ian. (1972). *Escape from Warsaw.* New York: Scholastic.

Shalant, Phyllis. (1991). *Look what we've brought you from Mexico.* Englewood Cliffs, NJ: Messner.

Shamir, Ilana, & Shavit, Shlomo (eds.). (1987). *The young reader's encyclopedia of Jewish history.* New York: Viking.

Sharmat, Marjorie. (1970). *Gladys told me to meet her here.* Illus. Edward Frascino. New York: HarperCollins.

Sharmat, Marjorie W. (1981). *Nate the great and the missing key.* New York: Putnam.

Sharon, Lois, & Bram (compilers). *Elephant jam* (rev. ed.). Illus. David Shaw. New York: Crown.

Shaw, Nancy. (1988). *Sheep in a shop.* Illus. Margot Apple. Boston: Houghton.

Shea, Pegi Deitz. (1991). *Bungalow Fungalow.* Illus. Elizabeth Sayles. New York: Clarion.

Sheffield, Margaret. (1973). *Where do babies come from?* Illus. Sheila Bewley. New York: Knopf.

Shemie, Bonnie. (1990). *Houses of bark: Tipi, wigwam and longhouse.* Plattsburgh, NY: Tundra.

Sherman, Eileen Bluestone. (1986). *Monday in Odessa.* Philadelphia: Jewish Publication Society.

Sherman, Josepha (reteller). (1988). *Vassilisa the wise: A tale of medieval Russia.* Illus. Daniel San Souci. San Diego: Harcourt.

Shimin, Margarethe. (1988; o.p.). *The little riders.* New York: Putnam.

Shore, Laura Jan. (1986; o.p.). *The sacred moon tree.* New York: Bradbury.

Shorto, Russell. (1990). *David Farragut and the great naval blockade.* Boston: Silver Burdett.

Showell, Ellen Harvey. (1991). *Our mountain.* New York: Bradbury.

Shub, Elizabeth. (1982). *The white stallion.* Illus. Rachel Isadora. New York: Greenwillow.

Shulevitz, Uri. (1974). *Dawn.* New York: Farrar, Straus & Giroux.

Shura, Mary Frances. (1991). *Gentle Annie.* New York: Scholastic.

Shusterman, Neal. (1992). *Speeding bullet.* New York: Scholastic.

Shute, Linda (reteller). (1988). *Clever Tom and the leprechaun.* New York: Lothrop.

Sidney, Margaret. (1880; 1976 reprint). *The five little Peppers and how they grew.* New York: Lothrop.

Siebert, Diane. (1988). *Mojave.* Illus. Wendell Minor. New York: HarperCollins.

Siegal, Aranka. (1981). *Upon the head of a goat: A childhood in Hungary 1939–1944.* New York: Farrar, Straus & Giroux.

Siegal, Aranka. (1985). *Grace in the wilderness: After the liberation, 1945–1948.* New York: Dutton.

Siegel, Beatrice. (1985). *Sam Ellis's island.* New York: Four Winds, Macmillan.

Siegel, Beatrice. (1992). *The year they walked: Rosa Parks and the Montgomery bus boycott.* New York: Four Winds, Macmillan.

Silverstein, Shel. (1964). *The giving tree.* New York: HarperCollins.

Silverstein, Shel. (1974). *Where the sidewalk ends.* New York: HarperCollins.

Silverstein, Shel. (1981). *A light in the attic.* New York: HarperCollins.

Simon, Seymour. (1979; o.p.). *The secret clocks: Time sense of living things.* Illus. Jan Brett. New York: Viking.

Simon, Seymour. (1980). *Einstein Anderson: Science sleuth.* New York: Puffin Penguin.

Simon, Seymour. (1980). *Einstein Anderson shocks his friends.* New York: Puffin Penguin.

Simon, Seymour. (1981). *Einstein Anderson makes up for lost time.* New York: Puffin Penguin.

Simon, Seymour. (1982). *Einstein Anderson lights up the sky.* New York: Puffin Penguin.

Simon, Seymour. (1983). *Einstein Anderson sees through the invisible man.* New York: Puffin Penguin.

Simon, Seymour. (1987). *Uranus.* New York: Morrow.

Simon, Seymour. (1988). *Volcanoes.* New York: Morrow.

Simon, Seymour. (1990). *New questions and answers about dinosaurs.* Illus. Jennifer Dewey. New York: Morrow.

Simon, Seymour. (1990). *Oceans.* New York: Morrow.

Simon, Seymour. (1991). *Neptune.* New York: Morrow.

Singer, Isaac Bashevis. (1966). *Zlateh the goat and other stories.* Illus. Maurice Sendak. New York: HarperCollins.

Singer, Isaac Bashevis. (1974). *Why Noah chose the dove.* Illus. Eric Carle. New York: Farrar, Straus & Giroux.

Singer, Marilyn. (1989). *Turtle in July.* Illus. Jerry Pinkney. New York: Macmillan.

Sis, Peter. (1991). *Follow the dream: The story of Christopher Columbus.* New York: Knopf.

Skira-Venturi, Rosabianca. (1990). *A weekend with Renoir.* New York: Rizzoli.

Sleator, William. (1975). *Among the dolls.* Illus. Trina Schart Hyman. New York: Dutton.

Sleator, William. (1988). *Duplicate.* New York: Dutton.

Slepian, Jan. (1989). *The broccoli tapes.* New York: Putnam.

Slepian, Jan. (1990). *Risk n' roses.* New York: Putnam.

Sloat, Teri. (1989). *From letter to letter.* New York: Dutton.

Sloat, Teri. (1990). *The eye of the needle.* New York: Dutton.

Slobodkina, Esphyr. (1947). *Caps for sale.* Glenview IL: Scott, Foresman.

Slote, Alfred. (1973). *Hang tough, Paul Mather.* New York: HarperCollins.

Slote, Alfred. (1978). *My trip to Alpha I.* New York: HarperCollins.

Slote, Alfred. (1982). *Rabbit ears.* New York: HarperCollins.

Slote, Alfred. (1983). *Omega station.* Illus. Anthony Kramer. New York: HarperCollins.

Slote, Alfred. (1989). *Make-believe ball player.* New York: HarperCollins.

Slote, Alfred. (1991). *Finding Buck McHenry.* New York: HarperCollins.

Slote, Alfred. (1990). *The trading game.* New York: HarperCollins.

Smalls-Hector, Irene. (1991). *Irene and the big, fine nickel.* Illus. Tyrone Geter. Boston: Little, Brown.

Smith, Barry. (1991). *Minnie and Ginger.* New York: Crown.

Smith, Doris Buchanan. (1986). *Return to Bitter Creek.* New York: Viking.

Smith, Doris Buchanan. (1987). *Karate dancer.* New York: Putnam.

Smith, Doris Buchanan. (1989). *Voyages.* New York: Viking.

Smith, Janice Lee. (1981). *The monster in the third dresser drawer.* New York: HarperCollins.

Smith, Janice Lee. (1984). *The kid next door and other headaches.* New York: HarperCollins.

Smith, Janice Lee. (1988). *The show-and-tell war: And other stories about Adam Joshua.* New York: HarperCollins.

Smith, Janice Lee. (1989). *It's not easy being George.* New York: HarperCollins.

Smith, Marya. (1991). *Across the creek.* Boston: Arcade, Little, Brown.

Smith, Marya. (1990). *Winter broken.* Boston: Arcade, Little, Brown.

Smith, Robert Kimmel. (1989). *Bobby Baseball.* New York: Delacorte.

Smith, Ronald. (1990). *Sea otter rescue: The aftermath of an oil spill.* New York: Dutton.

Smith, T. H. (1986). *Cry to the night wind.* New York: Viking.

Smith, William Jay. (1980, 1987). *Laughing time: Collected nonsense.* Illus. Fernando Krahn. New York: Farrar, Straus & Giroux.

Smith, William Jay, & Ra, Carol. (1992). *Behind the king's kitchen: A roster of rhyming riddles.* Illus. Jacques Hnizdovsky. Honesdale, PA: Boyds Mills.

Smothers, Ethel F. (1992). *Down in the piney woods.* New York: Knopf.

Smucker, Barbara. (1979). *Runaway to freedom.* New York: HarperCollins.

Sneve, Virginia Driving Hawk. (1989). *Dancing tepees.* Illus. Stephen Gammell. New York: Holiday.

Snyder, Diane. (1988). *Boy of the three-year nap.* Boston: Houghton.

Snyder, Zilpha Keatley. (1986). *The Egypt game.* New York: Dell.

Snyder, Zilpha Keatley. (1990). *Libby on Wednesday.* New York: Delacorte.

Sobol, Donald. (1990). *Encyclopedia Brown and the case of the disgusting sneakers.* New York: Morrow.

Sobol, Donald. (1991). *Encyclopedia Brown takes the cake.* New York: Scholastic.

Solotareff, Gregoire. (1988). *Don't call me little bunny.* New York: Farrar, Straus & Giroux.

Solotareff, Gregoire. (1990). *Noel's Christmas secret.* New York: Farrar, Straus & Giroux.

Soto, Gary. (1991). *Baseball in April and other stories.* San Diego: Harcourt.

Soto, Gary. (1991). *A fire in my hands.* Illus. James M. Cardillo. New York: Scholastic.

Soto, Gary. (1991). *Summer life.* New York: Dell.

Soto, Gary. (1991). *Taking sides.* San Diego: Harcourt.

Soto, Gary. (1992). *Living up the street.* New York: Dell.

Soto, Gary. (1992). *Neighborhood odes.* Illus. David Diaz. San Diego: Harcourt.

Soto, Gary. (1992). *Pacific crossing.* San Diego: Harcourt.

Souza, Dorothy M. (1991). *Insects around the house.* Minneapolis: Carolrhoda.

Souza, Dorothy M. (1991). *Insects in the garden.* Minneapolis: Carolrhoda.

Speare, Elizabeth George. (1958). *The witch of Blackbird Pond.* Boston: Houghton.

Speare, Elizabeth George. (1961). *The bronze bow.* Boston: Houghton.

Speare, Elizabeth George. (1983). *The sign of the beaver.* Boston: Houghton.

Sperry, Armstrong. (1940). *Call it courage.* New York: Macmillan.

Spiegelman, Art. (1986). *Maus I* New York: Pantheon.

Spiegelman, Art. (1991). *Maus II.* New York: Pantheon.

Spier, Peter. (1961, 1989). *The fox went out on a chilly night.* New York: Doubleday.

Spier, Peter. (1967). *The legend of New Amsterdam.* New York: Doubleday.

Spier, Peter. (1967). *To market! To market!* New York: Doubleday.

Spier, Peter. (1977). *Noah's ark.* New York: Doubleday.

Spier, Peter. (1982). *Rain.* New York: Doubleday.

Spinelli, Jerry. (1990). *The bathwater gang.* Boston: Little, Brown.

Spinelli, Jerry. (1990). *Maniac Magee.* Boston: Little, Brown.

Spinelli, Jerry. (1991). *There's a girl in my hammerlock.* New York: Simon & Schuster.

Spinka, Penina Keen. (1992). *Mother's blessing.* New York: Macmillan.

Spyri, Johanna. (1884; 1984 reprint). *Heidi.* New York: Knopf.

Staines, Bill (author/composer). (1989). *All God's critters got a place in the choir.* Illus. Margot Zemach. New York: Dutton.

Stanek, Muriel. (1989). *I speak English for my mom.* Illus. Judith Friedman. Morton Grove, IL: A. Whitman.

Stanley, Diane. (1986). *Peter the great.* New York: Macmillan, Four Winds.

Stanley, Diane, & Vennema, Peter. (1988). *Shaka: King of the Zulus.* New York: Morrow.

Stanley, Diane, & Vennema, Peter. (1990). *Good Queen Bess: the story of Elizabeth I of England.* New York: Four Winds, Macmillan.

Stanley, Diane, & Vennema, Peter. (1992). *Bard of Avon: The story of William Shakespeare.* New York: Morrow.

Staples, Suzanne Fisher. (1989). *Shabanu.* New York: Knopf.

Steele, William O. (1990). *The perilous road.* San Diego: Harcourt.

Steele, William O. (1979; o.p.). *The magic amulet.* San Diego: Harcourt.

Steig, Jeanne. (1988). *Consider the lemming.* Illus. William Steig. New York: Farrar, Straus & Giroux.

Steig, William. (1969, 1988). *Sylvester and the magic pebble.* New York: Simon & Schuster.

Steig, William. (1971). *Amos and Boris.* New York: Farrar, Straus & Giroux.

Steig, William. (1976). *The amazing bone.* New York: Farrar, Straus & Giroux.

Steig, William. (1977). *Caleb & Kate.* New York: Farrar, Straus & Giroux.

Steig, William. (1982). *Dr. DeSoto.* New York: Farrar, Straus & Giroux.

Steig, William. (1985). *Abel's island.* New York: Farrar, Straus & Giroux.

Steig, William. (1986). *Brave Irene.* New York: Farrar, Straus & Giroux.

Steig, William. (1988). *Spinky sulks.* New York: Farrar, Straus & Giroux.

Steig, William. (1992). *Doctor De Soto goes to Africa.* New York: HarperCollins.

Steiner, Jorg. (1972). *Rabbit Island.* Trans. Ann Conrad Lammers. Illus. Jorg Müller. San Diego: Harcourt.

Steptoe, John. (1969). *Stevie.* New York: HarperCollins.

Steptoe, John. (1988). *Baby says.* New York: Lothrop.

Steptoe, John. (1984). *The story of jumping mouse.* New York: Lothrop.

Steptoe, John. (1987). *Mufaro's beautiful daughters: An African tale.* New York: Lothrop.

Stevens, Janet. (1984). *The tortoise and the hare: An Aesop fable.* New York: Holiday.

Stevens, Janet. (1987). *The town mouse and the country mouse: An Aesop fable.* New York: Holiday.

Stevens, Janet. (1987). *The three billy goats gruff.* San Diego: Harcourt.

Stevens, Janet. (1990). *How the Manx cat lost its tail.* Reteller & Illus. Janet Stevens. San Diego: Harcourt.

Stevenson, James. (1986). *When I was nine.* New York: Greenwillow.

Stevenson, James. (1988). *We hate rain!* New York: Greenwillow.

Stevenson, Laura. (1990). *Happily after all.* Boston: Houghton.

Stevenson, Robert Louis. (1883; 1981). *Treasure Island.* Illus. N. C. Wyeth. New York: Scribner's.

Stevenson, Robert Louis. (1885; 1985). *A child's*

garden of verses. Illus. Michael Foreman. New York: Delacorte.

Stevenson, Robert Louis. (1905). *A child's garden of verses.* Illus. Jessie Willcox Smith. New York: Macmillan.

Stevenson, Robert Louis. (1926; 1990). *A child's garden of verses.* Illus. Henriette Willebeek le Mair. New York: Putnam, Philomel.

Stevenson, Robert Louis. (1988). *The land of nod: And other poems for children.* Selector & Illus. Michael Hague. New York: Henry Holt.

Still, James. (1977; o.p.). *Jack and the wonder beans.* Illus. Margot Tomes. New York: Putnam.

Stock, Catherine (author/illus.). (1990). *Armien's fishing trip.* New York: Morrow.

Stolz, Mary. (1989). *Storm in the night.* Illus. Pat Cummings. New York: HarperCollins.

Stolz, Mary. (1990). *Bartholomew fair.* New York: Greenwillow.

Stolz, Mary. (1991). *Go fish.* Illus. Pat Cummings. New York: HarperCollins.

Stoutenberg, Adrien. (1976). *American tall tales.* Illus. Richard M. Powers. New York: Puffin.

Stoutenberg, Adrien. (1976). *American tall tale animals.* New York: Puffin.

Stow, Jenny. (1992). *The house that Jack built.* New York: Dial.

Stowe, Harriet Beecher. (1966 reprint). *Uncle Tom's cabin.* New York: Dutton.

Stratemeyer, Edward. (1898). *Under Dewey at Manilla.* Boston: Lee & Shepard.

Strauss, Gwen. (1990). *Trail of stones.* Illus. Anthony Browne. New York: Knopf.

Strommen, Judith Bernie. (1990). *Grady the great.* New York: Holt.

Sufrin, Mark. (1991). *George Catlin: Painter of the Indian west.* New York: Atheneum.

Suid, Murray. (1991). *Demonic mnemonics: 800 spelling tricks for 800 tricky words.* Carthage, II: Fearon Teacher Aids.

Sullivan, Charles. (1991). *Children of promise: African American literature and art for young people.* New York: Abrams.

Sutcliff, Rosemary. (1958; o.p.). *Warrior scarlet.* Illus. Charles Keeping. New York: Walck.

Sutcliff, Rosemary. (1959; o.p.). *The lantern bearers.* New York: Walck.

Sutcliff, Rosemary. (1960; o.p.). *Knight's fee.* New York: Walck.

Sutcliff, Rosemary. (1979; o.p.). *Song for a dark queen.* New York: HarperCollins.

Sutcliff, Rosemary. (1980). *The light beyond the forest.* New York: Dutton.

Sutcliff, Rosemary. (1981). *The sword and the circle: King Arthur and the knights of the round table.* New York: Dutton.

Sutcliff, Rosemary. (1982). *The road to Camlann: The death of King Arthur.* Illus. Shirley Felts. New York: Dutton.

Sutcliff, Rosemary. (1983, 1992). *Blue remembered hills.* New York: Farrar, Straus & Giroux.

Sutcliff, Rosemary. (1987). *The eagle of the ninth.* New York: Oxford University Press.

Sutcliff, Rosemary. (1989). *Flame colored taffeta.* New York: Farrar, Straus & Giroux.

Sutcliff, Rosemary. (1990). *The shining company.* New York: Farrar, Straus & Giroux.

Suteyev, Vladimir. (1972, 1988). *Chick and the duckling.* Trans. Mirra Ginsburg. Illus. Jose Aruego & Ariane Dewey. New York: Macmillan.

Sutherland, Zena (selector). (1990). *The Orchard book of nursery rhymes.* Illus. Faith Jaques. New York: Orchard.

Sutherland, Zena, & Livingston, Myra Cohn. (1984). *The Scott Foresman anthology of children's literature.* Glenview, IL: Scott, Foresman.

Svedberg, Ulf. (1988). *Nicky the nature detective.* Illus. Lena Anderson. New York: Farrar, Straus & Giroux.

Swann, Brian. (1988). *A basket full of white eggs: Riddle poems.* Illus. Ponder Goembal. New York: Orchard.

Sweet, Melissa. (1992). *Fiddle-i-fee: A farmyard song for the very young.* Boston: Little, Brown, Joy Street.

Swift, Jonathan. (1726; 1952 reprint). *Gulliver's travels.* Illus. Arthur Rackham. New York: Dutton.

Tackach, Jim. (1991). *Hank Aaron.* New York: Chelsea.

Tadjo, Veronique (reteller). (1989). *Lord of the dance: An African retelling.* New York: HarperCollins.

Tafuri, Nancy. (1983). *Early morning in the barn.* New York: Greenwillow.

Tafuri, Nancy. (1984). *Have you seen my duckling?* New York: Greenwillow.

Tafuri, Nancy. (1987). *Do not disturb.* New York: Greenwillow.

Tafuri, Nancy. (1988). *Spots, feathers, and curly tails.* New York: Greenwillow.

Talbert, Marc. (1992). *The purple heart.* New York: HarperCollins.

Tashjian, Virginia. (1969). *Juba this and juba that: Story hour sketches for large or small groups.* Boston: Little, Brown.

Tashjian, Virginia. (1974). *With a deep sea smile: Story hour sketches for large or small groups.* Boston: Little, Brown.

Taylor, Ann, & Taylor, Jane. (1804; 1977 reprint). *Original poems for infant minds.* New York: Garland.

Taylor, C. J. (1990). *How Two-Feather was saved from loneliness.* Plattsburgh, NY: Tundra.

Taylor, Judy. (1987). *Beatrix Potter: Artist, storyteller, and countrywoman.* New York: Warne.

Taylor, Judy. (1988). *Beatrix Potter 1866–1943: The artist and her work.* New York: Warne.

Taylor, Judy. (1990). *Beatrix Potter's letters.* New York: Warne.

Taylor, Judy (compiler). (1992). *Letters to children from Beatrix Potter.* New York: Warne.

Taylor, Mildred. (1976). *Roll of thunder, hear my cry.* New York: Dial.

Taylor, Mildred. (1981). *Let the circle be unbroken.* New York: Dial.

Taylor, Mildred. (1985). *Song of the trees.* New York: Dial.

Taylor, Mildred. (1987). *The friendship.* New York: Dial.

Taylor, Mildred. (1990). *Mississippi bridge.* New York: Dial.

Taylor, Mildred. (1990). *The road to Memphis.* New York: Dial.

Taylor, Paul D. (1990). *Fossil.* Eyewitness series. Photos by Colin Keates. New York: Knopf.

Taylor, Sydney. (1951). *All of a kind family.* Chicago: Follett.

Taylor, Sydney. (1958). *All of a kind family uptown.* New York: Taylor.

Taylor, Sydney. (1973). *All of a kind family downtown.* New York: Taylor.

Taylor, Sydney. (1973). *Ella of all of a kind family.* New York: Taylor.

Taylor, Theodore. (1969). *The cay.* New York: Doubleday.

Taylor, Theodore. (1991). *The weirdo.* San Diego: Harcourt.

Tchudi, Susan, & Tchudi, Stephen. (1984). *The young writer's handbook: A practical guide for the beginner who is serious about writing.* New York: Scribner's.

Tejima, Keizaburo. (1987). *Owl lake.* New York: Philomel.

Tejima, Keizaburo. (1990). *Ho-limlim: A rabbit tale from Japan.* New York: Philomel.

Terban, Marvin. (1983). *In a pickle and other funny idioms.* New York: Clarion.

Terban, Marvin. (1984). *I think I thought and other tricky verbs.* New York: Clarion.

Terban, Marvin. (1986). *Your foot's on my feet! And other tricky nouns.* New York: Clarion.

Terban, Marvin. (1987). *Mad as a wet hen!* New York: Clarion.

Terban, Marvin. (1988). *Dove dove.* New York: Clarion.

Terban, Marvin. (1988). *Guppies in tuxedos: Funny eponyms.* Illus. Giulio Maestro. New York: Houghton, Clarion.

Terban, Marvin. (1990). *Punching the clock: Funny action idioms.* Boston: Houghton.

Terban, Marvin. (1991). *Hey, Hay!: A wagonful of funny homonym riddles.* New York: Clarion.

Terban, Marvin. (1993). *Time to rhyme: A rhyming dictionary.* Honesdale, PA: Boyds Mills.

Thayer, Ernest L. (1888; 1988). *Casey at the bat.* Afterword by Donald Hall. Illus. Barry Moser. New York: Crown.

Thayer, Ernest L. (1888; 1989). *Casey at the bat.* Illus. Wallace Tripp. New York: Putnam.

Thesman, Jean. (1990). *Rachel Chance.* Boston: Houghton.

Thesman, Jean. (1991). *The rain catchers.* Boston: Houghton.

Thomas, Joyce Carol. (1986). *Golden pasture.* New York: Scholastic.

Thompson, Kathleen. (1993). *Pedro Menendez de Aviles.* New York: Chelsea.

Thurber, James. (1943, 1990). *Many moons.* Illus. Marc Simont. San Diego: Harcourt.

Tilly, Nancy. (1985). *Golden girl.* New York: Farrar, Straus & Giroux.

Titus, Eve. (1990). *Anatole.* New York: Bantam.

Tobias, T. (1973; o.p.). *Isamu Noguchi: The life of a sculptor.* New York: HarperCollins.

Todd, Kathleen. (1982). *Snow.* Reading, MA: Addison-Wesley.

Tolan, Stephanie. (1992). *Sophie and the sidewalk man.* New York: Macmillan.

Tolhurst, Marilyn. (1991). *Somebody and the three Blairs.* Illus. Simone Abel. New York: Orchard.

Tolkien, J.R.R. (1938). *The hobbit.* Boston: Houghton.

Tolkien, J.R.R. (1979 reprint). *The lord of the rings.* Winchester, MA: Allen & Unwin.

Tomlinson, Theresa. (1991). *Summer witches.* New York: Macmillan.

Tompert, Ann. (1988). *The silver whistle.* Illus. Beth Peck. New York: Macmillan.

Townsend, John. (1986). *Tom Tiddler's ground.* New York: HarperCollins.

Travers, Pamela. (1934; 1972 reprint). *Mary Poppins.* Illus. Mary Shepard. San Diego: Harcourt.

Trease, Geoffrey. (1989). *Flight of angels.* Minneapolis: Lerner.

Trease, Geoffrey. (1966; o.p.). *The red towers of Granada.* New York: Macmillan.

Treseder, Terry Walton. (1990). *Hear O Israel: A story of the Warsaw ghetto.* Illus. Lloyd Bloom. New York: Atheneum.

Tresselt, Alvin. (1947). *White snow, bright snow.* Illus. Roger Duvoisin. New York: Lothrop.

Tresselt, Alvin (reteller). (1989). *The mitten: An old Ukranian folktale.* Illus. Yaroslava. Retold from version by E. Rachev. New York: Greenwillow.

Trimble, Stephen. (1990). *Village of blue stone.* Illus. Jennifer Owings Dewey. New York: Macmillan.

Trimmer, Sarah. (1786; 1976 reissue). *Fabulous histories.* New York: Garland.

Trotman, Felicity. (1985). *Davy Crockett.* Milwaukee: Raintree.

Troughton, Joanna. (1986). *How rabbit stole the fire: A North American Indian folktale.* New York: P. Bedrick Books.

Troughton, Joanna. (1986). *How the birds*

changed their feathers: A South American Indian folktale. New York: P. Bedrick Books.

Troughton, Joanna. (1990). *How stories came into the world: A folk tale from West Africa.* New York: P. Bedrick Books.

Tsutsui, Yoriko. (1987). *Anna's secret friend.* Illus. Akiko Hayashi. New York: Viking.

Tunis, John R. (1989). *World series.* San Diego: Harcourt.

Tunis, John R. (1990). *Highpockets.* New York: Morrow.

Tunis, John R. (1990). *Keystone kids.* San Diego: Harcourt.

Tunis, John R. (1990). *Rookie of the year.* San Diego: Harcourt.

Tunis, John R. (1991). *Go, team, go!* New York: Morrow.

Turkle, Brinton. (1976). *Deep in the forest.* New York: Dutton.

Turkle, Brinton. (1981). *Do not open.* New York: Dutton.

Turnbull, Ann. (1990). *Maroo of the winter caves.* New York: Clarion.

Turner, Ann. (1985). *Dakota dugout.* New York: Macmillan.

Turner, Ann. (1986). *Third girl from the left.* New York: Macmillan.

Turner, Ann. (1987). *Nettie's trip south.* Illus. Ronald Himler. New York: Macmillan.

Turner, Ann. (1987). *Time of the bison.* Illus. Beth Peck. New York: Macmillan.

Turner, Ann. (1989). *Grasshopper summer.* New York: Macmillan.

Turner, Ann. (1990). *Through moon and stars and night skies.* Illus. James Graham Hale. New York: HarperCollins.

Turner, Ann. (1992). *Katie's trunk.* Illus. Ron Himler. New York: Macmillan.

Turner, Ann, & Blake, Robert J. (1992). *Rainflowers.* New York: HarperCollins.

Turner, Dorothy. (1986). *Florence Nightingale.* New York: Watts.

Turner, Robyn M. (1991). *Georgia O'Keeffe.* Boston: Little, Brown.

Turner, Robyn M. (1991). *Rosa Bonheur.* Boston: Little, Brown.

Twain, Mark. (1876; 1989 reissue). *The adventures of Tom Sawyer.* New York: Penguin.

Twain, Mark. (1888; 1986 reissue). *The adventures of Huckleberry Finn.* New York: Penguin.

Uchida, Yoshiko. (1978). *Journey home.* Illus. Charles Robinson. New York: McElderry.

Uchida, Yoshiko. (1981). *A jar of dreams.* New York: McElderry.

Uchida, Yoshiko. (1983). *The best bad thing.* New York: McElderry.

Uchida, Yoshiko. (1985). *The happiest ending.* New York: McElderry.

Uchida, Yoshiko. (1985). *Journey to Topaz.* Illus. Donald Carrick. San Francisco: Creative Arts.

Uchida, Yoshiko. (1991). *The invisible thread: A memoir by the author of the Best Bad Thing.* Englewood Cliffs, NJ: Messner.

Udry, Janice. (1961). *Let's be enemies.* New York: HarperCollins.

Ungerer, Tomi. (1958). *Crictor.* New York: HarperCollins.

Updike, John. (1965, 1991). *A child's calendar.* Illus. Nancy Ekholm Burkert. New York: Knopf.

Uttley, Alison. (1981). *A traveler in time.* Illus. Phyllis Bray. Winchester, MA: Faber.

Van Allsburg, Chris. (1979). *The garden of Abdul Gasazi.* Boston: Houghton.

Van Allsburg, Chris. (1981). *Jumanji.* Boston: Houghton.

Van Allsburg, Chris. (1982). *Ben's dream.* Boston: Houghton.

Van Allsburg, Chris. (1983). *The wreck of the Zephyr.* Boston: Houghton.

Van Allsburg, Chris. (1984). *The mysteries of Harris Burdick.* Boston: Houghton.

Van Allsburg, Chris. (1985). *The polar express.* Boston: Houghton.

Van Allsburg, Chris. (1986). *The stranger.* Boston: Houghton.

Van Allsburg, Chris. (1988). *Two bad ants.* Boston: Houghton.

Van Allsburg, Chris. (1991). *The wretched stone.* Boston: Houghton.

Van Laan, Nancy. (1989). *Rainbow crow: A Lenape tale.* Illus. Beatriz Vidal. New York: Knopf.

Van Laan, Nancy. (1991). *The legend of El Dorado.* Illus. Beatriz Vidal. New York: Knopf.

Van Leeuwen, Jean. (1987). *Oliver, Amanda, and Grandmother Pig.* Illus. Ann Schweninger. New York: Dial.

Van Leeuwen, Jean (1989). *Dear Mom, you're ruining my life.* New York: Dial.

Van Leeuwen, Jean. (1990). *Oliver Pig at school.* Illus. Ann Schweninger. New York: Dial.

Van Leeuwen, Jean. (1992). *Going west.* Illus. Thomas B. Allen. New York: Dial.

Venezia, Mike. (1988). *Picasso.* San Francisco: Children's Book Press.

Venezia, Mike. (1988). *Rembrandt.* San Francisco: Children's Book Press.

Venezia, Mike. (1991). *Francisco Goya.* San Francisco: Children's Book Press.

Ventura, P. (1991). *1492: The year of the New World.* New York: Putnam.

Ventura, Piero. (1984). *Great painters.* New York: Putnam.

Ventura, Piero. (1989). *Great composers.* New York: Putnam.

Verdy, Violette. (1991). *Of swans, sugarplums and satin slippers: Ballet stories for children.* New York: Scholastic.

Vincent, Gabrielle. (1984). *Merry Christmas, Ernest & Celestine.* New York: Greenwillow.

Vining, Elizabeth (Gray). (1962). *I will adventure.* New York: Viking.

Viorst, Judith. (1969). *I'll fix Anthony.* New York: HarperCollins.

Viorst, Judith. (1971). *The tenth good thing about Barney.* New York: Atheneum.

Viorst, Judith. (1972). *Alexander and the terrible, horrible, no good, very bad day.* New York: Atheneum.

Viorst, Judith. (1974). *Rosie and Michael.* Illus. Lorna Tomei. New York: Atheneum.

Viorst, Judith. (1990). *Earrings!* Illus. Nola Langner Malone. New York: Atheneum.

Voigt, Cynthia. (1981). *Homecoming.* New York: Atheneum.

Voigt, Cynthia. (1982). *Dicey's song.* New York: Atheneum.

Voigt, Cynthia. (1983). *A solitary blue.* New York: Atheneum.

Voigt, Cynthia. (1985). *The runner.* New York: Atheneum.

Voigt, Cynthia. (1986). *Izzy willy-nilly.* New York: Atheneum.

Voigt, Cynthia. (1987). *Came a stranger.* New York: Atheneum.

Voigt, Cynthia. (1988). *Tree by leaf.* New York: Atheneum.

Vos, Ida. (1991). *Hide and seek.* Boston: Houghton.

Waber, Bernard. (1965). *Lyle, Lyle, crocodile.* Boston: Houghton.

Wadsworth, Ginger. (1991). *Rachel Carson: Voice for the earth.* Minneapolis: Lerner.

Wagner, Jane. (1972). *J. T.* Photos by Gordon Parks. New York: Dell.

Walker, Alice. (1974). *Langston Hughes, American poet.* New York: HarperCollins.

Walker, Paul Robert. (1988). *Pride of Puerto Rico: The life of Roberto Clemente.* San Diego: Harcourt.

Walsh, Ellen. (1989). *Mouse paint.* San Diego: Harcourt.

Walsh, Ellen. (1991). *Mouse count.* San Diego: Harcourt.

Walter, Mildred Pitts. (1990). *Justin and the best biscuits in the world.* New York: Knopf.

Wang, M. L. (1989). *The ant and the dove: An Aesop tale retold.* San Francisco: Children's Book Press.

Waters, Kate. (1989). *Sarah Morton's day: A day in the life of a Pilgrim girl.* New York: Scholastic.

Waters, Kate. (1991). *The story of the white house.* New York: Scholastic.

Waters, Kate, & Slovenz-Low, Madeline. (1990). *Lion dancer: Ernie Wan's Chinese new year.* New York: Scholastic.

Watkins, Yoko Kawashima. (1986). *So far from the bamboo grove.* New York: Lothrop.

Watson, Clyde. (1971). *Father Fox's penny-rhymes.* Illus. Wendy Watson. New York: HarperCollins.

Watson, Clyde. (1972). *Tom Fox and the apple pie.* New York: HarperCollins.

Watson, Clyde. (1991). *Father Fox's feast of songs.* Illus. Wendy Watson. Honesdale, PA: Boyds Mills.

Watson, Harvey. (1991). *Bob war and poke.* Boston: Houghton.

Watson, Wendy. (1989). *Wendy Watson's Mother Goose.* New York: Lothrop.

Watson, Wendy. (1991). *Thanksgiving at our house.* New York: Clarion.

Watts, Isaac. (1715, 1866). *Divine and moral songs for children.* London: J. Nisbet.

Weidt, Maryann N. (1989). *Presenting Judy Blume.* Boston: Twayne, G. K. Hall.

Weil, Lisl. (1986). *Pandora's box.* New York: Atheneum.

Weil, Lisl. (1990). *Let's go to the library.* New York: Holiday.

Weiss, Nicki. (1962). *On a hot, hot day.* New York: Putnam.

Weiss, Nicki (illus.). (1987). *If you're happy and you know it: Eighteen story songs.* Music arranged by John Krumich. New York: Greenwillow.

Weissberg, Ed. (1991). *Arthur Ashe.* New York: Chelsea.

Wells, Rosemary. (1979). *Max's first word. Max's new suit. Max's ride.* New York: Dial. [Boxed set of board books]

Wells, Rosemary. (1980). *When no one was looking.* New York: Dial.

Wells, Rosemary. (1985). *Max's bath. Max's birthday. Max's breakfast.* New York: Dial. [Boxed set of board books]

Wells, Rosemary. (1989). *Max's chocolate chicken.* New York: Dial.

Wells, Rosemary. (1991). *Max's dragon shirt.* New York: Dial.

Wells, Rosemary. (1992). *Shy Charles.* New York: Dial.

Westall, Robert. (1991). *Echoes of war.* New York: Farrar, Straus & Giroux.

Westall, Robert. (1991). *The kingdom by the sea.* New York: Farrar, Straus & Giroux.

Wettasinghe, Sybil. (1987). *The umbrella thief.* Brooklyn: Kane Miller.

Whaley, P. (1988). *Butterfly & moth.* New York: Knopf.

Whelan, Gloria. (1987). *Next spring an oriole.* New York: Random.

Whelan, Gloria. (1992). *Goodbye Vietnam.* New York: Knopf.

Whipple, Laura (compiler). (1989). *Eric Carle's animals animals.* New York: Putnam, Philomel.

White, Alana. (1990). *Come next spring.* Boston: Houghton.

White, E. B. (1952). *Charlotte's web.* Illus. Garth Williams. New York: HarperCollins.

White, E. B. (1970). *Trumpet of the swan.* New York: HarperCollins.

White, Ryan, & Cunningham, Ann Marie. (1991). *Ryan White: My own story.* New York: Dial.

White, Sandra, & Filisky, Michael. (1988). *Sterling:*

The rescue of a baby harbor seal. New York: Crown.

Whitfield, Philip. (1991). *Why did the dinosaurs disappear? Questions about life in the past.* New York: Viking.

Wibberley, Leonard. (1986). *John Treegate's musket.* New York: Farrar, Straus & Giroux.

Widerberg, Siv. (1989). *The big sister.* Illus. Cecilia Torudd. Translated by Birgitta Sjogren. New York: Farrar, Straus & Giroux.

Wiesner, David. (1989). *Free fall.* New York: Clarion.

Wiesner, David. (1990). *Hurricane.* New York: Clarion.

Wiesner, David. (1991). *Tuesday.* New York: Clarion.

Wiggin, Kate Douglas. (1903; 1962 reprint). *Rebecca of Sunnybrook Farm.* New York: Macmillan.

Wild, Margaret. (1991). *Let the celebrations begin.* Illus. Julie Vivas. New York: Orchard.

Wilder, Laura Ingalls. (1953). *The little house in the big woods.* Illus. Garth Williams. New York: HarperCollins.

Wilder, Laura Ingalls. (1953). *Little house on the prairie.* Illus. Garth Williams. New York: HarperCollins.

Wildsmith, Brian. (1963; o.p.). *Brian Wildsmith's ABC.* New York: Watts.

Wildsmith, Brian. (1984). *Daisy.* New York: Pantheon.

Wildsmith, Brian. (1987). *The little wood duck.* New York: Oxford University Press.

Wilkinson, Brenda. (1975). *Ludell.* New York: HarperCollins.

Willard, Nancy. (1981). *A visit to William Blake's Inn.* Illus. Alice & Martin Provensen. San Diego: Harcourt.

Willard, Nancy. (1987). *Voyage of the Ludgate Hill: Travels with Robert Louis Stevenson.* Illus. Alice & Martin Provensen. San Diego: Harcourt.

Willard, Nancy. (1989). *The ballad of Biddy Early.* Illus. Barry Moser. New York: Knopf.

Willard, Nancy. (1991). *Pish, posh, said Hieronymous Bosch.* Illus. Leo & Diane Dillon. San Diego: Harcourt.

Williams, Barbara. (1975). *Kevin's grandma.* Illus. Kay Chorao. New York: Dutton.

Williams, Garth. (1958). *The rabbit's wedding.* New York: HarperCollins.

Williams, Karen Lynn. (1990). *Galimoto.* Illus. Catherine Stock. New York: Lothrop.

Williams, Margery. (1922; 1991 reprint). *The velveteen rabbit.* Illus. William Nicholson. New York: Doubleday.

Williams, Sherley Anne. (1992). *Working cotton.* Illus. Carole Byard. San Diego: Harcourt.

Williams, Sue. (1990). *I went walking.* San Diego: Harcourt.

Williams, Vera. (1982). *A chair for my mother.* New York: Greenwillow.

Williams, Vera. (1988). *Stringbean's trip to the shining sea.* Illus. Vera Williams & Jennifer Williams. New York: Greenwillow.

Williams, Vera. (1990). *"More more more," said the baby.* New York: Greenwillow.

Williams-Garcia, Rita. (1991). *Fast talk on a slow track.* New York: Dutton.

Willow, Diane. (1991). *At home in the rain forest.* Illus. Laura Jacques. Watertown, MA: Charlesbridge.

Wilson, Beth P. (1990). *Jenny.* Illus. Dolores Johnson. New York: Macmillan.

Winckler, Suzanne. (1991). *Our endangered planet: Population growth.* Minneapolis: Lerner.

Winfield, Arthur M. (1899). *Rover boy* series. Boston: Stratemeyer, Mershon.

Winner, David. (1990). *Desmond Tutu.* Ridgefield, CT: Morehouse.

Winter, Jeanette. (1988). *Follow the drinking gourd.* New York: Knopf.

Winter, Paula. (1987). *The bear and the fly.* New York: Crown.

Winter, Paula. (1988). *Sir Andrew.* New York: Crown.

Winthrop, Elizabeth. (1983). *A child is born: The Christmas story.* Illus. Charles Mikolaycak. New York: Holiday.

Winthrop, Elizabeth. (1988). *Bear and Mrs. Duck.* Illus. Patience Brewster. New York: Holiday.

Winthrop, Elizabeth. (1989). *The best friends club: A Lizzie and Harold story.* Illus. Martha Weston. New York: Lothrop.

Winthrop, Elizabeth (adapter). (1991). *Vasilissa the beautiful.* Illus. Alexander Koshkin. New York: HarperCollins.

Wiseman, David. (1981). *Jeremy Visick.* Boston: Houghton.

Wisler, G. Clifton. (1983). *Thunder on the Tennessee.* New York: Dutton.

Wisniewski, David. (1989). *The warrior and the wise man.* New York: Lothrop.

Wisniewski, David. (1992). *Rain player.* New York: Lothrop.

Wisniewski, David. (1990). *Elfwyn's saga.* New York: Lothrop.

Withers, Carl (compiler). (1988). *A rocket in my pocket.* Illus. Susanne Suba. New York: Henry Holt.

Wittman, Sally. (1985). *A special trade.* Illus. Karen Gundersheimer. New York: HarperCollins.

Wolf, Bernard. (1987). *In this proud land: The story of a Mexican-American family.* New York: HarperCollins.

Wolf, Bernard. (1988). *In the year of the tiger.* New York: Macmillan.

Wolkstein, Diane. (1981). *Banza: A Haitian story.* Illus. Marc Brown. New York: Dial.

Wood, Audrey. (1984). *The napping house.* Illus. Don Wood. San Diego: Harcourt.

Wood, Audrey. (1987). *Heckedy Peg.* Illus. Don Wood. San Diego: Harcourt.

Wood, Audrey. (1989). *Little Penguin's tale.* San Diego: Harcourt.

Wood, Nancy. (1974). *Many winters.* New York: Doubleday.

Woolf, Felicity. (1990). *Picture this: A first introduction to paintings.* New York: Doubleday.

Worth, Valerie. (1976, 1986). *More small poems.* Illus. Natalie Babbitt. New York: Farrar, Straus & Giroux.

Worth, Valerie. (1987). *All the small poems.* Illus. Natalie Babbitt. New York: Farrar, Straus & Giroux.

Worth, Valerie. (1987). *Small poems.* Illus. Natalie Babbitt. New York: Farrar, Straus & Giroux.

Wosmek, Frances. (1985). *A brown bird singing.* Illus. Ted Lewin. New York: Lothrop.

Wright, Betty Ren. (1984). *Ghosts beneath our feet.* New York: Holiday.

Wright, Betty Ren. (1989). *Rosie and the dance of the dinosaurs.* New York: Holiday.

Wright, Betty Ren. (1991). *The scariest night.* New York: Holiday.

Wrightson, Patricia. (1986). *The Nargun and the stars.* New York: McElderry.

Wrightson, Patricia. (1989). *Balyet.* New York: McElderry.

Wynot, Jillian. (1990). *The Mother's Day sandwich.* Illus. Maxie Chambliss. New York: Orchard.

Wyss, Johann. (1812; 1949 reprint). *The Swiss family Robinson.* Illus. Lynd Ward. New York: Grosset.

Yacowitz, Caryn (adapter). (1992). *The jade stone: A Chinese folktale.* Illus. Ju-Hong Chen. New York: Holiday.

Yagawa, Sumiko (reteller). (1981). *The crane wife.* Trans. Katherine Paterson. Illus. Suekichi Akaba. New York: Morrow.

Yarbro, Chelsea Quinn. (1984). *Locadio's apprentice.* New York: HarperCollins.

Yarbrough, Camille. (1981). *Cornrows.* Illus. Carole Byard. New York: Putnam.

Yashima, Taro. (1955). *Crow boy.* New York: Viking.

Yashima, Taro. (1958). *Umbrella.* New York: Viking.

Yashima, Taro. (1962; o.p.). *Youngest one.* New York: Viking.

Yashima, Taro. (1977). *Momo's kitten.* New York: Viking Puffin.

Yee, Paul. (1990). *Tales from Gold Mountain: Stories of the Chinese in the New World.* New York: Macmillan.

Yenawine, P. (1991). *Line.* New York: The Museum of Modern Art. New York: Delacorte.

Yep, Laurence. (1975). *Dragonwings.* New York: HarperCollins.

Yep, Laurence. (1977). *Child of the owl.* New York: HarperCollins, Zolotow.

Yep, Laurence. (1979). *Sea glass.* New York: HarperCollins.

Yep, Laurence. (1984). *The serpent's children.* New York: HarperCollins.

Yep, Laurence. (1985). *Mountain light.* New York: HarperCollins.

Yep, Laurence. (1988). *Dragon of the lost sea.* New York: HarperCollins.

Yep, Laurence. (1989). *The rainbow people.* Illus. David Wiesner. New York: HarperCollins.

Yep, Laurence. (1991). *The lost garden: A memoir by the author of Dragonwings.* Englewood Cliffs, NJ: Messner.

Yep, Laurence. (1991). *The star fisher.* New York: Morrow.

Yep, Laurence. (1991). *Tongues of jade.* Illus. David Wiesner. New York: HarperCollins.

Yolen, Jane. (1980). *Commander Toad in space.* New York: Putnam.

Yolen, Jane. (1982). *Dragon's blood.* New York: Delacorte.

Yolen, Jane. (1986). *The lullaby songbook.* Arrangements by Adam Stemple. Illus. Charles Mikolaycak. San Diego: Harcourt.

Yolen, Jane. (1987). *The girl who loved the wind.* New York: Harper Trophy.

Yolen, Jane. (1987). *Owl moon.* Illus. John Schoenherr. New York: Putnam, Philomel.

Yolen, Jane. (1988). *The devil's arithmetic.* New York: Viking.

Yolen, Jane. (1988). *The emperor and the kite.* Illus. Ed Young. New York: Putnam.

Yolen, Jane. (1988). *Piggins and the royal wedding.* Illus. Jane Dyer. San Diego: Harcourt.

Yolen, Jane. (1989). *Best witches: Poems for Halloween.* Illus. Elise Primavera. New York: Putnam.

Yolen, Jane. (1989). *Things that go bump in the night: A collection of original stories.* New York: HarperCollins.

Yolen, Jane. (1990). *Birdwatch: A book of poetry.* Illus. Ted Lewin. New York: Putnam.

Yolen, Jane. (1990). *Dinosaur dances.* Illus. Bruce Degen. New York: Putnam.

Yolen, Jane. (1990). *Sky dogs.* Illus. Barry Moser. San Diego: Harcourt.

Yolen, Jane. (1990). *Tam Lin.* Illus. Charles Mikolaycak. San Diego: Harcourt.

Yolen, Jane. (1991). *All in the woodland early.* Illus. Jane Breskin Zalben. Honesdale, PA: Boyds Mills.

Yolen, Jane. (1991). *All those secrets of the world.* Illus. Leslie Baker. Boston: Little, Brown.

Yolen, Jane. (1992). *Eeny, meeny, miney mole.* San Diego: Harcourt.

Yolen, Jane. (1992). *Encounter.* Illus. David Shannon. San Diego: Harcourt.

Yolen, Jane. (1992). *Jane Yolen's Mother Goose songbook.* Illus. Rosekrans Hoffman. Music by Adam Stemple. Honesdale, PA: Boyds Mills.

Yolen, Jane. (1992). *A letter from Phoenix Farm.* Photos by Jason Stemple. Katonah, NY: Richard C. Owens.

Yolen, Jane. (1992). *Street rhymes around the world.* Illus. native artists. Honesdale, PA: Boyds Mills.

Yolen, Jane. (1993). *Sleep rhymes around the world.* Illus. native artists. Honesdale, PA: Boyds Mills.

Yolen, Jane. (1993). *Weather report.* Illus. Annie Gusman. Honesdale, PA: Boyds Mills.

Yorinks, Arthur. (1986). *Hey, Al.* Illus. Richard Egielski. New York: Farrar, Straus & Giroux.

Yorinks, Arthur. (1989). *Oh, brother.* Illus. Richard Egielski. New York: Farrar, Straus & Giroux.

Yoshida, Toshi. (1989). *Young lions.* New York: Philomel.

Young, Clarence. (1899). *The Motor Boys* series. Boston: Stratemeyer, Mershon.

Young, Ed. (1983). *Up a tree: A wordless picture book.* New York: HarperCollins.

Young, Ed. (1991). *The other bone.* New York: HarperCollins.

Young, Ed. (1992). *Seven blind mice.* New York: Philomel.

Young, Ed (trans./illus.). (1989). *Lon Po Po: A Red Riding Hood story from China.* New York: Philomel.

The Youth's Companion magazine. 1827–1929.

Zak, Monica. (1992). *Save my rain forest.* Illus. Bengt-Arne Runnerstrom. Trans. Nancy Schimmel. Volcano, CA: Volcano.

Zane, Polly, & Zane, John. (1989). *American women: Four centuries of progress.* Berkley: Proof.

Zeitlin, Patty. (1982). *A song is a rainbow: Music, movement and rhythm.* Chicago: Scott Foresman.

Zelinsky, Paul. (1991). *The wheels on the bus.* New York: Dutton.

Zemach, Harve, & Zemach, Margot. (1975). *Mommy buy me a china doll.* New York: Farrar, Straus & Giroux.

Zemach, Margot. (1973). *Duffy and the devil.* New York: Farrar, Straus & Giroux.

Zemach, Margot. (1977). *It could always be worse: A Yiddish folktale.* New York: Farrar, Straus & Giroux.

Zemach, Margot. (1979). *Self-Portrait: Margot Zemach.* Reading, MA: Addison-Wesley.

Zemach, Margot. (1981). *Hush, little baby.* New York: Dutton.

Zemach, Margot. (1988). *Three little pigs.* New York: Farrar, Straus & Giroux.

Zheleznikov, Vladimir. (1990). *Scarecrow.* Trans. Antonina W. Bouis. New York: HarperCollins.

Zhensun, Zheng, & Low, Alice. (1991). *A young painter: The life and paintings of Wang Yani—China's extraordinary young artist.* Photos by Zheng Zhensun. New York: Scholastic.

Ziefert, Harriet. (1992). *Big to little, little to big.* Illus. Susan Baum. New York: HarperCollins.

Ziefert, Harriet. (1992). *Clothes on, clothes off.* Illus. Susan Baum. New York: HarperCollins.

Ziefert, Harriet. (1992). *Count up, count down.* Illus. Susan Baum. New York: HarperCollins.

Ziefert, Harriet. (1992). *Empty to full, full to empty.* Illus. Susan Baum. New York: HarperCollins.

Zindel, Paul. (1968). *The pigman.* New York: HarperCollins.

Zindel, Paul. (1992). *The pigman and me.* New York: HarperCollins.

Zolotow, Charlotte. (1962). *Mr. Rabbit and the lovely present.* Illus. Maurice Sendak. New York: HarperCollins.

Zolotow, Charlotte. (1963). *The quarreling book.* New York: HarperCollins.

Zolotow, Charlotte. (1966, 1987). *I like to be little.* Illus. Erik Blegvad. New York: HarperCollins.

Zolotow, Charlotte. (1969, 1989). *The hating book.* Illus. Ben Shecter. New York: HarperCollins.

Zolotow, Charlotte. (1972). *William's doll.* Illus. William Pène Du Bois. New York: HarperCollins.

Zolotow, Charlotte. (1974). *My grandson Lew.* Illus. William Pène Du Bois. New York: HarperCollins.

Zolotow, Charlotte. (1978). *Someone new.* Illus. Erik Blegvad. New York: HarperCollins.

Zolotow, Charlotte (1980). *Say it!* Illus. James Stevenson. New York: Greenwillow.

Zolotow, Charlotte. (1987). *Everything glistens and everything sings.* San Diego: Harcourt.

Copyrights and Acknowledgments

Illustration Credits

Chapter 1

15 Facsimile of a hornbook, reproduced by permission of The Hornbook, Inc. **16** From the Rare Books and Manuscripts Division, The New York Public Library, Astor, Lenox, and Tilden Foundations. **17** From the Rare Books and Manuscripts Division, The New York Public Library, Astor, Lenox, and Tilden Foundations. **22** © The Pierpont Morgan Library, 1993. **24** © The Pierpont Morgan Library, 1993. **25** From the General Research Division, The New York Public Library, Astor, Lenox, and Tilden Foundations. **26** The Bettman Archive. **30** From *Madeline* by Ludwig Bemelmans. Copyright 1939 by Ludwig Bemelmans, renewed © 1967 by Madeline Bemelmans and Barbara Bemelmans Marciano. Used by permission of Viking Penguin, a division of Penguin Books USA, Inc. **34** Jacket painting by Rene Ade from *Missing May* by Cynthia Rylant. Copyright © 1992 by Rene Ade. Used with permission of the publisher, Orchard Books, New York. **35** From *Mirette on the High Wire,* copyright © 1992 by Emily Arnold McCully. Reprinted by permission of G. P. Putnam's Sons. **36** © The Pierpont Morgan Library, 1993.

Chapter 2

41 From *Where the Wild Things Are* by Maurice Sendak, copyright © 1963 by Maurice Sendak. Reprinted by permission of HarperCollins Publishers. **45** From *Pat the Bunny* © 1940 Dorothy Kunhardt, used by permission of Western Publishing Company, Inc. **47** Illustration and accompanying text from *What Game Shall We Play?* by Pat Hutchins. Copyright © 1986 by Pat Hutchins. By permission of Greenwillow Books, a division of William Morrow & Company, Inc. **49** From *The Summer of the Swans* by Betsy Byars, illustrated by Ed CoConis. Copyright © 1970 by Betsy Byars. Used by permission of Viking Penguin, a division of Penguins Books USA, Inc. **51** Courtesy of John and Sarah Lewis, Cambridge, Mass. **51** Courtesy of Harcourt Brace and Company. **52** Photo courtesy of L. Rosenblatt. **60** Courtesy of Harcourt Brace and Company. **67** From *Chicken Soup with Rice* by Maurice Sendak, copyright © 1962 by Maurice Sendak. Reprinted by permission of HarperCollins Publishers. **73** Courtesy of Rosemary Lufrano's 4th grade class, John Daly School, Port Washington, NY.

Chapter 3

81 Photo by Alan S. Orling. **84** Reprinted with the permission of Charles Scribner's Sons, an imprint of Macmillan Publishing Company from *I'm in Charge of Celebrations* by Byrd Baylor, illustrated by Peter Parnall. Text copyright © 1986 Byrd Baylor. Illustrations copyright © 1986 Peter Parnall. **84** From *Jumanji* by Chris Van Allsburg. Copyright © 1981 by Chris Van Allsburg. Reprinted by permission of Houghton Mifflin Company. All rights reserved. **85** Excerpt and illustration from *Moon Rope,* copyright © 1992 by Lois Ehlert; Spanish translation copyright © 1992 by Harcourt Brace & Company, reprinted by permission of the publisher. **85** From *Saint George and the Dragon* by Margaret Hodges; illustrated by Trina Schart Hyman. Text copyright © 1984 by Margaret Hodges; illustrations copyright © 1984 by Trina Schart Hyman. By permission of Little, Brown, and Company. **86** Illustration by Mike Wimmer, reprinted by permission of Philomel Books from *Flight* by Robert Burleigh, illustrations copyright © 1991 by Mike Wimmer. **86** Illustration from *Aïda* by Leontyne Price, illustration copyright © 1990 by Leo Dillion and Diane Dillion, reprinted by permission of Harcourt Brace & Company. **87** From *Animal Alphabet* by Bert Kitchen. Copyright © 1984 by Bert Kitchen. Used by permission of Dial Books for Young Readers, a division of Penguin Books USA, Inc. **87** Illustration from *Dawn* by Uri Shulevitz, copyright © 1974 by Uri Shulevitz. Reproduced by permission

of Farrar, Straus, & Giroux, Inc. **87** From *Give A Dog A Bone* by Brian Wildsmith. Copyright © 1985 by Brian Wildsmith. Reprinted by permission of Pantheon Books, a division of Random House, Inc. **88** Illustration from *The Napping House* by Audrey Wood, illustration copyright © 1984 by Don Wood, reprinted by permission of Harcourt Brace & Company. **89** From the book *Strega Nona* by Tomie de Paola, copyright © 1975. Used by permission of the publisher, Simon & Schuster Books for Young Readers, New York. **89** From *The Stinky Cheese Man and Other Fairly Stupid Tales* by Jon Scieszka, illustrated by Lane Smith. Copyright © 1992 by Jon Scieszka, text. Copyright © 1992 by Lane Smith, illustrations. Used by permission of Viking Penguin, a division of Penguin Books USA, Inc. **91** Illustration from *Where the Forest Meets the Sea* by Jeannie Baker. Copyright © 1987 by Jeannie Baker. By permission of Greenwillow Books, a division of William Morrow & Company, INc. **91** From *Dots, Spots, Speckles, and Stripes* by Tana Hoban, copyright © 1987 by Tana Hoban. By permission of Greenwillow Books, a division of William Morrow & Company, Inc. **93** From *All Around Us* by Eric Carle, Picture Book Studio, Saxonville, MA, 1986. **93** From *Red Dancing Shoes* by Denise Lewis Patrick. Text copyright © 1993 by Denise Lewis Patrick, illustration copyright © 1993 by James E. Ransome. By permission of Tambourine Books, a division of William Morrow & Company, Inc. **93** Illustration from *Working Cotton* by Sherley Ann Williams, illustration copyright © 1992 by Carole Byard, reprinted by permission of Harcourt Brace & Company. **94** From *Mirette on the High Wire,* copyright © 1992 by Emily Arnold McCully. Reprinted by permission of G. P. Putnam's Sons. **94** Illustration from *Jumanji* by Chris Van Allsburg. Copyright © 1981 by Chris Van Allsburg. Reprinted by permission of Houghton Mifflin Co. All rights reserved. **94** From *How A Book Is Made* by Aliki. Copyright © 1986 by Aliki Brandenberg. Reprinted by permission of HarperCollins Publishers. **94** From *Arrow to the Sun* by Gerald McDermott. Copyright © 1974 by Gerald McDermott. Used by permission of Viking Penguin, a division of Penguin Books USA, Inc. **96** Copyright © June, 1966, by Kirtley Perkins, The National Audubon Society Collection/PR. **96** Painting from *Wings Along the Waterway* by Mary Barrett Brown. Copyright © 1992 by Mary Barrett Brown. Used with permission of the publisher, Orchard Books, New York. **98** From *Heartland* by Diane Siebert, paintings by Wendell Minor, text copyright © 1989 by Diane Siebert, illustrations copyright © 1989 by Wendell Minor. Reprinted by permission of HarperCollins Publishers. **100** Illustration from *Eeny, Meeny, Miney Mole* by Jane Yolen, illustration copyright © 1992 by Kathryn Brown, reprinted by permission of Harcourt Brace & Company. **100** Reprinted with the permission of Bradbury Press, an Affiliate of Macmillan, Inc. from *Buffalo Woman* by Paul Goble, copyright © 1984 by Paul Goble. **100** From *Amazing Grace* by Mary Hoffman, illustrated by Caroline Binch. Copyright © 1992 by Mary Hoffman for text. Copyright © 1991 by Caroline Binch for illustrations. Used by permission of Dial Books for Young Readers, a division of Penguin Books USA, Inc. **101** From *My Great-Aunt Arizona* by Gloria Houston, illustrated by Susan Condie Lamb, text copyright © 1992 by Gloria Houston, illustrations copyright © 1992 by Susan Condie Lamb. Reprinted by permission of HarperCollins Publishers. **102** From *Possum Magic,* illustrations by Julie Vivas, text by Mem Fox. **104** From *The Tale of Peter Rabbit* by Beatrix Potter, copyright © Frederick Warne & Co., 1902, 1987. **105** From *The Tale of Peter Rabbit* by Beatrix Potter, copyright © Frederick Warne & Co., 1902, 1987. **105** From *The Tale of Peter Rabbit* by Beatrix Potter, copyright © Frederick Warne & Co., 1902, 1987. **106** From *The Tale of Peter Rabbit* by Beatrix Potter, copyright © Frederick Warne & Co., 1902, 1987. **107** From *The Tale of Peter Rabbit* by Beatrix Potter, copyright © Frederick Warne & Co., 1902, 1987. **123** Photo by Sean Kernan.

Chapter 4

128 From *Inner Chimes,* copyright © 1993, Boyd Mills Press. **135** Courtesy Little, Brown, and Company. **136** Courtesy Thomas V. Crowell. **137** Piper Productions. Reproduced by permission of HarperCollins Publishers. **139** Photo by Marilyn Sanders. **140** Photo by Bachrach. **141** Reprinted by permission of Houghton Mifflin Company. **145** Copyright © 1974 by Robert Froman. **147** Both illustrations from *In The Eyes of the Cat: Japanese Poetry for All Seasons,* Selected and illustrated by Demi. Translated by Tze-si Huang. Copyright © 1992 by Demi. Reprinted by permission of Henry Holt & Company. **152** From *And the Green Grass Grew All Around* by Alvin Schwartz, illustrated by Sue Truesdell, text copyright © 1992 by Alvin Schwartz, illustrations copyright © 1992 by Sue Truesdell. Reprinted by permission of HarperCollins Publishers. **155** Photo of Lilian Moore by Glen Weston, used courtesy of Atheneum Publishers, an imprint of Macmillan Publishing Company. **157** Courtesy of HarperCollins Publishers. **158** Photo © by Temple Studios.

Chapter 5

168 Reprinted with the permission of Atheneum Publishers, an imprint of Macmillan Publishing Company from *Turtle Knows Your Names* retold and illustrated by Ashley Bryan. Copyright © 1989 Ashley Bryan. **169** Illustration by Tomie de Paola reprinted by permission of G. P. Putnam's Sons from *Giorgio's Village,* copyright © 1982 by Tomie de Paola. **170** Photo by Jerry Bauer. **172** From *The Rough-Face Girl,* text copyright © 1992 by Rafe Martin, illustrations copyright © 1992 by David Shannon. Reprinted by permission of G. P. Putnam's Sons. **173** From *The Rough-Face Girl,* text copyright 1992 by Rafe Martin, illustrations copyright 1992 by David Shannon. Reprinted by permission of G. P. Putnam's Sons. **175** From *Three Little Kittens* by Paul Galdone. Copyright © 1986 by Paul Galdone. Reprinted by permission of Clarion Books/Houghton Mifflin Company. All rights reserved. **175** From *The Mother Goose Book* by Alice and Martin Provensen. Copyright © 1976 by Alice and Martin Provensen. Reprinted by permission of Random House, Inc. **176** From *Book of Nursery and Mother Goose Rhymes* by Marguerite de Angeli. Copyright © 1954 by Marguerite de Angeli. Used by permission of Doubleday, a division of Bantam Doubleday Dell Publishing Group, Inc. **179** From *Anansi Goes Fishing* by Eric Kimmel. Illustration copyright © 1992 by Janet Stevens. **182** Photo courtesy of Penguin USA, Inc. **184** Illustration from *Moss Gown* by William H. Hooks. Illustration copyright © 1987 by Donald Carrick. Reprinted by permission of Houghton Mifflin Company. All rights reserved. **193** Illustration by Diana Der-Hovanessian from *Street Rhymes Around the World,* edited by Jane Yolen. Copyright © 1992 by Wordsong, Boyds Mills Press, Inc. Reprinted by permission of Wordsong, Boyds Mills Press, Inc. All rights reserved. **196** Illustration by Jan Brett, reprinted by permission of G. P. Putnam's Sons from *Goldilocks and the Three Bears,* copyright © 1987 by Jan Brett. **197** Chart by Sandy Stoessel.

Chapter 6

203 Photo © by Avi. **204** Jacket cover art from *Tuck Everlasting* by Natalie Babbitt. Reproduced by permission of Farrar, Straus, & Giroux, Inc. **206** From *The Fortune Tellers* by Lloyd Alexander, illustrated by Trina Schart Hyman. Copyright © 1992 by Trina Schart Hyman, illustrations. Used by permission of Dutton Children's Books, a division of Penguin Books USA, Inc. **207** Photo by Shulamith Oppenheim. **208** From *Taran Wanderer* by Lloyd Alexander. Copyright © 1967 by Lloyd Alexander. Used by permission of Dell Books, a division of Bantam Doubleday Dell Publishing Group, Inc. **209** Reprinted with the permission of Margaret K. McElderry Books, an imprint of Macmillan Publishing Company from *The Grey King* by Susan Cooper. Jacket illustration by Michael Heslop. Copyright © 1975 Susan Cooper. **211** From *Martin's Mice* by Dick King-Smith, illustrations by Jez Alborough. Text copyright © 1988 by Dick King-Smith. Illustrations copyright © by Jez Alborough. Reprinted by permission of Crown Publishers, Inc. **211** Illustration from *The Borrowers* by Mary Norton, illustration copyright © 1953, 1952, and renewed 1981, 1980 by Mary Norton, Beth Krush, and Joe Krush, reprinted by permission of Harcourt Brace & Company. **212** From *Hey, Al* by Arthur Yorinks, illustrated by Richard Egielski, text copyright © 1986 by Arthur Yorinks, pictures copyright © 1986 by Richard Egielski.

Reprinted by permission of HarperCollins Publishers. **215** Jacket art from *Children of the Dust* by Louise Lawrence, jacket art copyright © 1985 by Judy Glasser, jacket copyright © 1985 by HarperCollins Publishers. Reprinted by permission of HarperCollins Publishers. **216** From *Among the Dolls* by William Sleator, illustrated by Trina Schart Hyman. Copyright © 1975 by Trina Schart Hyman for illustrations. Used by permission of Dutton Signet, an imprint of New American Library, a division of Penguin Books USA, Inc. **217** Reprinted with the permission of Macmillan Publishing Company, a division of Macmillan, Inc., from *The White Mountains* by John Christopher. Jacket art by Roger Hane. Copyright © 1967 John Christopher. **218** Illustration from *The Green Book* by Jill Paton Walsh, illustrations by Lloyd Bloom, text copyright © 1982 by Jill Paton Walsh, pictures copyright © 1982 by Lloyd Bloom. Reproduced by permission of Farrar, Straus, & Giroux, Inc.

Chapter 7

224 Photo by Jill Paton Walsh / courtesy of HarperCollins Publishers. **228** Illustration from *Bridge to Terabithia* by Katherine Paterson, illustration by Donna Diamond (Thomas Y. Crowell), copyright © 1977 by Katherine Paterson. Reprinted by permission of HarperCollins Publishers. **230** Photo courtesy of Harcourt Brace and Company. **232** Illustration by John Schoenherr, reprinted by permission of Philomel Books from *Owl Moon* by Jane Yolen, illustrations copyright © 1987 by John Schoenherr. **233** From *Hurricane Harry* by Judith Caseley, copyright © 1991 by Judith Caseley. Printed by permission of Greenwillow Books, a division of William Morrow & Company, Inc. **234** From *The Snowy Day* by Ezra Jack Keats. Copyright © 1962 by Ezra Jack Keats, renewed © 1990 by Martin Pope. Used by permission of Viking Penguin, a division of Penguin Books USA, Inc. **234** Jacket illustration copyright © 1989 by Ondre Pettingill. **235** Cover of *The Accident* by Carol Carrick. Illustrations copyright © 1976 by Donald Carrick. Reprinted by permission of Clarion Books/Houghton Mifflin Co. All rights reserved. **236** Jacket art by Wayne Windfield from *The Moves Make the Man* by Bruce Brooks, jacket art copyright © 1984 by Wayne Winfield, jacket copyright © 1984 by HarperCollins Publishers. Reprinted by permission of HarperCollins Publishers. **236** From *Aldo Applesauce* by Johanna Hurwitz, copyright © 1979 by Johanna Hurwitz. By permission of William Morrow & Company, Inc. **241** Cover illustration by Joyce Hopkins from *Unclaimed Treasures* by Patricia MacLachlan, copyright © 1984 by Patricia MacLachlan. Reprinted by permission of HarperCollins Publishers. **244** From *Everett Anderson's Goodbye* by Lucille Clifton, text copyright © 1983 by Lucille Clifton, illustrations copyright © 1983 by Ann Grifalconi. By permission of Henry Holt & Company. **244** From *Stevie* by John Steptoe, copyright © 1969 by John L. Steptoe. Reprinted by permission of HarperCollins Publishers. **248** Jacket painting by Rene Ade from *Monkey Island* by Paula Fox. Copyright © 1991 by Rene Ade. Used with permission of the publisher, Orchard Books, New York.

Chapter 8

257 From *Roxaboxen* by Alice McLerran, text copyright © 1991 by Alice McLerran. Illustration copyright © 1991 by Barbara Cooney. By permission of Lothrop, Lee & Shepard Books, a division of William Morrow & Co., Inc. **261** From *Roll of Thunder, Hear My Cry* by Mildred D. Taylor, Puffin cover illustration by Max Ginsberg. Copyright © 1991 by Max Ginsberg, cover illustration. Used by permission of Puffin Books, a division of Penguin Books USA, Inc. **263** Photo by Jack Ackerman. **266** From *Door in the Wall* by Marguerite de Angeli. Copyright © 1949 by Marguerite de Angeli. Used by permission of Doubleday, a division of Bantam Doubleday Dell Publishing Group, Inc. **268** Photo by Sarah Conrad / courtesy of HarperCollins Publishers. **270** Illustration from *Encounter* by Jane Yolen, illustration copyright © 1992 by David Shannon, reprinted by permission of Harcourt Brace & Company. **273** From *War Comes to Willy Freeman* by James Lincoln Collier and Christopher Collier. Copyright © 1983 by James Lincoln Collier and Christopher Collier. Used by permission of Dell Books, a division of Bantam Doubleday Dell Publishing Group, Inc. **274** Reprinted with the permission of Macmillan Publishing Company, a division of Macmillan, Inc., from *Nettie's Trip South* by Ann Turner, illustrated by Ronald Himler. Illustrations copyright © 1987 Ronald Himler. **275** From *Going West* by Jean Van Leeuwen, illustrated by Thomas B. Allen. Copyright © 1992 by Thomas B.

Allen, illustrations. Used by permission of Dial Books for Young Readers, a division of Penguin Books USA, Inc. **278** From *When I Was Young in the Mountains* by Cynthia Rylant, illustrated by Diane Goode. Copyright © 1982 by Diane Goode, illustrations. Used by permission of Dutton Children's Books, a division of Penguin Books USA, Inc. **280** From *The Lily Cupboard* by Shulamith Levey Oppenheim, illustrations by Ronald Himler, text copyright © 1992 by Shulamith Levey Oppenheim, illustrations copyright © 1992 by Ronald Himler. Reprinted by permission of HarperCollins Publishers. **282** From *The Wall* by Eve Bunting, illustrated by Ronald Himler. Text copyright © 1990 by Eve Bunting, illustration copyright © 1990 by Ronald Himler. Reprinted by permission of Clarion Books/Houghton Mifflin Company. All rights reserved. **284** © UPI/Bettman.

Chapter 9

293 Photograph by Charles Osgood. Copyright © 1988, Chicago Tribune Co. Used by permission of Clarion Books. **294** From *Lincoln: A Photobiography* by Russell Freedman, National Portrait Gallery, Frederick Merserve Collection/Art Resource, New York. **296** From *On the Day Peter Stuyvesant Sailed into Town* by Arnold Lobel, copyright © 1971 by Arnold Lobel. Reprinted by permission of HarperCollins Publishers. **298** Photo by Jill Krementz (1939). **299** From *Why Don't You Get A Horse, Sam Adams?* text copyright © 1974 by Jean Fritz, illustrations copyright © 1974 by Trina Schart Hyman. Reprinted by permission of Coward, McCann & Geoghegan, Inc. **300** From *Aunt Harriet's Underground Railroad to the Sky* by Faith Ringgold, copyright © 1992 by Faith Ringgold. Reprinted by permission of Crown Publishers, Inc. **302** © UPI/Bettman. **303** Photo copyright © 1992 by Lawrence Migdale. **304** Front book cover of *War Boy* by Michael Foreman, reprinted courtesy of Little, Brown & Company. **306** From *Shaka: King of the Zulus* by Diane Stanley Vennema and Peter Vennema, text copyright © 1988 by Diane Stanley Vennema and Peter Vennema, illustrations copyright © 1988 by Diane Stanley Vennema. By permission of William Morrow & Company, Inc. **306** Reprinted courtesy of Chatham Hall. **309** From *A Letter from Phoenix Farm* by Jane Yolen. Photographs by Jason Stemple. Richard C. Owens Publishers, Inc., P.O. Box 585, Katonah, NY 10536. Reprinted with permission. Photograph reprinted by permission of Curtis Brown, Ltd. Copyright © 1992 by Jason Stemple. **309** From *Jackie Robinson, He Was The First* by David A. Adler. Illustration copyright © 1989 by Robert Casilla.

Chapter 10

317 From *New Questions and Answers About Dinosaurs* by Seymour Simon, text copyright © 1990 by Seymour Simon, illustrations copyright © by Jennifer Dewey. By permission of William Morrow & Company, Inc. **318** Illustration from *Antarctica* by Helen Cowcher, copyright © 1990 by Helen Cowcher. Reproduced by permission of Farrar, Straus, & Giroux, Inc. **319** Photo © by Catherine Noren. **324** Illustration courtesy of NASA. **325** From *Backyard Hunter: The Praying Mantis* by Bianca Lavies. Copyright © 1990 by Bianca Lavies. Used by permission of Dutton Children's Books, a division of Penguin Books USA, Inc. **328** Courtesy of the Library of Congress. **332** Illustration and accompanying text from *The Doorbell Rang* by Pat Hutchins. Copyright © 1990 by Pat Hutchins. By permission of Greenwillow Books, a division of William Morrow & Company, Inc. **332** From *Many Luscious Lollipops,* copyright © 1989 by Ruth Heller. Reprinted by permissions of Grosset & Dunlap, Inc. **334** From *The Laura Ingalls Wilder Songbook* by Eugenia Garson, illustrations by Garth Williams. Original text copyright © 1968 by Eugenia Garson, musical arrangements copyright © 1968 by Herbert Haufrecht, illustrations copyright © 1953 by Garth Williams, illustrations copyright renewed 1981 by Garth Williams. Reprinted by permission of HarperCollins Publishers.

Chapter 11

347 © Jacob Lawrence/VAGA, New York 1993. **348** From *Mufaro's Beautiful Daughters* by John Steptoe, copyright © 1987 by John Steptoe. By permission of Lothrop, Lee & Shepard books, a division of William Morrow & Company, Inc. **349** From *Aunt Flossie's Hats (And Crab Cakes Later)* by Elizabeth Fitzgerald Howard. Illustration copyright © 1991 by James Ransome. Reprinted by permission of Clarion Books/Houghton Mifflin Company. All rights reserved. **353** Illustration by Ed Young reprinted by permission of Philomel Books from *Yen-Shen, a Cinderella Story from China,* retold by Ai-Ling Louie, illustrations copyright © 1982 by Ed Young. **354** Photo by Deborah Storms. **358** From *The Crane Wife* retold by Sumiko Yagawa, and illustrated by Suekichi Akaba. Text copyright © 1979 by Sumiko Yagawa/English translation © 1981 by Katherine Paterson. Illustrations copyright © 1979 by Suekichi Akaba. By permission of Morrow Junior Books, a division of William Morrow & Company, Inc. **359** From *Tortillitas Para Mama and Other Nursery Rhymes, Spanish and English,* selected and translated by Margot C. Griego, Betsy L. Bucks, Sharon S. Gilbert, and Laurel H. Kimball. Illustrated by Barbara Cooney. Copyright © 1981 by Margot C. Griego, Betsy L. Bucks, Sharon S. Gilbert, and Laurel Kimball. Illustrations copyright © 1981 by Barabara Cooney. Reprinted by permission by Henry Holt and Company, Inc. **361** Cover illustration by Nivia Gonzales. Cover design by Lorraine Louie. Courtesy of Vintage Books. **364** Photo by Carol Bruchac. **365** Reprintd with the permission of Macmillan Publishing Company, a division of Macmillan, Inc. from *Dr. Coyote: A Native American Aesop's Fable* by John Bierhorst, illustrated by Wendy Watson. Illustrations copyright © 1987 Wendy Watson. **367** From *Arctic Memories* by Normee Ekoomiak, copyright © 1988 by Normee Ekoomiak. By permission of Henry Holt & Company, Inc. **371** From *The Remembering Box* by Eth Clifford. Copyright © 1985 by Eth Clifford Rosenberg. Reprinted by permission of Houghton Mifflin Company. All rights reserved. **374** Illustration by James E. Ransome from *All the Lights in the Night* by Arthur A. Levine. Copyright © 1991 by arthur A. Levine. Illustration copyright © 1991 by James E. Ransome. By permission of Tambourine Books, a division of William Morrow & Company, Inc. **375** From *The Year of the Perfect Christmas Tree* by Gloria Houston, illustrated by Barbara Cooney. Copyright © 1988 by Barbara Cooney, pictures. Used by permission of Dial Books for Young Readers, a division of Penguin Books USA, Inc. **377** From *From the Hills of Georgia* by Mattie Lou O'Kelley. Copyright © 1983 by Mattie Lou O'Kelley. By permission of Little, Brown and Company. **378** From *Hopskotch Around the World* by Mary D. Lankford; text copyright © 1992 by Mary Lankford, illustrations copyright © 1992 by Karen Milone. By permission of William Morrow & Company, Inc. **379** Cover of *The Year of Impossible Goodbyes* by Sook Nyul Choi. Jacket art © 1991 by Marie Garafano. Reprinted by permission of Houghton Mifflin Company. All rights reserved. **382** From *Ronia, th eRobber's Daughter* by Astrid Lindgren, cover illustration by Trina Schart Hyman. Copyright © 1983 by Viking Penguin Inc., cover illustration. Used by permission of Puffin Books, a division of Penguin Books USA, Inc. **383** From *Hiroshima No Pika* by Toshi Maruki, copyright © 1980 by Toshi Maruki, by permission of Lothrop, Lee & Shepard Books, a division of William Morrow & Company, Inc.

Chapter 12

396 From *Dicey's Song* by Cynthia Voight, illustrator, James Shefcik. **398** Photo by Carolyn Soto. **399** Painting by Peter Catalanotto from *All I See* by Cynthia Rylant. Copyright © 1988 by Peter Catalanotto. Used with permission of the pulisher, Orchard Books, New York. **402** Photo © by John Gilbert Fox. **404** Illustration and text from *Berlioz the Bear* newsletter by Jan Brett. Reprinted by permission of Jan Brett. **405** From *Brown Bear, Brown Bear, What Do You See?* by Bill Martin, Jr., pictures by Eric Carle. Copyright © 1967, 1983 by Holt, Rinehart, and Winston, illustrations copyright © 1983 by Eric Carle. By permission of Henry Holt & Company, Inc.

Author and Title Index

Numbers in *italic* indicate the pages on which illustrations appear.

Subject Index

For entries on children's authors, illustrators, and children's books, see Author and Title Index. Numbers in *italic* indicate the pages on which illustrations appear.

Jean deBrunhoff, *The Story of Babar*, 1931

Laura Ingalls Wilder, *Little House in the Big Woods*, 1932

Marjorie Flack, *Ask Mr. Bear*, 1932

Kurt Wiese, illus., *The Story About Ping* by Marjorie Flack, 1933

Arthur Rackham, *The Arthur Rackham Fairy Book*, 1933

J. R. R. Tolkien, *The Hobbit*, 1937; *The Lord of the Rings*, 1954-55

Ludwig Bemelmans, *Madeline*, 1939

Esther Forbes, *Johnny Tremain*, 1939

Virginia Lee Burton, *The Little House*, 1943

Robert Lawson, *Rabbit Hill*, 1944

C. S. Lewis, Narnia series: *The Lion, the Witch, and the Wardrobe*, 1950

E. B. White, *Charlotte's Web*, 1952

Mary Norton, *The Borrowers*, 1952

Roger Duvoisin, illus., *The Happy Lion* by Louise Fatio, 1954

Dr. Seuss, *The Cat in the Hat*, 1957

Ezra Jack Keats, *The Snowy Day*, 1962

Maurice Sendak, *Where the Wild Things Are*, 1963

Lloyd Alexander, *The Book of Three*, 1964